Comanche Ethnography

STUDIES
IN THE ANTHROPOLOGY OF
NORTH AMERICAN INDIANS

Editors
Raymond J. DeMallie
Douglas R. Parks

COMANCHE ETHNOGRAPHY

Field Notes of E. Adamson Hoebel, Waldo R. Wedel,
Gustav G. Carlson, and Robert H. Lowie

Compiled and Edited by
Thomas W. Kavanagh

Published by the University of Nebraska Press
Lincoln and London

In cooperation with the American Indian Studies Research Institute,
Indiana University, Bloomington

Library of Congress Cataloging-in-Publication Data
Comanche ethnography: field notes of E. Adamson Hoebel, Waldo R. Wedel, Gustav G. Carlson, and
Robert H. Lowie / compiled and edited by Thomas W. Kavanagh.
    p.   cm.—(Studies in the anthropology of North American Indians)
Includes bibliographical references and index.
ISBN 978-0-8032-2764-4 (cloth: alk. paper)
1. Comanche Indians—History—Sources.   2. Ethnology—Fieldwork—Great Plains.
3. Ethnology—Fieldwork—Southwest, New.   4. Hoebel, E. Adamson (Edward Adamson),
1906–1993.   5. Wedel, Waldo R. (Waldo Rudolph), 1908–1996.   6. Carlson, Gustav G.
7. Lowie, Robert Harry, 1883–1957.   I. Kavanagh, Thomas W., 1949–   II. Indiana University,
Bloomington. American Indian Studies Research Institute.
E99.C85C473   2008
978.004′974572—dc22
                                                                2008026882

Contents

Photographs

(Following page 31; all photographs cropped)

1. The Field Party
2. Teneverka in front of his house
3. Rhoda and Herman Asenap
4. Quassyah, Ralph Linton, and unidentified Comanche man
5. Norton Tahquechi (right), and Pauau
6. "Comanche Orchestra" and Post Oak Jim
7. Frank Chekovi and Pedahny
8. Tahsuda
9. Niyah
10. Brush Dance. The dancers start away from the arena and dance towards it
11. Brush Dance. The singers, wearing cowboy hats, can be seen behind the women
12. Brush Dance. Several dancers are shading themselves from the sun with their fans
13. Brush Dance. The dancers have reached the arena
14. Brush Dance. The woman by the singers holds her hand to her mouth in ululation
15. Dance. Here only women are in the center ring while a few men are outside
16. Dance. Returning to their seats, the men and women move separately
17. Two dancers. Both men wear deer-hair roaches with single eagle feathers
18. Five women dancers
19. Two dancers. From the doubled mescal-bean and silver bandoliers, these men appear to be Gourd Dancers
20. Quermah

Figures

Preface

Two sets of unpublished field notes underlie much of the ethnographic understanding of the Comanche Indians. The earliest are Robert Lowie's brief notes of his 1912 Comanche fieldwork, the basis of the Comanche part of his "Dances and Societies of the Plains Shoshone" (1915). The second are the much more extensive and much more influential notes of the 1933 "Field Training Course in Anthropological Field Methods," also known as the "Field Party," sponsored by the Santa Fe Laboratory of Anthropology. Those latter notes are the basis of almost a dozen publications on the Comanches by members of the Field Party (Carlson and Jones 1940; Hoebel 1936, 1939, 1940, 1941, 1954; Linton 1935, 1936; Linton in Kardiner 1945; Wallace and Hoebel 1952; Wedel 1977) and countless secondary publications. Both sets of notes are presented here in full.

My interest in these documents began in the early 1980s, when I made a close reading of E. Adamson Hoebel's *The Political Organization and Law-Ways of the Comanche Indians* (1940) for background material for a dissertation proposal on modern Comanche politics. I had read *Law-Ways* before, albeit cursorily, but in that later reading I realized that one of my acquaintances at the Smithsonian Institution, Waldo R. Wedel, Curator of North American Archaeology, had been a member of the Field Party (Hoebel 1940:5). In the winter of 1983, while on a Christmas visit back to Maryland, I took the opportunity to meet with Waldo to ask him about his Comanche experiences. During the conversations that followed, he showed me his original notebooks and allowed me to cite them in publications (Kavanagh 1985, 1986).

In 1987 I returned to the Smithsonian on a string of grant- and contract-based projects. In an off hour, I approached Waldo about the possibilities of working up his material culture notes for publication, using the collections of the National Museum as illustrations. He liked the idea; indeed, he had begun to do it himself years before. He allowed me to photocopy all of his original notebooks and his various attempts at "working them up."[1] He also allowed me to copy

---

1. For the processing of Wedel's notes, see below, page 18.

the original negatives of his 1933 photographs.[1]

Although, the illustrated project was not feasible, my examination of Waldo's original materials confirmed a suspicion raised during our earlier conversations: they contain extensive ethnographic data about the Comanches that had not been reported in the publications of the 1933 Field Party. I wondered whether the other students' notes might also contain data not in the published materials, and I envisioned an expanded project, covering not just Waldo's material culture notes, but the entire corpus of the 1933 notes.

Both Waldo and his wife, Mildred Mott Wedel, were enthusiastic. With their encouragement, I sought out the notes of the other surviving members of the 1933 Field Party and additional documentary materials from the Laboratory of Anthropology, now a part of the Museum of New Mexico, and from other anthropologists who worked with the Comanches. I wrote to Edward Adamson Hoebel, retired from the University of Minnesota. He directed me to the Library of the American Philosophical Society (APS) in Philadelphia, where he had deposited his notes; the APS later photocopied them for me.[2] In later correspondence, Hoebel provided photographs and other reminiscences about the Field Party. I thank him for his assistance. I also wrote to Field Party member Gustav G. Carlson, retired from the University of Cincinnati. He graciously sent me all of his surviving materials.[3] Dr. Willow Roberts, former archivist of the Museum of New Mexico, provided copies of the administrative papers of the Field Party. Of the other members of the Field Party, little trace of them or their notes has been found.

1. Wedel later deposited those materials in the National Anthropological Archives, Smithsonian Institution.

2. American Philosophical Society, Collection 43 (Accessions 1985-924ms, 1987-1563ms, 1993-1749ms, 1994-771ms, 1995-960ms, and 1995-1180ms). For the processing of Hoebel's note cards, see below, page 18.

3. After making photocopies of those fragile original pages, I deposited them in the National Anthropological Archives. For the processing of Carlson's notes, see below, page 19.

PART ONE

The 1933 Comanche Field Party

Introduction

In late June 1933, six anthropologists—one professor and five male graduate students[1]—met at the Hotel Midland in Lawton, Oklahoma (Linton 1933b). They would spend the next six weeks recording traditional Comanche culture as remembered by eighteen Comanche elders.[2]

The six anthropologists came from diverse academic backgrounds and had diverse research goals. The leader, Ralph Linton, at that time on the faculty of the University of Wisconsin, was an established anthropologist.[3] He had carried out archeological fieldwork in New Jersey and the Southwest, ethnographic fieldwork on a number of Pacific islands, and published several articles and pamphlets on the Pawnee Indians. However, this was his first, and apparently only, Native American ethnographic fieldwork (Linton and Wagley 1971).

1. Besides the five male graduate students, two females were associated with the Field Party: Hoebel's wife, F. Gore Hoebel, and Martha Champion (later Mrs. E. P. Randle), a recent graduate in anthropology from the University of Wisconsin, Linton's academic home. Their presence was the cause of some concern in Santa Fe because in 1931 a female anthropology student studying the White Mountain Apaches in Arizona had been murdered (Woodbury 1987). Although that was not a Laboratory of Anthropology field school, it did result in a ban on female students participating in Laboratory-sponsored field parties.

Gore Hoebel had a semi-active role in the Field Party interviews. According to one of Hoebel's note cards, she served as recorder; in addition, Wallace and Hoebel (1952:260) states that she participated in the interviews with Herkeyah. Nothing further is known of her as an anthropologist.

Martha Champion, other than being mentioned in Linton's final report (Linton 1933d), has no presence in the Field Party documentation. She received a Ph.D. in anthropology from Columbia University in 1946, and published a number of works on the Iroquois and on Fox peyotism (Slobodin 1966), but she never published anything about the Comanches. My thanks to Richard Wilsnack, David Price, and Mike Pavlik (p.c. 2002) for biographical information on Champion.

2. Linton stated: "The Comanche were selected for study partly because very little ethnological work had previously been done with this tribe and partly because it contained many individuals who had been reared under aboriginal conditions" (Linton 1933d). If "individuals reared under aboriginal conditions" meant reaching adulthood before 1875, perhaps only one-third of the adult Comanche population in 1933 so qualified. Of the consultants interviewed by the 1933 Field Party, only two, Tahsuda and Teneverka, qualified.

3. Wallace and Hoebel (1952:x) cites Linton as being from Yale University, but he did not go to Yale until 1946.

Gustav ('Gust') Gunner Carlson was a first-year graduate student at the University of Michigan. He admitted that his participation in the Field Party was "premature" (p.c. 1990). He would spend his entire academic career at the University of Cincinnati. Aside from his ethnobotanical study (Carlson and Jones 1940), he did not publish further on the Comanches.

James Nixon ('Nick') Hadley was a graduate student at Columbia University. He had been on the previous year's Field Party to the Oklahoma Seminoles, and he had obtained special funding through Franz Boas and Alfred M. Tozzer to attend the Comanche session (Linton 1933a). Of Hadley's academic career after the Field Party, little is visible. He did some work for the Bureau of Indian Affairs in the late 1940s (Hadley, Young, and Morgan 1948), but any further institutional affiliations and publications are unknown. None of Hadley's Comanche notes have been located.[1]

Edward Adamson ('Ad') Hoebel was also a graduate student at Columbia. His participation in the Field Party was explicitly to gather materials for a doctoral dissertation on "primitive law" (Hoebel 1940:5). Although still a graduate student at Columbia, Hoebel was already teaching at New York University and he remained there through 1948. Later, he taught at the University of Utah (1948–54) and at the University of Minnesota (1954–68). He served as president of the American Ethnological Society (1946–47) and the American Anthropological Association (1957). He became a member of the American Philosophical Society in 1963. Hoebel was the most prolific of the 1933 Field Party students with six works directly derived from that fieldwork (Hoebel 1936, 1939, 1940, 1941, 1954; Wallace and Hoebel 1952); the latter work has been through at least ten printings without revision, although Hoebel added a new preface for the ninth printing in 1986.

Henry Claiborne ('Clay') Lockett was a graduate student in archaeology at the University of Arizona. Why he applied to the Field Party is not known. According to Field Party documents, he focused on religion and doctoring in his Comanche interviews (Linton 1933c). After the Field School, he did not pursue an academic career. Instead, he managed an Indian arts and crafts store in Tucson and later the store at the Museum of Northern Arizona in Flagstaff (Wedel, p.c. 1990). Although I conducted an extensive telephone correspondence with his family, we were unable to locate any of his notes.

Waldo Rudolph Wedel entered Bethel College in Newton, Kansas, and after two years transferred to the University of Arizona, where he received a B.A. in 1930. He earned an M.A. at the University of Nebraska in 1931; his thesis was an analysis of historical Pawnee artifacts in the university's collection. He then enrolled in the doctoral program of the Department of Anthropology at the University of California, Berkeley. Wedel applied to the Field Party on the advice of Alfred L. Kroeber, who wanted him to get more experience in ethnology. Before joining the Field Party in Oklahoma, he spent the spring of 1933 on a survey of ancestral Pawnee sites in southwestern Nebraska. In later years, Wedel became the dean of Central Plains archaeologists, spending his entire career, 1936 to 1990, at the Smithsonian Institution. Other than his reminiscences he never published on the Comanches (Wedel 1977).

1. My thanks to Phillip Young, Christopher Pound, and Samuel Stanley (p.c. 2002) for information on Hadley.

The 1933 Consultants

The Field Party's notes acknowledge seventeen Comanche consultants by name, with at least two unidentified consultants.[1] Hoebel's note cards include a list of sixteen consultants, and Hoebel (1940) provides brief biographies of twelve "primary" consultants. The seventeen named consultants are:

Herman Asenap

Herman Bluefoot, ésənap.[2] Born of a captive Mexican father and a full blood Comanche mother, Herman served as our chief interpreter and go-between. Highly respected for his leadership abilities he was ideal in his role, for he never obtruded his personality upon the informant, but served always as a skillful transmitter of ideas between Comanche and ourselves. Age 50. [Hoebel 1940:143]

According to the Family Record Book, seconded by Herman (June 30–July1), his father was a "Mexican captured when a child,"[3] but whether "Mexican" meant Euro-American, Mestizo, or Mexican Indian is unknown. Herman's mother, Tahchockah,[4] was born about 1858. They were affiliated with Coby's[5] Kwaharʉnʉʉ local band.

---

1. My identifications of the consultants and other individuals mentioned in the notes are based on interviews with Comanches and on several sets of records, particularly the Comanche censuses, 1876–1939, and the Family Record Book at the Kiowa Agency Office of the Bureau of Indian Affairs. The earliest extant name-based Comanche census dates from July 1876, recording the Penatʉhka local bands of Tosawa and Esihabit, then residing at the Wichita Agency north of the Washita River at modern Anadarko. These two lists, and the Comanche-wide censuses from 1879, 1881, 1883, 1885, 1889, 1892, and 1895, are at the Oklahoma Historical Society and available on microfilm rolls OHS-KA 1 and 1a. The annual lists from 1899 to 1939 are at the National Archives, microfilm publication M595, rolls 211–23. The 1879–92 lists are essentially organized by local band (by the band chief's name, although not in divisional order), and then in family order within the band. (However, the order of the bands, and of the families within them, varies from census to census.) From 1892 to 1929 the same order is maintained, but band chiefs are not explicitly recognized. The lists after 1929 are in alphabetical order by head-of-family patronym.
   The Family Record Book was compiled at the time of allotment (1901-2), apparently as an aid in resolving heirship problems. It lists all allottees and their parents in the order of the 1901 census. It sometimes also lists the adult's siblings and other relatives as comments. Although individual names are based on the 1901 census, parental and other names, especially those of the deceased, were not correlated with previous lists for spelling. Thus, it is often difficult to establish definite links with names on previous lists. A fair typescript photocopy of the Family Record Book is in the Genealogy Room of the Lawton Public Library (Murphy 1991).
   2. *esi* 'gray' *napʉ*; the latter can be variously 'lower leg', 'foot', 'shoe', or 'moccasin'. The 1879 census has Gray Moccasin. Wallace and Hoebel (1952:xi, 123) gives this name as Gray Foot.
   Asenap may be an old Comanche name. In 1899, Noah Smithwick, who had been a Texas Ranger in the 1830s, recalled that one of the men present at the Comanche village he had visited in 1836 (some 60 years earlier) was named Esanap (Smithwick 1983:125). Except for the censuses, the name does not occur in any other document that Smithwick might have seen.
   3. The Family Record Book estimates the elder Asenap to be forty-seven years old in 1901; thus he would have been born, and then captured, in the mid-to-late 1860s.
   4. Possibly *tsatUkarʉ* 'shoot'. Corwin (1959:95) gives it as Shoots Something.
   5. *kobi* 'mustang, wild horse'.

The Family Record Book gives Herman's age in 1901 as fifteen, born about 1886; he would have been about forty-eight in 1933. His Comanche name was Nahdahtissuwah, untranslated in the agency records, but according to Lawton journalist Hugh Corwin (1959:95), it was Dancing to Sleep. That translation has not been confirmed.

In 1893, at age eight, Herman was enrolled in the Fort Sill Indian School, where he obtained his knowledge of English. He served as interpreter for the Post Oak Mission, the agency, and the army at Fort Sill. In addition, he was an interpreter for George Herzog and David McAllester (1939) and, in 1940, consultant and interpreter for Joseph B. Casagrande (1954–55, I:140).

Rhoda Asenap

Rhoda Bluefoot. Wife of Herman Bluefoot, daughter of a well-known medicine man and warrior. Too young to have had a great deal of knowledge in the old culture, most of her information was secondary. Her services were as interpreter when working with woman informants.[1] Age 45 (?). [Hoebel 1940:143]

According to the censuses, Rhoda, also known as Rose, was born in 1890; she would have been forty-three in 1933. She was the daughter of Pahdopony[2] and Mamanetah,[3] and the older sister of Ernest Wallace's 1945 consultant John (also known as Mack) Pahdopony (Wallace and Hoebel 1952: xi).[4] Her parents belonged to Quanah's Kwaharʉnʉʉ local band.

Atauvich

The Family Record Book lists Atauvich[5] as the son of Coby and Ternahvoney[6]; he was twenty-nine in 1901, thus born about 1872, and sixty-two in 1933. His father was an important Kwaharʉnʉʉ divisional leader. Atauvich's mother must have died shortly after his birth, because all of the early censuses list him as living with his maternal grandmother, Hopahrah,[7] in Quanah's Kwaharʉnʉʉ local band. His older half-sister Weckeah (same mother, different father) was Quanah's second wife.

Hoebel lists Atauvich (spelled It)bits) on his note-card index of consultants. Carlson attributes several notes to him, dated August 7, 9, and 14. Hoebel has four note cards (one double, three single) attributed to him, two of which parallel Carlson's notes. There is a single reference to Atauvich in Hoebel (1940:121) where the name is spelled Itoβits. George Herzog

---

1. Although there is no direct evidence in the notes that Rhoda served as interpreter, she is cited as a consultant by Wedel (July 7, 12) and Hoebel (Undated).

2. *paaʔroponi, paa* 'water', *punitʉ* 'see'. The census gives it as Water Measurer. Wallace and Hoebel (1952:x) translates it poetically as See How Deep The Water Is.

3. No translation given. According to the Family Record Book, she was the daughter of a captive.

4. Ernest Wallace's papers at Texas Tech University apparently do not include any notes of his 1945 interviews (Texas Tech University Southwest Collections/Special Collections Library, S 1133.1).

5. *ata* 'other', *pitsI* emphatic modifier, i.e., a 'foreigner'. McAllester (1949:33) comments that the term was "'foreigner' in the sense of 'other Indian' not 'white man'."

6. No translation given. Otherwise unidentified.

7. No translation given. Otherwise unidentified.

and David McAllester interviewed him in 1939; in their field notes, they spell the name ʔiTovic, while McAllester (1949) spells it Itovic.

Frank Chekovi

Breaks Something, tʃíkoβa.[1] His information centered mostly about his own personal experiences as a medicine man and in damage settlements. A most conscientious informant who provided valuable material. A member of the Antelope band. Age (?). [Hoebel 1940:143]

The 1892 census lists Frank as thirty-one years old, giving a birth year of 1861, and making him about seventy-two in 1933. The Family Record Book lists his parents as Mocho[2] and Meahka.[3] The 1879 census lists him as a member of Coby's Kwaharʉnʉʉ local band, as do later censuses, although by his own testimony he lived for a while with the Yapainʉʉ near Saddle Mountain (Frank Chekovi, Undated III).

Frank had a total of five wives, but children by only two of them. The name of his first wife is not remembered. The second was Nauni,[4] with whom he had three children; they separated in the early 1890s. Frank's third wife was Wifeper,[5] with whom he had a son. By the mid-1890s, they had separated. Wifeper then married George Koweno, and Frank married Mahken-abitty,[6] remaining with her until her death in January 1923. He then married Pedahny, half-sister of George Koweno, with whom he was living in 1933 (see Pedahny below).

Frank was elected to the Kiowa-Comanche-Apache Business Committee in 1914, but because he was a peyote man, the agent did not accept him and apparently he did not serve. He was present at the celebratory peyote meeting led by Post Oak Jim in 1918 after the defeat of anti-peyote legislation; that meeting was also attended by James Mooney (1918). He was one of Günter Wagner's consultants (1932b).[7]

1. The 1879 census gives this name as Broken Dagger. Mooney (1918) spells it Chikova, and gives it as 'broken off'. Wallace and Hoebel (1952:xi) spells it Chikoβa. However, rather than being based on one of the several Comanche verbs meaning 'break', this name is probably based on the second element in his Comanche name, *kwihnaitsukuhpʉʔ*, *kwihnai* 'eagle', *tsukuhpʉʔ* 'old'.

2. Possibly *motso* 'beard'. Otherwise unidentified.

3. No translation given. Otherwise unidentified.

4. This name is not linguistically transparent, but it has historical importance. In 1852, Robert S. Neighbors suggested that the term *"na-ü-ni,"* signifying "first or live people," was the Comanches' own name for themselves (1852:126). However, it is difficult to get from that to *nʉmʉnʉʉ*, the actual Comanche self-designation. In the same article, Neighbors identified a component band as the "No-na-um, because they live in the high prairie where there is no timber or running water, and never leave that kind of country" (1852:128). This is reminiscent of the ethnonyms (group names) "Nonah" and "Noonah" used in 1846 by U.S. agents Pierce M. Butler and M. G. Lewis (Butler 1846; Butler and Lewis 1846). The former is not translated, but the latter is given as "People of the Desert." These latter three terms are close to *nōnī*, the modern Comanche pronunciation of Nauni. In the 1885 census, the name Nauni is given as 'young girl', but that is probably a confusion with *naiʔbi* 'young woman'. The present-day Nauni family, paralleling Neighbors, suggest it means 'Ridge People' (Raymond Nauni, Jr., p. c. 2004).

5. *waiʔpʉ* 'woman'. See below, Frank Chekovi, Undated III.

6. Translated as 'grasping'. Robinson and Armagost (1990) gives 'grasp' as *matsarʉ*.

7. Günter Wagner was a German anthropologist who visited the Comanches in 1932. He had previously conducted research on the peyote religion in eastern Oklahoma (1932a). He intended to make a major comparative study, but could not get the necessary funding. His Comanche research, he wrote,

Herkeyah

Carrying Her Sunshade, həkiyáni.[1] Captured as a seven-year-old child in a Comanche raid upon her schoolhouse in old Mexico, she has lived through a fantastic life history, and at the age of 90 survives with her very active 75-year-old daughter, born of a Comanche chief. A capable informant. [Hoebel 1940:144]

The censuses do not mention Herkeyah before 1889. There she is recorded as the wife of Esahaupt,[2] who ten years earlier was listed as the "headman" of a group of eight people in two families. The 1892 census lists her as forty-four years old, giving a birth year in the late 1840s, and a capture year in the mid 1850s; she was about eighty-five in 1933.

Hoebel (1940) gives no divisional affiliation for either Herkeyah or her husband, nor do any of the agency records. Richard Pratt's notebook on the Indian prisoners at Fort Marion[3] (1875–77) states that Esahaupt was the "brother of White Wolf"; Esarosavit, White Wolf, was Yapainʉʉ, suggesting that Esahaupt was as well. Herkeyah herself said that she "switched from the Noyʉhka to the Kwaharʉnʉʉ band" (August 14).

According to the Family Record Book, Herkeyah had two daughters, though with different men. The first was Weyahbitty,[4] born about 1865, who would have been about sixty-eight years old in 1933; there is, however, no record of her after 1901. The other (with Esahaupt) was Pahvoput,[5] born in 1884 and thus forty-nine years old in 1933.

George Koweno

Kowíno, (?) Yap eater, now deacon of the Mennonite Church, only slightly useful as an informant. [Hoebel 1940:143]

George Koweno,[6] apparently also known as Big George,[7] was born in the early 1870s. The 1885 census lists him in the family of Werkoni[8] and Puhawitsi,[9] along with a younger half-sibling, Pedahny. The Family Record Book lists his parents as Chenahvony and Chanah,[10] and,

---

"consisted of two parts, (a) a study of the traditional Comanche culture, today of a prevailing historical nature, and (b) a study of present day conditions.

"As to the traditional culture, I have obtained most material on certain aspects of social life (dances, warfare, chieftainship, birth and death-customs, games) and religious life (the vision-quest, religious symbolism and medicine believes [sic] and practices)" (1932b:4).

Of Wagner's fourteen Comanche consultants, six would later work with the 1933 Field Party. Unfortunately, he did not write up his Comanche materials and his notes were lost during World War II. My thanks to Jason Baird Jackson for information about Wagner.

1. Robinson and Armagost (1990) gives *hʉʉkI* 'shade' and *yahkatʉ* 'hold, have something in the hand'. Hoebel's notes give her name as Holding Something up for Shade. Hoebel (1940:97) has Carrying A Sunshade.

2. *isa ohaptU* 'yellow wolf'.

3. My thanks to Wahnee Clark for bringing the Pratt notebook to my attention.

4. No translation given. Otherwise unidentified.

5. *pahvo* 'clear' or 'white'.

6. No translation given.

7. From a comment on one of Hoebel's note cards.

8. Given on the census as Ring.

9. Literally, 'hunting for medicine'.

10. Both otherwise unidentified; the latter is probably *tseenah* 'wolf'.

in several side notes, indicates that he and Pedahny were the nephew and niece of Puhawitsi, rather than her children.[1] This seems to imply that George and Pedahny, were orphaned at an early age and grew up in the household of their aunt. They were associated with the Yapainʉʉ local bands of Tatchymotohovit[2] and later, Howeah.[3] In the 1920s, George was interviewed by Grace Hebard as part of her historical research on the possibility that Sacajawea had Comanche connections (Hebard 1932). He was also one of Günter Wagner's consultants (1932b).

In the mid-1890s, George married Wifeper, also known as Mary Kiowa and Mary Koweno, and he adopted the son she had with Frank Chekovi. The son became known as Felix Kowena,[4] and he was one of Günter Wagner's interpreters (1932b).

Frank Moetah

Hoebel lists Frank Moetah[5] on his note card index of consultants. Carlson attributed one dated note to him; Hoebel attributed several note cards to him, none of which parallel Carlson's note. Carlson interviewed him on August 16, probably at the dance north of Walters. It is not known when Hoebel interviewed him.

Moeteh was born about 1863, the son of Kerpaquechy and Naevite,[6] associated with Neithkawoofpi's[7] local band. Although he was married several times, he apparently had no children who survived to adulthood. By 1933, Moetah had long been involved in political activities. Beginning in the1890s, he, along with Quenatosavit[8] and Mamsookawat[9] were often

---

1. Those same notes state that Frank Chekovi was also a nephew of Puhawitsi.

2. *tatsunuupl* 'star'; *tuhupl* 'black', Black Star.

3. *hu* 'wood', *wia* 'worn away spot', usually translated as Timber Gap.

4. His surname is spelled with a final "a" to distinguish it from Koweno. He was also known as James Pedicks, that surname from the Comanche pronunciation of Felix. See below, Frank Chekovi, Undated III.

5. *mo* 'nose'. It is sometimes translated as Roman Nose or Pug Nose. Wallace and Hoebel spells it Moeta (1952:275) .

6. Both otherwise unidentified. The former is possibly based on *ke* 'no, not', *pa* 'water'. The latter may be *nai'bi* 'young woman'.

7. *neki'* belt', *kwibukitʉ* 'whip', Belt Whip. His divisional affiliation is unclear.

8. On the reservation censuses his name appears as White Eagle. He was also known as Isatai (variously spelled), often translated as Rear End of a Wolf or as Coyote Droppings. The latter is incorrect—that would be *isakwita*—but the former is essentially correct, although delicate, for it omits the wolf's gender (see Tahsuda, Undated). He was the prophet of 1874, and it is sometimes said that the name Isatai was bestowed on him in ridicule after the failure of his *puha* at the Battle of Adobe Walls, June 27, 1874 (e.g., Mihesuah 2002:3). If true, it occurred very soon after the battle, for a little less than a year later, in May, 1875, Dr. J. J. Sturm, sent by the army to persuade the Comanches to surrender, met with "Isah-tite," who was, arguably, the *paraivo* of the Comanche group (Sturm 1875:14; Wallace 1978:237). In 1879, he was the leader of the fourth-largest local band, with 91 people in his group (Hunt 1879). He was one of Lowie's consultants in 1912.

9. This name has been spelled variously. The 1879 census spells it Mamsookawat, which is followed here. The earliest published version of the name that I know of is a photograph caption in Babb (1912:35), which has it as Charley Mumcyki. I know of no other similar spelling, nor any other reference to a first name. The Bureau of American Ethnology photograph of him, taken during the 1918 Congressional anti-peyote hearings, is captioned "Mumshukawa." Although Wallace and Hoebel uses that caption (1952: facing page 271), and that is the spelling that is indexed, their text gives the name as "Mʌmsɜka."

in political opposition to Quanah (Hagan 1976:244).

Niyah

> Slope, náyia.[1] Easy going, genial, a Comanche who sees all life in its humorous aspects. Generously helpful with the information he possesses (except the nature of his secret herbs), with his interest in people and things he can provide much anecdotal material. Of Those Who Turn Back From Raids band.[2] Age 57. [Hoebel 1940:143]

The Family Record Book lists Niyah, also called Emerson Niyah, as the son of Habbywake[3] and Yahpoyah,[4] but there is no mention of him on any census before 1889; the 1892 census lists him as thirteen years old, born about 1879, and about fifty-four in 1933. He was a consultant for Günter Wagner (1932b), and later for David McAllester and George Herzog (1939; McAllester 1949:47).

The 1885 census translates the name as Lawless. Robinson and Armagost (1990) and the Comanche Cultural Committee (2003) give *masukaa* as 'feel around with the hand', -*waitᵤ* 'similar to', a translation given to me independently. At the same time, Robinson and Armagost (1990) gives *momᵤsaka* as 'firetender in a peyote meeting.' That he was, but it was his ritual role, not a translation of his name, nor conversely, the title of the role of firetender.

As with his name, there is some confusion about his age. The 1885 and 1892 censuses give his age as 36 and 44 respectively, suggesting a birth year of either 1848 or 1849. Later censuses record ages that indicate a birth year of 1838. Therefore, he would have been between 85 and 95 years old in 1933 (see below, Unidentified Consultant, Undated).

The Family Record Book gives his parents as Kokey and Yayake (both otherwise unidentified) and describes him as "7/8 Comanche, 1/8 Mexican." Mamsookawat himself commented at a council meeting at Fort Sill on January 2, 1926: "It was over seventy years ago that I was captured" (Buntin 1926) implying that he himself was a captive, rather than a captive three generations removed.

In the nineteenth century, Mamsookawat was a member of Tomichicut's Kwaharᵤnᵤᵤ local band. In 1908, he was appointed to the KCA Business Committee (Hagan 1976:289). After Isatai's death in 1915, Mamsookawat "desired to assume leadership over the band of Comanches living along Beaver Creek" in southeastern Cotton county, east of Walters (Stecker 1915). He was a member of the 1918 delegation to Washington to protest the anti-peyote bill before Congress (when his portrait was made by the Bureau of American Ethnology).

1. The censuses, Hoebel (1940), and Wallace and Hoebel (1952:xi) spell this name Niyah; Wedel and Herzog and McAllester (1939:2) spell it Naiya; McAllester (1949:47) spells it Naya. The censuses do not give a translation. Robinson and Armagost (1990) gives *naᵖᵁyatᵁ* and *nahᵤyaᵁ* as 'sloping'.

2. Presumably, "Those Who Turn Back From Raids" is the same as Hoebel's "Those Who Turn Back" (Hoebel 1940:13; Wallace and Hoebel 1952:26), i.e., Nokoni. Niyah identified himself as Tanimanᵤᵤ (see below, Niyah, July 6).

3. Probably *habi* 'lying down' *weeki* 'look for', Looking for Sleep. Habbywake was J. J. Sturm's guide to the hostile Kwaharᵤnᵤᵤ camps in the spring of 1875 (Sturm 1875; Wallace 1978; Kavanagh 1996: 450–51), but he must have died about the time of Niyah's birth, for he is not listed on any Comanche census.

4. No translation given. Otherwise unidentified.

Nemaruibetsi

'Get Your Neighbor', nɜmɜɹuiβetsi.[1] An effective woman informant from the Swift Stingers[2] band. She gave much comprehensive information. Age (?). Her name is also translated as "Visits her Relatives." [Hoebel 1940:144]

According to her own testimony, in 1933 she was "over seventy years old," born about 1862. She did not remember either her father or mother, although the Family Record Book lists them as Nemahsie and Chahmunny (both otherwise unidentified). The Family Record Book also states that her father was a Shoshone. According to her life story, after a harsh childhood, she ran off with Quanah, ultimately staying with his Kwaharʉnʉʉ local band for the rest of her life.

Ohataipa

Although Hoebel lists Ohataipa[3] in his note card index of consultants, and his cards include a single note attributed to him, he is otherwise unidentified, and there is no comparable name on the census lists.

Pedahny

Pedahny[4] was Frank Chekovi's wife in 1933. She was born about 1877, the daughter of Pahwoonard[5] and Chanah,[6] and was George Koweno's half-sister. Both parents were affiliated with Esananaka's[7] and later Attocknie's[8] Yapainʉʉ local bands, although Pedahny herself was also affiliated with several other Yapainʉʉ local bands.[9] Carlson identified her as the source for two notes on August 11, although Wedel's parallel notes do not indicate a change of speaker from Frank.

1. This name is not listed on any census before 1889, where it is recorded as Nemadooahvische. Although I generally follow the agency spelling of names, here I have decided to use the form given by Hoebel. Besides Get Your Neighbor, Hoebel, in his appendices, identifies her as She Invites Her Relatives (1940:146) and Visits Her Relatives (1940:147). The former is more correct. According to the Rev. Reaves Nahwooks, present holder of her allotment, the name is *nʉmʉrʉi* 'lady friends', *petsʉ* 'invite'(p.c. 2002).
2. Presumably, Swift Stingers is the same as Hoebel's Quick-Stingers (Hoebel 1940:13; Wallace and Hoebel 1952:25). Nemaruibetsi herself stated that she belonged to the Penanʉʉ (Nemaruibetsi, July 31).
3. *oha-* 'yellow', *turepu* 'infant'.
4. No translation given.
5. Given on the 1879 census as Tall Man, although this has not been confirmed. The Family Record Book lists him as a Mexican captive. See Wallace and Hoebel 1952: 260.
6. Possibly *tseenah* 'wolf'.
7. *isa* 'wolf', *nanaka* 'noise, sound'. The 1879 census gave it as Howling Wolf. Hoebel translated it poetically as Echo of the Wolf's Howl. He was Parʉasʉmʉno's stepson.
8. *ata* 'other', *kahne* 'house'. His wife was Esananaka's niece.
9. 1885: Tatchymotohavit; 1889: Howeah; 1892: Sowe.

Post Oak Jim

Post Oak Jim.[1] (?) An active, unusually extroverted Comanche with a colorful and notorious history, now a famous Peyote leader and singer. A willing and self-regarding informant, but not reliable on all respects.[2] Of Those Who Turn Back From Raids. Age 64. [Hoebel 1940:143]

Post Oak Jim was the principal source for the 1933 Field Party, contributing about twenty percent of the total number of notes.[3] Indeed, many modern Comanches recognize Post Oak Jim as a major conduit for their knowledge of traditional Comanche culture. Yet, paradoxically, for one so important in the transmission of Comanche culture, there is relatively little documentary evidence about him. He is not clearly identifiable on any census before 1901. According to the Family Record Book, Post Oak Jim was thirty years old in 1901, born about 1871, so he would have been about sixty-three in 1933. The Family Record Book gives his Comanche name as Tahkahper, *takahpʉ* 'poor person', although according to his own testimony (July 18), his Comanche name was Towoibita or Toboibita[4]; neither of those names appears in the agency records.

Jim married one of Coby's daughters, but none of his children survived to adulthood.

Jim sponsored the celebratory peyote meeting in 1918 after the defeat of the anti-peyote bill in Congress (Mooney 1918), and he was one of Günter Wagner's consultants (1932b).

Quassyah

Eagle Tail Feather, qwásia.[5] A member of the Those Who Move Often Band. Quiet, responsible and respected, one of the most reliable of Comanche informants, inclined however, to resist rapport with whites. Age 56. [Hoebel 1940:143]

According to the censuses and the Family Record Book, Quassyah was born between 1862 and 1865 and therefore, between sixty-eight and seventy-one years old in 1933.

The Family Record Book lists his father as Pahkeah,[6] corroborated by Post Oak Jim (July

1. The post oak (*Quercus stellata*) is a medium sized tree, about thirty feet tall, common in western Oklahoma. La Barre (1975:52) calls him Jim Post-oak.

2. Unfortunately, Hoebel did not indicate which features of Post Oak Jim's comments he felt were "unreliable."

3. According to Thurman (1982:243), Post Oak Jim was cited forty-one times (twenty-one per cent of identified consultant citations) in Wallace and Hoebel (1952). Based on the concordance in Appendix B below, which tallies uncited references as well, his contribution to that work was closer to twenty-five percent.

4. Translated as 'bunch of people standing' (Wedel) and 'a group of men standing on a hill' (Hoebel). Robinson and Armagost (1990) has *toboʔkatʉ* 'stand'.

5. *kwasi* 'tail', *sia* 'feather'. The 1879 census has the name as Tail Hold. There is nothing in the name specifically about holding or eagles.

6. This is the agency spelling from the 1879 census. The Family Record Book spells it Packyer; Wedel's notes spell it Paxkia; Hoebel's notes spell it Paxkih&. It is translated on the 1879 census as Hard Robe. Wedel's notes have it as Stiff Robe. Robinson and Armagost (1990) gives *pahkipʉ* as 'rawhide'. Pahkeah was born about 1809 and died after 1892.

Nye (1969:9) states that Quassyah was the son of Pah-kah, one of the signers of the Camp Holmes Treaty of 1835. That treaty translates that name as The Man Who Draws the Bow, possibly from *paka* 'arrow'. Whether Pahkah and Pahkeah were identical is unknown.

14), and his mother as Sahvora.[1] In contrast to Hoebel's attribution of Quassyah to the Noyʉhka division, both Pahkeah and Quassyah were associated with Yuniwat's, and later with Pahdi's, local Yapainʉʉ bands. Quassyah married Toarchi,[2] daughter of the early modern peyote man, Poewat,[3] but apparently none of his children survived beyond 1920.

In the 1890s, Quassyah was a member of the Kiowa Agency police, and possibly chief of police in 1901.[4] He was elected to the Kiowa-Comanche-Apache Business Committee in 1916. That year, the agent said of him:

> [He is] connected with the Peyote eaters and is looked upon as a leader. I believe he will not be antagonistic to government policies if permitted to serve as committeeman. [Stinchicum 1916]

However, the business committee was disbanded the next year as unnecessary with allotment.

Quassyah was a most experienced consultant: he was interviewed by Robert Lowie in 1912 (see Part Two, below); by Günter Wagner in 1932 (1932b); by Wilbur Nye in 1933 (1969); and by George Herzog and David McAllester in 1939 (1939).

Tahsuda

> That's It, tasʉɹa.[5] One of the finest of all possible informants, unassuming, intelligent, and versed with an astounding knowledge of Comanche ways and events. Entirely cooperative and appreciative of the purpose of the study. One of the few surviving members of the Water Horse band.[6] Age 79. [Hoebel 1940:143]

The 1879 census lists Tahsuda as a member of Tomichicut's Kwaharʉnʉʉ local band[7]; he was associated with several other Kwaharʉnʉʉ local bands before 1892.[8] Based on his own testimony[9] and the censuses, he was the son of Wahatoya[10] and Chieyah,[11] and the grandson of EkamokUsa.[12] The 1885 list gives his age as twenty-eight, born about 1857, and was about

1. No translation was given, and no similar name appears on the censuses.
2. No translation given.
3. No Eyes; he was blind. He was present at the 1892 peyote meeting photographed by James Mooney; the photos are in the National Anthropological Archives (Kavanagh 1993).
4. See below, Quassyah, July 5.
5. The 1879 census translates this name as Kidney Fat, possibly derived from *taʔkiʔ* 'kidney', *yuhu* 'fat'. The translation as That's It has not been confirmed.
6. The Field Party notes are the only documentary occurrence of this ethnonym. This does not invalidate it, but suggests that it was a local band name rather than a major political division.
   Hoebel's notes spell it Pahuraix. Given the translation, it apparently derives from *pa* 'water', *tʉhʉya* 'horse', that is, 'elk.' Given the normal internal sound shift of *t* to *r*, *patʉhʉya* produces *parʉhʉya*, which could further reduce to *parʉa*. However, this causes confusion with the homophone *parʉa* 'bear'. The Comanche Cultural Committee (2003) spells 'elk' as *parʉhya*, which I follow here. (To get Pahuraix, I can only guess that Hoebel somehow switched the consonants *r* and *h*).
7. If Tomichicut's local band was the Parʉhya, Mamsookawat was the only other survivor in 1933.
8. 1883: Tocas; 1885 Kodose; 1892: Todoessy.
9. See below, Tahsuda, Undated.
10. Two Mountains. This name is also the Comanche toponym for the Spanish Peaks, the double mountain in southern Colorado, just north of Raton Pass.
11. No translation given.
12. *ekapI* 'red' *makwUsàʔ* 'sleeve', possibly the Red Sleeve killed in 1847 (Mooney 1898:286).

seventy-six in 1933.

Despite Hoebel's glowing report, Tahsuda provided relatively few notes as compared with Post Oak Jim or Niyah. Moreover, some his more interesting materials, such as his story cycle, were not used in any of the Field Party's publications.

Teneverka

Gets To Be a Middle-aged Man, tɛneβɜkə.[1] An obstinate and tantalizing informant, he is the "greatest" of the living Comanches, for he is the sole surviving member of the band of five warriors who stole all 121 horses from the U.S. Cavalry at Fort Sill in 1871.[2] Buffalo Eater Band. Age 89. [Hoebel 1940:143]

The 1879 census lists Teneverka as a member of Taboconavische's[3] local band, but by 1885, he was the leader of a small group of his own. The divisional affiliation of either of these bands as Kutsutɨhka is not directly attested.

Documentary details about Teneverka are confused. According to his headstone in the Deyo Mission cemetery, he was born in 1835 and died in 1945, aged 110. The unreliable 1885 census lists him as thirty-five years old (i.e., born about 1850). The Family Record Book gives his age as forty-five in 1901 (i.e., born about 1856). According to the Family Record Book, he was the son of Ekakorohko[4] and Tosee.[5] Although married several times, Teneverka apparently had no children.

His is an old name: the 1835 Treaty of Camp Holmes lists one signer as Tennowikkah, translated as 'The Boy Who Becomes a Man' (Kappler 1972:39).

Norton Tahquechi

Skinny and Wrinkled, tekwitʃi. Interpreter. A Carlyle graduate.[6] Age 45. [Hoebel 1940:144]

It is unclear why Hoebel included Norton in his list of "primary" consultants, since he contributed little ethnographic information and his "interpreter" functions are only briefly directly attested (Norton Tahquechi, Undated).

Norton was born in 1894, and thus was thirty-nine years old in 1933. He was the son of

---

1. *tenahpɨʔ* 'man', *pɨhka* 'become.' This name is given on the censuses as both Teneverka and Tenawerka. The latter form was used by Nye (1969).

2. It is not clear where Hoebel got the specific data on the theft of the Fort Sill horses. There is no mention of it in Teneverka's one interview with Hoebel (Wallace and Hoebel 1952:317). The 1871 date of the raid given in Hoebel (1940:144) is incorrect, as is the date 1878 in the photograph caption in Wallace and Hoebel (1952:opposite 334); the event occurred in June 1872 (Nye 1969:155; Richardson 1933:349). Richardson, citing agency documents, gives the number of horses taken as fifty-one; Nye, citing army documents, gives the number as fifty-four. Wallace and Hoebel, without citation or comment, gives the latter number (1952:316).

3. *tabúʔkinaʔ* 'rabbit', *kenatsɄwitɨ* 'weak', translated as Poor Rabbit.

4. *ekapl* 'red', *koruhko* 'necklace'.

5. No translation given.

6. Carlisle Indian Industrial School, in Carlisle, Penn.

Noyobad[1] and Tahquechi,[2] the daughter of Watchsuah.[3] His father had been a member of Peahnavonit's[4] Nokoni local band, and his maternal grandfather had been a member of Esarosavit's Yapainʉʉ local band.

As noted, Norton had gone to Carlisle Indian Industrial School, and he served as interpreter for a number of interviews. In addition to his own interview on August 16, Norton made a number of comments while serving as interpreter for other interviews that were recorded by Carlson and Hoebel. In 1941, he was elected to the Kiowa-Comanche-Apache Business Committee, serving off and on until 1960.

Howard White Wolf

Although Howard White Wolf is named on Hoebel's note card index of consultants, he is not included on the list of "primary" consultants. That absence is very strange, for Howard was the principal source for political matters in both Hoebel (1940) and Wallace and Hoebel (1952).

According to the Family Record Book, Howard White Wolf was the son of Toyapoi[5] and Wunnaotah (otherwise unidentified). Born around 1867, he was about sixty-six years old in 1933.[6] His father was killed at the Battle of Adobe Walls in 1874, and he was raised by his uncle, Esarosavit, White Wolf, from whom he got his English surname. His personal name was Chowop.[7]

Howard attended the Carlisle Indian Industrial School around 1880 (Hagan 1976:163). After he returned, he became active in tribal political affairs. At a council in 1898, he served as secretary (Hagan 1976:226), but he was never elected to the council itself. He was another of Wagner's consultants (1932b), and Weston La Barre interviewed him in 1936 (1938:3).

THE FIELD PARTY'S METHODS

A few days after the rendezvous at the Hotel Midland, the Field Party moved some twenty miles west to the small village of Indiahoma. There, the Post Oak Mennonite Mission[8] served as the dormitory, and the students worked out of the nearby home of Herman Asenap. Herman served as consultant and interpreter, and arranged for other consultant visits, all of whom were paid three dollars per day (Linton 1933a).[9]

---

1. *noyo* 'testicles', *-wahtʉ* 'without'.
2. Robinson and Armagost (1990) gives *takwi-* as 'wrinkled'; it is also related to 'hunger'.
3. Dodger, said to have been a captive. See below, Post Oak Jim, July 25 and Herkeyah, Undated.
4. *pia* 'big'; *na* 'reflexive', *punitʉ* 'see', Big Mirror.
5. Possibly *toya* 'mountain', and either *puʔe* 'road, or *pui* 'eye'. Several writers give the father's name as Tsa-yat-see, but without citation (Nye 1969:191; Haley 1976:75). Otherwise unidentified.
6. Wallace and Hoebel gives his age as 80 (1952:334).
7. The 1885 census gives this as Throwing Away, but that has not been confirmed.
8. The name of the mission is only coincidentally related to the name Post Oak Jim.
9. This choice of location was no doubt influenced by correspondence the previous May between Linton and Günter Wagner. Wagner had used Magdalena Becker (Mrs. Abraham Jacob Becker), wife of the missionary at Post Oak Mission, as interpreter, and six of Wagner's consultants would serve the Field Party. Further, the consultant and interpreter fee schedule used by the Field Party was that suggested by Wagner (Linton 1933a).

According to Wedel, during the initial sessions, Linton, Asenap, and that day's consultant sat at one end of the kitchen table, while the students sat around the rest of the table taking notes. Although Linton asked the questions, he took no notes (Wedel, p.c. 1990).

There does not seem to have been a specific schedule of questions to ask or of topics to investigate. Indeed, the notes often have a rambling character, topic to topic. Linton commented, "I am now using anecdotes and personal histories, asking for explanations of points as they come up and feel that we are getting a real inside view" (Linton 1933c). Hoebel explained:

> the method of inquiry was to put pump-priming questions to the informant, who was encouraged to expound to the limit of his knowledge on all subjects where it appeared that he had knowledge. [Hoebel 1940:7]

There is little direct evidence of those "pump-priming" questions; the closest is a loose page in Wedel's papers with the questions:

How many tipis did a family own?
Size of villages. Ever camp in a tipi alone?
Buckskin manufacture?
Animal snares?
Were all leading men called *paraibo*?
How many per band?
Size of Yapai?

However, the page is undated, and it is not clear where the questions fit in the overall record of the Field Party. Similar questions are scattered throughout Wedel's notes, but they often have little relation to nearby statements.

Wedel also noted:

> Linton was at pains to impress on us the need for checking closely on what the Comanche informants were telling us. By repeated questioning and rephrasing, he was able to bring out the often wide gap between precept and practice among the Indians. . . . an extension of this point, of course, was the need for constant re-checking of all the statements made by our informants. [1977:4]

While there is a degree of repetition in the notes suggestive of "repeated questioning and rephrasing," they did not always result in clarification.

After the first several weeks,[1] the students went to work independently—or in smaller

---

Another result of this choice of location was that most of the early consultants were from the western part of the old reservation (Indiahoma/Cache), and that the southern and southeastern (Temple/Walters/Geronimo/ Faxon), central (Lawton/Apache), and far northern (Anadarko) areas of the old reservation were barely represented.

1. The dating of this separation is somewhat problematic. On August 3, Linton reported:
During the first *three* weeks [my emphasis] the group worked more or less as a unit, using a single interpreter with one or more informants and for the past week I have had them working independently. [1933c]
However, a month later, on Sept. 3, he wrote:
During the first *two* weeks [my emphasis] the whole group worked together with a single interpreter and informant . . . Following this, the students worked separately or in groups of

groups away from the Mission—with their own consultants on their own topics. It was during this time that Clay Lockett formed a fast friendship with Post Oak Jim,

> [a] leader of the Peyote cult, and the best-known living medicine man. Lockett and he have a natural affinity and Lockett has been working with him for . . . two weeks and is now away with him visiting a four-day dance of which Jim is leader. He goes as Jim's guest, whites being otherwise excluded. [Linton 1933c]

Similarly, Wedel worked with Howard White Wolf. He later remembered

> an unforgettable evening under the ramada, balmy with a full moon, with Howard White Wolf . . . where I lived alone for a week. . . . When I feigned inability to comprehend the details of travois construction, Howard's wife[1] disappeared to return after a time leading the family mongrel who, in turn, trailed an improvised but thoroughly functional travois put together from sticks, laths, and binder twine. Around one of the ramada posts were piled a number of large flat side-scraper-like implements of stone resembling in every observable detail the hide-scrapers we had shortly before been digging up on Pawnee sites; and the lady of the house answered my query as to their function by seizing one and drawing it towards herself across a nearby cowhide.[2] [Wedel 1977:5]

During this period Carlson met with Atauvich, and Hoebel met with Tahsuda and Teneverka.

To coordinate these individual efforts, the group, according to Linton, "assembles at headquarters on week ends to exchange material and I expect to have them all together for four or five days next week to correlate findings and see if anything has been overlooked" (1933c). As with the dating of the separation of the group into individual researchers, these re-groupings are problematic. Although there are a few parallels among the later field notes indicative of shared "findings . . . or anything overlooked," there is very little evidence of extensively shared notes.[3] Certainly, Wedel must have shared his notes from his interviews with Howard White Wolf, since those were solo interviews and the parallels in Hoebel's notes, and the citations to White Wolf in Hoebel (1940) and in Wallace and Hoebel (1952), must have come from Wedel. Conversely, neither Hoebel's interviews with Tahsuda, Teneverka, and Herkeyah, nor Carlson's solo interview with Atauvich, are paralleled in Wedel's notes.

At the close of the summer, Linton had hopes of continuing the Comanche work and to spend at least one more summer to produce a joint monograph with the students (Linton 1933d, 1933e; Nusbaum 1933). However, the Laboratory's next season went to the Kiowas and the planned monograph did not materialize.

---

two or three. [1933d]

As to the notes themselves, Wedel's, Hoebel's, and sometimes Carlson's, notes generally overlap from the beginning, June 30, to about July 27, four weeks into the session. Thereafter, they generally do not.

1. Clara Tahtissytocker, daughter of Chenevony and Iuka (both names untranslated), who were associated with Cheevers' local Yapainʉʉ band.

2. See below, Howard White Wolf, July 31.

3. According to Wedel, "I'm sure we compared notes when some didn't get a story. It was pretty informal, conversational" (p.c. 1990).

THE NOTES

Waldo R. Wedel

Wedel's manuscript notes are in six stenographer's notebooks, numbered 1 through 6, each of sixty leaves written on both sides. The first two are generic (Jasper Super Premium School Series), and the rest have a Lawton stationer's imprint (Goodner Book Store). The interviews are dated from June 30 through August 14, 1933; two undated interviews with Frank Chekovi are embedded within the text.[1] The entries are apparently consecutive, although during the July 6 interview with Niyah, Wedel skipped the lower half of a page, and when he discovered that omission a page later, he went back and filled in the blank page.

At some point, Wedel had the first five of his notebooks transcribed by a typist. For the most part, the typescript is accurate, although at least once the typist missed several manuscript pages and, in a few cases, misunderstood the manuscript. These have been corrected and footnoted. Also, Wedel began to synthesize his notes into topical commentaries. Most of these are clear quotations or paraphrases of identifiable notes, and I have not attempted to correlate any variations in them with the original notes.

Scattered in Wedel's notes are a number of references to Pawnee ethnology and material culture that do not appear in the other student's notes. The source of those comments is uncertain, as both Wedel and Linton were familiar with the Pawnee literature: Wedel from his M.A. thesis on Pawnee material culture and his recent survey of ancestral Pawnee sites; and Linton from his Pawnee publications. Beyond noting them, I have not attempted to make a definitive attribution for those comments.

E. Adamson Hoebel

Hoebel's notes consist of some 800 three-by-five inch file cards in two file boxes, arranged by subject.[2] According to Hoebel:

> My method of note taking in the field was rather idiosyncratic and quite unorthodox. Field notebooks were the thing, but I preferred notecards which I could categorize by subject as they were recorded. This greatly helped, I found, to assist me in my provisional analysis and development of lines of inquiry in situ. [p.c. 1990]

Hoebel's cards are composed in a numbered (or occasionally, lettered) outline format (see figs. 1 and 2). Each card identifies the consultant by a number keyed to a separate card, but the cards do not show the interview dates, and except for multiple-card topics, there is no indication of their original sequential order. However, cross-checking with Wedel's and Carlson's dated notes allows most of them to be ordered. This is not the case with the interviews with Tahsuda and Teneverka, which are therefore presented in an arbitrary order.

Hoebel provided subject titles for his cards (not always consistently, see Editorial Considerations).

---

1. These are herein titled as "Frank Chekovi, Undated I," and "II"; a third undated interview with Frank Chekovi is in Hoebel's notes, titled "Undated III."
2. Over the years, the note cards have become disarranged, and in several cases cards are obviously missing; these latter cases are footnoted.

Like Wedel, Hoebel later began to make typed copies of his cards. Apparently, he then discarded the original, as there is only one example of duplication between a manuscript card and a typewritten card.[1] Also like Wedel, Hoebel began to synthesize data from different consultants onto a single card. A few cards have the same data under different subject titles. There are also a few cards with notes from publications, which I have not included in the present text.

Shortly after the Field Party left Oklahoma, Linton sent a graduate student to copy Hoebel's cards (Hoebel, p.c. 1990). Linton's most obvious use of them is in "The Comanche Sun Dance" (1935), which follows the order of Hoebel's numbered cards, but not the chronological order of Wedel's notes. Weston La Barre also made use Hoebel's cards, citing them in *The Peyote Cult* (1938). His citations are usually as "Hoebel" or "Hoebel Comanche Field Notes." I have been able to identify many, but not all, of the sources of those citations; they are footnoted.

Gustav G. Carlson

Carlson's records consist of several kinds of material, none primary. First, there is a set of dated manuscript stories with attributions; these are full grammatical compositions, not raw notes, and are therefore secondary. Then, there is a set of undated typescript stories that are not duplicated in the manuscripts. These are also full compositions, many with editorial interlineations, again showing that they are secondary. Finally, there are dated, typewritten extracts from multiple consultants on specific topics.

Many of Carlson's notes, particularly stories, are duplicated in the notes of the others. As he wrote to me, "I should point out that not all of the tales are ones which I collected, but since this was my designated responsibility the ones collected by others were turned over to me" (Carlson p.c. 1990). It is not clear what he meant by "my designated responsibility."

Carlson's notes do not include any of the materials used in his pioneering ethnobotanical study, *Some Notes on the Uses of Plants by the Comanche Indians* (Carlson and Jones 1940); however, about one-half of Carlson and Jones's botanical terms are paralleled in Wedel's notes.

EDITORIAL CONSIDERATIONS

To create the present text, photocopies of the typescripts of Wedel's Notebooks 1 through 5 were passed through an optical character reader. That output was checked against the original manuscripts. Wedel's notebook 6 was transcribed separately. The resulting text formed the "main file."

1. George Koweno, July 21.

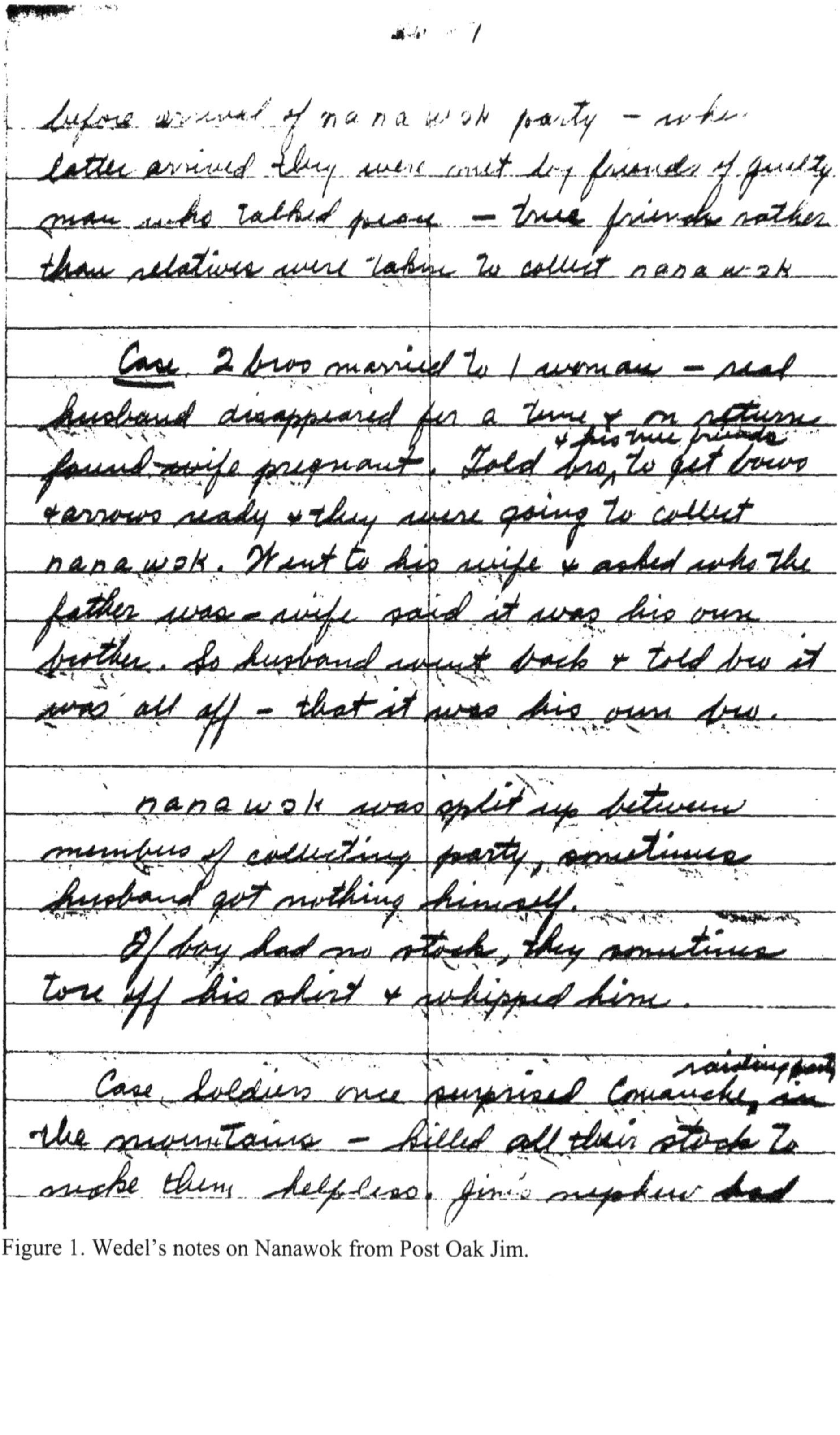

before arrival of nanawok party – when latter arrived they were met by friends of guilty man who talked peace – true friends rather than relatives were taken to collect nanawok

Case. 2 bros married to 1 woman – real husband disappeared for a time & on return found wife pregnant. Told bro, & his true friends to get bows & arrows ready & they were going to collect nanawok. Went to his wife & asked who the father was – wife said it was his own brother. So husband went back & told bro it was all off – that it was his own bro.

nanawok was split up between members of collecting party, sometimes husband got nothing himself.

If boy had no stock, they sometimes tore off his shirt & whipped him.

Case Soldiers once surprised Comanche raiding party in the mountains – killed all their stock to make them helpless. Jim's nephew had

Figure 1. Wedel's notes on Nanawok from Post Oak Jim.

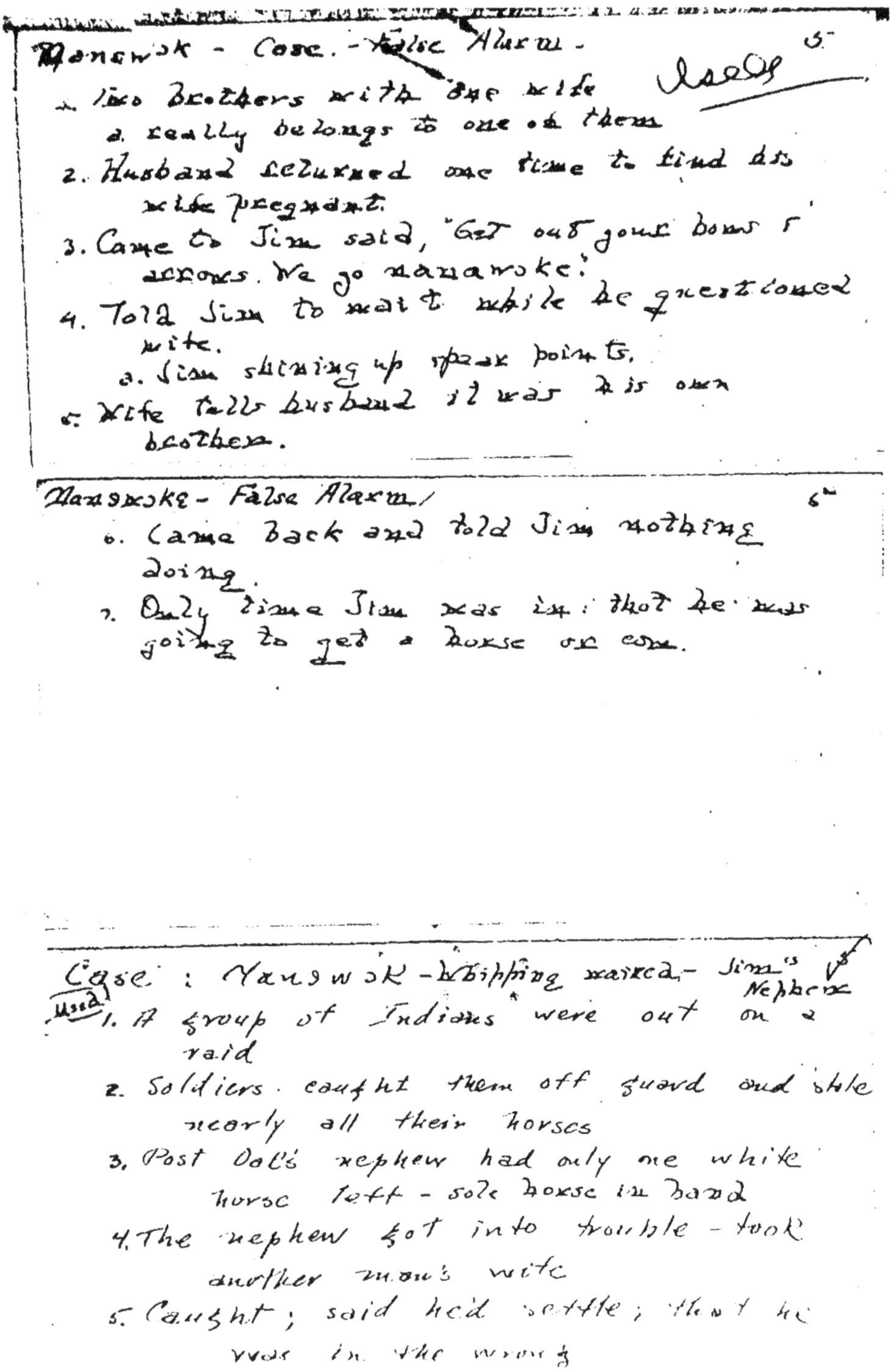

Nanawok - Case. - False Alarm.
1. Two brothers with one wife _Used_
   a. really belongs to one of them
2. Husband returned one time to find his
   wife pregnant.
3. Came to Jim said, "Get out your bows &
   arrows. We go nanawoke."
4. Told Jim to wait while he questioned
   wife.
   a. Jim shining up spear points.
5. Wife tells husband it was his own
   brother.

Nanawoke - False Alarm/
6. Came back and told Jim nothing
   doing.
7. Only time Jim was in: that he was
   going to get a horse or cow.

Case : Nanawok - Whipping waived - Jim's
Used Nephew
1. A group of Indians were out on a
   raid
2. Soldiers caught them off guard and stole
   nearly all their horses
3. Post Oak's nephew had only one white
   horse left - sole horse in band
4. The nephew got into trouble - took
   another man's wife
5. Caught; said he'd settle; that he
   was in the wrong

Figure 2. Hoebel's notes on Nanawok from Post Oak Jim.

Similarly, photocopies of Carlson's original typescript pages were read through an optical character reader and the output checked against the photocopies. Carlson's manuscript pages were transcribed separately. A duplicate set of photocopies of Carlson's typed topical extracts were cut up and rearranged by consultant and date, and merged into the main file.

Hoebel's note cards presented a much more labor-intensive project. The APS had photocopied Hoebel's cards, slightly reduced, eight to a page of legal size paper. These pages were themselves photocopied and, with the originals set aside as a backup, cut into individual slips and arranged by consultant. Each consultant stack was then correlated with the main file. Variations from the main file were entered by hand (see below).

This process identified words, sentences, and complete notes recorded by one student that are not directly paralleled in the other's notes. Some of these are simply points given in a slightly different wording. Where deemed significant, these variations are placed in the main file set off with brackets []. For the most part, these are from Hoebel's notes and are not further identified. Notes from Carlson which provide significant variations are also set off in brackets and are identified in footnotes. In addition, there are a number of cases in which the variations are distinct enough that they deserve to be reproduced in full. These are identified in the title line in braces, e.g., "Social Control: Murder {Wedel}" followed by "Social Control: Murder {Hoebel}." Finally, there are notes recorded by one student that are not paralleled in any of the other's notes. These represent solo interviews that were not shared with the others. They are placed after the dated notes and in arbitrary order. There are a few cases where the notes recorded by one student directly contradict those recorded by others, of that interview or as stated in publications. These are footnoted with the designation "contra."

I have assumed that the consultants spoke grammatical Comanche that the interpreters rendered into grammatical, albeit colloquial, English. However, except for the "worked-up" materials by Wedel and Carlson, all of the present text began as ungrammatical notes. Wedel's notes are brief semi-sentences and semi-paragraphs punctuated by hyphens; Hoebel's are semi-sentences in numbered or lettered outlines.

In order to make the notes readable and more useful to researchers, I have attempted to turn the raw notes into grammatical English using the following protocol:
- The syntax and word order of the original are retained
- Standard English capitalization and punctuation are added where necessary
- Articles (a, an, the, these, those) are added where necessary
- Sentences are standardized into the past tense
- Sentences are standardized in the third person, with the word "informant" replaced by the consultant's name
- Underlinings are retained
- Parenthetical words and phrases are retained
- Abbreviations, symbols, and other time-saving inscriptions are converted to text without notation
- Unless they provide information, strikeouts are not retained or noted
- Interlineations in the original note, either as a replacement for a strikeout or as a later elaboration, are retained where placed, but not noted
- My own additions in the text for clarity are enclosed in braces {}

The Field Party members were inconsistent in their methods of personifying the characters in animal stories. Wedel generally used a lowercase initial letter for all characters, e.g., "fox," while Hoebel and Carlson usually capitalized only the protagonist, "Fox," with the other characters lower-cased. I have capitalized all primary singular characters, while plural characters (e.g., "the raccoons," "the quails") are lower-cased.

The Field Party used a phonetic alphabet developed by Daniel Jones for the transcription of England's regional dialects (Jones 1917). With the help of Jean Charney, Robinson and Armagost's *Comanche Dictionary and Grammar* (1990), and the recently published *Taa Nʉmʉ Tekwapʉha Tʉboopʉ* by the Comanche Language and Cultural Preservation Committee[1] (2003), I have attempted to standardize spellings to the orthography used by contemporary Comanches.[2] Except for personal names and ethnonyms (group names), which are given in roman type with the initial letter capitalized, all Comanche words are given in lower-case italic. Some words recorded by the Field Party cannot be confirmed by the Comanche language references or by modern speakers. These range from forms that seem probable to forms that are unlikely. The former are presented in italics as given. The latter are in roman type and enclosed in angle brackets ⟨⟩ on their first use in a note.

Many Comanche individuals are mentioned in these notes. I have tried to identify them through interviews with modern Comanches, by reference to Comanche history, and by reference to the Comanche censuses and other records. This has been generally successful, but because individuals may have had several names, identification has not always been possible. For all identifiable personal names, I have used the spelling from the agency records, since this is generally the spelling used by their descendants.[3] Wherever possible, at the first occurrence of a name, I have footnoted it and given a normalization. The general format is: the Comanche morphemes in italic, followed by an English gloss in roman type enclosed in single quotation marks (e.g., *parʉa* 'bear', *sʉmʉno* 'ten', Ten Bears). For those known individuals who died before the censuses, most notably Parʉasʉmʉno, I have used the normalized form in the text. However, Parʉasʉmʉno is also an exception to the above general rule, for he is referenced in the original texts not only in Comanche, but also in translation as Ten Bears and several other variants. In his case, the references in Comanche have been normalized, while the other references are given as in the original. Other personal names that cannot be normalized or identified have been left as spelled in the notes and noted as "otherwise unidentified."

---

1. Hereafter cited as Comanche Language Committee.

2. The exceptions are primarily in the use of the barred *ʉ* rather than the barred *i* used by Charney (1993) and McLaughlin (in Kavanagh 2001), and the use of a capital vowel rather than an underlined vowel for the voiceless vowels (Canonge 1958). There are also some differences in how vowel lengths are represented between Robinson and Armagost (1990), Charney (1993), and the Comanche Language Committee (2003). Generally, I have followed the Committee's usage.

3. Although he recorded personal names in the Comanche language, Hoebel almost always used an English translation in his various publications. Inasmuch as the Comanches are one of the few Indian groups whose personal names were not translated into English patronyms, that approach is particularly infelicitous. Translations of some of the names of the consultants, e.g., Niyah, 'slope', are in the notes, indicating that they came from the consultants themselves or from the interpreter. Translations of most of the other names are not in the notes and it is not known where Hoebel obtained them.

The Field Party—or the Comanche consultants—were inconsistent in their usage of ethnonyms. Sometimes they used the Comanche marked plural (suffix -nʉʉ) and sometimes they used the unmarked singular. That is, they sometimes recorded ethnonyms in the plural, as in Yapaina *yapainʉʉ*, Penane and Penanur *penanʉʉ*, and Kwaharene *kwaharʉnʉʉ*.[1] In other instances, they used the unmarked singular form, e.g., "the Yapai band." However inconsistent, I have retained the original usage, although normalized.

For the first few interviews, Wedel made marginal notations of the subject, but he soon dropped that procedure. Hoebel's note cards provide subject headings throughout, and his cards are filed by these headings. I have borrowed that idea for this presentation. However, neither Wedel nor Hoebel were consistent in their nomenclature; there are variant headings, such as "Joking" and "Joking Relations." Through the convenience of computer indexing, I have standardized the headings, but they should be considered only as an arbitrary finding aid. Certain general notes may have more than one subject heading.

There are a number of comments throughout the notes. I have left these in place and footnoted them. Editorial footnotes have been added to provide etymologies of Comanche words, identify individuals, historical events, and geographic locations, and cite published works that made use of a particular note.

THE CONTENTS OF THE NOTES

During the course of the summer, the group examined "all phases of Comanche culture except the language . . . modern conditions . . . [and] Physical Anthropology" (Linton n.d.). In his final report at the end of the summer, Linton summarized in one long paragraph Comanche culture as recorded by the Field Party:

> The culture is a mixture of plateau[2] and plains elements, with the latter coming in varying degrees in the different bands.[3] War is the center of interest and war practices are the most formalized.[4] The man with many coups to his credit can do almost as he pleases, although restrained by informal public opinion. Little attention is paid to property, as the successful warrior could always get more from the enemy and internal disputes are almost always concerned with wife stealing. There is no real governmental control even in the band.[5] Power seems to be about equally divided between great warriors and great medicine men. An individual who is both is unassailable. Malevolent magic is well known, but not particularly feared.[6] They have the bilateral family, with no trace of clan organization, no

---

1. It is interesting that some ethnonyms—Yapainʉʉ, Penanʉʉ, Kwaharʉnʉʉ, and others—occur in the plural in the notes and in other historical records, while others—Yamparʉhka, Kutsutʉhka, Penatʉhka, and Noyʉhka—do not.

2. While Linton consistently derived Comanche culture from the Plateau, Hoebel consistently derived it from the Basin.

3. Since the Field Party obtained relatively little band-specific comparative information, this statement is problematic.

4. See Index: War.

5. See Index: Camp Organization.

6. See Index: Medicine: Sorcery.

mother-in-law avoidance, and a weak development of formalization in all family relationships. Marriage is limited only by actual blood relationships and shows little correlation with relationship terms. A man can and often does marry a women whom he calls sister, mother or aunt.[1] Brothers hold their wives pretty much in common.[2] In religion, we have gotten . . . accounts of the Sun Dance, said to be lacking among the Comanche, accounts of a multitude of other ceremonies and dances, some of them quite elaborate, and a great deal of information on medicines, powers, etc. The most important powers are obtained by dreaming on high lonely places (general Plains pattern) but at his death the man who has obtained such power is usually buried at the place where he received it and becomes a sort of genus loci. Other men desiring the power pray to him when they sleep there. The main power is the Sun, followed by the Earth, but neither of these give medicines. Oaths are sworn by them and untruth is always fatal within a year.[3] Lesser powers are the eagle, bear, buffalo, beaver (mainly malevolent). [Linton 1933c]

While reflective of the variety of material collected, this broad statement summarizes only a small portion of it and a few points (e.g., "successful warriors") cannot be specifically identified in the notes.

Kinship and Social Organization

The Field Party recorded relatively little information on kinship terminology, only eight direct notes, although there is terminological and behavioral information in several other notes.[4] Nemaruibetsi (July 31, Aug. 1, Undated) commented on the behavioral differentiation between matrilateral and patrilateral relatives, e.g., *ahpʉ*[?] (father and father's brother) and *ara*[?] (mother's brother), *toko*[?] and *kʉnu*[?] (maternal and paternal grandfather), and *kaku*[?] and *huutsi* (maternal and paternal grandmother).

Beyond kinship terminology, there are numerous notes on marriage (including polygamy[5]) and residence.[6] The consultants generally described a normative patrilocal residence pattern, sometimes giving the pragmatic rationale that should the father die, the son must look after his stock, something he could not do from his wife's place (Niyah, July 7). A few statements, however, take cognizance of situational variation, as when Howard White Wolf noted that "sometimes {a man} would leave his people and go to live with his wife's people rather than give up the girl" (August 4), and Frank Chekovi commented that his married brother lived with his wife's people, "not his own relatives" (August 3). Perhaps reflecting Hoebel's interest in law, there are at least thirty-six notes on *nanʉwokʉ*, the collection of damages for adultery.

There is little direct information on family structure or organization for either nuclear or extended families. The most explicit statement came from Frank Chekovi: "Frank's father and mother, brothers and sisters and cousins formed an extended family group. There were three tipis in the group" (Undated I).

1. See Index: Life Cycle: Marriage.
2. See Index: Life Cycle: Marriage: Polyandry.
3. See Index: Oaths.
4. See Index: Kinship Terms.
5. See Index: Life Cycle: Marriage.
6. See Index: Life Cycle: Marriage: Residence.

Despite the American Museum of Natural History's publications on Plains Indian sodalities (Lowie 1915; Wissler 1912–16), and Hoebel's own interest (Hoebel 1936), the Field Party recorded only a few notes on the subject. These may be arranged as a series. At the lower end of the scale were unorganized friendships—"all Eagle medicine men had friendly feelings toward each other, they were bound together by the common source of power" (Post Oak Jim, July 14)—through the somewhat more formalized "medicine societies" organized around a leader who shared his power with others (although there was some confusion about that latter point). Post Oak Jim said (July 14) that there would have been no more than twelve members of a medicine society and that a man could belong to several such groups, but George Koweno (July 21) reported that there would have been only six members and that a man could belong to only one group. At the top of the scale were the major warrior societies, the Tuwikaaʔnʉʉ 'Crows' or 'Ravens'[1] of the Yapainʉʉ (Howard White Wolf, July 31; Frank Chekovi, August 11); and the Tʉepukunʉʉ 'Little Ponies' (Post Oak Jim July 11, 14, 17; Atauvich, August 7) and Piviapukunʉʉ 'Big Horses' of the Kwaharʉnʉʉ (Howard White Wolf, July 31). Unfortunately, the Field Party—and/or the consultants themselves—often confused the groups per se with their dances (e.g., Post Oak Jim, July 11, July 14; Howard White Wolf, July 31).[2]

There are a few notes on the *pukutsi*, the contrarys (Frank Chickovi, Undated II, August 10; Frank Moetah, August 16; Herkiyah, undated). Hoebel (1940:33–34) attributes his discussion of the *pukutsi* to Nemaruibetsi. Hoebel (1940:33) used the term "Crazy Dogs," but except for the comment "(Cf. the Crazy Dogs of the Crow)" there is nothing in the Field Party's notes to directly support that attribution.

Socio-Political Organization

The notes contain little direct information on Comanche socio-political structure and organization. Although ethnonyms are common throughout, and a number of band lists were recorded (Quassyah, July 5; Howard White Wolf, July 30; Tahsuda, Undated; Nemaruibetsi, Undated), very little about how those groups were structured was recorded. At best are the comments of Tahsuda (Undated) that the *paraibo* was "a father, 'kind to the people; he didn't try to be brave; he was generous.'" This, of course, is to be expected: the local band was not just a random gathering of unrelated people, it was an extended family, with the head of the core family being the *paraibo* (Kavanagh 1996:41).

A number of Comanche terms for socio-political statuses were recorded. The term *paraibo*, generic for 'chief',[3] was used by several consultants, including Nemaruibetsi (August 8), who used it in the form *paraibo kwʉhʉʔ* 'chief wife'. Howard White Wolf (August 1) implied that the term *nomʉne* denoted the 'war leader'.[4] He also used the locution "war *paraibo*" (August 4).[5] A set of political status terms based on *tekw-* 'talk' were recorded. Most common in the

1. Sometimes called Black Knives, from *tu-* 'black', *wi* 'knife'.
2. As did William P. Clark (1885), following E. L. Clark (1881), and Robert Lowie (1915).
3. Contra Hoebel 1940:18.
4. Robinson and Armagost (1990) gives *nomʉnewapʉ* more generically as 'officer' or 'leader'.
5. Gatschet (1893) has war chief as "maimiana paraivo," that is *mahi* 'war', *miana* 'go'.

notes is *tekwⱯniwapɪ*,[1] usually given as 'brave man' (passim), although Frank Chekovi (Undated III) gave it specifically as 'war leader' (as distinct from *paraibo* 'peace chief'), a distinction followed by Hoebel (1940:19, 26). Similarly, Wallace and Hoebel argues for a "constitutional separation" of civil and military leadership (1952:210), implying that there were clear cultural distinctions between those roles. However, the notes have a large degree of overlap and indeterminacy among them, and there is no explicit discussion of a "constitutional" separation of these roles.

Several consultants (Post Oak Jim, July 18; George Koweno, July 21) implied that the Smoke Lodge was an informal nightly gathering of the village elders, though Tahsuda (Undated) described a much more formal occasion. Hoebel (1940:40) and Wallace and Hoebel (1952:147) generally follow Tahsuda's version.

Economics

There are a number of comments about the importance of the buffalo in the Comanche economy, e.g., "The Indians thought they would have buffalo for a long time, but then they suddenly disappeared" (Niyah July 7), but there are relatively few notes about the actual operations of a buffalo hunt. Niyah's description is the most explicit, and forms the basis of Hoebel's (1940:15) and Wallace and Hoebel's (1952:55–61) accounts of Comanche buffalo hunting. Niyah himself, however, noted that he had never actually seen a buffalo butchered. What he described was the way a cow was butchered.[2]

Nevertheless, according to Niyah, the winter meat supply was obtained in the fall, "when the buffalo were fat, the hides were good and thick, and the flies weren't bad."[3] He also noted that "if buffalo were run hard, especially in hot weather, the meat didn't keep well."

The hunters took light tipis, "small plain duplicates of the large tipis, made solely for use in hunting." After scouts located a herd, the men met to decide the plan of attack. The chief appointed "watchers" to prevent early hunters from stampeding the herd.

Niyah described the running hunt, in which the men lined up "as for a race" and, at the chief's signal, rode up from downwind to get as close as possible to the herd and then charged. Both Niyah and Howard White Wolf (August 4) dismissed running buffalo over cliffs as "inadvertent," rather than as planned efforts.

Kills were identified by arrow marks. Another man could claim a quarter by striking it, and the hunter was "legally entitled to only the hide, not the meat" (Herman Asenap, June 30–July 1).

The initial butchering was performed by the men, with the women doing the finer cutting and drying of the meat back in the camp. On the return to camp, a variety of people might have a claim on the meat, such that the "hunter himself might have none left." However, the only specific relationship described is that between the hunter and his father-in-law: "a man always

---

1. The other terms are *tekwⱯnitⱯ* 'announcer' (Niyah, July 10) and *tekwawapɪ* 'interpreter' (Howard White Wolf, August 4).

2. Niyah was born in 1879, a year after the "last" buffalo hunt. The oldest consultant, Teneverka, was apparently not even asked about hunting.

3. Wallace and Hoebel has "at certain seasons . . . during the summer . . . and during November and December" (1952:55).

divided up game with his father-in-law, he always had a certain choice piece of meat . . . and asked his wife to take her father's portion to him, he never took it himself" (Niyah July 7).

Two accounts of magical antelope drives were recorded, one by Niyah (July 7), the other by Post Oak Jim (Undated); neither were firsthand accounts. Niyah explicitly said he had only "heard of" a medicine man who had this power. Wallace and Hoebel (1952:67) generally follows Niyah's version, although the climax, "the people then piled in and killed them all" is from Post Oak Jim's account. On the other hand, they left out Niyah's account of the medicine man's injunction that "the biggest buck belonged to him, no one else should get it," a significant statement of an authoritarian appropriation of labor.

Post Oak Jim (July 12, July 26) and Howard White Wolf (August 3) provided important lists of plant foods, roots, nuts, and berries that augmented the animal protein. There are also several lists of medicinal plants (passim, see Index).These formed the basis of Carlson and Jones (1940) and Wallace and Hoebel (1952:73–74).

Relatively little information on food preparation was obtained. Herman Asenap (July 7) had never heard of stone boiling, and though Post Oak Jim (July 12) had heard of it, he offered no further comment. This may be expected; as Post Oak Jim also commented (Undated), the Comanches had obtained copper kettles from traders very early. Post Oak Jim (Undated) described roasting meat. There is no mention of fry bread.

The three other ethnohistorically recognized economic resource domains—trade, raid, and political gifts (Kavanagh 1996)—received little comment in the notes. Herman Asenap (June 30–July1) and Post Oak Jim (July 11) mentioned trade with "Mexicans"; Post Oak Jim (July 11) mentioned trade with Pueblo Indians, "the only friends of the Comanches." Post Oak Jim noted (July13) that "horses were the principal objectives of a raid."There are several comments about the way war booty was divided among the members of a raiding party (Herman Asenap, June 30-July 1; Quassyah, July 5; Post Oak Jim, July 13; Howard White Wolf, August 1).[1] After the return of a war party, further distribution of resources came through the "Shakedown Dance." Post Oak Jim (July 13) implies that it was indeed a "shakedown" of the returned warriors by the village women for goods, horses, blankets, etc., in return for honors and prestige. A good description is in Tahsuda's story (Undated) in which the hero's family, after each successful exploit, gave away increasing amounts of wealth. The presence of captives was freely acknowledged, but there is no mention of selling them or taking them for ransom. The only mention of a political gift is Paruasumuno's horse, "Washington" (Post Oak Jim, July 11).

Religion

Central to Comanche religious concepts is *puha*, 'power' or 'medicine'. The notes contain numerous references to *puha* and its role in both war and health. As Niyah said, "There were no men who won great honors without having medicine" (July 6). The basic source of power was through the vision quest, *puhahabitʉ* 'lying down for power' (Frank Chekovi, Undated

---

1. On a related matter, Wallace and Hoebel, citing Post Oak Jim and Howard White Wolf (both without dates), state that Quanah was not always "liberal towards his followers" in the distribution of booty (1952: 267). This is not evidenced in the extant notes.

III). Of the Comanches interviewed, only Frank Chekovi described his own experience (Undated III).

According to Niyah (July 7), young men began to consider seeking power at about age twenty.[1] Most emphasized that the importance of the quest lay in the sleeping/dreaming; as Post Oak Jim said, "If you expect to get medicine, you can't get it by sitting and watching, you must get it in sleep" (July 14).[2] They emphasized the "testing" aspect of the process, and that the faint-hearted might be driven away by the terror of their visions. They also emphasized that the seeker must know the specific power he was seeking; those who did not could be led into "evil thoughts" (Post Oak Jim, July 14). The other form of acquiring power was by transfer from an established medicine man.

Four major ceremonies were described in 1933: the Beaver Ceremony, *pianahuwitɄ*[3] 'Big Doctoring'; the Sun Dance; the Peyote ritual; and the Ghost Dance. As described by Post Oak Jim (July 13) and George Koweno (July 21), the Beaver Ceremony was a curing ceremony specifically for tuberculosis. Post Oak Jim said that it was also used to discover the source of sorcery. The Comanche Sun Dance was the subject of a number of notes. Post Oak Jim's accounts (July 17, July 19) were the fullest,[4] with less extensive remarks by Niyah (July 6, July 8), Herman Asenap (June 30-July1), Howard White Wolf (August 1), and Teneverka (Undated). The purpose of the ceremony was generally described as "curative" (Herman Asenap, June 30–July1; Niyah, July 8), although Teneverka (Undated) commented that the purpose was for "revenge." Interestingly, although Isatai is mentioned several times in the notes, no one made an explicit linkage of his 1874 ceremony with the Sun Dance.[5] The use of peyote was mentioned many times; the then contemporary ritual was described most completely by Post Oak Jim (July 12). The Ghost Dance among the NoyɄhka Comanches was discussed by Post Oak Jim (July 18). Sorcery was the subject of numerous notes.[6]

Material Culture

There are numerous comments on material culture, including hide work, utensils, including wooden bowls, wood and horn spoons, skin containers, parfleches and bags, bow and arrow making,[7] clothing, including shirts, dresses, leggings, robes, and moccasins, personal

1. Contra Wallace and Hoebel, "at puberty" (1952:156).
2. Contra Wallace and Hoebel, "at his watch"—that is, awake—"for four days and nights" (1952:158).
3. This is the form as recorded by the Field Party. It probably should be *pia natɄsuʔwaitɄ, pia* 'big', *natɄsuʔu* 'medicine', *waitɄ* 'appear, resemble'.
4. There is, of course, some question of the validity of Post Oak Jim's account, as he admits that he was only a small boy when the "last" dance was given.
5. Contra Hoebel 1941.
6. See Index: Medicine: Sorcery.
7. Interestingly, although there is a comment by Herman Asenap that "formerly they had sinew backed bows [with a sinew sheath over the center part]" (June 30–July1), and by Niyah that "[t]he cord from the bison's neck was placed along a bow to strengthen it" (July 7), there is no clear source in the notes for Wallace and Hoebel's (1952:100) multi-sentence description of the process of making a sinew-backed bow.

adornment, hair care, face paint, and earrings. Considering the Comanche's interest in horses, there is relatively little on horse care.

Sports and Games

There are multiple notes on sports and games, such as various forms of kickball, arrow throwing, arrow shooting for distance and at a mark, the hand game, and horse racing.

Oral Traditions

A number of histories, stories, and myths were recorded. These include: personal histories or "Life Stories" (Herkeyah, Undated; Nemaruibetsi, Undated); "tribal" histories, such as the various histories of Paruasʉmʉno (Herman Asenap, June 30–July1; Niyah, July 6); stories of war and power about unnamed individuals (Post Oak Jim, July 17; Niyah, July 6; Howard White Wolf, August 3); trickster stories (Niyah, July 7, July 8, July 10; Post Oak Jim, July 17; Tahsuda, Undated); and elements of a longer transformer cycle (Niyah, July 10; Tahsuda, Undated).

There are a large number of historical persons mentioned in the notes; wherever possible, I have identified them in footnotes. There are also a few direct or inferred mentions of historical events, such as the 1867 Treaty of Medicine Lodge Creek (Quassyah, July 5), Paruasʉmʉno's 1872 trip to Washington (Quassyah, July 5), and the 1874 Battle of Adobe Walls (Post Oak Jim, July 13; July 26). Whenever possible, details have been included in footnotes.

Photographs

Most of the photographs reproduced here were taken by taken by Wedel and originally processed in a Lawton photography studio. The prints reproduced here were made by Victor Krantz of the National Museum of Natural History. Except for the photographs of the August 16 dance at Walters, they are undated.

APPENDICES

Appendix A is a concordance linking information published in E. Adamson Hoebel's *Political Organization and Law-Ways of the Comanche Indians* (1940) with its source(s) in the Field Party notes. Hoebel is inconsistent in the citation of sources. Although specific legal cases are given attributions, few of the other ethnographic statements are identified. Wherever possible, they are here identified.

Appendix B is a similar concordance identifying the sources of materials in *The Comanches: Lords of the Southern Plains*, by Ernest Wallace and E. Adamson Hoebel (1952). As with Hoebel, Wallace and Hoebel are inconsistent in their methods of citation. Sometimes they directly identify their source in a footnote. However, if they state in the text, for example, "From Post Oak Jim we have . . . " (1952:161), they do not give a further citation. Further, if the information had been published previously in Hoebel, they cite that work, rather than the original source. If the material is not a direct quote, oftentimes no source is given at all. Still, the original source can often be identified. Where the relationship between the notes and the publication is clear, I have footnoted it in the text as, for example, "Wallace and Hoebel 1952:26," and noted it in Appendix B. Where the relationship is possible, but not definite, I have noted it as "Wallace and Hoebel 1952:123(?)." In those cases where the notes directly contradict published material, I have footnoted it as, for example, "Contra Wallace and Hoebel 1952:26" and noted it in Appendix B with an asterisk.

Appendix C provides a similar concordance for Gustav G. Carlson and Volney Jones, *Some Uses of Plants by the Comanche Indians* (1940).

I have not attempted a full correlation of the notes with either Hoebel's *Law of Primitive Man* (1954) or of Linton's various publications, although obvious sources are noted.

Appendix D is a lexicon of all the Comanche words recorded by the Field Party, with brief glosses.

1. The Field Party. From left: Gustav G. Carlson; Waldo R. Wedel; F. Gore Hoebel; E. Adamson Hoebel; J. Nixon Hadley. (Photograph either by Ralph Linton or Clay Lockett, using Wedel's camera; summer 1933.)

2. Teneverka in front of his house. (Photograph by E. A. Hoebel; summer 1933.)

3. Rhoda and Herman Asenap. (Photograph by E. A. Hoebel; summer 1933.)

4. Quassyah (left), Ralph Linton, unidentified Comanche. (Photograph by W. R. Wedel; Walters, Okla., August 1933.)

5. Norton Tahquechi (right), and Pauau. (Photograph by W. R. Wedel; Walters, Okla., August 1933.)

6. "Comanche Orchestra." Post Oak Jim (right). The dance arena seems to have been ringed by seating benches of sawn lumber on lengths of post-oak logs. A special section, probably on the west of the arena, was made for the singers. In the background is possibly a concession stand. While the Field Party's photographs show young people in attendance, they do not show their participation in the dance. (Photograph and caption by W. R. Wedel; Walters, Okla., August 1933.)

7. Frank Chekovi and Pedahny. Chekovi wears an otter-skin doctor's cap, buckskin shirt, neckerchief, mescal-bean necklace, a sheet *piksʉkwinaʔ*, a long trade cloth breechcloth, side-tab leggings, and moccasins. Pedahny wears a buckskin dress (with American flags beaded on the bodice), a cloth sash and calico *piksʉkwinaʔ*, and high moccasins. (Photograph by W. R. Wedel; Walters, Okla., August 1933.)

8. Tahsuda. (Photograph by E. A. Hoebel; summer 1933.)

9. Niyah. (Photograph by E. A. Hoebel; summer 1933.)

10. Brush Dance, said to be a survival of the old Sun Dance, when dancers brought willow boughs to cover the dance arbor. In more recent times it is done to Gourd Dance songs. The dancers start away from the arena and dance towards it. See Post Oak Jim, July 17. (Photograph by E. A. Hoebel; Walters, Okla., August 1933.)

11. Brush Dance. The singers wearing cowboy hats can be seen behind the women. (Photograph by W. R. Wedel; Walters, Okla., August 1933.)

12. Brush Dance. Several dancers are shading themselves from the sun with their fans. The two women on the right carry *nahaikoruko* spears. (See Quassyah, p. 391.) (Photograph by W. R. Wedel; Walters, Okla., August 1933.)

13. Brush Dance. The dancers have reached the arena. In the course of the dance, the women have passed their spears to others as the young lady on the right—the youngest dancer—carries a spear formerly held by the woman to her right. (Photograph by W. R. Wedel; Walters, Okla., August 1933.)

14. Brush Dance. The woman by the singers holds her hand to her mouth in ululation. (Photograph by W. R. Wedel; Walters, Okla., August 1933.)

15. Dance. Here only women are in the center ring while a few men are outside. The use of a center pole in the arena may be another survival of the Sun Dance. (Photograph by W. R. Wedel; Walters, Okla., August 1933.)

16. Dance. Returning to their seats, the men and women move separately. (Photograph by W. R. Wedel; Walters, Okla., August 1933.)

17. Two dancers. Both men wear deer-hair roaches with single eagle feathers. Both wear buckskin shirts with a wide V-back collar and twist-fringe at the shoulders; the dancer on the left has inserts of fringe across the back below the shoulders. Both wear *piksʉkwina*, but only on the left dancer is there evidence of a buckled belt. (Photograph by W. R. Wedel; Walters, Okla., August 1933.)

18. Five women dancers. On the left is Yannytashchi and to her right is Taddahki (see Kavanagh 2001: fig. 5). They all wear buckskin dresses with long sleeve fringes, and, except for Taddahki, they all wear otter-skin headdresses with beaded medallions around the hat and down the trailer; some have fluffy feathers in the hat. The dresses have loom beaded bands across the back (and presumably across the bodice), with pendant ribbons. All wear *piksʉkwina*. The use of quilts and blankets to pad the hard benches, as well as to claim one's place, is evident. (Photograph by W. R. Wedel; Walters, Okla., August 1933.)

19. Two dancers. The man on the left wears an otter-skin cap with short trailer, beaded medallions, and feather. He wears a yoked calico shirt with doubled mescal-bean and silver bead bandolier; an eagle plume is apparently tied to the bandolier at his left shoulder. He wears a patterned fringed shawl as a *piksƱkwinaʔ*; details of his leggings and moccasins are unclear. The man on the right wears a deer-hair roach with silver spreader and a single eagle feather; the roach trail is a multi-colored cloth strip. The man wears a long dark yoked shirt (probably black), a *piksƱkwinaʔ* or trade-cloth sash under a beaded belt and beaded moccasins. From the doubled mescal-bean and silver bandoliers, these men appear to be Gourd Dancers. (Photograph by W. R. Wedel; Walters, Okla., August 1933.)

20. Quermah. She wears an otter cap with an eagle feather and ribbon decorations. Her hair is braided but not wrapped. She wears a cotton print as a *piksᵾkwina*ʔ over a three-piece buckskin dress. It is bound by a leather belt with conchas, and a studded drop. There are beaded awl, knife, and needle cases on her belt. (Photograph by W. R. Wedel; Walters, Okla., August 1933.)

The 1933 Field Party Notes

HERMAN ASENAP
June 30–July 1, 1933

Etiquette   One said *hahaitsI* 'friend'[1] (in greeting). A visitor first stated his business, and then inquired as to his host's affairs. Indians are now suspicious.

Economy: Trade   There was trade with Mexico; horses for nuts, etc.; ten to twenty dollars per horse.

Horses   The early Comanches had family-owned brands for stock[2]; all stock was turned out on the range. Comanches gelded horses.

Captives   Herman's father was captured [while gathering beans] as very small boy, along with his two brothers [boys], and was later adopted into a Comanche family. [He was given full tribal status.]

Captives were adopted by families that had no children.

Herman's father was a Mexican (?). As an adult, he was given the chance to return to his old home, but he refused. [He was returned to Mexico by the Indians, but he refused to leave the tribe. He participated in raids.]

Political Organization: Chiefs: Leadership   Leadership was achieved through bravery in war only. Old braves were very rare. Leadership was never attained by generosity or sagacity alone.

War: Cowardice   Cowardice in battle was a deep disgrace.

Captives   Adopted children had the same privileges of attaining leadership as did full bloods.

---

1. Literally, "Hello, friend."

2. It is not clear if pre-reservation Comanches branded horses. They must have been aware of them, for there are several Mexican period edicts prohibiting the purchase of branded horses from Comanches (Kavanagh 1996:207–8). For the reservation period, James Inkanish's (a Caddo) brand book for the Kiowa, Comanche, Apache-Wichita-Caddo-Delaware Agency, 1879–1888, is in Box 29 of the C. Ross Hume papers in the Western History Collection at the University of Oklahoma.

War: Values   It was better to die than to retreat.

Medicine: Vision Quest   An Indian could attain protective medicine, for example, by visiting alone to a medicine man's grave and praying to the sun and earth (?). There was no fasting so far as Herman knew.

Life Cycle: Family Boys   Boys were desired rather than girls, as protectors [and to bring honor to the family].

Life Cycle: Adolescent Lodge   At age eighteen, a boy was given a separate tipi for a sleeping place. His mother was his housekeeper, and his sisters must keep away. [This was his first home after marriage.]

[If there were several unmarried sons, they all lived in one tipi; when one married, another tipi was built.]

Life Cycle: Marriage   A girl's husband was selected by her father. Marriage was not at an early age. A girl's brother could give his sister to a close personal friend, with or without her father's consent. The Comanches always wanted harmony (social control).

Social Roles: Slaves   There were no slaves among the Comanches.

Captives   [Captive women often belonged to the men who captured them.]

Etiquette: Gifts   Gifts, publicly made, were influential in overcoming stubbornness or criticism among Comanches. (cf. Stacey Matlock[1]—Republican Pawnee—with gift of horses). Gifts brought favors.

Quanah Parker   Quanah Parker was disliked by full bloods, but he had a great heart.

Social Control: Murder {Wedel}   A half-blood and gambler was suspected of paying attention to another man's wife and the latter (Cruz[2]) arranged to have the offender killed. (Quanah Parker took one of his wives[3] away and went to Washington.)

The Indians were seated at the Indian agency to receive meat or hides from the government when the old man shot the offender with a pistol.

---

1. Stacey Matlock, a Kitkihahki (Republican) Pawnee, had been a consultant for a number of anthropologists in the 1920s and 1930s, including James Murie and George Dorsey. This is probably a comment from Linton based on his work with the Murie and Dorsey manuscripts in the Field Museum.

2. Cruz Portillo was also known as Kodose. The 1885 census gives his English name as 'Cross', but that is simply a translation of the Spanish *cruz*, not a translation of *kodose*; the meaning of that latter name is unclear.

There is a good deal of confusion about Cruz/Kodose. The Family Record Book lists him as full-blood Comanche, with his father listed as Quenakesuit (*kwina* 'eagle', *kesuatɻ* 'mean', Bad Eagle), his mother as Chahwabitty (no translation given). Neither name appears on any census. Joe Attocknie (MS) states that he was full blood Comanche. Frank Chekovi (August 4) states that he was a Mexican captured by Comanches. Still others, such as Wedel here, call him a "half-blood" or "breed."

Cruz was first listed on the 1885 census as leader of a small (twenty-four people) local band. At one point he was married to the sisters Tonarcy and Erksey, until Quanah stole Tonarcy about 1891.

In this note, Wedel recorded that Cruz was a "scout against the Mexicans," while in the next note, Hoebel recorded that he was a scout "with the Mexicans." Joe Attocknie (MS) says that he was captured by the Mexicans, served in the Mexican Army against the Comanches, and ultimately returned to them.

3. This was Tonarcy; see Index.

The killer was a Mexican, an old man who had been staying with the breed. The victim was a full blood.[1]

The former was sent to Fort Sill, then to the penitentiary. His son was Herman's brother-in-law.[2]

The killer was very old. It was a free-lance job; he did not kill on his own account.

The man whose wife was suspected was a Comanche scout against the Mexicans.

Social Control: Murder {Hoebel}   This was the only case of murder in forty-seven years.[3]

A man suspected his wife of adultery. He called upon his Mexican friend, seventy years old, to kill the suspect.

They were gambling at the beef issue. The assassin came up behind him and pointed a gun at the victims's head; the gun misfired.

People thought he was joking.

He shot again and killed the victim.

The Indians, angry, pushed him around.

The victim was a full blood and popular.

The trial was at Fort Sill; he was sent to the penitentiary.

At the time of allotment[4] the murderer was blind, and the officials desired to release him. They called on his son to come and get him, but the Indians all refused, saying, "He killed a good man." He died in prison.[5]

No action was taken against the instigator, although "some talked against him."

He was a Comanche who was a scout with the Mexicans for some years against his own people. Later, he came back to live with the Comanches. There were no hard feelings. His name was Cruz.

Life Cycle: Marriage: Adultery   Infidelity was punished by killing the wife, cutting off her nose. [Adultery was a lack of obedience to her father. Her husband might force a confession by holding her over burning coals.[6]] If the wife was guilty, her parents could make no objection to punishing her, but if the wife had been maltreated, her father might take her away, to be remarried later.

Life Cycle: Marriage: Wife Desertion   Braves on raids were sometimes accompanied by women. [A woman could attach herself to the leader of a war party for protection on leaving her husband.]

Herman's father once went on a raiding party. A woman went with another man because she was dissatisfied with her husband.

1. This is apparently a reference to the murder of Secose (possibly the young man listed on the 1895 census as Secoah, aged 26) by Miyacky (given as Evening, a member of Tahpony's Yapainʉʉ local band), a captive Mexican, aged 76. According to eyewitnesses, Secose was a bystander at a card game in a stable behind the trader's store at Fort Sill when Miyacky came up behind him with a pistol. Miyacky pulled the trigger twice, but the gun misfired; on the third try, it discharged (Burton 1895).

2. Herman's sister, Tahchay, married Miyacky's son, Codopony ('Gray Eyes', -*punitʉ* 'see').

3. If this case was the Secose murder of 1895 (see above), it had been thirty-seven years earlier.

4. 1901.

5. Miyacky is listed on the 1895 census, but not that of 1899.

6. Hoebel's notes attribute this comment to Mrs. Becker.

The potential leaders announced a raid and immediately left, regardless of the time of day.

The husband pursued the party and approached the man who "stole" his wife. He spoke civilly. [The husband promised to treat her well] and the party decided to give her back; (the party was obligated to support its own members in this case).

The man and wife returned, but the wife endeavored to escape and to return to the war party. She missed the crossing over a difficult creek and was shot by her husband.

In this case, there was no comeback for her parents. Most of the killings in the tribe were of this nature; murder was very rare.

Life Cycle: Marriage: Polygamy   Some men had two or three wives. There was sororate and levirate.

Social Control: Theft   Theft was very rare in the tribe.[1] Herman knew of no instances.

[Mrs. Asenap knew of none among themselves. Horses stolen must have been stolen by enemies (Cheyennes or Arapahos probably).[2]]

Life Cycle: Marriage; Social Organization: Bands   Marriage was within or between bands[3]; families were at liberty to change their band affiliation.

Could the chief of a band buy families out of other bands?[4]

Social Organization: Bands   [Bands were non-exogamous; they were loosely organized. A member might leave at will. There were no internecine wars].[5]

Political Organization: Chiefs: Subchiefs   [There was one chief and assistants.] An aged chief could step out and turn the chieftaincy over to a younger brave. Leaders settled disputes.

Life Cycle: Marriage: Divorce   A father dissatisfied with his daughter-in-law could cause his son to give up his wife; parental wishes were generally carried out by their children.

Kinship Relations: Avoidance   A wife was more free to the man's parents There were no strict mother-in-law restrictions, [there was "a kind of feeling against it, but no customary avoidance."] (cf. Apache[6]).

Kinship Relations   The father's brother was called by the same name[7] as the father, and he commanded nearly as much respect. At the father's death, the father's brother or sister assumed control over the children. The oldest son was most highly regarded.

Did younger sons get tipis?[8]

[Grandparents and grandchildren had a close relationship. They have the same kinship term.]

1. Wallace and Hoebel 1952:240.
2. This note is handwritten on one of Hoebel's typed note card citing Herman Asenap. Since there are no parallels in the two other interviews Rhoda Asenap gave (July 7 and 12), I have placed it here.
3. Hoebel 1940:12; Wallace and Hoebel 1952:140.
4. This question is in the body of Wedel's notes, but since it is not answered immediately, it is not clear what was intended.
5. Since there are no other parallels in interviews with Herman Asenap, this note has been placed here.
6. This is probably a comment by Linton.
7. That is, the same kinship term.
8. The source of this question is unknown.

Kinship Terminology: Woman Speaking

son[1]	*tua⁷*
son's children	*huutsI*
elder brother	*pabi⁷*
younger brother	*tami⁷*

Life Cycle: Marriage   Marriage was not permitted between kin.[2] In the case of an inadvertent union between relations, the parties separated when the ties were discovered.

[In one case about 1930, a boy married his second-cousin. They found out about it later and they separated.] Adopted children were subject to the same marriage restrictions as natural children.

Etiquette   Kinship terms were used in ordinary address in preference to personal names. They carried more respect [more polite].

Names: Naming   Names were given a) in memory of an outstanding achievement or event, b) in honor of some friend of the father, or c) in recognition of some infantile peculiarity.

The name was first used in a public place.[3] Names were given after the first war exploit by a brave.

If a young child was dying, it was given a name to bear in the afterlife.

Names were given soon after birth, but might be changed by men after a war exploit [special deed or event]; they might be changed by women occasionally, not necessarily at marriage.

If a woman gave birth to frail children, she sometimes gave them the name of a brave warrior to strengthen them in hopes of their surviving.

Did they pay the same respect to a captive as to own son?[4]

Social Roles: Gender Roles   Women did the housework.

Material Culture: Utensils: Mortars; Food: Food Preparation: Mortars   Meat was ground in wooden mortars hollowed out with fire out of a knot, provided with a handle.

Food: Pemmican   There was no pemmican.

Material Culture: Utensils: Spoons; Bowls   They had wooden spoons and bowls.[5]

Material Culture: Crafts   There were no baskets[6] or quillwork.[7]

Material Culture: Tipis   Tipi covers were <u>staked</u>[8] down, with the door always toward the east.[9] Camps were located for water and wind protection.

---

1. This entire note is crossed out in Wedel's manuscript notes, and it does not appear in his typescript notes. The terms, however, are correct, so I have retained the note.

2. Hoebel 1940:140.

3. Wallace and Hoebel 1952:121.

4. The source of this question is unknown.

5. Wallace and Hoebel 1952:91. See also Frank Chekovi, August 10.

6. Contra Wallace and Hoebel 1952:91.

7. In 1812, New Mexican Pedro Pino commented that the Comanche's "long shirts and tunics have roses, carnations, animals, etc., embroidered on them; the shades of color are made with the quills of porcupines" (Carroll and Haggard 1942:129).

8. None of the tipis in the photographs of Medicine Creek village in the winter of 1872–73 seem to be staked (Kavanagh 1991).

9. Wallace and Hoebel 1952:88.

Material Culture: Crafts: Hide Work   The southern Plains peoples (Comanches) used long, fine fringe.

Material Culture: Craftsmen   There were special craftsmen, (e.g., women saddle makers).[1]

Economy: Trade   They traded products for other commodities.

Material Culture: Utensils: Pottery   Comanches made no pottery

Food: Food Preparation: Cooking   Meat was roasted or eaten fried, or dried and pounded.

Life Cycle: Marriage: Residence   At marriage, (there was no ceremony), the bride moved into the groom's sleeping tipi, near his mother's lodge.[2]

Life Cycle: Death: Disposition of Property   At death, all of the deceased person's property was destroyed and his name was never recalled.[3]

Social Roles: Gender Roles   The man was the boss in the home.

Economy: Trade   There was no selling; it was all trade.

Names: Taboo   A young man named Bacon Po?ro?[4] died [recently]. Thereafter, bacon was called 'pig'.[5]

　　　If a person died, the name taboo was overcome by using a nickname for the article for which his name stood; all memory of the deceased was wiped out.

Life Cycle: Death; Disposition of Property   A medicine man's paraphernalia was thrown into water at his death.[6] [Medicine articles may be given away or inherited by a son.]

Economy: Trade   Hides were traded to Mexicans for sugar and flour. They used the sign language.

Relations with Other Tribes: Kiowas   The Comanches were unfriendly to the Kiowas.

Economy: Trade Life Cycle: Death: Mourning   Women gashed themselves freely at the death of a husband or other member of their family; men seldom imitated this at the death of a woman.[7] [(Sometimes for a child.) A woman might cut her hair off short, uneven. Men might cut a braid off.]

Life Cycle: Death: Burial   (There was no fear of corpses.) The corpse [dressed in a buffalo robe, wrapped in shrouds, extended[8]] was placed in a hole or in a cave [crevice] in a rocky canyon with his personal [useable] possessions. If they were on a raid, the body was thrown into a gully and covered; the bodies were placed prone. [The spirit stayed there and prays if buried.[9]]

Relations with Other Tribes: Tonkawas   Tonkawas were called "man-eaters" by the Comanches.

---

1. Hoebel 1940:120; contra Wallace and Hoebel 1952: 96.

2. Wallace and Hoebel 1952:136. The implication of matrilocal residence is unexplained.

3. Hoebel 1940:120; Wallace and Hoebel 1952:152 (?).

4. The only documentary occurrence of this name is on the 1889 and 1892 censuses, where he is listed as a young man, aged 11 in 1892, son of Tahchachi (also known as Timbo), and thus grandson of Paruakuhma (see Index), and Weckpiti. He is not listed on any later census.

5. Robinson and Armagost (1990) glosses *po?ro?* as 'pig'. They do not give a separate term for 'bacon'. Casagrande (1954-55, II:229) suggests it is from the Spanish *puerco*.

6. Hoebel 1940:121; Wallace and Hoebel 1952:152.

7. Wallace and Hoebel 1952:151 (?).

8. Contra Wallace and Hoebel 1952:150.

9. This sentence is as given in Hoebel's notes. Presumably, this meant "and one prays to it."

Material Culture: Tipis   Women built the tipis. The poles were obtained from the Wichita Mountains. The covers were painted.

Economy: Hunting   Bison hunts were in the fall for prime hides, robes and moccasins.

Medicine: Vision Quest   Neophytes slept[1] beside a dead medicine man's grave until they dreamed; they couldn't become medicine men by their own power.

Medicine: Powers   medicine men could heal the sick [heal wounds], turn bullets [their "body was just as hard as rock," strike a horse to win a race], etc. Different men for different medicines.

Medicine: Bullet Proof   Bullet-proof medicine men couldn't protect others on the same war party.

Medicine: Taboos   Medicine men must observe definite taboos. [A medicine man couldn't eat the heart of an animal. People might give him heart to break his power without his knowledge.]

Medicine: Vision Quest: Women   Women got medicine or spirits in the same way, by a vision.

Medicine   A man with strong medicine was dangerous.

Medicine: Duration   Powers didn't last forever. Why not?[2] [Powers did not last for life; medicine got weaker as a man grew older.[3]]

Medicine: Medicine Women   [A medicine woman could go into the tipis of older medicine men.][4]

Medicine: Curing: Broken Bones   Broken bones were set with splints of rawhide.

Medicine: Payment: Smoking   Healing doctors were paid for their efforts. If a doctor smoked with a man, he was obliged to go and heal the sick person; if the smoke was rejected, the doctor didn't go to cure. [He probably wouldn't go on the first call, and he might refuse later if people didn't observe the rules of his medicine.] The subject came and smoked a few puffs, extending the cigarette. Then the medicine man asked his business, and they both smoked. Acceptance of the smoke meant acceptance of the call.

Medicine: Sun Dance   The Sun Dance was for curative purposes, especially as a final attempt to save the dying.

Cosmology   The sun was the father; the earth was the mother

Medicine: Peyote   [Peyote was used in the old days.] The Comanches were the first to have peyote (or possibly preceded by the Apaches). Peyote was used as a war medicine; it was used in prognostication [on war parties to foretell events.] If a tipi wasn't available, the ceremony could be held in the open. Peyote came from Texas. The Kiowas (but not the Comanches) used the Bible in the peyote ceremony.

Quanah Parker   Quanah Parker was the last chief.

1. Contra Wallace and Hoebel's "watched" (1952:158).
2. Question by Wedel.
3. The notes do not state whether this was an answer to Wedel's question, but Hoebel did credit it to Herman Asenap, and it does seem to fit here.
4. Hoebel 1954:140.

Life Cycle: Marriage: Divorce   In the old days, incompatibility was followed by separation through mutual agreement. Women had no recourse if their husbands were unfaithful. A divorcee returned to her parents with her property.

Life Cycle: Death: Disposition of Property   A woman's property was destroyed at her death.

Life Cycle: Marriage: Bride Price   [There was no bride price.] A young man could give presents to the father of a girl he wished to marry, but couldn't recover these in the event of divorce.

Life Cycle: Marriage: Divorce: Reconciliation   The fathers on each side decided in case of divorce.

Life Cycle: Marriage: Polygamy   The first married wife had the greatest authority.
      [Wives called each other "sister", *patsiʔ* or "younger sister", *namiʔ*.]

Life Cycle: Marriage: Divorce   A man might say, *miaruʔinʉ*, "I want to leave." The father usually acceded to his son's wishes.

Life Cycle: Abandoning Aged   The aged and infirm were never abandoned to die during hunts, etc.[1] (cf. Apache[2]).

Games: *tohpeti*   Formerly, the Comanche had a stick game. Six sticks were held in the hand and brought down forcefully on a flat rock. The count was taken from the way the sticks fell. Women gambled as much and as often as the men. A man could gamble away the household possessions, sometimes causing a domestic split.[3]

Horses: Races   Comanches bet heavily on horse races.

Games: *nahiwetʉ*   The hand game was played with four game sticks. Any number of players could play. There were two sides, each with four sticks. One side concealed a stick in one player's hand, while the other side guessed. If he guessed wrong, they lost one stick of their four. Each side had chants and song leaders who used drums (?) Each side gambled on the outcome. When one side had all of the other's sticks, they were returned and a stick was taken from the scorekeeper. When all of the score-keeper's sticks were gone, the game ended.

Games: Kickball   A soft rag ball was kicked by women.[4] Each woman hopped along on her left foot, kicking the ball with the instep of her right foot. The ball was not allowed to touch the ground. If it did, then another woman tried. A good player could go seventy-five to one hundred yards without dropping the ball. There were three players; one kicked until she dropped the ball, then another took it over and continued. The total combined yardage was what counted. It was a hard game. It was too hot now.

Games: Shinny   It was an old game that used a curved shinny club and ball. It was a woman's game, formerly popular.[5]

Games: Lacrosse   There was no lacrosse among the Comanches.

Games: Wrestling; Boxing   There was wrestling, but no boxing. When a man fell, he was down.

1. Contra Wallace and Hoebel 1952:149.
2. Comment probably from Linton.
3. Wallace and Hoebel 1952:116 (?).
4. Wallace and Hoebel 1952:115.
5. Wallace and Hoebel 1952:114.

Games: Hoop and Spear   There was the hoop and spear game.

Games: Javelin   There was also javelin throwing, a feathered javelin, for distance or at a mark.

Names: Changing   A woman sometimes changed her name if her children died young.

Case: A certain woman lost several children at early ages. At the birth of another child, she took precautions. The woman's mother and another woman lived in the same tipi. The cure was to take down their tipi last when breaking camp. The second woman had interviewed the medicine man and she hid the baby. The child was hidden in the brush when camp was being moved, and was then "found" by its mother. Thus it did not appear to be the child of its real mother and was protected. The boy was named Esikono (the child was named "They found a boy").[1]

Life Cycle: Death: Disposition of Property   The tipi was sometimes destroyed at the death of a young child.[2] [All personal property was destroyed at death. It was either burned or thrown in a flooding river. The tipi was destroyed on the death of either sex (sometimes for a child)].

Names: Taboo   If two men in the tribe had the same name and one died, his kin would never use the name in speaking to or of the other.[3]

Names: Family Names   There were no family names.

Live Cycle: Marriage: Divorce   If a man let a woman go without a struggle even though she was unfaithful, he was looked down upon.

Social Roles: Gender Roles: Female Warriors   Women sometimes fought in war parties.

Material Culture: Slings   Herman thought slings were formerly used; now they are just boys' playthings.

Material Culture: Arrows   Dogwood was used for spears and arrows.

Material Culture: Arrow Straightener   Arrows were straightened with the teeth.

Material Culture: Bows   Osage orange (bois d'arc[4]) and mulberry were used for bows. The bow and arrow had a range about 200-400 (?) yards. Formerly they had sinew-backed bows [with a sinew sheath over the center part].[5]

War: Shields   Shields were round, rawhide, about eighteen inches in diameter, with a central loop handle. Shields were not to be brought into the house. They were strengthened by medicine. The shield was decorated according to some dream or by kin [they could be inherited through the generations]. Each man made his own from the neck hide.

---

1. This gloss given by Asenap is unclear. Robinson and Armagost (1990) gives *esikono* as 'Gray Box' (*esi* 'gray', *koono* 'cradle, box, resting place'). Esikono was listed on the1879 census as 'Gray Thighs', born about 1859. He was listed as a member of Youniacut's and later Tabeyetchy's Yapainʉʉ local bands. The Family Record Book lists his father as Wetooahpap (otherwise unidentified) and his mother (unnamed) as a Mescalero Apache. His allotment was west of the Post Oak Mission in Indiahoma. He lived at least through 1923, but apparently had no children. He was an important early modern peyotist.

2. Wallace and Hoebel 1952:152 (?).

3. Wallace and Hoebel 1952:123.

4. Bois d'arc is pronounced "bow dark" in Oklahoma; in Comanche, the tree is *ohahuupi* 'yellow wood'. Carlson and Jones (1940:523) give it as *Maclura pomifera*.

5. Wallace and Hoebel 1952:100.

Life Cycle: Death: Disposition of Property   A medicine man's paraphernalia was never destroyed by fire, but by water (in flood times?) or passed on to a son.[1] A medicine man could, while living, turn over his magic to another.

Life Cycle: Childhood: Discipline   Children were never whipped or scolded, [but disciplined by persuasion, "just by talk"]. They were kept in line while young by threats of Mupits[2] who was so large that it made holes when it walked (owl?) monster (large fossil bones). [Some old people claim to have seen it.] Bad children were sometimes frightened into obedience by disguised adults. [An older person might cover his head with a sheet to frighten them.[3]]

Medicine: Curing   Fossil bones[4] were ground or chewed up fine and applied to injuries as a cure.

Rat manure was used as a cathartic.

Bat skin stew was used as an external lotion.

Social Roles: Gender: Men and Boys   Horses were tended by men.

Boys had horses, which were saddled after breakfast by their parents, then the boys went out hunting, etc. They had few real duties. When a boy first killed game, he made an offering. He brought the bird in on an arrow, and was rewarded with a gift by the first person he met, usually his father.

A father took his son on first war party; a boy could not go without his father's consent. If a boy went on war party as a stowaway, he was turned over to his nearest kin.

Life Cycle: Puberty Ceremonies   There were no puberty ceremonies for boys or girls.[5]

Life Cycle: Marriage   Girls were not married before seventeen or eighteen in the old days.

A man sometimes requested the father of promising youth [an "honorable boy"] to give him as a son-in-law.[6] [The marriage was consummated on the agreement of the parents.]

Some men didn't want to marry, but they did at their father's insistence.

A groom made a gift to the bride's brother. It was not a "purchase."

Life Cycle: Marriage: Bride Service   A son-in-law had certain duties toward his father-in-law. [The son-in-law does all the work for his father-in-law when they were together.] A daughter-in-law was under less obligation. A man gave a portion of the kill to his father-in-law, usually the best of the game.[7]

Hunting: Division of Hunt   The hunter grabbed the tail of a kill and got the hide. If anyone else touched a quarter or shoulder, etc., he received it. The hunter was legally entitled only to the hide, not the meat. [The quarter attached to the leg touched by those who came upon the hunter's quarry went to that person. The only part in such cases going to the hunter was the hide. {The hunter asserted his right by} seizing the tail.][8]

1. Wallace and Hoebel 1952:152.
2. The name of the ogre is usually given as Piamupits.
3. Wallace and Hoebel 1952:124.
4. Wallace and Hoebel 1952:171. There are fossil bone beds over much of southwestern Oklahoma, e.g., the Domebo mammoth find north of the town of Stecker on the old reservation (Leonhardy 1966).
5. Wallace and Hoebel 1952:125.
6. Wallace and Hoebel 1952:138.
7. Wallace and Hoebel 1952:134 (?).
8. Hoebel 1940:119.

Adornment: Mescal Beans   Red beans {*Sophora secundiflora*} were used as beads.

Life Cycle: Marriage   A youth could ask permission of a girl's father to marry her, on his own initiative.

Life Cycle: Marriage: Divorce   In case of divorce or disagreement, the fathers of the young couple decided who was right. If they were unable to decide, they called on the chief for a final verdict. [Herman knew of no cases where the chief's decision was disobeyed.]

War: Division of Loot   The booty from a raid was divided up in a rote order. The leader selected his portion first, then the others in the order set by the leader. [The leader observed the industry of the men on the party, which one got wood most willingly, carried water, aided in camp activities. After the raiders were safely away from the enemy, he picked the two or three most industrious for first choice. Then his assistants got to pick. The chief got the last choice, though if there was not enough to go around a second time, he may get the balance.][1]

Political Organization: Chiefs: War Leader   In a raid, the leader appointed scouts, commissary leader, etc.

Medicine: War   The leader sometimes made magic, and always took an important part in the fighting. There was always a medicine man along. If game was scarce, the medicine man went out to an isolated place for a vision.

Medicine: Taboos   Some medicines were very dangerous. That from the American eagle {*sic*, bald eagle?} required the holder to arise before sunup and eat breakfast, to keep shadows off the tipi, and to let no one walk behind him. He had to keep the tipi shut while eating, etc.

Medicine: Animal Powers: Eagle   The eagle gave medicine for pain or sickness.

Kinship Relations: Joking and Avoidance   A man could joke with his brother's wife or his sister's husband or his wife's sister. A son-in-law couldn't joke with his father-in-law, nor could a daughter-in-law joke with her mother-in-law nor a brother with his sister.

[A sister avoided her brother's lodge.] A girl never entered a tipi where her brother was eating.

Life Cycle: Adolescent Lodge   Boys were given a tipi when they went on and returned from their [first] raiding party.

War   A man could go alone on a raid.

Life Cycle: Abandoning Aged   In one case, an aged woman was abandoned to her fate because she was hopelessly sick.[2]

Medicine: Sorcery   A young man was paying too much attention to one wife of a bigamous husband [one of another's two wives] and the latter put the bee on the former so he became mentally deranged, but he was harmless. [He wandered on foot, never rode]. He was cared for by his relations, but wouldn't talk to people. He was feared [though they never did anything to him; they especially closed the doors of their tipis at night to keep him out.][3]

1. Hoebel 1940:25.
2. Wallace and Hoebel 1952:149 (?).
3. Wallace and Hoebel 1952: 236.

[Once Herman's family was moving. They camped at a creek one night. Their dog chased a mule around and around, then they saw the crazy boy.]

Another youth talked to himself continually. He was also harmless.

Medicine: Curing: Blindness   Blindness has become more common since the introduction of the wash basin.

Animals: Dogs   Dogs were used to watch only, not for hunting.

Dove was regarded as lazy because it built a poor nest, hence it wasn't eaten because they didn't want to inherit laziness. [Its nest had only a few sticks, therefore she didn't care for her young.]

Eagle feathers were obtained by trapping the birds.

Comanches were afraid of snakes, they never ate them.

Comanches never ate ⟨mambuma⟩[1] a blue lizard with a yellow head. ["The Indians were scared of him."] Once some boys threw stones at one. They were on horseback and were pursued by the mambuma that got big. [It caught up with them, climbed up on the rump of the horse and bit the boys], hence they were afraid of it and wouldn't kill it.

Comanches ate terrapins, and used the shells for beads, etc.

Comanches bred for pintos. Horses nearly always followed the sire.

Notes on a Comanche Funeral, Deyo Mission
July 1, 1933

(1) The ceremony began about 4:00 P.M. with a song (hymn?) in the native tongue, mostly by older men and women.[2]

(2) An English hymn, "What a Friend We Have in Jesus."

(3) A prayer led by an Indian in the native tongue.

(4) Another English hymn.

(5) The funeral address (by Gilbert[3]) with the aid of an interpreter.

(6) Then there were speakers, two male, one female, two male. There was a native chant by a woman. And then more speeches, one male, one female, two male. Three of the speakers, including two men and one woman, were kin of the deceased. One woman (the daughter of the deceased) was under great emotional stress, the interpreter less so. All the addresses save one (by the interpreter) were in the native tongue.

(7) At the close of the speech making, the body was placed in the hall and people filed past. The female kin of the deceased lamented very audibly. The daughter collapsed, and

---

1. Both Wedel's and Hoebel's notes initially gave this term. However, both sets of notes have emendations suggesting that they later realized that "manbuma" was a mishearing of the English folk name "mountain boomer" for the lizard that Robinson and Armagost (1990) identifies as *ebimuutaroo³* and *ebipaboko³ai³*, both based on *ebi* 'blue'. Conversely, while Robinson and Armagost gives *paboko³ai* as 'lizard [timber variety]', they do not identify the meaning of *muutaroo*.

2. Deyo Baptist Mission is at Cache, Okla. The deceased was Pahkahwah, a former Indian scout, age 87, who died July 1 from the effects of a fall (see Lawton, Okla., *Constitution,* July 2, 1933).

3. Rev. H. F. Gilbert, pastor of Deyo Mission.

required the attentions of three or four older Indian women. Finally, an old blind man was led to the coffin. He was a lifelong friend of the deceased. He passed his hands over the features of dead man. Then, in a high penetrating voice,[1] he delivered a fifteen-minute funeral oration in Comanche, recalling all that the deceased had done for him, ("he was his eye when he became blind") and urged him (the deceased) to seek for the speaker in the hereafter as the latter would seek for the former, etc. As he finished his voice broke, then he began a few low syllables of an ancient wail. At the same time he stooped and started to embrace the corpse but was led away before the act was completed. After the body had been replaced in the hearse, a delay ensued due to the collapse of the deceased's daughter. During the wait, another old man placed his left arm on the orator's right shoulder, rested his head thereon, and began another lament, in which he was quickly joined by the orator. After a very few minutes, a third Indian approached, spoke to the sorrowers, and they promptly quieted down. Both of the old men wore their hair parted in two braids wrapped with green cloth. The orator also wore silver ear ornaments.

QUASSYAH
July 5, 1933

Names: Quassyah Quassyah meant 'Eagle Tail Feathers.' He was sixty-seven years of age.[2]

Names: Comanche *nʉmʉ* meant 'Indian'.[3] (Its plural was *nʉmʉnʉʉ*.)

"Comanche" was not Indian,[4] but was the name applied by the whites, its meaning was unknown. *nʉmʉnʉʉ* was their own name. It meant "the people."[5]

[The general Comanche name was *nʉmʉnʉʉ*, which meant people. It was derived from *nʉmʉ* 'Indian'.]

Social Organization: Bands: Band Lists The different bands had different names.

(1) The Yapainʉʉ[6] were the northern band. It was the name of an edible herb, similar to the potato, *yap* {*Perideridia gairdneri*}. It meant "a root eater." [They were under Parʉasʉmʉno[7] {Ten Bears}.]

---

1. In 1867, Henry Stanley described Parʉasʉmʉno's oratorical style at the Medicine Lodge Treaty Council of 1867 as a "shrill voice" (Stanley 1967:282).

2. See Introduction.

3. Robinson and Armagost (1990) gives *nʉmʉ* as 'our'; with the plural suffix -*nʉʉ*, *nʉmʉnʉʉ* is 'our people' and thus, by extension,'Comanche'.

4. That is, not Comanche'; the name derives from the Ute language (Opler 1943).

5. Wallace and Hoebel 1952:22.

6. The form *yapainʉʉ* is a shortening of the ethnonym *yamparʉhka* 'yampa eaters'. For the last century of recorded Comanche history, the latter (as Yamparika) was the usual form. To date, the earliest record of *yapainʉʉ* is Garcia-Rejón's vocabulary (1866:5). It is interesting that none of the 1933 consultants used the older form.

7. Although he is well-know historically, there are in the literature several degrees of confusion about this individual and his name. In these notes his name alternates between the Comanche appellations Parʉasʉmʉno, Sʉmʉno, and Wasape (all normalized), as well as the English appellations Ten Bears and Ten.

(2) The Kwaharʉnʉʉ were the western band. They moved west into the plains.[1] They were named after the antelope. They were also called KwahihʉʉkInʉʉ[2] because they turned their backs to the sun; they were "the people who used their backs for shade" [They were sometimes called the KwahihʉʉkInʉʉ after the "back shades" worn by them].

(3) The Noyʉhka were called "those who moved camp often" because they changed camp more frequently than the others. This was Quassyah's band.[3]

[a. Tʉtsʉnoyʉhka[4]]

(4) Penanʉʉ[5] meant 'wasp'; like wasps, they raided and immediately disappeared, to sting you right now and get away.

[bee?];

[a. 'quick stingers' or 'raiders']

[(5) ⟨tanomai⟩[6]]

A search for the Comanche word for 'bear' produces several historical and linguistic problems. Robinson and Armagost (1990) gives only *wasape* for 'bear' (although by implication, they recognize *parʉa* as 'bear' via Parʉakuhma 'Bull Bear'). Jean Charney (1993:41) describes *wasape* as a borrowing of the Osage word for 'bear'. Other historians, ethnologists, and linguists, notably Berlandier (1844), Steward (1938:274–83), and Casagrande (1954–55, III:9), give other terms such as *parʉa*, *wʉra*, and *ohamukweyahr*, the latter literally, 'something yellow smeared on his nose'. Casagrande suggests that these terms might refer to separate species (1954–55, II:9 n. 137) . This comment finds some resonance in Berlandier's comment:

> In Texas there are two varieties of black bear; one is wholly black . . . the other is more aggressive, has a yellowish snout . . . Both . . . This animal, known as huira [*wʉra*] by the Comanches. [1844:181]

Although Berlandier said "both," he gave only one name, "huira," clearly *wʉra*, while his notation of a "yellowish snout" presages Casagrande's *ohamukweyahr*.

There is also a temporal dimension to these terms. From the mid-eighteenth century the Comanche element *parʉa* is translated in Spanish documents as *oso* 'bear' and no other 'bear' word as a name element appears in these documents. The element *wʉra*, 'bear', has its earliest documentary appearance as a Comanche name element in 1845 in the name Tunawooraquashi, glossed as 'Bear with a Short Tail', probably 'Bear with a Straight Tail' (*tuna* 'straight' [Robinson and Armogast 1990]) (Kavanagh 1996:273).

Meanwhile, apparently based on a homophonic confusion between *parʉa* 'bear' and *parʉabi* 'dogwood stick', the 1853 Treaty of Fort Atkinson translated Parʉasʉmʉno's name as 'Ten Sticks'. In another homophonic confusion, the single lexeme *parʉa* 'bear' has been confused with the compound lexeme *parʉhya* 'elk' (*pa* 'water', *tʉhʉya* 'deer'), which could reduce to *parʉa* (see p. 13, note 6, above). Thus, Wallace and Hoebel (1952:281) translates the name Parʉakuhma as 'Bull Elk', rather than 'Male Bear', and Robinson and Armagost (1990) glosses Parʉasʉmʉno as 'Ten Elks'.

1. This directional movement is particularly problematic, given that the earliest documentary mention of any ethnonymic form similar to *kwaharʉ* was around 1860, long after most of the other ethnonyms had been recorded. This apparently passing comment may be a reference to an historical event.

2. *kwahi* 'back', *hʉʉkI* 'shade'.

3. See Introduction.

4. This ethnonym appears as a manuscript addition to Hoebel's typewritten notes under Noyʉhka; he does not give a gloss/translation. It is glossed by Mooney (1896:1044) as 'Bad Campers' (*tʉ* 'bad'). It does not occur in any prereservation documentary source.

5. *pihna* 'sweet'.

6. Only Hoebel's notes give this name; it is probably the same name that Niyah (July 6) later gave as Tanimanʉʉ. The last four ethnonyms are handwritten on the otherwise typewritten card and were thus added later.

[(6) Nokoni,11,[1] 'Those who turn back before reaching their destination.'[2]]

[(7) Penatuhka, "honey eater" (same as Penanuu).]

[(8) Kuhtsueka,[3] "meat eaters"]

[(9) KwahihuukI "Carrying Sunshade on Back."]

Political Organization: Chiefs: Paruasumuno   Ten Bears treated with the whites at Medicine Lodge (Kans).[4] He was one of the main speakers and represented all four bands,[5] but was actually the chief of one only. He was also tribal representative at Washington. He had several wives, also a stepson.[6]

At Ten Bear's death, he passed on his government certificate of chieftainship[7] to his stepson, Esananaka, 'Echo of the Wolf's Howl', who was Ten Bears' son [stepson].

Political Organization: Chiefs: Inheritance   Chieftainship was <u>customarily</u> handed down in family. It was a great thing for a man to give chieftainship to honor his stepson thus.[8]

The Yapainuu were first to make friends with the whites. They remained faithful to their promises. They were first located in the north, and later drifted south.

Esananaka had his stepfather's desire for peace.

After the southward movement all {. . . [sic]}.

(The Shoshone belong to the Comanche tribe. The Shoshone left the Comanche because of an outbreak of smallpox that necessitated the scattering of groups over the Plains.)

The four bands met in council, and Esananaka called upon the chief of each band; each band was ordinarily autonomous. [He called the first general meeting of all Comanche chiefs.] The purpose of the council was to verify his chieftainship.[9]

---

1. The "11" indicates consultant 11, Howard White Wolf, and this is a quotation from him from Wedel's notes of July 31.

2. *koni* 'turn or return'.

3. As written, this is literally 'red buffalo' (*-eka* 'red'); 'buffalo/meat eater' is *kuhtsutuhka*. The use of the two terms as near-synonymous ethnonyms dates back to 1786, with "Cuchanee" and "Cuchantica" (Thomas 1932:294). Kuhtsueka is the normalized form used by Hoebel (1940:13) and Wallace and Hoebel (1952:26).

4. The Medicine Lodge council was held in October 1867 at Medicine Lodge Creek in southern Kansas. It was not the first time that Parausumuno had treated with Americans. He had already signed the1853 Fort Atkinson Treaty and its 1854 amendment. He went to Washington in 1863 and would go again in 1872.

5. "Four bands" is consistent with Quassyah's listing of Yapainuu, Kwaharunuu, Noyuhka, and Penanuu. However, the Kwaharunuu were not represented at the Medicine Lodge council (Kavanagh 1996:411–12).

6. Parausumuno had three sons and/or stepsons: Kotsoekavit (*kuhtsu*ˀ 'buffalo', *ekapI* 'red', 'Red Buffalo'), who died before the reservation; Esananaka (see next note); and Hightoastischi (*haitutsi* 'Little Crow'). He also had a daughter whose name is not remembered (Kavanagh 1996:47).

7. There is no record of the United States government issuing "chief's certificates" to Comanche leaders. This may be an inference from the "chief's certificate" issued to the Kiowa chief, Ahpeatone, around 1891. See below, Post Oak Jim, July 18.

8. Hoebel 1940:20 (?); Wallace and Hoebel 1952: 211 (?).

9. Hoebel (1940:11) and Wallace and Hoebel (1952:214) imply that this occurred at the Medicine Lodge treaty council in 1867. However, there is no documentary evidence that Esananaka spoke at all at that council; Parausumuno was the principal Comanche speaker. Although Esananaka signed the ensuing treaty, he played a relatively invisible role in Comanche relations with the United States (Kavanagh 1996).

Life Story: Paruasumuno {Wedel}   The band was drifting from place to place. They met whites and were almost destroyed; Ten Bears was a very small boy at the time.

All but he were killed.

A raiding party on its way home stopped at a spring. One man unloading the horses discovered the footprints of a child. The man trailed the child and found Ten Bears beside his dead mother, with numerous corpses scattered about. The child was taken, washed and wrapped in a small shirt made from the cloth cover of a shield. He was adopted by one of the warriors and taken home by the party.

When the party arrived back at the camp, they inquired as to which families had gone hunting, raiding, etc. and thus found out who the slain Indians were.

The leader of the war party, childless and young, wanted to adopt the boy, and after some deliberation, he was given him. The party that was annihilated had been gone about ten days from camp, so the boy was called simply *sumuno* 'ten'.

He was very well loved by his foster parents.

His aging stepfather wished the youth to gain honor and respect among the people.

One day he went out to get the horses and met another young man, who urged him to join his (the latter's) war party. Ten went home; he wanted to go on the raid but lay down on his bed without saying anything.

His mother asked his father what he had done to the boy, but his father denied doing anything. The youth finally said he had been asked to go on raiding party, but feeling that his parents might disapprove, he had said nothing and was merely lying around.

The stepfather sent his wife out to see whether the young man seriously intended to go on a raid. Sumuno's stepmother asked the young man to come over to Sumuno's place. Sumuno, at his stepfather's request, fixed a seat of honor for guest at the west (opposite the door-way), so as to gain a reputation for generosity.

The visitor came in and sat down and the stepfather questioned him. He said he didn't want his son to be a coward, but to be brave. The young man promised to look after Sumuno.

There were only those two men in this party.

(Parties may be of any size—it was free for all.)

They planned to go to a certain hostile village, which had just moved, leaving arbors[1] under which they rested.

Presently, they noticed an Indian[2] returning to the abandoned village. He picked up a mirror, without seeing them. Utes were the hostiles.

The man returned to his village and reported the presence of the Comanches. The Ute chief prepared to meet them.

The two Comanche warriors rode on and unexpectedly came upon the Ute camp.

Ethically, they couldn't turn back now.

---

1. In Oklahoma, the term "arbor" refers to the brush-covered structures, either domed or flat-roofed, used for summer sleeping quarters.

2. At this point in Wedel's manuscript notes, there is an arrow from the next page indicating the insertion of the sentence: "The man who retrieved the mirror rode a spotted horse." But given the sense of the sentence, the insertion should probably be in the next line.

The Ute camp was in a circle with two painted ceremonial lodges in the center. The Ute medicine man knew that two men were coming and had given orders that they were <u>not</u> to kill the strangers.

The two Comanches rode straight to the central tipis, to be met by a chief. They were asked to dismount. They were given seats of honor and through an interpreter, they were asked their business. Sʉmʉno's companion said they sought friendship.

Another Ute medicine man arrived in the tipi. He saw the two Comanches and asked the people to be calm. Communication was through a Comanche captive who spoke Ute.

The captives entered the tent with the chiefs and medicine man.

The tipi was surrounded by Ute braves. The Comanches were asked their business by the medicine man. They replied they were seeking peace. The Comanches could hear the outsiders urging that the visitors be killed. The interpreter inquired as to how they knew the location of the village, and they related their experience at the abandoned village.

The medicine man assured them that all would be all right; he was very powerful among the Utes. He said he too desired peace. He lit a peace pipe and handed it to Sʉmʉno's companion, then to Sʉmʉno, who blew the smoke upward.

Another medicine man rubbed his palms on the ground before smoking, because he wanted all people to live together on this earth.

The pipe was <u>always</u> passed to the <u>left</u> "with the sun" (clockwise) in all ceremonies. The men who were allowed in the lodge were already honored, hence there was no discrimination in the smoking order. The smoke was blown first up, then down to the earth (not, as among the Pawnees, to the four directions)[1] by both the Utes and the Comanches. After passing the pipe, it was agreed to make peace. The visitors were asked to eat, and after some debate, they accepted. They ate in the medicine man's own lodge where no one had ever eaten before.

They were then asked how long they wished to stay in the village; they answered, four days.

The shaman told his people he wanted no trouble.

At the expiration of the period, the chief gave them new horses to ride, plus a fine black pinto as a gift. They were also presented with goods. An old war bonnet hanging in the tipi was given to Sʉmʉno's companion, and another was brought in for Sʉmʉno. Then the visitors left with assurance that they would be unmolested. The black horse was loaded with gifts and led. They returned to the Yapai band.

The Utes added 'Bear' to Sʉmʉno's name, thus 'Ten Bears'.

On the return of the men, a crier called the people together. Sʉmʉno's stepfather asked the older of the returned men to relate what had happened. The latter did, and referred to the gifts for proof. This was how Ten Bears got his name and became a chief.

Ten Bears was a peacemaker all his life. He called a council and went to Washington. From a camp northeast of Oklahoma City, seven Comanches rode horseback to St. Louis.

1. This is probably a comment from Linton.

They were aided by whites by train.[1] They told the President they wished peace, etc. They returned to St. Louis and were presented with horses and other gifts by government officials, and then returned to the Comanches.

The treaty with the Utes was broken in Ten Bears's old age by other Comanches. Ten Bears made peace with other tribes. He was also great war leader. He became great through following the teachings of his stepfather, who often accompanied him on raids.

Ten Bears went on a raid against the Osages. He had an American flag. He went to make peace and friendship. He had a letter from the government. Ten Bears showed his letter to the Osages and made peace.

Next he had a special meeting up north with the military. During the council Sumuno had a knife at his belt. An army officer and Sumuno disagreed; the latter drew his knife and plunged it into his own wrist to show his nerve and bravery, thereby winning over the officer.

Ten Bears also went out to act as mediator for the Kwaharunuu.[2]

Life Story: Paruasumuno {Hoebel}   Ten Bears was chief of the Yapainuu.

A war party met whites in battle. Many Indians were killed, all but a small baby boy. A second war party happened on the battle field several days later. They found the baby boy nursing on the breast of his dead mother. She had been dead several days. The leader said he would adopt the baby. They took the cover from a rawhide shield and wrapped the baby up in it. The men carried it home in their arms.

When they got to camp, they learned who was out on the raid; his parents were dead.

The leader said he had no child, and said if the chiefs were willing, he would adopt the child. The council said, "OK."

How would they name him? One spoke out and said, "The people were gone ten days, call him 'Ten', sumuno."

A friend wanted to take him on the warpath. He met the boy out hunting. The boy said he had better find out what his stepfather had to say. He went back to his camp, but instead of going to see his father direct, he sulked in his bed and talked to no one.

His stepmother came in, and said "What's wrong?" She said his father must have mistreated the boy. "No, that's not it."

He said he wanted to go on the warpath.

His mother informed the father, who sent her for the boy. He instructed him to fix the sacred place in the tipi for their guest. (The father could have done it himself, but he wanted his son to learn the "honorable ways.")

---

1. This is probably a reference to Paruasumuno's 1872 trip to Washington (his 1863 trip apparently included only Paruasumuno and 'Prick on the Forehead' [Kavanagh 1996:395]). The other Comanches on the 1872 trip included: Cheevers and his wife; Timber Bluff; Quitsquip, (kutsukwipU, translated as 'Chewing' or 'Chew-up', sometimes as 'Elk's Cud' or 'Chewing Elk'); Esahabit and his wife; Onawia (ona 'salt', wia 'worn away spot', known as 'Salt Gap') and his daughter; Tosawa (tosa 'white', wi 'knife' 'White Knife'); a young man named Jim and another named Buffalo Hump, the latter two otherwise unidentified.

2. There is no documentary evidence that Paruasumuno "acted as mediator for the Kwaharunuu." This is possibly a confusion with Paruakuhma's activities in 1868–73 (Kavanagh 1996:425–48).

They invited in the man. They asked the man if it was true he wished to take the son on the warpath. The father wanted the leader to be an honorable and brave man who would teach their son the bravest way. The man would do it, so the father gave his assent.

The two set out. They arrived at their objective, a Ute camp, and found it had been recently abandoned. The arbors were left standing. They dismounted and looked about.

While doing this, a Ute came back towards the camp. He picked up a mirror he had lost. He saw the pair, and rode away to tell his people. There was excitement in the Ute camp, but the chief told the people to wait to see what would happen.

The pair followed the fugitive and came upon the Ute camp before they expected it, and were surprised. They could not turn back, so they rode directly into the camp. The Utes had a camp circle with two lodges in the middle. They rode straight to those lodges.

The Ute medicine man had had a dream prophesying the arrival of two strangers and had warned the chief to protect them.

The chief came out and signed for them to get down and come in. He sent for a captive Comanche to be the interpreter.

He asked, "What do you want here, you who are enemies?"

The older man said, "We want to make friendship."

The leader sent for the medicine man. The people were gathered around the outside of the tipi talking of killing them. The medicine man came, and asked them how they knew the camp was there. They answered that they had followed the Ute on the spotted horse from the other site.

The medicine man said he wanted peace too. He was tired of trouble, He filled and lit his pipe, then gave it to the companion of Sumuno, who smoked and prayed and blew to the Sun and the Earth. Sumuno smoked next so, and passed the pipe on around the circle. Finally, it came to the medicine man, who rubbed his palms on the ground (let all people live peacefully on the earth), smoked, and made a prayer. They agreed on peace.

The medicine man then asked them if they had eaten. They didn't know what to say, and hesitated a minute. But they said, "Yes."

Usually meals were never served in this tipi, but the food was brought right in. They ate.

Then the medicine man asked them how they felt now. They replied that they were pleased and satisfied.

He asked them how long they would like to stay, and they replied, "Four days." They stayed through this period and the medicine man kept the people quiet.

When they were about to leave, the medicine man said their horses were in poor shape. They should pick two of the best horses that suited their fancy and for remembrance of the incident that lead them in, also the spotted horse that the man they followed was riding. Each was given a present of a war bonnet from the wall of the tipi and other presents that were loaded on the spotted horse.

Their band, the Yapai, were looking for their arrival, for they were overdue. When they got home, Sumuno's father sent about the crier to call the people together. There he announced his son's deeds and the gifts were shown in evidence. Thus he became a chief.

The Utes added *parua* ('bear') to his name, hence Paruasumuno.

Life Story: Paruasumuno {Carlson}   The family group of Ten Bears was moving about from place to place. In their wanderings, they were one time met by the enemy (the whites). In the battle that ensued, all were killed except one little boy (Ten Bears). A returning raiding party of Indians discovered the massacred group, and found the boy lying near his dead mother nursing.

The boy was too young to talk but old enough to understand what had taken place. Some of the members of the party picked up the child, washed him, and made a cloak for him from the cover of a shield.

The chief of the raiding party wanted to adopt the little boy as his own. Finally, after getting the boy ready, the party started on its return journey to the camp.

When the party arrived at camp, they found that the massacred group had left the camp about ten days previously. The leader of the raiding party was anxious to keep the young boy, and he consulted the other camp chiefs about the matter and he was permitted to keep the boy.

The next thing to be done was to give the baby a name. It was thought that the boy should be given the name "Ten Days" since it was ten days since the party had left camp. However, from that time, on he answered only to the name 'Ten' (Sumuno).

The young boy grew up to be a nice-looking young man. His stepfather and stepmother were very proud of him, and they had learned to love the young man as their own son. His grandfather felt old age creeping up on him and he was eager that the young man be honored in some way.

One day, while tending the stock (horses), the young man met a friend of his. They talked with each other. The young friend was eager to go on a war party and to have the stepson accompany him. The young stepson did not agree to his plan as he felt that he must first consult with his stepfather.

He returned home to get his father's permission, but instead of asking him directly, he lay down on his bed and sulked and was silent.

The parents saw that something was wrong. The mother asked the father if he had mistreated the boy in any way. The father replied that he had not. Finally, the young man told this parent the cause for his sulking, and of his desire to go on a war party. The parents immediately inquired about the other young man. The mother said she would go and see the young man, and ask him to come and talk with the stepfather about the matter, which she did.

The young friend came. The stepfather told his son to make a place for the guest, which was a special honor to the son. A place was prepared by the stepson on the west side of the tipi, which was the place of honor. The stepfather could have done it, but wanted his son to get a name for generosity and kindness.

The stepfather spoke to the young man. He told him that he was anxious for his stepson to be a brave honorable man, and was not willing to have him disgraced in a raiding party. He was anxious for his son to make good on a raiding party and he wanted a brave man.

The two young men finally agreed that all things were satisfactory for the two men to go on a raiding party. Just those two young men went on the party.

On their first day out, they visited a recently abandoned Indian camp (Ute). They stopped there to rest. While resting in the camp, they noticed an Indian brave riding toward them on a pinto horse. When the Indian had come a certain distance, he bent down and picked up a mirror that he had apparently lost or forgotten.

The riding Indian noticed the two young men. He turned quickly and rode back to camp. He told the people what he had seen. The chief of the camp, who was also a medicine man, told the people not to be alarmed, as no harm would come to them.

The two young warriors followed the Ute. The two men came upon the Ute camp very unexpectedly. Since it was a disgrace to turn back and retreat from danger when on a warpath or raiding party, they must go on directly into the camp of the enemy.

They noticed two tents in the center of the camp. They rode directly toward them. They were the ceremonial tents of the medicine man, who was also the chief. Before the chief had ever been told that the two young men were coming, he had known it, since he had a dream in which he had learned of their coming. He told his people not to harm the young men or attempt to kill them.

When the two men stopped before the ceremonial tipi, one of the leading men came out from the tipi and told them to dismount, which they did. They were then told to go into the tipi, which they also did.

Within the tipi, they were given seats as honored guests. The two young men were questioned by some of the leading men of the tribe, who were within the tipi. The elder of the two young men replied (Ten Bears' friend) that they wanted to be friends of the Utes. A medicine man came in and said that they were enemies.

The two groups had difficulty understanding each other since they spoke different languages. They found a Comanche captive who acted as interpreter. The medicine man told the interpreter to find out from the young men the true nature of their intentions.

The older boy replied that they sought friendship.

The tipi was surrounded by Ute braves who were shouting, "Kill them!"

The interpreter inquired of the young men how they had known the location of the camp. They replied that they had simply followed the young Ute warrior who had returned to the deserted camp to look for his mirror.

The medicine man assured the young men that they had nothing to fear, that their lives would be spared, saying that he desired peace. The medicine man lit the peace pipe, smoked, then passed it to Sɨmɨno's companion on his left, then to Sɨmɨno. When it came to another Ute medicine man, he rubbed the palms of his hands on the ground before smoking, as a sign that he wanted all people to live together on this earth in peace.

After the pipe had passed around, peace was concluded. The visitors were then asked whether or not they had eaten. They replied that they had not, but were at first hesitant about accepting the invitation to eat. Finally, they consented, however, and food was brought into the tipi. The food was not prepared in the tipi because it was the ceremonial tipi and was never prepared in it.

After eating, they were asked how long they wanted to remain. They answered that they wished to remain four days and that they did. The medicine man (or chief) then told his people that he wanted no trouble and all was to be peaceful as long as the visitors were in their midst.

At the end of four days, the men prepared to leave. They were each given a new horse to ride by the chief. He said that their own horses were in pretty bad shape. They gave them also the black pinto of the young man whom they had seen returning for the mirror. This pinto the Utes loaded with gifts. To the older of the two men was given a war bonnet hanging in the tipi. They brought in another war bonnet that was given to Sumuno. Finally, the two young men left the camps of the Utes and returned to their band, which was the Yapai. The Utes added the word 'bear' to Sumuno's name, and henceforward he became known as Ten Bears (Paruasumuno).

When the two young men returned to their camp, all of the people were gathered together to hear the exploits of the two young warriors. When the whole camp had assembled, Ten Bears's stepfather told Sumuno's friend to recount their exploits, which he did. As a result of this experience, Sumuno became an important man in the tribe.

All through his life, Ten Bears was a peacemaker. When he became chief, his band was located northeast of what is now Oklahoma City. Later, Ten Bears and six other Comanches, with a guide, rode horseback as far as St. Louis. There they were assisted by whites and proceeded to Washington to visit the President. In the interview with the President, they told him they desired peace with the government. They later returned to St. Louis and were presented with gifts of horses and other things by government officials. After this they returned to their people.

The treaty with the Utes was kept until Ten Bears was an old man. It was finally broken. Ten Bears made peace with many other tribes. He was a great war leader.

Ten Bears went out against {illegible} his warriors together and took with him an American flag. He went out to make peace. He showed the Osages some kind of letter from the government. Ten Bears showed his letter to the Osages and thus established peace with them.

One time, Ten Bears was in council with some military men, He disagreed with the chief officer of the military group on some matter or other. To show his nerve and bravery, and his contempt for life, Sumuno, in the presence of the officer, plunged a knife into his wrist. This act impressed the officer so that he was won over to Sumuno and a settlement was made. At this council, Ten Bears was acting as representative for the Kwaharunuu band.

Paruakuhma   Paruakuhma[1] was the [war] chief of the Kwaharunuu. He gave up his chieftaincy to a younger man, [Wild Horse {Coby}, at the time the Indians were placed on the reservation] because he couldn't adopt and apply white man's ways.[2] Paruakuhma means 'buffalo bull'. ⟨parewa⟩ means 'marrow'.[3] (?)

Wild Horse   The leadership was taken by Wild Horse; Paruakuhma said he would act as assistant. During a sudden attack by hostiles, Paruakuhma was rescued by Wild Horse, and in consequence, the latter was given the chieftaincy.[4]

Tomichicut   Tomichicut, 'Mustache',[5] was a subchief under Wild Horse. He became chief when Wild Horse grew old. [Wild Horse outlived Tomichicut so he never became head chief.[6]]

---

1. *parua* 'bear', *kuhma* 'male'. He was sometimes called He Bear, or Bull Bear. Wallace and Hoebel (1952:281) gives his name as Bull Elk (see above, page 45-46, note 7).

2. Paruakuhma died in 1874 en route to the Adobe Walls and before the move to the reservation.

3. In Robinson and Armagost (1990), marrow is *turana'ipU*.

4. There is no other documentary evidence of this incident.

5. *tu-*'black', *motso* 'moustache', *kutU* 'possessor'.

6. Based on the censuses, Tomichicut died about 1883 (he is listed on the 1879 census, but not that of 1885) and Wild Horse died about 1890 (he is on the 1889 list, but not the1892 list).

Political Organization: Chiefs: War Chiefs   The warriors usually selected their chief[1] or leader; the rest of the village had little or nothing to do with it. [The people did not have much to say about it.] A son would have to be brave.

Esahabit {Wedel}   {Esahabit[2]} 'gray cloud strip' (Milky Way) was the head chief. Terheryaquahip,[3] 'horse's back', was subchief of the band.

Esahabit went on a raiding party south (into Texas) and was shot through the stomach. He fell on his face and was given up for dead. His widow went alone into the prairie to weep. She faced south; she stood facing the wind. Esahabit rode up from behind. He listened to his widow lamenting. Then she turned and saw him, and ran toward him. The two rode back together into the camp where his relatives were mourning his death. He was already a chief, but gained much prestige through this adventure.

Esahabit {Hoebel}   'Gray Skin Between The Legs' was the chief of the Noyʉhka (the third band).

He was the leader of a war party to the south. He was shot in the abdomen, and was left by the party for dead. The party returned and told his wife he was killed. She went out on the prairie to mourn for him, weeping and talking. Esahabit came up behind her down the wind. She didn't hear him. He heard her words of sorrow over him. Then he spoke. She turned and ran to him and he said he did not know she loved him so. He told her to get on the horse behind him and they rode back to camp together. This event gave him more prestige.

Esahabit {Carlson}   "Gray Streak in the Cloud" was chief of the Noyʉhka band.

One time, Esahabit went on a raiding party into Texas. The party that he was with was attacked and Esahabit was shot in the stomach. His friends, thinking him dead, left him on the battlefield when they retreated. When they returned home to their band, they told what had happened and that Esahabit had been killed. Esahabit was a married man and when his wife heard of his death she was overcome with grief. One morning she went out on the prairie to mourn the death of her husband. Gray Streak had not been killed, however, but had recovered from his wound and returned to his band. When he returned, he discovered that his wife was out on the prairie mourning his death. He rode out to her, approaching from behind so she did not see him. Esahabit was almost overcome with joy. He said to her that he had not realized that she loved him as much as she did. Both mounted his horse and rode to camp. Esahabit, who was already a war chief, had his power and reputation greatly enhanced by this raiding exploit.

---

1. Wallace and Hoebel 1952: 216 (?).

2. Both Wedel and Hoebel spelled this name "esihaβi:t." In the 1860s and 1870s, there were at least two men with very similar sounding names, usually spelled Asahavey, and it is very difficult to tell them apart. One is Esahabit (*isa* 'wolf', *habiitU* 'lie down', 'wolf lying down'), associated with the Nokoni/Noyʉhka. The other is Esihabit (*esi* 'gray'); although literally 'gray lying down', it is variously translated as 'gray cloud strip' or, as from Frank Chekovi (August 10), 'gray strip in the sky', both metaphorically the Milky Way. Robinson and Armagost (1990) gives it as 'gray streak, gray flat lying object.' Esihabit was associated with the Penatʉhka. Both men apparently died soon after 1879.

While the present notes clearly refer to Esahabit, the Noyʉhka, the translations refer to Esihabit, the Penatʉhka. The source of the confusion is unknown.

3. *tʉhʉya* 'horse', *kwahipU* 'back'. He was the principal Nokoni chief in the prereservation period. He died between 1885 and 1889 at about age 70.

Social Organization: Bands: Noyɯhka   Quassyah belonged to the Noyɯhka band; the number of band members was unknown. There were about ten old men like him, at age sixty-seven.

The Noyɯhka and Penanɯɯ had the same chief.[1]

Political Organization: Chiefs   A *paraibo* was a chief. There was no separate term for subchief, of whom there were two or three in each band. All chiefs were *paraibo*. If the principal chief was absent, one of the remaining subchiefs was appointed as acting chief. His acts stood even after the return of the principal chief.[2] People abided by the chief's ruling in olden times. He acted as judge in all disputes X.[3]

Life Cycle: Marriage: Divorce   If either party in a divorce was dissatisfied with the chief's judgement (after the respective fathers disagreed as to who was right) {. . . [*sic*]}

If both parties desired a divorce, the chief was powerless to keep them together.[4] If one party only wanted a divorce, the chief tried to persuade them to live together, but he could not use compulsion. [He did not give gifts to bring the recalcitrant party into line. He had no further powers.]

Social Control: Disputes   In the old times, if two men were in dispute (e.g., had threatened each other), the chief called in two other warriors to get testimony as to the past behavior of each of the disputants. If one had a bad record, the other was usually supported by the chief and the weight of authoritative approbation.

The commonest cause of dispute was theft[5] (rare), adultery, wife stealing.

War: The Public Value of a War Record {Wedel}   Case: Just before the allotment of Indian lands, one of two men beat the other to a certain choice half-section[6] of land. The one who had the claim threatened to kill the other if he caused any disturbance. The latter countered with another threat of violence.

The case was settled by Quanah Parker, who called in two old warriors in an effort to determine the war records of the respective parties to the dispute. One warrior was late in coming, so Parker sent the Indian Police to see him for his record. One of the disputants accompanied the policeman. The warrior said that the other disputant was the braver of the two. He had fought a hostile party on foot single-handed. {He} urged number 1 to give up the dispute or run the risk of a beating or death.

---

1. It is not clear what Quassyah intended by this comment. Although it is likely that the Noyɯhka and Penanɯɯ/Penatɯhka shared a common political ancestry in the early nineteenth-century Kutsutɯhka, by Quassyah's own time, some one hundred years later, they had long been politically distinct. Quassyah's statement may be an example of the blurring of political boundaries during the reservation period.

2. In 1829, the southern Comanche chief Parɯakevitsi (*parɯa* 'bear', ɯkɯbitsi 'little' 'Little Bear') traveled from San Antonio to Santa Fe. In his absence, he left his subchiefs Keyuna ('chicken', from the Spanish *gallina*), El Ronco (The Deaf One), and Toyoros (meaning unclear) to act in his stead (Kavanagh 1996:200).

3. This sentence is underlined and marked with an 'X' in both Wedel's manuscript and typewritten notes, but it is not crossed out and it is unclear what Wedel intended by those emendations.

4. Hoebel 1940:19 (?).

5. Wallace and Hoebel 1952:240.

6. The notes of both Wedel and Hoebel record this as a dispute over a "half-section" allotment. However, Comanche allotments were all quarter-sections, 160 acres. In his book, Hoebel corrects the allotment size (1940:55), yet Wallace and Hoebel retains "half-section" (1952:341).

The man with the best record for bravery won the decision and the loser gave up his claims to the land. In this case, if the latter could have shown braver deeds, he could have kept the land.

War: The Public Value of a War Record {Hoebel}   Case: At the time of allotment, one neighbor beat another to a claim wanted by the second, for a half-section of land. The second protested and contested. The first party threatened to kill the second if he should lose the land because of the objection. The second threatened to kill the first for beating him out.

Quanah Parker decided the case on old lines. He called for two warriors to find out the war records of the disputants. One of them was late in coming, so he sent out the informant, Quassyah, who was then the chief of the Indian police,[1] to get the record from this man.

The first party asked to go along to confront the witness. There, he said to the warrior, "Which is better, I, or this other fellow?" (thinking that thus asked, the warrior would give him the credit).

"All right," said the warrior, "You asked me, I'll speak out plain. This other fellow is the better man. I was in a battle where I saw him get off his horse and help a dismounted comrade from the midst of the enemy. He is a brave man and did a great deed. You better look out or he'll whip you or kill you."

With this report taken back to Parker, it was necessary for the first party to come out with the true account of a braver deed or give up the land and abide by the decision. He could not do this. With the Chief and two warriors deciding for the second party, he had to relinquish and keep quiet.[2]

Life Cycle: Marriage: Wife Stealing {Wedel}   If a chief, no matter how brave, took a man's wife, the aggrieved man's brothers or cousins took up the matter, and if their record for bravery was good enough, the chief desisted.

Life Cycle: Marriage: Wife Stealing {Hoebel}   A chief might want a man's wife. He might get away with her if the man was not a brave fighter. However, the man's brother and cousins might take up the case if they were brave. "The chief better look out and go slow." If the man was not a renowned fighter, the chief might simply appropriate her. If the chief or brave went too far, "people would band against him." If asked nicely for a thing, people would probably give it to him.[3]

Social Roles: Warriors   A very brave warrior had things very much his way in the village. He could not deprive others of their property by force without the loss of his reputation. If he asked quietly for the property, e.g., a horse, it was usually given him.

Social Organization: Prestige: Competitive Feasting   If a man were throwing a feast, a braver man could come and stand by and tell the people of his bravery. Then he asked the promoter of the feast if he had anything better to boast of. If he did, the latecomer retired. Otherwise, if the second had the bravest feats to his credit, he took over and promoted the feast, getting the honor at the actual giver's expense. (Cf. Sioux: among the Sioux, the giver

---

1. This has not been confirmed.
2. Hoebel 1940:55; Wallace and Hoebel 1952:341.
3. These notes on wife stealing from Hoebel are on two separate typed cards. Most of the second card is a summary of the two cases involving Cruz and is not included here.

could get the feast back[1]).

War: Coup   The <u>most</u> honorable man was he who had killed most enemies in fighting.[2] It was also very honorable (but less so) to carry off one's wounded friend while under fire.

Political Organization: Chiefs   The leader of a war party was also *paraibo* or *tekwⱵniwapɪ* 'brave man'.

Social Roles: Club Man   [A few men in each band had a notched wooden stick with a leather lash as an insignia of bravery. The bearer of the stick may not retreat in battle. At a social dance, he may use it to strike male onlookers, who must then enter the dance. An onlooker who saw the coach coming for him would usually hop to get in before he was struck.]

   One of the disputants in the foregoing land case saw a man (the man who won the case) ride past a fallen comrade without paying attention. Later at a dance, he {the rider} whipped those who failed to dance.

   {There were three men} (a) the one dismounted, (b) the one who rode by, and (c) the rescuer and litigant. (b) was the "coach" of a dance and whipped warriors to put them into the dance. (a) saw (d) {someone} in a dance with a stripe from a flogging and recognized (b). Thereupon, he related the coach's act in battle and shamed him thus.

   [The coach in a dance whipped an onlooker viciously, and the man danced. When they were through, the man noticed that he had a welt about his waist. Angry, he announced to the assembly that in the battle referred to in the case under dispute over land, this man had ridden over him while he was prostrate and had failed to give him aid, and he was saved by the man to whom the decision in the case was given; the coach was disgraced.]

War Parties: Returning   Upon the return of a war party, there was no speech-making as among the Cheyennes and Arapahos.

War: Scalps   Scalps alone counted and helped a warrior to greatness.[3] The scalp was taken by the warrior who slew the man, or by his friend, but the latter could not boast of killing the victim.

Dances: Scalp Dance   Scalp Dances were held only when a party returned from a successful raid, not for just any foray. [Not after every raid, but only when they were satisfied with success, meaning a sufficient number of enemies had been killed with no great casualties of their own.] There was <u>no dance</u> unless an enemy was killed; even the capture of many horses did not call for a dance, nor did the capture of enemies, as, e.g., of children. [There was no dance for captives, no dance for horses.] There was a Victory Dance only if the number killed was satisfactory. [Handsome women danced with scalps on tall poles.]

War: Division of Loot   When the party reached a safe distance, the leader picked his men as follows: the cook's helper, as the hardest worker, was first; then came the hunters and their assistants; and afterward, the rabble. The <u>hardest workers</u> got first choice of loot. The <u>leader</u> of the party had the <u>last</u> choice in the division. He may get not much more than glory, and could claim nothing.

---

1. This is probably a comment by Linton.
2. This echoes a comment made almost two centuries earlier by New Mexico Governor Francisco Marín del Valle: "Their leader is the one who had killed the most enemies" (Kavanagh 1996:29).
3. In 1912, Quassyah had told Robert Lowie, "Scalping was not prized." See Part Two, below.

Political Organization: Chiefs: War Leader   The leadership of raiding parties was "inherited" (learned). Youths were carefully watched, and as soon as one showed promise and ability, he was slated to lead parties of his own.

Political Organization: Chiefs   When the chief became old, he retained civil duties, his son took over war tasks.[1]

War Parties   Sometimes men were directed in dreams to go on a raid. Quassyah knew of no case where one waited for supernatural direction.

The leader gave out word that a party was about to take off and was assembling at such and such a place, and anyone who wished to join congregated there. The party rode through the villages to show the people who was going.

A good leader could get a great following, a poor leader had to be satisfied with a small party. The chief never interfered with a poor leader [in whom he personally had no confidence. Any man might go who could raise a following].

A party might split after getting under way, if some of the members were dissatisfied with the leader. [If the men on the raid lose confidence in their leader, the party may split up.]

If the chief felt that the party should not go against a particular tribe {. . . [*sic*]}.

If a medicine man in a dream foresaw bad luck for the expedition it might be given up until signs were more auspicious. [If a medicine man had a dream of ill omen, he might stop the war party from going out.]

War Story   A raiding party, while returning, passed people sitting on the prairie and warned them of the enemy nearby. The sitters laughed and remained sitting, and were killed. Don't be too skeptical.

NIYAH

July 6, 1933

Names: Niyah   Niyah means 'slope of land'.[2]

War Story: Comanches and Arapahos {Wedel}   An Arapaho leader, Kuhtsuʔnabo,[3] wanted to go to war with the Comanches to make slaves of Comanche children, to capture the children so that when they grew up they would carry water, etc.

The Arapaho chief had a conference with the Cheyennes so that the two tribes could fight together. The Cheyennes knew the reputation of the Comanches, that they were hard to whip, and they were kind of afraid of the Comanches. He told the Arapaho chief that he loved his young men, and that he knew the reputation of the Comanches and wouldn't let

---

1. This was probably a comment by Linton rather than a statement by Niyah. As given, this echoes a comment made by Josiah Gregg in 1844: "When a chief becomes old and care-worn, he exercises but the 'civil authority' of his clan while his son, if deemed worthy . . . assumes, 'by common consent', the functions of war chief" (1844, 2:308).

2. See Introduction.

3. *kuhtsu* 'buffalo', *nabo* 'paint'. Wedel spelled it "Koatsanaβo."

any of his young men go to war. He told the Arapaho to fight by himself, because he knew he would lose most of his men. The Cheyenne begged the Arapaho chief not to fight the Comanches.

The Cheyennes and the Comanches were enemies at the time, but the latter, the Cheyennes were afraid to attack.

The Arapahos at that time were looking for the Comanches to attack them.

The Kiowas and Comanches were camping together, at the forks of a certain river with lots of oak trees, to celebrate the Sun Dance. At that day, the Arapahos were to make a surprise attack while most of the Comanche men were away hunting and getting food.

The women went to the creek to eat the sweet inner bark of slippery elm—they had no candy in those days. Some of the women were out at the creek when the Arapahos came upon them. This was the first time the Comanches noticed them. The Arapahos killed quite a few of the women and young men. Two young men and two young women were together; the young men had no weapons, but tried to protect the women.

The Arapahos attacked from over the hill, the Kiowas and Comanches were camping in the valley. Those who had stayed behind armed themselves and went out to meet the Arapahos; they had to fight hand-to-hand.

The Arapaho chief rode a pinto and so he could be noticed. The Arapaho chief told his men to fight as long as he was alive, and if he fell, the fight was to end.

By this time, the hunters were returning and the Arapahos attacked them as they came in. The hunters didn't know the Arapahos were in the camp, although fugitives from camp had tried to go out and warn the hunters.

The battle lasted about two days. The warriors were very tired by this time. The Arapaho chief's pinto was about to give out. Two Comanche warriors on one horse noticed him and attacked him from behind. As he turned his back to them to run, his horse stalled and the Comanches speared the chief. The Arapaho chief called for help when he was attacked.

Two warriors rode together to help each other; one could jump off and fight on foot while other stood by to help if necessary.

When the chief fell, the Arapahos turned and fled, pursued by the Comanches; quite a few Arapahos were killed in the flight.

One of the Arapahos left and returned to the Cheyenne village to report the outcome of the fight. The Cheyenne chief was kind of expecting news of how the Arapahos came out. He was watching a certain hill. The messenger was to dismount on the hill, walk a short way, and hit the ground with his blanket. Each time he hit the ground, the chief piled up small tally sticks to record the slain. Soon, he had a big pile of sticks. "Are they all killed?" he said to himself.

It was the chief's place to notify the people. The Cheyenne chief called the people together in a shady place. When the messenger came, the chief told him to tell the whole story of battle, from first to last. The messenger told everything. When he was finished, the Cheyenne chief rose, told of his efforts to dissuade the Arapaho chief, and pointed out what had happened to him.

Niyah's grandmother was in the Comanche village at the time. No Cheyennes were in the war.[1]

sube²tɨ[2] means 'it is finished'.

War Story: Comanches and Arapahos {Hoebel}   An Arapaho chief, Kuhtsuʔnabo,[3] wanted to take Comanche children for slaves. He proposed an alliance with the Cheyenne for an attack on the Comanche.

The Cheyenne chief was afraid to attack the Comanche; he said he loved his young men, and he did not want them slaughtered in an attack on those fierce fighters. He said to Kuhtsuʔnabo, "If you take out any of my men in battle and lose some, I'll kill you for it." The Arapahos went alone.

The Comanches and Kiowas were camping together at the fork of a river for the Sun Dance. The men were out hunting for the big affair. The women were swimming in the creek and stripping slippery elm bark.

The Arapahos attacked and killed quite a few women and boys. Two young men with no weapons protected their two girls and fought their way out. The Comanches rallied and fought hand-to-hand.

The returning hunters were attacked by the Arapahos. Sallies from the camp helped them to break through.

The battle lasted two days. The Arapaho chief could be seen on a spotted horse. He had told his braves to fight as long as he lived. The warriors were all very tired and the Arapaho's horse was about to give out.

Two Comanches on one horse attacked the chief as he turned away from them. They drove with long spears. The chief's horse faltered, they were on him. He hollered for help; they drove him through.

The Arapahos broke, pursued by the Kiowas and Comanches.

An Arapaho left during the battle to carry the news. The Cheyenne chief was expecting him. He had arranged for him to appear on a certain hill and signal victory or defeat: a downward stroke of the blanket for each man lost. For each casualty, the Cheyenne chief dropped a tally stick. There was a big pile piled up. The chief said, "Are they all dead?"

The Cheyenne chief called his people together in a shady place. He told the messenger to tell the battle from the start.

"Now," said the chief, "I told him not to go and you see what has happened."

(This was told by Niyah's grandmother who was in the Comanche camp.)

War Story: Comanches and Arapahos {Carlson}   One time, an Arapaho chief, Kuhtsuʔnabo[4] by name, desired to have a war with the Comanches as a means of getting captive children who could be used as his slaves when he became old. He would need them to wait on him, carry water, etc.

---

1. This is probably an account of the 1838 Battle of Wolf Creek, between the Comanches and Kiowas on one side, and Cheyennes and Arapahos on the other (Mooney 1898:271; Powell 1981:38–41; Kavanagh 1996:243–44).
2. Robinson and Armagost (1990) gives this as "That's all (narrative closing; end of story)."
3. Hoebel spelled this "kwóats&anna:Bo."
4. Spelled by Carlson, "kɔatsənaβ."

The Arapaho chief, not wanting to tackle the job himself, entered into a conference with the Cheyenne Indians. The Cheyenne chief, however, knew from experience in the past the great fighting ability of the Comanches. The Cheyenne chief said that he loved his young men too dearly to permit them to go out and be killed by the Comanches. Moreover, the Cheyenne chief said that if the Arapaho chief went out and fought the Comanches and lost a lot of his braves, he (the Cheyenne chief) would kill the Arapaho chief.

The Kiowas and Comanches were gathered at the forks of two creeks to have a "Sun Dance" (together). On the day that the Arapahos made their attack, the majority of the Comanches and Kiowas were away hunting food for the "Sun Dance." Some of the women of the camp were out at the creek, gathering the sweet inner bark of the slippery elm, which they ate. These women were there when the Arapahos arrived. The Arapahos killed practically all those who were on the creek. There were two young men and two women there also, who saved their lives by making, in some way, the enemy think they had weapons.

The Kiowa-Comanche camp was in a valley. The Arapahos attacked the camp from over the hill overlooking the camp.

The Arapaho chief, who was riding a pinto, told his men to continue fighting as long as he (the chief) was alive. The battle was a furious one— almost hand-to-hand combat.

After the battle had gone on for a certain time, the Kiowa and Comanche hunters began to come in from the hunt. The camp group tried to get the hunters into camp so they would be safe. The Arapahos attacked the hunters as they were coming in.

This battle lasted for two days. At the end of this time, the warriors were very tired. The Arapaho chief's horse was about all in. Two Comanche braves mounted on a single horse noticed the Arapaho chief and attacked him from behind. The chief started to run from his assailants, but his horse balked. The chief called out for help, but he was not heard and he was killed by the two warriors. (The two rode together so that in case they had to battle the chief on the ground, they would have a better chance.) When the chief was killed, the Arapahos retreated. The Kiowas and Comanches followed them, in their retreat and killed a large number of them.

The news of the battle had been carried to the Cheyenne chief in the following way. An Arapaho warrior had mounted a high hill that was in sight of the Cheyenne camp. The sign of defeat (as decided beforehand) would be for the brave to dismount from his horse, wave his blanket before him, up and down, and every time the blanket hit the ground it counted one dead. The Cheyenne, watching from his camp, each time that the blanket went down tossed a tally stick into a pile to keep a record of the number dead.

After sending the message, the Arapaho messenger descended to the Cheyenne camp. When he arrived, the Cheyenne chief called his people together in a shady place. The chief then instructed the messenger to recount the battle from beginning to end, which he did. After the messenger had finished his story, the Cheyenne chief told his people that he advised against this battle. Also, the outcome of this battle went to show what would happen if they fought the Comanches.

(Niyah's grandmother told him this story. She was in the Comanche camp at the time this happened.)

War Parties   When a raiding party was organized, a council was held between the party members to decide where they would attack (they usually attacked Mexicans), how many will go, etc.?

They can't go on horseback all the way through, but they must go afoot part way. They made extra moccasins, bows and arrows, rawhide ropes, etc. While some of them were prepared to go any minute, others were not, so they gave them two or three days to prepare.

[No matter how small a war party was, one of them must be the leader of the rest. The group decided how many would go and what the objective would be. Several days are allowed for preparation.]

War Parties: Parade   When the party was organized and ready to go, toward evening, they went on horseback through the camp to show the people they were prepared and who was in the party. The men going on the party were dressed in the way they would meet the enemy. "They acted like they were going to meet enemies."

They loped through the camp, kind of like a rehearsal. [The afternoon before the dance, all in the party rode through the camp at a lope in full regalia.]

War Parties: Dance   When evening came, just before the departure of the party, the members staged a dance. The young men usually invited their lady friends, possibly also a few other women to lead the songs. Only the men danced, but they could invite their friends to attend.

[There was a war dance the night before leaving. Only the braves going on the raid participated. Each male selected a young girl. Some women helped to lead the songs.]

War Parties: Departure   Probably early the next morning the party would leave. The warriors could sleep with their wives on the last night. [There was no taboo on sleeping with one's wife that night.]

War Story: The Last Raid {Wedel}   On the last raiding party, a certain young man, who had never been to war before, had been talking to a certain young woman and asked her to marry him. She promised to marry him if he killed an enemy.

He went home to his uncle and just lay down without saying anything. His aunt said to her husband, "Did you ask this young man what was troubling him?"

His uncle asked him why he was so quiet, would he like to go on a war party? His aunt had raised the point.

The uncle had a war bonnet, a fast pony, spear, and all the accoutrements of a warrior, and the uncle agreed to let the boy go and to use his war horse, weapons, etc. He told the boy that he should lead the horse, to ride him only in the actual war, and not to let his brother, who was also in the party, ride the war horse.

The party had already left, and the young man caught up with them at noon when they were eating lunch. The boy's uncle was a warrior and advised him to take off his saddle when they camped, to take off and dry the blanket, to keep his arrows straight, etc.

The party took two days to reach their destination. After two days, they met two Indians afoot, maybe Navajos.

When they saw the Navajos, they put on their costumes and prepared to fight. The young man's brother wanted to ride the war horse, but the young man refused to let him.

They all rode a short distance so as to get an even start as in a race.[1] The young man was on a good horse and took the lead. He got to the enemies first. His horse ran into the first man and he killed the second with his spear. The leader of raiding party said, "It's no use going farther, we have what we want, now we can go home and have the victory dance."

They returned from the raid with two scalps and something to celebrate. The scalps were hung on the bridle of the successful warrior's horse to honor him. They shot guns to announce their successful return.

The boy's uncle hadn't had confidence in him, so he was just laying on his bed when the party returned. They were leading the boy and singing a victory song. Usually they led a warrior back and forth across the front of the party.

The boy's aunt recognized the horse and called his uncle, who came out and began to sing and dance and shout when he saw the horse. As was customary, the returning party rode through the village. A big fire was started and the dance began. The uncle was proud of the boy and gave him good clothes, and when night came, he was ready to dance with the others.

The boy had no father and was reared by his uncle. That's how the boy won a wife.

War Story: The Last Raid {Hoebel}   A youth wanted to go on the war party. He asked a woman to be his wife; she said not until he had taken the life of an enemy.

The boy went to the tipi of his uncle (his parents were dead), saying nothing. He lay on his bed, sulking. His aunt said to his uncle, "Did you wrong this young boy? What is the matter with him?"

The uncle went to the boy and asked the question that had been brought up by his aunt, "What is the matter?"

The boy stated his wish and the uncle agreed that he could go. (The boy's father was dead; the uncle, the father's brother, was called *ahpʉ*.)

The uncle was a brave warrior and had all of the equipment. He lent his arms to the boy and offered his best and favorite horse to him to use, with the injunction that he ride it only when they were going into the fight, and that he not lend it to his brother to ride.

The party being already gone, the boy followed out on their trail and reached them at the noon camp. The uncle had enjoined the boy on procedure: come into camp, take off the saddle; dry the saddle blanket in the sun; look to the arrows, keep them straight.

It took two days for the party to reach the area it was seeking.

They came on two Navajos walking. The band prepared itself. The brother tried to get the horse, but the boy said, "No, my uncle instructed me that I alone should ride him into battle."

They lined up and all started at once, so that each had an equal chance. The boy, on his uncle's fast horse, got in the lead. He charged the first man with the horse, knocking him down. He rode on and speared the second. Both were killed.

The leader decided that this was success enough and ordered the party to turn back home for a Victory Dance.

---

1. Hoebel (1940:16) has an unattributed comment about hunters lining up before a running hunt "to get an even start," paralleling this comment about warfare.

They took scalps and hung them on the horse's bridles. The men lead the horse and sang the Victory Song. Coming into camp, they shot guns for announcement, leading the boy back and forth in front of the approaching band. All in the camp made a great noise.

The uncle, not having great confidence in the boy, had taken to sulking and lay in his bed with his head covered. The aunt saw the horse and recognized the boy. She ran and told the uncle to get out of bed. He came out, saw, and then shouted and danced.

They built a big fire and danced. The uncle gave the boy new clothes and the woman married him.

War Story: The Last Raid {Carlson}   During the time of the last raiding party, a boy who had never been on a raiding party asked a certain young girl to marry him. But she refused him, saying he must first kill an enemy before she would have anything to do with him. The young man's maternal uncle was a brave warrior and had all of the paraphernalia for going on a war party (fast horse, weapons, war bonnet, etc.).

After being turned down by his ladylove, the young man returned home, lay down, and sulked. The foster-parents were annoyed by the young man's actions. The uncle finally asked him what the trouble was, and would he like to go on a war party, saying his aunt had raised the point.

The boy replied to his uncle, saying that he wanted to go on a raiding party.

The uncle said to the boy that he could go on a war party, and that he could take his (the uncle's) equipment, including his horse. The uncle told the young man that he must not ride the horse continuously, but only when he met an enemy. The uncle also said that the boy's older brother would probably want to ride the horse, but that he should not be permitted to do so. He told the young man other things also, to keep his arrows straight, saddle blankets dry, etc.

The young man was late in starting, so he had to follow up the party. He overtook them as they were resting at noon.

The party traveled for two days, and at the end of that time, came upon two Indians on foot (Navajos, Niyah said). When they sighted the Indians, they began to prepare for war. The brother, as the uncle had said, wanted to borrow the horse, but he was refused.

Before attacking, the party all lined up as if preparing for a race, and thus charged. The young man had the fastest horse and consequently, reached the enemy first. He did not strike the first man, but his horse ran into him and killed him. The second man he killed with his spear.

With the enemy dead, the leader of the party said it was no use to go any farther, they had what they wanted. They would return home now and celebrate a Victory Dance. The party started for home with two scalps tied to the bridles of the young man's horse.

As they neared the village, the successful warrior's horse was led by the bridle to honor him. They fired guns to announce their return.

The youth's uncle didn't have much confidence in the young man, so he lay on his bed at home with his head covered.

They were leading the boy's horse and singing the Victory Song. He was being led back and forth in front of the returning warriors.

The boy's aunt recognized the horse, ran into the house and called the uncle. He came out and saw the horse and began to shout and dance and sing.

The returning party, as was the custom, rode through the village. A big fire was started and a dance began. The uncle was very proud of the boy. He gave him good clothes and when night came, the youth was ready to dance with the others.

That's how the young man won a wife.

Dances   There were two different kinds of dances: one was on the return from a raid, the other was when men were whipped.

Social Roles: Club Man   A brave man wielded a whip or club and compelled other warriors with the whip or club to get into the dance. The club was a sign of great honor—the club man couldn't retreat in battle—and the others couldn't resist the greater warrior. When they saw him coming, they ran to get into the dance. [The others, like a private to an officer, couldn't speak back; they must do what he said.] The club was the weapon he used on enemies. It was a great big club.

Herman saw one with notches, maybe to denote the number of the warrior's victims.

The right to use the club in enforcing the dance was limited to a very few of the bravest warriors. These men did not have police rights. [No power to keep people out of the dance went with the whip.] It was just at a social dance, not at the return of a war party.

Dances: Victory Dance   The other dance was different, it was a Victory Dance after the return of a war party. A woman usually danced with a scalp or scalps on a pole. They danced at night. Usually the handsomest woman danced, but they were not necessarily related to the braves of the party.

War: Scalps   Comanches took the whole scalp,[1] cutting a strip through the forehead and peeling the scalp off, accompanied by expressions of glee.

[The killer might take it, or leave it, or leave it for a friend to remove, but the friend could not claim the killing.]

Scalps with long hair were sewn on buckskin shirts to make the fringe along the under side of sleeves,[2] or were kept as keepsakes. Sometimes they were attached to shields.

War: Shields   Shields were made from the bison neck hide, stretched and dried on a hoop. The thickest part of the hide was used. Some shields were made of two plates of hide, with (feather) padding between. *topʉ* is 'shield'.

Medicine: Shields   If a medicine man wanted to transfer his shield medicine, the recipient [novice] had to have the same colors and pattern on his shield.

Medicine: Vision Quest   Powers were obtained in lonely burial places, in hills, etc.[3] There was medicine for pain, war, bullets, etc.

1. Hoebel 1940:21; Wallace and Hoebel 1952:246.
2. Wallace and Hoebel 1952:79 (?). There are no known Comanche scalp shirts in museum collections. However, an H. R. Robinson photograph, dated 1892, shows Esarosavit in what appears to be a hair-decorated shirt. If so, it is the only known example. However, the headdress worn by Esarosavit in that photograph also appears in several Robinson photographs of Quanah Parker, a political opponent of Esarosavit. This raises the possibility that the headdress—and by extension, the shirt—were neither Esarosavit's nor Quanah's, but rather Robinson's props. The headdress is now in the Hearst Museum at the University of California, Berkeley, where it is attributed to Quanah.
3. Wallace and Hoebel 1952:157 (?).

Medicine: Shields   Shields could be made anytime, but they were only decorated after the power was received. He had to follow the command of the dream before he could decorate the shield. The shield could be made before, but was not painted until after a dream.

Medicine: Transfer   A medicine man retained his power even after transferring it to another.

Sometimes powers were freely given, or they could be bought with gifts. One could ask a man for his medicine, and if he was willing, then one made a gift. The request was always granted. The person had to smoke with the medicine man, and the latter, if he smoked, couldn't refuse the request. A man <u>might give</u> a horse to get a good medicine.

In the old times, they might have smoked a pipe. Niyah rolled a cigarette of leaves.

Medicine: Curing   The caller lit and smoked the cigarette first, then handed it to the doctor, and if the doctor smoked, he was obligated to go cure. While the caller had no set rules, the medicine man had to observe certain rules of procedure, e.g., puff the smoke up and down.

When he accepted the invitation, the caller informed him of the proffered price. If the cure failed, payment might not be forthcoming, but as a rule, payment was made, and if made, it was not returned even if the cure was unsuccessful. An unpaid doctor might make medicine against the client, although ordinarily he was above such practice. ["An honorable medicine man would forget it."[1]]

The gift of medicine was passed on to sons, not to women, but to boys. A man usually passed his power to his favorite (not necessarily, but usually the oldest) son, who was generally most capable.

Life Cycle: Adoption: Captives   Childless couples adopted children, usually a captive, who was raised as a warrior. Captive children might be given away or obtained by gifts. The consent of the tribe was not needed to sanction the adoption of a captive. Couples might also adopt native Comanche children with their parent's consent. In that case, a young child usually forgot its natural parents.

Life Cycle: Marriage   So far as relations were known, intermarriage was always forbidden; the actual kin of adopted children were still regarded as kin.

Once the grandchildren of two half-sisters married, but they separated when the relationship was discovered. Such marriages were avoided because of the fear of public disapproval and ridicule. Niyah didn't know if there would be "something wrong" with the children of such unions.

Medicine: Fertility   Some women didn't have children in the old days. [It was fairly common.] There was no medicine for unfruitfulness, so far as Niyah knew. The man was sometimes blamed; at other times, it was casually accepted as unavoidable. [There was no particular theory as to whose fault.]

Social Organization: Bands   Niyah belonged to the Tanimanʉʉ[2] band.

Mowway   Mowway was the chief of the band.[3]

Names: Niyah   Niyah was the name given to the informant. The Comanches were fighting

---

1. Hoebel 1940:127; Wallace and Hoebel 1952:167.
2. Wedel spelled this "Ta'nɛmɜnɜ." Hoebel (1940:143) states that Niyah was Nokoni; see Introduction.
3. Here Niyah implies that Mowway was Tanimanʉʉ, although he was usually identified as Kutsutʉhka.

Navajos on a sloping hill of sandstone. One Comanche speared a Navajo when the latter fled on the sandstone slope. Niyah's father was on the party {and asked the slayer to name his child. The latter then[1]} His child was named in memory of this warrior's exploit.

Names: Girls: War Names   Girls sometimes had war names given to them.

Material Culture: Tipis   Niyah was brought up in a tipi.

Names: Naming   The belief was that if a child was named after a true deed, it would have a long life; if it was named after a false deed, it would die young.[2]

Material Culture: Tipis   Tipis usually had about twenty-two poles,[2] usually [of cottonwood or cedar] (from the mountains) about eight inches in diameter when cut. They were trimmed down by the women. The green pole was laid on ground and straightened by driving stobs {stakes} on either side and forcing it to dry and straighten.

Comanches used a four-pole foundation, with a squarish base.[3] A rope was wrapped about the crossing of poles. The poles were pointed and set in small pits, but not laid in a definite sequence.[4]

It would stand strong winds. Guy ropes were used, one in front and one in the rear, fastened to the top to a stake.

The tipi cover was tied to the top of a pole at the rear middle of the cover. The sides were carried round by two women. This pole was one of the tent poles. One woman stooped and other got on her back to pin the cover. They used about eight pins, each about ten inches long and about three-eighths of an inch in diameter, to pin the edges of the cover together. An oval doorway, two feet by four feet, was covered by a flap with two or three crossbars that could be tied down at each end.

Camps: Tipis: Beds   Beds were of peeled withes fastened together with thongs, sometimes to give a "lazy back" effect. Sometimes the willows were painted. In permanent camps, beds were set on forked poles raised above the ground, sometimes with a straight leaning back. The crotches were of chinaberry. The crosspieces were slats of willow. A bison hide laid over the slats served as the mattress. Beds were of any width to accommodate one or several sleepers, and were raised about two feet above the ground.

Rawhide was placed at the base of the door to keep out mad dogs.

A large tipi might have two beds in the rear.

1. The material in braces was struck out in Wedel's original manuscript.
2. While one tipi at the 1872–73 Medicine Creek village had twenty-two poles, the average was seventeen (Kavanagh 1991).
3. Hoebel 1940:16. Wallace and Hoebel states:
Like the Blackfeet, Shoshones, Utes, Crows, Hidatsas, Omahas, and others, the Comanches used four poles as a foundation. . . . It seems evident from the fact that the Comanches used a four pole foundation . . . instead of the three pole foundation of the . . . other southern tribes, that they adopted the tipi while still in their northern environment. [1952:87]
Unfortunately for this argument, the Comanche four-pole tipi foundation is very different from the Northern four-pole framework (Laubin and Laubin 1977). It is essentially a three-pole base with a second door pole (Kavanagh 1991).
4. It is not clear what Niyah meant by this comment. The tipis at the Medicine Creek village, 1872–73, had a definite sequence of tipi poles, although they were equally divided between right- and left-hand order (Kavanagh 1991).

Camp Organization: Tipis: Sleeping Arrangements; Life Cycle: Marriage: Polygamy   The
father and mother always slept on one or the other of the side beds, usually on the north
side. The children, or surplus wives, slept on the rear bed.

     One man had four wives. He slept with one on the north, two others on the south bed,
and one on the west at the rear. [The husband kept them all in the same tipi and slept with
them in rotation to the left.]

Camps: Tipis: Ear Flaps   With a wind from the north, they lowered the south flap, and vice
versa.[1]

Camps: Tipis: Insulation   In winter, bundles of long grass were laid about the inside of the
base of the tipi to turn the wind.

Camps: Tipis: Rain Awning   In rainy weather, an awning was placed over[2] each bed to ward
off moisture.

Camp Organization: Tipis: Sleeping Arrangements; Life Cycle: Marriage: Polygamy   The
man with four wives slept in turn with the others; between the two in the south bed, then
to the one in the west bed. He once forgot where to go, so he stood at the door and asked
where he should go. All the wives called that it was their turn. The man would spend two
nights with each wife, but tried to divide up his time evenly.

Life Cycle: Marriage: Residence   Some men had two or three tents.

Adolescent Lodge   Boys at age twenty were given tipis. Girls sometimes also were given a
tipi.

Material Culture: Clothing   Clothing was hung over the rear of the bed.

Camp Organization: Tipis: Storage Racks   Articles were stored on racks of oak about two
feet long by three feet high, usually at the foot of each bed. A water rack was on one side
of the door. The water was in wooden buckets, formerly an animal paunch. There were
large racks for drying meat outside the tipi.

Camp Organization: Tipis: Fireplace   The fireplace was just <u>east</u> of the center of the tipi.
There were smoke wings on two poles at the rear to control the smoke vent, which was on
the <u>east</u> side of the apex of the tipi cover. The fireplace was slightly hollowed out. It was
not lined with stone slabs.

Food   The Comanches got dried pumpkins and corn from the Wichitas [Kiowas]. It was
roasted in the fire with the shucks on. Corn was dried.

Smoking: Tobacco   The Comanches traded for tobacco with Mexicans.

Relatins With Other Tribes: Wichita   Tukahni (-nʉʉ) "those under"[3] was the Comanche
name for the Wichitas.

---

    1. Wallace and Hoebel 1952:88 (?).

    2. At this point in Wedel's manuscript notebook, he had filled the upper side of a page. But rather
than continue on the lower side, he turned to the next page and started on that page's upper side. When
he realized what he had done, he went back and filled in the previous lower side, and then continued on
the next upper page, continuing in proper sequence. The typist apparently did not notice the change, but
there is a notation "next page" in Wedel's handwriting on the typescript, indicating that he understood
the situation.

    3. The "under" may be based on the suffix -*tuhka* 'under' (Charney1993:74). A more likely
derivation of the ethnonym is *tu*- 'dark' or 'black'*, kahni* 'house', referring to its dark interior, a form
given by the Comanche Language Committee (2003).

Relations with Other Tribes: Sheep Herders   The *kawidahkoniwapI* 'sheep herders' were not worthy foes. It was not honorable to kill one. *kawida* is 'sheep'.[1]

Quanah Parker {Wedel}   Quanah Parker had seven wives. He took one from Cruz and went to Washington with her; she was his favorite wife, Tonarcy.[2] Many people were pretty sore at his taking the wife, but did nothing about it.

Quanah always wanted peace.

Quanah Parker {Hoebel}   In the case referred to, Cruz had induced a Mexican friend to murder a man who was paying attention to one his two sororal wives.

Quanah Parker took Tonarcy, the handsomest wife, to Washington with him on one of his trips. Cruz was red hot and threatened Parker's life. Parker returned with the woman and ignored Cruz. Because of Parker's prowess, however, Cruz failed to do anything. "Some of the people were pretty sore at Parker."

Beliefs: Thunderstorms   The Comanches were very superstitious. During rainy weather they didn't move around very much. They were afraid of thunder and lightning, they laid around on their beds during thunderstorms.[3]

One medicine man understood that lightning made noise and kept his children quiet.

Nighthawk[4] was thought to have something to do with causing thunder [was instrumental in making thunder].

Medicine: Rain Making   {Wedel} Niyah knew of an instance where people were in need of rain.

A man who wanted rain went to a hill where a medicine man was buried. He had no medicine himself, so he went to the grave for help. The man went not asking for rain, but for something else.

Another medicine man had shown the seeker a trick, {and as a result} the seeker had the bean lodged in his throat and was unable to get rid of it, so he went to the grave.

He was uncertain of the grave's location and went to another place. They were advised in a dream while resting overnight that they were in the wrong place and were directed to go down and wash, then go to the grave in the correct direction.

The spirit told them that the medicine man's soul was gone but would return on the following night and they should wait for it. The directing spirit was the soul of another person.

The seekers were on the mountain dreaming the next night. The trees all about them acted as though the wind were blowing. They saw a big black bird (black eagle) whose wing beats caused the trees to quiver. While watching the eagle, he lit on a rock. All at once, the medicine man appeared on the rock with a rattle and a cane. The eagle was transformed into the shaman.

---

1. *tahkooniaru* 'round up herd', *wadI* 'agentive suffix'. The spelling of *kawido* is in the original. Detrick (1895) lists kahwoody as 'sheep, goat'. In Robinson and Armagost (1990), 'sheep' is *kabɨrɨɨ?*. The referent of this ethnonym is unclear. My thanks to Wahnne Clark for bringing the Detrick dictionary to my attention.
2. Quanah took Tonarcy about 1891.
3. Wallace and Hoebel 1952:129.
4. *Chordeiles popetue.*

The medicine man knew what they wanted. That bean (bead) that the man swallowed was gone and he was all right. The medicine man offered them his peyote medicine, but they refused.

It told them that when it was drought, when there was sickness in the country, if the country was droughty, the medicine man advised they should take the least tail feather on the north side of a west-facing right-hand-side eagle, dip it in water, sprinkle the water toward the sun four times, and a cloud would appear, growing larger.

In the old days, most medicine men had eagle feathers on hand.

The seeker refused the power because of the taboos and restrictions placed on the medicine man. "It was too hard."

The seeker's companion, Big Bear {otherwise unidentified}, years later tried the same stunt during a drought during the late tipi days. (They were told to specify whether they wanted a soft or a hard rain) but he forgot to specify. He asked his wife for a cup of water and he sprinkled it with the feather to the sun four times. A cloud appeared and grew larger. Wind appeared with rain and blew the tipis over. His wife got after him for not asking for slow, soft rain and for having tipis blown down.[1]

Medicine: Rain Making {Hoebel}   A man got a bead stuck in this throat while trying to learn a trick from another. He couldn't get it out.

He went with a companion, Big Bear, to the grave of a medicine man in the mountains, but they were at the wrong grave.

They slept; a vision (the ghost of the medicine man) appeared and told them they were at the wrong place. In the morning, they should go down the hill to a spring, where they would find clean water in which they should bathe.

It gave directions for getting to the right grave. They should wait there, because the spirit they were seeking was not in his grave at the time but would be back the next night.

The next day, they followed those direction. One of them looked on the mountain and noticed all of the trees moving as in a high wind. Flying above them was a big black eagle. It lit on a rock nearby and turned into the medicine man they were looking for.

He knew what they wanted without asking and told them that the bead was gone from the man's throat.

It asked them if they would like his peyote medicine. They refused. They didn't want it, it was too dangerous.

Then the medicine man told them how drought brought sickness and trouble in the country, giving them thereafter a rain medicine.

The black eagle has twelve tail feathers. Take the last one out on the side. Dip the feather in water and sprinkle towards the sun four times. A cloud would soon appear and shortly it would rain.

Some years later, Big Bear tried the same medicine when he was living in a tipi northeast of Cache. In using the medicine, the worker should ask for the kind of rain desired. Big Bear made medicine for rain with a little wind in it.

1. Wallace and Hoebel 1952:172.

Then came a cloud, which increased, then rain and a big wind, and his tipi was blown down.

"His wife got after him for not asking for a nice, soft rain."

Medicine: Rain Making {Carlson}   One time there was a great need of rain. One man was going to a lonely place where a medicine man was buried. This man had no medicine, so he went to the medicine man's grave for help. He didn't go to ask for rain, but for something else. Another man had gotten him to swallow a bead that stuck in his throat. He got another man to take him to this grave.

They weren't quite sure where it was, so the first night they were in the wrong place. It told them to go down the valley and wash, and then how to get to the medicine man's grave. This first spirit advised them that the medicine man's spirit was not in the grave just then, it had gone off somewhere, but it would be there the next night. This was the spirit of another corpse.

They were at the medicine man's grave. A voice advised them to look in a certain direction. The trees were shaking as in a great wind. They saw a big, black eagle flying along, and the wind from his wings was causing the trees to quiver. As they watched, the eagle flew towards them and lit on a nearby rock. Suddenly, it turned into the medicine man they sought, sitting there with his rattle and cane.

The medicine man knew what they wanted. He said that it was all right, that the bead had already disappeared. He told the other man he could have his peyote power if he wanted it. The two men refused to accept the power because they were afraid of the difficult taboos that it carried with it.

The medicine man told them that drought brought sickness. He told them how to bring rain in a drought. They should take the least tail feather from an eagle and dip it in some water. Then they should sprinkle it toward the sun four times. A cloud would come up and it would only be a matter of time until it rained.

<u>Big Bear</u> was the man who got the directions. A long time afterwards, when there was a drought in the land, he tried his rain medicine. The people were living in tipis at the time.

He had been told to ask for the kind of rain he wanted, a soft, gentle rain, or what.

Big Bear asked for a rain with wind. His wife brought a cup of water and he sprinkled toward the sun. A cloud sprang up. There was a strong wind and the tipis were blown over. <u>Big Bear's</u> wife got after him for not asking for a soft gentle rain.

Medicine: Eagle Medicine   The holder of Eagle Medicine or Rain-Making Medicine must <u>not</u> be touched by others with greasy hands, and they did not want any sort of shadow to fall upon them while they were eating. A man with such a gift from the Eagle, if he took care of himself and followed the directions, would have much power; otherwise, he didn't have much power. The power that the Eagle gives was for most any kind pain <u>except</u> where there was any blood.

Medicine: Buffalo Medicine {Wedel}   For bloody injuries, there was Bison Power.

Nowadays, in pastures, one sees bison wallows. A wounded man once lay in one of those wallows and died.

One of the bison (probably a bull) noticed that he had died there from a bullet wound—bulls like to wallow and they wanted no dead there—so all the bulls gathered around and bellowed trying to make medicine. Finally, they revived him and gave him power to cure injuries (bullet wounds, etc.) The buffalo medicine was thereafter passed on from man to man.

Medicine: Buffalo Medicine {Hoebel}   A wounded man died in a buffalo wallow. A buffalo bull saw him—buffaloes love these places—and so started to revive the brave. He danced around and made noises; he came to.

The buffalo leader then gave him the power.

There were no taboos on the buffalo flesh, perhaps on certain vital parts.

Medicine: Buffalo Medicine {Carlson}   Once there was a man who was out on the prairie. He was shot and wounded. He fell into a buffalo wallow where he soon died. There were many buffaloes standing around and a Buffalo Bull who was the chief noticed that the man had died. The buffaloes liked the wallow and didn't like to have any dead men about, so they made medicine and they revived him. The Buffalo gave him the power to cure bullet wounds. This medicine was later passed on to others. The only way to get Buffalo Medicine now would be to go the grave of a Buffalo Medicine Man.

Medicine: Vision Quest   If one wanted Buffalo Medicine, he would go to this man's grave. By going to a lonely spot, a medicine man's grave, a man could find what was in store for him, thus might be forewarned of disaster on a forthcoming raiding party. The seeker <u>must</u> sleep at the grave and get a dream. Otherwise, he couldn't foretell the future.

Medicine: Vision Quest: Peyote   Peyote was not eaten before going to a grave, so far as Niyah knew.

Medicine: Vision Quest {Wedel}   In looking for power, a man must have a strong faith and courage or else he wouldn't be successful.

One man went to a grave and lay down. Before he fell asleep, he heard a strange sound (a low groan) and he became terrified. It was a moonlit night on the hill. The seeker saw a specter with a large knife and a bloody scalp. He lost his guts and began to run, pursued by the specter until he reached home and collapsed, "slobbering." When he got home, he was treated with the cedar smoke cure for fainting.

Then he put on his cartridge belt, took his gun, and returned to the same spot as before. This time he went to sleep; this time the spirit came to him and said that because he carried a gun, he would make no gift this time, and he might as well go home. He never again tried for a vision.

Medicine: Vision Quest {Hoebel}   A neophyte must have strong faith and courage to get medicine.

A friend of Niyah's was at the grave of a medicine man. He heard a rumbling noise. In the moonlight, the medicine man appeared with a long knife in his hand. His head was scalped and bloody.

The man ran away. The ghost followed, keeping the same distance along.

The man was scared out of his wits. He fell in a faint when he reached his tipi. He was treated with cedar smoke and he revived.

Later on, he tried to get medicine at the same grave. He went armed with a gun and bullet belt. The medicine man appeared and told him that was no way to come; he didn't like the gun and that he should go back home. There was no medicine for him, and he never tried again.

Medicine: Vision Quest {Carlson}   In seeking medicine, a person must have strong faith in the one from whom he was getting it. He must also have courage.

Case: a certain person sought power and lacked faith and courage.

One man went to the grave and lay down. Before he fell asleep, he heard a strange sound, something like a low moan, which terrified him. Looking up the hill, he saw a specter with a large knife and a bloody scalp, whereupon he promptly lost his nerve and fled. Behind him came the specter, always staying at exactly the same distance behind hm. Arriving at home, the man finally collapsed slobbering all over. He was treated with cedar bark, the usual cure for fainting. Then the man put on his cartridge belt and returned to the same spot where they had been before. This time he went to sleep. The spirit then appeared to him, and said that because he carried a gift {*sic*, gun} he would get no gift this time and he might as well go home. The man did so and he never tried for a vision again.

Medicine   *puha* was power in a man, or spirit. A *puhakatu* was a medicine man or a doctor.[1]

Medicine: Curing: Pneumonia {Wedel}   Pneumonia was pretty hard to cure.

A certain person had this pneumonia. He had two medicine men. The first one tried for two days, then gave up the case. The second doctor then had two days, but before the end of the two days, the patient seemed to be worse. They called a third doctor, but before he arrived, the second doctor returned to work on the patient. They were doctoring the patient in a tent where there was a trunk. The second doctor's medicine was no good in the presence of finger rings, so he asked them to remove the trunk. Later, a woman looked in the trunk and saw a finger ring.

There were three persons in the tent: the patient, Niyah, and the doctor. The patient was prostrate; Niyah was at his feet, and the doctor was standing over his head. The doctor shook a bunch of feathers over the patient's head while standing erect. The patient felt something cool over his body; the doctor told him to move himself again and the patient felt no pain. Thus, the patient was cured with no internal medicine. While shaking the feathers, the doctor prayed, evidently to the spirit who gave him his power.

Medicine: Curing: Pneumonia {Hoebel}   The first medicine man worked for two days with no result. They called in a second medicine man. He worked for a day and a half. The patient was getting worse. The people were about to call in another.

The medicine man said there must be a finger ring about; this would nullify his medicine. He ordered a trunk removed from the tipi, then asked a woman to look in the trunk and search through it. She found a ring.

Then, with only three persons in the tent, the patient, the curer, and the agent who got the doctor (Niyah), the medicine man stood over the patient's head and shook an eagle feather bunch over the patient. He asked the patient if he felt anything. He said he felt something cold falling on him. He asked if he felt better. "Yes, the pain is all gone."

The medicine man was talking all the time he shook the feathers.

Medicine: Curing: Pneumonia {Carlson}   A certain man had pneumonia. A medicine man was called in. He worked for two days with no success. A second medicine man was called in. His two days were almost up so they sent for a third medicine man. But before the third

---

1. Wallace and Hoebel 1952:156 (?).

medicine man could get there, the second medicine man had a trunk removed from the tipi. It contained a ring that was taboo to his medicine.

After the removal of the trunk, there were just three people in the tipi, the medicine man, the patient, and Niyah.

The medicine man stood over the sick man and shook a bunch of eagle feathers over his head. The medicine man then asked the patient if he felt better. The patient replied that he felt cool. Finally, the patient's pains disappeared altogether and he got well.

While shaking the feathers, the medicine man talked and prayed to the spirit that had given him his power.

Medicine: Rain Making   The trick in the story a few pages back was to swallow a bead so as to learn more about peyote. The man later became a U.S. scout. His companion became possessor of rain-making power (Big Bear).

Medicine: Sleight-of-hand   Two boys, with a medicine man, went to the trading store. The boys wanted something. People nearby bought something and paid for it. The medicine man made two or three sweeping motions of his right hand and had a fifty-cent piece in his hand.

Niyah once saw a medicine man swallow and extract a long knife. (There was no arrow swallowing as among the Pawnee.)[1]

Medicine: Sorcery {Wedel}   A medicine man could cause another man to get sick by putting a breath feather, etc., into him. Then, another could draw it out and cure him (by suction, a la Asenap).[2] Niyah knew of an instance of this action.

A feeling over women might cause some such trouble.[3]

If people find that a medicine man was making evil medicine, they might band together and kill him.

A certain medicine man among the Noyuhka got so bad that all the people hated him. Finally, he drifted away west into the Plains Indians,[4] and located with a certain bunch. Soon after, another man got sick. The people called on another medicine man to cure him, and the second doctor knew at once that the other medicine man was responsible for the sickness.

The people kind of got it in for him, and they planned out that they wanted the guilty man to doctor a patient, then they would kill him when he came out after the doctoring. They killed him just the way they planned. They sneaked around the tent and shot him with bows and arrows as he came out.[5] He made just one jump and fell dead at the door.

Sometimes he took the evil off if he was threatened.

The medicine man was not always to blame. His spirit told him what to do and he had to do it, otherwise the sickness would come back on him.[6]

1. This comment is probably from Linton.
2. The reference of this sentence is not clear. Although there are several notes about "sucking cures," none are from Herman Asenap.
3. Wallace and Hoebel (1952:238)?
4. This opposition of the Noyuhka with Plains Indians is unexplained.
5. Wallace and Hoebel 1952:239.
6. Wallace and Hoebel 1952:238 (?).

Medicine: Sorcery {Hoebel}   A medicine man put an eagle breast feather in a man over a quarrel. Niyah saw another medicine man take it out.

A sorcerer would be killed if he did not withdraw a curse.

Case: A medicine man lived among the Noyɨhka band. The people hated him so he moved away; he went west, and located with another band. A man there got sick. Another medicine man took the cure and found that the first medicine man had caused the sickness.

The people plotted to kill the fellow. They arranged for him to doctor a person, then they would kill him as he came out from the tent. He did as they planned and they killed the man with bows and arrows. He made one jump and dropped dead.

This medicine man was not altogether to blame. The spirit forced him to do it, or else it would have come back on him and made him sick.[1]

Medicine: Sorcery {Carlson}   There was a medicine man who was with the Noyɨhka band. Later, he drifted westward to another band. Soon after his arrival in the new band, a certain man got sick. So they called on a medicine man to affect a cure. As soon as the medicine man began doctoring the patient, he knew that the new medicine man had worked evil medicine upon the patient.

The people became angry with the new medicine man for this doings. They planned out a way to kill him. They sent for the guilty man to come and doctor the patient, then when he came out of the tipi after doctoring, they sneaked around the rear of the tipi and shot him with bows and arrows. He made just one jump and fell dead.

Beliefs: Ghosts   The ghost, the spirit, of a bad medicine man, might enter a living medicine man and cause him to kill someone.[2] The living medicine man was at the mercy of the ghost of the deceased. A man could get bad medicine too, and might do so to work mischief on his enemies.

Medicine: Sorcery: Blackmail   The possessor of bad medicine never tried blackmail, because he didn't want his powers to be known. A more powerful medicine man might find him out. A good medicine man could find out who was responsible for sickness, etc.

[Niyah knew of no use of blackmail. {Medicine} must be kept secret always.]

Medicine: Sorcery   Niyah knew of a case where an evil medicine man tried to cause the death of a brave warrior. The doctor told the people who was responsible, but to prove it, they must have the evil magician there too. He later came and said that he had heard that he had been accused of causing the death of the warrior. If he was really guilty, he wouldn't live until the next fall, that lightning would strike and kill him. Before very long he was struck by lightning and killed. Thereupon the sick warrior became well.

Life Cycle: Death: Sorcery   In the old days, there were only two ways of dying: in battle, and from evil medicine men, of whom there were many.

[There were only two ways of dying. There was no illness; one died on the battlefield or by an act of sorcery.]

When found out, sorcerers were either shot or driven from the tribe. There were no diseases but those caused by evil magic, there was no natural death.

---

1. Hoebel 1940:79.
2. Wallace and Hoebel 1952:239 (?).

Medicine: Medicine Women   There were some medicine women. They went up on a mountain to get medicine the same as a man. The procedure was as with a man. A man could go to a dead medicine woman's grave.

Medicine: Competition   An Arapaho and a Comanche evil medicine men met and had a contest to see whose medicine was stronger.

One time, a Comanche camp was near an Arapaho camp, they were side by side.

The Arapaho were camped in a circle; the evil medicine man and his wife were farther to east. He was hated by his own people, who wouldn't go near him. The Comanche medicine man usually rode his horse with a rope around its neck. The Comanche medicine man went down to visit the Arapaho. Each one knew of the other's reputation.

As the Comanche was on his way, an Arapaho warrior approached and asked him where he was going. The Comanche said he was going to smoke with the Arapaho medicine man. The warrior warned him that he would lose his life.

The Comanche reached the tipi. The Arapaho came out and asked the Comanche what he wanted. The Comanche said he had come to smoke. He was invited into the Arapaho lodge and he accepted.

The Arapaho's custom was to invite in a visitor and have the guest sit on the west. The Comanche noticed the skin of an eel lying with its head to the east next to the fireplace. The Arapaho gave the Comanche a place to sit down, and then he lighted the pipe to smoke. They sat close together facing east.

The Arapaho sat on the right. He smoked and passed the pipe to the Comanche. As soon as the Comanche inhaled the smoke, the medicine in the pipe was to go all over his body. When the Comanche received the pipe, he inhaled and he felt something stick through him.

He knew what had happened. The medicine was a yellowhammer[1] feather.

He put[2] his own medicine (a thorn) into the pipe and returned it to the Arapaho. The Comanche's medicine was a barbed thorn, like from a cactus, which could not be pulled out.

The Comanche then left the Arapaho's tipi by request.

The Arapaho took the eel skin and went to the creek, which he jumped over four times and dived under to get rid of the evil magic. But he couldn't get it out of his body and on his return to his tipi, he fell down dead.

The Comanche removed the feather and was OK because he knew how.

The leading men of Arapaho picked out their best horse and other gifts and sent them to the Comanche out of gratitude for deliverance from the evil medicine man.[3]

Medicine   Some men had no medicine. They were afraid to go where there was great danger. Niyah knew of no men who won great honors without having medicine.

The young man who killed the two Navajos got no medicine from his uncle prior to the war party's departure.

---

1. There are a number of European and North American birds referred to as yellowhammers. The one whose feathers are used by Comanches is the yellow-shafted flicker, *Colaptes auratus*.
2. This is the end of Wedel's Notebook 1.
3. Hoebel (1940:81) attributes this note to Quassyah.

Medicine: War   Niyah knew of no men who could exert power against an enemy in war before a battle. [It was not used against the enemy themselves.]

Medicine: Transfer   Medicine men were often seen giving power to one another and encouraging members of their own party. [It was always used before a battle to pass powers among the fighters.]

Medicine   A man could try to get power at about twenty years.[1]

Adornment: Eyebrows   In the old days, men plucked their eyebrows and beards.[2]

Medicine: Animal Powers: Burrowing Owl {Wedel}   The burrowing owl also gave power or medicine. Sometimes it stood and beat its wings and it was hard to hit with bullets. It was proven that before a battle, if a man who received power stood and flapped his arms like an owl, he would be pretty hard to hit. If the soldiers lined up and an Indian with owl medicine could ride by in front of them flapping his arms and thumbing his nose, he would not be hit.

Once an Indian, who had no intention of going and getting medicine from the owl, was returning from a war party alone and afoot. He became very tired and dropped down to sleep beside a prairie dog town. An owl appeared in his dream; it thought that the man was in quest of power. He apologized for its poor home, but said that it would give him power to dodge bullets.

Niyah knew the man who derived this power, but didn't know of any attendant taboos and rules of behavior.

Medicine: Animal Powers: Burrowing Owl {Hoebel}   The burrowing owl gave the power of making bullets miss. The owl stands by its burrow and fluttered its wings; it was difficult to shoot.

Case: An Indian with such power stood before a line of soldiers. He fluttered his arms and the soldiers could not hit him.

Origin: A warrior returning from a raid on foot was so tired, he dropped down to sleep by a prairie dog hole. The bird was there in the hole. He was flattered by the visit, and appeared and told the man he was pleased to be in his so humble home. He had nothing to give him but would offer his power.

Niyah did not remember any taboos.

Medicine: Animal Powers: Hawk   There were two kinds of hawks: one brown-tailed, one gray. They usually flew along creeks and little birds scattered before them.

The hawk said to an Indian in a dream, "I'm going to give you this power so your enemies won't face you." [Little birds fled before the hawk. The medicine gave power to scatter one's enemy.]

---

1. Wallace and Hoebel 1952:156 (?).

2. Men were removing their eyebrows in this manner as recently as the 1980s. See also Lowie's notes in Part Two, below.

Rhoda Asenap
July 7, 1933

Rhoda Asenap's Father   Rhoda Asenaps's father was Pahdopony.[1]

Medicine: Charms: Childhood   Porcupine quills were broken into pieces, put in a bag, and placed about the neck of a sick baby as a charm.

War: Raids   Pahdopony and his brothers usually went together on raids. They stayed out until they had lots of horses[2]; there were always plenty of horses in their family.

Captives   Her father caught a Mexican boy but thought it was too much trouble to teach him the Comanche language, so he gave him away. Thereafter, he never kept any more captives.[3]

War Story   A large party, including four brothers, went out for a battle with the soldiers. All were killed save the father, his brother, and a cousin. Both of the latter were wounded. They stuck together and went into the mountains. Her father decided to stick there until they got well because the country was very dangerous. They made no fire because of the danger of discovery. They got water at night by cutting off the leg of a horse and skinning it out with the hoof on; this made a rotten water carrier, but serviceable. When the men could ride, they stole horses, then got a number more and rode in with lots of captured horses. They had a big dance, and then started out on a raid in the morning.

Medicine: Foretelling: Badger's Mirror   They killed a badger and slit the belly open and let it lie there until the coagulated blood formed a mirror. Then they jumped over it and performed various rites. Her father saw a prognostication of old age; [he didn't believe it since he was continually going on raids], and he lived to be seventy-five. All those slated to die, died in the raid (cf. Cheyenne practice[4]).

Medicine: War   A medicine for turning bullets was owned by her father. He was often hit, but the bullets left only a [red or] blue mark and a sting. Her brother was injured [and killed] once because he hadn't had time before the fight to work up the medicine as was required.

Two of the brothers were killed by Arapahos.

Niyah
July 7, 1933

Camp Organization   In the old times, Niyah never heard that the Comanches camped in a circle. The chief usually had a central place in the camp, regardless of its form or arrangement of the camp.

1. See Introduction.
2. Wallace and Hoebel 1952:44 (?).
3. Wallace and Hoebel 1952:260.
4. This comment is probably from Linton.

People usually retained the same neighbors from camp to camp; they were generally some relation to each other.

The camp was divided into band groups, if the tribe was together, because each band was more of an integral unit and better acquainted.

Acquaintances tended to gravitate to one another in the camp arrangements. In a large camp or gatherings, newcomers always stopped to locate their friends or acquaintances, then they camped with them.

[A camp might stay together for a year, depending upon the water supply, pasture, and game.]

Life Cycle: Marriage: Residence   When a married young man had living parents, he always took his wife to his own people. They lived near the wife's parents only when the man had no living parents. If the man's parents had accumulated much stock, he stayed and took care of the stock when they died; he remained in the same band. [If a father died, his sons must take care of his stock, therefore, he can't be with his wife's folks.] If his parents had little or no wealth, he might, at their death, transfer to his wife's band. [If a man's father was poor, the above did not hold, and he might move over if he wanted.]

If man has several sons, he tried to keep them and their families near his own lodge.

If there were several boys, one or more might go to live with their wife's people.

After the father's death, the sons usually stayed more or less together and kept their tipis together. [As a practice, brothers stay as close together as they can (see brothers of Mrs. Asenap).]

War   Sons [brothers] didn't go on the same raiding party, but usually scattered among several different groups.

Life Cycle: Death: Disposition of Property   This was Niyah's own experience; he also knew other examples, but didn't know if it was always so. If a deceased man had plenty of stock, his brother or sister had more right to the property than his children. Niyah's father's sister stepped in and took all of the deceased's stock, and left the boys with nothing.

Niyah knew of no case where a man, before death, could say who should get what. Sometimes it was understood that a child should inherit a certain piece of property, but there were no written wills. They simply said, in front of witnesses, that someone was to get certain property. This request was sometimes disregarded. But if it was disregarded, the deceased's soul didn't come back to haunt the disobedient. If a relation of the deceased was an honorable warrior, he might step in and compel people to follow the request of the deceased, but Niyah knew of no instance.

When a person died in a family, everything was destroyed in the way of household goods, usually by burning. If a warrior had certain favorite horses, they were killed; favorite stock was always killed, and all the household property was destroyed. The only property to be inherited was stock.[1]

---

1. Hoebel 1940:121.

Life Cycle: Death: Disposition of Property: Medicine   When a medicine man died, his shield and things were put into water and allowed to wash away[1]; it was feared that death or misfortune would happen if his property was burned.

Life Cycle: Marriage: Bride Service   A son-in-law's only work was to gather food. A man always divided up his game with his father-in-law and other kin.[2]

Horticulture   There was no horticultural work.

Life Cycle: Marriage: Bride Service   A man always cut a certain choice piece of meat from the kill for his father-in-law. He always asked his wife to take her father's portion to him. He never took it over himself.

Hunting: Division of Hunt   Game was split up among the people in the camp. Fresh meat was the principal food in those days. If a man brought back plenty of fresh meat, everyone in the camp was welcome to some, often the hunter himself might have none left for himself.[3]

Food: Food Animals   Bison was the most important because it was the most common; hides and meat were both used. Antelope and deer were secondary, former for clothing.

nɨmɨkuhtsuʔ	was bison, it meant 'Indian cattle'[4]
tasʔsiʔwooʔ	was also bison because it 'drags his feet' when running
kuhma	was the male of any animal
taʔsiʔwopiakuhma	was a big buffalo bull, *pia* was 'big'[5]
taʔsiʔwopiabɨ	was a 'buffalo cow'[6]
ekakúuraʔ	was a 'buffalo calf'; a buffalo calf was 'red' when it was born. *ekapI* is 'red'

Hunting: Buffalo   In the fall, when the buffalo were fat, the hides were good and thick, and the flies weren't bad, they went out for the winter meat supply. The children and old people were left behind in camp: "They didn't want to take any chances with them." Certain warriors and families were also left behind to guard the camp.

Everything was arranged. Arrows were prepared with big spikes for the buffalo, although generally they used what arrows they had.

They had special lighter tipis for hunting expeditions, leaving the heavy ones behind in the village. The parfleche was used for packing meat after it was dried. Whetstones were also packed in the parfleches.

There were special hunting ponies that were led until they were near the game, and were ridden only for the actual hunt.

1. Wallace and Hoebel 1952:152 (?).
2. Wallace and Hoebel 1952:134 (?).
3. Hoebel 1940:119.
4. With advent of the reservation, the meaning of *kuhtsu* evolved from strictly 'buffalo' to the more generic 'bovine', or, as given by Robinson and Armagost (1990), 'meat'. A term was needed for 'our cow', thus *nɨmɨkuhtsuʔ*.
5. *taʔsiʔwoorɨ*, literally 'to paw the ground with the foot', a common designation for buffalo, *pia* 'big', *kuhma* 'male'.
6. *piabɨ* 'female'.

The light tipi was not like the real tipi. It was much smaller than an ordinary tipi, made of cloth or skin; they were small, plain duplicates of the large tipis, made solely for use in hunting. They were not fancy.[1]

They called a meeting and decided when and where to go and who wanted to go. Anyone was welcome to the council. [The time was determined in a meeting in which leaders, war chiefs, take the important part, but everyone was welcome to listen.][2]

Once in a while, the buffalo get scarce or drift farther than usual. Then smoke was given to a medicine man by the chief to make him bring the buffalo nearer.

Someone (usually the chief) had to ask the medicine man to make medicine.

Hunting: Premature Hunting   Some people were selfish and wanted to go ahead and get the best of the game. The Comanche were not like that; no one wanted to go ahead and drive away the bison. The people stayed together and hunted even.

Hunting: Running Hunt   If buffalo were run hard, especially in hot weather, the meat didn't keep well.[3]

Hunting: Premature Hunting   Niyah heard of a man who took advantage of the rest. The people were waiting for the daylight. This man went out and shot, but didn't skin, a few animals, planning to do that later. The rest of the people came up and immediately knew who was guilty, so they took their knives and cut up the animal's insides and rendered them unfit for food. [The chief told everybody to keep an eye on the suspected man.][4]

Economy: Hunting: Premature Hunting: Watchers   They always tried to watch when they neared the bison to prevent prekilling; they especially watched doubtful characters if they were known. The chief appointed the watchers. There was no regular police.[5]

Economy: Hunting: Scouts   Scouts were sent out in advance to locate the herd.[6]

Economy: Hunting: Medicine: Taboos   Men with Buffalo Medicine could kill and eat bison, usually a certain part of the kill, but generally they didn't eat the heart, liver, and/or some part of the guts.

There was no medicine to make buffalo follow a man or to come near the camp (cf. Pawnee[7]).

Economy: Hunting   They always came up on the bison from the downwind side. Bison ran against the wind, not with it.[8]

Economy: Hunting: Scouts   The scouts, when they had located the herd, returned and told the people. Then the people left camp and went near the herd. The women led the pack animals to carry the meat and hides. The men rode their hunting horses. Some people were left to guard the camp.

1. Wallace and Hoebel 1952:56 (?).
2. Wallace and Hoebel 1952:213 (?).
3. Wallace and Hoebel 1952:57.
4. Hoebel 1940:82.
5. Hoebel 1940:82.
6. Wallace and Hoebel 1952:57.
7. This comment is probably from Linton.
8. Wallace and Hoebel 1952:57.

Economy: Hunting   The men lined up and the chief let no one take advantage of the others.[1]
They all lined up as for a race. The chief gave the signal, then they rode up (if possible, taking advantage of a hill) and got as near as possible without being discovered.

An old man would probably have some young man to do his shooting. At the last moment, he would tell him to notice certain things on the bison that would show that he was fat; Indians were great for fat.

The men were now among the buffalo. They would get right into the herd, getting as close as possible to the fleeing animals.

The only way to kill bison was to shoot diagonally behind the ribs and drive the arrow forward into the heart cavity.[2] One good shot might kill it.

The buffalo runs fast, so they needed fast horses because they had to be right close to the animal to kill it.

They usually killed two or three buffalo each, and then turned back and skinned the fallen animals.

Economy: Hunting: Arrows: Marks   A man recognized his kill by his own arrows. Each man knew the decoration on his own painted arrows; each man had a definitely-marked arrow.[3]

Economy: Hunting   They never tried to turn the herd. That was hard to do when the animals were stampeding.

Economy: Hunting: Division of Hunt   Men divided the kill if two shot the same animal, but this almost never happened.[4]

An old man was after buffalo. A boy come along and shot his animal and claimed it. The old man wanted no quarrel, so he quietly backed out of the argument and gave up his buffalo.

Economy: Hunting: Butchering   Men did the skinning. After the first few were killed, they stopped and skinned.

They slit it along the belly and along the inside of the legs and skinned it open. After skinning, they set the buffalo on its back. They first cut the brisket, then trimmed it off, peeled it off from the ribs. Then they cut the forelegs off through the shoulder, then cut off a piece from the shoulder to the hips along the back, and a piece from each side (loin) to save the sinew. The brisket and flank, with attached fat, were cut off in one piece. The hind quarter was unjointed at the knee and at the hip. They left the rump with the back.

Both hind quarters were taken separately.

The abdomen was cut open to get the guts with the buffalo still on its back,. If you don't do very good job, it was bloody. You stuck the knife into the belly, reached in, and pulled out the guts. Sometimes they come out easily, sometimes not. The ribs were split between the middle ribs, then the hind ribs were broken off from the backbone.

The loin was the best part of the meat; it looked like fish.

---

1. Wallace and Hoebel 1952:57 (?).
2. Wallace and Hoebel 1952:58.
3. Wallace and Hoebel 1952:59.
4. Wallace and Hoebel 1952:60.

Niyah never saw bison butchered; this was the Indian way of skinning a cow. Hump?[1]

Nearly all of the insides were eaten, with only a little bit left uneaten. The tail was skinned out and left on the hide.

Economy: Hunting: Selection   Young heifers were preferred, not bulls. The hide was kept intact.

Older bulls were killed to get skins for tipi covers. They left the meat as too tough.

Economy: Hunting: Butchering   Wood pins were slipped through the tendons and lashed together.

Economy: Hunting: Division of Labor   The men killed and skinned and helped cut up the meat. After their arrival back in camp, it was all was turned over to the women.

The meat was prepared in the temporary camp. The women sliced the meat and placed it on racks to dry. While it dried, they chopped up the bones and boiled them to bring the fat to the surface, then they skimmed it off and stored it in a paunch.

Economy: Hunting   On the first trip, they didn't kill too many, they killed only what they could handle. They might go out for more, if they wanted them.

The hide never went to waste. The meat was scraped off the hides, then they were pegged out with stobs {stakes} and dried. Then they wouldn't spoil.

Material Culture: Crafts: Hide Work: Flesher   They used a toothed, hide flesher of bone or steel covered with hide (cf. Pawnee[2]). *tohtsiyuʔ* was a hide scraper.[3]

Material Culture: Crafts: Hide Work   Brains of buffalo were rubbed into the hide to soften it.

Animals: Buffalo Fetus   They ate bison fetus on spring hunts.

Economy: Hunting: Duration   They didn't return to the village until they got all the game they wanted.

Food: Dried Meat   The meat dried in three or four days.

Food: Mesquite   Mesquite beans were pounded up and mixed with ground meat.

Economy: Hunting: Duration   After the first lot of bison, the kill was worked over. They went back and got more. They got all they could carry so as to have something to divide with the stay-at-homes.

Material Culture: Sinew   The sinew along the backbone was used for sewing, for bow strings,[4] etc. It was dried on a wall, etc., and moistened for sewing; it was twisted into bow strings.

Material Culture: Bows: Bowstrings   In wet weather, the bow string was removed and carried in a dry place on a person's body, e.g., under the arm pit.

The cord from the bison's neck was placed along a bow to strengthen it.[5]

1. This is probably a comment from Wedel about how would they deal with a buffalo hump.
2. Inasmuch as this comment related to material culture, it may have been from Wedel's own experience as an archaeologist rather than from Linton.
3. Robinson and Armagost (1990) gives *tohtsiyuʔitʉ* as 'scrape meat from a hide.'
4. Wallace and Hoebel 1952:101.
5. Wallace and Hoebel 1952:100 (?).

Economy: Hunting: Duration   It took two or three months to gather the winter supply of meat. The stay-at-homes were plenty hungry by the time the party returned, which was usually well into the winter.

Economy: Hunting: Danger   It was very dangerous to hunt buffalo, especially if a man fell off his horse.

The bulls were dangerous.[1] Niyah knew one man who was chasing buffalo and nearly fell off his horse. A bull tore the skin off his back but the man didn't die. Sometimes a bull gored the horse to death, hence they used specially trained horses.

[They were afraid to go alone; it was dangerous. They set a day and they all went together for protection. Several families were once killed by Cheyennes or Arapahos because they went alone. The whole family had to go, as the women prepared the meat.]

Economy: Hunting: Spring   There were no big spring hunts. Small parties only went to kill a few at time.

Economy: Hunting: Buffalo Movements   The buffalo moved north and south; at some seasons, there were no bison in this locality.

Economy: Hunting: Falls   Niyah heard of one instance where the buffalo were driven over a cliff by hunters.

Economy: Hunting: Antelope Drives {Wedel}   Niyah heard of a medicine man who rounded up antelopes so they wouldn't run away from hunters.

There was once a certain medicine man preparing for an antelope hunt. He gathered the men and said they would have to dance several days to get medicine. While the dance went on, the man got power.[2] He selected two men to stand, one on either side of the dance. They had been given power. One was to go around the antelopes each way; this would make a magical corral to enclose the antelopes. After they were driven into the corral, the people gathered around. The chief {*sic*, medicine man?} said the biggest buck belonged to him, no one else should get it. After the animals got tired, the medicine man removed the corral and the people had no trouble killing the antelopes. Only a certain medicine man had this power.

Economy: Hunting: Antelope Drives {Hoebel}   A medicine man called for a several-day dance to work up his power. He selected two men to whom he gave some power. They drew a large circle walking in opposite directions. This was a medicine corral. The Indians drove the antelopes into the corral. The animals ran around and around inside, but they could not step over the line. Finally, when they were tired out, the medicine man took off the corral. Then the people could easily kill them.

Economy: Hunting: Antelopes   Antelopes were hunted on horseback sometimes, but were never lured by flags or signals through their curiosity.

kwaharʉ   {is antelope}

*tosabI tohtsía*ʔ   is a white rump or tail.[3]

---

1. Wallace and Hoebel 1952:58.

2. It is not clear if this means that the medicine man got power from the dance, or that he went off somewhere else while the people danced.

3. Robinson and Armagost (1990) gives *pi*ʔ*tohtsía*ʔ (literally, 'bob-tailed white spot') as 'white-tailed deer'.

| *tosapI* | is white |
| *pi'to* | is bobtailed. |

Hunting: Rabbits   Comanches didn't eat rabbits; they had plenty of other game.

Hunting: Deer

| *arʉkaa* | is deer |
| *tu'arʉkaa* | is black deer (mule deer). |

Animals: Buffalo   The Indians thought they would have buffalo for a long time, but then they suddenly disappeared.

Story: Buffalo and Alligator{Wedel}   *nʉmʉ'yʉwi* 'swallows without chewing'.[1] Alligators have places where they stayed most of the time, usually deep holes in the water.

Certain warriors were going out on a raid. They stopped by this water hole to camp. While they were resting, they noticed a buffalo bull coming to the water. They noticed him entering the water until he was out of sight, and that was the last they saw of him.

They sent a man down to see what was wrong. He looked close and saw only the switching tail of the bull. An alligator must have got him.

He called his comrades. In the next few minutes, the bull got the alligator out of the water and started working on him, he put his horns to him. The alligator then turned the bull loose and went back to water. The bull went away a distance and died. Then the alligator came out of the water and crawled over near the bull and died; they had killed each other. This story was told as a true tale by some of warriors on the party.

Story: Alligator and the Buffalo {Carlson}   Alligators had a special place to stay in the water. Certain warriors were going on a raiding party. They stopped by this hole of water to camp. While they were resting, they noticed a buffalo bull coming to the water. He got in the water and then was out of sight. This was the last they saw of him.

They sent a man down to see what was wrong. He could not see the bull at all. Finally, he saw just the tail switching about above the surface of the water.

He notified his companions. Pretty soon, the buffalo bull had the alligator out where they could see him. The bull was working on him, putting the horns to him. After this fighting, the alligator turned the buffalo loose and went back to the water. The buffalo laid down and died. Pretty soon, the alligator came out of the water and went over to the buffalo bull and died too.

Animals: Buffalo   There was no tribal organization among the buffalo.[2]

Story: Fox and Meat   There was a big roll of meat drying. Fox smelled the meat, who asked Fox if he was hungry. Fox said, "Yes," so meat gave Fox one bite and left. Fox went ahead on the trail and waited. The meat asked Fox again, and gave him another bite. This was repeated twice more.

Animals: Prairie Dogs   Prairie dogs were eaten.

Story: Fox and Skunk {Wedel}   In a certain prairie dog town, Fox and Skunk once met. Fox called Skunk his brother, and said, "Brother, if you're hungry, I will show you how to get plenty to eat. Follow me and we'll have plenty."

---

1. Literally, 'swallows people'.
2. The reference of this comment is unknown.

Fox put a mark, like blood, on Skunk's side and had Skunk lie down near the dog town. Fox told Skunk, "We'll trick the dogs and kill all we want to eat."

Fox told the dogs that their enemy (Skunk) was alive {*sic*} and to have a victory dance. He told the dogs to close all their holes because there were some people about who would steal.

The dogs built a big fire near where Skunk lay. Fox then told all the dogs that while dancing, they must close their eyes, otherwise something would happen. The dogs were dancing with their eyes closed. Fox clubbed them as they danced past, until just one skinny dog was left. He opened his eyes halfway just as Fox was about to club him. He yelled and fled, shrieking to spread the news.

Fox and Skunk were going to roast the dogs; they put them into the fire with their tails sticking out. (The dogs had danced to celebrate Skunk's death).

Fox had another idea; he said, "Brother, while the meat is cooking, let's race around the hill and the best man will get all of the meat."

Skunk said, "No, I know I can't outrun you."

Fox said he would tie a big rock to his foot and drag it. So the race was agreed upon and began. When they first started, Fox led, then Skunk passed him and went around the hill. Fox turned around and went back while Skunk ran on around the hill and he ate up all the meat save for one skinny dog. Then he stuffed the tails back into the fire as they had been and he left.

Skunk came, and thinking he had beaten Fox, pitied him. He pulled out the thin dog, but threw it into water because it was too skinny. He began pulling out the tails and got no meat. Finally, Skunk went after the skinny one. He just about drowned in the deep water, but got no meat.

Story: Fox and Skunk Fool the Prairie Dogs {Hoebel}   Fox met Skunk in a prairie dog town. {Fox} was real friendly; he called Skunk, "Brother."

Fox said, "Brother, I'll get us something to eat, you just follow my directions. Now, I'll put a bloody mark on you. Now lie down here like you are dead."

Then he went and told the prairie dogs, "Skunk, your enemy, has died here. Let us have the victory dance. Be sure to stop up all your holes when you come out, there are too many people who steal about."

They built a big dig near the skunk. Fox said that all must obey him in the dance. He told them to shut their eyes and keep them shut while dancing in the circle.

He took a big club and hit them each over the head as they danced by. They were killed except one last, poor, skinny dog who peeked out with his eye and saw what was happening. He hollered for help and ran off.

Fox woke up Skunk and together they laid all the prairies dogs in the fire, each with its tail sticking out.

Fox proposed to Skunk, "Brother, Let's run a race while the meat is cooking, the winner to take all."

Skunk said, "No, I don't want to run with you, you can beat me easy."

"Well," said Fox, "We'll tie a big rock on my leg."

That suited Skunk.

They started with Fox in the lead, but soon Skunk passed him. As Skunk disappeared over the hill, Fox turned about and went back and ate up all of the dogs except one. He stuck all the tails around the fire as before and went off.

Skunk returned. He saw no Fox.

"Ha!" he said, "I have won." He felt sorry for Fox, who would have nothing to eat.

He took up the one poor, skinny prairie dog. He thought it too thin and threw it in the water.

He pulled out tail after tail—nothing to eat. He put his hand in the ashes and found nothing.

He dove in the water after the other one, nearly drowning.

Story: Fox and Skunk {Carlson}   Fox and Skunk once met in a certain prairie dog town. Fox called Skunk, "Brother."

Fox said to Skunk, "Brother, if you are real hungry, I'll show you how to get something to eat. You just follow my directions."

He then told Skunk that he was going to put a red blood mark on Skunk's side, and that, when the prairie dogs came in, he should pretend that he was dead. Fox said that then he would call the prairie dogs together and tell them that their worst enemy, Skunk, was dead.

Fox did this. He told the prairie dogs what had happened to Skunk. They decided that they must have a dance.

Fox told them to be sure to block up their holes, as there might be thieves around who would get in while they were away.

Fox soon built a large fire and laid down the rules for the dance. He said to the prairie dogs, "You must all dance with your eyes shut, otherwise something terrible will happen."

The prairie dogs began to dance with their eyes shut. As they danced, Fox hit one after the other with a club and killed them. He came to the last prairie dog, who was a little skinny one. This dog opened his eyes just as Fox was about to strike him. He ran to his hole, but the hole was closed and Fox killed him too.

The big fire that Fox had made was to cook the prairie dogs in. When the prairie dogs were dead, Skunk and Fox put them in the hot coals of the fire. They left just their tails sticking out.

While the prairie dogs were roasting, Skunk and Fox sat talking. Fox had something on his mind. Finally, Fox said to Skunk, "While the meat is cooking, let us run a race. The best man will get as his reward all the meat that we have killed. We will run around the mountain out there."

Skunk said, "No, it is no use for me to race with you, you will beat me."

"To make things more even, I will drag a big rock," said Fox.

Skunk said this was all right with him. The race was started with Fox taking the lead from the start. Skunk soon overtook Fox and got way in the lead. He got out of sight of Fox around the hill.

No sooner was Skunk out of sight than Fox turned and ran back to where the prairie dogs were roasting. He ate all but the poor little skinny dog. He took the tails of those that he had eaten and placed them in the fire as before. Then he went away.

Skunk finally returned after running around the entire mountain. He thought that Fox was still behind him and felt very sorry for him. He decided to start eating the dogs. The first one he took hold of happened to be the poor little skinny dog that Fox had not eaten.

"He is too skinny," thought Skunk, "I'll get a real fat one."

He threw the little skinny dog into the stream. Skunk then reached for a second tail and it was only a tail, as there was no body attached to it. He pulled out a third, a fourth, and all of them. There were only tails left.

He began to paw around in the fire. He found nothing and realized that he was tricked by Fox.

He remembered the skinny dog that he had thrown into the creek. He dove into the creek after it, but he almost drowned and had to climb out without the dog.

Story: Fox and Bear {Wedel}   Fox was organizing the different animals to dance. He saw a fat bear he'd like to eat.

Bear was awfully tender about his feet. Fox wanted to put a needle where Bear could step on it and, perhaps, die.

The dance started, with the bear in the bunch. Fox put the needle where Bear would step on it. Bear stepped on the needle and got sick. Fox called off the dance, saying they'd had a great misfortune and should quit dancing.

When Bear finally died, the animals asked Fox what to do with the body. Fox advised them to throw the corpse into water and let it be carried away, because if they buried it, it would hurt his feelings whenever he saw the grave. Fox cried until he was hoarse.

Fox had many children. He told them to go down and play at the stream and look for something black in the water.

He heard the children calling to him that there was something black floating downstream. Fox went down and pulled out the bear, skinned him, roasted him, and they had a big feast.

While they were feasting, a little bird lit on a branch overhead and asked for something to eat. Fox answered, very cross, and threatened to throw a stone at him if he didn't scram. The bird said it would tell the news and left. Fox dug a hole and buried the rest of the bear, and then painted himself and his wife with ashes on their faces and assumed a deep mourning attitude.

The bird brought the news to the people who, angry, went after Fox. Fox was too hoarse to talk when the people arrived. So the little bird told what had happened, that it had seen Fox and his little ones eating the bear. Fox thereupon wept at the thought of Bear's death. The rest of the animals looked at him and he looked so pitiful that they thought the little bird was lying, and they left.

After the departure of the people, Fox told his children to bring out the rest of the bear and they finished their feast.

Story: Fox Kills the Bear {Hoebel}   Fox was organizing the animals for a dance. He noticed a big fat bear that he would like to eat. He thought the bear had tender feet; maybe if he put a needle in the bear's foot that bear might die. Then he would get the people to throw the bear's corpse into the stream and it would wash down to where Fox had his home.

The dance got going. Fox planted the needle and the bear stepped on it and got sick. Fox said, "We will call off this dance. We have had a sad misfortune here." So the people stopped the dance.

Pretty soon the bear died. The animals asked Fox what should be done. Fox advised them that should throw the bear in the water. "If we bury him," he said, "I'll feel badly when I see the grave."

Fox felt so badly that he wept until he was hoarse.

Then Fox went home and told his children to go down by the creek to play. They should let him know when they saw something black floating down the water.

Thus, they found the bear. Fox pulled him out and they built a fire and made a big feast.

A bird came and sat on a tree while they were eating. It asked for something to eat, "I'm hungry," it said.

Fox was cross and said, "Go away, or I'll throw a stone at you."

The bird replied, "That is not a nice way to talk. I'll go tell the people what you have done."

Fox thought that it might do this, so his family ate all they could and then buried the remaining meat. Then he made himself and his children pitiful, cut their hair, rubbed ashes on their faces, etc.

Then the people came. There was Fox feeling badly, hoarse from crying. The people told him that the bird had said that he did this to the bear. When Fox heard of Bear, he put his hands on his head and wept copiously again. They thought he looked so sad that the bird must have told them a story. They went away and Fox dug up the meat and finished the meal.

Fox and the Bear {Carlson}   Fox organized all the different animals in a dance. Bear was in the group and Fox wanted to eat him, but was afraid to tackle him. Fox lived way down south by a stream. He was going to do have this dance and put a needle where Bear would step on it with his tender feet. That would kill the bear and Fox would get the animals to throw it into the stream where it would float down to his house.

Things went the way Fox wanted them to.

Bear stepped on the needle and got sick. Fox then said that they had better call off the dance. Pretty soon, Bear got very sick and died.

The other animals asked Fox what they should so with the body. Fox said, "Throw the body in the stream and let it be carried off. If we bury it here, my feelings will be hurt every time I see the grave."

They followed Fox's suggestion. Fox took the death hard. He cried until he was hoarse and then went home. He told his children to play in the stream and to keep an eye out for something black floating downstream. Pretty soon, he heard someone call him. It was his children, who shouted that there was something big and black floating downstream. It was the bear. They pulled him out and skinned him and had a big feast.

While they were eating, a little bird lit over their heads and asked for something to eat. Fox spoke very angry-like to the bird, and told him that if he did not go away, he would throw stones at him. The bird said that he would tell the other animals what Fox had done to the bear. The bird flew away.

Fox and his family ate all they wanted and buried the rest. Fox cut his hair and painted himself with ashes to look pitiful. His wife did the same. The bird told the other animals as he said he would. The animals came to get Fox. Fox looked very pitiful. He was so hoarse from crying he could scarcely talk.

The animals told Fox what the bird had said. When they talked about Bear's death, Fox took it hard. He put his hands to his face and cried and cried. He looked so pitiful that the animals said that bird must have lied. They left.

No sooner had they gone than Fox said, "Children, get out the meat. We will have another feast."

HERMAN ASENAP
July 7, 1933

Adolescent Lodge   If a man had more than one son and they were all single, they occupied the same tipi. When one married, he retained the tipi and the single ones moved out.

Life Cycle: Marriage: Divorce   If man didn't like his son-in-law, he could make his daughter divorce him.

Life Cycle: Marriage   The first wife usually stuck with a man through life despite the ease of separation.

Names: Naming   They always tried to get different names for different individuals. The same names were not used for a man and his wife in the same band.

Case: a man had the war name of Tisawawonu[1] ('loss of nerve in battle') and Herman also knew a woman who had the same name. Herman thought it was funny that a female had a male's name.

Captives   An adopted captive son was as much honored as a natural son if he was a good warrior. A brave man was respected for his ability, not for his ancestry.

Names   A puny child was named if it was thought that he was about to die.

They went to a warrior to have the child named after a true deed and thus get a long life. [It must be a true deed to avoid damage to the child or its family.]

A restless child, one that cried at night, was named by a great warrior in the same way as before. The child was named after great deeds actually done. They wouldn't go to a warrior in whom they had no confidence, because it was dangerous for the child.

Herman's nephew was very restless and cried a lot at night, so they hunted up a warrior. They gave the warrior a horse to name the child. He set up a special tipi like that for peyote. They went in first, before sunup, and the warrior gave the child a name that

---

1. This is probably the agency name Tissywahwoonard. In the late-nineteenth and early twentieth centuries, two people were listed with that name: a man (born about 1868), and a woman (born about 1878). The man's name was translated as Refuses to Shoot. Although similar to Loss of Nerve in Battle, it has been not been confirmed.

described very close combat ['Run Directly Against the Enemy'].[1] The child died of typhoid at about twenty-two [twenty-two to twenty-three] years.

Names: Naming After a Woman   [A child may be named something about a woman.]
Asenap meant 'gray foot'.[2] Herman's father [grandfather] was named as follows: a man and woman were crossing a stream, and while talking, the woman noticed her foot. She said, "Look at my foot, it's all gray." So Herman's father [grandfather] was named 'gray foot' to recall this incident. They did not give him the woman's name, but one that would recall her to mind.

Names: Unnamed Children   It was all right if a child died unnamed. [If a child died without a name, he was not given one.]

Beliefs: Soul   Souls didn't wander.

Material Culture: Utensils: Spoons   In the old times, the Comanche used bison horn spoons.

Food Preparation: Stone Boiling   Herman never heard of stone boiling in an animal paunch.

Material Culture: Tipis: Painted   The paintings on tipis referred to the warrior's exploits. They were sometimes related to medicine. Sometimes they were like cartoons.

Life Cycle: Courting   Courting was a very secret thing. {Young men} didn't go to a girl's home; in those times, the mother was very close guardian of her children.
Girls married when they were past twenty years old.
A young man didn't have much chance to talk with girls. He might sneak around at night and talk to the girl while her parents slept. The girl might go out and talk, or might talk through the tipi past a loose stob {stake}. They might get a chance to talk while the girl was [herb or] berry hunting. Boys were not allowed to come up and talk to girls in the daytime.[3]

Musical Instruments: Flutes   Youths played flutes in camp; they just walked through the camp. The flutes apparently were not definitely used in courtship.

Life Cycle: Marriage   Sometimes the young couple fixed things first; they would have known each other pretty well prior to marriage.
Sometimes a woman (outside of the family) [an intermediary (old woman)] acted as go-between, carrying messages from the boy to the girl and vice versa.[4]

Names: Taboo: Teknonymy   If a person died and had children, he was referred to as "father of so and so," or "husband of so and so," etc., never by his proper name.

Names: Taboo   Blood relations didn't repeat the name of the deceased; others might. The name avoidance was now less rigidly regarded due to its breakdown.

Life Cycle: Death: Mourning   People mourned anywhere from one day to three years. In the old days, if a person passed a grave, it renewed the feeling.[5]

---

1. Otherwise unidentified. Wallace and Hoebel 1952:121.
2. Wallace and Hoebel 1952:123. See also, Introduction.
3. Wallace and Hoebel 1952:133.
4. Wallace and Hoebel 1952:134 (?).
5. Wallace and Hoebel 1952:151 (?).

Women mourned the most and the longest. They cut their hair with a knife when in mourning.[1] Men also cut their hair, but not so short. Women are more nervy than men; the latter very seldom gashed themselves on the legs.[2]

Beliefs: Ghosts   The spirits of the deceased were thought to remain in high places near their graves. The fate of the ghosts of unburied slain was unknown.

Life Cycle: Death: Burial   In the case of stillborn children, there was only a very slight funeral, only the parents or grandparents were present, or only women. The body was wrapped and placed in a tree. Names were not given to stillborn infants. If a woman had a miscarriage, her child was buried in a tree.

Medicine: Duration   Power might leave a medicine man if he didn't follow its directions. If the power was very great, it didn't last very long, it disappeared.

Medicine: Peyote   Peyote was carried in little round bags suspended from the bandolier.[3] There were no charms in the bag or pouch, so far as Herman knew.

Medicine: Charms   Herman knew of no lucky stones or charms.

Adornment: Feathers   A breath feather might be worn on the top of the head by an Eagle Medicine Man. Sometimes a trimmed eagle feather was worn on top of the head, falling over the right side, as a sign that he belonged to the Eagle Medicine group.

Medicine: Curing: Cedar Smoke   If a person was sick or weak, he stood over a cedar fire, or tobacco, and had to inhale the cedar smoke to get strong. This was a great thing, they couldn't do without it and it was still used by the Indians today.

The Cheyennes used sage.

Medicine: Curing: Tobacco   There was no medicine without tobacco.

Smoking: Pipes   The Comanches used to smoke long pipes. Herman knew of a catlinite (?) pipe. The description tallied with the Siouan type.

Medicine: Curing   A medicine man wasn't told the caller's mission until after he had smoked; then he couldn't refuse. He usually had a suspicion as to why caller had come, and sometimes refused the call.

Medicine: Taboos   A man who hadn't much power could break his taboo and didn't suffer, but if he had much medicine, look out.[4]

Some medicine men can't eat buffalo heart or liver or something like that.

A man might feed a medicine man his forbidden food unbeknownst so as to break his power.

Medicine: Transfer   A medicine man might give power to another, who might not be able to use it so well, but the first still had it.

Social Control: Adultery   Herman knew of no case where an aggrieved wife attacked a woman who had alienated her husband's affections.

Horses: Horse Care   Captive boys or men's sons looked after the horses. [They were kept close to the camp to be easily procured.]

1. Wallace and Hoebel 1952:151 (?).
2. Wallace and Hoebel 1952:152 (?).
3. La Barre 1975:26.
4. Hoebel 1954:142.

Horses: Feed   Cottonwood sprouts and shoots [tender shoots and bark] were used as feed for choice horses in cold weather and deep snow.

Horses: Horse Care   Boys seventeen or eighteen years old tended the horses.

Life Cycle: Boys: First Kill   When a boy brought in his first victim (a bird, etc.) on his spear, the first person he met said to him, "You must make that good." Then he took it home and his father gave the man a present.

Animals: Dogs   A short-legged, long-bodied, hairless, lap-eared dog (Mexican hairless) was the first one remembered by Herman. They fixed dresses for them.

Kinship Relations: Joking   A man must respect his father-in-law and mother-in-law, a woman the same. No jokes were allowed. A man could joke with his brother- or sister-in-law, and an old man would joke with his grandchildren.

Life Cycle: Marriage: Polygamy   Jealousy between wives was seldom shown.

Social Roles: Friendship   Two men often formed a friendship for life. [They would go together on raids.]

Life Story: Paruasumuno {Wedel}   When Paruasumuno and his friend followed the Ute warrior into the latter's camp, they found the sick chief's son lung trouble. The Utes made arrangements with the two Comanche boys to kill the sick Ute boy so he wouldn't die a natural death. The two Comanche boys dressed in their war costumes. The boy was also dressed. Then they killed the Ute boy.

The Comanches were then given presents and asked to leave. It was more honorable to die at the hands of enemies than naturally. They gave the Comanches the Ute boy's battle horse, clothes, etc.

Life Story: Paruasumuno {Hoebel}   The chief's son was about to die, incurable.

They didn't want the boy to die a natural death, so they arranged for Ten Bears and his friend to kill him.

The two men dressed in their war togs ready to meet the enemy.

. The sick boy was also dressed for war.

They killed him, acting as if in battle.

The chief presented his son's horses to them, and his war clothes in gratitude.[1]

Etiquette   If a person ate with someone, they were friends. A young man who spoke too much was laughed at. Old men had priority of right in speaking.

The law of hospitality was based on eating together.

Food: Cooking on a Raid   Kidney, paunch, etc., were eaten raw when it was unsafe to build a cooking fire, on a raid, etc.

Camp Organization: Duration   A "permanent" village might last a year. It depended on the water supply, etc.

Honoring   The mother's brother honored the boy who had killed the two Navajos.

Life Cycle: Suicide   An old man might go on a war party to end his life, rather than die a natural death.[2]

Herman heard of one case of suicide.

---

1. Wallace and Hoebel 1952:279.
2. Wallace and Hoebel 1952:247.

A man had a tipi, while his sister stayed in the tipi with their parents. The girls preferred an honorable warrior and liked to go with him. They knew several honorable warriors and sometimes went to talk to them.

This man was in bed and was aware of a woman getting into his bed. He marked her on her back with red paint. The next day, at a shinny game, he saw the girl playing. His sister came up and he saw the red mark, and he knew that she was the girl.

He sharpened a stick on each end, and the next night when the girl came back, the warrior placed the double-pointed stick between them with the points to their chests and pulled her toward him, killing them both.

The next morning, when the boy didn't appear for breakfast, his parents got uneasy. They went into his tipi and found him dead with his sister. His mother was angry and cut her daughter to pieces.

Another woman had a grandson who went out root gathering with girls. The grandmother said she would kill herself if he did it again [she said he wouldn't find her alive on his return]. The boy disbelieved her, and on his return, she was gone. Later, they found her dead, hanging from a tree by the neck. It was a disgrace for the boy and the village had nothing more to do with him.

Kinship Relations: Brother-Sister   It was a very great disgrace for a sister to go into her brother's tipi or to be alone with him. A mother often slept with her daughter to guard her.

Life Cycle: Illegitimacy   Herman knew of no case of premarital pregnancy.

Camp Organization: Adolescent Lodge   Girls did not get separate tipis like boys (cf. Niyah[1]).

Medicine: Vision Quest   Only one man went to the grave for a dream, but sometimes he had a companion who would go part way up the mountain.

NIYAH

July 8, 1933

Story: War Party and Beaver {Wedel}   A party was out on its way and it was getting late, the sun was going down. They happened to camp at a certain place, a place like an island, but it was connected to the land on one side, with water around it.

In the party was a man who always joked, and he was telling the rest that it was very dangerous where they camped on the horseshoe-shaped land (spit?), a big beaver might cut them off, might put his tail across the spit or wrap his body about the island and cause the water to rise and cut them off from land. Another superstitious Indian told him not to talk about such things, that they might happen.

Such a party was usually up and away before daybreak. One man (the leader?) got up very early and saw that they were penned up. Beaver had placed his body about the island. The first thing he thought of was the man who had spoken of this, so he awoke the man and told him to find a way out because it was his fault.

---

1. See Niyah, July 6.

He said the only thing to do was for some brave warrior to talk to the beaver, to dress himself in his war costume as though he was going to meet enemies. He must take his weapons, mount his horse, and tell the beaver what deeds he had done. If his story was true, the beaver would open and give them a narrow trail just the width of a horse to get by.

The leader asked them all to go. The man who spoke of this thing was detailed by the leader to be the last one through. As the rest were getting out, the man who was to be left behind, who had badger power, began to dig a hole deep enough to hide himself. After the warriors had passed, the beaver left, not knowing that there was another man on the island. Then the remaining man crawled out of his hole and went on to join the party. The Badger Man didn't know what would happen when he was left behind, but dug himself in so as to be on the safe side.

Story: War Party and Beaver {Hoebel}   A war party camped one night on a peninsula by a beaver pond. A joker was present in the party. He told the others that they were in a dangerous place. If a beaver should get angry with them, he would trap them there; it would cut them off, would dam them up with his tail. Another Indian said he shouldn't talk like that, it was bad.

Their custom was to get up before daylight. The leader got up and saw that they were kind of corralled by that beaver. The first thing he thought of was about that fellow who had talked about this thing. The chief called on that man to get them out. The only thing to do was to have the brave dress in his war regalia and recite his brave deeds to the beaver; the brave told how he had killed an enemy. This being true, the beaver had to give an opening through the water. A passage the width of a horse appeared.

The chief made the man who had caused the trouble wait to be the last to go. This man was afraid to go through because he thought the beaver might close the passage on him. He had Badger Medicine, so he made a hole and hid. The beaver thought they were all gone and he got up and let all the water flow away. Then the man followed the others.

Story: War Party and Beaver {Carlson}   A war party was out on a raid. At sundown one day, they camped near a beaver pond. The place where they camped was a peninsula with water around it like a horseshoe.

In the party was a man who was always joking. He told his friends that this was a dangerous place to camp, and if that beaver who lived in the pond had a grudge against anyone in the party, he would place himself across the neck of the peninsula and their escape would be cut off. One of the men told the joker it was not good to joke like that, as talking and fooling about such things could make them come true.

The next morning, when the leader awoke, he found that they were corralled by the beaver just as the joker had said. He called to the joker and told him that this trouble was all his fault and that it was now up to him to find some way for them to get off the peninsula.

The joker said that some brave warrior should get on his complete rigging and then go to the beaver and recite his war deeds. If the warrior told the truth about the war deeds, the water would get shallow.

A warrior did this and immediately the water got shallow enough for the horses to pass off of the peninsula in a single file. Before they started, the leader said that the joker must go last as a punishment for his joke. The rest of the party began to leave the peninsula.

The joker had Badger Medicine and he dug a hole in the ground and crawled into it. When the rest of the party had left the peninsula, beaver looked around and seeing no one, moved away and the whole neck of the peninsula was free again.

The joker got out of the hole then climbed on his horse and joined his party on the mainland.

Jokers　〈isarenyet〉 was a joker; 〈isarenyekwit〉 were funny ways.[1] Niyah knew of no entertainers who told jokes or clowned when the people at a dance became bored, although he had seen it among other tribes.

Grave Robbery　There was a rich young man and a poor man. The rich man, who had good deal of good costuming, died, and, as was the custom, they buried him in his richest clothes. The poor man thought he should have the clothes, as he had very few of his own. He saw where the rich man was buried in a crevice in the rocks with all his clothes. The poor boy went to the grave and threw the rocks aside. First, he uncovered the head of the corpse. It was night. First, he got the beaverskin braid wraps, then the earrings.

The dead man came to and was trying to get his breath and free himself. He finally freed his hands and seized the grave robber by the wrist as he was working on the earrings. The robber got scared and cried out as loud as could for help.

Finally, he quieted down. The dead man said he wanted a drink. Anything he had, the poor men could have. He told the poor boy to go and tell his (the rich man's) relatives that the dead man had come to life and wanted a drink.

The poor boy followed the mourners and asked them to stop, he wanted to talk to them. He confessed to his grave robbing and said that the dead man had come to life and wanted water.

After the rich man's relatives returned to the grave, they gave him water and he recovered and was taken home. There they gave the poor boy all the good clothes he needed, also three good horses. That's how a joker got good clothes.

Niyah thought it was a true story.

Life Cycle: Death: Burial　In the old days, the dead were wrapped up at once in a blanket. They might come to and smother to death. Niyah saw one corpse wrapped in a blanket; he saw the blanket move, but refused to open it.

Grave Robbery　Comanches very seldom robbed graves, either their own or of other tribes.

(Quanah Parker's grave was once robbed. Also, a white man robbed a grave in the mission cemetery to steal the dead man's money.)

In the old days, the corpse was wrapped in a buffalo hide, later in a blanket. They put lots of stuff with him.

Life Cycle: Death: Disposition of Property: Medicine　A man's shield was not usually buried with him.

---

1. These words are otherwise unattested. They are possibly a combination of *isapʉ* 'liar' and *nohitekwarʉ?* or *nayanohitekwarʉ?*, glossed in Robinson and Armagost (1990) as 'joke' and 'joker' (with *tekwarʉ?* 'speak, talk to someone').

A medicine man's shield was thrown into water.[1] The shield was not supposed be passed on to relatives; other property was passed on. [It may be given away.]

If the shield or other of a medicine man's property was burned, it would bring bad luck.

Medicine: Shields   Shields were usually hung up while the party rested; they were not laid on the ground. Some shields with strong medicine were put as far as one-half mile away from camp. Nobody dared touch a shield so far from camp. [Menstruating women especially may not touch it, or a person with greasy hands.]

Medicine: Shields: Taboos   There were certain things in camp that a shield should not be near, for instance, menstruating women or children with greasy hands. If her husband was a medicine man, a menstruating woman had to leave his tipi. She might go to a friend's or to her mother's tipi. Most medicines forbade proximity to menstruating women. A man shouldn't drink from the same cup as a menstruating woman, nor put his foot in her shoe. The woman didn't have to go apart unless her husband was a medicine man or had medicine.

In old times, any such woman probably went aside during her periods.

Medicine   Usually all the male members of the tribe had some kind of medicine about their person.

Story: Fox and Raccoons {Wedel}   Some raccoons were digging roots out of a pond of water.

Fox saw them and asked how they did it. They told him it was their medicine.

He insisted he wanted the power.

The raccoons told him that he was too foolish and it might cost him his life.

Fox insisted, so they gave him the medicine.

He stayed around a while and dug with them, then he left to try the medicine elsewhere.

The raccoons instructed Fox to go into the water just so far, but Fox wanted to go deeper. Fox went deeper, going beyond his command.

He got his tail too far into the ground and he couldn't get it out. He worked himself skinny trying to get his tail out. He was about to give up when the people who gave him the power came along. He thought of their warning. Fox asked them to loosen him, that he didn't want the power anymore.

The raccoons jokingly said they'd leave him there to paddle his own canoe.

Finally, they dug him out and sent him on his way. Fox never wanted their medicine again.

Story: Fox and Raccoons {Hoebel}   Fox came upon raccoons digging waterlily roots with their tails. He asked them how they did it.

"It's a gift. We have medicine for it. You're too foolish. We can't give it to you. You'd lose it."

Fox insisted. They finally decided to give him the medicine. He got power to dig lilies with his tail like the raccoons. He left to try his luck alone.

He decided to put his tail in the water farther to get more; he put it in too far ("goes beyond his command").

---

1. Wallace and Hoebel 1952:152 (?).

His tail stuck, he couldn't pull it out. He pulled and pulled. He got thin for lack of food.

The raccoons came along and found him thus. They reminded him that they had known that he has too foolish to keep the medicine.

Fox only wanted to get loose. He didn't care about the medicine any longer.

They said they didn't care if he lived or died; finally they pulled him out.

He didn't care about the medicine.

Story: Fox and Raccoons {Carlson}   One day Fox in his wanderings came upon some raccoons digging waterlily roots with their tails. Fox asked, "How are you able to dig those roots with your tails?"

The raccoons said that they had the medicine and power for digging roots this way.

"Give me the medicine," said Fox.

But the raccoons said, "You are too foolish to have such power, it would bring you much trouble."

Fox begged and begged the raccoons to give him the power. Finally, the raccoons decided to give Fox their power. They gave him the power and, at the same time, told him not to put his whole tail into the ground in digging the roots.

After he got the power, Fox stayed around with the raccoons a few days and then went away to try digging by himself.

Fox was no sooner out of sight of the raccoons than he began digging by himself. But this time, he decided to stick his tail in the entire way. But when he did this, he could not get his tail out. He tried and tried to pull his tail loose, but it was no use. He simply could not get it loose. He pulled and tried so hard to get his tail loose that he became real skinny.

A long time afterwards, the raccoons came up to where Fox was trapped. They laughed when they saw Fox. "We knew you would be selfish and try to reach too far down," they said.

Fox groaned and said, "Take me out of this and take your power back, I don't want it any longer."

The raccoons only laughed at Fox. They told him that because he was so selfish, they were going to make him stay there. But after teasing him for awhile, they loosened him and let him go. Fox beat it.

Medicine: Returning   If a man had too powerful medicine and began to fear it, he could go back to the grave where he received it and could have it taken away again [ask it (spirit) to take the power back]. The paraphernalia was not put on the grave, but was thrown into the water to be washed away.

Story: Fox and Fishhawk {Wedel}   Fishhawk (Osprey) was married to Fox's sister. One day, Fox went to visit Fishhawk and Fishhawk was very glad to see his relatives. It became noon and they were hungry. Osprey told Fox he must go get some food. He left the room and flew upwards. He saw water below a bank. It was winter, but he dived through the ice, caught a fish, and came up again. He went home and they had good meal. Fox said he must leave, and invited Osprey to come out with his family and visit him sometime.

When Fox left, he noticed the location of Osprey's home in a bank and decided he wanted a home like that. Osprey went around to visit Fox, who came out and invited him in. Osprey noticed that Fox had a home like his near a pool of water. Osprey hadn't much confidence in Fox.

Fox said it was about noon and he was going out to get some food. Osprey went to watch him. Fox howled like a wolf, ran around in a circle, and then dived onto the ice and killed himself.

Osprey noticed that Fox was dead and his children were hungry, so Osprey dove through the ice, caught a fish, fed the children, and then went home. He was sorry he had caused all this trouble and Fox's death.

(Fishhawk and Kingfisher were intermixed in this tale.)

Story: Fox and Fishhawk {Hoebel}   Fishhawk was married to Fox's sister. Fox went to visit his brother-in-law's home, which was a hole in the bank. Fox was very nice and was glad to see his relatives. It came noon, and Fishhawk said it was time to eat; he would go out and get some food.

He flew over the water, which was frozen. He took a swooping dive and penetrated the ice to bring out a fish. He took the fish back to his house and they all had a good meal.

Fox then wanted to go and invited Fishhawk to come visit him someday and to bring his children.

One day, Fishhawk came to visit. He noticed Fox's house was like his own, with a pool of water nearby.

Fishhawk did not think much of his brother-in-law's ability.

At noon, Fox went out to get food. He ran around hollering like a dozen wolves. Then he took a high dive into the pond and killed himself on the ice surface.

Fishhawk fed the fox children and went home feeling very sorry.

Story: Fox and Fishhawk {Carlson}   Fishhawk was married to Fox's sister. One day, Fox decided to visit his brother-in-law and his family. Fox came early in the morning and when noon came there was nothing in the house to eat.

Fishhawk decided to go out and see if he could get something for dinner. Fishhawk lived in a bank overlooking a pond. Fishhawk flew out of the house and circled the pond. It was winter and the pond was frozen over. Fishhawk flew around over the pond for a while and then dove through the ice and came up with a fish.

Fox and Fishhawk had a good meal out of this fish. After dinner, Fox was ready to go and, as he was leaving, he invited his brother-in-law to come and visit him sometime and bring his family.

The home of Fox was in a bank overlooking a pond much like that of Fishhawk. When it was time to eat, Fox went out to get something to eat. He remembered how Fishhawk had caught the fish and decided to try the same way. As soon as he left the house, Fox began to howl like a wolf. After a while, Fox ran for the pond and took a dive at the ice, thinking that he would go through as Fishhawk had done, but he didn't go through and hit the ice so hard that he killed himself.

This accident made Fishhawk feel very bad, but his children had to be fed just the same, so he went out and caught a fish just had he had done before. After this, Fishhawk went home with his family feeling very bad.

Etiquette   A caller in the old days never knocked, but spoke out and announced his presence; he was then invited into the tipi by the host or his wife.

Medicine: Taboos   If a medicine man was eating and didn't want to be disturbed, he set a pole outside against the tipi to keep away visitors. There was also someone outside to warn away would-be visitors.

A medicine man should not be selfish; if a visitor came before mealtime, he was invited to eat with the host.

Medicine men washed their hands right after eating so as not to pollute his paraphernalia.

Food: Mealtimes   There were no regular mealtimes.[1] They ate whenever they got hungry, probably four or five [three or four] times daily in the old times. Dried meat was always ready to eat. A [open] parfleche was put in the center of a group as a platter is with us. All persons ate together, men, women and children; they were not segregated.

"Spongers" were not excluded. The meat was free. The poor were your friends if you fed them. [They didn't get tired of visitors.]

Borrowing   There was not much borrowing in the old days; a person just gave, never borrowed. Things were simply divided up.

If you have nothing a visitor wants, you get it from one of your relations.

If a single man had nothing, he generally made his home with a friend or relative.

Economy: Poverty   [A poor man who was alone would go live with someone.] A poverty-stricken family would be helped along through gifts from friends and relatives [so they could continue their own menage]. There was no fixed time for making gifts to the poor.[2]

Medicine: Sun Dance   Sun Dancers danced four days and four nights with no food or water; they only sucked slippery elm bark.

The dancers stood in one place and danced up and down, blowing on the whistle meanwhile. When a dancer was about to collapse for water, someone made a gift (a forfeit) of a horse loaded with goods to get the man out. The gift was given to the medicine man who started the dance. They had the same Sun Dance in the old days. The Comanche didn't tear skewers out of their breasts in their Sun Dance.

The Sun Dance was given to cure the sick.

Story: Fox and Lightning {Wedel}   Fox was getting too smart. He wanted to get into a contest with Lightning to see who had the most power. Fox went to the home of Lightning. Lightning asked whether Fox meant business and told him to take the lead in whatever he wanted to do. Lightning would have a little joke on Fox.

Fox began to howl and bark and jump about the room. Lightning said, "You pretty near scared me."

Fox had done his performance. Now it was Lightning's turn. Lightning raised his arm and Fox could see lightning all over. Then he batted his eyes and lightning flashed again. Fox ran to the door, scared, and wanted to end the contest. Fox dirtied all the floor. Then the contest ended. Fox was beaten at the game.

Lightning was like a big bird, probably?

1. Wallace and Hoebel 1952:74.
2. Variations from Carlson.

Story: Fox and Lightning {Hoebel}   Fox went to the home of Lightning for a contest. Lightning asked if he really meant business; Fox said, "Right."

Lightning told Fox to take the lead. Fox began to jump about the room and holler fiercely. Lightning said, "Oh, you nearly scared me out of the room."

It was Lightning's turn. He raised his arm and lightning came from under his armpit. Fox ran to the door. Lightning batted his eye and sparks flew. Fox begged Lightning to stop. He was so scared that he defecated on the floor.

Story: Fox and Lightning {Carlson}   Fox was getting pretty smart and cocky over his ability and power. He was anxious to match his power with that of Lightning. He went to the home of Lightning and challenged Lightning to a show of power. Lightning knew Fox's reputation for being a trickster and was suspicious of Fox's intentions.

Lightning said to Fox, "Do you really mean business this time or are you fooling as usual?"

Fox said, "I really mean business this time."

Lightning knew that he had more power than Fox, but he decided to have some fun with him.

Lightning said to Fox, "You show your power first, and when you are finished, I will show my power."

Fox agreed and began to go through a lot of crazy motions, thinking he could scare Lightning. Lightning pretended to be very much frightened at the actions of Fox. Lightning said, "My goodness, you almost scared me out of the room."

Then came Lightning's turn to show his power. He raised his arms and sharp flashes flew out in all directions. Then, he batted his eyes and the flashes became worse and the racket became terrible. Fox was scared and ran from the house yelling. He was so scared he made some dirt on the floor of the house as he left.

Story: Fox and Raccoon {Wedel}   Fox and Raccoon met one day to look for something to do for entertainment. Fox said, "Brother, I know what we could do." He suggested that they play like they were women.

Raccoon said, "No, your thing is too big."

He would play only if he got first chance.

Fox agreed to give Raccoon first chance, so he went to work. When Raccoon was finished, he was tired and wanted to rest before Fox's turn, but Fox seized Raccoon's wrist, he wanted to play right now.

Raccoon said "OK," but he got hold of the trunk of the tree and he wouldn't lay down. Fox got too anxious. Raccoon told him to back off and give him chance to stretch.

When Fox came up again, Raccoon ran up the tree out of Fox's reach. Fox was angry; he looked up and said, "Come down, you never fooled me before. I'll chop down the tree."

Fox went out and got a bison scapula and began hacking at the tree, pointing to the bone bits as {being wood} chips. Raccoon said to Fox, "Go away, I'm going to sleep."

Fox gave up and went to a camp nearby, where, on the east edge, an old woman was living. The woman asked what he wanted. Fox, without invitation, sat down and asked the woman whether she had heard any new stories.

She said, "No," but then suddenly remembered one and agreed to tell it.

"Lately," she said, "I had heard Fox was full of tricks, but heard someone had pulled this trick on him and had got away with it."

At that moment, Fox saw an old woman's knife laying nearby, so he picked it up and gave it to her as though it was a gift, then left.

Story: Fox and Raccoon {Hoebel}   Fox met Raccoon one day. They wanted to entertain themselves, so Fox brought up this question; he said, "Brother, let's play like playing with the women."

Raccoon answered, "No, your thing is too big, but if you let me do it first, I'm willing."

Everything was going all right. Raccoon got his share first, but was then tired and wanted to rest.

Fox wanted his turn right away, but Raccoon said, "Oh, no, let's wait awhile. You're just going to ruin me."

Fox insisted. Raccoon said, "Well, let me get hold of this tree, then."

Fox was too anxious and got too close. Raccoon said, "Give me a chance, get back a bit."

Then he jumped up the tree.

Fox looked up and said, "You've never done me before. If you don't come down, I'll chop down the tree,"

He went off and got a buffalo shoulder blade. Chips fell off the blade, and Fox said, "See how the bark is flying off. You had better get off of there."

Raccoon answered, "Go away, I'm sleepy."

Fox went off east where an old lady lived. He went to her camp. She asked what he wanted. He said, "Oh, nothing," and without waiting for invitation, he right into her tipi and sat down.

Fox asked her if she had heard any stories lately.

"Well, yes," she said. She didn't know if it was true but she would tell him. She had heard that some enemy had pulled this trick on Fox.

Fox saw the old lady's knife lying there. He picked it up and gave it to her as a present and went off.

Story: Fox and Raccoon {Carlson}   One day, Fox and Raccoon met. They wondered what they could do for excitement.

Finally, Fox said, "Let's do to each other what we do to the women."

Raccoon said, "No, your penis is too big for me. It will hurt me."

After a while, Racoon said, "If you let me do it first, it will be all right."

Fox agreed and Raccoon did it to Fox.

When Raccoon was through, he was all tired out, and he said to Fox, "You tire me out. Let me rest for a while before you start on me."

After a while, Raccoon walked over to a tree and took up a position as if ready for Fox to get his share. Fox was pretty anxious by this time and ran over to Raccoon. But Raccoon said, "Go on back, I'm not ready yet. I just want to stretch."

Fox moved back. As he did so, Raccoon ran up the tree. That made Fox very angry. "Come on down, Raccoon, and give me my turn. If you don't come down, I'll chop the tree down."

Raccoon answered back, "Go away, Fox, I'm tired and I want to sleep."

Fox began to chop on the tree, but it was no use, it was too big. Finally, Fox gave up and went away.

Fox went on until he came to a camp. He came to the tipi of a very old lady. The old lady asked Fox what he wanted. Fox said, "Oh, nothing," and sat down. Finally, Fox asked the old lady, "Do you know any stories that you could tell me?"

The old lady said that she knew of a story about Fox and Raccoon that happened recently. She then went on and told how Fox had been fooled by Raccoon. She told the very story to which Fox had been a party and in which he was fooled.

As she was telling the story, Fox noticed a knife lying nearby. He went over, picked it up, and gave it to the old lady as if he were giving her a present.

Fox then went away.

Kinship Relations: Joking   This story was told to a brother-in-law, not to one's sister or parents. In-law tricks were played on the same relatives to whom jokes were told.

Food: Fish   There was no fishing.

Directions   North was where the cold comes from. South was warm, east by sunup, west by sundown. South was known as 'hot wind' or as 'sun'.

tabeʔtoinakwɨ	'where the sun rises'	⎫ east
tabeʔtoipehtʊ	'toward where the sun rises'	⎭
yuʔanenakwɨ	'toward the warm wind'	⎫ south
tabeʔnakwɨ	'toward the sun' ['coming up']	⎭
tabeʔikanakwɨ	'toward where sun goes down'	south [west]
kwihnenakwɨ	'toward the cold'	north
panihputʊ[1]	'above' or 'up'	[zenith]
sokopehtʊ	'toward the ground' (*soko* 'ground')	[nadir]

Story: Sun   A true story. Medicine men had long pipes. A medicine man once lit his pipe several times by the sun. He would puff on the pipe several times toward the sun and presently the tobacco would ignite. The people marveled greatly.

[He did this many times to demonstrate his power.]

Numbers

one   *sɨmɨ*

two   *waha*

three   *pahitʊ*

Cosmology: Moon   *mua* was the Moon.

Story: Piamupits {Wedel}   Once there was a camp along a river. Children were playing. A little dog's bowels moved and it passed some beads. The biggest child sent the smallest one back to camp for sinew to string the beads. On the way back to camp, the child noticed that all of the camps had disappeared, no one was present. So the child returned empty-handed, bringing word that camp was gone.

The oldest child, disbelieving, sent an older child, then another, and all brought the same report. At last, the oldest child went in person and found the camp had been moved. So they decided to follow the trail made by the moving camp.

1. Robinson and Armagost (1990) translates *panihputʊ màʔbatɨ* as 'high, tall (literally, upward long)'.

They traveled quite a way, but night overtook the children. The youngest got tired and worried and cried for its grandmother. As they going along, they heard a distant voice asking for the crying child. They didn't know it was Mupits (big owl). The little child heard Mupits calling, and said, "It's my grandmother calling." The oldest child said, "No, it's Mupits, he would eat us."

The eldest child decided to go investigate. The children finally got to Mupits' home, a big hole in ground. Mupits told the children just where they should bed down for the night; each would have a separate bed, but the eldest child said they all should sleep together. The little dog could understand language, and he was told to stay awake and every time Mupits came near, he should run and tickle their feet. He did so, awakening the children.

Piamupits noticed the dog and asked why he always woke the children when he wanted to cover them, and he began to whip the dog.

Finally, came the dawn. Mupits told the oldest child to go get a bucket of water. The child wanted to take all of the children, despite Owl's protest. Owl told them to hurry back.

As they went after the water, the children noticed a big bullfrog. They went and told Frog that if Mupits called, Frog should answer that they were cleaning the youngest child's pants. Then they fled.

The creek was up. The children wanted to cross the creek. The eldest child asked Crane to lie down and bridge the creek. Crane asked the girl to pull a flea off its head and to bite it when they were across the creek. She did so and busted the bug.

Every once in a while, Mupits called to the children to hurry and Frog answered back. Finally, Mupits got sore of waiting and went toward the children, threatening them. He saw that the big frog was talking and got his club to kill Frog, but the latter dove into the water and escaped.

Then Mupits followed the children. He asked Crane to form a bridge. Crane gave the same directions about biting the bug. The bug was bitter and Owl spit it out, and the bridge collapsed. The next time, he followed the directions and got across and followed the children.

The children met a big eagle and asked him for assistance. He gave them a downy feather to drop in Owl's way if he got close. The children thought Owl was very near so they dropped the feather; then came a thick fog, so Owl couldn't find his way.

Owl finally got out of the fog and after the children. The children met Buffalo and asked him for help. At the bull's command, the children went around the bull four times, then started to run. Mupits clubbed the bull to death, then went on after children. There was no obstacle.

The children met a Bison Calf, who said he couldn't help much, but told them to go around him four times.

Owl came along. He didn't think much of Calf and told the children Calf wouldn't help much. Calf pawed the dirt, as though he were mad when he saw Mupits.

Mupits ran up to Calf and they fought. Calf threw Owl up into air, not far, and Mupits fell. Mupits charged again and was thrown a little harder. The third time, Calf threw Mupits up into the moon.

Look at the moon now and you see the picture of Mupits in the moon's face. And the bullfrog still says that children are washing the baby.[1]

Story: Piamupits {Hoebel}   There was a camp along a river. The children were with a little dog who defecated some beads. The biggest child sent a little one to get a string of sinew to string those beads. The child found the camp had gone. It returned. The older child didn't believe it and sent another. It returned with the same news. It sent the others with the same result. Finally, he went himself and saw, and decided to follow the trail.

They couldn't catch up before dark. The smallest child was tired and worried. It wanted its grandmother. It heard a voice from a distance asking them to bring the crying child over there.

They didn't know it was Mupits. The little child heard it and said, "It's my grandmother."

The oldest child said, "No, it's the Mupits. If you don't stop crying, he'll eat you."

The child didn't stop. They went over to see. They came to a big hole, the home of Mupits.

Mupits told them where to make their {beds. He} told the youngest to make their beds apart from the others. The older child said no, they would all sleep together.

The children had the little dog sleep with them that could understand talk. They told him to stay awake and, whenever Mupits came about, to tickle the bottoms of their feet. This he did.

Mupits saw the dog doing this and was angry; he beat him, saying "What do you mean by doing this when I come to cover the children up so they won't get cold?"

Daylight came and Mupits asked the oldest child to get a bucket of water. This child wanted to take the others with it. Mupits told them they must hurry back.

On the bank of the creek, they saw a bullfrog. The eldest asked the frog to call back when Mupits called that the youngest had dirtied his clothes and they were washing them.

{card missing}

Mupits saw that the frog had fooled him. He got out his club to hit the frog, but the frog dived in.

Mupits followed on to come to the crane. He asked him to make a bridge. Crane told him to take off the bug and bite it. Owl did so, but the bug was bitter and he spit it out and the bridge fell. Owl tried again and followed orders, this time getting across.

The children met Eagle. They asked him for help.

Eagle said, "Take my downy feather and when Owl catches up to you, drop if before him."

A child saw that Owl was on their trail and dropped the feather. It made a big fog. Owl lost his way. Finally, he got out and continued the pursuit.

The children met a buffalo. They told him they needed help. The buffalo said that he couldn't be of much assistance, but they should go around him four times and start to run.

Mupits came up and killed the buffalo with a club.

---

1. This is the end of Wedel's Notebook 2.

The children came to a buffalo calf and asked him for help. The calf said he didn't think he could be of much aid.

Owl came up to the calf. He didn't think much of it. The buffalo calf was angry and pawed the earth. Mupits came up and started to fight. The calf tossed it into the air with his horns. They fought some more. The calf tossed Mupits again. Finally, the calf tossed Mupits high into the sky up onto the face of the moon.

That is what you see in the moon, and that is what the bullfrog says.

Story: Piamupits {Carlson}   The Lost Children. One time, some Indians were camped along a creek. Some children left the camp one day to go for a walk. This group of children had with them a small child and a little dog. After the children had gone a little ways, the dog stopped and made dirt. In the dog's dirt, there were some beads.

The children noticed this. The oldest child of the group sent one of the younger ones back to get some sinew so they could string the beads. The child was gone a little while, then came back and reported that the camp was gone.

The oldest child would not believe this, so he sent another child, and soon this one came back with the same news. Finally, after sending all the children, the oldest child decided to go himself.

He went and found that the younger children were telling the truth. The camp was gone. The children decided to follow the trail.

After they had traveled for a way, night fell and the small child grew very tired and began to call for its grandmother.

Out of the darkness came a voice saying, "Bring the child here to me."

The child stopped crying and said, "Oh, it's my grandmother."

The oldest child said, "No, I think it is Piamupits, and he will eat us if we go to his house."

They decided to investigate and went in the direction of the sound.

At last they came to a cave. It was the den of Piamupits.

Piamupits was there. He said, "Come in and make beds for yourselves for the night."

The children hesitated at first, but finally went in and started to make their beds right close to each other.

Piamupits said, "No, don't make your beds so close together, spread out more."

But the oldest child said, "No, we are going to sleep right close together."

All of the children lay down to sleep. But before the oldest went to sleep, he told the dog to lick their toes if Piamupits started to come toward them during the night. Several times during the night, Piamupits started to come toward the children, hoping to get one to boil for food, but each time that he started, the dog would lick the children's feet and wake them up. This made Piamupits mad, and he said to the dog, "What is wrong with you, always waking up the children when I try to come over and cover them up." Piamupits beat the dog.

Finally, daylight came. At this time, Piamupits asked the eldest to go down to the spring and get some water. The eldest child said, "I'll go, but I want the other children to go with me."

Piamupits said, "Why don't you go alone."

The oldest child would not do this. He gathered all the children together and went down to the creek.

When they got down to the creek, there was a big frog sitting on the bank. The eldest child said to the frog, "When Piamupits calls, you answer him, and tell him that the baby has done in his pants and that we are changing his pants for him." The frog should also say that they would be along as soon as they had changed his pants. The frog agreed to do this.

The creek was very high at this time. There was a large crane on the bank. The eldest child spoke to him, saying, "Will you lie down across the creek so we can go across?"

The crane replied, "I will do this for you, but first you must pick a louse from my head and, as you are going across, you must hold it in your mouth." The eldest child did this and all the children got across over the crane's back.

At this time, Piamupits began to wonder what had become of the children and he began to call to them, and each time the frog would answer back, "The baby has done in his pants and they are changing him. They will come back as soon as they have changed his pants."

When the children did not return for a long time, Piamupits got very suspicious and went down to the creek to see what was keeping the children so long.

On his way down to the creek, he kept threatening the children out loud.

When he got to the creek, he found only the frog there, and he knew then that he had been fooled. He knew that the frog had been lying to him.

He got a club, intending to kill the frog, but just as he was about to strike the frog, he slid off into the water.

Piamupits saw the crane and asked him to make a bridge across the creek. The crane said he would, but Piamupits would have to take a louse from the crane's back and hold it in his teeth as he was crossing. Piamupits agreed to do this. He put the louse between his teeth and started across over the crane's back. When he was half way across, the louse began to taste kind of bitter so he spat it out. Just as he did this, the crane became limp and fell into the water carrying Piamupits with {page(s) missing} came up to the bull and clubbed him to death.

The children next met a buffalo calf. They asked him to help them. He told the children to run around him four times, which they did. By this time, Piamupits was right up close to them.

When he saw what the children were doing, he laughed out loud and said, "There is no use to do that, that little buffalo cannot help you."

The calf began to paw dirt upon himself.

Piamupits ran up to attack the buffalo, but just as he was going to grab the calf, the calf grabbed Piamupits instead and threw him a short distance into the air. The calf threw Piamupits into the air three times. The third time that he threw him into the air he threw him so high that he went to the moon.

And it is Piamupits that you see in the Moon now. The children found the camp all right after that.

{Carlson Note} 1. There seems to be no unanimity of opinion as to just what kind of creature Piamupits was. Some pictured him as a large owl-like creature, others as a huge man who ate people. The Comanches often frightened their children by telling that if they did not behave Piamupits would get them. In that respect, he would correspond to our bogey man.[1]

{Carlson Note} 2. The Comanches say that the frog, when he croaked, said, "The baby had dirtied his pants, and they are cleaning him. They will be along in a short time."

NIYAH
July 10, 1933

Story: The Owner of the Buffalo {Wedel}[2]   Fox once saved the people from starving. All the buffalo had disappeared in the old times. The people were getting very hungry because the buffalo was their principal food. A certain man had trapped all the buffalo and shut them up. He had plenty to eat, but made it hard on others. So Fox went out to free the buffalo.

One family that lived at one end of the camp was getting all the meat. There were the man, his wife and child.

A certain man went out one night. The wind was blowing, and as he passed their tipi, he smelled meat cooking. So he went back and told the rest of the people.

Fox was on hand, ready to help the people; he acted as chairman of the council. He promised relief if his instructions were followed. He said to move their camp. The captor of the buffalo had a permanent camp because of his trap, and he couldn't move.

Fox became a little puppy and stayed behind while the rest of the people moved away. The woman and child, walking through the abandoned camp, came upon the puppy. The child picked it up and fondled it and took it home.

The father was not home. When he came home, the child showed him the pup. He became suspicious and was displeased. The child decided to take the pup and show it the buffalo. It opened the trap door to the underground pen. The dog jumped out of the child's arms and went among the buffalo. He then became human and began yelling like a cowboy. The buffalo began milling about, running against the door and finally breaking through.

The father was furious and sat by the door with a club to kill the dog. The dog attached himself to the underside of the last buffalo and rode out unseen. Once outside, he jumped off and told the man that he had been starving people, now he himself would starve.

---

1. In a parallel to this comment, Charney notes that [-*pitsɄ*] "generally applies to 'fearsome beings'. In Comanche it is found in that role in the name for a monster. I assume that this name is to be analyzed as a single word: *mupitsɄ*. When it is translated—it usually is not—this word means 'monster, bogeyman'" (1993:96, n. 2).

It may be noted that both Wedel's and Hoebel's notes alternate between Piamupits (or Mupits) and Owl, and Carlson has the comment, "owl-like creature," suggesting that the 1933 consultants—or the interpreters—recognized the nominal owl-like affinity of the ogre. Going back farther, St. Clair (1902) translated the ogre's name, *mópic*, as 'owl'.

2. This is the start of Wedel's Notebook 3.

The man {Fox} then went back to the people happy and told them the buffalo were out now, and it was up to them to go get their meat supply. Fox remained human after this act.

Fox was called *ohaahnakatU*[1] from the bright yellow spot under his foreleg; *waani* was 'fox'.

isapU[2] was a joker, like Fox, in these stories.

Story: The Owner of the Buffalo {Hoebel}   The buffalo had disappeared, there were none to be found, and the people were hungry. Some man had trapped all the buffalo and kept them all shut up. He had plenty of meat for his small family.

One night a man passed their tent and he smelled meat cooking. He wondered where they got it, and went to camp and told the others.

Fox was at the meeting and heard the man. He told the people to follow his instructions.

He said the camp must be moved. Fox knew the people with the buffalo. They must stay behind with the buffalo trap and Fox would stay too, in the form of a little pup.

The woman and child walked through the old camp. The child saw the pup and picked it up; she liked it. She took the pup home. The father was not there; he was out for the day. He came home. The child ran up to her father with the pup. Father didn't like it very much; he suspected something.

The girl was so proud. She showed the pup the buffalo under the ground. She opened the trap door.

Fox jumped from her arms among the buffalo and changed to human form. He then whooped and yelled, stampeding the buffalo through the door.

The father was angry. He said he would club the pup, but Fox clung to the belly of the last buffalo and got out.

Fox stood off and hollered, "Now you can starve."

Fox was anxious to take the news to the camp that the buffalo were out and they could get their meat again.

Story: The Owner of the Buffalo {Carlson}   There was starvation among the Indians. All of the buffalo had disappeared and no one knew what had become of them. The Indians, however, were suspicious of one man who lived on the west side of their camp. This man and his wife and little girl always seemed to have plenty of meat. Their suspicions were confirmed when one day an Indian happened to be passing this man's tipi and smelled meat cooking. This man called the rest of the camp together and told them what he had noticed.

Fox was present at the meeting. He was acting as chairman. He made a speech to the rest of the Indians in which he said that if they would follow his instructions, all would be well and they would soon have meat again.

By way of instructions, Fox said the following, "Let us move our camp. This man has a very permanent camp established here and he will not want to move with us. He will be the only one left here after we have gone. When camp is broken and all of you are gone, I will change myself into a little dog and act as though I have been left behind. They will

1. Literally, 'he has yellow armpits', usually referring to Coyote, not Fox.
2. 'liar'.

pity me and take me to their home, and then I will find out if this man is really holding the buffalo back from us."

All of the rest of the Indians thought this was a good idea and carried out the instructions of Fox in full. Things worked just as Fox had hoped they would.

When everyone had left camp, the little daughter of the man was walking over the old camp site and discovered this little deserted dog. She liked the little dog and she picked it up and asked her mother if she could take it home. The mother said that she could. The little girl brought the dog home.

Her father was not at home when she came home. In the evening, the girl saw her father coming. She picked up the little dog and ran to meet her father. The father did not like the dog. He was suspicious, but the girl continued to keep the little dog.

One day, she picked the dog up in her arms and took him to a secret place in the ground. There were all the buffalo kept in a large corral and kept from getting into the world by a trap door. The girl carried the dog over to the trap door. She opened the door to look in, and as she did so, the dog jumped suddenly from her arms and ran into the corral.

Once in the corral, the dog changed into a man and began to yell at the buffalo to stampede them. All the buffalo began to run out of the corral through the trapdoor into the world.

By this time, the little girl's father had arrived upon the scene. He was furious and got himself a club in readiness to club the dog when he came out. But the man clung to belly of a buffalo and got out of the corral unseen by the father.

When the fox man was a little ways away, he got off the buffalo and yelled back to the father that now it was his time to starve.

The fox man returned to camp and told the people what had happened. They were very happy. The next day the entire camp went on a buffalo hunt.

Camp Organization: Breaking Camp   The breaking of camp was announced by a special crier at the chief's order, probably two or three days ahead of time. There was no particular order of departure, each family moving as it got ready, driving its own stock.

Camp Organization   Usually a family retained the same neighbors from camp to camp. The chief was in the center. Camps were very frequently moved if the water or grass gave out.

Camps: Brush Arbors   In the old days, small brush arbors were made of a series of bowed saplings set in the ground and covered over (cf. Shoshone[1]).

[They were not as big as those in use now because they didn't stay in one place long enough.][2]

Camp Organization: Scouts   Scouts were usually sent out in advance to pick the camp ground.

There might be some squabbles over tipi sites if two parties wanted the same spot.

Story: Fox Kills His Wife {Wedel}   Certain Indians were going out to trade tanned hides for food. They were met by Fox, who asked where they were going. They said they were going to get food by trading hides.

---

1. The source of this comment is not clear.
2. Wallace and Hoebel 1952:89.

Fox asked where their hides were and they told him they were packed up in a bundle. They said that sometimes they killed their wives, put them in bundles, and traded them off, then after seven days, they came back to life.

Fox asked where they were stopping for lunch, and then he ran home.

Fox went home. Fox had many children. He told them he would kill their mother, trade her off to get food, and in seven days she would come to life.

Fox did so and set out. He caught up with the people just as they were departing after lunch. He joined them.

When the people began to trade off their hides, Fox watched, but saw no wives unloaded. Someone asked him why he wasn't unloading and he said he hadn't seen any wives traded. He had killed his wife.

Fox went home sorrowful and told his children how he had been tricked into killing his wife. That's how Fox was fooled into killing his wife.

Story: Fox Kills His Wife {Hoebel}   Indians had some hides to trade for something to eat. Fox met them and asked them where the hides were.

They told him that they were packed in bundles and that they had killed their wives to get the hides. The women would come alive in a week.

Fox asked them where they would have lunch at noon; they told him on the river.

Fox ran home. He told his children he would get them something to eat, but first he must kill their mother, and she would be dead for seven days.

He killed her and put her on a pack horse. He caught up as the people were leaving. They went up to the trading place.

Fox didn't see anybody trading wives. One asked him why he didn't trade. He told him he had killed his wife. He felt badly and went home and told his children.

Story: Fox Kills His Wife {Carlson}   A group of Indians had tanned some hides and they were on their way to trade them for something to eat. On the way, they met Fox, who asked them where they were going. The Indians said that they were on their way to trade their hides for something to eat.

Fox asked them where their hides were. The Indians said that all the hides were in one bundle on one of the horses. The other bundles, they said, had the bodies of their wives which they were also going to trade for something to eat. They said that it was all right to kill one's wife this way, as she always returned to life after the seventh day.

Then Fox asked them where they expected to camp at noon that day. The Indians told him the place.

Fox then said to them, "Wait for me there. I have a little errand to run and then I will catch up to you and go in search of something to eat."

The Indians and Fox then separated. Fox went to his home and the Indians went on their way.

Fox had a large number of children. When he got home, he told his children that he was going out to get some food for them, but to get it he must first kill their mother. He told them not to worry, because she would return to them in seven days.

Fox then killed his wife, wrapped her up, put her upon a pack horse, and went to the camp of the Indians. They were just breaking camp when he got there. Fox joined the Indians and they went to the trader's camp.

When they got there, they took out their tanned hides and traded them for food.

After all the hides were traded, Fox stood by waiting for the Indians to trade some of their dead wives. But in all of their packs there were only hides and no dead wives.

The Indians wondered why Fox did not offer any of his goods for sale. One of the Indians asked him what the trouble was. Fox said that he had done as the Indians had said they had done: killed his wife for trade. All the Indians started to laugh and made fun of Fox for being so foolish. Fox then turned toward home very much broken up over the death of his wife.

Story: Fox at a Horse Race {Wedel}   People once were racing horses. Some whites were present. They were all betting. Fox came in leading a big gray mule that he wanted to enter in the race. The mule beat all the horses.

People gathered around talking; some wanted to buy his mule, but Fox refused, saying he would only sell it for a big price or trade it for horses. Fox finally traded the mule for horses and probably some money. Fox told the buyer not to let the mule loose, but at night to neck him to another horse. Fox was very anxious to leave. The next morning, the man wanted to see the mule. He saw the horse at a distance but no mule. The horse was dragging something, and when the man got up to his horse, he found it was a jackrabbit. Thus, he was tricked by Fox.

Story: Fox at a Horse Race {Hoebel}   Fox brought a big mule to race. He wanted to enter it. People thought he couldn't beat the horse, but he did. People gathered around and wanted to buy the mule; they offered big prices.

Fox finally decided to trade it for two fine horses and money. Fox told the buyer that he couldn't let the mule loose at night, but must tie him by the neck to a horse.

Fox was anxious to leave.

The man got up the next morning to see his fine mule. He saw the horse, but no mule. Something was on the horse. He came up and found a dead jackrabbit.

Story: Fox at a Horse Race {Carlson}   There were some horse races going on. There were many white people there. While the races were going on, Fox came up leading a mule. He wanted to enter the mule in the races but the people would not let him, as they said the mule was too slow and that he could never win anything.

Finally, Fox got the people to let him enter the mule. The mule was a very fast runner, and he won all the races that day without any trouble.

As soon as he won the races, many people wanted to buy the mule. At first, Fox refused to sell him. He pretended as if he did not want to part with such a fine animal as the mule. But finally, Fox gave in and traded the mule to a man for two very fine horses.

Fox told the man to keep the mule tied up, as he would run away if he didn't. He told him that when he got home, he should neck his mule to a horse. The man did this. The next morning, the man thought he would look at his new mule. When he got to the barn, the mule was gone. He went up close to the horse that had been necked to the mule and saw a dead jack rabbit hanging from the neck of the horse. He knew then that he had been fooled by Fox.

Economy: Trade: Horse Traders   The Comanches had no crooked horse traders; horses were not fixed up to sell to suckers. But Comanches were badly tricked by white horse traders in the early days. Niyah bought two teams from crooked Charley Thomas in Lawton.

Story: Fox and Man {Wedel}   A certain man once got tired of the way Fox always tricked him. He challenged him. He wanted to see how Fox tricked people, so that he wouldn't be tricked.

Fox wouldn't meet him in a crowd, but with one witness only. The man agreed. The man said to Fox that his companion wanted to know how Fox fooled people; he wanted Fox to show how it was done. Fox said he had left his paraphernalia for fooling people at home, and told the men that they should let him borrow their horse and let him go home and get his paraphernalia. Fox mounted and rode a piece. Then the horse stalled. Fox said there must be something horse wanted, so the man gave him his blanket. Fox started off again. The horse stalled again, until Fox had the men all undressed. Then Fox rode back to the men who were on foot and said, "Now you see how I worked you."

Story: Fox and Man {Hoebel}   A man got tired of Fox tricking people all the time. He sent a challenge to him to show his ways.

Fox demanded just one witness—no crowd.

The umpire told Fox how this man had been wondering how he always bests the people. He wanted to see it done on him.

Fox said, "I left my materials at home. If you lend me your horse, I'll go get it and show my stuff."

The man got off his horse. Fox mounted and rode a little way; the horse balked.

Fox {. . . [*sic*]}

Story: Fox and Man {Carlson}   Once there was a man who was fed up with Fox always getting the best of people. He thought that someone else should know how it was done.

One day, this man met Fox. When they met, the man said to Fox, "How is it that you are able to fool people so much? I think that you ought to show me in some way how it is done so I can fool some people. Why don't you fool me in some way now so I can see how it is done?"

Fox said to the man, "I would be glad to do you that favor, but right now I don't have my material along for fooling people. It is at home. But if you really want to see how I fool people, let me get on your horse and ride to my home and you can come along beside me on foot."

The man consented to this and got off from his horse. Fox got on the horse and they started for Fox's home.

After they had gone a short distance, the horse began to balk. Fox said to the man, "The horse doesn't know my clothes. You will have to give me your clothes."

The man took off his clothes and gave them to Fox. The man was all naked now.

Fox had no sooner put on the man's clothes then he spurred the horse and galloped off. As he was riding away, he turned to the man and said, "You see how I have fooled you. That is how I fool other people."

Horses: Names   Comanches gave special names to race horses and to a warrior's favorite war horse. Other horses were known only by a color name, (e.g., bay, etc.). War horses were named for special deeds, although Niyah knew of no specific instances.

Horses: Names: Color Names for Horses

tupIsikUmaʔ[1]	dark bay, between bay and black horse
ohaekapItɄ[2]	light bay, red-yellow
ekakUmaʔ[3]	bay
tukUma[4]	black
tuhuniya	yellow with black mane and tail
tosa	white
nahnhia	dun, light yellow
ebituesi	blue horse
otɄkUmaʔ[5]	sorrel
eka esi	roan
oha esi	yellow roan
ekasanaboʔ[6]	red pinto
tusanaboʔ	black pinto
etɄsanaboʔ	sorrel pinto (*sanabo*)
esikUmaʔ	gray horse
tosaʔesi	white gray
ekanakI	red ears, *nakI* is ears
tuhunakI	black ears
ohanakI	yellow ears[7]

Horses: Mares   Mares were not used in fighting. Prior to the automobile, an Indian man would be laughed at if he rode a mare. A young lady would rather ride a horse than a mare. [A mare was never ridden in battle and never when a boy or girl was out for show.][8]

Horses: Geldings   Castration was practiced; stallions could be troublesome, and they didn't want too many. Each Indian who had a herd of horses would have a stallion. Stallions were rarely ridden for hunting.

Horses   Niyah didn't know how the Comanches received horses.

Horses: Care   Horses were curried with dry cow turds in the old days. Medicine men applied herbs or roots to cure cholic among horses. Cedar was burned under the nose to cure distemper. Tender-footed horses had rawhide moccasins tied onto their feet,[9] but these were not used on raids.

Material Culture: Rope   Indians were pretty handy with ropes in the old days.

Story: Fox and Quail {Wedel}   Fox was wandering along a creek when he came to a quail's nest. He peeped in and saw young birds. He asked them what they were. They said they

1. *kuhma* 'male'.
2. Literally, 'yellow-red'. Robinson and Armagost (1990) has this as 'orange'.
3. Literally, 'red male'.
4. Literally, 'black male'.
5. Literally, 'brown male'.
6. *nabo* 'painted'.
7. Wallace and Hoebel 1952:46.
8. Wallace and Hoebel 1952:46.
9. Wallace and Hoebel 1952:47.

were children of the bird that scared (startled) people. Fox made fun of that, and said that he would never be afraid. He made water over the nest and the young birds.

When the mother bird came back, she smelled something and asked her children what it was. They told of Fox's visit.

She set out in the direction taken by Fox, gathering more quails en route. They saw Fox trotting along the creek bank and lit right before him. As he arrived just over them, they broke cover, scaring him so that he fell over the bank into a deep pool and almost drowned before he got out. After that, every slight noise scared Fox. That's why Fox was so nervous now.

Story: Fox and Quail {Carlson}   Fox was wandering about one day and he came to the nest of some quail. He looked into the nest and saw little children inside. He said to them, "Who are you?"

The quail children answered back, "We are the children of the bird that frightens people."

This made Fox laugh and he made fun of them. To show them that he wasn't scared, he lifted up his leg and urinated on the little quails. Then he went away.

Soon, the mother quail returned to her nest and as soon as she entered, she smelled something funny. She asked the children what it was and they told her. This made her mad and she asked the children in what direction Fox had gone. They told her.

She then flew away and met up with some other quails. All together, they flew away and kept going until they spotted Fox running along the river bank. They landed and hid themselves in his path. When Fox got up real close, they all flew out of their hiding place, making an awful noise. Fox became so frightened that he fell into the river and was almost drowned before he could drag himself out again. After this, he went along his way acting very nervous and scared. From that day on, Fox has been a scaredy animal.

Story: Throwing Eyes {Wedel}   Fox was still going on the same trip. He met four screech owls standing under a willow tree, looking up into the tree. They were throwing their eyes up into the tree, saying, "Fall in eye, fall in eye," and the eye returned to its socket.

Fox stopped and said, "Brothers, what are you doing?" and asked the owls to help him do it.

They said they didn't want to take any chances; they had no confidence in him. They finally agreed to give him the trick, but if he ever used a different kind of tree he would lose his eye. They gave him the trick.

Fox stayed around a while, and then left.

Presently, he stopped and said to himself, "These trees all look alike to me."

So he decided to try his luck. He threw his eye into a tree, but it didn't come back. Then he tried his other eye and it too stayed up in the tree. So Fox was without eyes.

Story: Throwing Eyes {Hoebel}   {first card missing} willow tree. Their eyes would come right back to their heads.

Fox looked up and asked sweetly, "Brothers, what are you doing?"

Four of them were doing that trick.

Fox asked if they would help him do that trick. They wanted to take no chances. "You aren't the right kind of fellow. If you would go throw your eye on the wrong kind of tree, you would lose it."

Fox begged, so that they taught him the trick.

Fox went on his way, looking at the different trees as he went. He stopped and said, "All the trees look alike to me."

He threw his eye at a tree, but it didn't come back. He thought he would try again, so he threw out his other eye. It didn't come back.

Story: Throwing Eyes {Carlson}   One day, as Fox was going along, he saw four screech owls under a willow tree. These owls were throwing their eyeballs into the air and catching them again in their eye sockets when they came down. Fox went up to the owls and said, "Brothers, show me how to throw my eyeballs into the air that way."

The owls said to Fox, "You are not the right kind of person to know this trick."

But Fox begged and begged the owls and finally they showed him how it was done. They told him not to throw his eyeballs into any kind of tree except a willow.

After Fox had learned the trick and practiced it a few times, Fox went on his way. As he was going along, he saw a tree that was not a willow. He thought he would try his new trick. He took out one of his eyeballs and threw it into the air and it landed on the tree and didn't come down.

Then he thought that if he threw his other eyeball into the tree, he might get both of them back at the same time. So he threw his second eyeball into the tree. Neither eyeball came back. That was how Fox lost his eyeballs.

Story: Fox and the Berries {Wedel}   Fox was wandering about as usual. He came into some berries and asked what they were. They say they made the butt itch. Fox disbelieved and rubbed the berries as directed on his butt, and then he went off. Presently he began to feel his butt; he would jump and say, "eee-e-e" and muttered slight sounds. He came to a rocky place, sat down, and dragged his butt until he wore himself raw.

Story: Fox and the Berries {Hoebel}   Fox came across some berries. He asked them what they were.

"Oh, we're berries," they said, "but we make the butt itch."

Fox didn't believe it, so the berries told him to rub them between his palms and spread it between the tail. He did this.

He went on his way. He yelped, "i, i."

He found some rocks and rubbed his end on them.

Story: Fox and the Berries {Carlson}   As Fox was going along one day, he came to a berry patch. He asked the berries who they were. The berries said that they were the berries that made the hind end itch. Fox did not believe this and laughed at them.

He then took some berries, broke them up in his hand and rubbed them on his hind end. After that, he went on his way and had gone only a short ways when his hind end began to itch. It got worse and worse and pretty soon it got so bad that he had to stop and rub his hind end on some rocks. In order to stop the itching, he had to run on the rocks so hard that he was all in a very short time.

This made Fox realize that he didn't know everything.

Beliefs: Reincarnation   Niyah often heard old people say that a man might become a woman (probably vice versa) in the hereafter. They would never become an animal. They were not reincarnated as such.

Beliefs: Revival of the Dead   Niyah's grandmother got sick. Different medicine men tried to doctor her but couldn't help her. She finally died. Usually they wrapped corpses; now they burned her things. They didn't wrap the corpse as usual.

She was going to the other world in a death dream. She was going to a creek with many oaks and cottonwoods. She noticed a great camp of dead people. First, before arrival, she noticed some horses between herself and the camp. She got to the horses and looked around. She saw someone coming towards her; it was one of her deceased relations, her aunt. The aunt was looking through the herd and saw a certain gray horse from her herd that had died. The newcomer roped the horse for her and told her to mount. Another fellow was hurrying her up. While trying to mount, she came to and opened her eyes. People were standing about crying.

She lived a long time after that, and finally died of old age, forty years ago. She was named Ya?ai ('to take something up in hand while on a horse and lope away').[1]

There was much game in the future world.

Mowway   Mowway[2] was a brave Indian. He was with the Mexicans for a time; he was an old-time warrior before he went to the Mexicans. He resumed the chieftaincy after his return.

Political Organization: Chiefs   In those days, a brave warrior was chosen leader by the bravest men in the entire tribe or band.

Political Organization: Chiefs   Leaders in Mowway's band included[3]:

m[4]	(1) Tabenanaka[5]	'voice', (or 'echo') of the sun
	(2) Esarosavit	'white wolf'
m	(3) Cheevers[6]	'male goat'
m	(4) Wild Horse	much white blood[7]
m	(5) Hightohavit[8]	

1. Wallace and Hoebel 1952:187. Wallace and Hoebel states that Ya?ai died in 1890, but she is otherwise unidentified.

2. In the late 1840s and early 1850s, one of the leading Comanche raiders in Mexico was called Maue (*ma-* 'hand') or Mano (Emory 1857; Smith 1970), probably the man later known as Mowway. In 1883, he told the Dutch ethnologist H. F. C. ten Kate that some forty years earlier he had gone far enough into Mexico to see the "little men, covered with fur and with long tails," the *kwasitaibo* 'tail-men' (1885:123).

3. Here Niyah has simply listed all of the well-known chiefs. Interestingly, most are Yapainʉʉ, rather than Mowway's Kutsutʉhka.

4. The meaning of the "m" notation is not known.

5. *tabe* 'sun', *nanaka* 'noise'. Robinson and Armagost (1990) gives it as Hears the Sunrise or Voice of the Sunrise. He was associated with the Yapainʉʉ.

6. Probably *tsibis* from the Spanish *chivo* 'goat', although Joe Attocknie (MS) insisted that the name was *tsii puhtse* Little Pitied One. He was Parʉasʉmʉno's grandson, and Joe Attocknie's great uncle.

7. It is not clear what this comment means. This is the only assertion that he had "white blood."

8. Black Crow. He is not mentioned in any prereservation document. However, in 1879 he was leader of a Yapainʉʉ local band of about twenty-five people.

(6) Onawia[1]   was Paruasumuno's friend and successor; (he was chief before Quanah.)

(7) Peahnavonit[2]   'Big Mirror'

Tabenanaka   Tabenanaka was called brave by some, not so by others. In one battle, a young man on his first trip ran ahead of the warriors, but lost heart before he closed and turned back. Tabenanaka was right behind and did the same. The third man then took the lead. Tabenanaka began whipping the man who turned back, blaming him for his own turning back. Witnesses had no respect for Tabenanaka thereafter.

White Wolf   White Wolf was Herman Asenap's daughter's grandfather on her mother's side.

Howeah   Howeah[3] was chief [medicine man] of a band, but failed to meet an army officer at a specified time. Cheevers went in his place, it being a tribal matter. Later, he became a chief, with Howeah fading out. [Howeah would have gotten the office by heredity.][4]

Political Organization: Chiefs: Qualifications   All chiefs had to be a *tekwUniwapI* first.

Social Roles: Announcer   *tekwUnitu* was the crier or announcer.

Quanah Parker   There was some jealousy among the different band leaders and chiefs. Most of the chiefs were against Quanah Parker because of his great influence with the whites.

Political Organization: Chiefs   A chief was for life, but he had to treat people good. A man's past life and behavior toward the people determined the success of his chieftaincy.

Quanah Parker   Quanah Parker's removal of Cruz's wife was resented by a few. Quanah was a Peyote medicine man.

Enemies   Comanches fought with Navajos, Pawnees, Wichitas, and Kiowas.

Shoshones   The Comanches never heard of the Shoshones until recently. The old people knew of some people far to the west who talked their tongue.

Isatai   Isatai should have succeeded Quanah as chief.

1. *ona* 'salt', *wia* 'worn away spot', known as Salt Gap. The earliest documentary reference to Onawia is his participation in the 1872 trip to Washington. He was Yapainuu.

2. *pia* 'big', *napuni* 'mirror' (*na*- reflexive, *punitu* 'see'). In 1879, he was listed in Hightohavit's Yapainuu local band, and in 1885 as chief of a portion of that group. In 1894, he was a delegate to Washington, where he was photographed at the Smithsonian, both individually and with fellow delegates Ahpeatone (Kiowa) and Apache John (Plains Apache), posing as a group of peyote ritualists. Peahnavonit died before allotment.

3. *hu* 'timber', *wia* 'gap, worn away spot', usually translated as Timber Gap. Robinson and Armagost (1990) gives his name as Refuse to Come, possibly referring to this incident. He was a Yapainuu local band chief.

4. Wallace and Hoebel 1952:281. While it is known that Cheevers was Paruasumuno's grandson, Howeah's relation to that family is unknown and so the implication of foiled inheritance is unclear.

The incident of the meeting with the "army officer" cannot be directly confirmed from existing documents, although it possibly refers to events in the years 1872–73. In the winter of 1872–73, Howeah and Cheevers were camped together north of Fort Sill (Nye 1969:164). In early October, 1873—it is not known where they were in the interim—after a tumultuous meeting with Governor Davis of Texas, Cheevers agreed to lead a party in search of the Kwaharunuu (Nye 1969:177; Kavanagh 1996:441). There was no mention of Howeah attending that meeting. The implication that the army chose Comanche leaders, or that Howeah displayed cowardice and was thus superceded by Cheevers, is not supported by other evidence. Cheevers died in 1899, Howeah in 1905.

[He was a rival to Quanah; he led the settlement at Walters. He was originally ten or fifteen miles south of Cache, but the land was not good enough so he moved further southeast.][1]

Quanah Parker   Quanah's father was not definitely known.[2]

Medicine   Some medicine men would swallow a human hair, then throw it up again as a snake.

Medicine: Foretelling   A medicine man could foretell the future or see what was happening at a distance through his dreams.

Some men once went on a raid. They were gone unduly long and the people began to wonder whether they had been killed. They went to the medicine man, smoked, and told him to locate the missing men because their kin were worried.

It was toward night when he was asked and he promised an answer by the next day. The next morning early, he said, a messenger who brought a cigarette should come alone and he would tell him. The messenger came in the morning and the medicine man told him that the warriors were safe and on their way home, and would arrive the next noon. He told what kind of horse each man rode, and when the warriors arrived, they rode the horses as forecast. They gave the medicine man a horse ridden by the son of the man who had made the inquiry.

Medicine men usually operated at night.

Beliefs: Soul   Niyah learned about the existence of the soul from whites.

[Niyah "never heard of the soul until he was grown up." Niyah can't say whether the spirit or body goes on.]

Beliefs: Revival of the Dead   A certain medicine man thought he had the power to revive the dead.

One time, a fifteen-year-old child died, and the people wept. Someone had heard the medicine man boast of his powers. He stopped the people from weeping and sent a man to him with news of the death, and to ask him to come and see if he could revive the deceased.

Once the custom was to wail, alone, especially for women.

The medicine man said to select the loudest women to mourn. While the medicine man worked on the dead, two women wailed for the dead. The dead person came to and got well.

Huuba⁷ 'coffee' was the medicine man.[3]

---

1. In 1895, Isatai (as Quenatosavit 'White Eagle') and portions of his local band were listed as living on the "west side of West Cache Creek, five miles south of Quanah Parker" (Long 1895). Six years later, in 1901, many of them took allotments far to the southeast along Blue Beaver Creek, about twenty miles east of Walters. After Quanah's death in 1911, Isatai aspired to the position of Principal Chief, but the agent, arguing that with allotment there was no longer a need for a "tribal" organization, refused to recognize the position. He died in 1916.

2. Quanah's mother was Cynthia Ann Parker, a young girl captured in Texas in 1836, and his father was reportedly a Comanche named Peta Nocona (De Shields 1886). The only prereservation documentary appearance of a name resembling "Peta Nocona" is in MacGowan (1865). As Niyah implies here, some Comanches questioned who Quanah's father was.

3. During the reservation period, there were a number of people whose names were some variation of 'Coffee', so this particular person cannot be identified with certainty from the documents.

Life Cycle: Death: Mourning   Men sang and cried differently than did the women, and Comanches mourned differently than did Kiowas. Mourning was very hard and people suffered by it. There was no difference who died in a family. Women took off their clothes and gashed themselves; men gashed their thighs.[1]

In the old times, Indians thought much of their hair,[2] but they cut it off in mourning. Sometimes they cut off the lobe of an ear; Quitsquip 'chewing' [who died recently][3] had his earlobes cut off, but he later covered them with hair.

If the kin returned to an old camp a year or so later, they renewed the mourning, sometimes as long as three years after.

They were ready to move the camp as soon as the funeral ended.

Life Cycle: Death: Burial   A warrior's favorite horse was killed, sometimes at the grave, but not always so. Niyah thought this was because the warrior might use the horse in later life. The corpse was dressed as for "big doings" or for war. They put red paint [red brown earth paint was crumbled up and sprinkled[4]] over his face. A father fixed his son's corpse, a mother that of her daughter. There was no feast. The corpse was not kept very long before burial.[5] It was put on a horse to get through the mountains, then deposited headfirst in a rock crevice. The corpse was removed from the tipi through the door.

Life Cycle: Marriage: Widow Remarriage   A widow might remarry when her hair was long enough to braid; before that she couldn't find a husband. A man didn't wait so long.

Life Cycle: Death: Burial   A certain man got sick soon after the opening of the country. He finally died and was buried. Another couple accompanied the widow to the grave. Upon their return from the grave, the widow went to live with the couple. It was not like that in the old days.

Life Cycle: Death: Mourning   A young girl would cut off her hair if her father died, but not herself.[6] If a widow or widower didn't cut his hair, people would talk.

Story: The Woman Who Betrayed Her Husband   There was trouble between the Utes and Comanches (?), with the Utes getting the best end of the deal. Finally, they caught one woman. The Ute chief claimed her. She had parents, two brothers, and a husband. The latter determined to follow and recapture her.

While seeking her, he was joined by his brothers-in-law. They traveled two or three days when they spotted the Ute camp along a creek where the ash trees were very thick.

The husband told the wife's brothers to wait while he went to the creek. He finally located the watering place nearby.

Presently, a woman came down to the creek and he recognized her as his wife. The man went to his wife and said how glad he was to see her and that her brothers were ready to

1. Wallace and Hoebel 1952:151.
2. Wallace and Hoebel 1952:152.
3. Quitsquip, *kʉtsʉkwipʉ̱*, usually translated as Chewing or Chew-up, sometimes as Elk's Cud or Chewing Elk. Although the form Parʉakʉtskwipʉ̱ does not appear in the historical record, he was a prominent Yapainʉʉ local band leader who died about 1883.
4. Hoebel (1940) attributed this note to Post Oak Jim.
5. Wallace and Hoebel 1952:149 (?).
6. Contra Wallace and Hoebel 1952:151 (?).

go. She made excuses that she had to take her bucket back to camp, that she had to get her shawl, etc.

This was in the morning. She went back to the camp and took a nap.

She awoke and called to her Ute husband's mother that she had dreamed of three men, two young men and one old one down by the creek. She described the older man; they were to capture him and kill the two young men. The Utes surrounded the grove and killed the two brothers and captured her husband.

He told her she had caused her brothers to be killed and he wanted to be killed, too. His wife interpreted falsely to the Utes: she told the old people to come and use awls to kill him.

The husband scolded his wife and renewed his request for immediate death. She told the Utes to get hay and burn him to death. Her husband didn't die and again asked for death. She interpreted that he wanted to be crucified. They crucified him, then they moved camp and left him hanging.

An old captive woman didn't move with the rest; she was wandering about the abandoned camp and saw the crucified man. She had lost her sons and remembered them. She took pity on him and cut him down, took him to her tipi and dressed his wounds.

The man appreciated her kindness. After a few days he could walk. He said the Utes would be attacked by his people in the spring and she should camp at the extreme east end of the village to be saved.

She gave him a horse and he returned home, bringing the news to his wife's people, and they set the time for a revenge attack.

In the spring, the war party went out and finally located the Ute camp. Early in the evening, the husband went out to locate the old woman's tipi to get her out before the trouble started, warning her to go east toward his people and not to run with the Utes.

They surrounded the Utes at daylight and killed many of them. He finally captured his wife back and led her back on foot. She began to call to her father and mother. They said they had no daughter. The husband began to mimic his wife's misinterpretation. He asked the old woman to use awls on her, then they brought grass to build a fire under her. Finally, they killed her. Her own parents made no objections, because she had caused own brothers to die.

sube²tʉ.[1]

Story: Capture and Recapture of a Woman   There were two tribes, but their names are unknown. One woman from one tribe was captured by two brothers from the other and taken as wife by the older [both slept with her, the woman between them[2]].

Her husband went in search of her. He found her camp, and ran into the tipi of another old captive woman. He said he was seeking his wife and asked if she had seen a captive woman. The woman said yes; she also said that the new husband was about same size as her (the stolen wife's) present husband.

1. Robinson and Armagost (1990) gives this as 'That's all (narrative closing; end of story)'.
2. From Carlson.

She said she was willing to help him get his wife back, so she dressed him like the present husband and told he to go into his tipi, leaving his shield outside. The husband would be gone on a raid. She gave him full instructions.

The wife's new husband had two tipis, one for living and one for sleeping. The seeker was to go into the former and sit down. On one side was tobacco; he should sit down and smoke. Afterward, he should go out and his wife would follow him to the bedroom {tipi}, where his wife slept between the two brothers. He should kill the younger brother and retake his wife.

The younger man slept next to the wall. During the night, he heard the man snoring and he cut his throat. Then he spoke to his wife in their own language. He asked her where the good horses were. She knew of a certain racehorse. They mounted the horse and rode to a high mountain from where, in the morning, they watched the camp.

The sun was high when the people in camp found the dead man. They thought the elder brother had killed the younger, so they buried him and moved the camp.

Meanwhile, the reunited couple rode back to their own village. When the elder brother returned from his raid, he was accused of killing his brother. He denied it and proved that he was innocent by the presence of his own shield apart from the imitation one.

Tipis: Domestic Arrangements   Comanches usually had two tipis each, one for eating and living quarters, the other for sleeping.

Life Cycle: Marriage: Polyandry   If a woman wasn't trusted during her husband's absence, his brother slept with her.[1]

Captives   Comanche women were afraid of being captured by Pawnees because Pawnee men piled up on them like roosters. Two men once caught a woman and shared her.

Medicine: Sorcery: Cannibalism   Some people once fed a medicine man some of his forbidden foods and made him crazy; the people were afraid. So he mounted his horse and rode away. People forgot about him then.

A raiding party coming by located a camp with a tipi, and a gray horse was tethered nearby. A member of the war party disappeared and the rest found that medicine man was killing and eating people.

Two men returning from a raid saw the tipi by a creek, and they recognized it as one of their people, so they went in to rest. The medicine man gave them a place to sit down, while the medicine man sat and made an arrow.

They saw human skulls and bones scattered about. The visitors became afraid and excused themselves, saying that they were scouting for a camp site and soon the rest of the people would come and camp beside him that night and tell stories. He excused them then.

Out of sight, the scouts began to run. The medicine man got on his horse and rode after them, but they got to their own camp all right and told their story. So the people decided to go and kill the medicine man. They got together and went out. As they approached, he rode toward them. They began shooting and killed him before he got near. The people went into his tipi and looked over the skulls and bones.

Niyah heard of no case of cannibalism by sane persons.

---

1. Wallace and Hoebel 1952:139.

Story: War: Rescue   Utes captured a Comanche, killing the rest of his party. They tied him up in a tree and began dancing below him. The captive's brother followed the Utes to rescue him. He found their trail and located their camp. He arrived early in the day and waited for a chance to enter.

At night he went into their camp. He had a Ute-like blanket so he mixed with them. Late at night, the people began scattering to their camps until only the dancers were left. The rescuer prowled about. Every once in a while, when the drums stopped, he heard a groan up in a tree and suspected that his brother was up there. So, while the drums were beating, he climbed the tree, stopping when the drums stopped. Finally, he found his brother, who was thirsty.

He cut the ropes and they descended to the ground. The captive sent his brother for water to the tipi where he had been imprisoned. The owner was a sound sleeper and the brother got water. Then he got a saddle and a bridle at another tipi. He got a horse and went to his rescuer's horse. Then they left and rode till daylight, climbed a mountain, and watched the people at the camp.

The Utes didn't miss the prisoner until the sun was high, then began to pull down tipis. They thought there must have been many Comanches, else they wouldn't have dared such a thing. Later, the boys descended the mountains and returned home.[1]

Captives   Niyah heard of the crucifixion of a captive Navajo boy, also of the killing of a diseased Navajo man. Comanches captured Mexicans, keeping the women as wives and killing the men. Niyah heard of no cases of torture of whites, though he did know of one Comanche who castrated his captives.[2]

Animals: Pets   There were no animal pets. Niyah knew one girl who had a pet beaver.

Life Cycle: Marriage: Wife Stealing   This was Niyah's own experience: Two warriors were good friends. While one was gone, the other took his favorite wife, who camped near him. The latter was told, and not knowing it was that wife, asked his brother why he hadn't come to visit. He soon got his wife back, but she ran away and was not recovered.

If the wife stealer was a stronger man, nothing was said.

The two camps were about two miles apart.

Story {Carlson}   A young boy visited a girl's tipi in another village [two and a half miles off]. He pulled up a stob {stake} and crawled in with her. Just before dawn, he left for home.

On his way, he met four enemies, who decided to kill him on the hill and name the hill after him, but they met a returning war party of his people. They had a battle and three of the enemies were killed, a fourth also, and they named the hill after him.

The boy got home safely.

---

1. Compare with Howard White Wolf, August 2.
2. Wallace and Hoebel 1952:260.

POST OAK JIM
July 11, 1933

Dances: Social Dances   Social dances were often held when people hadn't been together for some time.

Social Organization: Societies   The Horse Dance was the *tнeрикипнн*.[1]

Both women and men participated. Two or three men used gourd rattles. They were organized by a leader who carried a club. He handled the people like he wanted, "They were his horses."

He had another man to announce what he wanted done; the leader merely supervised.

If he wanted a certain man to get in and dance, he had the announcer call for him. If the warrior refused, but was physically able, the leader went after him with the club.

If he saw one standing about uncostumed, or astride a horse, the announcer went and told him to get into the dance. The announcer called absent members of the group by beating the drum and calling them by alluding to some act of theirs that were better untold, e.g., intimacies with an old woman, etc. This was very effective.

As the drums began to beat, the people arose, advanced, and danced; there was no ring or other formation.

If people didn't like a certain song leader, they needn't dance, but with a good leader they all danced.

If a woman wanted to dance with a certain man she could, but the women were not invited by the men.

Men sometimes admired a friend's dancing and gave a present to his friend and they danced together, usually with the latter's family accompanying out of gratitude.

[Women danced, too. A man and a woman might get together to dance. (There were no special invitations.) The warrior may give the girl a gift while dancing. Children and kinspeople of the girl might come up and dance with the pair to show appreciation of the gift.[2]]

There was no feast in connection with the dance. It was held during the late afternoon and night when it was cool. A tent was put up if the weather was cold; a large tipi of twelve to fourteen hides was used.

Musical Instruments: Drums   Drums were made by binding a flattened limb, three inches wide, in a circle, then stretching a green hide across the circle, sewing it with buckskin, and then allowing it to dry. Drum sticks were eighteen inches by one inch, with rags on the end, painted blue, black, red, etc., but there was no fixed color. Drums were about twenty-four to thirty inches in diameter, large enough for three or four drummers simultaneously. A large double-head drum suspended from sticks is used now.

Musical Instruments: Rasps   There were no wooden rasps (cf. Southwest[3]).

---

1. *tнe* 'little', *pнkн* 'horse', *nнн* plural, 'little horse group'. This is one example of the Field Party's confusion of the societies with their dances.

2. This form of honoring is still practiced in the Gourd Dance.

3. The source of this comment is uncertain.

Musical Instruments: Rattles   Gourds were late. [Rattles were used by the song leader.] Rattles were formerly made of rawhide from the scrotum of buffalo. They were filled with dirt and dried to mold the shape. The [buffalo] tail was used as a handle. Large trade beads were used inside the rattles. [Tin cans or gourds are used now.]

Dances   When the young men wanted to dance, they took it up with the chief, who then had the announcer told of the forthcoming dance, and he went out to call the men he wanted to dance.

Each camp had an announcer.

Each band had different dances.

If a warrior wanted to excuse himself from the dance, he first danced, then, if he could tell of a braver deed than the announcer [coach], the latter had to get out and dance.

Social Organization: Bands: Noyʉhka   Jim belonged to the Noyʉhka.[1]

Dances: Social Dances   [Social dances were held before a raiding party as a general party.]

The Noyʉhka (round) dance was called ⟨wekinai⟩. Women, men, everybody participated. They danced around in a mixed circle, from left to right, (clockwise).

The ⟨naredyad⟩ "move back and forth dance" [was a social dance]. Women line up on one side, the men on the opposite side. The women back up and the men follow, then they dance back, with the men backward, women forward. [There was a fire.]

The *otsinʉhka*,[2] from *otsi* 'knee'[3] (an obsolete term) meant "knees bent while dancing." The song leaders were in a group with drums. The men were in one group, women in another. The women came out, picked their male partners, and danced with them around the general fire. They danced back and forth until the music ceased, then they returned to their respective groups. They danced like whites did, clinched.

The ⟨wakenoweit⟩, from ⟨wakeno⟩, the back of buffalo neck (buffalo, when thirsty, lope to the creek) [⟨wakenoweyt⟩ Buffalo Hump Dance]. Men and women danced in couples, one behind the other, about a fire and the drummers.[4] If a couple got thirsty, they danced to the creek to get a drink, then danced back. If too many couples were gone, the drummers rested. It was sometimes held in winter, with the women dressed in buffalo robes. They danced until midnight.

[They stooped like a buffalo-hump while dancing.]

Dances   When people came together in a tribal gathering, each band had its own dancers and put on its own part of the show at the center of the encampment.

Medicine: Sun Dance   At the Sun Dance, each band danced one way, one from the east, one from the west, north, and south; each danced their own way.

Dances: Scare Dance   If a medicine man saw trouble ahead, or war, [if he had a dream or scouts saw the enemy], and the Indians felt uneasy, they held a "scare" dance ['fear dance'] *tuhunuhka*,[5] thus averting disaster.

---

1. See Introduction.
2. ten Kate (1885:128) gives "otchi-niskera," which he identifies as 'a circle dance'.
3. According to Robinson and Armagost (1990), 'knee' is *tanapʉ*.
4. This description seems to match the modern Two Step Dance.
5. Robinson and Armagost (1990) and the Comanche Cultural Committee (2003) imply that *tuhu* is 'anger'. See also Lowie's notes in Part Two.

While the people got ready, some young men got dressed in their war costumes. They waited in the shadows. As the music started, they ran through the firelight and back. Then they advanced and made a ring about the fire, making motions as if they were striking the enemy, dancing back and forth. The women cheered [*katatakitʉ*] as the men came out. At the drum, the drummers hollered and cheered the boys. After the drums stopped, the boys ran back into shadows.

Jim heard of a medicine woman who dreamed that soldiers were coming and advised them to hold a Scare Dance. So they had the dance and soldiers didn't come.

Economy: Trade: Comancheros   The only friends of the Comanches were Pueblo Indians.

Comanches also traded with some Mexicans. The Mexicans drove ox carts and brought in trade goods from the plains to the west. They were never attacked by Comanche war parties. Some Mexicans had bows and arrows like the Comanches. They traded flint to the Comanches for fire making.

Material Culture: Fire Making   Indians used a hand firedrill.

⟨kɔs:op⟩ was flint. Comanches got flint and steel and the striking method from Mexico. [When it was wet, the flint was no good, so they fell back on the firedrill.] The materials were kept in a container made of buffalo horn. Rotten wood [Spanish moss, or the inside of a bird's nest] was used as tinder. [Sometimes an old gun filled with rags was used.] ⟨naʔa⟩ was the "matchbox" of [buffalo] horn.

Jim remembered the use of the firedrill. They used a yucca stalk both for the drill and for the hearth. [They dropped the spark on buffalo chips or wood pulp.] The old people formerly lit cigarettes with this.[1]

Smoking: Cigarettes   In the old days, they smoked cigarettes of cottonwood or cat briar[2] leaves, [or the bark of a bush], and [large] leaf tobacco from Mexico.[3]

Smoking: Pipes   They used straight pipes of deer tibia. The bowl was made from the joint end and was wrapped with sinew. The *omotoi*[4] was the straight pipe. Stone pipes were made from a white soft stone obtained in the west [*ekatoi*[5]].

Pipes were of different sizes. Walnut pipe stems ⟨pitsim⟩ were used because of the large pith cavity; it was bored with a hot iron (wood borer technique with fire in the north). Osage orange was also used.

The stem was tightly fitted, sometimes lashed with rawhide to the pipe. The pipe was held with both hands to keep the stem from slipping out, with the projecting fore-end used for grasping with the left hand.

Pipes were bored with a [special] knife. Sometimes they were dyed with a red dye, *ekAsapU*, boiled for a time with grease. Walnut husks boiled with grease were used to make a black pigment for pipes.[6]

1. Wallace and Hoebel 1952:89.
2. Carlson and Jones (1940) identifies this as greenbriar, *Smilax* sp.
3. Wallace and Hoebel 1952:97.
4. Robinson and Armagost (1990) gives *omo* as 'lower leg from the knee down', *toi* 'pipe'.
5. Literally, 'red pipe'.
6. Wallace and Hoebel 1952:98.

Material Culture: Paint: Pigments   A red dye [*ekAsapU*] came from pokeberries. They mashed the pokeberries in a paunch, then put in feathers and buried the mass for four days. When it was dug up and rinsed, the feathers had a good color. They should be boiled in dye to get the best color. Red dyed feathers were used on arrows.

The root of *ohasapU*, a pond weed, when powdered and boiled, gave yellow. It was used for dying also by the paunch treatment.

[Walnut gave a black (brownish black).]

[Red and yellow vegetal pigments were used in the old days as above.]

There were four pigments from the earth in the old days:

Hematite was locally acquired [fifteen or twenty miles to the west] and was used by women [on their faces].

White ⟨eip:⟩ kaolin or marl was used for trimming moccasins because it wasn't greasy; it was also for buckskin suits.

Blue came in small lumps from some large river toward the west. Indians called it *tupusahunuʔbi*[1] or Black Paint River. It was a very dark blue azurite.

Yellow came from a clay, very soft, probably ochre. Water was added to the paint when buckskin was to be colored. [Eagle dung was important for painting medicine men, shields, and as a war paint.]

[Water was added to all earth paints.]

Material Culture: Paint: Paint Brush   Comanches used a bone paint brush made of a bison patella (cf. Pawnee[2]).

[Paint was pressed into the buckskin. Some colors were mixed (i.e., green).]

Adornment: Face Paint   These same paints were used for face painting. Young men painted just "to look pretty."

A medicine man, or another who had dreams, painted only as they were directed in dreams.

Medicine: Power: Paint   The bull has a very thick hide and bullets couldn't pierce him; some medicine men had this power also. [(A picture of a bison or cow head made them impervious to bullets like those animals are sometimes when they are mad.)]

When a man got a dream, he went to the creek and washed, and then he was ready to apply the paint. Comanches painted their faces only on special occasions, not at all times. A man painted his own face.

Adornment: Paint   No stamps were used (cf. Pawnee[3]).

A striped effect was made by painting lines across the palm of the hand, then pressing the hand to the face. They painted their bodies yellow or blue before going into battle. Brown hematite paint was applied to the body in stripes with fingers.

The method was also part of the medicine.

Medicine: Transfer of War Power   When a war party came in sight of the enemy, it stopped. A man might give power to a friend, and they could make other preparations for battle.

---

1. *tu* 'black', *hunubI* 'creek'. Its specific location is unknown.
2. It is not clear if this material culture note is from Linton or Wedel.
3. It is not clear if this material culture note is from Linton or Wedel.

War: Battle of Tipi Creek   The Tipi Creek Battle was one of last battles before the Indians surrendered.[1] The Wichitas had camped there. The army [Negro soldiers[2]] came and burned their camps. The soldiers went to the North Fork of the Canadian River. The Indians were prepared and were on the mountain looking on.

[Four Comanches were preparing to fight, two medicine men, Quanah Parker and his nephew.]

Two men who already had power wanted to give medicine to their two friends. The medicine man smoked and bear claws came out of his mouth. Another of the medicine men stripped and, taking a live coal, he drew a picture of a gun on the ground. He laid the live coal on the drawing. Presently, the gun drawing discharged with a loud report, burning the man who was getting medicine on the chest and leaving a big blue mark.

The medicine man then told them they had come some long ways to get the enemy. Now the four would try their strength with the soldiers. There were other Comanches in the mountains watching how the Noyʉhka would behave.

["Many times you walk many miles to find an enemy; today, they are right before you. We four are alone; other Indians are in the mountains watching us. We will show them what the Noyʉhka can do."]

One man (Quanah Parker's nephew[3]) who had received medicine fixed his horse up like a bear; he tied the ears down and the tail up short with a red rag. He wore a bearskin [hood, and his face] was painted like a bear [yellow, and blue-black], and he carried a long spear [revolver] fastened to his wrist by a loop.

One of the men who taught the power was Quanah Parker and his other nephew.[4]

They started toward the (Negro) soldiers and rode in front of them. The soldiers shot but couldn't hit them. The third man then rode by and escaped. The fourth man was old; he had a red hood with long [white] hair and rode a white horse. He rode by also and was unhit. This was late in the evening, because the smoke was settling. These four men alone did the fighting, shooting at the soldiers as they rode by. The rest of the Comanches watched from a distance.

The four men returned to the warriors.

The Negro troops crossed the river. Another man, without medicine, tried to imitate the others and was shot in the face. Another man tried to rescue him, but his horse was shot under him, and he had to be rescued by his brothers. [The brother's wife came out and took him in.] The wounded man ultimately died of his wounds.

Animal Powers: Bear   The bear had power to turn bullets.

Medicine: Transfer of War Power   War power would be transferred only for the current battle.

Quanah Parker's other nephew later disobeyed some of the rules of his medicine and was finally killed.

1. From the details, this is probably the battle of McClellan Creek, Sept. 29, 1872 (Nye 1969:160).
2. Ninth Cavalry from Fort Sill.
3. Otherwise unidentified. Inasmuch as nephew means 'sibling's son', and as Quanah had no adult siblings, this would have been a classificatory nephew.
4. Otherwise unidentified.

Medicine: Defilement   A medicine man who disobeyed his rules could make things good again by <u>prompt</u> action. He could go to a peyote meeting, tell his troubles, and ask for assistance. He had to roll a cigarette, hand it with an eagle feather to the peyote leader and tell him he was in trouble. This matter was taken up after midnight. He wanted someone with more power to tell him that to do. Word was then passed to the man that the trouble was settled and that he needn't worry.

They built a cedar fire and fanned the smoke toward him with an eagle feather. Thus, medicine men could atone for violations of taboos.

Prior to the peyote days, such a man would dress up [in war regalia] and go to a hill alone, to the grave of the man who gave him the power, and be fixed up. If relief didn't come at once, they could try again.

Medicine: Peyote   Peyote came from the western peoples in Jim's memory. Peyote was first used for evil purposes by the western tribes. It was finally given up by them.

Apache women at first took up with it and became so bad that the medicine men forbade it. Travelers to the western peoples brought peyote to the Comanches. Mescaleros used it for evil purposes; they used strong drinks and finally gave it up. Comanche used it right and were never harmed. Jim began using peyote as small boy.

Medicine: Sorcery: Medicine Man Causes Nosebleed {Wedel}   A medicine man tried to kill two men by nosebleed through peyote. He took four pieces of joint grass stem and put them into a hole in his tipi where the buffalo of the tipi had been shot, to show that what died would never heal. Those two men bled so much from the nose that finally they went to a peyote meeting.

The medicine man found who was causing the trouble; he saw the four sticks. They threatened that his medicine would come back on him if he didn't withdraw it, and in the fall of the year he became very sick [and died].

If medicine was used for good purposes, one lived long. This man was a cripple, but could get up and get around.

Medicine: Sorcery: Medicine Man Causes Nosebleed {Hoebel}   A medicine man caused a man's nose to bleed. He put four pieces of joint grass in an arrow hole (where the arrow had penetrated the buffalo) in his tipi as a sign that the wound would not heal.

A peyote meeting was held on the question. The medicine man worked on the question to find out about it. He revealed the culprit.

They went directly to this man and accused him of the deed. They told him that if he did not immediately recall his medicine it would come back on him.

He refused to remove the curse.

His victim got well and he died in the fall.

This medicine man was crippled, but when his power was on him, he could get up and walk. Jim saw him do this.

Medicine: Sorcery {Wedel}   Jim nearly lost his life because another medicine man used his medicine. Jim was in a peyote tipi, the other man was outside.

In a peyote meeting they need two men, one fireman and one leader. Jim was the fireman.

From the outside, Jim felt that he was shot. He noticed that he had spat blood. He ran outside, stumbled, and fell. He lay in the dew and bled a big pool of blood.

He came back in, breathing hard. While walking around the semicircle to the fire, the people asked what was wrong. Jim told them he was sick.

The leader told him to fix the fire, then come sit by him. The leader took a live coal, put it to his own mouth, and blew smoke into Jim's mouth, so that he felt better.

Jim went outside and rested. He aired his clothes four times, to the south, west, north, and east.

He felt better when he back came in. He was saved by the Peyote man.

The medicine man died the next fall. The medicine man was probably jealous and did not want Jim to live. Jealousy was the main cause of a medicine man's killing a person.

Medicine: Sorcery {Hoebel}   Jim was nearly killed by a medicine man (counteracted with peyote and the medicine man died).

Jim was the fire tender in a peyote meeting. The medicine man was outside. He was in the prime of life and his power was strong.

Jim suddenly felt like he was shot in the back. He spat blood; he thought he was going to die. He ran outside and fell on the grass. The dew was heavy (signifying the purifying effect of water?). He made a big pool of blood.

He re-entered and walked around the tipi to his place.

They saw him bleeding and asked what was wrong. He told them he wasn't feeling well.

The leader told him to fix up the fire and then come around and sit by him. The leader then picked a live coal out of the fire and put it in his mouth. He blew four times in Jim's mouth. Jim felt better.

Then he was instructed to go out and air his clothes to the four directions, south, west, north, east.

He re-entered and was purified with cedar smoke waved with an eagle feather fan.

The other medicine man died in the fall while feeding his horses.

Life Cycle: Death: Mourning: Dances   Mourners were excused from dances, but usually some member of the family danced a while. If the announcer saw such a person weeping, he excused him. Usually mourners worked back in by degrees.

If a family passed near a grave, it once more mourned, but less so than at first; sometimes they gashed themselves slightly. Nowadays people take it less seriously.

Beliefs: Revival of the Dead   Jim's mother died of a fever and was laid away, but she revived. She told the following tale.

When she died, an iron gray horse awaited her. She got on the horse and rode away along a path where people had moved, dragging poles. The horse acted as though it smelled something and then trotted along the trail, neighing. She looked around; the land was beautiful. She noticed a camp on a stream by a hill. The people were up farther on horseback. She looked closely and saw they were on foot, playing [old-time] games (hockey) [shinny].

Two horsemen left the crowd and began to run as if they were racing. Then she heard someone yell and the report of a gun.

Then she turned away from the hills and toward the creek. The creek ran south and the woman was riding east. She saw a spring. She dipped her hand in the water and tried drinking, but the water smelled too bad to drink. Some water splashed on her face and she awoke.

Her husband was making medicine over her and that was what she had felt as cool water. He gave her water to wash herself and she lived a long time.[1]

Life Cycle: Death: Soul/Spirit   When a person died, he just slept, the soul didn't leave.

The spirit of an evil man stays and worries living people, scares them and may bring sickness, but good spirits stay with the body.

[Good people just sleep.]

Beliefs: Ghosts   Jim had traveled much but had never seen a ghost.

Once he was on his way home from a trading post in the northwest. When he stopped to camp, two boys went back to town for supplies. Jim and another man went out and shot a buffalo calf. As they were returning to camp, crossing the creek, something hit Jim in the back. The other men spurred ahead, drew his gun, and challenged the ghost to come forth, but he didn't.

They had crossed the creek and noticed smoke moving toward them. The horses also noticed it and began to jerk away.

They headed back east and met another man who was waiting for the boys who had gone to town. Jim and his companion warned the man that there was something dangerous at the creek, but he didn't believe them and wasn't scared. He headed in that direction when suddenly the horse reared, turned, and rode back to where Jim and his companion were. The rider couldn't control his animal.

This was the first time he had ever noticed it. They later heard from other Indians that many Osages had been killed by Comanches on the creek years before and the apparition, the smoke, may have been the ghost of an Osage.

There were also tornados often along the creek that may have had something to do with it.

Animal Powers: Coyote {Wedel}   Jim and George Koweno went to get some meat when a storm came up. They had killed a small coyote (he thought that's what brought on the storm).

Finally, they found some cattle. They rushed in, rode, and killed a calf.

They had loaded the meat when the storm came. Jim was in the lead. The wind turned the load over and George called Jim back. Every time the lightning flashed, Jim saw small twisters. Jim turned back to help George reload. The ground was covered with water and it rained all night. He thought the little coyote or its mother had something to do with the storm.

When the rain ceased the next morning, it turned very cold. They nearly froze although it was summer. They crossed the overflowing creek by swimming.

(Coyote had the power to bring storms, especially if one mistreated its young.)

When a coyote howled close to a dwelling, he was trying to tell them something and some people could tell what he was saying.

After Jim rode along the creek, he noticed large trees were uprooted and a big hole in the ground.

---

1. Wallace and Hoebel 1952:187.

Animal Powers: Coyote {Hoebel}   Coyote had medicine; if you harmed it or its {young} it will get back on you in some way.

Case: Jim and George in a cyclone.

On a trip out west, they killed a coyote cub.

It was harder to find the cattle than they expected, but they came on the herd. Jim went in and roped a two-year-old. They knifed it and loaded it on a pack horse.

Pretty soon a big cloud came up and they ran. The wind blew a cyclone.

George was ahead with the load. The wind spilled it off. George called for help.

Jim thought his horse was spinning on its head. The rain was so hard that the horses nearly smothered.

The coyote's mother probably had made medicine.

It rained all night long and in the morning it was so cold that they nearly froze.

Once some raiders were caught in a terrific hail storm. The storm ruined the horses, blood was streaming from the animals, so they had to go on foot.

Medicine: Rain Making   Some men could produce rain.

Medicine: War: Peyote {Wedel}   A man was on a war party; he wanted to make medicine before a battle. He stopped in a buffalo wallow for a peyote ceremony. The cook had horse meat ready for them to eat as soon as they finished.

About midnight, they had some water and afterward heard a coyote howl to the east. One man understood him. He said that a coyote had been shot and crippled by one of the party. He had also lost a toe and wanted food.

Soon after, they heard another coyote howl to the west. He said that he had seen soldiers and would act as a scout, but he wanted food. The man woke the cook and said he should put out meat for the animals to the east and to the west.

Then, they went ahead and beat the drums and danced. There came a noise and lightning and it began to rain. The cook got wet; he came into the peyote meeting and saw that the men were dry.

About daylight, the cook came with breakfast; he had water in a paunch. He went around the tipi in the right direction. He went in and gave the food to the leader and wanted to know the good news.

The leader spoke to the coyote: "Last night, you were southeast of the camp yelling and we got a good bunch of horses."

So the party continued on their way. They took all day to reach their destination. Peyote had shown them their way.

So they traveled until nightfall. Then they saw the horses. They followed the directions but didn't find horses.

They crossed the creek to a high bank; it was near sundown. They watched the spot where they were to find the horses.

Presently, they saw the head of a man, which turned out to be two horsemen. As they watched, a covered chuck-wagon appeared and set up camp on the spot where the horses were to appear.

The warriors then gathered in a circle, heaped up their shields, put a peyote button on top, smoked, and told the peyote they had now reached the spot. Peyote gave them a new direction.

It was a moonlit night. It told them to follow a smoke cloud. There would be a gun fired. Some men had hobbled horses, and two men with raincoats would be watching the horses. The warriors started over; one brave began waving his whip and lightning appeared. One guard jumped off his horse and ran away, and they got the whole herd away, over one hundred horses.

The next day they divided the horses. This was the good news told to the cook. There was one good racehorse in the herd. This was about the best raid they had.

When the Indians were put on this reservation, there were many races won on the bay racehorse they caught. The government took it away and killed all of the horses.

Medicine: War: Peyote {Hoebel}   {First card(s) missing} Not long after, they heard another coyote. It said, "Some soldiers who went by here wounded me. I am on their trail. You must feed me and I'll be your scout."

The leader told the cook to put food on the east and west sides of the tent. He started the meeting again.

Pow! Came lightning and a big rain. The cook had a special tent. He got all wet.

(On the morning after the peyote episode figured by the coyote episode, above), the water bearer brought in a paunch of water at daybreak.

He brought smoke to the leader and asked for good luck.

The leader said, "You, I saw you last night over on the southeast hollering. You brought back many horses."

The dream gave directions as to how to get to a big herd.

Easy traveling brought them to the place by sundown, but the horses weren't there.

They turned to a big cliff to wait.

They saw a man's head appear in the timber, then a man on horseback, then a cow and a colt. A covered chuck-wagon followed and made camp at the very spot where the horses should be.

The Indians were puzzled. They set up a shield with a peyote button in the center.

They gathered in a circle about it.

They smoked and ate the peyote. They received new directions from the peyote: the moon would be up; a white cloud could come down from the moon to the place where the horses would be. One gun would be fired if the horses were there

On the raid, some of the horses were hobbled and there were people in raincoats watching them. The warriors dashed over; one cracked his whip, lightening flashed out; the guard fled. The party drove off one hundred horses. They left the whites only one.

This was about the last raid.

When on the reservation, the government took most of the horses and killed them.

Horses: Races   Jim's father owned horses, no mares, although his grandfather owned horses, mares, colts, etc.

A Noyʉhka had a very swift gray racehorse, one of swiftest known, but the bay beat it. The government finally killed the horses to keep the Indians on the reservation.

The race course was ten times as long as an arrow flight, which was 300 yards, i.e., 3,000 yards [ca. two miles].[1] There was a starter, men stationed at intervals to watch the contestants, and a finish judge.

They frequently ran a certain bay and a light black against each other; The bay usually won at more than 3,000 yards, the black at more than 3,600 yards by a neck.

There were judges at the finish.

They started from a standstill.

Some racehorses didn't get excited at a start, some horses over short distances reared at the start.

They bet horses, blankets, cattle, etc. Some men often backed out and refused to pay debts; they weren't trusted thereafter. [The bets were held by one man. Sometimes a man refused to pay up, and he lost the confidence of the others.]

War: Loot: Money   Indians once raided some wealthy people's house. They broke open a trunk, taking silver, but they scattered paper currency over the house and burned it; they didn't know its value.

Horses: Races   Captives and breeds were used as jockeys; little men were preferred. [The riders were often captives (small and industrious).]

No saddles were used, just a rope around the jaw, no bridle.

The horse's tail was tied into a knot for decoration.

A certain herb was given to the horses before the race to make them fast.

Women couldn't get near this medicine.

Right after the race, the horse was ridden to the creek and washed, and the jockey bathed, so as to get rid of the medicine. The herb was chewed and spat into the ear or mouth of the horse.[2]

Race horses were kept thin and weren't fed grain. They were staked in the shade at daytime to keep them thin. They were put out to graze at night. They were used only for racing.

Horses: Wild Horses   Wild horses were the fastest racers. When a herd was located, they surrounded them and ran them down. They were usually fat and could not run fast. Wild horses ran in a single file. The Indians rode up and fastened a rope around the neck; they didn't need to lasso them.

They tied a knot in the horse's tail and fastened a rope to it to guide it.

Sure-footed horses made good buffalo horses.

Horses: Breaking   Horses were broken by riding them in water or on sand where lighting was easy. Sometimes they tied a stubborn horse down for two or three days. They put something in its mouth to make it tender and easily guided. A horse was broken at about three years; Jim broke them as high as seven years.

Horses: Gelding   They were castrated at about three years.[3] Jim handled one horse alone. He roped the horse around the forefeet and tied them to a stake, then drew back the hind legs

---

1. Wallace and Hoebel 1952:50.
2. Wallace and Hoebel 1952:49.
3. Contra Wallace and Hoebel's "two years" (1952:46).

and cut. It was not proper to draw one leg back, as it might dislocate it. The younger they were at castration, the better they were to break.

Horses: Stallions   Some people once had a very bad sorrel stallion. Jim went to round up their horses. He got the first group without trouble. He tried to slip the next herd away and was chased by the stallion. Jim picked up a bone to use for a club. The stallion ran up and bit Jim's horse on the back of the neck. Jim hit the stallion on back of the head and knocked him down, but didn't kill him. A wild stallion was shot if he was too mean in the defense of the herd.

Horses: Names   Racehorses were named by their color or some physical peculiarity. Paruasumuno's horse given him at St. Louis was named "Washington."

Hunting: Buffalo   A buffalo got up, stood a while, then ran against the wind.

Buffalo horses were well-trained to dodge angry bulls. If a bison hit a horse, he usually killed it. For short distances, the buffalo was very fast.

Material Culture: Arrows   In the old days, arrow points were of flint, traded up from Mexico. Later, skillets, knives, or bells were cut up and made into points. Blunt arrows were used in tourneys. They were unmarked.

The Comanches used a three-feathered arrow.

The release between thumb and forefinger was hard on the feather. The release was against the second finger of the right hand. Jim shot arrows over his left hand. They did not put a finger over the arrow.

Barbed points were used in warfare; triangles in hunting.

Material Culture: Arrows: Poison   Arrows were poisoned with the scent from a skunk; they also used some sort of vegetal poison.

Relations with Other Tribes: Arrows   Cheyennes, Arapahos, Pawnees, Pueblos, and Navajos didn't know how to make arrows, but the Comanches and Wichitas did.[1]

Material Culture: Arrows   Dogwood was the best for arrows.

Material Culture: Arrows: Arrow Straightener   Arrows were straightened with the teeth or with a shaft straightener. First, the arrow was greased, then heated, and inserted into the rib and straightened. Uniformity was ensured by pulling it through a hole in a tin can or a rock.

Material Culture: Arrows Points   Arrow points were fastened into a slot on the shaft, cemented with mesquite gum, and fastened with sinew.

Material Culture: Arrows   Feathers were fastened with mesquite gum.

Material Culture: Glue   The big neck vessel, the beef jugular, made a good glue.

Material Culture: Arrows   The spike was inserted, covered with cement, and wrapped with sinew. Hawk and turkey feathers, also eagle wing feathers, were used, but not crow.

Material Culture: Bows   Bows were made of young bois d'arc; old wood would split in cold weather. Mulberry was also good if from the upland, but it was not as strong at bois d'arc. The wood was cut at any time and the bark allowed to peel off by itself. It was dried thoroughly. The heart of bois d'arc was the most durable.[2]

---

1. Wallace and Hoebel 1952:101–2.
2. Contra Wallace and Hoebel (1952:100).

Material Culture: Bows: Bowstrings   The bowstring was set to shoot at a certain tension. One end was adjustable, and loosened when not in use and kept dry.

Material Culture: Bow Case   The bow case and quiver were separate, with the latter reinforced at the bottom. The quiver was carried high over the left shoulder during a hunt. Ordinarily, it was allowed to swing at one's belt when not in use.

Material Culture: Awl and Knife Case   The "matchbox," awl in a special case, and knife case were secured to the quiver-bow case. They were all attached so that if a man lost his clothes in a hurry, he had material to make new clothes and to make out. The bow was about four feet long.

POST OAK JIM
July 12, 1933

Dances   One man in each band was usually the dance leader.

Music: Songs   Different bands had different dance songs. Scare Dance songs were mostly medicine men's songs obtained by vision. There were different songs for different dances. Very few new songs were made for dancers.

Dances: 49 Dance   Young people made up songs for the 49 Dance. [The only dance in which new songs were made up by the young people.]

It was a mixed dance, a modification of an old dance.

When the camp was more permanent, some men usually wanted to go on a raid. They would hold a council. The forerunner of the 49 Dance was held by the men going on the party.[1]

The men paraded on horseback among the tipis in their war costumes. On the last night before their departure, they went in a single file. [The last horse in line bore two men. The leader had asked each man in turn if he would ride double on the last horse. All must refuse unless] he had picked up a fallen companion in battle, hence the two riders on one horse, a sign of honor.

After the parade, the men went to the creek and washed. They returned and dressed in their ordinary costume.

The dance leader was announced. There were no drums in those days, they just beat sticks on a dry hide. (Good plains pattern.[2])

The kin of the men who were going on the raid gathered about for the dance. Everyone sang, but only the war party members danced.

Young men might join the party at the dance and go on the raid. They applied to the dance leader for permission.

---

1. This seems to be Lowie's ⟨ni′otsāīt⟩. See Part Two.
2. The source of this comment is unknown.

Warriors with clubs were standing about. The new members were told where the party was going. They went south to Texas against whites, west against Mexicans, north against other Indians.

Young girls might visit the warriors in their private tipis on the night before the departure.

Social Roles: Gender Roles: Female Warriors   Women sometimes went along on war parties.

Once a woman and three men went on a party. The men were slain by white soldiers and the woman was captured. She had a spear; it was later found by Indians with a bent and bloody point. The woman had probably killed some of the white soldiers and was in turn killed. Her body was also found.

Women usually carried knives, rarely spears.

[A woman who could not get along with her husband would wait until a war party was announced. That night she would creep into the tent of one of the members and say she wanted to go with him.[1]]

Social Roles: Gender Roles: Female Hunting   Some women used bow and arrow. Jim's mother was pretty handy. Sometimes she hunted small game.

Woman sometimes roped [and butchered] calves if the buffalo were plentiful.

Food: Food Plants: Roots   Women dug roots and hunted berries.[2] Women used flattened pointed digging sticks called *pooro*.[3] They dug onions, wild onions, in swampy land; they were sweetish. The onions were braided together, roasted, and eaten. Also, small onions were sometimes boiled.

tabahko[4] was ready in early February. The roots were made into soup. Its leaves were like the small wild onion.

siiko[5] grew in draws. Its leaves were also like wild onion. It had blue flowers. The roots were eaten.

tuhna[6] was a gray vine with a white tap root. It was eaten raw or peeled. It was sun dried, then pounded and made into a mush. It grew in dry habitats.

totohtu[7] was a root. It looked like a walnut and had a peeling, white meat. It died early in the summer. The vine looked like young tomato plant.

ekakoni[8] was a red, radish-like vine like the preceding. It was sweet, eaten raw.

ketanaruhka[9] 'hard to eat'. It grew in sandy habitats; it was a vine with a sweet potato-like root. It was roasted.

---

1. From Carlson. This dated note has no direct parallel in either Wedel's or Hoebel's notes, and is placed here arbitrarily.

2. Only one item on the lists of roots and berries below is duplicated in Hoebel's notes. None of Carlson's surviving notes include ethnobotanical information.

3. Wallace and Hoebel 1952:91. The Comanche Cultural Committee (2003) gives *pooro* as 'club, weapon, or tool'.

4. Carlson and Jones (1940) notes the use on this plant, but does not identify it. Robinson and Armagost (1990) identifies it as 'Indian tobacco', *Nicotiana rustica*.

5. Carlson and Jones (1940) identifies this as *Camissa escuelenta*, wild hyacinth.

6. Carlson and Jones (1940) identifies this as *Cymopterus acaulis*, plains springparsley.

7. Robinson and Armagost (1990) identifies this simply as an "edible tuber."

8. Carlson and Jones (1940) identifies this as *Psoralea hypogeae*, Indian bread fruit.

9. Possibly from *keta* 'don't!' *na* reflexive, *tuhka* 'eat'.

tsunʉsʉ[1] was sweet, not hard, and was dug with a stick. It was a deep-growing, gray vine with small thorns. It had a sweet potato-like root and was roasted after peeling.

pihtsamuu[2] was a round, brown root, sweet. Some were white, some were red. It had a grayish vine, with mesquite-like leaves, and yellow flowers. The roots were eaten raw or cooked.

toʔroponiiʔ had yellow flowers and round roots like the dandelion.

paiyapI was used to work gas off the stomach. The root was roasted or boiled. The plant was like a small sunflower.

sehetsitsina tasted and looked like an Irish potato. It was boiled or roasted.

The juice of *pakeetso*[3] root was sweet and it was eaten raw.

pakʉʉkA, *pa* 'water', *kʉʉkA* 'onion'.

tuekʉʉkA, 'small onion'.

Food Preparation: Stone Boiling   Jim had heard of stonecooking in a skin supported by poles from two old warriors. The skin burst and their wives tried the method again.

Food: Food Plants: Berries

tuʔamowoo, red haws,[4] were eaten raw; a man howled like a wolf before eating them, otherwise he would founder.[5]

tupokopI, black haws,[6] grew on a tree with thorns. *wokwekatU*[7].

mitsonaaʔ,[8] hackberry, was gathered and pounded fine, mixed with lard, rolled into "wiener" like rolls, and roasted on a stick, good.

natsohkweʔ, mesquite beans, were gathered in July. They picked out the best of the fallen pods (*namabitsooʔna*).[9] They were pounded into meal, white. They were very extensively used. A soup made from the seeds is very sweet. The seeds were put into cornmeal for shortening. The seeds were taken out after a short pounding and the pods were ground into meal. The meal was mixed with fat. They fed mesquite beans to horses; they were very fattening.

A hole was lined with a hide [a buffalo hide was pounded into this form], beans were pounded with long green mesquite pestles, two persons [women] pounded.

waapokopI[10] were juniper berries. It was a fall crop. Bears were fond of the berries. They were eaten raw when very ripe. Some are strong, others are sweet.

---

1. Robinson and Armagost (1990) identifies this simply as a "certain plant with edible tuber."

2. Carlson and Jones (1940) identifies this as *Hoffmanseggia jamesii*, Camote de raton. Robinson and Armagost (1990) says simply, "milky-rooted plant."

3. Carlson and Jones (1940) identifies this as *Petalsotemum purpureum*, purple prairie clover.

4. Carlson and Jones (1940) identifies this as *Crataegeus* sp, "locally called 'red haws'." Robinson and Armagost (1990) gives *tuʔamowoo* (*tuʔ* 'black') as 'thorn apple, black haw'.

5. Wallace and Hoebel 1952:203.

6. Carlson and Jones (1940) identifies this as *Crataegus* sp.

7. This seems to be a general term for any thorny plant—*wokwe* 'thorn', *katʉ* possessor—rather than a term for a specific plant.

8. Carlson and Jones (1940) identifies this as *Celtis laevigata*, southern hackberry.

9. Carlson and Jones (1940) identifies both of these as *Prosopis glandulosa*, mesquite.

10. *waapI* 'cedar, juniper', *pokopI* 'berry'.

wokweesi[1] fruit was eaten after the removal of the seeds. They were eaten raw or they were split open, the seeds were removed, and dried for winter use, then boiled to eat.

upʔai was the fruit of the tree cactus. It was eaten after a ritual; the juice was blood-like. The point was broken off the fruit and a line drawn across the forehead. One might founder if he ate too much.

ekamitsáaʔ was barrel cactus fruit. One had to make a cross on one's forehead with the juice before eating the fruit.

kusipokopI 'gray berry' was a bush with green leaves and black berries that were eaten raw.

tonopI was plum-like, small, very sweet, like a cherry.

poʔaʔpokopI,[2] wild currants. It was an early berry, eaten raw.

etɏai, mulberries,[3] were eaten fresh. *etɏ* 'bow'.

panatsayaaʔ, blackberries.

⟨kuxbara⟩, wild strawberries.[4] These were from the mountains only.

naséka,[5] wild persimmons. The juice was squeezed out and the meat was dried for winter use.

sɏkɏʔi, wild plum, was "bitter."[6] They used *natsomɄ*, dried and fallen raisin-like plums, picked up and dried for winter, then boiled and eaten.

natsomukwe were grapes.

nosinatsomukwe were big, wild, tree-climbing grapes; they were blue.

tɏbitsi ('real') was a small grape; its blue pulp was sticky like a newborn calf.

tue were late fall (coon) grapes.

Raisins were never made.

tɏahpI[7] was between the black haw and grape. It was a thornless bush. It grew in a mountain habitat. It was dried and kept. "You could eat all you wanted and never founder."

tuhnaséka[8] were black persimmons from Mexico; they were too sweet.

Story: The Man and the Bears {Wedel}   A man was returning afoot from a war party of which he was the sole survivor. He drifted to the mountains for safety. His moccasins were nearly worn out, his feet were sore, and he was unable to kill game.

---

1. Both Carlson and Jones (1940) and Robinson and Armagost (1990) identify this as prickly pear cactus, *Opuntia* sp. In addition, however, Robinson and Armagost also identifies it as *Echinocereus baileyi*, barrel cactus.

2. *poʔaʔ* 'bark, skin, cover', *pokopI* 'berry'. Wedel's notes spell this "puaβukɔ:." Carlson and Jones (1940) has the wild currant, *Ribes odoratum*, as "huaβoko." However, *waapokopI* is the juniper berry (see above).

3. Carlson and Jones (1940) has both *etɏhuupI* (literally, 'bow wood') and *soho boʔko* as *Morus rubra*, red mulberry. Robinson and Armagost (1990) gives both *huwaboʔkóo* and *soho boʔko* as 'mulberry'.

4. In Robinson and Armagost (1990), strawberry is *ekapokopI* 'red berry'.

5. Carlson and Jones (1940) identifies this as *Diospryros virginiana*, persimmon.

6. *sɏkɏ-* 'sour'. Carlson and Jones (1940) identifies this as *Prunus* sp.

7. Robinson and Armagost (1990) identifies this as Chickasaw plum, that is, *Prunus angustigolia* (Carlson and Jones 1940).

8. Carlson and Jones (1940) identifies this as *Brayodendron texanum*, Mexican persimmon.

He discovered a hole in the mountain with something moving in it. He got closer and recognized bear cubs. He thought it was no use trying to get away because the bear mother had already seen him. So he picked up the cubs and fondled them to show he was friendly. He took off his necklace and restrung it into four necklaces, one for each bear. He also removed his quiver and arrows and laid them outside. He was talking to the little bears, telling of his hardships and urging the cubs to tell their parents not to kill him.

The father bear come home, saw the man, and became mad. He fell on his back and rolled over. The cubs ran over and played over him to restore his good humor. The bear went and lay down beside the man, with his ears down. He began to lick the man's feet.

Night came and they went into the bear's home. There were many grapes, persimmons, and other fruits in the cave. The man ate with the bears. The next morning, the bear wanted to take the man home because the mother bear might return; she was very dangerous and might kill him. The father bear appreciated the man's gifts of necklaces to his cubs.

The mother bear was coming home. She smelled the man and became mad. When she got close to the cave, the father bear and the cubs ran out. She fell on her back, but couldn't be tamed. She snapped at the father, who became angry, and seized her by the throat and killed her.

The warrior stayed another night and the next day the bear took him home; he wanted to see the camp. The man rode on the bear's back. The bear paced and in two or three days reached the camp. The bear stopped outside the camp and sent the man to tell people to let him put his tipi on the south side. The bear was to give him medicine, and would return after a while and eat with him. The bear stayed all night in the tipi with the man. The man told a woman who came to the tipi to tell the announcer that the bear would eat with him, then leave. He wanted no harm to come to the bear.

The woman was a relative of the man. She came down to fix him something to eat. He told her to come around the tipi when she brought the meat in. She came in so and saw the bear and didn't know what to do. The bear disliked plums because they affected his power and made him want to show off. The bear grunted as he saw the dried plums.

When the meal was finished and the bear was about to leave, he gave the man a protective name against enemies so they couldn't shoot him. The name was Paruakoni, 'bear coming back'.[1]

The people noticed the bear leaving and didn't want to harm him. They were afraid to tackle the bear because it was too dangerous.

The man was brave, one of greatest medicine men in the tribe, and did many brave deeds. He lived many generations back.

Story: **The Man and the Bears** {Hoebel}   A man went on a war party. Everyone else was killed. He was on foot. He was tired and his feet were sore.

He headed towards the mountains. He discovered a cave in the mountain. He saw something moving in it. It was small bears.

He went in and took one baby bear in his arms to show that he was friendly. The parent bears were gone.

---

1. *parua*, 'bear', *koni*, 'turn or return'.

He took off his necklace and restrung the beads to make a necklace for each little bear.

He put his quiver outside the cave. He told the little bears of his hard time. He wanted them to tell the parent bears so they wouldn't harm him.

The father bear came in and saw him. He got mad and rolled around. The little bears came out and climbed around him. He appreciated what the man had given to the little ones.

The father bear paced towards the man with his ears down. The man laid down. The bear saw the sores on the man's feet. He licked them.

They went into the cave. There was plenty of food there, persimmons, grapes, etc. They had supper.

The father bear wanted to take the man home. He was afraid that the mother might come home and be very angry and eat {the man}. The father bear told the man that she must eat him before she could have the man.

The mother bear came home. She became angry. She was growling. When she got close, the father and the little ones went to meet her. She fell on her back and snapped at the father bear. He got her by the throat and killed her. He felt very sad.

That night the father bear said he would take the man back to his camp. The man couldn't walk; he rode on the bear.

It took two or three days to return. When they were near, the bear told him to go on alone and put a tipi on the south side of camp, that he was going to come and eat with them and give them power.

He did so. The bear came and stayed all night with him.

A woman came to the tipi. He told her to have the announcer tell the people that his friend, the bear, was staying with him, that he would leave at dinner time, and that no one should harm the bear when he was gone.

This woman was related to the man. She brought them food. He ordered her to fix the meat and bring it in from the south side.

When she went in, she was surprised to see the bear. She fixed the meat.

The bear didn't like plums; if he ate them, they affected his medicine so he felt like showing off. He grunted when he saw them. He ate the meal.

The bear told the man that he would have a new name to protect him from his enemies, Paruakoni, 'Bear Coming Back'.

The people in the camp saw the bear and did nothing to hurt him. The man got to be a heap big warrior and medicine man thereafter.

Story: **The Man and the Bears** {Carlson}   A man went on a war party. All his companions were killed and he lost his own horse. He was on foot. He wandered into the mountains. His moccasins were worn and his feet were sore from walking.

As he went along, he discovered a hole in the mountain. As he got closer, he noticed something moving in the hole. Finally, he saw that they were bears.

He went into the place where the bears were. As he entered the cave, he picked up one of the baby bears to show that he was friendly.

The father and mother bears were gone.

He had a string of beads. He took them off and made new strings for each of the four bears.

He took off his quiver and put it outside.

He explained his sad plight to the little bears. He asked them if they would ask the parents to do him no harm.

Finally, the father came home. He got sore when he saw the man, so he rolled on his back. The little ones came and played with him and put him in a good humor.

The papa bear came close and lay down by the man. The bear noticed the feet of the man and began to lick his feet. Finally, they ate grapes, persimmons.

The next morning, the father said that he had better let him (the bear) take the man home, as the mother was dangerous and she would want to kill the man.

The mother bear was on her way home, some distance from the cave. She smelled. The father bear could tell that his wife was angry.

When the mother bear got near to the cave, she made a noise to show them that she was mad. The father bear and the baby bears ran out to the mother. She was mad and rolled on her back, but the father and children could not humor her.

The mother snapped at the father. This made the father mad. He got the mother by the neck and killed her.

The man stayed another night with the bears.

The following day, the man got on the bear's back and the bear took the man to the outskirts of the camp. Then he let him off and told him to go to the camp and ask his people to place the young man's tipi on the south side of the camp. The bear then said that he would come to the tipi and give the young man power.

The next day, a woman came to the tipi and the young man told her to tell the announcer of the camp to tell all the people that the bear was visiting him and was going to leave at dinner that day, and to say also that the young man didn't want any harm to come to the bear.

The woman who told the announcer was a relative of the young man.

She returned home to cook for them.

The bear gave the man medicine, protection from enemies. The man got to be a great warrior.

Plants: Yucca   *mumutsi²* was yucca.

Medicine: Herbs: Sage   Wild sage was used with any other kind of medicine which wasn't good without it. It was used in peyote meetings for people to sit on, covered with blankets; the peyote button also sat on a small pile of sage.

Medicine: Peyote {Wedel}   The members walked around the lodge and from the north side they entered the tipi from the east. Then they walked about the fireplace and seated themselves in a horseshoe about the fireplace.

There was an altar of earth about six inches high in a semicircle on the west side of the fireplace and a fire by cribwork at right angles, with the ashes pushed against the altar.

The leader sat on the west; he was the first to enter. He announced the purpose of the meeting, unless it was a regular meeting.

Everyone chewed sage leaves, spat them in their palms, and rubbed it over their face and arms. (Definite curative value.[1])

The fireman acted as janitor.

They smoked cigarettes. Then they each had a peyote meeting.

The headman sang four songs. Then he passed the rattle to the drummer who sang four songs while the man on his left drummed.

Then the man who was drumming sang four songs while the next man drummed. Finally, everyone had sung four songs.

The time to drink was about midnight, so the fire tender, with an eagle feather, went out for water using the bucket. If the fireman went a long way, the leader sang a song or two with his whistle. If he went only a short distance, everyone waited.

The fireman, on his return, walked about the outside of the tipi once clockwise, then entered. The bucket was set down just inside the entrance. At the leader's permission, and not before, he brought the bucket to the leader and then he went and sat.

Cigarettes, not paper, were passed to the fireman.

The leader talked, telling how God made cedar and placed it among the Indians. The leader made a wish that all live to be a hundred years old. The leader had placed cedar on the fire so members were inhaling the smoke for purification.

When the talk was finished, the fireman went around the inside of the tipi clockwise and handed the cigarette to, first, the drummer, who smoked and handed it to the leader. He gave {illegible} the privilege of talking to the leader.

The stub of the cigarette was laid on the semicircle of ashes about the fireplace.

{The leader took} an eagle feather, and made a cross as with a pencil in the water bucket (first the east to west, then the south to north). The whistle was drawn crosswise in the water.

The feather was taken out by the leader and given to the drummer and fanned through the air by the drummer to dry. Now he put the feather against the back wall behind the leader.

The leader got about four swallows of water, no more. The bucket was passed about the circle clockwise. The old custom was that they drank out of the bucket, nowadays they use a cup in common. When the last man had drunk, the fireman got the bucket, took it outside, and hung it on a tree.

When he came in, he walked around the tipi leftward and sat down again beside the door.

The leader went outside, taking his whistle, while the drummer sang. He went out, blew his whistle to the east.

The leader went out, blew his whistle to the east, then to the south, west, and north. He came back inside and, standing at the back, placed cedar on the fire and fanned himself with cedar.

Any man had the privilege of fanning himself with the cedar.

---

1. The source of this comment is unknown.

Any man could go out only by walking around leftwise. He can't walk in front of a singer.

Cigarette stubs were placed on the south of the fireplace by the fireman in cleaning up.

Women could join the group.

Each man had his own songs, but a person couldn't sing a song that had been sung by another previously.

The Kickapoos, Shawnees, and Poncas learned peyote from the Comanches.

There was a semicircular curb about the west half of the fireplace, against which the ashes were banked.

The morning song was sung about the time the morning star rose. After singing, they went outside singing.

The woman brought water before they left the tipi. She gave a cigarette to the leader; she may talk and sing. The woman prayed at the door. The next person to speak was the leader. Any man may speak, for instance, to ask help for sick relative. If he had something to say, but he must smoke first, afterward handing the cigarette to the leader.

Women brought in the breakfast. There were three different kinds of food and water. One woman took two dishes, the other took two. There was sweetened roasted Mexican corn in water, rice or mush, pounded meat, and water in separate containers; salt was forbidden.

The leader usually started. The water was first, to be followed about the circle by the other foods. Sometimes they started to the left of the door (but not if Jim led). They got four swallows each; there was sometimes a second round.

It started from the door with some (Jim's father).

Women couldn't sing four songs, but could join a man in his songs; they couldn't drum.

People might eat from four to a hundred peyote buttons as needed.

The drum was a skin-covered kettle, half-full of water, with four pieces of live coal inside.

They used gourd rattles.

Before breakfast, the drum was untied.

People stretched themselves to relieve the muscles.

All the paraphernalia was taken out by the fireman, after more cedar had been thrown on the fire and the things were purified.

The woman outside took the dishes after breakfast.

The fireman was the first to leave. He stepped out of the tipi, turned completely about once, then went to the east.

The peyote was chewed up, spat into the hand, and in a circular motion of hands to the left, and then swallowed. It was used green or dried.

The drum was taken out first.

Peyote and medicine go together among the Comanches.

Medicine: Peyote {Hoebel}   The fire tender was the first to enter the tipi. He started the fire before the others arrived.

The leader and drummer took their positions. The participants entered and went clockwise about the tipi to their places. They did not stop to greet the leader.

The participants washed themselves with rubbed sage leaves.

If it was a special meeting (for a cure or for mourning), the leader announced the purpose.

There was an introductory smoke. Blackjack[1] {oak} leaves were used to roll it[2]; paper was taboo. The cigarette started with the drummer and passed to the left. The stubs were carefully placed around the outside of the horseshoe.

Then they were ready for the peyote. They started with four buttons each.

The leader started with four songs. He made a circular motion with his staff clockwise. Then he passed the staff to the left. A complete circuit was made this way around to the leaders, each person singing four songs.

At the midnight pause, the fire tender took an eagle feather and exited with the water bucket. If he had to go far for the water, the leader might sing a sing with his whistle. Returning, the fire tender must circle the tent. He set the bucket down at the door and awaited the order from the leader.

The fire tender placed the bucket between the peyote button and the leader, resuming his place, where he was given a smoke.

While the fire tender smoked, the leader put cedar in the fire, praying. He told of how God made cedar to purify man. Each person asked for a blessing and for 100 years of life.

When they were all through, the fire tender walked around the tipi to the left and gave the smoke to the drummer. He took a few puffs; if he had any prayer, he then gave it. The stub was passed to the leader who put it to the west of the peyote button.

The leader took an eagle feather and drew a cross in the bucket of water, with points from east to west and then south to north.

The leader blew his whistle across the bucket marking a cross as above.

The leader took the feather out of the water and handed it to the drummer, who put it against the back of the tipi to dry.

Now they were ready to drink. The leader was first, taking four swallows. It was passed to the left, with each taking four swallows. The fire tender took the bucket outside the door. He re-entered passing about the circle.

The leader went out and blew his whistle to the east, south, north, and west. He returned and placed cedar on the fire.

Anyone who wished to leave could go then. He got permission from the leader to leave after some person had finished his set of songs. The exit was to the left about the circle.

Before the midnight pause, the fire tender swept all of the butts into a small heap before the fire.

They resumed singing.

Any person might speak when so moved, after getting permission from the leaders.

The morning song was sung at daybreak.

A woman cook brought in water. She talked or prayed and then gave a smoke to the leader. The leader then smoked again.

Four different foods were prepared. Salt was taboo. They were served by two women.

---

1. Carlson and Jones (1940) identifies this as *Quercus marilandica*. In Robinson and Armagost (1990) blackjack oak is *tuhuupi* 'black wood'.
2. Wallace and Hoebel 1952:97, 181.

Water, roast corn, rice, and meat. It was usually served from the chief to the left, each person taking four bites. (Jim had it go around twice since he couldn't get enough in four only.)

Before eating, the people all stretched. They untied the drum and put it outside. Then all the other paraphernalia was removed by the fire tender. The woman outside took away the used dishes.

The fire tender was the first to leave. He took one step outside the door. On the second step, he turned completely about and continued on his way. The others made a straight exit, going about to the left of the tipi to reach the door.

The peyote was chewed into a round ball, spat out into the palm of the hand, rubbed in a circle to the left, and then swallowed.

The peyote drum was a round-bottomed kettle, half filled with water. They put in four pieces of live coals. The head was lashed over pebbles around the edges. It was shaken intermittently.[1]

Medicine: Curing   *natsaakʉsi*[2] `was 'sneezing medicine'. It was good for headache [head colds] if sniffed into the nostrils, also for hiccoughs.

Jim cured a friend in Ponca City in one hour after a hospital treatment had failed. It was also good for heart trouble. [For heart trouble, it was thrown into a fire; you took four whiffs.]

Medicine: Lightning {Wedel}   Jim's father was struck by lightning; the spirit of peyote must have had something to do with it.

The lightning told him in a dream it wanted to give him power. It showed him how to paint himself: blue-black on his back for the sky, yellow on the belly for the sun; the sun in a blue sky. From one leg up and over the chest and down the other leg was a zigzag line of many colors (like a rainbow). The horse had to be pure white—he pointed to a certain white cloud and said, "That's the horse." Its mane was painted blue-black. A side tail feather was tied to the tail (not realizing that it had power).

When the Indians were driven onto the reservation, some went back out to hunt meat, including Jim's father. On their return, his father washed his horse and turned it loose. When the horses were rounded up next morning, a group of men were sitting together in discussion. That's what attracted Jim's attention. When he had washed the horse the night before, there were no signs of paint on him, but on his return in the morning, he was painted, with red around the eyelashes, yellow beside the eyes, a buffalo head on the hips, and lightning down the legs. He had been painted overnight by the thunder.

The horse was the white cloud. When Jim's father got on the painted horse and was in the prescribed costume, he was the lightning riding on a cloud. Enemies could shoot at him, but it was like rain striking him, there was no effect. This was the only manifestation of his father's power that Jim recalled.

Medicine: Lightning {Hoebel}   Jim's father was one time struck by lightning. The lighting told him in the form of a dream that it had wanted for some time to give him this medicine.

---

1. La Barre 1975:53.
2. Carlson and Jones (1940) identifies this as *Helenium microphalum.*

It told him how to use paint. Paint the back black, the middle chest yellow, a rainbow paint in zigzags down the legs and across the chest to represent lightning. It pointed to a certain cloud and gave him a pure white medicine horse. The edge of its mane was black with a small tail feather of the eagle tied at the edge.

After the tribe was on the reservation, Jim once heard some men talking about the powers of this horse. His father gave a demonstration. He washed the horse clean and turned it loose in the pasture. The next morning, the horse came in all painted up. This had been done by the lightning. There was a red dash under the eyes surrounded by a yellow circle. On his haunches was a buffalo head, with lines like lightning down its legs.

When Jim's father got on this horse in war paint, he was lightning on a cloud. The bullets were just like rain, they could never touch him.

Medicine: Peyote   Peyote was Jim's main reliance.

Story   Jim was mean, hence he was once hit by a bullet.[1]

Story   Jim was once caught afoot by a longhorned steer. They were weighing steers at the station. Jim had gotten off his horse, which, being gunshy, turned and ran. The steer was coming at him. It had broken off one horn. The steer got its head under Jim's arm and rushed him three times. Other Indians were standing by. On the steer's third rush, a young man came and got between Jim and the steer, saving Jim.

Animal Powers: Buffalo: Buffalo Breath   Jim was once caught on the Salt Fork {of the Red River} by a buffalo bull.

At certain times of the year, bulls went off by themselves. The bull was in a creek, digging in a bank, maybe trying to shed its horns. Jim came riding along and didn't see the bull, but the bull came after him. Bulls are mad all the time, just ready to attack a person.

The bull came along the gully; it was so big it could hardly get through. It must have had a drink of water. Its head was like a lion, an awfully big bull.

Neither Jim nor the bull saw the other until they were close together. Meeting so close, Jim's horse wheeled and fled back to the camp. When it arrived there, Jim was all in. The buffalo bull's breath must have had some effect on him. Old people came around, blew water on him, and got him over the spell. Jim was a boy at the time. Buffalo had some power, it could blow on a person and produce bad effects.

Social Relations: Joking   [Post Oak Jim was telling the story of the mad buffalo on its haunches, panting. ____ {sic} said, "That's just like Jim when he has fits. Only he doesn't froth, he bawls like a baby."

____ {sic} told Jim to talk so those boys can understand. "Don't talk like when you're with women."]

Animal Powers: Buffalo {Wedel}   Some people went on a raid. They came to a little house. They were looking around when soldiers surprised them and the Indians had to run. Two men were riding double. The man on the rear had a painting on his body, a human face in front and one at the rear. The soldiers were shooting at the rear. They hit the nose of his back painting, pierced his chest, and came out through the eye of the chest painting, hitting

---

1. Wallace and Hoebel 1952:162 (?).

the shoulder blade of the man who was riding in front. The front man had on a cloth shirt, which was torn by the bullet, but it dropped to ground harmlessly.

The men changed places. The wounded man was dying, so they rode down into a draw. The pursuers didn't follow them any further. They got off their horses by the creek and rested.

The *tekwɄniwapI* called for someone to come to aid the wounded man. A certain man came, but soon gave up. The wounded man was getting weaker. The *tekwɄniwapI* rode up and asked how the patient was. He was worse, so he called for another medicine man (TanapɄ, 'knee'[1]) and begged him to doctor the patient. He told the medicine man that if he cured the victim, he would ride over to the enemy and kill one of them. The medicine man agreed. So the *tekwɄniwapI* rode away a piece. He fixed his horse's ears like a bear, tied its tail into knot, put white (lead) on his hair, black and yellow on his face, and a bearskin over his shoulder as a hood.

The medicine man was using the power of the buffalo, sucking on the wound, spitting out the pain and like blood {*sic*}. Once in a while, he would mimic the bellow of a bull and butt the patient front and rear. The wounded man revived.

The *tekwɄniwapI* had a pistol on his arm and a bow and arrow. The medicine man laid his own shield (which had a buffalo tail attached to it) on the ground, and mimicked the buffalo. He took off his blue-bordered bandanna. Singing his medicine song and wiggling the bull tail, he stretched his handkerchief. He inhaled sharply and the kerchief disappeared. He was approaching the patient all the time. The medicine man was ready to doctor. A man was still supporting the patient's head. The doctor got a piece of ice from his kerchief and blew on it. The patient revived and began to talk to his comrades.

The *tekwɄniwapI* was off addressing[2] and asking to die before the patient if he didn't kill an enemy. The *tekwɄniwapI* started for the enemy camp, stalking like a bear. The others took good cover and watched to see his bravery. The *tekwɄniwapI* sang his death song, others watched to show bravery. The soldiers saw him coming and knew what he was after. They dismounted, held their horses by the bridles, and began to fire at the approaching *tekwɄniwapI*. He went on unaffected, bullets falling all about the rest of the party. The smoke was so heavy, they could hardly see. The soldiers saw they couldn't kill him, so they remounted and beat it back for the creek.

The *tekwɄniwapI* rode after them, shooting. One soldier wore a white shirt. The *tekwɄniwapI* saw a blood stain on his shirt and the rest of men gather about, so he felt that he had hit him.

It was about sundown. The Indians traveled a short way, then camped and built a small fire. The *tekwɄniwapI* said he would take the wounded man home, as he was responsible. Some of the men debated whether to go on or not. Probably they all finally returned home. The man was well taken care of and recovered. He lived a long time and died a few years ago.

---

1. According to Robinson and Armagost (1990), 'knee' is *tana*. A man known as Tounip or Tonips, glossed as 'knee cap', was a member of Esarosavit's YapainɄɄ local band in 1879–80. He is not listed on any later censuses.
2. This is as given, probably intending "addressing his medicine."

Animal Powers: Buffalo {Hoebel}   On a raid, Indians were one time surprised by soldiers. The Indians broke in flight. Two braves were riding double. The one in the rear had a human face painted on his back and chest. A bullet struck him from the rear, coming out through the eye of the face painted on the chest. Its force spent, it did not penetrate the cloth shirt of the man in front. They changed places and drew into a draw to hide out. The army gave up the pursuit and took up a position a ways off.

The chief called for a medicine man to stop up the wound. One tried and failed. The man was getting weaker. The leader rode up again and asked how he was coming. They told him it was pretty bad. He then called to TanapƱ ('knee') to doctor the case.

The chief made an oath to kill a white soldier if the man was cured. He rode off to one side to fix up his medicine power for the fulfillment. He tied down his horse's ears like those of a bear. He tied its tail up in a knot. He painted his own face and body, smearing white paint on his hair. He threw a bear robe over his shoulders.

The medicine man acted like a buffalo. He butted the patient from the front and back. He sucked red paint from the wound. The man revived.

He took off his shield and removed the buffalo tail from it. He removed a handkerchief from his neck, and stretching it out before him in both hands, he sang a medicine song. He swallowed the handkerchief, waving the buffalo tail all the while. He took a piece of ice (quartz crystal) and blew it into the patient's mouth. The patient talked and was saved.

{The chief}, a brave man, talked to the sun, and said that if he failed to meet the enemy, he wanted to die before the sun went down.

He started towards the soldiers singing his war song. All the other Indians were watching. The soldiers drew a bead on him and shot a fusillade; one could hardly see for the smoke. The brave man paid no attention. He was not scathed by a shot. The soldiers, fazed by their inability to hit him, broke and retreated across the creek. The warrior rode up to the bank and shot across, hitting a man. Having done his deed, he turned back.

It was then about sundown. The Indians went on and made camp. The people wanted to go on and finish their raid, but the chief said they would go back to get the wounded man home, since he was responsible for this attack.

RHODA ASENAP
July 12, 1933

Medicine: Charms   Porcupine quills were burned and put in a beaded bag about a child's neck to ward off evil [children's diseases].

Nanʉwokʉ   A man could take the horses of a man who had stolen his wife; the former {sic, latter?} had no recourse. Otherwise, if a man demanded his wife, he might have to kill the wifestealer.

[A wounded husband might steal some of the warrior's best horses in their absence. The rule was that the warrior could do nothing about this on his return, not even if he didn't know she was going beforehand. If the husband demanded his wife back, the warrior might send him horses and goods instead; if he won't accept the gifts and wanted only the woman, there would be trouble. The husband may try to kill him.]

Social Control: Adultery   A husband could [kill her], cut up the soles of a woman's feet, cut off her nose and ears, or hold her over the fire.[1]

Life Cycle: Marriage: Wife Desertion   (1) Rhoda's father's wife deserted her {first} husband to join a war party led by his older brother and refused to return. The brother wanted to keep her and sent back a gift of horses that had to be accepted. The brother (husband) was later killed and Rhoda's father took her as his wife.

[A woman deserted her husband by joining a raid of which her father's older brother was the leader. The older brother took her as his wife. On their return her husband "did nothing to get her back" (He was afraid of them).

He sent an old woman to plead for her.

They wanted to keep her. They sent back a gift of horses and goods, which he had to accept. Later the brother was killed and Rhoda's father took her as his wife.]

(2) Rhoda's mother's brother's wife ran away with a man on a raid. The man wasn't good enough to keep her, so her husband and a friend took her away. They cut up the soles of her feet and made her walk; she couldn't crawl because her husband made her walk.

Life Cycle: Marriage: Wife Stealing   A full blood could take a captive's wives unless the latter was a powerful warrior.

[Full bloods had more power than captives. "Full bloods could take a captive's wives when they wanted them."]

[If he was a brave warrior, he could protect himself. Otherwise he had no recourse.]

Life Cycle: Marriage   Sweethearts never married. ["They didn't marry sweethearts in those days."]

[Rhoda's father and mother were not sweethearts when they were married. Her father was wealthy and had many horses. His wife had died, so Rhoda's mother's brother gave her to him as a present.]

There was a twenty-seven to thirty [thirty to thirty-five] year difference between mates. [The reason was that some men liked to raid and didn't like the responsibilities.]

Life Cycle: Marriage: Polygamy   The oldest wife was supreme; she could make life miserable for the other wives. [The oldest wife was in charge of the others. The younger wives work for her. "She only has to sit around and eat." An older woman might tell lies about the other wives to get them beaten.] Only one or two men were kind to their wives.

Life Cycle: Menstruation   Menstruating women ate no meat, it was bad for the blood. At the end of her period, [no matter how cold], she went to the river and washed. [This also applied to captive women.][2]

---

1. Wallace and Hoebel 1952:234 (?).
2. Wallace and Hoebel 1952:144.

POST OAK JIM
July 13, 1933

War: Motives   Horses were the principal objectives of a raid. If the enemy resisted, they fought, trying to kill man for man.

Dances: Victory Dance   If there was no trouble, no enemy's lives were taken, they just came home with no excitement going on. If they have taken lives, they showed some excitement; they might have a Victory Dance. Most of the warriors would be painted with blue paint.[1]

War: Scalps   Sometimes the interior of the scalp was painted red or blue. Poles about an inch thick were peeled and the scalp was attached at the top like a flag. The cane was probably painted blue.

Dances: Victory Dance {Wedel}   When they got near the camp, they stopped; they might camp overnight. The stop was to get ready, clean up, and get the scalp fixed to the pole.

When they got near the camp, they shouted and fired their guns. They came into camp singing a Victory Song. As the people in the camp heard the shouting, they knew what it meant. They began to dance in camp. Everyone came out of the tipis and danced right where they were, there was no fixed arrangement. The returning party rode around the camp to the farthest east side and stopped (tipi doors faced east). Then the party broke up and each man went home. The dance was given after the men had gone home.

Another bunch organized the dance. They wanted some gift from the returning warriors. The dancers dressed up the young women's faces like men. They put a straight feather on their heads, and braided their hair like men. They painted their faces in imitation of men. They wore bear claw necklaces like men. They wore the long female dresses.

The warriors were expecting something. They came up and stopped at a distance. The women called each warrior by name. They said they're expecting something from him. The dance party had a spokesman selected from the group, not the regular announcer. When the warriors appeared, he told them that they have wished them good luck, that none of the party has been killed, and now they expected a gift, maybe an arrow, a blanket or a horse, something the warrior didn't need.

The dance was started by the men who led the music. The women danced while the warriors looked on. The women went to the warriors and took them about the neck. The warrior then gave the woman a Navajo or Mexican blanket or a horse for a souvenir.

After the gifts had been made, the dance quieted down. Then, one of the men came forward, named the gifts, and thanked the warriors for the gifts. He also told of any brave deeds done by the warriors and whose son had performed it.[2] Probably the young ladies then borrowed the scalps and danced with them. Sometimes the mother or grandmother of a returned brave joined the dance and carried the scalps (probably the mother of the man who had taken the scalps).

1. See Richard Petri, "Plains Indian Warrior in Blue" (Texas Memorial Museum, accession #2197), and Kavanagh 1999: cover.
2. That is, he named the warrior's father.

The dance was given only if nobody in the party was killed. If the party lost a man, but gained many horses, no dance was given.

Dances: Victory Dance {Hoebel}   The Victory Dance was held only when enemies were killed.

They stopped outside camp to fix up. They painted their bodies blue. They painted the inside of scalps red or blue. They hung the scalps on blue poles.

They rode in whooping. They entered the camp singing a Victory Song. They rode around the camp to the point farthest east and dismounted and disbanded.

People heard them coming and danced in joy.

The Victory Dance proper was performed by a separate group of dancers.

Young women dressed up like men. They painted their faces like men. They put a feather in their hair. They wore men's headdresses. They wore men's necklaces of bear claws, etc.

The drum was sounded. The dancers came up near the warriors and stopped in hearing distance. The dancers called the warriors by name, saying they were expecting success from them. The dancers had a spokesman who told them they wished them good luck. They were glad they all returned safely.

The spokesman told them they expected gifts, blankets, horses, etc.

The song was started by the men. The women danced. The warriors looked on.

During the dance, a woman might dance up to a warrior and take him around the neck, whereupon the warrior may give her a blanket or a horse that he got on the raid.

The women dancers might dance holding scalp poles, or the mother or grandmother of the warrior might do so.

The spokesman announced the gifts received by the dancers and thanked the warriors. He recited special deeds performed, mentioning the warrior's father during the recital.

War: Division of Loot   The horses were divided. If a warrior has been killed <u>before</u> the division, the family got no animals; if he died after the division, his family claimed his share.[1]

War Parties: Roles   The leader and his assistant and cook were the three most important members of a war party. The cook carried and looked after all the food, he carried the water. If his horses were lost, he carried it all on his own back. If they got too few horses to go around, the cook got first pick because he needed them for his work.

War Parties   The party stayed up maybe two or three nights hunting horses. They might hide in the mountains to catch up on their sleep. They rode around to the north side of a mountain, climbed part way up, and hid, sending two scouts to the summit to watch back along the trail, thus giving the warriors time to get away if pursuers got too close.

Pursuers sometimes used trail hounds, but the rocks in the mountains rendered them useless.

They might go two or three days without food, then they might kill a beef. They cut off a portion of meat without skinning it, then threw the whole piece into the fire. They took a strap of green hide after the meat was done and beat off the burned outside with a stick, then passed the strap through a hole in the meat and swung it over the horse or across the cook's shoulder. If it was carried on a horse, the side with the hide was put next to the horse to keep the meat clean. Thus, if they got too close to an enemy's camp, they needed no fire, lunch was already prepared.

They hid in the mountains or in the timber near a hostile camp to eat, spreading green branches for a table. The meat was cut up and eaten. Each man carried salt.

After the meal, two of the men went to call in the sentries and replaced them; one man was always on guard.

They all traveled at night and the party hid during the day. If water was scarce, the leader called on two men to get some. They used buffalopaunch containers. [They had to go when ordered.] This was hard work and dangerous.

Horses might be taken out of a barn or a corral. [They set scouts by the nearest doors to kill anyone who appeared.] If from a barn, they were led away on their own halters. Rail corrals were entered to look for the bell mare. The bell was stuffed with grass and the horses led a distance, then were driven away. [From a pasture being watched by boys, they would take them away from them, then drive them off.]

War: Division of Loot   They didn't stop to divide them until the party got far away.

The leader got the first choice, then some others as called upon by the chief. The cook always got his share. If it was a big herd, each man might get from three to seven animals.

Horses: Mules   Mules were tougher than horses, their feet didn't get thin and slippery like horses' hooves did in the summer on grass.

War: Water   Some people not familiar with the country could get awfully thirsty. There were many springs south in Texas, but not many to the west in Mexican country.

War: Motives   {If} people wanted horses, they simply took them, e.g., from the big herds in Texas.

War: Motives: Revenge   If an honorable warrior was killed, the leader went to his family to mourn with them, and might give them horses.

War: Scalps   If a man of the party was slain, and an enemy scalp was obtained in retaliation, the scalp was given to the family of the deceased.

War: Battle of Adobe Walls   Quanah Parker's nephew[1] was killed in Texas. Quanah didn't retaliate at once. Later, he took the pipe around among the people to organize a return party. He came to a certain leader's house and they smoked. Quanah told him they were going back to avenge the death.

1. Otherwise unidentified.

Quanah had something to do with Adobe Walls.[1] A certain medicine man[2] told the people that if they attacked those hunters, their guns wouldn't fire. [As the medicine man made medicine to silence the guns of the whites in the fort, he assured the Indians of the lack of danger.]

Several tribes went together. They attacked early in the morning. Most of the people were not yet out of bed. When they awoke, they broke holes in the wall and began firing with long-range buffalo guns [the first time they were used]. It didn't happen like the medicine man promised. The hunters killed Indians right and left with their rifles. There was much damage to the Indians.

A young man was sleeping outside in a wagon.[3] He was attacked by two Indians, knifed by one but shot the other with a rifle. The mother of a youth killed in Texas climbed into the wagon and killed the man with a hatchet.

[At Adobe Walls, a white man was sleeping in a wagon outside the stockade. Two Indians attacked him with knives. He got his gun and shot one of them. While fighting with the other, an old woman climbed in the wagon and killed him.]

A bullet struck Quanah Parker's powder horn and glanced off.

The Cheyennes liked to have killed the medicine man, who was a Comanche (Isatai), but he lived until a few years ago. [He later got to be chief however.]

Howard White Wolf's father was shot and wounded, but couldn't be rescued because the Indians were afraid to approach the Adobe Walls; Jim thought he finally died there.

Isatai was on the ground, but probably not active in the fight.

Cheyennes, Arapahos, Comanches, and Kiowa-Apaches were in the Adobe Walls battle.

War Parties: Roles   The cook was selected for industry, activity, alertness, and willingness to do what was needed. Most of the time it was probably a Mexican or other captive. Jim would have been a cook in the old days.

Food: Salt   Salt was obtained from the Salt Fork, west of Mangum, OK.[4]

War: Shields   Shields were made from the back of a buffalo's neck. A large circular piece was cut out with the hair left on. It was pegged out to dry, then the hair was worked off; it was not shrunk. After drying, it was trimmed into a circle. It was pierced (about the edge?) with small holes for lacing. No forms were used. The buckskin cover was laced to the hides. A short strap was fixed as a handhold in the back center.

1. The Adobe Walls were the remains of a series of trading posts originally built by William Bent about 1842 on the Canadian River northeast of modern Amarillo, Texas. The first Battle of Adobe Walls was on November 10, 1864, when Colonel Kit Carson and Federal troops attacked adjacent Comanche and Kiowa villages near the old post (Pettis 1908). The second Battle of Adobe Walls took place on June 27, 1874, when a war party of Comanches, Kiowas, and Cheyennes attacked a group of buffalo hunters who had reoccupied and rebuilt the structures. All of the references to the Adobe Walls in the notes refer to the second battle.

2. Isatai, also known as Quenatosavit, White Eagle. Isatai was a local band leader before and during the reservation period. See p. 9, note 8 above.

3. Two brothers, Ike and Shorty Shadler, were sleeping outside the buildings in a wagon; both were killed (Haley 1976:69).

4. Mangum is a small town just north of the Salt Fork of the Red River in Greer County in far southwestern Oklahoma.

The shield was painted all over with white pigment with sticks used as paint brushes. A good painter decorated it. The warrior told the painter how to decorate the shield. After the application of the design, the top, a strip of buckskin, or cover (case), was likewise decorated. The strip was semicircular, sewn to the upper edge of shield, and fringed with feathers and bells. It opened from the bottom. Strings with feathers hung down from each end of the diameter.

It was slung at the left waist by horsemen from a shoulder strap, or at the shoulder [over the heart in war] by a footman.

Shields had different designs; one shield had a cross.

War: Shields: Painting by Peyote   A young boy had a shield, but he didn't know how to paint it, so on a friend's advice, he went to a peyote meeting. He gave a smoke to the leader; he had to carry a feather, too. The leader told him to leave the shield by the door near the fireman. After the midnight drink, the leader came around, picked up the shield, put cedar on the fire, and held the shield in the cedar smoke [and shook it]. The shield owner was on the south side of the tipi. He got the shield, [made a circle], and placed it behind him. He was told he would get instructions on how to paint it in the morning. [The boy thanked him.]

[The leader could give directions at the meeting or afterwards.]

The leader told the young man in the morning to get someone [an artist] to decorate the shield. Also, that the design would mean something and he should not be afraid. If he wanted to know the meaning of the design, he should go alone to a lonely place, rest and sleep, and the shield itself would reveal its meaning.

["The design would be alright. Do not be afraid. If you want to know about the shield, go to a lonely place some night and the shield will tell you about it."]

Medicine   Everything with medicine was handed about the circle clockwise.

War: Shields   [Shields were kept away from the house. To get it, one went out of the tipi one way, moved the shield in a circle, then returned to the tipi from the other direction to complete the circle.]

Jim's mother walked about the outside of the tipi clockwise, took down the shield, and walked around the tipi again, then entered and set down the shield. There was probably the third cover over the shield. Jim saw a peyote with red flowers on green ground with thirteen marks on his father's shield cover. There was a cowface on buckskin of the shield proper. Jim's mother often carried his father's shield. Jim also.

Some shields had a feather padding between the buckskin cover and the shield proper. Things were sometimes carried between the buckskin and the hide of the shield, e.g., herbs, smoking mixture of tobacco, and _____ {sic}, etc.

Smoking: Tobacco   There was no kind of smoke in the old days. Tobacco came from the Mexicans. There were two kinds, dark and light. The leaves were cut into strips, then the two kinds were blended and mixed with other [sumac] leaves, then greased slightly, and smoked in pipes of stone and clay.

Smoking: Pipes   Women used clay pipes mostly, with a straw or cane stem.

Medicine: War   A young man didn't go to battle until after he had a dream and got medicine.

Medicine: Vision Quest   Lonely places were visited for medicine before the peyote days.

Weapons: Bow and Arrow   In the old days, all boys and men carried weapons. Jim's father wouldn't make him any arrows because of his quick temper, but said he could make them himself. His father and nephews were good at making arrows. Jim tried to make arrows and cut himself on the wrist.

Jim got a mulberry branch from the creek and peeled off the bark. He had to oil or grease the bow and heat it to make it the right shape.

Material Culture: Bows: Bowstrings   The bowstring was made from spliced sinew. Jim's father and uncles advised him to make three strings to be sure to have enough. The two- or three-ply bowstring was twisted by rolling it on the thigh; those to be spliced were made small and pointed. One end was fastened to a tree, then the string was rolled on the thigh. A sinew string was no good in wet weather, the splices pulled apart. In the old days, they used horsetail hairs for the bowstring because they were long enough not to need splicing and were unaffected by wet weather. Bear guts made the best bowstring, you couldn't break it.[1] Lately, sometimes they used binder twine.

Weapons: Bow Guard   The rawhide bow guard was laced up inside, trimmed with silver buttons, feathers, and paint. This was needed especially on a bow.[2]

Life Cycle: Boys and Bows   Little boys were never around camp in the old days, but went to the creek and made bows of dogwood. *witakwena* was a straight weed used for arrows.

Boys killed grasshoppers, pulled off their legs, and put one through the point of the arrow for each victim. [They used grasshopper legs for the points.[3]] Sometimes they got mud and put it on the shaft about two inches above the point to give it weight. They would go to a pool, camp all day and shoot anything, bullfrogs, lizards, snakes.

They never shot horned lizards. Horned lizards were asked in old times where the buffalo were because they have horns like the buffalo. They were asked, *kuhtsutubini?*[4] "where is my buffalo" ["asking about your stray buffalo"]. Then the lizard would run in the direction of the buffalo.[5]

[After a while boys would get tired of temporary arrows and would get real arrows.]

Older boys killed larger game, small animals, birds, etc.

Little boys killed doves, but they were never kept as pets or eaten.

They ate cowbirds, snow birds, squirrels.[6]

Social Relations: Joking   Boys would sit around the watering pool until some old fellow appeared, then would rush down and drive the stock into water; the old man would ask them to wait until the horses were through drinking.

Story: Rattlesnake and Horned Toad   Jim once saw a rattlesnake approaching a horned toad. The toad just lay down and the snake swallowed him. Later, Jim noticed that the toad must

---

1. Wallace and Hoebel 1952:101.

2. This sentence is in Wedel's typescript but not in the manuscript. It does not appear in his written-up synthetic notes. Its source is unknown.

3. Wallace and Hoebel 1952:128.

4. Robinson and Armagost (1990) has this as simply 'horned toad'. Casagrande (1954–55, II: 221) has *kuhtsuvininA* as 'ask about the whereabouts of buffalo'. Possibly based on *kuhtsu* 'buffalo', *turubinitu* 'ask about'.

5. Wallace and Hoebel 1952:61.

6. Carlson attributes this note to July 12.

have gotten mad, and got out probably by cutting his way out with his horns that were sharp as a knife. Jim saw the horned lizard cut off the rattlesnake's head with his horns, and its young ran up and began eating the snake.

Story: Skunk and Snake   Skunk handled snakes as he wanted. Jim once saw a skunk come toward a snake. The snake began to coil. The skunk pawed the earth, turned, and pawed again. The snake tried twice to strike but the skunk shot the snake, then bit the snake on the back of head and ate it.

Story: Buzzards and Snakes   Buzzards often helped skunks eat snakes. Buzzards were bad after snakes. When they located a snake, they would light and walk up to it, using their wings as a shield, and they would "spear" the snake's head with the spur on their wing.

Medicine: Curing: Snake Bite: Amulet   [A man captured a snake. He cut out its] gall [poison sack] and laid it on a buffalo chip to dry. He called the boys playing on a nearby creek to bring a [small] buckskin [bag] for medicine. He cut the gall open and gave each boy a little piece of the gall tied to the leg of the buckskin. It was tied to the legging to ward off snakebite. The boys run about in the grass; if it was slightly damp, the gall would begin to smell and the snake wouldn't strike them.

If they were bitten, the victim chewed and rubbed the root on the injury, drew a red circle about the bite to limit the swelling, and the cure would follow.

Medicine: Snake Medicine   Jim's uncle had strong snake medicine. He could put a snake about his neck and was immune to the bite.

Medicine: Love Medicine {Wedel}   Jim's father got medicine to make women love him. It came from the "red fin" minnow. It was dried to a powder, cut up and mixed with medicine, willow limb or root, red paint, and something from inside of a beaver.

A certain medicine man wanted a certain woman. He brought out smoke and a feather and went to Jim's father for aid. He told him to go to a certain stream flowing south and dive in four times, then to return. The seeker promised a good present if he got this woman.

Upon his return, Jim's father put some of the medicine on the tip of his tongue, gave him a willow piece to eat, a bit of bark. Then he told him to go to a certain spring, to go from the north, not from the south, to spray water through his teeth four times, and go back to creek where he had made the four dives, there wash off the paint, and then go home. There, he was to put cedar in the fire and smoke himself.

He was through with the medicines, so he wrapped up the rest of it, took it out and tied it to a tree west of his house.

The medicine must not be approached by menstruating woman.

The woman that the medicine man wanted went to the spring, smelled the medicine and it began to work all over her. She thought of him all the time. The woman was going to try all the time to see the man.

In the second washing, the man removed the worry lines from the forehead down his legs.

Medicine: Love Medicine {Hoebel}   This was possessed by Jim's father. The potion was the red fin of a minnow mixed with red paint. A yellow something from the inside of the beaver was added.

You went to the creek and dove in four times and returned to see the medicine man. The medicine man put a bit of the potion on the tongue. You bit a piece of bark and chewed this with the medicine.

You then went to a certain spring and approached it from the north. You took a drink of this water and spat it out four times, then went back to the creek and dove into the pool four times once more to wash off the paint. Then you returned home and smoked with cedar.

You took the remaining medicine and tied it on a tree where women did not frequent.

The desired woman went to the spring for water. She smelled the medicine there, inhaling it all over. It reminded her of the man. She could not get him out of her mind.

The man never gave any sign of wanting to talk to the woman. But she was always approaching him after that.

Medicine   If he was quite a medicine man, people who came must give him a cigarette of cottonwood leaf.

Medicine: Rain Making   Some medicine men could cause rain by nightfall, even if the sky was clear in the morning.

[a) They went to the medicine man and asked him to make medicine. He went into his tipi and made his secret medicine. At sundown, he came out and sat facing the setting sun with sage, cedar, and feathers. He blew four clouds of heavy smoke to the west; they turned into rain clouds.]

[b) They strung peyote buttons on yucca leaves for a necklace for the medicine man. He sat under a mesquite tree, smoked and prayed.]

[They all ate twelve buttons each. They got on their horses and rode until they were dizzy. They got off and slept with a quiver for a pillow. They heard an eagle scream four times and saw lightening four times. Rain came.]

Medicine: Transfer {Wedel}   Jim's father left him no medicine, but his uncle told him how it was done.

Medicine: Transfer {Hoebel}   Jim's father, a powerful medicine man, never left him a power. The "Love Potion" apparently went to his father's brother.

Jim's father did not leave this medicine of his to Jim. His uncle had it, however, and Jim asked him for it.[1]

Material Culture: Clothing: Headdress: Otter Cap {Wedel}   Jim chewed a piece of willow and dived into the creek. He wanted a certain otter, so he set a trap and left.

A week later he heard of an Indian near Faxon[2] who had caught one, so he went to see after his own trap. The trap was gone and the chain led him to the land, and he found the otter frozen to death. He skinned the otter carefully and threw the body back into the water, because he appreciated what the medicine had done.

So Jim knew the medicine was good. He made a headdress of the otter skin and gave it as a war bonnet to his brother, who sold it for $60.

1. The two paragraphs of this section are on separate Hoebel manuscript note cards.
2. Faxon is a small town southwest of Lawton. Wedel had it as "Taxson." Casagrande (1954–55, II:230) notes that in Comanche it would sound like *paksʉn*.

Material Culture: Clothing: Headdress: Otter Cap {Hoebel}   Jim wanted an otter skin for his
hair. He followed the pattern given for the Love Medicine. He set a trap in a pond.

He went away a while. He came back and heard that another Indian had caught an otter
and he thought it was his.

He went to the place and took off his clothes. The trap was gone. Then he saw the chain
over a log. There was the trap and a fine otter.

That showed that the medicine worked.

He skinned the otter carefully and dropped the body in a deep part of the creek.

He only had the power for this once.

Food: Food Plants   Comanches ate a few acorns, from both oak and blackjack {oak}, boiled
in water. The reddish acorn came from blackjack, the yellow acorn came from oak.

Pecans were mixed with corn. Peyote corn was mixed with these, it was very rich.

Acorns were mixed with dried corn for winter use.

They traded for corn with the Mexicans. [Comanches didn't raise corn when Jim was
a boy.]

Comanches never ate mushrooms. They were called "Mupits' paint" when dried up.
[They ate pumpkin seeds.]

Black walnuts were eaten like pecans. They grow along creeks and rivers.

There were no flavorings or seasonings save salt, rarely pecans.

Weapons: War Clubs   *wɨpitapuʔni* were stone-headed clubs. The head was about the size of
a large egg. Sometimes they were made from the tail bone of a buffalo. The rawhide was
soaked and fastened in the grove while wet, and then sewn on. Sometimes a wood handle
was provided. It was heavy; it was used a long while ago. Weapons themselves had no
medicine to kill an enemy.

Medicine: Duration   A person's medicine sometimes failed; it was not entirely foolproof.

War: Defense   Comanches never built protective walls about their camps because of the
impermanent character of the villages. Sentries were posted if they were in danger of
attack. White people never got back this far, but other Indians caused much trouble to the
Comanches.

Food: Storage   Comanches had no underground caches. All meat was stored in parfleches.

Material Culture: Containers: *oyóotɨʔ*   The *oyóotɨʔ* was a hide container. It was like a
pillowslip with a laced opening in the center. It was used to pack meat. It was loaded at
either end and slung across the saddle to pack meat. A slightly more ornate form was used
for a clothes bag, in which was put some sort of perfume.

Material Culture: Crafts: Hide Work: Parfleches   Women did all the leather painting on
parfleches, etc. Two straight sticks were cut for rulers in making the long straight lines.

Material Culture: Paint: Pigments   Walnut stains were for the black color, it was color fast.
tuhupI was the black stain.

Material Culture: Containers   *naboo oyóotɨʔ* was a painted container.

Material Culture: Crafts: Hide Work: Robes   The hair side of a buffalo pelt was worn inside,
the other surface was painted. Some paintings were plain—lines, squares, etc.—sometimes
with war scenes [near the top].

Material Culture: Containers: *oyóotн* The *natsahk*[1] *oyóotн* was pillowslip-like container.

Material Culture: Calendar Comanches had no picture calendars.

Calendar: Month Names

1. *tomomнa* 'fall moon'[2] (leaves are falling) ['after leaves fall off moon']. [*mнa* was 'moon']. *tomapU* was the year in general.

2. *tнe'нtsн'imua*[3] 'getting cold moon' ['slightly cold moon'].

3. *piamнa* was the 'big moon'; this was the first of the year, about Christmas.[4]

4. *kwe'yarнmua*[5] was the shedding moon (for animals) ['buffalo shedding moon'—spring].

5. *paasitsI* was sleet; February.

6. *nahotitнkнtU*[6] means part of the days are cold and part are warm ['cold-hot moon'].

7. *tatsatUmнa* was a summer month.

Post Oak Jim remembered no more names although there might be more.

There was no story as to why the moon changes.

These names are not necessarily in their correct sequence.

Material Culture: Rope The long hair from the back of the buffalo's neck was sometimes made into rope or horse girths. It made good rope, strong, but it was too light for heavy roping.

Rawhide strips were tied to a tree, then twisted into rope. It was greased to make it limber; it was pretty strong.

Another lashing rope was pulled tight by stepping on it.

Horses: Pack Horses A pack horse was never broken for riding. It was loaded by women. Jim didn't know how it would act if a man tried to load it.

Horses: Travois Holes were cut through each tent pole, through which straps were passed and fastened in front of the saddle horn, about one fourth of the way down. The poles were lashed together to keep those on each side in a solid bundle.

The tipi was thrown over the saddle. The saddle was secured with a crupper and chest strap, and the tipi was then lashed to the saddle. Baggage was carried on the saddle only, not between the poles behind the horse; the horse already had a load on the saddle.

[Baggage carriers: They took the tipi poles and put straps through holes {bored} for that purpose. They fastened the poles to the saddle horn in front. Luggage was tied on between the poles with a pole across to hold it on. The tipi was put on top. All was held securely with a rope.]

A very sick person was sometimes slung in a net [hide] behind a gentle horse; this ordinarily required heavier poles than regular tipi poles.

Relations with Other Tribes: Kiowas Kiowas were too poor to afford horses, so they used dogs for hauling.

1. Robinson and Armagost (1990) gives *natsahk* as 'cut or gash'.
2. According to Robinson and Armagost (1990), 'October, fall month' is *yнbamнa*.
3. Literally, 'little cold month'.
4. Robinson and Armagost (1990) has this as July. They also note that December is *piaнtsн'imua* 'big cold month'. Compare with previous entry.
5. *kwe'yaru* 'shed'.
6. In Robinson and Armagost (1990), 'hot or cold month' is *nana'butнikatUmнa*.

Animals: Dogs   [Comanches had dogs only as pets.]

Camp Organization: Moving   In the old days, camp movements were easily followed by the marks of the dragging tipi poles.

Meat and water racks were also moved on the horses. The camp was quickly broken; the women had the system down pat.

[It didn't take long to move.]

The announcer announced early in the morning that the camp was to break. The herders went out to gather in the horses [before daylight].

Camps were moved only ten, twelve, or fifteen miles, to get there before noon.

Camps didn't wait for anybody; each family moved when it was ready.

Jim never heard of a moving village being attacked en route.

On the move, men would gather into groups, they didn't stay with their families. Young men might stop and race while the woman set up the tipis. The men had to be content with the site where the women pitched the camp. Wranglers took over the horses as they were unloaded, and drove them off for water.

Good sites might be reused year after year. [Sometimes they came back to the same place repeatedly.]

Winter camps were made where resources were plentiful, and they seldom moved. [If it was a good place, they might remain all winter. Most movements were in the summer.]

Camps: Tipis: Windbreak   There was a fence around each tipi as a windbreak only in the winter; it was made of sunflower-like stalks.

Camps: Tipis: Summer   The stobs {stakes} were pulled out and the tipi cover was raised in the summer for a draft.

Camps: Brush Arbors   If a camp was set for several days, an arbor (lean-to?) was made.

Beliefs: Thunder   There was no first thunder celebration in the spring.

If a storm came up, the medicine man would take a handful of dirt, motion with it four times in the direction he wanted the storm to go, and thus could send it around the village. Everyone kept quiet during the thunder and lightning, otherwise they might be hurt.

The sandstorm that preceded a rain was thought to drive it away or to prevent a heavy storm.

Thunder and lightning had no sympathy for anyone. ["Lightning ain't got no pity for them as talks back."][1]

Jim [and his bunch] was once branding cattle for a white man. At breakfast, a storm came up. A tough cowboy was going to have a contest with lightning. He walked away from the crowd and, as lightning flashed, he fired and it thundered. Lightning flashed again and he shot once more. At the third shot, the lightning struck close and scared everyone, and the braggart dived under a wagon [and the lightning killed him]. Jim wouldn't let anyone talk about lightning now.

Thunder was probably a big bird. It had lots of power, maybe like dynamite. When Jim was a boy on Tipi Creek,[2] a shower came up, a big black cloud. There was a tall cedar on

1. Wallace and Hoebel 1952:199.
2. Probably not the same Tipi Creek as the site of the 1872 battle (see Index: Locations).

a hill that they could see. Steam, or a white cloud, dropped on the tree and burned it up. So Jim thought thunder was like dynamite.

Lightning made a very small hole where it hit, but you don't find arrows or other missiles there.[1]

Jim's father was crossing a certain creek near Cache. He must have known what it meant, so he sent his two wives away.[2] Lightning struck a cottonwood and then the eye of his mule while it was drinking, knocking it down and putting its eye out, but it didn't harm the rider. Without power, he would have been killed.

Never fool around with a mirror while it was lightning and thundering, because thunder likes to look into mirrors, too. Among the Poncas, a woman was braiding her hair before a mirror and was struck in her mouth and killed.

Another woman was braiding rope during a thunderstorm. She was warned to quit, but continued to work. Lightning struck the post to which the rope was attached, followed the rope, and killed her. [A woman was making rope. Lightning told her not to do it there. She continued. She was struck by the lightning.]

Sometimes lightning knocked a fellow unconscious. The quickest remedy was to put him in cold water. [A woman was knocked unconscious by lightning. She was put in a tub and came to.]

Lightning struck a fence on the 4-6 Ranch in Texas near which thirty steers were standing, killing them through their ears.

There was no good antilightning medicine. Cedar smoke might help.

Lightning and Thunder were like humans, sometimes they wanted to play with people. [It likes to make fun of people.] [Jim was out riding.] Lightning and Thunder [a shower] came up. He got off his horse and hid his head in the grass [he got down among some weeds]. Lightning struck near him several times. He decided it was [they were] only playing [making fun of him], so he got up, gave a war whoop [in defiance], mounted, and rode away. Lightning struck a couple of times nearby and then quit. It was just having fun with him.[3]

Deer head, elk head, a turkey wing could protect against lightning. The turkey was the best friend of lightning. [It "knows all about it."] It had every mark of lightning; its head turned blue when a storm came. A gobbler answered "*paraibo*" whenever it thundered.

Story: Buffalo   About two years after the Indians were put on the reservation, some went back out on a hunting trip.[4] The buffalo were drifting westward, with dust rising clear to the sky. On the Red River, the buffalo were plentiful and the Indians were just going along. They noticed the river was bank full.

They were looking for camping places, watching the buffalo go down to the river. The bulls were first in; they swam across the river. The cows were in close, trying to get the

---

1. This was possibly in answer to a question about "thunder stones."
2. There seems to be an incident missing between this sentence and the previous sentence.
3. Wallace and Hoebel 1952:199.
4. For the first few years after 1875, buffalo hunts were allowed on the western portion of the reservation, and numerous buffalo were taken. However, by 1879, few buffalo were taken and by 1882, the Kiowas were unable to find any for their Sun Dance (Mooney 1898:349).

calves on their backs. Quite a few were carrying calves when they got to the opposite shore.

River Crossing: Fording   At the Red River, North Fork, and Pease River (Texas), they crossed in high water. A man swam across ahead to check the course. Sometimes the pack horses got bogged down and had to be rescued.

Material Culture: Rafts   No rafts or boats were used, but *sahkI*[1] were. You got a forked log, placed your belongings across the fork, stripped, and swam over, pushing the log first. Comanches did not use bull boats. In the old days, all Indians could swim.

River Crossing   Once a cattleman had to ship about two thousand cattle, first crossing a flooded stream. Jim swam his horse across first, narrowly escaping quicksand. Then came the chuck wagon, cowboys, and the cattle.

POST OAK JIM
July 14, 1933

Social Organization: Societies   Dancing "clubs" were organized with the leader handling all business. There were no clubs or societies in the old days.

Medicine: Peyote   The young men who went to peyote meetings raised money to pay the expenses.

Social Organization: Medicine Societies: Eagle Men   All Eagle Medicine Men had friendly feelings toward each other; they were bound together by their common source of power.

Dances: Horse Dance   The Horse Dance has disappeared.[2]

Social Roles: Club Man   Two men were left with the right to wield the club during the Horse Dance (one Apache and a scout); now both are dead.[3]

Social Organization: Medicine Societies {Wedel}   A medicine man could give power to no more than twelve other persons, who formed a group.[4] If the giver passed away, the most capable of the others would be elected to the leadership.

If anyone who wished to join asked the leader, the others got together to discuss the candidate's reputation, etc. If favorable, he was given the medicine and taken in.

To take in new members, they required a special tipi on the south of the camp. The group met and the members told him their ways, what things they could not deal with. The leader went with the candidate to the lonely place where the first man of the group received his power. They went at night.

---

1. Robinson and Armagost (1990) glosses this as 'canoe'.

2. It is not clear if this refers to the *тʉерикипʉʉ*, the Little Ponies, or to another institution called the Horse Dance (see above, Post Oak Jim July 11, and Lowie's notes in Part Two, below. In 1979, I was told that the original Little Ponies "went down" in the 1920s (Kavanagh 1980:102).

3. Post Oak Jim was probably referring to Chebatah (also spelled Chivato) and his brother, Penaro (or Dinero or Dinero's Boy, the latter the source of Hoebel spelling, "Pinedapoi" [Nancy Minor, p.c. 2004]). Both were Lipan Apaches, and both were Club Men. Chebatah died after 1923, but Penaro was still alive in 1933 and, indeed, the Field Party photographed him at Walters in August, 1933.

4. Hoebel 1940:40; Wallace and Hoebel 1952:165.

They might notice nothing the first night. During the day, they went to a shady place (if their camp was distant), or to the camp for a rest, first going to the creek for a bath and paint up. In the evening, they washed again, painted and went up to the solitary place.

Four nights was the limit. The neophyte got a revelation of what not to eat, what rules to obey, etc., and was accepted into the ring.

The novice got four sages, black or white eagle feathers, and a whistle of eagle wing bone.

The two men may ride horseback if they are to go a long way. They rode around the place clockwise, tied their horses, and entered the place. They didn't go to bed, but smoked on the solitary place and prayed to the grave. The medicine man slept at the head of the grave, the neophyte at the foot. They had to have their heads covered up; they didn't come to look but to listen.

The noise of anything sounded dangerous, but they were not to be scared. If one of the men was scared and the power saw he was awake, he got no medicine.

In this case, a sound like the wind blowing came over them four times, then they went to sleep. The power appeared in the form of a dream to both men, and told them what the man should do. The power came at night only. The power sent them back home to wash themselves and blow cedar smoke over their bodies. They could eat and rest during the day, they were not under any restrictions.

Certain things were forbidden, the same to each member of the group.

Social Organization: Medicine Societies {Hoebel}   The transfer of medicine was limited to twelve persons. Each would have the same power. Each had the same prohibitions, etc.

If the original member (leader) died, the other eleven elected the most powerful of their group to be the leader.

They did not proselytize. If a man wanted the medicine, he might ask to join. If he was honorable and suitable, they might take him into membership.

{There was a} medicine tipi on the south of the camp. The initiate came there. He sat and listened while they told him their ways, taboos, etc.

The leader of the group then took the new member to the grave where they first found their medicine at night.

The procedure at the grave in the lonely place was this: they sat and smoked, and prayed to the dead; they laid down at the grave, the leader at the foot, the novice at the head; they covered their heads (they were there to hear, not to look); they did not move, no matter what the sounds; they had with them four sages, an eagle feather, and sometimes an eagle bone whistle.

Maybe nothing happened the first night. They left during the day to go to a shady place; they went back to camp if it was not too far. On reaching that place, they bathed again and painted up. They returned to the grave.

If one was scared and wakeful, no power would come. The power would notice it. It would make a sound like blowing wind over them four times. Then they went to sleep.

They must repeat this until they received a vision, or for four nights.

Taboos, injunctions, instructions were given in the vision.

They returned home, purified in the bath, burned cedar and sage.

Medicine: Restrictions; War Parties: Roles {Wedel}   The cook on a raid knew how to act; he was very careful not to touch anyone with his greasy hands, for he doesn't want to break anybody's power. Hence the cook got the first choice of plunder. Medicine was a warrior's protection, so the cook had to watch very carefully not to weaken it. He passed water around afterward so all could wash their greasy fingers.

Medicine: Restrictions; War Parties: Roles {Hoebel}   The cook knew the taboos of the medicine of the society, e.g., the Eagle Society. He knew that if he touched them with greasy hands that they would be injured, or the whole bunch would get wiped out. He passed water after the meal for a finger bowl.

Medicine {Wedel}   A man might have two medicines, but one was always stronger.

If he had a friend who wanted his medicine, they went to a peyote meeting and smoked. The older man may give some of his weaker medicine to a young man, but he never gave it all.

Medicine: Transfer {Hoebel}   A medicine man might have more than one medicine. He liked to keep his favorite that he did not use often. If a young man offered smoke and asked for medicine, he would withhold the favorite and give him another.[1]

Medicine: Vision Quest   If you expected to get medicine, you couldn't get it by sitting and watching, you must get it in sleep.

Medicine: Competition   Today's medicine men have no power, it's not in him. [Present day medicine men can't do miracles.] But in the old days, a group could get together and compare powers.

Jim's father would put a feather crosswise in his mouth like a tooth brush, then blow on the palm of his hand, and he would get a lead spot on his palm. The lead color represented eagle dung. [He would paint his face with this.] This would show a medicine man's power.

Medicine: Curing {Wedel}   Certain sicknesses on a man could be cured.

If a woman couldn't pass water and got bloated, the medicine man took the outer feather from an eagle tail. The patient was placed at the back of the tipi. The medicine man entered, walked around the tipi clockwise. He drew the feather across his mouth right to left four times, inhaling as did so and on the fourth time he blew vigorously on the feather. Sometimes he also blew water on the patient's head if water was still difficult to pass.

Medicine: Curing {Hoebel}   One procured the services of a medicine man with a feather in the right hand and a smoke offering.

The medicine man walked about the tent in which the patient lay. He entered and smoked with the patient. The patient told of the trouble.

He did not touch the patient.

He drew the eagle feather across his teeth from left to right three times; he blew his breath through it. On the fourth time he drew his breath in and expelled it forcibly.

The patient might faint. The medicine man might blow water on his face to revive him.

Life Cycle: Childbirth: Medicine: Otter Medicine   Otter Medicine was for the relief of a

---

1. Wallace and Hoebel 1952:160(?).

difficult childbirth. They called on a medicine man with a feather and a cigarette.

An otter hide was used for this purpose, also four wild sages. Another pregnant woman should not call during the doctoring; also they couldn't expect relief from the medicine man.

He drew the otter skin across his mouth four times (not inhaling), then he dragged it down the right side of the woman's body. After the third time, he fanned the patient with the feather, starting at the head and moving down the body. On the fourth time, he stood out to the side, heard [made] music faintly, then ran to the door and jumped out. As his feet touched the ground outside, the child was born.[1]

There was no power like this today. Jim was not certain whether or not the eagle gave this power; it came from some force in the air.

Medicine: Duration   Sometimes a medicine wasn't very strong, at other times it was very strong; it was variable from time to time in an individual.

Social Organization: Medicine Societies   A medicine man could belong to two medicine societies ("parties") simultaneously.

If he wished to leave one society for another [which would give him more power], he would take his shield and regalia out to a lonely place and give up his power in that society, or he could go to the grave where he got it and surrender it there.

[He would go to the head of his group and give him his shield and paraphernalia. The Medicine leader put them out in the mountains away from camp. This corroborates Niyah's report on the return to the grave from which the medicine was received.[2]]

Medicine   A young man had to have some kind of medicine in the old days.

Relations with Other Tribes: Osages   Osages ("cut throats") were especially dangerous. The Comanches early got up a fear of them. *wasási* means "cutthroats," Osages.[3]

Medicine: Transfer {Wedel}   A young man[4] was advised by his parents that he was grown and that to be honorable and live, he had to have some medicine.[5]

{There was a} medicine man whose power was desired. His mother went to the medicine man's wife and asked how to get at him. She was told to bring sage, a feather, a horse with a good saddle, bridle, and a saddle blanket. It didn't make any difference how much the medicine cost. The mother returned and reported to the father.

He got a pipe or a cigarette and went to the medicine man. He got his horse and loaded it with presents, tethering the horse just east of the tipi where the medicine man would see it. The father went alone. He walked around the tipi and entered, handing the medicine man the pipe or cigarette.

The medicine man promised to have a new tipi immediately to the south the next time, and invited the father to bring his son to it. The next time, the boy went also. They entered the same way as before and discussed things. The medicine man agreed to give the boy

1. Wallace and Hoebel 1952:143.
2. See above, Niyah, July 10.
3. *wazaze* is the Osage's own name for themselves. In the sign language, they were often referred to by a sign implying cut (or shaved) hair (Bailey 2001:493).
4. Wallace and Hoebel (1952:162) implies that this was Post Oak Jim's own history.
5. Contra Wallace and Hoebel, "without any prompting from their elders" (1952:156).

some medicine.

MasiitotopɄ,[1] Painted Bear's Claws on a Shield, was the name of the medicine man's pipe.[2]

Everyone saw the tipi and knew. They said, "That's where it's going to take place."

The medicine man was going to shoot the neophyte with an arrow, so they asked for arrows from another young man. Also, they looked for a long spear to use on the young man. When everything was ready, the young man who gave the arrows and the medicine man stood at the back, side by side.

The seeker stood outside the door on the east. Both went around the tipi, came in and walked around inside, and stood to the south of the door, stripped to the breechcloth.

The medicine man stopped to the north.

He blew four breaths across the room, preceding this by singing his medicine song.

The young man with the medicine man was told to shoot an arrow as hard as he could, using his knee to gain greater force. The young man tried the bow three times, shooting on the fourth. The knife-pointed arrow struck the neophyte, turned and went upwards; the neophyte made a noise like a bear.

Then the young man advanced with the spear, tried three times and thrust on the fourth. The spear blade turned aside. The neophyte was still making a noise like a bear.

The medicine given was to protect against bow and arrow and spear.

The medicine man's name was Keekiwa.[3]

Medicine: Transfer {Hoebel}   The mother of a boy might arrange for his first medicine transfer.

She went to the wife of the medicine man. This woman told her what her husband would want for this service, what the sort of horse, blankets, and bridle her husband would prefer. No matter what it cost them, they were going to have the medicine.

The mother told the boy's father what was needed. The father loaded a horse with the proper gifts and tied the animal a short way east of the medicine man's lodge. He walked around the tipi to the left and then entered the door. He offered smoke, and told of the desire.

Preparations were made for the ceremony.

A new tipi was raised by the medicine man on the south side of the camp.

He got a young man with good arrows. He got a young man with a spear.

The medicine man and his helpers stood at the rear of the tipi. The neophyte stood at the door outside. He circled the tipi to the left. He entered and circled the inside as above.

He took his place to the south of the door. He had only his breechclout on.

He assumed a stooping posture facing north.

The medicine man sang his medicine song. He blew his breath across the room four

---

1. *masiito* 'fingernail', *topɄ* 'shield'.

2. Hoebel's notes (see next note) and Wallace and Hoebel (1952:161) identity "MasiitotopɄ" as the name of the man rather than his pipe. I know of no other references to pipes being named. Otherwise unidentified.

3. Otherwise unidentified.

times.

He told the arrow assistant to make his shot, to shoot as hard as he can. Using his knee to help bend the bow, the assistant took three practice pulls and then let fly on the fourth. The steel-pointed arrow struck the neophyte, the point was bent, and the arrow flew upwards towards the top of the tipi.

Then the spearman took his turn. He ran up to the neophyte, took three practice thrusts and jabbed full force on the fourth. The spear point was bent, but the candidate was not fazed.

During the entire proceedings, the neophyte made grunting noises like a bear. The power of this medicine man was very strong as demonstrated.

His name was MasiitotopU, Bear Claw Marks on a Shield.[1]

Medicine: Blackmail   A medicine man could extract money from a man without the latter knowing it.

Medicine   The younger generation made better medicine man.

Material Culture: Slings   Slings were used as toys on nighthawks.[2]

The nighthawk has something to do with lightning. He carried a chunk of ice [hail] on each wing and had a big mouth. He went to the lake for a swallow of water, then sat in it until evening.

He was shot with slings, *taʔkɯbuuʔ*. It had a square pocket of rawhide and a string of buckskin. It was used by the Mexicans, and the Comanches probably learned it from them. Formerly, they had [a thong and a bone].

Medicine: Bull Roarer   Medicine men used a bullroarer, *yuʔanee*[3] 'warm wind', of cedar at time of war.

A bullroarer was sometimes used instead of a whistle [by some medicine men] but never in a Peyote meeting.

Medicine men with the Beaver Medicine used the bullroarer in curing sick patients.

The slats sometimes had notches on one edge to represent the beaver's tail.

Musical Instruments: Flutes   Flutes were made of cedar.

Medicine: Bull Roarer   The "warm wind" went with the Beaver Medicine.

Medicine: Beaver Ceremony {Wedel}   The Beaver Medicine used an extra big tipi with the door on the east. {see fig. 3} A gravelike ditch was outside the door, beside which was a ten-foot pole from which waved an eagle feather. The grave was about two feet deep. In curing the patient, {gap of several lines} fireplace, lined with willow shoots, and a mud beaver was outside the lane north and south of the hearth.

A cottonwood tree was west of the fireplace.

The patient was on the west wall, with his feet to the fireplace. There were women to the north and the medicine man to the south.

The medicine man was ready outside. He was dressed as directed by the beaver. He

1. Hoebel 1940:127; Wallace and Hoebel 1952:161.
2. Wallace and Hoebel 1952:128.
3. Robinson and Armagost (1990) glosses *yuʔanee* as 'south wind', but 'bull roarer' as *wekɯbupɯ*.

went to the east side of the tipi, swung the bull roarer and called to the people, who knew what it meant, that he was inviting them.

The fire was already built and the patient was inside the tipi. A whole bunch gathered outside; anyone in the crowd who felt puny jumped into the grave, and then out. After walking about the tipi, then they went into the tipi clockwise. They sat wherever there was room. All rings must be taken off by an attendant, there was no metal allowed.

The drummers came in after the people and placed themselves on the south, next to the door. The song leaders [carried rattles] and sat immediately to the west of the drummers; they were the last in, after they jumped into the ditch. The song leaders and rattlemen sang four medicine songs, the first to entertain. Then they drifted among and intermingled with the drummers.

The two women were the ones who went after the doctor. The medicine man directed the drummers and song leaders. The drummers hit the drums four times before they started to sing.

The medicine man stopped the singers when enough songs had been sung.

The women loaded the pipes and had someone light them with an ember from the fireplace.

The women took a puff and then passed it to the medicine man.

Probably he smoked or talked or prayed as instructed by the beaver.

He took four puffs and handed it back to the women, who cleaned it and laid it in front of them.

The medicine man went through a performance with a feather.

He went to the lake on the north, then around the fireplace to the south lake; he probably dipped his feather in the water. He came back to the patient and fanned the patient with the wet feather.

While the doctoring was done, the women smoked, passed the pipe to the doctor who smoked and returned it, and the women again cleaned it out.

The medicine man stood at the foot of the patient making medicine with herbs. He threw off his robe and climbed the tree to put his head out of the top of the tipi, then he descended. He ran around the fire, then stepped into the fire from the east, stood and flapped his arms like a burrowing owl.

Then he came out and ran back to his place.

He got willow bark from the south lake shore, chewed and spat it into the air.

Then the beaver perfume filled the tipi.

When he was through, he gave a signal to the drummers and singers, and the people all started to sing a song.

Sometimes, the fire was put out and they sang in the dark, men, women, and children, mingled in the dark.

Young men and young women took part in the meeting. It broke at midnight and they went home. They quit at midnight and started again in the morning; those who wished might come again. The ceremony was kept up for two days and two nights. It started in the evening always.

They went in the same order the next morning, and stayed till noon.

When the people left the tipi, they went outside into the ditch first.

The last song at the end of the ceremony was sung four times as a benediction.

The stobs {stakes} about the tipi were loosened just before the last song, and everybody dropped to the ground and ran out as they pleased.

It ran evening to midnight, morning to noon, evening to midnight, morning to noon; it ended at noon of the second day.

Beaver Medicine was used to cure tuberculosis, but it didn't hardly work. It was also for detecting evil magic.

It was called *pianahuwaitʉ*[1] 'big doctoring'.

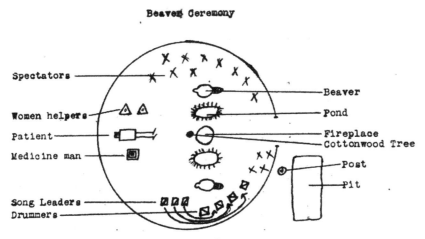

Figure 3. Wedel's diagram of the Beaver Ceremony

Medicine: Beaver Ceremony {Hoebel} An extra large tipi was set up facing east.

The fireplace was slightly east of the center.

There were two ponds, one north, one south, of the fireplace. One pond faced the sun, the other, shadows.

A beaver effigy made from earth was on the far side of each pond, facing west.

West of the fireplace and in the center of the tipi was a large cotton wood tree reaching to the top of the tipi.

Just outside the tipi, to the south of the entrance was dug a pit, two feet deep, six or seven feet long. The long axis was north and south. At the northwest corner of the pit was a vertical pole with an eagle feather at the top. The pole was about ten feet high.

The patient lay at the extreme west of the tipi.

Two women assistants stood north of the patient facing him.

The medicine man's place was south of the patient.

The drummers and song leaders occupied the southeast quadrant, south of the entrance.

---

1. This is the form as recorded by the Field Party. It probably should be *pianatʉsuʔwaitʉ* (*pia* 'big', *natʉsuʔu* 'medicine', *waitʉ* 'appear, resemble').

Spectators filled in the vacant space, concentrating on the north side.

The patient was brought in and the fire lit. The medicine man, dressed according to his medicine, approached the tipi from the east. He swung the bullroarer and called to the people, inviting them in. The medicine man then circled the tipi in a clockwise direction. He jumped into the pit from the east and out on the west and entered the tipi.

All of the people who wished to be spectators (everybody was welcome, although sickly or puny ones were most likely to participate) gathered around and did the same as the medicine man. They must first remove all metal from their persons, rings, buckles, etc.

The drummers and song leaders entered also, circling the tipi and jumping into the pit.

Anyone going to the north side of the tipi to sit down must circle the fire clockwise to get there.

The medicine man ordered the music to start. The drummers beat four times and shouted. The song leaders sang four songs (singing special Beaver Medicine songs). The medicine man ordered the song leaders to cease; the song leaders mingled with the drummers.

The assistants (who summoned the medicine man) loaded the pipe; it was lit with an ember given them by a spectator by the fire, and smoking a puff each, they gave the pipe to the medicine man. The medicine man smoked four times and prayed (in accordance with the dictates of his medicine). He returned the pipe to the women, who cleaned it and laid it on the ground before them.

The medicine man took his feathers, dipped them in the north pond, then in the south pond (circling in a clockwise direction always), and fanned the patient with the wet feathers.

The two assistants again lit the pipe, smoked and passed it to the medicine man, who smoked it and returned it. They cleaned it and laid it down again.

The medicine man then stood at the feet of the patient and doctored with herbs.

The medicine man then threw off his buffalo robe and climbed the cottonwood tree, sticking his head out of the top of the tipi. He descended and ran around the fire. He stepped into the fire from the east and fluttered his arms like a burrowing owl. He stepped back out of the fire to the east and took his place again, going to the south to complete the circle.

The medicine man went to the south lake. He took some willow bark, chewed it and blew upwards, blowing out the perfume of the beaver.

The medicine man then ordered the drummers and song leaders to start a song in which everyone present joined.

The fire was extinguished and the people all mingled in the tipi. It lasted until midnight.

Everybody jumped into the ditch after leaving the tipi (after each day's performance).

The next day, the medicine man got up early. He announced when they would start. The procedure was the same as above, ending at noon.

The entire ceremony lasted two days and two nights, ending at noon of the third day.

Before the people left the tipi at the end of the last day, they sang a closing song four times. The tipi stobs {stakes} had been loosened. At the close of the song, while still singing, they lifted up the tipi cover and ran out in all directions.

The Beaver Ceremony was to cure tuberculosis and to detect sorcery.[1]

Games   Children hunted for a rough place to play. They tied ropes to a piece of rawhide and pulled themselves downhill; they went fast like an automobile. If one side of the hide wasn't held fast, they spilled.

Animals: Beaver   Beaver was *piakwasi* 'big tail'.

Medicine: Beaver Ceremony   The Beaver Ceremony was used to determine who was guilty of causing sickness. The latter would then be visited by relatives of the sick man and asked to withdraw the evil medicine. If he denied his guilt, he had to swear by the Sun. If he swore falsely, he soon died. If he refused to withdraw the evil magic, he was publically threatened. When he swore, if denying, he raised his right hand toward the sun, "If certain things are so, may it come back on me."

It might take a year for him to die. If he admitted his guilt, but withdrew the magic, no grudge was held; if he denied guilt, and didn't die within a year, he was held innocent of guilt.[2]

Medicine: Sorcery   One man could pay a medicine man to kill a third party for him. If the medicine man withdrew the curse, the blame was attached to the person who paid him, and he lost the friendship of the people.

Medicine: Vision Quest   If a person kept going to a lonely place with no definite idea of what he wanted, his mind may be led into evil thoughts.

Medicine: Sorcery   A certain man was nice-looking and attractive, but some people didn't like him, so they put boils on him, on different parts of his body. The man knew what was up, so he undertook to cut off the boils with a knife. He cut off a piece of bone from his chest, and also a bone out of his little toe.

This might arise from jealousy over women.

A woman used evil medicine upon a man other than her husband. A certain young man was brave, honorable, and nice-looking; his wife was not so nice-looking. The young man went out as the leader of a war party. His wife took up with another man. While they were lying down, her sister-in-law saw her. The young man's father was bragging about his daughter-in-law's fidelity. This made the young man's sister angry and she said, "No, she isn't good," and she promised to tell the man upon his return.

It was the custom in those days that a childless couple would take down their tent while the husband was away on a raid, and the wife went to her parent's-in-law. This was true here also.

[In a family where there were no children, when the husband went on a raid, <u>the wife went to live with the husband's parents</u>. Their tipi was taken down and stored until his return was expected.]

Upon the husband's return, the tipi was set up and they spent the first night together. The next day, after breakfast, the warrior's sister came in and said she had something to tell him. She told him not to take it hard; he was an honorable and brave man. His uncle said that she spoke the truth, but for him to take it easy. She then told the warrior of finding his

1. Wallace and Hoebel 1952:175–76.
2. Wallace and Hoebel 1952:175.

wife abed with another man. He didn't seem to take the news very hard because he was a brave, kind-hearted man, but he said they would separate and he would give her eight head of horses.

The wife was Kwaharʉnʉʉ; her people were camped at a distance. Before leaving, the warrior picked another woman to be his wife. As they rode along driving the horses, the divorced wife carried his muzzle-loader across her saddle. The man got off to do something and the woman shot at him, trying to kill him, but missed. The man came around and was mad. He said that her uncle had cautioned him to go easy and now she had tried to kill him, so he was going to kill her. He threw her down, sat on her, drew his knife and cut off her nose. The warrior and the new wife returned, leaving the ex-wife unconscious from the loss of blood. Finally, she recovered and drove her horses on to the Kwaharʉnʉʉ.

A few days after, the warrior gathered some men and went off on another raid, leaving his new wife at home. The old wife got home and told her troubles to her folks, who were surprised to see her in that shape, which made her folks mad. They went to an evil medicine woman and asked her to do something. She went to a lonely place, cut off a piece of her flesh, and told the Great Spirit that she wanted the warrior to be killed on this raid.

The warrior was on a raid into Texas. As they went along, they got to their destination, but the people noticed them and dodged off, so they stopped to rest. The warrior slept; he had a dream that was against him and woke up. They were close to the whites. It began to rain toward dawn.

Jim's father was in the party. They had a few horses already. They saddled a young horse for Jim's father to see if it was bucky, and he was promptly bucked off. The horses went back to the whites with Indian saddles on, warning the whites.

It was the custom to try out young horses so.

The Indians drifted off into the mountains and heavy cedars. The leader thought of his dream. Two Apaches were in the party. They stopped and told the cook to rustle fire and prepare food. While preparing dinner, they were surprised by whites who charged them. The warrior was riding a brown horse. He ran toward it when the whites attacked. He had a pearl-handled six-shooter, which was rare with the Indians then.

These were Mexican soldiers. The Indians didn't resist, but fled through the sloping cedar scrub. The warrior collided with a soldier, each shooting at the other. Jim's father and another man saw the warrior fall, but didn't know he was shot, so they started to get off. Then they found he was dead, so they remounted and fled. They were pursued across a deep creek. Most of the Indians and the Apache women were killed.

Two Indians got across the creek and saw an old man and a boy [Comanches or Comanche captives] with the soldiers shooting at them. The man was shot through the side and fell. The warriors rode on up a steep bluff; they rode over the bluff and rode by some houses. They could see the washing.

The soldiers didn't follow beyond the bluff. The two warriors stopped in a grove beyond the houses and rested.

The soldiers returned the next day and the warriors rode up into mountains. As they rode along, they saw the old man with the captive boy, whom they thought were killed. The two warriors rode over after them; they knew who they were and began to talk about their companions who had died and wondered who had escaped. The old man thought almost everyone had been killed. He advised them not to return to the battlefield because the soldiers might be laying in wait.

Since they had some horses already, they went back with the sad news. They told just how it had happened. Soon after the question came up, a certain young woman was talking about how fine and brave the slain warrior was.

The man was brave, kind, good-looking; the husband had these honors. The woman who caused the warrior's death and extermination of the war party wasn't punished.

Different tribes gathered in the west and were drifting this way along the creek. Before his death, the warrior had been in this group.

Young men liked to show off and this warrior liked to show off with earrings, breastplate, silver bridle, and a silver mounted saddle, riding along where he could be seen when the camp was moving.

The Comanches often forgave an erring one; Apaches were not like that.

The medicine woman probably inserted a needle into her arm, lifted it, and cut off flesh; this was customary.

Life Cycle: Death: Mourning (Kiowa)   If an enemy killed a man's brother among the Kiowa, the man cut his finger off. If a brother died, a woman cut off a finger joint.

There were some women with no first finger joints on their left hands.

This was a Kiowa, not a Comanche custom.

Medicine: Flesh Sacrifice   Kiowas and Cheyennes cut off bits of flesh to make medicine, the Comanches did not. The chests of some people in other tribes were all scarred.

Jim had seen a Cheyenne with ropes through the skin on his back, dragging buffalo skulls about the camp until they tore out. Comanches did not do this. Comanche made no vows as far as he knew.

Medicine: Bull Roarer   The Warm Wind was carried near the shield in time of war, whirled in time of danger to feel power. When in action, a bullet would come straight but miss them.

Medicine: Beaver Ceremony   They were forbidden to have any metal near the Beaver in the ceremony.

Medicine: Cows   Cows had medicine too.

Two men on horseback were going to kill a bull. Its owner said it was getting along in age. It was an awfully big bull, black with a yellow back stripe. They were coming up on him. As he crawled up on a cow, they shot it through the heart with a forty-five, but the bullet only penetrated an inch and the bull breathed smoke out of his mouth. The second shot glanced off; the third burnt hair; the seventh showed no mark at all.

The bull was not very wild, so they drove it toward the creek. The bull began to twist among the bushes and the bank caved in, throwing the bull on its head. Then an Indian, Quassyah's brother, jumped off his horse and cut the bull's throat.

Jim's brother and another Indian came riding up and noticed the bull. They said the bull was very fat. They asked why they had shot the bull so many times. They told him they couldn't kill him.

The old man asked for the bull's tail. They cut off the bushy tip and gave it to the old man. He called a young companion up and said he would show him that the old bull had medicine that he could give him for three or four days. He told the young man to stand a little distance away and put the tail in his mouth. He wheezed and pulled the tail out of his mouth; you could see blue paint slobbering down his chin. He flicked it towards the young man and spattered his shirt. He told him not to wash the shirt because in four days the spots would disappear and for four days no bullets could hit him.

The old man got his power from Mt. Scott.[1]

Medicine: Vision Quest   Pahkeah[2] 'stiff robe' was the old man in the above story. He was Quassyah's father. He went up to Mount Scott while young, hunting for power. [Many people tried to get power from the mountain and failed.] In a dream, the mountain refused to give him power up to the third night, but he stayed with it nine days without food or drink. Then, he got up in the morning without a vision and turned toward the sun, praying. The mountain said, "You have been faithful [you have stayed with me]; look toward Medicine Bluff; it is sharp as a knife."

It told him to decorate his shield a certain way. He must use blue paint in blue lines, drawn with spread fingers from the top downward to imitate the rock strata. It told him to look around and see how the falling raindrops were harmless; his enemies' bullets would be the same way to him. The medicine man told him to go to a certain place and show the power, but not to kill anybody. He was to ride a yellow horse with a black mane, to ride four times from left to right across a firing line of soldiers. He did so and was unhurt.[3]

People would sometimes go to lonely places for power. This was not necessarily to a grave. If a medicine man died near the place where he got power, he was buried there, otherwise not.

Names   *tuhʉyatai* means 'pussy of a horse'.[4] He was Quanah Parker's nephew.

Beliefs: Ghosts   A young man was going out on a raid to the west. There were about ten in the party. The man had a special medicine to give strength to horses so they wouldn't give out. The horse's tails were braided with buckskin near the end, and an eagle feather was also inserted. The medicine gave a person or a horse strength so they wouldn't give out so easily.

He met a very strange human on the trip. The top of his head was all bloody. He probably was scalped. The man could hardly keep from running away. The belief was that you can't run from a ⟨pɛ:kewat⟩.[5] If you ran away {. . . [*sic*]}.

The young man happened to go out into the brush and there he met the pɛ:kewat. It ran to meet him and he grabbed and killed it. He went back to his people and told them that he had killed the pɛ:kewat. He stood and told the brave deeds he had done, that now he wished to live to a ripe old age. The man had power to walk as far as he wanted without tiring.

1. Mount Scott is the tallest peak in the Wichita Mountains, northwest of Lawton.
2. See Introduction.
3. Wallace and Hoebel 1952:161.
4. *tuhuya* 'horse, *tai* 'vagina'.
5. *-wahtʉ* 'without'.

Medicine: Foretelling: Badger's Mirror   The party went on and met a badger. The people had heard what people said about the badger. They wanted to kill it and prove what they had heard about badger. They killed the badger in the afternoon, cut down the belly, removed the viscera, but left the blood. They sprinkled dirt over the blood and laid him wide open, with the head to the west.

The next morning early, a man, not very honest, came up first, hit it, told of the brave deeds he had done, and asked what would happen. He looked into the mirror of badger blood. The badger said ___, {*sic*} which meant something very bad. The man saw blood in his mouth and on the right chest. Then he jumped over the badger. Next came a young man. He saw his image as an old, wrinkled man. He said to the badger, as was the custom, "You lie," and then jumped over the badger. The other men didn't want to look; they were afraid because the mirror always tells the truth. The young man grew to be very old, so old that he had to be helped at his last peyote dance. He had an otter skin headdress, etc.

Beliefs: Ghosts   The ⟨pɛ:kewat⟩ was the same as the Pawnee ghostman.[1]

Social Organization: Bands: Nʉmʉkiowa   The Nʉmʉkiowa was a mixed band of the Comanche. It meant "part Kiowa."[2]

Post Oak Jim
July 17, 1933

Dances: Blow Away Dance[3] {Wedel}   (*poʔayanʉhka*[4]) was a social dance, the "blow away" dance (*poʔahimarʉ*, 'blow away'.) It was a social dance held when the different bands had been away from each other for a long time and finally got together. It was held at any season. It was held at night. The announcer spread the news of the coming dance. They had a fire. The dance started as a circle, later each man had a female partner. Toward midnight, the couples "blew away" and rested awhile. The drummers and song leaders had to stay and keep up the music.

After a while, the couples came back. It was mostly for single people; if a married woman was present, she didn't blow away. If a young man wanted to dance, he picked someone other than his wife. Parents didn't object to their unmarried daughters dancing if they were grown.

The dance continued until about midnight, then the dance was stopped. There were no special dates to hold this dance. If the moon was bright, no fire was necessary.[5] There were no regular full moon dances.

1. This comment was probably from Linton.
2. In the early 1870s, there was a mixed group of Comanches and Kiowas on the Staked Plains under the leadership of Patchoconi (Kavanagh 1996:429; see also, Index: Individual Names). It was later referred to as *nʉmʉkiowa* (Gatschet 1893).
3. This is the start of Wedel's Notebook 4.
4. Robinson and Armagost (1990) gives *poʔayaʔ* as 'blown away object'.
5. Wallace and Hoebel 1952:56.

Dances: Blow Away Dance {Hoebel}

po²ayanɨhka ⎱ 'blow away'
po²ahimarɨ ⎰

It was a social dance. It was held any time of the year, at night, with a fire.

It was announced by the crier in advance.

It started in a circular formation. There were partners.

Later, they "blow away together." The drummers and song leaders continued.

The participants were usually single. Married women did not blow away. Grown girls and separated women took part.

Duration: until about midnight.

If there was a full moon, the fire was unnecessary.

Dances: Fox Dance   The Fox Dance was something like the Horse Dance. It usually preceded some big event, as, for example, the Sun Dance, etc. It was held just at the start of the Sun Dance.

Medicine: Sun Dance {Wedel}   They put up a big arbor, which represented the nest of the eagle.

The Sun Dance was usually put on about the middle of the summer. There was a big forked pole in the center of the arbor, from which rafters radiated outward to rest on horizontal poles carried by a circle of lower forked poles. The arbor was built and covered with nothing but cottonwood leaves. They cut small straight cottonwood brush and set it about the sides to form a wall. They wove the brush wall basketwise, like wattle. The doorway on the east was the only opening. There was a wall of cedar trees reaching to the ceiling across the west side of the arbor. There were beds behind the cedars for the dancers to rest on. The cedars were brought in before the arbor was built.

The cutting of the center pole was a woman's job. Only a certain woman could cut it, probably a captive woman, truthful and decent. There was something to the center pole, but Jim didn't know the story.

The center pole was cut in a creek and the bark peeled off. Ropes were passed under the pole and it was carried, <u>not</u> dragged. Everyone took part in carrying the pole, even children helped. People sang and danced as they carried it. They might stop three or four times en route. The pole might be fourteen feet long; it was put in a post hole about three feet deep, dug out with knives. They made four attempts to raise the pole, and on the fourth time everyone sang and shouted and they raised it with forked sticks. The chief blew his whistle to accompany the raising. All the other poles and brush were already cut and at hand, ready for erection as soon as the center pole was raised.[1]

The dance had a preparation period of four days. During the four days, there was no law and everybody was allowed to do as they pleased.

Everyone could go to the timber, married women and all. A man who had a horse picked a woman partner and they went to the creek for brush to drag in. Usually, a big bunch[2]

---

1. In Wedel's manuscript, this paragraph appears farther down on the page, after the paragraph about receiving rations. But there is an editorial emendation indicating that it should be placed here, and it is so placed in the typescript.

2. In Wedel's typescript, this is given as "brush."

went out to the timber. They made big headdresses of leaves or sage. The partners came back with leaves and brush. If a man had no horse, he tied a rope about his waist and dragged timbers that way. As they came in, they sang songs. They had four days to build the arbor, so they were in no hurry to finish it. In those days, the Indians had nothing to worry about, plenty of game and food.

The Indians were on the reservation at the time of this particular dance and used government rations.[1]

Then, after the completion of the arbor, they went out and killed a three-year-old buffalo bull. The forepart was skinned out to include the legs, shoulders, and head, then stuffed with willow and put on top of the center pole at the peak of the lodge, facing to the east. The eagle ate the buffalo, "They're feeding him." The arbor was now completed.

The cedars for the partition were cut the same way as the other brush.

Anyone could take part in the dance.

A special medicine man who had power was giving the dance.

A spot for the arbor was selected when the camp was made. The camp was arranged in a moon shape about the arbor, with the open side on the east.

When the people were coming to the dance, they didn't come direct, but stopped and pitched camp maybe four different times before reaching the spot.

When the arbor was finished, four or five clowns appeared. Some men were covered with mud (*sekwitsipuhitsi*,[2] the mud men). They wore headdresses of leaves open at their faces, with big noses of mud, and carried shields of willow and clubs. Their horses were also covered with mud so that people couldn't recognize them. They acted as clowns. They couldn't get off their horses. They might chase around the camp and whip dogs. Perhaps they chased bathing women out of the creek so they could wash off the mud. Nobody knew who they were.

The shield was woven of peeled willows fastened together by bark, with the ends of the bark left hanging like a fringe.

A bunch of men went out to the timber. They cut brush and built a shelter, like a rail fence, where they could hide from the people. Someone went down and located them, returned, and told the people that the enemy was there. Then the warriors went out in their war costumes with their muzzle loaders and beat up on the bunch. Old people, women and children also in the shelter where the men were. People yell and mimic a real battle. After cleaning up on them, they rode back to camp singing victory songs.

Two men were selected as announcers. They went along the village on the fourth night and announced the dance.

Each band was going to dance its way.

Each band had its own location in the camp; the dance was a tribal affair, but there was no definite orientation of the bands in the circle.

Dancers from each band danced from their camp to the cleared space before the door of the arbor. They all started at the same time from their camps.

---

1. This implies that Jim was describing a specific ceremony, rather than providing a general overview.

2. *sekwi* 'mud', *puhipʉ* 'leaf'.

The groups went a short way, followed ("driven") by the man with the club.[1] He stopped them every so often to quench their thirst by telling them of some brave deed of his. He told them it wasn't true, but it really was. Each time he killed a man in a story a drum sounded.

The groups would stop maybe four times. Each time the leader told of his brave deeds.

They started up again at the beat of the drum, one beat the first time, two beats the second time, etc.

Each group was singing as it approached.

Each time the song ended, the group stopped and the leader recited a brave act of his. The groups didn't stop simultaneously.

When the bands got in front of the arbor, they stopped. They were told that the dance would start early the next day, they must get things ready.

They said that so many buffaloes had been located near camp that a scout had been sent out and he had found them. A certain warrior was picked out the next morning to run the buffaloes into the arbor. The warrior had bows and arrows in his right hand, a flaming torch in his left hand.

The warrior started the buffalo toward the arbor. The buffalo were people in disguise, wearing robes, but with sticks for horns and a tail fastened behind. One bull was chased around the arbor clockwise four times before he entered; the other buffaloes entered the arbor at once.

taʔsiʔwooʔ ketsiha,[2] an old buffalo bull who looked lousy and scabby (was the one who ran around the arbor).

They were then through with the buffalo. They left the arbor soon and went home.

It was about noon. The dancers were about ready to commence. Anyone could join the dance.

The act of driving the buffalo was to show that the buffalo belonged to the Indians as food, that they were taken with bow and arrow, and eaten with fire.

The announcer announced the dance right after dinner. The dancers, with their female kinfolk (wife, sister, etc.), went in and made up their beds of sage covered with blankets, with pillows. Thereafter, the dancers and the medicine man only were permitted there.

The dancers went four days without food or water (except plums or slippery elm bark). A man might give out after two days. He sent word to his father who took it up with the medicine man leader, but he couldn't get out without paying a fine or forfeit. The father went directly and talked to the medicine man without smoking; he said his boy couldn't finish and paid maybe a horse to get the boy out. The boy was told to go wash in the creek before returning to camp; he was told to dive into the creek upstream four times, to wash his mouth first but not to drink. After he got home, he could drink all he wanted. The boy packed his stuff and went out the door.

Those of strong constitution went there for four days. The dancers were allowed to chew slippery elm bark and eat plums, but no water.

1. This seems to be a description of the Brush Dance.

2. *taʔsiʔwooʔ* 'paws the ground' a common term for buffalo. Robinson and Armagost (1990) gives *ketsihanakenitu* as 'starving (extremely hungry, without food)'.

They danced until midnight every night. They started early in the morning and stopped at noon for a brief rest. Finally, the dancers could only stand and move their bodies up and down, blowing on their eagle whistle each time they went down. (The dancers made a flapping motion with their arms and whistled to represent young eagles crying to leave the nest. The eagle whistle represented the cry of a young eagle.)[1]

The fan was made of roadrunner tail feathers.

The medicine man blew on the fan, then made a horizontal circular motion clockwise toward the dancers, beginning in front of the left arm, to speed them up. Dancers sometimes got frightened and ran, falling over the spectators; it was something like hypnotizing, some kind of medicine behind the fan. The medicine man danced with them for the four days.

Drummers and songsters sat just to the south of the door. Visitors sat about against the north and south walls.

Dancers raised their arms toward the sun as they danced and looked toward the sun. The dancers were naked save for a breechcloth.

Toward the last day, people came forward and placed offerings at the foot of the center pole, or tied them to the pole. Soon the pole looked like a Christmas tree. Sometimes young boys shot arrows into the top of the pole inside the arbor. The {gift} givers prayed for long life. When they beat the drums, everyone joined in the song. Some drummers had rattles.

The dancers were painted; one man seen by Jim had a terrapin on the back of his neck (a charm against thirst?).

(A medicine man once took his knife and punched his throat until the blood ran. Then he blew on the knife and the blood ceased. The medicine man who gave this dance was feared because he made evil magic.)

The Sun Dance ended on the morning of the fourth day.

No one dared to take the gifts placed at the center pole, everyone was afraid. But a visitor from a different tribe could take something from the pole, leaving some gift of his own in exchange.

Jim and some companions once wandered to a Kiowa camp where a Sun Dance had been held. There were drums and rattles lying about. Jim's grandfather was a good singer, so he told the boys to dance. Then they removed their breechcloths and exchanged them for new ones from the gifts at the center pole. Upon getting home, the old man told their people, and they liked to get them for their act.

The Sun Dancers went down and took a bath, diving four times against the current to wash themselves. The dancers did this, made the sacrifice, to obtain a long life. After the dance, the people moved away.

The man who represented the bull above passed out from thirst. He came to grasping the center pole and said he had seen a white man with long hair and a beard, Christ. This was before we had heard of Him. (This was fifty-seven years ago, about 1875.)

---

1. In Wedel's manuscript, this parenthetical sentence appears later on the page, but there is editorial emendation indicating it should go here, and it is so placed in the typescript.

After the dance, people packed up and left at once. There was no feast.

The center pole had to be cut by a very truthful woman.

Drummers and song leaders were under no food restrictions.

Anyone in the camp who was sick could ask the medicine man to pray for him in the Sun Dance. All people had faith in the Sun Dance. When the camp broke up, they felt that all the sick were cured.

The same medicine man gave a dance on another occasion, too.

Soon after the buffalo disappeared, the dance was given up.

If a man told things that weren't true, the Sun Dance wasn't good.

Medicine: Sun Dance {Hoebel}   The general site was selected in advance.

The camp was broken and groups moved by easy stages to that locale. Four stops, with overnight camps, were made on the way.

The time was usually midsummer. It lasted eight days.

The ceremonial camp was pitched in a semicircle about the site of the dance arbor.

It officially began with the bringing in of materials for the arbor. All must be brought in before the work commenced.

In the gathering of the materials, a man invited a woman to ride behind him on his horse to the creek for materials. They wore headdresses of wild sage.

The brush was dragged back with a rope. Men without horses would pull it back on foot. They were in no hurry at all; the people sang as they went. They probably stopped three or four times to rest and sing.

The center pole must be cut by a captive woman who was virtuous, "true." It was a single piece, one foot by fourteen feet. It was peeled of bark and carried up to the location slung on ropes. There might be twenty-five or thirty in number. Everybody helped. They stopped four times on the way.

{In raising} the center pole, there were three unsuccessful mock attempts to raise the pole. On the fourth trial, the pole was raised. The pole was set in a hole two or three feet deep. A forked stick was used to help hoist it. The leader blew an eagle bone whistle in unison with their attempts.

The outer circle of uprights were set. To these were fastened the roof rafters radiating outward from the crook in the center pole.

They covered the whole structure with cottonwood branches with the leaves attached. Cottonwood was used throughout the structure.

One door was left opening to the east.

A row of cedars was planted across the west side of the circle. This was a screen for the beds of the dancers. On the morning of the dance, the wife or female kin entered and laid a sage mattress on the bed.

They killed a three-year-old buffalo bull. They cut off the head and the top of the chest and skin. They stuffed it with willow. The animal was then placed on the top of the center pole outside, facing east. This was food for the eagle. The entire arbor represented an eagle's nest.

The motion of the dancers represented small eagles (?). Herman Asenap.[1]

1. What Hoebel meant by this reference to Herman Asenap is not known.

During the four-day period of construction, there was no law; general rules of propriety were relaxed.

Clowning by the Mud Men (*sekwitsitpuhitsi*[1]). When the arbor was finished, four or five clowns appeared. Those men had prepared themselves down by the creek. They smeared their faces, bodies, and hair with mud. They build large false noses on their visage, with leaves about their bodies. They wore willow helmets and carried willow-withe shields decorated with strips and fringes of willow bark. They carried clubs of willow-withes in a bundle form. They rode into camp on horses, whipping whoever they saw. The people can't remonstrate, but they might dodge into the tipis. The Mud Men couldn't follow them on horses. They chased dogs around and generally acted funny.

On the afternoon of the fourth day, when all the work was done, some men had built a fort, like a rail fence, down by the creek. They retired to this defense. A man who had served as a scout in a real war went out and discovered it, reporting back to camp. The warriors in camp put on their regalia and sallied back to attack. Each man attempted to reenact his deeds performed in real fighting. The women and children looked on and got frightened by the realism. They returned to camp singing the victory song. This symbolized the triumph of the Comanches over their enemies.

On the evening of the fourth day, the crier went through the camp telling the bands to get ready. Each band started from its location in the camp at the same time, doing its favorite dance as it came. They sang as they came. The dance coach drove them from behind with his whip. When the song was done, he told them to stop, he had something with which to quench their thirst. He recounted his war deeds, which he assured them were not true. The drum was sounded for each man killed. The people knew that these stories were true, for he was a brave. This was repeated four times, with one song between each stop.

The bands approached from both sides of the arbor and stopped in front of the door at the east. Here, they clustered about, dancing with a slow, stomping step.

The announcer told them that the dance would begin in the morning, that the herd of buffalo had been located, a scout had found them.

The dance began the next morning with the roundup of the bison. An outstanding warrior had been selected to drive them in. He carried a torch in his left hand and arrows in the right. The bison were impersonated by people dressed in buffalo robes. The warrior whooped and chased them through the door into the arbor. One old buffalo bull was hard to get in and ran four times about the arbor before entering. *taʔsiʔwooʔ ketsiha* means "an old scabby buffalo bull who looks scaley and lousy." The herd was then released.

The bison symbolized food for the people. The arrows symbolized the hunt, the torch symbolized the fire for cooking.

The dance proper started before lunch. It was in the complete control of the medicine man who got it up.

After the sage mattresses were laid by the women, no one but the dancers could go behind the cedar screen.

---

1. *sekwi* 'mud', *puhipʉ* 'leaf'.

Eight to twelve dancers might participate. There was nothing to keep anyone who had impersonated a bison from joining. The dancers had to dance four days without food or drink. They rested at certain periods. Wild fruits and slippery elm were allowed.

The medicine man had the announcer tell everyone to take a morning bath before entering the arbor. The dancers prepared themselves with paint behind the cedar partition. They might help each other.

The dancers began with their arms stretched to the sun, but as time progressed, they merely moved their shoulders in a shrugging movement with exhalations of breath. This causes short blasts on the eagle bone whistle that each had in his mouth (represents young eagles in the nest?).

The drummers sat near the fireplace and the door. They were older men and led the singing. They were also equipped with rattles.

The spectators sat three or four deep around the outside. When certain Sun Dance songs were sung, all the spectators could join in, rise and dance, too.

The medicine man remained behind the screen most of the time, but occasionally came out and, with a circular left-right motion of his fan, blowing on it at the time, speeded up the dance. The fan was of the tail feathers of a roadrunner. It had a strong medicine, and some men faint at it.

The usual procedure was to dance until noon, stop for a rest for the dancers and lunch for the people, then dance until supper. They resumed again later and danced until midnight.

The dancers were repainted every day.

They might wear sage leaves if they desired.

Spectators made offerings at the center pole. They prayed, while doing so, for a long and happy life.

Small boys shot arrows up into the pole as their offerings.

The offerings were sacred and might not be touched—when the dance was done, they would be left there. (Jim was with three other boys and his grandfather when they found an old Kiowa arbor. The old man told them to change their breechclouts for some left there. When they got back to the Comanche camp, people said they were untruthful for doing such a thing.)

Visitors from other tribes might put up an offering and take down something in exchange.

Jim said that if a boy couldn't stand it, he could get his father to arrange for his release. The father went directly to the medicine man, without making a smoke offering, and offered him a gift for the release of the boy. If the medicine man accepted, he would tell the father to have his son go to the creek and wash his mouth, then dive against the stream four times, wash his mouth again, and go home. The boy wrapped up his bed and did those things.

(Mrs. Asenap said that was impossible. A man knew what he was in for and would be disgraced if he quit.)

The medicine man might do tricks. Jim saw him put a knife down his throat and bleed. He drew out the blade, blew on it, and the blood disappeared.

This was an evil medicine man whom the people feared.

Visions might come to the dancers. The man who impersonated the buffalo bull became so exhausted, he started for water. He lost his senses and clung to the center pole. When he came to, he said he had seen a white man with long, white, curly hair. This was Jesus, but it happened before the Comanches had heard about Him.

Sick people might ask for special help from the medicine man during the dance.

All the spectators also benefitted from the ceremony; they went away well-pleased.

The dance ended on the eighth morning. The camp was broken and the people moved away, leaving the arbor behind.[1] The last dance was held about 1874–76. Jim was five years old. There was an eclipse of the sun that year.[2]

Social Control: Disputes   Most of the time, women were the cause of hard feelings and some people drifted away to another group.

Medicine: Sun Dance   The Sun Dance was not necessarily given every year.

Dances: Fox Dance   No woman with her nose cut off[3] could enter the Fox Dance. If any such woman approached, the dancers scattered and the leader with club had a time rounding them up. *wotsia*[4] was the Fox Dance. Dancers jumped {see fig. 4} up and down.

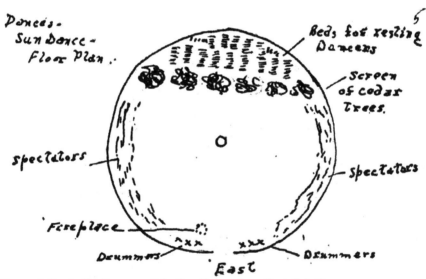

Figure 4. Hoebel's diagram of the Sun Dance from Post Oak Jim

1. It is apparent, based on comparison of Hoebel's numbered typewritten note cards with Wedel's chronological notes, that Hoebel's notes on the Sun Dance are probably a synthesis of separate interviews. The order of events in Linton (1935) generally follows that of Hoebel's cards. I have not attempted to distinguish those parts of Hoebel's notes based on this interview with Post Oak Jim from the later interviews.

2. See Introduction. There was no eclipse during those years, but there was one on July 29, 1878.

3. That is, an adulterous woman.

4. This is as given. ten Kate (1885) lists "wautcheah-niskera [*wotsia nuhkaru*]" as 'la danse du renard [fox dance]'. Robinson and Armagost (1990) has 'fox' as *waani*, and the Comanche Cultural Committee (2003) glosses *wotsia* as 'snowhair rabbit'. *Wantsi* and *wotsi* are probably survivals of the old Shoshonean pre-nasalization pattern, and/or variant transcriptions of the glottal stops in *waaʔneʔ* (ibid.:144), leading to modern Comanche *waani*.

Medicine: Sun Dance   The fireplace was in front and just south of the doorway of the arbor. It was used to light cigarettes smoked by the dancers during the rest periods; most of the spectators had pipes.

It may have been customary to leave the drums and rattles in the arbor after dances, as did the Kiowas in the above story. Sometimes they made new drums and rattles for the dance, but old ones could be used over again.

The medicine man stayed behind the cedar trees most of time, only came out to speed up the dance.

There was no feast in connection with the dance. People retired to their homes after the dance to eat, then break camp.

The center pole was raised into position with crotched sticks, steadied by hand. The center pole was about twelve inches thick.

Sometimes people prayed to the Sun (Father) as it came up; in the Sun Dance, they prayed to someone above.

There were eight to twelve men in the Sun Dance.

If a visitor exchanged presents for those placed by the center pole by a Comanche, the latter could take the visitor's gift. Articles placed by the center pole were regarded as thrown away.

Kinship Relations: Joking   A man could joke with the wife of any man whom he called brother.

Social Roles: Club Man   The only place the club bearer wielded his club was in enforcing dances. He had to be a brave warrior.

Political Organization: Chiefs: War Leader   (A man who was kind and generous got to be a war leader.)

Social Roles: Club Man   One or two men in each band could carry the club. If there were two club bearers, one usually stood on either side in a dance. They danced also. Between dances, they told of their brave deeds. If the people disbelieved, he swore by the sun and the earth that the deed was true. (The earth was called Mother because we grow up on it. An untruthful man wouldn't live long.)

If a club man died, another succeeded him. His club was hung up in a tree, or else allowed to wash away.

The successor's club was made like that of the deceased. Anyone who knew how could make a club; [it wasn't] made by the club bearer. The *pianʉʔʉpaiʔi* was the big whip.

[An Apache man had a club that was passed on to his brother.[1]]

It was also called a "peace club."

The tribal (or band?) leaders got together in awarding the peace club. They considered likely candidates on the basis of their warlike accomplishments.

The successor was nominated by the leaders. A man could not assume a club on his own responsibility. [Jim didn't know who gave the right to use the club.]

Sometimes they had to wait a long time to fill a vacancy left by the death of the club bearer in the absence of any qualified man.

---

1. This may refer to passing rights to the club, but not the club itself. Chivato's club was significantly different than Pinero's (see fig. 7, p. 479, below).

Deserving persons did not seek this honor, but were sought out. If the *paraibo* had enough honors, he might be a club bearer.

Social Organization: Societies   If a stranger came along and was asked to join a warrior's group, he {they?} couldn't refuse. The warrior then appeared before the people and told what brave deeds he had done to become a member. If the warrior killed an enemy in the absence of witnesses, he had to swear by sun and earth. If the warrior's deed was in battle, other witnesses were called in to testify on the matter.

Dances   No one could be kept out of dances.

Social Organization: Society Dances   Each honorable man had his bunch.

Each group was named after its leader.

In the dance, they would call the leader's name and tell him to round up his "horses." He would come forward and tell his brave deeds.

The announcer would call the names of persons present, and call on them to come out and tell their brave deeds. He said, "Only the eyes of the people are on them, they wouldn't be hurt" [he said, "The people's eyes are on you; don't be afraid of them."] He called on the most notable to be honored.

Kinship Relations: Joking; Social Roles: Club Man   A certain captive had been shot in the right temple and in the knees. He later became a club bearer. It was customary for brave warriors to joke with one another.

At a big dance, the captive leader was in charge. He was going to call on a full blood, a bashful friend of his. The latter, very attractively costumed with shell necklaces, deer roach, etc., stood watching the dance with a lady standing beside him.

The club bearer called out that the dance would soon be over.

He talked about a battle where the Comanches had attacked and made the Mexicans (his own people) run. The Comanches had used lariats, and also lances; when the Mexicans started to run, Misura[1] (the captive), using his spear, made four runs and killed a Mexican each time.

Then he called on the full blood, saying "My sister will tell you the rest." ["Ask my sister over there, wasn't it true?"]

The full blood was terribly disconcerted [because he had been present at the battle]; he told Misura to wait until after the dance. Afterward he ran around, seized the Mexican by the hair and began beating him up playfully. The Mexican said, "Let me loose, dear husband."

These men were not related to each other, but both were great warriors. They were both related to Jim.

There were no jokes of this sort between blood kin.

Two men who would joke thus must stick together in battle or during any crisis. They were closer than brothers. [When two brave men joked, it meant that if they met the enemy, one couldn't run off and leave the other. They have to aid each other in trouble.][2]

1. A man named Misarah, about 60 years old, was listed on the 1892 census as being in Tabeyetchy's Yapainuu local band. He is not listed on any other census, and there is no indication that he was a captive.

2. From Carlson.

Another joking relationship was something different. Women played jokes on their brothers-in-law. Jim's sister-in-law stuck a knife two inches into his instep once, playfully. "There aren't many of them who joke like this."

[A brother-in-law and a sister-in-law joke. The joking between brother-in-law and sister-in-law was just fun, it didn't mean anything. Jim's sister-in-law threw a knife in his instep as a joke. It was pretty rough, though.[1]]

A man would joke with his older sister's husband. Women joked with their older sister's husband. [You joked with your elder brother's wife, or your elder sister's husband.[2]]

Jim's sister-in-law took a twenty-dollar ring away from him and sold it for six dollars. It cost Jim seven dollars to recover it.

If Jim's sister-in-law surprised him talking to another woman, "it was rough on him." [If your sister-in-law saw you talking with another woman, she would pull something on you to punish you.[3]]

In the old times, men gathered and told stories, joked, etc. They never fought like they do today. It was a very serious thing if two Indians got angry with one another.

Story: Origin {Wedel}   There were two Indians at a big double camp; there were two camps. Every night the young men got together to have fun, running races, etc. Sometimes they would divide up and have contests kicking one another. One young Indian kicked another above the stomach. He knocked the breath out of him and he died.

The deceased was the son of a chief of the west camp. There was crying all night in his camp. The east camp was all quiet. The next morning, the boy was buried. Upon their return, the father decided to settle the matter by battle. He told the announcer to announce the battle loudly enough so the other camp could hear. The bereaved father said he loved his son and was going to settle it by war. There were quite a few brave warriors on each side.

The chief of the east camp told his men to get to their horses and prepare for the fight. He told the women and children to prepare for flight.

The hostile warriors from each camp came close together and formed two lines at the center. The chiefs must meet first at the center.

While they waited, a poor man started from the east camp and walked to the center. He stopped and cried. He said it wouldn't be right for them to fight each other. One old man from each side came out and comforted him. He said that the boys had been youngsters only, that they had plenty of enemies to fight, and that a battle could mean only suffering for the children. He asked them to arbitrate.

The chief of west camp said he hadn't known what he was doing, and that he would accept payment. So the old man returned and the east camp paid compensation of horses, blankets, etc., to the father of the slain boy.

The camps decided to separate for a while until their feelings had calmed. Then smallpox arrived. The Comanches split; two parts went west, one part went north, and one part stayed there. The people who went west mixed with Mexicans and now talk their

1. From Carlson.
2. From Carlson.
3. From Carlson.

language. Two groups mixed with Pueblos. The group that went north were the Shoshones, now they call themselves Yapainʉʉ.

Story: Origin {Hoebel}   There was a large camp divided into two groups. Each group had a leader. Every night the young men held games, races, etc.

They were having a kicking game (they kicked each other). One man kicked another over the stomach so hard that he died of it.

The man killed was from the west camp; he was the son of a chief. The west camp cried all night; the east camp was silent. The next day, the boy was buried.

The boy's father had the announcer announce a fight to see which camp was the best to settle the question of his son's death. There was big excitement. There were good warriors on both sides.

The east camp ran for their horses. They were ready to fight: "if they really mean what they say, then kill us."

The two sides lined up. The chiefs met at the center.

An old man from the east camp came into the center and told them that it wasn't right to fight among themselves like this. He cried. They took pity on him. Other old men gathered with him. They said they had plenty of enemies to fight. They were just boys; they shouldn't take it so seriously, it would be a bad example to children. The old men said they would do whatever the chief said to keep the peace (in payment for killing his son).

The chief called it off. The east camp paid the chief of the west camp horses, etc.

The chief had the announcer tell them that it was time to move camp; they had bad luck here, bad feelings.

While they were still there, smallpox broke out. Then they broke up. Two groups went west, and one group went north (Shoshones).

Two groups went west, Mexicans (they lost the language); one went north, Shoshones; one was here, Northern Comanches (Parʉasʉmʉno's group).[1]

War Story: Comanches and Pawnees {Wedel}   Pawnees stole some horses and were pursued by Comanches. There were only a few Comanches on the reservation, so they went west and got their brothers. The Pawnees preferred to travel on foot. When the Comanches caught up with them going west, they had a fire going, cooking a horse maybe. The Pawnees had built a stone wall for protection. The Comanches put on their war costumes and rode down toward the Pawnees. As they approached, the Pawnees shot at them, but couldn't hit them.

A certain captive near the back of the Comanches loped easily along; he wasn't worried. He came up and asked what the trouble was. He was told that the Pawnees were shooting and it was dangerous to attack, so he drove his horse away.

He took his knife and shield and ran down to the Pawnees, crawling over to the wall even though they were shooting at him. Presently, Pawnees could be seen crawling out over the wall. It was on a prairie, and the Comanches ran them down and killed most of them. Two Pawnees escaped by running west and climbing a mountain.

They got back and told their people, who then got it in for the Comanches. The Pawnees united with Osages, Poncas, and Otoes for revenge. They came down the next fall. The

---

1. Wallace and Hoebel 1952:9. The final paragraph is from another card with the same title.

allies came up to the mountains. They used field glasses and finally located smoke. The Comanches and Wichitas were camping together at the time, not expecting any trouble.

A certain young man up on the mountain noticed a dust storm and saw buffalo running, and behind them, he saw people running, quite a bunch of them. The young man hurried down the mountain and told his people that a big bunch of their enemy was coming. The announcer went through the camp and told the people that a fight was coming.

It was now late in the afternoon. They got their horses ready for the fight on the next day. They wanted to fight away from their own camp because of the presence of the women and children. In their excitement, they forgot to notify the Wichitas, who were camping across Otter Creek.

The next day, the Comanches rode out from their camp to meet their enemies, but missed them and circled back to their own camp. They saw fresh manure as they returned. The Wichitas had been attacked in bed, and the allies had done quite a bit of damage to the Wichitas, cutting their throats before they knew what had happened. The allies began drifting across the creek, fighting the Comanches. They were already tired when the returning Comanche warriors came into the camp. They fell upon the allies and killed every one of them.

This was told to Jim by some old folks.

War Story: Comanches and Pawnees {Hoebel}   Pawnees came and drove off Comanche horses when most of the tribe was out west.

The Comanches went west and got their people. They hurried back on the trail. There had been a heavy rain that made tracking easy.

They came upon the Pawnees behind a rock fortification. They were not expecting many Comanches waiting up for them.

The fight started after the Comanches put on their regalia.

A captive came riding down. He said, "let's see if those people are so brave."

He took a long knife from under his shield.

He climbed over the breastworks and chased the Pawnees out alone. The Comanches pursued and killed all but two Pawnees, who got to the mountains. Those two got home and informed their people.

The Pawnees, Poncas, Osages, Caddos, and Otoes planned a next fall revenge.

A young Comanche in the mountains saw a big herd of buffalo. He noticed something shining, Indians! He notified the Comanches.

The crier went through the camp. They did not expect an attack before morning.

The people got ready. The Comanches went out before daybreak to meet the enemy away from camp. They missed them.

The Pawnees struck the Wichitas, who were camped across the creek unaware. They did quite a little damage.

The Comanche horsemen swung about and attacked the rear. They killed all the Pawnees.

Social Control: Murder {Wedel}   A captive and a full blood joked with one another. They were going on a raid together. They came to some plums, pulled off some and threw them at each other. The leader told the boys they must begin to look for a camp site. As they were going along, they stopped for dinner. The captive stopped and fixed his saddle. He asked the boys not to pick on him any more, as they were near enemies and were in a dangerous place. Right after dinner, one of the boys asked the captive, who was still working on his saddle, in a silly way, what he was doing. The captive answered that they should leave him alone.

As they were coming along in the morning, he had nearly speared one of the other boys who joked with him, threatening to kill someone if they didn't leave him alone.

One of the boys threw a knife and just missed him. The captive picked up a bow and an arrow, advanced close to the knife-thrower, gave a war whoop, and shot, the arrow lodging just over his heart. The captive tried to draw out the arrow, but couldn't. The boy pulled a six-shooter and shot the captive in the hip. He was going to shoot again, but he was dying and missed, shooting into the air.

The brother of the full blood got his gun. He missed the captive the first time, but shot him in the head on.the second shot. They left the captive lying there. Jim's father was on the party. They wrapped the full blood in a blanket. They took him back to a canyon and put him in a crevice. The captive's clothes had caught fire somehow, and he was left burning.

The captive and his victim had thrown plums, etc. at each other during the morning.

The captive couldn't get any help; even his captors couldn't protect him because the full bloods were influential people and brave warriors. The dead full blood already had a brave deed to his credit. The leader of the party decided to turn back after this trouble, not to go on.

Social Control: Murder {Hoebel}   A captive, Po'saraibo,[1] and a full blood, Sokonumu,[2] were in joking play. They were out on a raid. They picked plums and threw them at one another.

The leader told them to go ahead to seek a camp site.

The party stopped for noon. The captive was fixing his saddle. One teased him. He said, "Don't do that here, this is a dangerous place. The enemy is near."

After lunch, he was still working on his saddle. One of them came along and teasingly asked what he was doing.

The captive said, "I'll kill one of you fellows, if you don't take care. I ran a spear through the blanket of one of those fellows this morning."

One of the boys threw a knife at him. The captive took up a bow and his single arrow and shot the fellow (war whoop) coming towards him in the heart.

The captive tried to pull the arrow out, but the point came off.

The wounded man pulled his six-shooter and shot the captive in the hip. The second shot was in the air. He died. The captive ran off.

Someone told the dead man's brother. He took a gun and shot twice, hitting the captive in the back of his head.

Jim's father said, "The best thing to do is to drop him in the canyon we came through."

They left the captive, laying a fire on the plains.

The captive got no help from his captors. The Indian he killed was quite a brave warrior. The leader turned the party back.

---

1. Probably *po'sa* 'crazy', *taibo* 'man'. He is otherwise unidentified.
2. Possibly *soko* 'land', *numu* 'Comanche'. He is otherwise unidentified.

Social Control: Disputes   Most troubles arose over women misbehaving. Men talked roughly to each other, but they didn't often come out and fight.

War   Young men didn't vow to kill an enemy or not return from their first raid.

Story: Fox and the Young Girls {Wedel}   Some young girls were playing in creek sand, and Fox came to them. The girls began to plan what they should do. They finally decided to make a cradle for him and fasten him in it.

They made a cradle and fastened him in it. They set him up against a tree.

The girls decided to play at married life. One would be the father, another would be the mother, and Fox would be the baby. So they built tipis.

They named Fox Tsiʔtsi.[1] Each night a girl took care of him. Finally, one girl noticed that Fox looked like a grown person in the face.

Story: Fox and the Young Girls {Hoebel}   Girls were playing in the creekbed. Fox appeared. The girls decided what to do. They made a cradle and fastened Fox in it.

The girls played "married folks," one father, one mother, Fox was to be their baby.

They made a play tipi. They named the baby Tsiʔisi.

At night, one girl, caring for the baby (Fox), said, "Why Tsiʔisi, you look a like a grown person."

Fox got out of his cradle.

Story: Fox and Meat {Wedel}   The people were camped at a certain place; they were nearly starving. Something appeared and told them it would bring them something to eat.

Dried Meat, with plenty of fat, came blowing along. Fox, who was gaunt and lean and had escaped from the children's cradle, was the first to meet the roll of Dried Meat.

Dried Meat took pity on Fox and said, "I'll give you four bites, there are many other people who I must feed."

Fox took four bites, then said, "As you go south, you'll meet many more people hungrier than I am, maybe lying down."

As soon as Dried Meat was gone, Fox ran around the hill and lay down, thin and panting, with his belly drawn in. Dried Meat came along, and pitying Fox, gave him four big mouthfuls.

As soon as Dried Meat was gone, Fox ran around ahead and lay down. He tried to draw in his stomach to appear skinny, but couldn't. Dried Meat asked him to get up, and gave him four more big mouthfuls.

Fox went around again. Dried Meat called to him and said it wanted to see his teeth. Fox showed his teeth, with meat and fat still clinging to them.

Dried Meat accordingly rolled on into the creek. He made it very greasy and looking like soup. Fox went to look for a rawhide to skim out the soup.

Meanwhile, Bobcat came along and scooped up the fat and, eating it, he splattered himself: that's how Bobcat got his markings.

When Bobcat was through, Fox returned with a dry hide. Bobcat asked him whether he was going to sole his shoes with it or not. Fox announced it was to skim off the fat. Then he saw that the fat was gone. He asked Bobcat what he had done. Bobcat said, "I ate it."

So Fox got left.

---

1. Possibly from *tseena* 'fox'.

Story: Fox and Meat {Hoebel}   It was summer and there was not much meat supply. They received news that soon food would come. They looked and saw to the south something coming (being blown by the wind). It was Dried Meat coming.

Fox (he got out of the cradle) was the first to meet the meat.

Meat told Fox that he can have four bites (there were plenty of people hungry).

Fox swallowed meat before he chewed it. He told Meat that there were people starving.

Fox then ran ahead and got down in front of Meat. He lay down, breathing hard, and with his stomach all drawn in.

The roll of Meat came over the hill and saw Fox so starved, he gave him four more bites.

This was repeated. Fox had trouble holding his stomach in to look starved; he was too full.

Meat was coming along. He said, "Get up!"

Fox could barely get up. He got four more bites.

On the fourth time Meat came, he said he'd like to see Fox's teeth. He saw meat on his teeth and went on.

Meat went on and fell into water. That made the water greasy.

Fox came and wanted the grease. He went for a hide.

Bobcat came and got the grease in his paws (on his fur; that's what made his fur spotted).

Fox came back with his hide. Bobcat said, "What are you going to do with that, make shoes?"

Fox said he was going to skim the grease off the water. Then he looked and saw it was gone. Fox asked Bobcat, "What did you do with it?"

Bobcat said, "I ate it."

That's how Fox got left.

Cosmology: Star Lore   Herman Asenap knew of no instance of anyone shooting at stars.

Kinship Relations: Affines   When a girl got married, her mother helped her fix a tipi. Her brother and her husband got the hides.

A son-in-law was treated like a son. A husband's parents did things for their daughter-in-law, but not so much.

POST OAK JIM
July 18, 1933

Dances: Ghost Dance {Wedel}   The Indians here didn't really know what it meant; it was brought in from the north.

Many Comanches joined because the organization said that all of their deceased would return if they joined.

Each person had to have the medicine; they had to paint their faces and bodies with brown, earthy paint, and also inhale some of the paint mixed with medicine. Thus, they became a member.

The dancers moved circularly in a clockwise direction, with their hands interlocking.[1]

Anyone could join the dance, but only members were affected. The inhaled medicine had some certain effect. Pretty soon, they began to grunt, and after a while they passed out. It soon developed that some of these people were putting it on.

The dance came first to the Kiowas, Wichitas, and Caddos, then to the Noyʉhka band.

Ahpeatone,[2] a Kiowa, went to visit the northern tribes in search of the Ghost Dance. He became chief after his return.[3]

There was no fixed date for the rising of the dead.

The whites were not to be wiped out.

The dance took up too much time among the Noyʉhka. People were worried and didn't tend to business. It did more harm than good.

The inhaling medicine was brought down from the north.

When the Ghost Dance reached the Noyʉhka, it spread south through the Comanches. A dance was held in this community two miles south and one-half mile east of Jim's; another was held east of Niyah's.[4]

A woman brought the dance into this country.

The dance worked on the minds and systems of participants, so it was gradually given up. The dancers, when they collapsed, dreamed of the dead and talked to them. The dance didn't do anyone any good. If it had, it wouldn't have been given up.

Dances: Ghost Dance {Hoebel}   It was originated by a Paiute. It came through the Kiowas, Wichitas, etc., to the Noyʉhka.

Comanches didn't really understand what it meant. Quite a few Comanches joined before they understood what it was. They were told that it would bring back all the old people who had died.

They had a medicine paint initiation. Red-brown earth was smeared on the face and body. They inhaled this paint. This was a mark of membership.

They danced in the round dance style, holding hands.

The dance and the medicine were intoxicating. Soon they staggered around, breathing heavily, gasping, and fell to the ground.

It was revealed later that some people were putting it on.

1. See Mooney 1896:920.

2. Wooden Lance. This is the agency spelling. Mooney (1898) spells it several ways, varying in the diacritical markings, but mostly as Aʹpiatañ.

3. After Ahpeatone's negative report about his trip to see Wovoka, the Ghost Dance prophet (Mooney 1898:221), he was given some sort of "chief's' certificate." Its exact nature is unclear, but on the basis of that certificate, Ahpeatone attained a certain authority in Kiowa-Comanche-Apache politics. In 1914, Agent Ernest Stecker, replying to a demand by Kiowa Bill for a new council, stated, "As far as Ahpeatone, you cannot remove him by vote. He was appointed by the Commissioner . . . and nobody can remove him except the Commissioner" (Stecker 1914).

4. If this refer to allotments, Jim's allotment was south of Indiahoma, while Niyah's was to the far south and west of Walters. These dance locations contradict Mooney: "The Messiah doctrine never gained many converts among the Comanche, except those of the Penateka division and a few others living on the Little Washita and other streams on the northern boundary of the reservation" (1896:901). They also contradict Wallace and Hoebel, which echoes Mooney: "Almost the only Comanches to become converts to the new Ghost Dance religion were the Wasps and a few others on the northern edge of the reservation" (1952:345).

Ahpeatone, a Kiowa, went as a delegate to the prophet. He was later a chief. No Comanches went, however.

It caused quite a bit of trouble among the Noyʉhka, not with the government. It worked on their minds, and they forgot everything but dancing. "Some of them just went around crying, worried."

Infusion: It drifted in from the north. Dances were held north of Cache in the timber up west of Post Oak.[1] It was brought to this district by a woman. "It sounded so nice they couldn't resist. The medicine was prepared in the north."

Finally, they got scared of it. It worked on their minds.

They would see the dead in their catatonic faints.

The Ghost Dance came though the Kiowas and Caddos and Wichitas to the Comanches (Noyʉhka). "Just like a wind blowing, it blew right through the tribes of Indians."[2]

Story: Loco Weed   A certain weed grew out west that was very dangerous to stock. It was a gray weed growing in bunches, with red and white flowers, *esitariwʉ* "loco weed."[3] It was the source of the medicine in the Ghost Dance.

[Jim thought loco weed might have been mixed in the medicine (*esitariwʉ*). It grew to the west of the Comanches. It was habit-forming to stock. Jim saw a blind steer with its head twisted, its mouth slobbering, while hunting.]

At a certain camp out west where Indians were hunting deer, there was another camp, up on a hill on the Salt Fork. Early one morning, they saw a big steer coming straight for the camp. It was not turning aside, but its head was twisted to one side and it was slobbering.

Dogs began to bark and to chase it. The steer ran into the bluff as though it was blind, then fell into the creek, crossed, and got out on the other bank. It blundered through the cottonwood brush, unseeing. They thought it finally died. Some of the people were afraid, and ran and hid under the bluff. Jim thought this weed might have caused the trouble.

Animals: Coyotes: Mad Coyotes/Mad Dogs   Mad coyotes were more dangerous than mad dogs [usually during mating season, when they fought each other (males)]; there were many of both in the old days.

Animals: Skunk   A skunk once came into Jim's tipi smelling meat. It got under his covers while he was asleep. He thought it was a cat so he gave it a kick. The skunk bit him on the leg, so he got up and threw it into the fire.

Animals: Dogs: Mad Dogs   A mad dog bite was cured by coyote medicine, but if a medicine man was not near, the victim often died.

In the old days, if a dog bit someone, the dog was disposed of so he wouldn't bite anyone else. Ordinarily, if a victim killed a biting dog, nothing was said, but if the dog was a valuable animal or had belonged to a deceased member of the family, something might be done.[4]

Small dogs were sometimes carried by women on horseback when moving.

1. Probably referring to Post Oak Jim's allotment; see previous note.
2. These last two sentences are from a separate note card titled "Diffusion."
3. According to Robinson and Armagost (1990), 'loco weed' is *esinʉʉparabi*.
4. Hoebel 1940:119.

Dogs were sometimes used to kill wild turkeys. They were trained not to eat them. They hung around outside the tipi and waited for slop. They were watchdogs.

[There were ten dogs at Jim's house; they weren't considered very valuable or important. They were often given away to friends or relatives, and if a person died, sometimes they were killed.]

Jim's dogs located snakes when he was rounding up horses, etc., so he could kill them.

One of Jim's dogs nursed him while he was a small child. [It watched over him and was sad when Jim got into trouble. The family had a dog who would go from camp to camp.]

Before the reservation days, Jim's uncle had a bobtailed dog called *wasape* 'bear'. Jim's parents camped apart from the uncle, and the dog visited back and forth between the camps. The dog would stay around when rations were issued. Everyone about Anadarko knew the dog; it was a good sized animal. He liked to lie about where people were gathered.

One day, a warrior goosed the dog with a stick. The dog knocked the warrior down, then stood over him growling. But he never bit anyone.

Old dogs died with sores on their ears and back. Dogs were not often killed unless one had to.

Food: Dogs   [They never ate dog meat.]

Horses: Racehorses   Injured racehorses were usually killed.

Animals: Dogs   They didn't kill dogs because such a deed might cause the death of children or other members of the family, or bring other bad luck.[1] [They sometimes killed dogs in old age, but not often.] Jim was fond of dogs as a child, but since he grew up, he did not care for them; he felt they brought him bad luck. [Jim killed one after he was married. Since then, his life hasn't gone so well.]

Dogs were frequently given names. Makwitspai [Makutsrai][2] had a ration ticket and was drawing government supplies. The name was thought by the agents to be that of an Indian.[3]

Hunting: Coyotes   Coyotes were killed for fur. If they wanted many hides at once, Indians would dig a large deep pit from which coyotes could not jump out. They placed beef lung or other bait [guts] in the pit. They burned fat outside the pit so the smell would lure the coyotes. When they came, they would jump into the pit for the bait. Sometimes ten or twelve coyotes would be caught at once. They might get on each other's backs and escape. [They also chased them with horses.]

Hunting: Traps   The trigger gun (*nakihtura?*[4]) was used, with beef as bait. *tseenahauru?*[5] was the pit trap.

Hunting: Wolves   Lobos were hunted on horseback. They couldn't run very fast, but they were usually gotten with trigger guns.

---

1. Hoebel 1940:119.

2. Hoebel (1940:119) has 'Mákkutavai'. Robinson and Armagost (1990) notes that Makutabai was a "dog hero (notorious in stories)."

3. There are no such names on any of the censuses. The closest is the name Mahkersey, a female in Pahighpeop's Kuhtsutuhka local band, 1885–95.

4. *naki* 'ear', *tura* 'pop'.

5. *tseena* 'fox', *huaru?* 'trap'.

Beliefs: Horses: Coyotes   There was a belief that if a coyote [chased on horseback] wasn't caught, the horse would become lame; conversely, if they did catch the coyote, the horse would become a good racehorse.

Hunting: Eagles   Eagles were sometimes choked. [Eagles can't swallow during the day without bringing bad luck.]

If men saw an eagle in a tree, it might drop to the ground and they could get it.

In winter, eagles were sometimes caught when sleet on their wings made it impossible for them to fly.

Animals: Birds   Smaller birds, such as hawks, were trapped; eagles were not. Hawks were snared with horse hair loops. Fresh meat was surrounded by stobs {stakes} and when the hawk walked around it, he would get tangled in the loops.

Animals: Birds: Eagles   Eagles usually had two young, one white and one black.

Jim once went eagle hunting with an army officer. They located a large eyrie on the face of a cliff. They shot at the birds flying over them. They wondered how to get down to the nest.

Marksmanship   Jim shot at a man who was stealing wood, at 500 yards. He missed.

Animals: Birds: Eagles   The army officer wanted the young eagles, so he {Jim} removed his shoes, coat, and hat, and fastened a rope about his waist. Securing it to a cedar at the top of the cliff, he started down. When he reached the nest, he turned around and grasped a young bird by the wing in each hand. The flapping of the bird's wings seemed to help him get back up. Later it was put in a park.

If a man's intention was good, no harm would come from robbing an eagle's nest. Eagles didn't want anyone to walk behind them while eating, so they ate back to back. [Nobody could go behind an eagle while it was eating. The eagles Jim captured for Fort Sill finally got to eating with their backs together to avoid this.][1]

Medicine: Sun Dance   There was no medicine doll or hereditary sponsorship of the Sun Dance.

Medicine: Curing: Tuberculosis {Wedel}   The sweat house was not used for tuberculosis victims.

In the old days, they had a cure for tuberculosis if it was not too far advanced. It was an herb medicine but something else went with it.

Jim's father had a cure. He built a special tipi. The patient washed before entering, dressed in white, clean clothes. The doctor was similarly dressed and washed. The doctor took the patient into the tipi early in the morning. He made the herb tea and gave it to the patient to drink.

Every time he gave the medicine, he went to the medicine lodge. If the disease was caught in time, it could be cured. The patient stayed at least two days; two days was the limit for a doctor. If there were signs of improvement, there might be two days more later.

Some of the tea was put on the patient's hands and again <u>rubbed</u> over his body, then he faced the sun and was <u>rubbed again</u> over his body. There were three treatments daily: in the morning, the patient faced east; at noon, south; in the evening, west—always toward the sun.

1. Wallace and Hoebel 1952:159.

Tuberculosis was regarded as contagious. If a person died, other persons of the same family sometimes died too. They knew this from actual experience.

In any sickness, the patient was isolated, used separate dishes, etc.

Medicine: Curing: Tuberculosis {Hoebel}   First, there was the Beaver Dance.

The medicine man and the patient went to a special tipi away from the camp. They took a bath (the patient and the medicine man). They put on clean white clothes (the patient and the doctor).

They boiled herbs and made a tea. The patient drank it (done early in the morning).

They treated early, before the disease had gotten far. Later, it was incurable.

The medicine man put tea on his hand and rubbed {the patient's} head and chest.

The treatment lasted two days. If the patient improved, they might have two more days later.

The patient faced the sun for each treatment (in the morning, to the Sun; at noon, to the south; in the evening, to the west).

At the end, they bathed again.

Tuberculosis was thought to be catching, because when one member of a family died of it, frequently others did too.

Medicine: Curing: Smallpox   There was no medicine to prevent smallpox [to avoid the spread of smallpox. There was medicine to make the case light.] Prairie dog fat was smeared over the body to make the pox disappear.

Medicine: Curing: Peyote   Peyote juice, ⟨patarub⟩, ([dry] peyote was soaked in water to make tea) was drunk and rubbed over the body.

Economy: Hunting: Prairie Dogs   Prairie dogs were shot with bows and arrows. Sometimes they were drowned out with water. Rarely were they snared with horsehair loops. That was difficult because of the shape of their bodies.

Animals: Insects: Dragonflies   Dragonflies were lassoed with horse [tail] hair snares put on sticks [with a loop at the end of it. They were roped by the wings.] They were lassoed for sport only.

Wild Horse had their power to dodge bullets. He had a beaded dragonfly on either shoulder as an epaulet (?) and a cross (conventionalized dragonfly[1]) painted on his chest, also a necklace.

Medicine: Sulfur   [Sulfur was protection against bullets. One could be shot at all day and never be hit.]

They burned sulfur, fanned it with a black- and red-bordered kerchief. A ball was made from the wadded kerchief. A man could shoot at the kerchief with a pistol and afterward couldn't see where it had been hit.

Sulfur was gotten as exudings from volcanos, somewhere [in the west] in Mexico. (?)

[The Comanches didn't know what it was. They thought it was medicine because it breathed.]

A yellow horse allowed to breathe some sulfur was then rubbed all over four times; it was no use shooting at such a horse, you couldn't hit it, or if you did hit it, the bullet did not penetrate.

---

1. Comment probably by Linton.

Men were also rubbed thus. You could shoot all day at such a man and not hurt him. [If a man had it on when another wanted to harm him, that fellow would turn around and forget to make it.]

Medicine: Herbs   Comanches got many herbs from Mexicans.

Relations with Other Tribes: Pawnees, Utes, Navajos   Pawnees never hollered for help when fighting. Utes and Navajos hollered for help every time.

Names: Naming {Wedel}   At the birth of a child, the people looked for names. An honorable warrior must christen it to give it long life.

Post Oak Jim, when given a name, was restless all night and wouldn't sleep. The next day, he was taken to another warrior, who said that the deed after which he was named was untrue. (The first man could do nothing to the warrior who had done more deeds.) He told them to come back the next morning for a new name.

His grandmother took him in her arms. She walked around the warrior's tipi clockwise. The medicine man was inside the tipi, putting on his costume like he was going to battle. He came out with spear and told Jim's grandmother to stand a little south of, and outside, the door of the tipi.

The sun was just rising. The medicine man called upon the Sun, Earth, Eagle, etc., to bear witness that what he said was true.

He told how had met enemies on a hill. He was poor at the time, he had a poor horse and was the last to arrive on the scene. Other Comanches hadn't done anything and were retreating.

He asked his friends what they had done. They said, "Nothing, because the enemies were dangerous."

So he used his spear on one enemy.

When they returned, they gave the victory dance.

Towoibita[1] means "a bunch of people standing." Jim was named after this incident.[2]

The Medicine man dabbed black paint on Jim's cheeks.

He made motions as if spearing to remind the Sun of the deed.

If a young man was sickly, he might be given a name at any time to make him stronger.[3]

Names: Naming {Hoebel}   Jim's mother and father took him to a warrior for a name.

Jim was restless; he cried all night. His parents took him to another brave to find out what was wrong.

He told them the deed was false. The other man could do nothing; he hadn't sufficient war deeds.

They asked him for another name.

He circled the tipi. He said he couldn't give it then, they should come back in the morning.

His grandmother took Jim down. The medicine man said, "Don't come in, look to the rising sun."

1. In Robinson and Armagost (1990), 'stand' is *tobo^ʔikayʉ*.
2. Wallace and Hoebel 1952:122.
3. Wallace and Hoebel 1952:121(?).

He fixed himself up in his war regalia and came out with his spear, just as the sun was coming up.

He went south and east of the tipi, and spoke to the Sun: "You, Sun, you can't do anything to me. This thing I did was true. Earth has seen me. The Big Bird (eagle) has seen me. You can't dispute my word."

The medicine man then recalled his deed.

He saw the enemy on a hill. The braves outstripped the warrior who named him (his horse was slow because the man was poor). He came up to the battle, the last arrival. The warriors there did nothing. He asked, "How goes it?"

They told him the enemy was too strong and brave.

He rode in and killed a man with his spear. He got a victory dance for that.

He turned around and went back.

Jim's grandmother was holding him in her arms when he named him *toboibita* "Group of Men Standing on a Hill."

Names: Naming {Wedel}   Once a little girl was sick with high fever; she was very sick in bed. A medicine man tried but failed to help her. The girl's grandfather met Jim and asked him to try. He said he had no money, but promised to pay ten dollars when he did have some.

On the second day, the child was better; she smiled at Jim, which she had never done.

Jim went out to the arbor to rest. A man who had never seen the child came and told Jim the child looked bad, so Jim went into the house. The child's mother said it was much better.

Jim chewed peyote. The next day when Jim returned, the child was playing in the tipi and was well.

Later, when Jim was in Lawton,[1] the child's grandfather came up to him and gave the ten dollars and said the child was well.

When he came home, Jim went to a peyote meeting and told of curing the child. Then, the idea for a name came, even though the child was absent. He named it Makwitso?aitʉ, which meant 'saved something'.[2]

Naming: Names {Hoebel}   Once a little girl had a high fever (at Walters[3]). A medicine man tried and failed. Her grandfather met Jim. He said he had no money, but he would give Jim ten dollars any time he could.

Jim doctored.

The next day {when} he came, the child looked better and smiled.

---

1. Lawton was not founded until 1901, six years after the last census mention of the girl (see next note).

2. Robinson and Armagost (1990) gives *makwitso?aitʉ* as 'save someone, rescue, prevent death.' A girl, Mahquitsowitebitten (-*pitʉnʉ* 'arrive') is listed on the 1889, 1892, and 1895 censuses (born about 1883) as the daughter of Patchokotohovit (Black Otter) and Tovah (no translation given), members of Coby's and Tooahvonie's Kwaharʉnʉʉ local bands. Tovah was herself a daughter of Coby, and thus, Jim's sister-in-law, and the girl, his niece.

3. This reference is unclear. Although Comanches had been living along the southern Cache Creek vicinity for some time (Kavanagh 1989:103), the town of Walters was not founded until 1901, six years after the last census mention of the girl. Moreover, Patchokotohovit's own allotment was in the west, near Cache.

Jim went out to the arbor to rest.

A man came and told Jim that he didn't think the child looked good.

Jim went back. He chewed peyote and gave it to her.

The next morning the child was playing.

Later, the grandfather met Jim in Lawton and gave him ten dollars.

When Jim got home, there was a peyote meeting. Jim was telling them what he did. It occurred to him to name the girl. He called her Makwitso'aitʉ, 'saved somebody'.

Names   The medicine man told the announcer that a person had been given a new name because he hadn't been happy under the old name. The announcer then told the village. But you could call the person by the old name and no harm was done.

P.M.

Omens: Raven {Wedel}   Raven brought good news to the people, telling them there was a big bunch of buffalo nearby. Raven was hungry and wanted something to eat, hence he told the people.

Omens: Raven {Hoebel}   Raven always followed bison to eat off the bugs. It would circle over the camp four times higher up, craning and dipping its head. It was telling the Indians where the herd was; it would fly off and show the way.

A raven making noise meant that buffalo were in the vicinity. It meant that he was hungry and wanted carrion food.

Omens: Coyote {Wedel}   Coyotes sometimes barked near a house; they brought bad news.

Omens: Coyote {Hoebel}   When coyotes came close to a tipi, it meant they were bringing news. Some people could understand them.

A war party stopped at sundown for its night camp. They ate some peyote to forestall trouble; they had a regular meeting. At the midnight pause, they heard a coyote. It said, "Today, one of your people took a shot at me; he knocked out a toe. Now, I can't walk. I can't get food. You must feed me."

Not long after, they heard another coyote. It said, "Some soldiers who went by here wounded me. I am on their trail. You must feed me and I will be your scout." The leader told the cook to put food on the east and west side of the tent. They started the meeting again. Pow! Then came lightning and a big rain. The cook had a special tent. He got all wet.

Omens: Black Cat   A black cat meant bad luck. One once crossed before Jim and his wife when they were going on a visit. It followed them and finally jumped on a gate post in front of them and meowed. Jim took a club and knocked it off and it ran away.

On the way home after the visit, his wife stooped to pick up some sunflower stalks for kindling and was seized by a fit of chills. She had bad chills for four years before finally dying.

Another time, Jim and a companion were walking at night and heard a cat calling, as though starving. Finally, they found the cat dead, very lean. Later, Jim's companion died of tuberculosis; the cat had forecast his death.

Medicine: Foretelling {Wedel}   A certain war party was gone a long time. The people asked a medicine man to find out about them.

A special tipi was placed on the west side of camp.

The medicine man wanted a fire built in the tipi at about eleven o'clock at night.

He had seven selected men to accompany him. They went in about midnight, smoked, and the men told the medicine man what they wanted. They told him to bring in a night prowler (a ghost) to tell them what had become of the war party.

After everyone in camp was abed, they went into the special tipi and became quiet. The leader advised the fire tender to put the fire out with ashes, then to go outside and close the "ears" of the tipi. The medicine man covered himself with a robe and went outside, away from the tipi, and made a wailing noise. Presently, he heard an answer. He called again, then got a second answer. He called and got third and a fourth answer.

At the fourth answer, the medicine man returned to the tipi. He went in, sat down, and covered himself. He told the others to be quiet, the ghost was coming. Then the ghost flew up like a bird; it made a rushing sound, like wings. He lighted on one of the poles. The medicine man talked to the bird from inside. He told the bird what they wanted to know about the war party. The bird answered in falsetto (ventril[1]) that they were killed.

After that answer was received, they brought up another question. A puny man was present, and they asked how long he would live. The bird replied that he would die in the fall.

They asked the bird who and what he was. The ghost was of a powerful, evil medicine man who had died of tuberculosis.

After awhile, one man went out to open the "ears." He then came in and started the fire. Then they heard the bird flying away and making the same sound as when he approached.

Medicine: Foretelling {Hoebel}   A war party was gone for a long time. They cleaned up a pleasant place on the ground for a special tipi on the west side of the camp. They selected about seven special men to go in the tipi with him (the medicine man).

He told the camp to be quiet.

He had a fire built.

They went in before midnight.

They smoked and told him what they wanted.

The medicine man told the fire tender to put out the fire, and to go out and close the wind vent.

The medicine man put on a blanket and went off some ways. He made a call. An answer came back one time. On the second time, it was closer; a third time; a fourth time.

He went back into the tipi. He sat down and told all to be quiet, a ghost was coming; it was his call that was heard.

The ghost, in the form of a bird, lit on the top of the tipi. They could tell that it was heavy.

The medicine man talked from inside the tipi, "What we want to know is what became of those people on the war party. You are wonderful. You know everything."

The answer came in a strong voice, "They are killed."

Then they asked if the sickly man with them would get well.

Answer: "You will die in the fall."

They asked the bird who he was.

---

1. Ventriloquism?

After a while, one went out to open the flaps of the tipi and came back in to light the fire.

They could hear the ghost calling as he went away. The bird was the spirit of a medicine man who had died of tuberculosis. He had used evil medicine.[1]

Beliefs: Ghosts   Medicine men's ghosts alone could return.

Ghosts prowled at night. Timid persons might be frightened thereby.

Paralytic strokes were caused by meeting a ghost.[2] They were only dangerous on dark nights and were invisible at short range. At a distance, they might look black or white.

Sometimes one saw only a light there.

Animals: Owl   One kind of owl (Great Horned?) made a noise just like a ghost.

Beliefs: Ghosts   Jim believed that if one whistled at night, ghosts would come.

Story: Ghosts: Phantom Campers   There was a camp at certain place. Late at night, the people heard a noise coming. It sounded like tipi poles dragging, women talking, etc. They knew there were people moving down to their camp. They didn't come into the camp, but set up their tipis southeast of the village. They could hear sounds of stobs {stakes} being hammered.

Presently, someone came and asked for a kettle, then for coals to start a fire. They were told through the tipi wall where to get these things. The next morning, they went over to visit the new camp and found kettles, coals, and old stobs, but no camp. They guessed they were ghosts of people who had been killed in a camp there several years before.

Story: Ghosts: Phantom Hunters   A single warrior returning saw some buffalo sitting in a hollow where there were mesquite trees. Northeast of them, he saw a person's head sticking out. At the same time, this latter person rode out, beckoning his companions to follow him. They stopped and changed to their buffalo horses; the warrior was always watching them.

The buffalo saw the new arrivals; they got up, and looked. Then they rode in and began killing the buffalo. One buffalo ran up the hill and was killed by two men near the warrior. They put it on its back.

The latter went down to eat with them. He asked the men who were skinning the animal where their village was, etc. He looked up at the sun; it was late in the afternoon. When he looked back, all the people and the buffalo were gone.

People often saw ghosts in that neighborhood.

Story: Ghosts: Phantom Soldiers   Some warriors were setting out on a war party. Near the scene of the preceding story, they saw a spring and decided to camp for dinner [late lunch]. The horses were loosened. After dinner, the men were sitting around resting. It was getting along toward sundown.

One of the party spoke up, saying there was some danger near. They got up quickly and ran to their horses. They could see what looked like soldiers on gray horses coming toward them. As soon as the soldiers were in sight, the warriors ran to a hill, near Salt Fork, in some timber. They left much of their belongings behind. They looked back from the hill,

1. Wallace and Hoebel 1952:172.
2. See Jones 1972:85–90.

but saw nothing following them. They stayed there all night with their horses tied nearby, but they saw nothing all night.

They got up early and sneaked around through the creek to the spring. They saw everything just as they had left it. They couldn't find any tracks of the soldiers either.

Many Kwaharʉ had been killed there by soldiers before that, and it was probably the soldier's ghosts returning to the scene of the battle.

All ghost events were in the country where big battles had taken place.

Story: Lost Stirrup {Wedel}   Two boys were going on a war party alone. They stopped to camp not very far away, not in dangerous country. They ate a late supper and went to bed.

The buffalo smelled the boys and came down and surrounded them. A big buffalo bull stepped into the stirrup of one saddle; he got his hoof through it, and dragged the saddle away. The more he ran to get away, the worse he was scared. Finally, he tore off the saddle and galloped away with just the stirrup. The boys found the saddle the next day, all torn and battered, minus a stirrup.

The boys went on and finally came back home. They told what the buffalo had done to them. The next fall, another party of warriors passed through the same place. While going by the river, they saw some buffalo sitting there. They stopped to camp and decided to get a buffalo for fresh meat. There were all bulls. They got right up to the buffalo before it could see them. Two Indians shot one bull and drove him, wounded, toward the camp. Finally, he laid down and died. They started to skin it, calling to the others to bring knives and help them. One of the men found the lost stirrup on one leg of the bull, all worn slick inside. They unjointed the leg and removed the stirrup.

Story: Lost Stirrup {Hoebel}   Two boys went on a raid. They traveled all day and made camp and went to bed. At night, some buffalo smelled them; the buffalo came and smelled around, saddles, blankets, etc. One big buffalo bull got his hoof in a stirrup when he stepped on a saddle. It got stuck. He ran and caused a stampede.

The buffalo bull ran, dragging the saddle until it fell off. The saddle got smashed and the stirrup stayed on his foot.

The boys came out the next day and found their saddle thus. They went on anyways.

On their return, they told the story to their people.

The next fall, another war party going through this same place located some buffalo by this river. They needed meat and decided to kill a buffalo.

Those two boys were along. They went out to shoot buffalo.

The buffalo ran away, sat down, and died.

They skinned it, and they found their stirrup on the buffalo's leg.

Material Culture: Horses: Stirrups   Stirrups were made of willow, greased, heated, and bent into shape. The lower portion was the heaviest. Sinew was wrapped at the top. A strip of rawhide was passed around the stirrup, and the edges sewn together.[1]

Material Culture: Horses: Saddles   Saddles were made of two wooden forks to fit the horse's back, covered on each side with a leather strip.

1. Wallace and Hoebel 1952:97.

The woman's saddle was deeper with projecting pieces, the man's had a straight front and back. Women's saddles were decorated with brass-headed tacks and fringes.[1] *wa'ihpɨ'narɨnoo'* was the women's saddle.

narɨnoo' were men's saddles of elk horn.

pika[2] was the piece of hide on either side of the horse, fastened by straps near either end. A blanket was thrown over it for riding; there were no stirrups or girth.

piksikarɨ was riding a horse back on its hips. It was the only way to heal a saddle-sore horse.[3]

Horses   A colt's ears were sometimes cut off short and the tail trimmed to the bone (a docked tail was called was *kwasi*[4]). This was done by young men to attract attention and to make people laugh.

Kinship Relations: Joking   A man would cover up with a blanket so as not to be recognizable, then he would ride to the creek and chase the women in fun. They would throw sand at him.

Games: Boys Horsing Around   When camp was being set up, boys would ride ahead and locate the watering hole.[5] They made lariats out of some climbing weed and would rope the colts when a man brought his herd down to water them. Then they rode off on these for a while.

Boys very early became good riders.

[Twenty-five or thirty] boys would steal saddle straps to use as bridles from the camp. They would go out a ways and run races at night on good racehorses. If someone came out to check up on them, they simply scattered. Sometimes this deterred would-be horse stealers.

[They began to ride as soon as they could walk.]

At about seventeen to eighteen years of age, they gave up this sort of playfulness and began paying attention to girls.

Boys and young people played together while young, they played in sand, built arbors, etc.

Games: Children's Games: Bear Game   They made a hill of sand to represent sugar. One boy laid face down on his arms and was dragged around the hill by his legs by two other boys to make a circle about the mound. The bear then chased the other children. If he got one inside the circle, he would tickle them. Children lined up behind the largest, who was the mother, who must protect them against the bear. They dodged back and forth, their hands on the shoulders of those in front, trying to get the sugar. The bear must protect the sugar and, at the same time, try to catch a child and tickle it.[6]

Games: Guessing Games   Thirty or forty children sat in a row, their feet all in the same direction. The children all said, "*nɨe, nɨe, nɨe*," "me, me, me," when the man came. The man felt at their feet and picked one out. He then turned his back and carried the child

---

1. Wallace and Hoebel 1952:96 (?).
2. Robinson and Armagost (1990) defines *pika* simply as 'leather'.
3. Hoebel 1940:120.
4. Literally, 'tail'.
5. Wallace and Hoebel 1952:128.
6. Wallace and Hoebel 1952:129.

away on his back, head down. He carried the child around and returned to the line. Each child asked him a question:

"What have you got?"

"Have you got horses?"

"Suspenders?", etc.

The man always answered, "Yes."

When tired of asking questions, one child said, "We'll eat him."

Then they all attacked the man, pulled the child off his back, and tickled it.[1]

Children generally played alone, without adults.

Games: Guessing Games   Two older boys got up the game. They went to the top of a hill where one was stationed as guard. Children laid down on the ground and were covered by blankets. The guesser came from over the hill. He took a stick, went to the covered children, touched each in succession and guessed who the individual was.

⟨naquɜxki⟩ was the name of the game [nánípɄka, 'guess over the hill'].[2]

Political Organization: Council: Smoke Lodge Mischief Makers {Wedel}   Two men were just full of mischief; they were kin of Jim's.

The central tipi was called the "smoke house," where men met, talked, smoked, etc. The men were to have a meeting that night in the smoke house.

One of the leading men called out to the camp that he was going to have a meeting that night to discuss the next camp and general business.

A captive kept up the fire in the tipi and sat near the door. The men left their war robes outside.

The mischievous boys of the camp came around. They might take their knives and cut up the robes.

All the men smoked one pipe. It was lit by the fire tender with a coal from the fireplace. No one spoke until the pipe was lit. The leader, opposite the doorway, smoked first.

During the day, the boys would think up some devilment. They might catch a skunk and liberate it in the tipi. They might send the skunk in the door, goose it, and close the ventilator flaps.

The men in the meeting gave up and decided to finish their meeting later. They went out and picked up the remnants of their robes. Often moccasins were also left outside; one of each pair might be taken.

In winter, the boys might slip a colt in and poke it so that it would kick the men inside, etc. All this deviltry was while the men couldn't talk.

A war party was starting off. The two boys were going along. The men announced that they were meeting that night. The boys returned that night on an old mare. They rode her to where men were meeting, then kicked her in the ribs, and broke up the meeting.

A war party didn't go far the first night so girls would come out to their camp.

Another time, the boys made a mess, covered it with dirt, and left. Medicine men would rub their hands in dirt and then smear it over their faces.

1. Wallace and Hoebel 1952:129.
2. Wallace and Hoebel 1952:129.

Again, the boys did the same trick. They rubbed weeds in the mess and whacked each man over back of head as he left the tipi. One of the men got home, his wife smelled it, and asked him what was up. The man couldn't figure it out because they thought the pranksters were out of town.[1]

Tsaka?ai was the leader of these boys, Tumumeai was his lieutenant.[2]

The council was the regular village council, composed of brave, but senile, warriors.

At the first meeting in a new camp, each man wanted to find out how many times he had been on war parties. They had straws for counting.[3] They would ask a certain man how many times he had gone on a war party and returned before meeting the enemy, or how many times he had divorced his wife. They asked dishonorable questions.[4]

If a woman misbehaved, a man was compelled to pay *nanuwoku*. The questions came up, "How many times have you been compelled to pay {illegible}?," "How many times have you helped collect *nanuwoku*?", or "How many times have you taken a woman on war parties?"

Sometimes, when the boys were gone to war, the council had a peaceful meeting.

The boys would stick their hind end through the door when no one was supposed to speak; if someone spoke while the pipe was passing, they had to refill and pass the pipe again. They might shoot a speaker with a thorn-tipped straw arrow. These boys were Jim's cousins (*ara?*); one was a good warrior, the other was a good cook.

Political Organization: Council: Smoke Lodge Mischief Makers {Hoebel}

There were two mischievous men. There was the smoke house near the middle of the camp where men smoked as in a club.

The crier called for a meeting for that night.

East of the door was a captive who tended the fire.

Sometimes they left their war robes outside; sometimes they took them in.

The two jokers came and cut the robes into strips.

They had one pipe to smoke. It was lit by the fire tender. (Tobacco was scarce in those days.) While the pipe was being smoked, no one might speak. The two mischief makers slipped a skunk into the tipi while the smoking progressed. Another time, they would close the smoke flap. The men couldn't stand it any longer and had to stop before they were ready.

1. Hoebel 1940:40–44; Wallace and Hoebel 1952:148.
2. Neither of these two young men is otherwise identified.
3. There are two other documentary mentions of Comanche counting straws. In 1851, Lieutenant Colonel William J. Hardee "induced [several chiefs] to bring in bundles of sticks to make the number of men, women, and children in their respective tribes" (Hardee 1851). In 1868, Dr. Edward Palmer collected for the Smithsonian several bundles of grass-stem "census-sticks" (National Museum of Natural History, Department of Anthropology, catalog numbers 6930–33), representing the number of warriors, women, children, and lodges of the Nokoni. Unfortunately, he did not record the numbers, and in the ensuing years, the grass stems have become brittle and broken and their exact counts cannot now be determined. See also DeMallie and Parks 2001, fig. 2.
4. Jean Louis Berlandier noted, "It is at these meetings that they exchange their deepest secrets and it is here that an adulteress is usually discovered. The guilty man is almost never killed; the aggrieved husband usually thrashes him and takes some of his horses and mules" (1844:178). In 1848, Robert Neighbors attended a smoke lodge, where they spent the evening discussing "war and women" (Neighbors 1848).

They had to take off their moccasins to enter the club.

Another time, they put a colt in the tipi. The jokers poked it with stick. It kicked all over, but the men couldn't say anything.

Those two boys went off on a raid. They didn't go very far, close enough to get back. They brought back an old mare with a sore back, backed her up to the tent and flanked her so she kicked.

They made a mess on the ground and covered it with dirt. The medicine men smeared dirt on themselves, and they rubbed their hands in it.

They made a mess in weeds. The meeting let out when {illegible}. They smeared it on the heads of the men as they came.

The ringleader of the pair was Sako?ai, his assistant was Demonokai.[1] They were nephews of Jim's father. They were "brothers."

They[2] had a lodge meeting to decide about supremacy.

They had a handful of straws.

They asked questions of a dishonorable nature: "How many times have you been divorced?" "How many times have you turned back from a war party without meeting the enemy?" "How many times have you taken a woman on a war party?" etc.[3]

Kinship Relations: Joking {Wedel}   Once, on a raid, these boys went along. A brave warrior, too. Each of the men lost his younger brother on the raid and cut off his hair, but they got many horses.

The brave warrior was sorrowful. The mischievous brother comforted the warrior, urging him to set an example to the other people and not weep.

The warrior told the men to drive the horses on a ways, then stop and camp and kill a fat horse for fresh meat. The warrior was riding a mule; the mischief maker was ahead of him. As they rode along, the warrior began to weep again. The trickster slipped off his horse behind some bushes and waited until the warrior came by. Then he threw a robe in front, startling the mule so that he threw his rider. The warrior got up laughing. He said if the trickster's brother hadn't been killed, he (the warrior) would have killed the trickster for his act. The joker said that he had done it so the warrior's weeping wouldn't spoil supper for the others. The warrior promised not to cry anymore.

Kinship Relations: Joking {Hoebel}   Two young men were killed on a raid; one was the brother of the leader, the other was the brother of one of Jim's jokers.

They got lots of horses, but the leader wailed on the way back.

The leader had a camping place in mind. He send some ahead to kill a fat horse and prepare a meal.

The joker didn't take the death of his brother as hard as did the chief. The wailing annoyed him. He told the chief not to make so much noise.

The chief kept it up.

---

1. Hoebel translates these names as Leader and Through (1940:42). These translations are unattested, and neither man is otherwise identified.
2. The following is from a separate card.
3. Wallace and Hoebel 1952:147.

The joker rode ahead and hid behind a bush. As the leader rode by, he jumped out and flapped his blanket. The chief's horse balked and threw the chief.

The leader was angry. He said, "If you had not lost your brother today, I'd kill you."

The joker explained, "I did this for the others. You cry all the time. It will make them feel bad. They will not be able to eat and they are hungry."

Political Organization: Council: Smoke Lodge {Wedel}   The council was composed of men too old for war parties. They met to talk, smoke, talk over the moving of the camp, reminisce, and discuss dishonorable deeds, etc.

Political Organization: Council: Smoke Lodge {Hoebel}   A special tipi was near the center of the crescent camp. It was a social lodge for smoking.

There was one big pipe.

There was a taboo on talking. They must clean and relight the pipe if anyone spoke.

The members were old warriors too old to fight.

There was a captive for the fire tender and pipelighter.

There were pranksters.

They discussed moving the camp.

It was like a Chamber of Commerce.[1]

Nanɨwokɨ   *nanɨwoku* was the fine levied by a husband upon an adulterer.

POST OAK JIM
July 19, 1933

Medicine: Curing   Jim used axle grease and sugar to heal bad cuts. He was once kicked by a mule under the left eye and cured himself this way.

Medicine: Sun Dance   The clowns (Mud Men) performed in the Sun Dance on the last day before the dance opened. There were usually five in number. The arbor should be completed by that time. The dance proper began next day. *sekwitsipuhitsi*[2] were the Mud Men.

The Mud Men didn't function at any other time.

The mock battle was before the dance proper, if possible, on the same day as the Mud Men. In the evening of the same day as the battle, all the bands staged the preliminary Fox Dance. The arbor was completed on this day.

Buffalo impersonators might join the main Sun Dance. They had to wash first and get into other costumes, only one or two usually did this.

The last Sun Dance was given two years after the last buffalo hunt, which was fifty-seven years ago. The hunt was staged in the year of a total solar eclipse, the last dance was in 1878.

The fire tender in the Sun Dance was a brave warrior.

---

1. Hoebel 1940:44.
2. *sekwi* 'mud', *puhipɨ* 'leaf'.

There were four drummers, each with a small drum about fourteen inches across. There were three or four rows of spectators about the tipi wall who didn't take part in the dancing.

The dance was suspended for one hour at each meal to allow the spectators and the drummers to eat. They were called back by the medicine man. It started about nine o'clock in the morning. Everyone had to take a bath in the creek daily before entering the tipi. Whoever wanted to could wear leaf wristlets of sage (?), but it was not required.

The Sun Dancers prepared right in the arbor behind the cedar screen. There was no special individual to do the painting. They painted as they wished. They must wash daily and repaint, going to the creek to wash.

Jim didn't believe the dancers went four days without drinking water.

The custom was to dive upstream four times to wash off, especially in connection with dances.

A Mud Man could take part in the dance.

The total ceremony took eight days, four to build the arbor and four to dance.

The willow bark headdress was on a frame, open at the face. The shield was made by bending a limb circularly and crossing the circle with willows. It was equipped with bark fringes. The mock battle was an imitation of some real battle, each man acting as he had in some actual fight. The scout was a real war scout.

Incest rules were not broken during the four-day license preceding the Sun Dance.

The Mud Men used straight willow sticks with the twigs left on the upper end and bound into a bundle like a switch; they were thrown away after using. (Cf. Pueblo clowns.[1])

Life Cycle: Marriage   An old man might take a young woman where he went. It was not a voluntary marriage on the woman's part. She sometimes bit her husband. A girl was often teased by others during her husband's absence. Captive girls were often given to old warriors.

Life Cycle: Marriage: Arranged {Wedel}   A man with two or three sisters would try to marry one of them to an industrious man, so that his brother-in-law would provide him with game, etc.

If a father was getting old and needed someone to support him, his son would interview the parents and tell them he had a certain young man in mind who he wanted in the family. The parents always consented.

The son then went to some gathering or something. There, he took his friend aside and told him he wanted him in the family. If the friend refused, it was all off. If he accepted, the son would take his sister to the friend's tipi and they were considered married.

If the son-in-law was industrious and good to his parents-in-law, he would be given the younger sister of his wife in compensation. The son-in-law lived near his wife's parent's in this event.

Life Cycle: Marriage: Arranged {Hoebel}   A young man with a sister or two might give one to an industrious acquaintance to get him to lighten his own work, and to provide for his aging parents.

---

1. This comment was probably by Linton.

The brother went to the young man after getting his own parent's consent.

He went to the boy and said he would like to have him in the family.

If the other accepted the gifts, it was OK; if not, it was all off.

If so, he brought his sister in that night.

If the son-in-law was industrious and the folks appreciated it, they might give him an extra sister to wife.

The girl's parents did most of the setting up of the household.

Life Cycle: Marriage: Arranged {Carlson}   A young man had two sisters. His father was getting old and the son knew that he had to have some assistance, and the way to get it was to marry a sister to a young, energetic man.

He went to his parents and said that he couldn't care for them all the time, that he had to go out on war parties, and that he had a young man in mind that he wanted as a brother-in-law.

The parents consented.

The young man took the man he had in mind aside and told him he would like to give him his sister.

The man either accepted or refused outright.

If he accepted, the young man would take his sister to the man's tent that night.

The provider, they will feel that one daughter was not enough and they would give him another as a thanks offering.

Life Cycle: Marriage {Wedel}   The mother would help her daughter develop her household, e.g., equipping the tipi, curing meat, making clothes, etc.

Life Cycle: Marriage {Carlson}   When a girl got married, her mother helped her fix the tipi. Her brother and her husband got the hides.

A husband's parents do things for their daughter-in-law, but not so much.[1]

Life Cycle: Marriage: Affinal Relations   A matrilocal son-in-law was treated just like their own son. [A son-in-law was treated like a son.[2]]

Marriage established a friendship between the parents of young people; it was not a joking relationship. [A couple's parents respected each other and did not joke.[3]]

Social Roles: Friendship   Two very close friends might call each other "brother"; consequently, they could not marry each other's sisters, they couldn't even talk about them.

Two close friends calling each other brother were never to desert each other in battle. If one was killed, his father treated the survivor just like an adopted son.

The survivor would say on his return, "The horse has come," and would tell what took place. He would tell of the place where the battle was, and how his "brother" died in action. The father of the deceased was named so he could feel satisfied that his son had died like a brave man. The family of the survivor came and mourned for the deceased as they would for one of their own family. *tubitsinahaitsInuu* were 'true friends'.[4]

---

1. This note is dated July 17.
2. From Carlson, dated July 17.
3. From Carlson, dated July 17.
4. Possibly *tubitsi* 'real', *na* reflexive, *haitaI* 'friend', *nuu*, plural.

Post Oak Jim's father was a great friend of a Cheyenne. The friendship probably began on a battlefield. Both men were good-looking; they favored one another. At gatherings, they were always together. They went out together with girls, on war parties, etc.

In a certain battle, they were separated and the Cheyenne man was killed. Post Oak Jim's father heard of his friend's death. The Cheyennes were camped at some distance, but Post Oak Jim's father went to visit and mourn with them. The family of the deceased had several daughters, but no sons, so they said they would regard him as their son. They gave the deceased's horse to Post Oak Jim's father, a medicine man, who wouldn't let anyone ride the horse. He paid seven visits to the family of the deceased later and got a horse each time.

The Cheyenne man was a pretty notable man. The last time Jim saw him was while his father still lived. Mahakits was the name of Cheyenne man, it meant 'old'.

Jim and his family went to a certain fort to visit the Cheyennes. At the fort, they were asked what they wanted. An officer there was the Cheyenne man's son-in-law (?). Post Oak Jim's father said he wanted to see the Cheyenne, it might be the last time, as he was getting old. The next morning, his father and the old man's son went out to kill a beef. They rounded up the cattle and drove them near a house. They butchered four beeves, and hauled two wagonloads of meat back to camp. This was the last time Jim ever saw the Cheyenne. They prepared the meat and took it to their camp.

The Cheyennes got out all of the costume of the deceased warrior, shell necklace, breechcloth, moccasins, leggings, etc., and offered it to Post Oak Jim's father. He refused it, saying they should keep it in remembrance of their son.

Such "brothers" would fight against each other if war broke out between the respective tribes.

Jim called Mahakits his *kʉnuʔ* {paternal grandfather}. Mahakits' children were his *araʔ* {mother's brother}.

Mahakits's son-in-law (the officer) wanted to make friends with Jim, just before they left the Cheyenne. Post Oak Jim had a five-year-old dark sorrel and a twelve-year-old smoky. He offered the officer his choice. The officer selected the five-year-old because he was a good saddle horse. Jim was twelve-years old at the time.

Social Roles: Friendship {Hoebel}   *tʉbitsinahaitsIna*. Two young men became friends. They called each other "brother." All avoidance relations and taboos for sisters held. They were in a joking relation with each other.

The death of one in battle called for equal mourning from both families.

Similar relations held for women.

Jim's father and a Cheyenne were friends. Both were good-looking and looked alike. They did everything together.

The friend got killed in a Cheyenne battle when Jim's father wasn't with him.

His father heard it and went to the Cheyenne camp. He mourned with the parents. Then he said, "You have no more boys. I'll be your son now."

He made seven different visits and every time they gave him a horse.

The last time, his brother-in-law killed four beeves for him.

There has been no Cheyenne-Comanche war since.

Jim wanted to make a *haitsI* of the brother-in-law of his father's *haitsI*. He gave him a horse, the pick of two. He would use *pabiꞌ* {elder brother} and *tamiꞌ* {younger brother} terms.

These friendships often started through going with girls.

Kinship Relations: Use of Address Terms   Two friends, if they knew each other well, would use relative age names, taking cognizance of each other as older and younger.

If they were of different tribes or villages, they might call each other *hahaitsI* only.

Two women might be staying together, one going with each of two boys. The boys would take up with each other as a result. Young people also formed these close friendships; such a girl's brother's friend had to respect her {*sic*, his?} "sister" just like herself.

Life Cycle: Marriage   If a man had a daughter and his "brother" had a son, the two children might <u>not</u> marry in the old days, now they can. They would call each other brother and sister.

[Children of two friends could not marry. They would call each other brother and sister.]

Life Cycle: Marriage: Polyandry   Two brothers could share the same woman. [Of course, the wife really <u>belonged</u> to <u>one</u> of the men.]

But if one "brother" was married and the other was single, the latter couldn't ask to sleep with the former's wife, but if the former was a true friend, he would offer the bachelor his wife. The single man might decline, saying he didn't want to strain their friendship. Then the wife might say that he didn't care for her, and thus, force him to stay with her.

If both were married, they might sleep with each other's wives, but as this caused trouble, it wasn't done very often.

[It was not a good thing for two married brothers to allow each other the use of their wives. It might break up their friendship. There were two friends now alive {in 1933} who used to let each other have the use of the other's wife, but it didn't work out very well and they weren't friends any more.[1]]

An elder brother sometimes let his younger brother sleep with his wife[2] (cf. Pawnee polyandry[3]).

Jim's younger brother married before Jim. Jim made his home with them, but his brother didn't offer him the use of his wife. Finally, the couple didn't get along very well and broke up. Then Jim married; he didn't say anything to his younger brother because he figured he wouldn't live long. The younger brother died young. [Jim allowed his younger brother access to his wife.[4]]

If two brothers married, they might exchange wives, but wife exchange between "brothers" often caused hard feelings.

A single woman might take pity on an old man, "A kiss would make you feel good."

Nowadays, even if he couldn't get a nice-looking, well-formed woman, he often thought of her. His friends wouldn't let him stay with them long. They would ask him why he

1. From Carlson.
2. Wallace and Hoebel 1952:132.
3. It is not clear whether this reference to the Pawnees is from Linton or Wedel.
4. From Carlson.

didn't marry, then they would be better friends. He said he was afraid to get married, his friends might get it back on him. Jim was afraid of girls when he was young. All Jim could get out of young girls now was to kiss them and feel around.[1]

Life Cycle: Sex   The kiss was different in the old days.

Older girls started young boys out.

[Boys were very bashful. They were usually started by older women.[2]]

[Young boys were afraid of women. They generally had their first sex experience with an older woman.[3]]

P.M.

Social Roles: Friendship   "True friends" were closer than actual brothers, especially in time of battle, because if a man lost something belonging to himself, he was less bothered than if he lost something belonging to someone else. So long as there was any life left in a fallen warrior, his "brother" couldn't desert him in battle.[4]

Story   Two friends stood back of the fireplace, hands together, while Jim, the leader, prayed, asking that these two be friends through life, and that they might live to be a hundred years old.

Beliefs: Handedness   *ʉ ʔ tʉbitsinakʉ*[5] was your right hand. *ʉ ʔ ohininakʉ* was your left hand.

The right hand was luckier because it was more accomplished; left-handed men never made success of anything.

Words   *tabe* was both watch and sun. *kuna* was both wood and fire.

Beliefs: Physical Deformities   There were quite a few cross-eyed people in the old days, but it was not particularly unlucky if they looked at you. Sometimes ghosts were blamed for crossed eyes.

It was unlucky if a person with a cut-off nose looked at you. A cut-off ⟨giharerkup⟩ nose was due to the activity of worms during pregnancy.

If a woman saw a corpse during pregnancy, the child would be born blind; that's why pregnant women were not permitted to attend funerals.

tʉnoorʉ 'carry something', i.e., a hunchback. There were some in the old days.

Jim saw a Cheyenne with two heads, one body, two pairs of legs. He was born so.

Life Cycle: Childbirth: Twins   Parents of twins often gave one of the pair away; Jim did not know the reason.[6]

Life Cycle: Childbirth: Navel   The navel [*siikU*[7]] was regarded as the stem of the child, the sprout. The seed (child) grew underground in the woman's body. Indians believed conception was the result of sexual intercourse. [The men had nothing to do with it.[8]]

---

1. Linton 1936:136; Hoebel 1939:447.
2. From Hoebel.
3. From Carlson.
4. Following this sentence there is a gap of 14 lines in Wedel's manuscript.
5. Literally, 'your real hand'.
6. From Carlson, dated July 12.
7. From Carlson.
8. From Carlson.

Animals: Cattle: Hermaphroditic Cattle   Jim had seen hermaphroditic cattle. They noticed a cow coming, bellowing like a bull. The next morning, he saw it in the herd, taller and thinner than other cattle. Its seeds were smaller than those of a bull, and its horns were twisted. He heard of no such case among buffalo.

Animals: Buffalo   ⟨daiβ⟩ *kuhtsuʔ* is a fat "razorback" buffalo.

Animals: Buffalo: White Buffalo   Jim knew of an Arapaho Indian who carried a bone of an albino buffalo about in his belt. Every once in a while, he blew on [in] the bone and blood dripped from it. He also carried a small bottle along with the bone.

The Arapaho was watching a gambling game; a [Comanche] boy standing by came and cut off the bone and the bottle and threw them out into the gaming crowd. This was bad for the medicine and soon after the Arapaho died.

Questions[1]

Names: Naming   Jim's mother's mother held him while he was being christened.

Camp Organization   The camp was sometimes in a semicircle; it <u>had</u> to be so arranged for the Sun Dance. Otherwise, it was often strung out in a straight line with the special tipi to the southeast.

Political Organization: Council: Smoke Lodge   The special "smoke house" was not always set up. Sometimes a council of old-timers met in a cleared space without the special tipi.[2] The men smoked every night in this group.

Representatives of different bands met to talk. [There were a few representatives from each band.] Sometimes the chief was also there. Sometimes young men attended.

The announcer was present to see what was going on. The next morning, he announced the plans, that their move was put off two or three days. Then the chief would get out on the last morning and help announce.

Social Roles: Announcer   The announcer might get in the habit and would get out every morning and announce.

Camp Organization: Moving   It was the old men's job to decide when the camp should move.

If the chief wasn't ready to move, he and his immediate friends could stay behind while others went on.

Sometimes disagreement over moving was settled in a compromise.

Political Organization: Council: Smoke Lodge; War: War Parties   The old men might persuade a war party to give up a projected raid against a powerful enemy.

Not all the old men in the tribe belonged to the council. Some of the members had brave deeds to their credit, others were more or less obscure. Any old person who wanted to could attend the meeting, it was open to all, but not everyone went because there wasn't

---

1. This word is centered on the line, implying that the following comments were in answer to specific questions, but those questions are unknown.
2. Wallace and Hoebel 1952:147.

enough room. The same persons didn't come every night. ⟨napomopetseru⟩[1] was the council.

Life Cycle: Marriage   Riding double was a sign of intimacy.[2] An old man with a young wife might ride double to keep an eye on her.[3]

GEORGE KOWENO
July 21, 1933

George Koweno   [Big George] was a full blood, belonging to the Yapainʉʉ band. He was sixty-two years old and had been a church member since the age of forty. [He joined the church twenty years ago.]

Medicine: Beaver Ceremony {Wedel}   The patient occupied a place against the west wall of the tipi. The spectators filed in clockwise and seated themselves about the wall. The medicine man sat just east of the patients.

There were two patients in this case (tuberculosis). Two persons (a man and a woman) went after the medicine man. The man went alone to his tipi, then joined by the woman. They smoked.

He also carried an eagle tail feather and sage plants pulled out by the roots.

The drummers entered the lodge, circled it once clockwise, and seated themselves against the south wall of the tipi toward the rear.

The announcer was outside. He then called the people in. He wanted no metal and nothing red.

After everything was fixed, the man and woman smoked and told the medicine man what they wanted.

The drummers and song leaders then sang a special song in slow measure. While they sang, the doctor doctored the patient. The doctor had a finger ring in his mouth. He sucked on the body of the patient where the pain was and spat at the end of each inhalation into a cup.

The ceremonies were early in the morning and late at night.

Finally, he lifted the ring out of the cup, with phlegm hanging from it like an icicle, and replaced it in his mouth. He made a sucking noise, then drew the clean ring from his mouth and put it in his pocket.

The singing continued while the doctoring went on. The doctoring lasted about two hours; two sessions were required.

The substance spat into the cup was what caused the sickness.

---

1. This may be *na-* reflexive prefix, *pahmuʔ* 'tobacco', *tʉsuʔʉrʉʉ* 'give counsel'.
2. A similar belief was apparently what led to the murder of a female student among the Apaches in 1931 (Woodbury 1987).
3. This note is from Carlson.

The man who went to get the doctor retained the eagle feather, sage, and tobacco. The medicine man got the eagle feather after the ceremony.

The central eagle feathers were too valuable to give away.

When the man went to get a doctor, he handed him a cigarette with his right hand and it was received with the right hand. This was the Beaver Medicine, used for tuberculosis. Very few people had the power to give this ceremony.

Medicine: Beaver Ceremony {Hoebel}   Beaver Cure of Later Times

It was in an ordinary tipi. It was a cure for tuberculosis.

The patients lay at the west end (there were two in this case). The medicine man was to the east of the patients.

A man went alone to get the doctor. After all was set in the tipi, the man and the woman smoked with him. The man had an eagle feather (from the side of the tail) and four sage plants torn up by the roots.

The drummers and dancers entered and took their places to the south and east of the patients.

The announcer selected by the medicine man called out from the front of the lodge, inviting all to come. He warned them not to wear red or any metal.

After all entered, they danced and a special song was given. Drums and rattles were beaten to an extra slow measure.

The medicine man sucked in with his mouth against the patient at the infected points. He had a finger ring in his mouth. He spat after each inhalation(retaining the ring in his mouth) into a cup. The medicine man picked the ring out of the cup, with phlegm adhering to the ring. The medicine man put it back into his mouth and took the ring clean from his mouth and put it in his pocket.

This was done early in the morning and at night. It lasted only two hours.

There was music and dance all the time.

The person engaging a medicine man must carry an eagle tail feather and four sage plants pulled up by the roots. The tail feather was from the side. The sage plants were unbroken, pulled up by the roots.

Smoke must be offered with the right hand and accepted in the same.

The same intermediary was used by all the people to get a medicine man. George was intermediary for Beaver Doctors.

The person who went for the medicine man expected a gift after the cure, something that had been given to the medicine man for the cure. Other people could also ask for his things. They might ask him for his gifts before he went to make the cure. It depended upon how much nerve he had. He couldn't refuse them.[1]

Medicine: Transfer {Wedel}   This medicine man asked George whether he would like to

have his power; George usually worked with this medicine man and knew the ropes, e.g., if he went for a bucket of water and there was no cup, the man had to drink all the water directly from the bucket. George refused to take the power because of this taboo. The medicine man explained that if he did take the medicine and he had to drink a bucketful of water, it wouldn't fill him up. This man had Buffalo Medicine.

1. Wallace and Hoebel 1952:175.

Medicine: Transfer {Hoebel}   The medicine man who gave the beaver cure described by George wanted to pass it to George. This was unsolicited by George.

The medicine man asked him if he would like it. George was the intermediary used by people to get this doctor.

George wouldn't take it because of the taboos. The holder had to empty at one pull any vessel he drank from. The medicine man said that if he should drink so, he wouldn't get full. {He had} buffalo medicine so a big drink would not fill him.

Medicine: Ghost Sickness   [Later this medicine man made a cure for convulsions.]

There was a camp north of Lawton. Two children, one Comanche and one Apache, were seized with spasms caused by ghosts. They both called on the same doctor, who healed them both. George wanted to get his medicine, but he refused to give it because of George's refusal to take the proffered buffalo medicine. [Later, George and a friend went over to horn in on gifts the doctor had received. The man refused because George had not accepted his medicine when offered.]

Medicine: Transfer   George's father was a medicine man, but didn't pass it on to George.

Medicine: Transfer: Snake Medicine {Wedel}   The medicine man offered George some snake medicine. This was a herb, dug out of the ground. The medicine man gave him this herb and told he to take the root home and put it under his pillow. The medicine would tell him what to do, maybe not the first night, but eventually.

He was not to eat beef gut or the power would vanish. He liked this food but kept away from it.

One day his son was bitten by a snake and his wife told him he had this medicine and should cure the boy.

George hadn't yet received the directions from the medicine as to how to work it. George's companion asked who had given him the snake medicine. Then he went ahead because he knew something of it himself.

So he marked out a snake on the ground. He picked up a little dust, spat on it, and made a paste. Then he drew lines along the wound and one above the bite to keep the swelling from spreading, and so cured it. (The root was chewed up and spat into the dirt.)

George liked gut more than he did the medicine, so he threw the herb away.

A certain man who was friendly and knew a medicine man's taboos generally acted as a sort of go-between when someone wanted a cure.

Medicine: Transfer: Snake Medicine {Hoebel}   Another time, he tried to give George snake (*sisinobits*) medicine.

He had the root in his pocket. He gave it to George and told him to take it home and put it under his head at night; it would give directions in a dream.

The medicine man gave taboos: no gut of beef.

George's son was bitten by a snake one day. His wife said, "You've got snake medicine, doctor your son."

George hadn't dreamt yet, so he didn't know what to do.

A man with him asked who gave him the medicine. He said he knew something about the medicine. He told George to get the herb. He smoothed a place on the ground. He drew a snake on the ground in a circle. He chewed the herbs. He picked up some loose dirt, spit on it, and drew a line across the arm; he drew lines at right angles on the bites. The swelling would not cross the lines.

George didn't keep this medicine long. He liked beef gut too much.[1]

Medicine: Sorcery {Wedel}   A certain medicine man once lived among the Apaches. He wanted a certain women (who finally settled among Comanches.) She would have nothing to do with him, so he used evil medicine on her and caused her sickness. The people wanted to investigate the medicine man when she became sick. Another medicine man discovered eagle-down feathers in the sick woman's chest and treated her for it. Nothing was done to the offending medicine man.

Medicine men often used their medicine against each other, or against women who rejected their advances.

Medicine: Sorcery {Hoebel}   A Comanche medicine man lived among the Apaches. An Apache put sickness on a woman who refused him. The Apaches called on the Comanche to doctor her. (He was a Beaver man.) He discovered an eagle breath feather in her breast. He found it by listening. He removed it and the woman recovered. She lives here today. Nothing was done to the Sorcerer.

Medicine: Curing   A medicine man sometimes dreamed that a certain woman should come after him to cure a sick person. Then he would tell her that he wanted to be friends and if she agreed the patient would get well.

[In this case, she could not refuse to do his bidding.]

[A method of getting a woman to come to him.]

George didn't believe a dream would instruct a medicine man thus.[2]

Medicine: Payments   Payments for doctoring were not usually returned, even though the patient might die.

Medicine: Transfer {Wedel}   If a man wanted power from a medicine man, he went to him with sage, feathers, and a smoke. After smoking, the medicine man couldn't refuse, but if he didn't want to give the power, he refused to smoke.

A medicine man could tell by his power what a caller wanted, so he knew whether he wanted to smoke with him or not.

Correction: A caller would come in, light up, smoke, and extend the cigarette to the medicine man. As he extended it, he stated the purpose of his call, also the amount of his fee or gift. By accepting or rejecting the cigarette, the medicine man indicated his acceptance or rejection of the call.

Medicine: Transfer {Hoebel}   A person came for help. He brought sage, eagle feathers, and a smoke.

The person lit the cigarette, puffed a few puffs, and told the medicine man what he wanted.

The medicine man could accept or refuse to smoke.

Gifts: Relatives didn't have to offer gifts.

1. Wallace and Hoebel 1952:162.
2. Hoebel 1940:127.

The person told the medicine man what he could expect as a gift before the medicine man smokes acceptance.

Pihune _____[1] was the medicine man's name.

Medicine: Specialization   Some medicine men specialized [pneumonia, stomach pains, etc.].

Medicine: Curing: Hypochondria {Wedel}   A certain woman was sick and they couldn't find out what was wrong. She was taken to a peyote meeting and was given peyote. During the night, she got out of her head and was taken out of the tipi.

Another doctor was called in, but he couldn't help much.

Finally, George was sent after Pihune. He couldn't find him at home, so he trailed him and finally located him, sitting around with a bunch of fellows, gambling. There was a big crowd there. George went up to him, lit a cigarette, smoked, and handed it to the medicine man without saying what he was after. The medicine man smoked, then asked George whether he was in a hurry and George said, "Yes."

The medicine man sent George ahead and George rode fast. Finally, the medicine man called him back and took the lead himself, and they rode along. The medicine man told George he had known George was coming and what he wanted. He knew of the sick woman and that she was in no danger.

The patient was on a bed against the south wall of a tipi. The medicine man sent George after a cup of water. The patient was watching the medicine man; she called him an untruthful man.

On the way over, the medicine man had told George that the woman would be scared. She was out of her head.

The medicine man didn't deny that he was untruthful. He told her to drink from the same cup he had used, and then the effects of the peyote would be cleared away.

She began to fight him. He told George to help hold her. She again called him untruthful. He told her to wait and drink again from the cup and the feeling would disappear. He gave her a drink and she quieted down. He laughed at her, said he had cheated her with the drink and she got all right.

The medicine man had made no medicine at all, he just gave her a drink of water. When the woman talked out of her head, the medicine man had George tell her that he was no good, etc.

Medicine: Curing: Hypochondria {Hoebel}   Hysteria(?) A woman was ill, but they didn't know what it was.

They took her to a peyote meeting. She ate peyote. During the night she was delirious, "out of her head."

They went for another doctor. He didn't help her.

She said she didn't expect to live until the next morning.

They sent George for Pihune. He was not home. He found him gambling with other men.

George told of his mission. The medicine man asked if he was in a hurry. George said, "Yes."

---

1. There is a blank in Wedel's manuscript notes where a translation would be. Pihune is otherwise unidentified.

They rode back together, loping. The medicine man asked George to stop. He came up to him and said that this sickness wasn't serious. He knew George was coming for him. He knew from a dream what was going on and their route to the woman. He said the woman would be frightened on their arrival.

They came to the tipi where the sick woman was.

George gave him a smoke.

The medicine man asked for a drink of water. The patient watched the medicine man closely. She called him "an untruthful man." He confessed she was right.

She was to drink after him. He told her that she would then be no longer delirious. She started to fight him. George held her hands. She called him untruthful again. He told her to drink again and she would get better.

The medicine man gave her two drinks. She gradually got quiet.

He laughed at her, "Now I have cheated you and you have come to."

She got well. He stayed until night.[1]

p.s. When she talked in delirium, the medicine man told George to say that the medicine man had no power, to deny his power, that she really was well.

Smoking: Cigarettes   Cigarettes were used only when a person wanted some doctoring done or wanted some power.

Medicine   George didn't know where Pihune got his power. He thought medicine men didn't visit more than one grave for power.

Medicine: Duration   He thought one could not renew his power if it began to weaken. [When it got gradually weaker, there was no strengthening it. George never knew of a medicine man going back to the grave that gave him power in order to reinvigorate the power.]

Medicine: Skin Sacrifice {Wedel}   Pieces of flesh were cut off one's body (usually the chest) while praying to the rising sun. Afterward, they were buried. This was for strength or to harm or kill another person. The skin was lifted with a needle and cut off with a knife.

This sort of power didn't last long. It might come back on the family. George heard of several cases where this medicine came back on the family of the man and resulted in the death of other members of the family. The medicine was no good against enemies in war, it was only good against one's tribesmen.

Medicine: Skin Sacrifice {Hoebel}   One prayed to the rising sun and cut a raised piece of flesh from the breast. It must be buried in the ground. If sorcery, this meant the enemy's body was buried under the ground.

George used it to pray for strength.

Such medicine was not lasting and was very dangerous. It might come back on one's family. George didn't know about any attempt to expose this practice, and he didn't think anything would be done if exposed.

The use of this sorcery is likely to come back on one's family.

Medicine: Sorcery {Wedel}   One Indian drew a picture of a woman on the ground: she did not want to be friendly with him. He drew in her heart and put a pin in her heart and waited for her to die. "She never did die."

1. Wallace and Hoebel 1952:168–69.

Sometimes they would put a feather in the heart instead of a pin. This may have been the usual way of putting feathers, etc., into people. George was not certain.

Medicine: Sorcery {Hoebel}   A woman refused to take a man. He drew a picture of her with her heart. He stuck a pin in it and waited for her to die. She lived very well. "He had no medicine."[1]

Medicine: Peyote   About three years ago, a white man came to investigate peyote. He went to Niyah's, and questioned George, and wrote down a lot of stuff. Then he went east and died.[2]

Nanʉwokʉ: Champion-at-Law {Wedel}   If a poor man had been deprived of his wife by a brave man, he could go to a braver warrior, present his case, and have him talk to the wife-stealer. The two warriors would talk things over. If neither would back down, they might (rarely) kill each other.

Nanʉwokʉ: Champion-at-Law {Hoebel}   "Where a *tekwʉniwapI* wronged a poor man, how does he get redress?"

He must get a braver man than the offender to go to him and talk. The first warrior must listen because the go-between had more brave deeds to his records than he. They talked it over. If there was no agreement, "a serious fight is on." If neither would retreat, they would kill each other.

Nanʉwokʉ: Champion-at-Law {Wedel}   A brave warrior was going on a war party. He decided to take a woman along, so he took the wife away from a poor captive. The captive talked it over with another warrior, and they followed the party. After two or three days, they caught up with the party at rest. Some of the men on the party recognized the woman's husband and told her. She said she didn't want to go back.

When the two men got closer, they recognized the warrior wife-stealer; he was worried. The two men were asked to dismount and eat dinner. The woman was surly, but her paramour talked and joked. He had no intention of keeping the woman because the warrior who accompanied her husband was a braver man.

The party was already on their way back.

After dinner, the braver warrior told the wife-stealer to give the woman all her clothes, they were going to take her back, they were going back.

Night was falling and the husband wanted to sleep with the woman, but she would have nothing to do with him. Before they got home, enemies attacked them and the war party also caught up with them. The wife-stealer was killed. Word came to the husband and his companion went to see about it. One was to ride in front, the other to pick up the body and bring it back. When the woman heard of her paramour's death, she began to cut her hair and gash herself. They buried the warrior and she left much of her stuff there.

They went on their way. The husband asked his wife to wash off the blood and come to bed. She became angry and said she wouldn't sleep with him. The two lived together though, after they reached camp.

---

1. Wallace and Hoebel 1952:238 (?).
2. It is not known who this person might have been, perhaps Günter Wagner.

Nanɨwokɨ: Champion-at-Law {Carlson}   One time, a brave warrior going on a raid decided to take a lady friend. He took the wife of a captive. The captive wanted his wife back again, so he went to another brave warrior. They decided to follow the party.

They followed for two or three days and finally caught up. The party was resting and noticed the pair approaching. They saw that one was the husband. They saw that the other man was a brave warrior. It worried the man who had taken the wife.

The two came up and were asked to get off and eat. The woman acted as if she was mad, sulking in the background, but the man she had gone off with laughed and joked. He knew that he could not keep the woman because the captive's friend was a bigger warrior than he.

The war party was at the time on their way home.

After they had eaten, the warrior asked the man who had taken the woman to give her all her clothes and fix her up, that they wanted to take her back to camp.

The two men started back with the woman. Night overtook them before they got back to camp, so they camped out. The captive wanted to sleep with his wife, but she'd have nothing to do with him.

They went on. Before they arrived home, they were attacked by an enemy war party. The Comanche war party was just behind them and joined in the fight.

The man who had taken the wife took an important part in the battle. Finally, word came to the captive and his warrior friend that their brother[1] had been killed. They went out to get the body. One stayed at the head as a guard and the other got off and put the body on a horse.

When the woman heard that her lover was dead she took it hard. She cut her hair and gashed herself and threw away a lot of her clothes. That night, the husband asked her to wash the blood off and come to bed with him. She said no, she loved the other man and now he was dead.

They got home. Nothing was done. The woman continued to live with her husband.

Nanɨwokɨ: Champion-at-Law   A poor man didn't have to get a brave relative to help recover his wife, any brave man would do.

War: Revenge {Wedel}   If some of a poor man's relatives were killed by the enemy, he could go and smoke with a brave warrior (like in doctoring) and the warrior might help organize a return party.

War: Revenge {Hoebel}   {version 1[2]} Where a loved one had been killed, one went to a warleader and offered smoke. If it was accepted, the leader would organize a party.

The announcer would inform the camp. He said the people didn't care if they got killed, they wanted revenge.[3] One scalp would be sufficient. Then they would have a victory dance. This would assuage the mourning.

{version 2} If the enemy killed a relative whom you wanted to revenge, {you went} to a *tekwɨniwapI* and offered a smoke, a pipe. If it was accepted, he would lead a party for

---

1. "You called a man who has stolen your wife 'brother'." See below, Atauvich, August 9.
2. There are three versions of this Hoebel note: the earliest is handwritten and the later two are typewritten.
3. Wallace and Hoebel 1952:256.

you. He would announce it to the camp. One scalp for a Scalp Dance was sufficient. The dead man's father felt better, he had a clear conscience.

{version 3} A son killed in battle must be mourned until an enemy scalp had been taken in return.

War: Revenge {Carlson}   When a relative was killed by the enemy, you wanted revenge, so you went to a warrior and offered him a pipe. If he accepted, he would lead a war party for you and it would be announced to the camp.

If you killed one man, it was enough, and you took the scalp home for a Scalp Dance.

Then the dead man's father felt better. He had a clear conscience. A family must mourn a son killed in battle until they killed an enemy. Then the mourning stopped.

Nanɨwokɨ: Champion-at-Law   It was not necessary to smoke with a brave to get him to help recover a wife.

Nanɨwokɨ   *nanɨwokɨ* was recovered from an adulterer. If he refused to pay, his horses might be taken or killed. This sort of thing often happened. A revenge party, on recovering the wife, asked for what the lover valued most, usually a horse. If they were refused, it might be killed.

A great warrior wouldn't be fooled with.

nanɨwokɨ couldn't be collected while the warrior was gone. [A man could not come and take possession of the abductor's property in his absence.]

P.M.

Material Culture: Clothing: Moccasins   *tsomonapU*[1] were beaded moccasins.

Life Cycle: Marriage: Wife Desertion {Wedel}   A certain woman ran away. Her young husband went to his mother and asked whether he should follow her or wait till she returned. His mother told him to follow and get her, but to treat her kindly. He was a very brave warrior, and he followed the party and recovered his wife. Her paramour didn't resist because he wasn't as brave a man. Upon their return to the village, he again asked his mother what to do. This time she advised him to kill her. So he killed the woman.

Her people didn't object because he was a brave man and the woman had been in the wrong.

Life Cycle: Marriage: Wife Desertion {Hoebel}   Brave Kills His Wife. The son of a widow, Punitɨ,[2] had respect for his mother. His wife ran away with another. He asked his mother what he should do about it. His mother said he should follow her up.

What should he do if he found her? "Treat her good as you always do."

He found her with the man. Because he was a brave warrior, the absconder gave her up to him.

He took her back to camp. He asked his mother what he should do with her. She said, "Kill her." He did this.

Nothing was done to him because he was a brave warrior.

---

1. *tsomo* 'bead', *napU* 'shoe'.
2. Wedel's manuscript has Bonita, but this is unlikely. Both Hoebel and Carlson have Punitɨ 'eye'. Otherwise unidentified.

Life Cycle: Marriage: Wife Desertion {Carlson}   Once there was a young man whose father had died, and whose mother was still alive. His wife ran off with another man. The young man went to his mother and asked what to do. Should he go after his wife or wait until the pair came? His mother told him to go after them.

He asked what he should do when he got her. His mother told him to treat her as before. He had been good to his wife.

He was a brave warrior.

He caught up with the raiding party. The other man put up no resistence because he knew the husband was a braver warrior. The young man got his wife without any trouble and brought her back, treating her well.

Then he asked his mother what he should do with her now. His mother said to kill her, so he did.

Nothing was done about it. The woman had done wrong and the young man was a brave warrior.

Nanʉwokʉ {Wedel}   Punitʉ, a very handsome youth, was accused of going with three women. Their husbands investigated and found it was true.

Punitʉ's father had a fine herd of horses. The women's husbands demanded some horses in payment, but the father refused to pay the horses. So the youth was arrested and sent to Anadarko, where he had to work at cutting *piapunitʉ* 'big eyes', weeds, etc. for a year. His father never did pay over the horses.

Nanʉwokʉ {Hoebel}   Punitʉ was the best looking Indian Herman had ever seen. He was accused of going with three married women. Their husbands went to the father of Punitʉ. He had many horses. The men demanded the horses. The father refused to give them up. They went to the agency. Punitʉ went to jail for a year. They used to see him chopping wood.

Nanʉwokʉ {Carlson}   If a man took your wife, you got your brothers to go with you to demand *nanʉwokʉ* payment.

Sometimes you got mad. The other man had done wrong, and you had the right to do what you wanted to do. You asked for what you wanted. You always asked for something the young man really loved. If he refused to give up that horse, you could shoot it. The injurer had no comeback against a *nanʉwokʉ* payment.

There was a young man named Punitʉ who was a fine-looking fellow. He went with three different women. Their husbands found out. Maybe the women got mad with each other and one gave the others away.

The husbands investigated and found out it was true, so they went to Punitʉ's father. The father had plenty of horses.

The men demanded a lot of horses as *nanʉwokʉ*. The father refused, so they had Punitʉ put in jail.

Oaths   In the old days, Indians were pretty truthful and they didn't have to swear in a case like the preceding.

But women might become angry and give one another away.

[Polygamous wives might get jealous and tell on each other.]

Nanʉwokʉ: Collective Liability {Wedel}   The father was held liable for his son's paramours, his brothers also. If they refused to pay, the young man might be killed.

Nanɨwokɨ: Collective Liability {Hoebel}   If the offending son was poor, his father would have to give up stock to make it right, for fear of them killing his son. The brothers and the whole family were responsible. Conversely, brothers would aid in collecting or feud.

Nanɨwokɨ: Collective Liability {Carlson}   In the old days, the father would probably have been forced to give his horses or else see his son killed. A brother would be equally responsible. All blood relatives were responsible.

Life Cycle: Marriage: Adultery: Disowning {Wedel}   After one such offense, the parents would talk to the boy and he would generally watch his step thereafter. The <u>father</u> was the first to reprove the youth. Then the <u>grandfather</u>, the paternal uncle, elder brothers. George heard of none being disowned and cast out.

Life Cycle: Marriage: Adultery: Disowning {Hoebel}   The father and {paternal} grandfather (*kɨnuʔ*) warned the boy first. Then the father's brother. Then his own brothers. Then the mother.

The boy was thus soundly lectured, but he was never thrown out. He would likely come to in time.

The father never disowned a boy for cowardice, but if the father were brave, the people would talk of the father's bravery and ignore the boy.[1]

Life Cycle: Marriage: Adultery: Disowning {Carlson}   Probably when a boy was troublesome that way, his father and *kɨnuʔ* would talk to him. He would listen to them if he would listen to anybody.

War: Cowardice {Wedel}   A man who was afraid to go on a war party was ridiculed, but he never suffered any violence. The worst thing was to turn back before the party struck the enemy. There were few cowards, due to early conditioning in childhood.

War: Cowardice {Hoebel}   Cowardice was controlled by ridicule. There were only a few cases. Children were brought up from the beginning in the pattern of war, bravery, etc.

Story: Tahpony's Story {Wedel}   A certain young man who was afraid once started to go on a war party. After starting, he began to think of his wife and how he could get back to her gracefully. So he began to play sick; he said he had pneumonia. The leader was called and told the man to go back before they were too far away.

The man's name was Tahpony.[2]

Some women were playing a stick game. They saw the youth's wife standing red-eyed from crying and thought she must be crying for her husband. That night, her husband came home.

His wife was staying with her parents, but upon her husband's arrival, his parents called her. That night, in bed, she told of being at the game and how the women had talked.

Her husband said, "Do you really love me?"

She told him, "Yes."

---

1. Wallace and Hoebel 1952:233 (?).
2. Wedel spelled this name "daxpɔni," Hoebel spelled it "tapɔnɛ," and Carlson spelled it "taxp)ne." Presumably, this is the man listed on the censuses as Tahpony, translated as Mark Time. Casagrande (1954–55, I:148) gives it as 'test with the foot' or 'try on shoes' (*ta-* 'with the foot', *punitɨ* 'see'). If so, the events described here occurred when he was a fairly young man (born, according the censuses, between 1844 and 1859), for, from 1879 on, he was listed as the leader of a Yapainɨɨ local band. He died in the 1899 measles epidemic.

He said he didn't believe her, and finally he told her to leave the tipi. She didn't want to because she loved him, but he insisted and she finally left.

It was moonlight, and summer, and the young man had his tipi up at the bottom. He watched his wife go to her parent's tipi and then return to his, but he again sent her away to her parents. He lay and looked toward her parent's tent.

The camp began to break the next day. The young man was staying with his parents. Presently his wife's mother came over and asked whether it was true that he had sent his wife away. He said it was, and that he didn't want her anymore. So the mother-in-law went back.

The camp set up in a new place, with the man's people and his wife's close together. They[1] set up his tipi.

He raised the lower edge of the cover and watched. Presently his wife came again and said she wanted to stay. She put her hands on him, but he brushed them off and without speaking she left again.

It was night and the man watched for her; he did not sleep all night. In the morning, he went to his own mother and asked her why she hadn't taken up for him and gone to his wife's mother to bring his wife back.

The camp was moving again, scattering to different directions. He didn't see his wife for a year or two until the camps again reassembled. He went down to the watering place and waited until his wife came down. Then he asked her whether she would return. She put it up to him and he was willing. He presented her with his only horse, and she came back to him; he was very glad. He had just been trying her to see whether she loved him.

Story: Tahpony's Story {Hoebel}   A war party was organized. One young fellow went with them. On the way, he thought of his wife and wanted to return. He played sick, pneumonia. He called the leader. He advised that the fellow turn back to avoid future trouble.

The people were playing stick dice. One woman pointed his wife out; she said she had been crying, she must miss her husband, and that he would come home. That night he came.

In his absence, she was staying with her parents; they called her home. That night, she told him how the woman had predicted his return.

He asked her if she really loved him. She said, "Yes."

He didn't believe her and told her to leave the tipi. Finally, she left.

There was moonlight. She wandered around; he watched her. She returned and said she wanted to live with him, that she loved him. He sent her away again. She went to her parent's tipi and stayed there.

The next morning the camp was to move. Her mother came to see him. She asked if he sent her daughter away. He said, "Yes, he didn't want her anymore."

They all moved to a new camp. He rode there alone. Her parent's tipi was near his (he raised his tipi to see). It was his idea, to prove her love. She came again; again he sent her away.

That night, he watched for her all night, but she didn't return.

1. His own family? Compare with Carlson's version in which he set up the tipi himself.

He went to see his mother. He told her to go tell the girl's mother to bring her back, he would keep her.

Later, they moved again, in small groups. He didn't see her for one or two years. He missed her.

The camps came together again. He went to the stream to see her. He asked her back. She came. He was so glad that he gave her his only horse.[1]

Story: Tahpony's Story {Carlson}   There once was a young man named Tahpony who was afraid to go on a war party. One time he went. He went a ways, and then thought of his wife at home.

He played sick, saying he had pneumonia and could not ride, so the leader told him he thought he'd better turn back.

In the meantime, while the people at home were playing stick dice, Tahpony's wife looked on. She was crying because she was lonesome and the people made fun of her.

He came home. His wife was living with her parents, but his parents sent for her. They went to their own tipi and talked. He told his wife that he had left the war party because he got to thinking of her. She told of how the people made fun of her.

He said, "Do you really love me?"

She said she did, but he didn't believe her and kept questioning her. Finally, he told her to get out. She said she didn't want to go, but finally he forced her to leave.

It was good moonlight. Her people lived close, and Tahpony watched her from under the raised tipi cover. It was summer and the tipi cover was raised for air.

He kept looking. After a while, she came back. He said, "Why do you come back?"

She said, "I don't want to leave you."

He forced her to leave. This time she did not return. Tahpony lay there and kept looking at his father-in-law's tent.

The next morning they were going to break camp. His wife's mother came over. She said she wanted to talk to her *monahpʉ*.[2] She said her daughter came home the night before, and said that he had turned her out. She wanted to know if this was so. Tahpony said it was so. His mother-in-law said that was all she wanted to know and left.

They moved and camped again. Again, the wife's people were close.

While they moving, Tahpony rode alone. He set up his own tipi and put the cover up.

His wife came and put her hands on him. He pushed her away. She went back to her own people. It was night; all night long he looked for her, but did not see her.

He went to his mother. He said, "Why don't you take up for me?" He wanted his mother to tell his mother-in-law to bring his wife back, that this time he would not leave her.

Again the camp moved, this time scattering. It was two years before the two parts drifted together again.

Tahpony hid by the watering place. His wife came. He went to her and asked her to come back. She said that it was up to him, that he had sent her away. He was so glad, he gave her his only horse. He had done what he did to prove she really loved him. The last time she went off, he cursed himself, big nose, ugly, etc.

1. Hoebel included Tahpony's story with the above note "War Parties: Cowardice."
2. Daughter's husband.

Life Cycle: Marriage: Exchange   Brother and sister sometimes married sister and brother. [An unmarried men may ask their brother-in-law for his sister.][1]

Life Cycle: Marriage: Lovers {Wedel}   Lovers sometimes married.

Life Cycle: Marriage: Lovers {Hoebel}   "Do couples love each other when mated by others?"

They may have trouble during the first few weeks, but they got used to each other.

Life Cycle: Suicide   George knew of no Comanche suicides.

Medicine: Transfer   Medicine men didn't necessarily hand down their powers to their sons.

Life Cycle: Marriage: Levirate/Sororate   If a widow refused to marry the brother of the deceased, but married someone else, the brother would *nanɨwokɨ*. Either younger or elder brother, according to widow's choice, was suitable mate.

Kinship Relations: Joking {Wedel}   A man could joke with his wife's sister or friends. A man's *haipia*[2] would say, "Take me plum-hunting with you alone," etc. The jokes were only for amusement.

Kinship Relations: Joking {Carlson}   You joked with all your mate's siblings. Jokes were in fun; they were not practical. Your wife's friend was also called *haipia*. She would come up to you before a crowd and say, "Let's go off somewhere, just us two." That would make the people laugh.

Life Cycle: Courting {Wedel}   If a young man wanted a certain girl, he would go out and kill some game, then take it up to her tipi. The girl's parents, seeing this, would suspect his designs. Some men got wives this way.

A young man might give bow and arrows to the brother of a desirable girl and say he wanted him for a brother-in-law. The latter would go to his father and show him the things. The father would appreciate this and never refused such a request.[3]

Life Cycle: Courting {Hoebel}   A young man might go out and shoot a deer and take it to her family. The family suspected that he wanted their daughter as his wife. They arranged it.

A young man might take some arrows to the girl's brother and tell him to tell his father that those arrows were given to him by a fellow who called him "brother-in-law" and wanted to marry his sister. Her father would not refuse; he was flattered.

Life Cycle: Courting {Carlson}   A young man wanted to marry a girl. He killed a deer or some similar thing and took it to the girl's parents. The old man knew that there must be a reason for such a gift and realized that the young man must want to marry his daughter. That's how some young men got wives.

The young man might give a younger brother of the girl some bows and arrows, calling him "brother-in-law" and telling the boy to tell his father he should have the girl.

See also Nemaruibetsi's life story.[4]

1. Wallace and Hoebel 1952:132 (?).

2. Opposite sex sibling-in-law or opposite sex cousin. Robinson and Armagost (1990) has *haipia* as 'opposite sex cousin (parallel or cross)'.

3. Wallace and Hoebel 1952:134 (?).

4. Although Nemaruibetsi's life story survives in Hoebel's notes (see below, Nemaruibetsi, July 31), it survives only in fragments in Carlson's notes. There are no clear parallels between the contents of this note and either Carlson's or Hoebel's versions of Nemaruibetsi's life story.

War: Revenge   A war party for revenge was led by a brave warrior and included some kin of the slain person. As soon as a scalp had been obtained, the party was ready to return. The father and grandfather of the slain would feel better, although mourning was continued. Every time a Comanche was killed, an enemy had to be killed in return.

War: Coup   A warrior whose deeds hadn't been witnessed by others was believed only in proportion to his general truthfulness.

War: Coup: Transfer   If two men went on a war party, and one took a scalp and then was killed, the other had a right to take the scalp and count war honors on it.

War: Scalps; War: Coup {Wedel}   If the first man struck a fallen enemy and a second killed him, the killer took the scalp. Only two men could count war honors upon one victim.[1]

War: Scalps; War: Coup {Hoebel}   If a friend took scalps off an enemy and was later killed, his comrade could bring back the scalp and possess it as if he had struck the body with his spear.

In a double coup, the first man had struck the enemy, while the second man killed him and took the scalp.[2]

War: Fighting {Wedel}   In-fighting was preferred, because the first man to close with the enemy and kill one was highly honored.

The killer would take none of victim's possessions, save his spear and other weapons.

War: Fighting {Hoebel}   Fighting was always close in. People would talk about a man who didn't meet his enemy.

They would take weapons, but no moneys or ornaments.

Medicine: Bullet-Proof   A man with antibullet medicine might ride past a firing line three times and on the fourth time he would dash in.

Social Organization: Medicine Societies {Wedel}   A medicine man could give power to not over six others (cf. Post Oak Jim {July 14}). Each of these would have the same shield decorations. A man would belong to only one of these clubs.

Social Organization: Medicine Societies {Hoebel}   George thought that six men with one medicine was the limit. Their shields would be all alike.[3] The man who distributed the power would be the leader.

Medicine: Animal Powers: Buffalo   Gun- or arrowshot wounds were cured by Buffalo Medicine.

Social Organization: Medicine Societies   Clubs might meet occasionally to get more power [for their medicine].

Medicine: Sulfur   Sulfur was smeared over the body as a protection against bullets.

Animal Powers: Bear   Bear also gave protective medicine [to stop bullets; possessors wore bear's ear's].

Medicine: Ghosts [and Eagle]   Ghosts [and eagles] gave power to cure pain.

Medicine: Eagle Medicine: Taboos {Wedel}   There could be no shadow on the possessor. One could not walk behind him. He had to eat before sunup, and no one could enter his

---

1. Hoebel 1940:22.
2. Wallace and Hoebel 1952:248.
3. Hoebel 1940:40.

lodge while he was eating. A man with many children could not have this medicine. Its possessors were very watchful, like an eagle.

Black eagle medicine was more powerful at night. White eagle medicine was more powerful in the daytime

Medicine: Eagle Medicine: Taboos {Hoebel}   It was dangerous. The owner must eat before sunrise. No shadow must fall on his tipi while he was eating. No one could pass behind him while he ate. If he ate in the tipi with the door shut, no one could enter (there was no particular sign set out, one knew).

The holder could not have many children; they would touch him with greasy hands or break other taboos.

White eagle's medicine was more powerful in the daytime; black eagle more powerful at night.

Black eagle feathers were dangerous. They were used only in fans. One must wash the hands after touching them before one could eat. If they were hung in a tree, one couldn't sit under it.

One could not get rid of Eagle Medicine, but it would gradually wear off.[1]

Material Culture: Clothing: Headdress: Roach   The roach was worn by warriors in a headdress. [There was the eagle roach.]

Animal Powers: Beaver   Beaver gave no medicine. [Beaver had power to cure disease, i.e., tuberculosis.]

Medicine: Curing: Herb   Herb remedies involved no power [Herb doctoring was without medicine.]

Medicine: Sacred Places: Medicine Hills   There was a *puhaku?e* south of Cache.[2] It was probably where a medicine man was buried; it was a residual mound.

Kinship Relations: Parents   If a man really loved his parents, he did what they said.[3]

Kinship: Sibling Attitudes   If a man really loved his brother, he wanted to share everything with him.

Adornment: Hair Care   Braids were worn down the side.

The sweetheart lock[4] was braided and attached behind the others.

Social Control: Adultery: Punishment   A woman might have her nose cut off by her husband for unfaithfulness. She was then free to marry again (when divorced or he died). She isn't likely to find a husband, however. The Horse Dancers left her alone.[5]

Medicine: Peyote: Fans   In the old days, only the leader brought a medicine fan with him. Now, many young men brought them who had no special business to.[6]

1. This note is a combination of three note cards, one typewritten, two manuscript.
2. Robinson and Armagost (1990) gives *ku?e* as 'top, summit', and Canonge (1958), 'roof, tipi opening, top of mountain'. It is one mile west and a quarter mile south of Cache. About 1982, I was told that some time before, an entrepreneur thought to open a race track there, using the slope of the hill for the grandstand, but no one would attend. The remains of the grandstand could still be seen.
3. This note and the next are from Carlson. They are dated July 21, but are not directly paralleled in Wedel's main text, and so are placed here.
4. This "sweetheart lock" is an otherwise unknown term.
5. This and the next three notes are from Hoebel and are undated. Since George Koweno was interviewed only once, I have placed them here.
6. La Barre 1975:69.

Political Organization: Chiefs   "I am going on the warpath. I am going to put so and so (*haitsI*) in charge."

He left her his *haitsI* and announced, "Look here my friends, here is my wife. Pitch your tents close to her so that you may tell the rest of the people what you intend to do. She has full instructions. I have left all my plans with her. I want you to help her carry them out. She knows everything I want done and how I want it done. And she will tell you."[1]

The *haitsI* was to provide meat.[2]

Nanʉwokʉ: Champion-at-Law   A brave warrior was called upon to help a man get his property back (i.e., only his wife captured by a warrior.) He didn't have to be a relative. Some brave warrior took pity on the person and agreed to help him out. Brothers might go out to collect a gift. They could take it by force (*nanʉwokʉ*) or ask for what they wanted.[3]

POST OAK JIM
July 24, 1933[4]

Material Culture: Crafts: Woodwork   Cedar, mulberry, walnut, bois d'arc were used for cradles.

Adzelike gouges, ⟨narino?ai⟩, were used for hollowing meat grinders, etc. [wooden bowls]. They had a wooden handle and a steel blade.

Material Culture: Cradles   The cradle was of soft buckskin, cut in an oval shape with perforated edges.

Material Culture: Cradles: Night Cradle   For the night cradle, they used a young buffalo hide with the fat scraped off. The hair was scraped off and placed in a cloth. It was sewn up and used for a pillow. The underfur was left on the inside of the cradle. There were loops of rawhide on either side, laced up with a hide thong. In winter, it was laced up, all except for a small place for breathing.

---

1. These exact words are duplicated in Hoebel, but attributed to Jeanette Mirsky's field notes (see Appendix A). Hoebel then comments:
    Such a practice would have been of most unusual occurrence. Aside from its not having been recorded in the investigations of the . . . Field Group, it does not fit comfortably into the Comanche setting. It may be noted, in this respect, that *haits* were reputedly always together when one of them took to the warpath. [1940:20]
It is not clear what part of this statement Hoebel was objecting to: putting the wife in charge, or the *haitsI* remaining behind. It may be noted that in 1829 the southern Comanche chief Parʉakevitsi (*parʉa* 'bear', *ʉkʉbitsi*, 'little', Little Bear) left his three subchiefs behind to act in his stead while he traveled from San Antonio to Santa Fe (Kavanagh 1996:200).

2. Hoebel's note card has the consultant notation, "6, 20." George Koweno was consultant number 6, but the numbered consultants only go up to sixteen, so it is not clear who number 20 was.

3. In the place of the usual consultant number, Hoebel's note card has the initials F.G.H., presumably F. Gore Hoebel. The specific notes parallel comments recorded by Wedel, but are not paralleled on any other of Hoebel's cards.

4. Wedel's notes indicate that someone named Gordon was the interpreter for this session, but it is not known who he was.

Finely scraped buffalo calf hide was used for diapers in the old days. They were washed and dried after each wearing. They were cut square or triangular.

Life Cycle: Childbirth   A special tipi was erected for childbirth. The mother entered the tipi. They heated a large flat stone and put it on one side of the mother. They covered the stone with sage and she lay down, placing the stone on her abdomen. Sometimes she lay face down and the stone was placed on her back. The treatment was continued every morning for eight or ten days, then the patient went to the creek and bathed and was through. She bathed in quiet water.

Matrons were present at childbirth to assist. Some men were permitted to come in to visit, but mostly they stayed out because of the danger to their medicines.

The navel was squeezed free of blood, doubled up, laid in a pile, and tied up with a deerskin thong. A cottonwood leaf was wrapped around the navel. It was placed over the fire and warmed to make the sap flow from the leaf. White and red clay were mixed and smeared over the navel. Eventually, the navel dropped off and was then placed in a tree to insure long life.[1]

[The umbilical cord was not severed. It was smeared with salve, a grayish clay and red paint mixed with cottonwood sap. After three to five days it would drop off.]

The afterbirth was wrapped in deerskin, then buried or placed in the crotch of a tree.[2] The mother or some female kin handled this, <u>never</u> a man.

The stone was heated in a dug fire pit.

After the woman had bathed, she must begin to exercise. She took hold of a horse's tail and was made to run for 300 yards or so, repeated from time to time until she had regained her strength.[3]

After the mother had exercised, she went back to the tipi, got dressed in her best clothes, and was fed; she had eaten nothing but soup during the period of the heat treatment. Cedar sprigs were placed on a hot stone and the woman inhaled the smoke. The mother was exercised and inhaled the cedar smoke on the day after the heat treatments ended.

A mother should not sleep with her husband for a month after the birth of her child.

If the baby was a boy, his mother's parents gave the father a rifle painted with red ocher, so if he went after buffalo, he would always get blood, i.e., kill game. If they had no gun, they would present a bow and arrows. The same presents were given if a girl was born, because in those days either a man or a woman could jump on a horse and get game. Those presents were given at the birth of the first child only. If there was more than one wife, the parents of each made a present when their daughter had her first child.

Life Cycle: Marriage: Polygamy   The first wife was the highest, the others had authority according to their rank. The first wife's consent was not necessary for additional wives. The man was supreme in the house.

Life Cycle: Sex: Premarital Sex   If a young man got a girl in the family way, he might marry her.[4]

1. Wallace and Hoebel 1952:144.
2. Contra Wallace and Hoebel 1952:144.
3. Wallace and Hoebel 1952:126 (?).
4. Wallace and Hoebel 1952:240.

Life Cycle: Marriage: Sororate   If he was a good provider, he would be given all of the daughters of all the wives of his father-in-law.

Life Cycle: Illegitimacy   There were very few bastards in the old days.

    The mother wouldn't marry for long time.

    If the real father wanted the child he could have it.[1] The father of the girl rarely resorted to violence; they usually settled the matter satisfactorily.

Nanɨwokɨ {Wedel}   *nanɨwokɨ* was only for adultery.

    They might shoot him down like a dog if they caught the offender, or else take his property or kill his choice horses.

    They were very strict in this respect.

    Sometimes they killed the woman.

    If the adulterer was a greater warrior, the husband tried peaceful methods first; then, if unsuccessful, a feud would break out. The husband would gather his true friends, they smoked together, then went in a group to collect *nanɨwokɨ* or to kill the adulterer or his horses. The adulterer was given a warning before the arrival of the *nanɨwokɨ* party. When they arrived, they were met by friends of the guilty man who talked peace. True friends, rather than relatives, were taken to collect *nanɨwokɨ*.

Nanɨwokɨ {Hoebel}   If a man took another man's wife, the injured man might take the other's horses; he might kill the other man's horses; he might kill the other man (?); he might kill the woman or both.

    If the man who took the wife was a braver warrior, the injured man came to talk it over.

    If there was no agreement, "war broke out between the two families."

Nanɨwokɨ {Wedel}   Two brothers were married to one woman. The real husband disappeared for a time and on his return he found his wife pregnant.

    He told his brother and his true friends to get their bows and arrows ready and they were going to collect *nanɨwokɨ*.

    He went to his wife and asked who the father was. She said it was his own brother. So the husband went back and told his brother it was all off; it was his own brother.

    nanɨwokɨ was split up between the members of the collecting party. Sometimes the husband got nothing himself.

    If the boy had no stock, they sometimes tore off his shirt and whipped him.

Nanɨwokɨ {Hoebel}   Two brothers with one wife, who really belonged to one of them.

    The husband returned one time to find his wife pregnant.

    He came to Jim and said, "Get out your bows and arrows. We'll go *nanɨwokɨ*."

    He told Jim to wait while he questioned his wife. Jim was shining up his spear points. The wife told her husband that it was his own brother. He came back and told Jim, "Nothing doing."

    This was the only time Jim was in {on a *nanɨwokɨ* party}; he thought he was going to get a horse or cow.

    Sometimes there wasn't enough *nanɨwokɨ* to go around among the accompanying friends and the husband got nothing. If the offender had no horses or cattle, they might take his shirt off and whip him.

---

1. Wallace and Hoebel 1952:240.

See the case of Youniacut,[1] whipping waived.[2]

Nanʉwokʉ {Wedel}   Soldiers once surprised a Comanche raiding party in the mountains. They killed all their stock to make them helpless.

Jim's nephew had a fine white racehorse left. He got into trouble with a woman. A *nanʉwokʉ* party came to get the horse. The boy and all his friends went to catch it. The horse stepped into a hole, tripped and fell, and was roped by the *nanʉwokʉ* party. The horse then died of a broken neck.

The leader of the friends then said that the only thing to do was to take the boy's shirt off and whip him.

The leader of the *nanʉwokʉ* party said that since they had tried to pay, and since the boy was willing to take the whipping instead, they would let him go if he promised not to let it happen again. The boy promised and the affair was ended.

Nanʉwokʉ {Hoebel}   Whipping Waived; Jim's nephew. A group of Indians were out on a raid. Soldiers caught them off guard and stole nearly all their horses. Post Oak Jim's nephew had only one white horse left, the sole horse in the band.

The nephew got into trouble and took another man's wife. He was caught, He said he would settle, that he was in the wrong. The nephew was going to give them his white horse, which was extremely hard to catch. All the friends and relatives ran out to catch him. The horse was caught finally and got down, but its neck was broken in the process.

The nephew's relative said to the party, "Well, we intended to do right. Now we have nothing left to do but offer to let you whip him."

The offender took off his shirt to get ready. A man spoke up for the other side. He said, "We see that your intentions are good. He is a young and fine man; we want you to be good in the future."

He promised not to do it again and the case was settled.[3]

Nanʉwokʉ {Wedel}   A band of Comanches was on a trip. A boy did another man's wife wrong. Nothing was done until they got back. Then, two of the aggrieved man's friends went to talk it over with the boy. While talking peacefully, another young man called to them to kill him and quit fooling around. The boy then got angry, got up, and knifed the speaker. He was then set upon by the two others and they began to cut him up.

Nanʉwokʉ {Hoebel}   A band was on the warpath. An adulterer was along. They refrained from action because of the danger. They had a *nanʉwokʉ* party on their return. One emissary was talking kindly. The aggrieved husband got impatient. He said, "That's no way. Why don't you beat him up? Kill him."

The culprit got sore. He jumped from his horse and stabbed the husband in the hip. The friends of the husband killed the attacker.

Nanʉwokʉ: Feud   When a *nanʉwokʉ* feud began, the chief usually stepped in and tried his best to quiet things down. Usually they exacted life for life, always the life of a killer. The feud continued until an equal number of men were killed on each side.

---

1. *yuni* 'hair', *kutʉ* 'possessor', Has Hair. Hoebel (1940:145) gives this name as Yóniakat and translates it as Buffalo Robe. Youniacut was a Yapainʉʉ local band leader, 1879–92.

2. See below, Nemaruibetsi, Undated.

3. Hoebel 1940:58.

[In cases where one was killed, it was sure to come that his true friends would get the other. They would ambush him when his protectors had left and they felt it was all blown over.

The chief might try to prevent direct action.

They said no words to cause heat unless they have made no progress. This used to happen frequently; "lots of people got hurt, lots got killed." Jim was never in one, but saw some long distance fighting. There were four men on the claimant's side, but he couldn't see the others. Relatives did not participate, only true friends.]

Social Control: Adultery   If a woman found her husband gone, she might take up with the husband of her husband's paramour. Here, the offenses cancelled one another.

Political Organization: Chiefs: War Leader   A war party was under the command of one man. [There was a chief over all.] He had several sub-officers to whom he gave orders and who passed them on to the warriors. The chief called his inferiors, "brothers." [They were war bonnet wearers.] The chief was called "big brother."

If two brothers became chiefs, they were treated as one. They couldn't desert each other in battle.

[Two brothers might be chiefs; they were considered as one chief. They must help each other in warfare.]

War Parties   If a war party went out, they left word for the village not to wait for their return, but to move without them. They would follow if they weren't killed.

Political Organization: Chiefs   The chief's word was supreme, because of the danger of dissension. [Braves never failed to follow orders.]

War: Battle of Navajo Mountain {Wedel}   The Navajos had possession of the highest hills in this country. They camped on the top for one winter and one summer, and couldn't be driven out because there was only one entrance. Finally, a tribe [band] came in and camped at the foot of the trail. They killed a buffalo, put up their tipis, turned their stock loose, and showed themselves fearless. The Navajos slipped down, rounded up their horses, and drove them up the trail.

One young man had his horse staked out and wanted to follow the Navajos. Another young man wanted to use his horse, so they had a row and the horse broke loose.

The Indians then followed on foot. They tangled with the <u>Navies</u> {*sic*}. While they were fighting, the young man slipped in, recovered the horses, and single-handedly drove all the horses away from the Navajos and back to his (Comanche) people. The Navajos shot at him, but couldn't pierce his shield.

The young man later went to Rainy Mountain and told all the people there that [they had fought the Navajo and that] he was the only survivor, and he was greatly honored. But the next day, the rest of the Comanches come up after traveling all night. The chief of the Rainy Mountain people had to apologize to his people for his own announcement.

War: Battle of Navajo Mountain {Hoebel}   The Navajos had a high hill. It was impregnable, with only one entrance. They lived there summer and winter. A band of Indians got in and camped. They killed and skinned a bison. They let the horses loose. The Navajos came down and cut off the horses. There was just one horse staked out.

They started the pursuit; they quarreled about who should take the horse. It escaped. They went on foot.

One brave got the horse (the man who owned it). He rode in and drove the other horses back without being killed. He then shot his shield full of holes and rode quickly to the main camp by Rainy Mountain. He told the people there that they had fought the Navajos and he was the only man left alive.

The chief has his brave deed announced.

In the meantime, the rest were traveling back. They all arrived in the morning. It showed that the young brave had been fooling them. The chief had to explain it to the people.

P.M.

Material Culture: Clothing: Headdress   There were two kinds of headdresses, one for doctors, the other for brave warriors [*tekwᵾniwapɪ*]. Doctors had to be well-known and strong.

Weapons: Spear {Wedel}   Brave warriors carried a spear with their bonnets. The whole spear was beaded; it was one and a half inches in diameter by six feet long, with crow feathers at the top, and an eagle feather. This belonged to the chief. There was a buffalo hide case to carry the spear. There was only one spear per band, carried by the chief. It was carried only in time of danger. At his death, the spear was placed in a tree; his descendants must earn their own spears, it was not inherited.

Weapons: Spear {Hoebel}   A spear went with the paraibo. It was six to seven feet long, one and a half inches in thickness. It was beaded the entire length. There was just one in the band. It had a bunch of crow feathers and one eagle feather.

Material Culture: Clothing: Headdress {Wedel}   For each brave deed, a young warrior got an eagle feather. Mere membership in a party didn't get a feather. Killing an enemy, stealing horses were brave acts.

The headdress was tied under the chin and about the body.

If a warrior retreated, he first untied the headdress and threw it down, thus losing all of it at once; he had to surrender it before retreating.

Feathers were presented by the chief.

Someone else could pick up a fallen bonnet on a bow or spear, carry it back, and set it against a tree. If the battle was still on late in the day, he could charge against the enemy four times as near as possible, and if he escaped, he was then entitled to the bonnet. There were a limited number of bonnets to each band.

A doctor's headdress was small, with a few feathers and with buffalo horns on the side of the head.

There was no way for a warrior to win back a bonnet he had once thrown down.

It took four eagle's tails of twelve feathers each (i.e., forty-eight feathers) to make a bonnet.[1] Sometimes they alternated feathers from different species of eagles. There was no specific meaning for different feathers.

In giving feathers, a number of warriors with headdresses met and discussed the merits of the candidate. They sat about the chief and smoked and invited the candidate to smoke the pipe also. The special tipi was erected and the announcer called the warriors in. Each

---

1. The only known prereservation Comanche headdress in a museum collection has forty-three feathers in a straight row (Kavanagh 2001:897).

man as he came in got a seat by the door, with the rest moving around clockwise to make room. The chief was in the center

The chief said he would make a comparison to see if the man was worthy. The first four feathers were awarded after a man had four brave deeds. The rest were awarded in a second ceremony after the remainder of the brave deeds were done.

The candidate smoked and was given the feathers by the chief, and was then a member of the warrior's society. He left the tipi with the other warriors. Warriors with feathers must lead in the attack.

All of the villagers were present. The announcer got up and told them the man was now of the elect. The bonnet was made when a full complement of feathers was presented.

Material Culture: Clothing: Headdress {Hoebel}   The headdress was worn only in time of danger.

There was a feather for each war expedition in which one or more brave deed was performed by the man concerned.

He must untie and throw down his bonnet before he could retreat from his position.

The feathers were presented by the *paraibo*.

Recovery of a bonnet lost in battle: Anyone who saw an abandoned hat may charge in and pick up the hat with a bow or spear. He returned and placed it on a pole. If the fighting continued when the sun was setting, he could put it on and charge the enemy four times. If he came through alive, the bonnet and its honors were his.

It took the feathers from four eagle's tails for one bonnet. There were twelve feathers to a bird, forty-eight total.

Presentation of feathers: Certain men who have bonnets were selected by the chief. They formed a committee considering the worth of the candidate. After the man had four deeds he was eligible. They met in a special tipi. The chief sat in the center west. Each man to enter sat next to the door crowding the others down.

The announcer invited the candidate in. The man was told the duties and dangers. They first smoked and then gave the feathers. "From that point his rank was raised."

He must always be in the front rank, those who gave the orders from a chief on raids. Should he fail, he lost the bonnet.

There was a second and more important ceremony when the forty-eight feathers were won. None were worn until all forty-eight were gained.[1]

Material Culture: Clothing: Headdress: Shaming {Wedel}   If a young man boasted of brave deeds and complained of being slighted, the women made a bonnet and sold it to him for a horse or a cow. If he couldn't afford to buy some, his kin got it for him. Then, he must carry it into battle and prove his bravery; everyone watched to see if he was brave.

Material Culture: Clothing: Headdress: Shaming {Hoebel}   If a man boasted of exploits, saying he should have a bonnet too, the women were told. They made him a bonnet and took the bonnet to him. He had to buy it. He wore it and all watched him in action. If he was brave, he could keep it as deserved; if a coward[2]

---

1. Hoebel 1940:29.
2. Hoebel 1940:30; Wallace and Hoebel 1952:273. Hoebel's note ends abruptly here.

Material Culture: Clothing: Headdress: Otter Cap {Wedel}   Caps were made of otter skins wrapped about the head with the tail hanging down behind. This was the highest badge of honor; the wearer was above the war bonnet men. He could go and come as he pleased. After getting this cap, a man must go along on every raid made by the group of cap wearers.

Material Culture: Clothing: Headdress: Otter Cap {Hoebel}   The highest bonnet wearers had to go to war all the time. They were greatly respected. It was made of otter or beaver furs. It was wound around the head, one hanging down back. It was one stage beyond the war bonnet. They could go and come as they pleased. The highest one came decorated with buffalo horns.

Material Culture: Clothing: Headdress: Shaming   People who didn't like to go to war were made otter skin caps half as large as those of the highest warriors, open at the top, to set themselves off. Other people sang ludicrous songs about them and ridiculed them.

War: Cowardice   Persons who refused to go on a party or turned back [or liked to go to peyote meetings] were razzed as cowards. Men who never went to war could be distinguished by poor horses, lack of good blankets, and general poverty.

War: Loot: Clothing   Well-dressed warriors were stripped of their clothes when they fell in battle.

War: Mutilation   Others were simply scalped and had a limb or nose cut off for good measure.

War: Loot: Weapons   Spears were always repossessed from the fallen enemy because of the difficulty in making them; arrows were not always recovered. [They were pulled or cut out of the enemy, but not if they were broken.]

[Twelve-shot[1]] repeating rifles were taken from fallen foes; pistols were not because of the danger of their exploding[2] and of the shortage of ammunition.

Material Culture: Clothing: Headdress   A man could wear a war bonnet taken from an enemy, but it didn't mean anything unless he proved his bravery.

When a man died, his war bonnet was put in a tree or buried.

The bonnet was kept in a rawhide cylinder, hairside inside, with the top bound up like a duffle bag.

Medicine: Charms: Crow Feather {Wedel}   A crow feather was tied to a lance to keep away evil spirits. They were also tied on bed posts to quiet children and keep away ghosts. Small feathers were used for small children, with the largest for older children.

Medicine: Charms: Crow Feather {Hoebel}   Crow feathers were combined with eagle feathers to ward off evil spirits (i.e., war bonnet).

A crow feather was tied to a child's cradle[3] or forelock for the same purpose.

This evil spirit was a ghost.

The longest wing feather was for a walking child, a pin feather for a baby.

---

1. This probably refers to the twelve-shot 1873 Winchester carbine.
2. The treaty goods for the 1867 Medicine Lodge Treaty council included revolvers made by the Union Arms Company, several of which exploded on first firing (Jones 1966:136).
3. Wallace and Hoebel 1952:160.

Beliefs: Ghosts {Wedel}   Some warriors were on their way to a battle when spirits met them one night as they were passing an isolated tree on the edge of a small grove. A voice told them to go on, that the best part of existence was life on earth. He must have been a bad man on earth to talk like that.

Beliefs: Ghosts {Hoebel}   Warriors were out; it was moonlight. They came to a tree and heard a voice, "Friends, keep on going. I'm through, you keep on."

The spirit spoke again, "The best part of life was the part on earth."

He said that he'd like to live on earth again.

He was probably a bad man who was killed, because he talked thus.

War Parties: Returning   Returning warriors didn't have to stay outside the village to be purified.

Relations with Other Tribes: Pueblos   Pueblo Indians were called *tebo*.

Captives   Skilled captives were used [forced] to repair guns.[1]

[They frequently snuck into the camp to give themselves up. They came from some poor tribe where there wasn't enough food.]

Material Culture: Slings   Mexicans used slings; they could hit a man at 200 yards.

Material Culture: Crafts: Silver Work   The Indians removed silver from Mexican saddles and bridles and reworked it after heating. Comanches learned about turquoise from the Navajos.

[Silver work was learned from the Mexicans. The Comanches took the tools off of captives. They heated pure silver and beat it into shape. There was no turquoise until they had contact with the Navajos.]

Material Culture: Crafts   A skilled craftsman would give his product to his kin or swap them with others (e.g., saddles for silverwork).

Dances: Pipe Dance {Wedel}   Two or three girls get together to get a young man in the morning while he was still asleep. Another gang got another young man. They brought him {them?} to the dance.

(Another man threw the subject over his shoulder, another took his feet, and they carried him to the dance.)

He was then decorated for the occasion by some old warrior. It was very embarrassing for the young man because he hadn't won the honor. One of the young men was the black eagle, the other was the white; the white eagle came from the south and is always on top. They danced about with eagle feathers along their arms and carried gourd rattles.

There were two sides, north and south.

Calico, blankets, pumpkins, perfumes, and money to be given away were all in a pile in front of either side.

A man got up on one side and spoke of a man on the other side, telling of the man's brave deeds, and he told him he was giving him a horse, which may be good or very bad. The donor also handed over a pipe and told where the horse might be found. The recipient went out to a post and pointed to it as if an enemy. Then he went away, mounted the horse, and rode by the post with his lance. He "killed" it and scalped it as the enemy.

1. As early as the 1780s, several captives, including Pedro Vial, acted as gunsmiths for the Comanches (Loomis and Nasatir 1967:265).

When the speaker was through, the other man got a choice of the goods. Then the others got a choice until the goods are gone. One man once went out to get fine horse and found a mule that he couldn't approach.

This took place when two different tribes came together.

Formerly, the two Eagle dancers went until noon, then the announcer called out the end of the dance. Then the dancers were set upon, stripped, and left. This was now replaced by an exchange of gifts between the two sides. Dancers were formerly stripped in punishment for a similar act toward a captive white. They didn't want the Indians to torture prisoners thus.

Dances: Pipe Dance {Hoebel}   (Put on for a visiting tribe.) This was like capturing an enemy in war.

Two or three girls snuck up on a man while he was sleeping. They got two men simultaneously. He knew what they were about and went along.

They went out to where the dances were. An honored brave would decorate him in imitation of his own deeds.

The two parties represented the white and black eagle. One came from the north, one from the south (the white eagle). They had a gourd rattle in one hand and a bundle of feathers in the other.

They were carried into the dance on the shoulders of a warrior.

White eagles always flew above black eagles. In the dance, {when} they passed, the black eagle passed under the spread wings of the white eagle.

In old times, it was over at noon. They were thrown down and the people pulled all their clothes off.

There were two sides, north and south. There was a pile of blankets, cloth, pumpkins, perfume, in between. Piles of stuff on both sides.

A man got up and presented an ancient horse to one (he made a speech about a fine horse). The man gave the fellow a stick with which to go out to get the horse. (It may be an old plug, or it may be a good horse; maybe a mean one.)

The man had the singers stop. He wanted to tell a brave deed he had done. He rode in on a horse with his spear. He speared the enemy (a dummy) or wrestled with him and took his scalp (the people all watched). He had a choice of goods laid out. Another man did the same performance, and so on until all the gifts are gone. Once a fellow chose a fine horse, he found a very bad mule when he got outside.

They wanted to see who had done the bravest deed. First came the warriors from the home tribe; then it was open for the visitors to act out their deeds.

In the old days, the dance ended at noon. The clothes were taken off the men. This was done as punishment to men who had completely undressed an enemy. It was not supposed to be done. Later, this undressing act was considered too rank. Then they left them dressed after the eagle dance, and continued with individual performers.

Relations with Other Tribes: Intertribal Peace   A common hatred toward the Whites brought the Indians peaceably into union with one another.

Trouble over women caused disruption. Intermarriage ended the taking of captives; it was a cohesive factor in tribal and intertribal factors.

POST OAK JIM
July 25, 1933

Material Culture: Clothing: Headdress: Doctor's   The doctor's headdress was an otter skin cap with feathers; ther e were no horns. Horns were only on the caps of those warriors who went hunting trouble.[1]

The doctor went and got power, then returned to the village and was given the otter skin and feathers at the same time in a ceremony like that for a warrior. A medicine man's power was proved by his invulnerability in warfare and power to cure the injured.

Material Culture: Clothing: Headdress: Doctor's: Number in Band   A small band might have four or five doctor's cap wearers; there were [no more than] ten in the Noyʉhka.

Medicine: Curing: Women Doctors   Women doctors cured rheumatism, headache, stomach ache, [pneumonia, etc.].

Medicine: Curing: War Doctors   War doctors were buffalo doctors. They used different parts of the buffalo to cure wounds, according to the portion (e.g., the liver, gall, etc.) which was revealed as curative by their vision. A cut vein was mended by tying it into place with a section of vein excised from a buffalo, using sinew from the spine to secure it.

A doctor had to prove that his medicine was strong before he was thought of as a candidate for a bonnet; the doctors were awarded their bonnets.

Medicine: Curing: Women Doctors: Payments   [They made an agreement beforehand as to price. She didn't seek patients, she was called on]

If a patient's family refused to pay the fee to a woman doctor after a cure, she would never help them again. A male doctor might put a curse on the delinquent family, but a woman never would.

Material Culture: Clothing: Headdress: Women Doctors   Doctoresses couldn't wear bonnets, but tended to home medicines only, both in their own and other households.

Material Culture: Clothing: Headdress: Doctor   A young man didn't have to have a bonnet before curing persons outside his own family.

Social Organization: Medicine Societies   After a young man had been accepted by the doctor's "society," his parents presented a horse or blanket.

The initiate to the "society" brought his parents, who gave presents of horses, blankets, etc. He sat on the south side of the door. The big man sat against the west wall of the tipi. The servant sat just north of the door.

The men filed in clockwise and seated themselves against the wall. The men smoked and laid the butts of their cigarettes about the fireplace. Before any could leave the tipi, the servant had to sweep the floor with sage and pile the cigarette butts and sweepings just east of the fireplace.

Various men got up and recommended the candidate formally. He was then awarded the bonnet.

Villagers gathered about the tipi, as there was no room inside.

Medicine: Sweat Lodge: Children {Wedel}   A buffalo skull was set in front of the door, outside, facing west into the tipi. There was red paint on the front of the skull, blue on

---

1. Wedel's notes state that Gordon was again the interpreter. See above, July 24, 1933.

either cheek. The tipi was built up of willows tied at the top, covered with a heavy robe. Jim was about ten years old when he gave this.

He took grass in bunches and started a fire outside, piling wood on top. Everyone filed in, laid down as near the fireplace as possible, and raked in the coals, making a great pile.

The door was closed and the tipi was made airtight.

Jim prayed a while. Then he threw water onto the coals. Nobody was allowed to say "Gee, it's hot"; they all had to say, "Gee, it's cold" and slap themselves.

He threw on a second cup of water and they nearly passed out.

Another man came on the outside and crushed the tipi down on top of them. Then it caught fire and they all had to run out.

In the old days, they didn't crush the tipi down.

Medicine: Sweat Lodge: Children {Hoebel}   (Six to ten years old.) A skull of a buffalo was set at the door facing west. It was painted red between the eyes and blue on the cheeks.

They brought up willow poles, two and a half inches thick, and tied them at the tips. They covered it with a tight buffalo robe.

They built a fire of prairie grass and cactus spines.

They undressed completely.

The fire chief piled coals up; Jim, acting as the fire chief, gave the orders.

Jim told them to get in their places. They went in. It was airtight and dark.

Jim prayed.

Jim then took a cup of water and poured it over the coals; there was a great steam.

They couldn't mention the heat. They had to pat their arms and say, "Gee, it's cold," and "Thank you, thank you."

At that point, an adolescent came along and squashed the hut over their heads. It caught fire and they all ran.

Medicine: Sweat Lodge: Men's {Wedel}   The men entered the tipi, sweated, then raised the tipi cover and cooled off. Then they sweated again, and raised the cover. They repeated this four or five times, and then went out and took a dip in the river.

The sweat lodge was used to cure headaches, pneumonia, rheumatism.

In curing pneumonia or rheumatism, the doctor went in with the patient, and while steam was floating about, he touched them with a bundle of grass where the pain was.

It was also used as a general tonic.

The lodge was large enough for four to six men.

Sweatbaths were held at sunrise or sunset, not at noon. On a war party or other strenuous occupation, they were used to limber up the muscles, etc.

They were like the children's, but no one pulled down the lodge at the end.

Medicine: Sweat Lodge: Men's {Hoebel}   It was done at sunrise or sunset.

There were four to six men.

They took turns.

It was for:

    a) general health;

    b) relieve fatigue;

    c) cure migraine, pneumonia, rheumatism.

The procedure was like the children's, but no one pulled the lodge down at the end.

They poured water three or four times (and let in air in between). They jumped in the creek afterwards.

In curing, the medicine man took a bundle of grass and tapped the patient over the infected places.

Medicine: Curing {Wedel}   For headache, they dug a trench long enough for the man's body. A fire was built in the trench until the ground began to crack from the heat.

The coals were raked out and a thin layer of sage was spread over the hot ground, and they poured water over the sage to get steam.

The patient was placed in the trench and entirely covered with blankets to induce a thorough sweating.

This was also used for women after childbirth, but only in the summer. In the winter, hot stones was used in the tipi for new mothers.

Medicine: Curing {Hoebel}   For rheumatism, headache, or after birth, they dug a trench for the patient.

They built a fire until the ground was so hot it cracked.

They raked out the fire and covered it with sage.

They poured on cold water.

They felt it if it was not too hot.

The patient lay in the trench, covered with a buffalo robe or blanket, and steamed.[1]

Medicine: Curing {Wedel}   A rich man in Texas had a child with paralyzed legs; he could stand, but not walk. He spent much money on specialists, but they were unsuccessful. Jim thought he could cure it by steaming in the trench, rubbing herbs on his legs, and taking it to a peyote meeting. He had seen worse cases cured, but Jim didn't get a chance to cure the child.

Medicine: Curing {Hoebel}   There was a child paralyzed from birth (Texas). It could stand, but couldn't take a step.

It's parents were rich. They tried every treatment.

Jim was <u>sure</u> he could have healed him as follows:

a) rub his legs with herbs;

b) give the trench sweat treatment;

c) peyote ceremony.

Jim had seen worse cases cured this way.

Medicine: Curing {Wedel}   Jim was called by a Ponca to cure a three-year-old child who was congenitally blind. They said they had tried two specialists, but failed. Jim felt the pulse, veins, and legs of the child.

Jim took two different kinds of roots and chewed them while the child's mother bathed the child. Jim then went in, chewed some sage with the roots, and put the juice on the legs of the restless child. Jim then went to a peyote meeting.

The next day, he had the child brought over and repeated the treatment, blowing on the child and massaging it. Suddenly, the child jumped out of its mother's lap and ran out of tipi, cured.

It was now a strong and healthy child.

---

1. Wallace and Hoebel 1952:170.

Jim got a fine blanket, valued at about twenty dollars for this.

Medicine: Curing {Hoebel}   Jim was called on by a Ponca to cure a child of three years who had never had the use of its legs. (They previously had two specialists who gave no help.)

Jim felt the child's legs; he said he could cure him.

The procedure:

a) he took two kinds of roots, chewed them with sage;

b) the mother washed the boy; Jim applied the liquid from the chew to his legs and blew on them;

c) he let him sleep, and went to a peyote meeting. The next morning he repeated the treatment, massaging.

d) on the second treatment, the child jumped from his mother's arms and ran out of the tipi (peyote meeting). The child was still well.

Payment: Jim asked for none; he left it to them, They gave him a new blanket worth twenty dollars.

Medicine: Curing {Wedel}   Medicine men were not as effective as in the old days.

If a man had pneumonia, for example, and had hypodermic injections, and then a medicine man tried to cure by suction, the latter was apt to get sick from the effects of the injection.

Medicine: Curing {Hoebel}   Curing used to be much better than now. Medicine men were not so successful nowadays. The reasons might be that they haven't had the full ceremony, or that the patients took too much white medicine.

They used to be able to cure tuberculosis, but now they can't. "We never used to have that disease."

Medicine men were now afraid to treat people who had previously taken white medicine. If a medicine man sucked it out, he might get sick himself from the medicine given by the white doctor.

Medicine: Curing {Wedel}   A medicine man had to be ready to go anywhere, anytime.

Jim once rushed over and cured a wealthy Shawnee who was expected to die. Jim cured him and was paid $300 by the Shawnee, who was still healthy but old. The exact nature of his disease was unknown, but no white doctors could cure him. They tried to get other Indian doctors and finally settled on Jim.

Jim decided to put on a peyote meeting; the patient provided a special tipi and a beef.

All the Indians were asked to attend. Jim told the patient he would do his best and trusted God to help him through. So they had the meeting. The next morning, the man brought him fifty dollars. Jim distributed it among the others present, retaining none for himself.

Then they moved a ways off, put up another tipi, and held a second meeting, but still he didn't cure him. Then they moved up to Shawnee country.

After the fifth meeting, the patient felt better. He rolled a leaf cigarette, smoked a couple of puffs, and handed it to Jim, who took a couple of drags, praying to God and to earth, "If it's your will, may this man be healed." Then they prayed to the peyote power.[1] The man

---

1. Wedel's typescript omitted the following two manuscript pages.

seemed like he was let out of one room into another.

The next morning, he told the members he was cured and paid Jim $300. He was still living.

It was not Jim's power that cured him but that of the Almighty. The patient had been suffering from fear that someone had put a spell on him. When he placed confidence in Jim, he became cured.

Jim formerly thought he had power to cure anything; when he reached the point where couldn't cure, he became discouraged. Peyote offered an additional hook-up with the Great Power. He saw the light at about twenty-five years of age.

Cosmology   The sun was the great father, the source of power in the old days.

⟨ɔrənánsɜwɜkai⟩
atsabiʔ[1] } was the 'Great Spirit'

Medicine: Curing {Hoebel}   A Shawnee man was diagnosed by several doctors differently. He was treated for four years, but no one cured him. He gave up on the white doctors.

He came down to where Indians were camped. There were several Indian doctors there.

They didn't want the case. They got together and chose Jim to take the case.

Jim gave a peyote meeting. The patient furnished the beef and the money for the tipi, etc.

Jim said he didn't know what was wrong with him, but he would do his best.

Procedure: He gave a peyote meeting. All the doctors were present.

The next morning, the man gave Jim fifty dollars. He passed it around to the other medicine men. He got none himself.

Later, they had another peyote meeting here. He was still no better.

They went to the Shawnees and had more meetings (five altogether).

The patient smoked, gave it to Jim. Jim smoked and prayed, "God, if it is your will, let this man live. Earth, if it is your will, let this man live on you. Peyote, if it is your will, cure this man."

He gave him peyote. The effect was as though he had entered a new room alone; he was healed. He gave Jim $300 in gratitude.

Theory of Jim: It was not his personal power, but the power of God working through him.

Jim's diagnosis (he had a vision). The patient thought sorcery had been worked on him. He worried himself weak. He was really not sick. The patient believed Jim and got over his fear. Jim said he'd thrown all his money away; he was really not sick at all.

By age twenty, Jim thought that he was acting through his own power, but by about age twenty-five, he recognized the outer power, the Great Spirit, ⟨ɔronánsɜwɜkai⟩, *atsabiʔ*. This was the spirit of the sun and earth, particularly of the sun.[2]

Story: Creation {Wedel}   In the old days, people had no creation idea. However, they

---

1. Robinson and Armagost (1990) glosses this as 'Creator, Holy Spirit'.
2. This last paragraph is from an untitled and unidentified card, although it clearly parallels Wedel's notes from the July 25 interview with Post Oak Jim, and thus is placed here. Hoebel's other cards from that interview are numbered 1 through 6, but this card is numbered 6 and 7, implying that there were other cards in the sequence that are now missing.

thought they were the only people placed on earth by the Creator, until the white people arrived. Old timers never understood where the whites came from. Some thought they came from the sky, etc. Tribes from the east finally told them that where they had come from was the sea.

Story: Creation {Hoebel}   People never gave much consideration to creation. "We knew we were here."

Thought was mostly directed to understanding the spirit.

They thought they were the only people. They never did understand where the whites came from. Old folk thought they came from the sky.[1]

Medicine: Peyote: Prayer   In peyote, they recognized the earth as their source, and prayed, "Bless me now, [that] I was formed from the dust of the ground and was given breath just same as this herb; you have been given life by God and so have I."

This was prayed first to the Sun, then to Earth.

Medicine: Vision Quest {Wedel}   The power that a medicine man got from a lonely place was the same as the Great Spirit emanating from the sun.

Medicine: Vision Quest {Hoebel}   {The Great Sprit} was the same spirit that entered a man when he had a vision and received power.

Medicine: Vision Quest: Story of Nappywat {Wedel}   A young man had been on war parties, but his parties always lost men, so he figured his turn might come. So he went to a medicine man and asked what hill he should visit to get protection. The medicine man told him where to go, and to take a buffalo robe and a whistle of eagle wing bone. He was to spread the robe hair side up, sit down facing east, and just as the moon was coming up, blow the whistle and then tell his wishes[2] to the moon. The hill would hear his wishes and grant him the power.

He said it would take lots of nerve to go up on the hill alone. He told him to pray for invulnerability, protection against bullets, etc.

He told him to lie with his head to the east and his feet to west.

Before blowing the whistle, he was to fill up the pipe and smoke. The pipe was lit by striking two flints together.

The man was naked, his body smeared (Watchsuah[3] was the Comanche's best sniper) with gray-white clay.

He went on horseback part way up. The moon was coming and so was the Great Spirit. The spirit carried a long dagger and had just been scalped. He was uttering a low, groaning sound, and came walking toward the man.

As he approached, he said, "I'm glad this time I'm going to get my revenge."

The horse was beginning to snort because it noticed the apparition. The seeker became frightened, jumped up, grabbed his pipe and robe (but left the feathers), got on his horse and fled from the hill.

1. Wallace and Hoebel 1952:194.
2. Here Wedel's typescript picks up again.
3. Watchsuah, translated as Dodger, was a Mexican captive, born around 1830. He was a member of Esarosavit's Yapainuu local band, and became a local band leader himself in 1883. It is not clear why this comment is inserted here.

When he got far enough away, he stopped and could still hear the spirit's voice, so he picked up again and ran. He made four stops, and each time, he heard the spirit and fled. Finally, he reached his village. He was on his way to the special tipi where he was to meet the warriors. He got there just at daybreak. He lay there covered with gray clay and dozed off to sleep.

The apparition appeared at the door of the tipi and said, "You're an awful coward. I almost killed you on the hill, but you got away, now I've got you."

He then promised to give him the power of invulnerability and courage. He became a very brave man and a great warrior and was never afraid again.

Once this man dreamt that he was in battle, and wondered if he was actually invulnerable, so he placed a rifle against his chest and fired. The bullet glanced off harmlessly, so he knew his medicine was good.

He was married to an Apache woman. One day, he was beating her with a whip, holding a rifle in the other hand. The rifle went off and injured his wife in the arm. In remorse, he tried to shoot himself in the head but the bullet glanced off and he was unhurt.

His name was Nappywat[1] 'without legs' because was once shot through the heel on a buffalo hunt.

He was to tie a red cloth halfway up his horses tail and on the mane, and also tie a red cloth on himself, otherwise the spirit wouldn't be with him. He was shot because he hadn't made the horse up this way and the sprit wasn't there to help him.

Medicine: Vision Quest: Story of Nappywat {Hoebel}   Nappywat meant 'without legs'. He was once shot in the heel and wounded.

How could he have been wounded when he had medicine against wounds?

On that occasion, he was unprepared. To be prepared, he must:

-tie a red cloth on himself;

-tie a red cloth on his horse's mane;

-tie his horse's tail halfway up and wrap it in red cloth.

A youth had been on several war parties. Every time, a companion had been killed. He thought his time might come if he had no medicine.

He went to a medicine man and asked for a recommendation as to a vision place.

The medicine man knew a good place, but it was mighty dangerous; he would need a strong heart. He had to smoke a pipe. He had to take a *huukU*[2] (eagle bone whistle) and a buffalo robe, a pipe, and feathers.

He laid the robe fur side up.

He sat down, facing east for the rising moon. When the moon came up, he was to blow the whistle and then tell the moon what he wanted, so the hill could know what he wanted and it would give it.

Then he was to lie down with his head to the east and his feet to the west and wait for the power to come. He wanted power to turn bullets.

He was naked and was painted (before going up the hill) over his whole body with gray

1. This is the agency spelling. *napʉ* 'shoe' 'foot' or 'leg; *wahtʉ* 'without'. He was a member of Coby's Kwaharʉnʉʉ local band.

2. Robinson and Armagost (1990) gives *huukU* as 'collarbone'.

clay.

He had come up on a horse. He tied it a little ways off.

At the same time as the moon came up, the spirit came up. He had an arm's length knife in his hand. He was scalped from the ears up. He groaned as he came. He said, "At last, I get my revenge."

The horse noticed it and began to snort.

The man got scared and grabbed the pipe and robe and ran off, leaving the feathers. He stopped, heard the voice behind him, and sped off. This happened four times.

He finally got to camp, to the special tipi that had been prepared for him where the heads go to meet all the braves. He lay down in the tipi and slept.

The vision came to the door and talked, "Oh, my, you're an awful coward. I almost killed you on the hill. Now I've got you in my power. I've changed my mind. You are an awful coward, but I will give you power anyhow."

He became a great warrior.

He dreamed in an engagement to test his power. He placed the muzzle against his left collar bone and shot. The bullet glanced off.

He quarreled with his wife and accidently shot his wife in the wrist. He tried to shot himself in the head, but the bullet turned off.

He died in 1931.[1]

Animals: Birds: Crow {Wedel}   Crows were once pure white, the king of birds, even higher than the eagle. After the flood, Crow was sent out to see whether the waters had subsided. Instead of returning to the Great Spirit and reporting, he pecked the eyes out of the corpses scattered about.

Word reached the Great Spirit of this, and he told Crow that he would be black, disliked by all, and an enemy of everyone.

He sent another bird with a leaf in its mouth; this was the red-legged dove. This bird was to be loved by everyone, to be king and not work too hard. Dove was above eagle. When the dove landed with the leaf before the people, the seasons were established.

Animals: Birds: Crow {Hoebel}   Crow was the smartest bird. He was considered the king bird, above the eagle. During the flood, the Great Spirit sent the crow to see if the water was down.

He found the people drowned. Instead of going back, he stayed here and plucked their eyes out and ate their flesh.

Crow had been pure white; the Great Spirit sent his voice. He told Crow he would be black from then on. The Great Spirit said Crow had been the king bird, but now he would be an enemy, and he was sending a new king bird with an olive branch in his mouth (red-legged dove). The king dove would be loved by all and not have to work as hard as others, (he used only a <u>few sticks</u> in his nest; it was easy to make).

Animals: Dove and Snake   The dove was brother-in-law of the snake. Snake was killed, and the dove still mourns for his slain brother-in-law [it had a sad coo].

Animals: Snakes {Wedel}   The rattler was now king of snakes. *tsipitoko* was formerly the

---

1. According to agency records, Nappywat died April 4, 1930, at the age of 88. This note is a combination of two separate Hoebel note cards.

king, but was now extinct. He had a face like a bulldog, with an upturned nose, and was very deadly, a sidewinder. This was dove's brother-in-law.

Formerly, when this snake was shot, the arrow wasn't reused; it was as deadly as the snake's bite when used.

Jim once caught one of these snakes. He cut the rattles off with a knife and didn't wash the blade. Years later, he was skinning a cow and the knife slipped when he got to the udder and he cut his hand. Before he could stop the flow of blood, his arm was swollen clear to the shoulder.

Animals: Snake {Hoebel}   Snake was dove's brother-in-law. Rattler was the king snake now.

The king snake used to be *tsipitoko*. *tsipitoko* was now extinct. It was a sidewinder. It was of a small size, poisonous, and gray striped.

To kill a sidewinder, one shot it and left the arrow in; if the arrow was used again, it was poison. (One knife poisoned a man three years after it had touched a snake; it didn't kill him.)

Story: Flood {Wedel}   The flood destroyed the world. There were some Indians in it. They believed that something was going to happen but didn't know what. They saw a white (smart?) man building a boat so they knew it meant a flood.

The Indians killed a great many buffalo and dried the meat, then cut a number of cottonwoods into blocks. When the water came they floated away on the raft of blocks. But the flood lasted so long their food gave out and they all starved to death.

The flood was caused by the power from the sun. It was sent because the Indians were so cruel, they raided camps, scalped people, took their clothes, cut off their limbs, etc.

Story: Flood {Hoebel}   There was a flood in olden times (white man's flood). There were some Indians on earth then. They knew something awful was going to happen, but didn't know what.

They saw a white man making a boat and wondered what to do to save themselves. They killed lots of buffalo and dried the meat. They made a raft of logs and put the meat on it.

They lived until the meat was gone, then all of them starved to death.

The flood was caused by the Great Spirit because the Indians were so cruel. The Great Spirit got angry and punished them with the flood.

Material Culture: Fire Making   Flints that got wet in the rain were no good for starting fires. Then they used a fire-drill with Spanish moss for tinder, cow flops also.

Sometimes they used a muzzleloader with a light charge of powder and cloth wadding to start a fire.

Nɨnɨpi {Wedel}   Spears were already made by the *nɨnɨpi*, or little people; they made spears and scattered them wherever they went.

Jim was once traveling with a band of Indians about thirty-two miles northwest of Cache. They were camped at the forks of a creek. They camped four days so they had to kill four cows (i.e., they always had one per day). Presently, they heard the cattle stampeding. The cattle came rushing by, and they saw a big Brahma steer run out of the herd with something after him. As it came closer, they saw one of the little men throw a spear into it.

Jim's people yelled and the little man turned and disappeared. The steer ran a few steps farther, coughed up a few chunks of blood, and collapsed. The Indians didn't touch it because it was poison to them. Later, they went to a watering hole. The horses came by much frightened, and presently Jim began to cough up blood. Then they knew that this was the little man's home, so they moved the camp.

Jim once saw the skeleton of a little man; it was just like a human, but smaller.

The little men used spears tipped with alligator bone.

Nunupi {Hoebel}   There was a family of Indians, *nunupi*. They were little men (pygmies). They went around shooting spears everywhere. Later, Comanches came and found those spears around, already made.

Post Oak Jim, when he was young, saw one of those little men (thirty-three miles northwest of here). They camped there four days. They killed four beeves. [If they camped four days, they needed four beeves. If they camped thirty days, they needed thirty beeves, etc.]

They heard a herd of cattle coming, being driven. They saw little men jump aside and shoot spears. They killed an animal. (The little people all ran away.)

When a beef was killed by the little men, they couldn't touch it; they would be poisoned if they did.

Later, some men were out. They saw a herd of horses stampeding. One horse, separated from the others, coughed blood and died. Thus, they knew that the little men lived there and took this way of showing them that this was their territory.

Post Oak Jim had seen the skeleton of one. It was very small and just like a human (a hundred bones).

Their spear heads were made from the backbones of alligators.[1]

Animals: Alligators {Wedel}   Alligators, like fish, came down with the rain.

So long as the alligators were in a deep hole, it never went dry. Alligators all went to deep pools.

They had medicine to keep the water from going dry. If drought threatened, the alligators gathered on the bank, held a session, wiggled their tails, opened their mouths, and made a bellowing noise. Presently clouds would appear and the rain would fall.

There were lots of alligators formerly in the Wichita Mountain area. They came up the creeks in floodtime from the Red River.

Animals: Alligators {Hoebel}   Baby alligators came down in the rain. They lived in holes around. There was always water in those alligator holes.

They had medicine. When the water was low, they came out, wiggled their tails and opened their mouths. Then clouds would form and rain would came down.

They came up from the Red River when it was in flood. (There really were some here.)

Story: Alligator and the Buffalo {Wedel}   A warrior strolled away from a war party once. He got on top of a high bank and saw a beautiful clear pool below him. Presently, he saw a big buffalo bull come all alone. It must have been mean. The bull waded out to drink. An alligator seized the bull by the throat and pulled him to the deep water, clear out of sight, with only bubbles to show the spot. Then, the bull backed out and got in shallow water, and the alligator let go to run back to deep water. The bull tossed the alligator three times,

---

1. Wallace and Hoebel 1952:174.

then made his way up to the bank and died.

The warrior went down to see the alligator; its side was ripped open. Then he looked at the bull; he had a great wound on the side of its head. That's when he found that the alligators and little men were related. He found an arrow in the buffalo's heart when the warrior cut him open. That's why alligators were so much cussed, just like the little men.

Story: Alligator and the Buffalo {Hoebel}   On a camping trip, an old warrior strolled away. He came up on a cliff and saw a beautiful, clear body of water below.

He lay there watching. He saw a lone buffalo bull come along. The buffalo bull put its head in to drink. An alligator came out and grabbed him.

They struggled. The buffalo backed out of the water.

The alligator headed towards the water, but the buffalo picked him up and flipped him several times. Then the buffalo threw him out of the water.

The Indian went down to look. He found both animals badly gashed.

During the fight, a little man had shot the buffalo with a spear (alligator and little man were of the same family).

Alligator and pygmy were very dangerous.

The warrior opened up the buffalo and found the pygmy's spear in its heart. He knew they were of the same family as the alligator.

Story: Nʉnʉpi and Mupits {Wedel}   The little man outclassed everything else, he had no match. One day <u>Mupits</u> came walking along and met *Nʉnʉpi*.

Mupits said, "Aw, you're nothing. Jump on my hand."

Nʉnʉpi jumped up in his hand and Mupits looked him over and ridiculed him. He let him down and took up his war club and hit a big stone, shattering it completely. Then he hit a still bigger stone and broke it, showing what he might do to little *Nʉnʉpi*.

Now it was *Nunʉpi*'s turn. He shot an arrow into the stone and buried it to the feathers. Then he repeated it, driving the arrow clear through another rock. So Mupits cleared out, he was completely outclassed.[1]

Story: Nʉnʉpi and Mupits {Hoebel}   The little man met no equal until he met Piamupits (who was like a giant).

Mupits was out walking. The pygmy came along. Mupits said, "You are nobody; come get up on my hand."

Piamupits showed the pygmy his *wʉpitapuʔni* (war club). He smashed up two big stones with it to show what he could do.

He asked the pygmy, "What can you do?"

The pygmy pulled out his bow and arrow (made of buffalo rib) and shot two big stones. The arrow went up to the feathers in one, and clean through the second.

Piamupits was scared. He went away. He said the little man was stronger than he was.

Medicine: Nʉnʉpi {Wedel}   *Nʉnʉpi* gave medicine to a man.[2]

The man's arrow {*sic*, bow?} was to be no longer than his forearm, with an arrow half as long.

He cautioned him not to shoot promiscuously because every shot would cause death.

---

1. Wallace and Hoebel 1952:175.
2. Contra Wallace and Hoebel 1952:175.

If a man with this medicine dreamed of a death, he <u>had</u> to go out the next day and kill something. If he dreamed of killing a man, he <u>had</u> to kill him.[1]

This medicine was so powerful and dangerous that not many men wanted it. The medicine was acquired by going on certain hill with the sole intention of getting this power from the little man.

Medicine: Nʉnʉpi {Hoebel}   The little man gave an Indian power.

He told him to have his bow.

He told him to have his arrow, half as long as the bow.

He told him not to shoot around carelessly, as he would kill something with every shot. If he shot a buffalo, the arrow went clean through it.

The Indians didn't like this power. It was too strong. They couldn't shoot except to kill.

If an Indian had this power, he must not misuse it in any way; he "must learn to love it."

Pygmy power was procured in the same way (vision, etc.).

One went to get it specially; to have it in mind when sought.

It was not wanted anymore; it was too strong.

Medicine: Competition {Wedel}   At certain times, the tribe gathered so the medicine men could show their powers.

Once a man with *nʉnʉpi* power came along. He said he would do his power at night. So they gathered at a lodge late one night. The man took his bow and arrows, and the *nʉnʉpi* touched each one. Then he sent a man outside to shoot four arrows in any direction.

The man shot the arrows.

Then the *nʉnʉpi* man went out to get them. A streak of lightning pointed at each one, and each shaft was illuminated. One was fired in each direction. The man got all but the east one, which was stuck in a tree; he said they would get it the next day.

The next man stuck an eighteen-inch stick in the ground and put a blanket over it. He then pulled the blanket off and a big plum tree loaded with plums sprang forth. This man had power for doctoring pregnant women, he couldn't approach a menstruating woman.

The third man sent a man to bring in a large grape leaf and laid it on the ground beneath the knee of the preceding magician. Then he told the latter to lift it up. He did so and found a baby under the leaf. Crestfallen, he promptly crawled out of tipi on his hands and knees and left.

Here, the meeting was interrupted by a medicine man who wanted a peyote meeting because he didn't believe in it. So he put up a tipi and held a meeting. He went into the tipi when the moon came up.

The man who wanted the meeting sat beside the chief on the west wall. He said he saw a man with a big knife and a bloody scalp come into view as the moon rose; the higher the moon, the nearer the apparition. The man was terribly frightened. He tried to tell the chief, who was singing, that he wanted to get out and go home. At the end of the meeting, the chief put sage leaves on the fire and smoked the lodge up. The man was finally brought around; he said he still didn't think anything of peyote, but he didn't care to go through the experience again.

1. Wallace and Hoebel 1952:175.

Medicine: Competition {Hoebel}   The Indians had certain gathering times to show their power to each other.

One Indian had *nꭐnꭐpi* power. At night, in a special tipi, he demonstrated his power to the medicine men. He touched arrows at the tips (put medicine on them thus).

The man owning the arrows took them outside; he shot one to the north, one to the east, one to the west; one to the south.

The medicine man said he would go and get them.

The *nꭐnꭐpi* medicine man went out. There was a light on each arrow to show where it was. (The light made a streak in the air when they were thrown.)

He gathered the north, south, and west arrows. The one on the east was up in a tree. He said he would get it tomorrow. He went out the next day and got it.

The next man to perform put an eighteen-inch stick in the ground, with a blanket over it. He pulled the blanket off and threw it away. There stood a tree loaded with plums.

This man, the medicine man for pregnant women, was not supposed to go near menstruating women.

The next medicine man told a medicine man to bring in the largest grape leaf he could find.

He laid the leaf next to the former medicine man, who had just performed.

He told him to remove the leaf. He did so and found a baby there.

The former medicine man grunted and crawled from the tipi (sick).

The meeting was interrupted after these three had performed.

A man wanted to know about the power of peyote, so they stopped and had a peyote meeting.

The skeptic who inquired sat next to the chief. They started eating peyote. The skeptic man received peyote.

He looked out of the tent and saw the moon rising. He saw a man coming up with the moon with blood and a knife, coming for him.

He was scared. He wanted to leave.

They wouldn't let him go. The chief continued singing and drumming.

At the end of the meeting, the chief threw a handful of cedar on the fire. All inhaled it. The man came out of the trance. He believed in peyote after that.

Medicine: Competition; Dances: Deer Dance {Wedel}   There were four dancers naked to the breechcloth. Each man took some sage and an eagle feather. Each had a pole and a gourd rattle containing seeds. They danced in a large tipi with a central fireplace.

The dancers were on the south, the spectators on the north, and the singers sang.

The chief was the leader.

Each man wore a deerskin apron.

The first doctor danced around.

The next doctor took sage, dipped it in the fire until it ignited, then put it in his mouth.

Then he chewed up some sage and haw root, and extracted from his mouth a wild red bean.

While he held the bean, another doctor blew in his hand and extracted the bean from the holder's hand. He may give it to a drummer or singer or keep it; the possessor knew who took it, but had to find out who had it.

Another doctor, maybe, had a grudge against the last one. He came out and made a sawing motion with an eagle feather and pretty soon, his victim faltered and collapsed and everyone applauded.

A lady doctor was a friend of the big man who was throwing the party. She was the chief's grandmother. The next doctor made the chief and the lady come together hunching before all the people. The chief supposedly had the greatest power.

This made his grandmother mad. She pulled off her moccasins, walked to the fireplace and stood over it. She shook a black handkerchief over the fire, brushed through the air with a feather, then stepped into the fire and danced. The people thought someone had attacked the camp because of the sound of the dancing woman.

The people were all amazed because she had proven who had the greatest power.

There were always women present during these Deer Doctor meetings.

The dance was performed to draw all the people together.

If someone was sick in the stomach, they mixed medicine with water and put it in a big bowl, then they got hollow reeds and each patient sucked up some of the medicine. They had holes dug near by, and people went to these and heaved. Soon they got well and the holes were covered up. *kusiwʉʉnʉ*[1] (black haws) was the medicine put in the bowl.

Any one of the Deer Doctors could put on the dance if he thought he was the most powerful of them. The medicine was good for pneumonia or other internal ailments.[2]

Medicine: Competition; Dances: Elk Dance {Hoebel}   Four (or seven) Elk Medicine Men undressed except for a deerskin apron.

Each took a bunch of sage and an eagle feather. Each had a gourd rattle.

They sat down facing the crowds. They sang and rattled while others danced.

The place was a large tipi. The medicine men sat on the north side facing the fire. Spectators sat all around the sides.

The chief medicine man got up first to dance. He danced up around the fire. He put his feather through the smoke and blew it towards another dancer. (It caused him to turn a flip.) This was his demonstration of power.

The spectators applauded the various stunts.

The next medicine man dipped his sage branch in the fire. When it caught, he put it in his mouth, burning. He pulled it out and blew. He had a red bean in his hand. This wild bean was made out of sage leaves and chewed black thorn bark.

Another dancer from the other side of the fire blew. He had the bean in his hand. He might throw it outside or give it to a drummer or spectator, etc. The man who lost it was looking for it.

Another dancer (medicine man) took his eagle feather and shook it in a motion as though cutting off a man's head. The man he was motioning towards staggered and fell.

The chief's grandmother was present. The next medicine man took his feather and drove the chief and his grandmother together (thus getting it back on the chief for wanting to show that he had the most power). The chief was thus embarrassed.

1. Robinson and Armagost (1990) defines *kusiwʉʉnʉ* as 'sage-like plant'. Post Oak Jim (July 12) has black haws as *tupokopI*.

2. Hoebel calls this the "Elk Dance." See next note.

The grandmother was angry. She wanted to show her power. She shook her moccasin off. She took off the black handkerchief from her neck and shook it over the fire. She jumped in and danced without being burned. The fire popped like guns, She made motions like an elk or deer. The people were afraid; they thought the pops were enemies outside. She won the dance; she had the most power of all.

Occasion: It was put on by one of the Elk Medicine Men who wanted to show that he had the most power in his group.

Idea: Each dancing medicine man tried to outdo the others in magic feats. It was a social dance to amuse the spectators; also for curing.

Medicine: Anyone sick (e.g., stomach) was brought. Medicine was cut. The next day, the medicine men put their medicine in a bowl of water. The sick people drank it out of straws. They had holes dug all around.

When the medicine worked, they went and vomited in the holes. It made them well. The holes were then covered. *kusiwᵾᵾnᵾ* (black thorn bark) was this Elk Medicine. It was good for stomach troubles. Also pneumonia.[1]

Medicine: Curing: Pneumonia {Wedel}   A young woman was dying from pneumonia, and every time she coughed, she gave up chunks of blood. She was brought home after doctors gave her one day to live. Jim sucked out a needle that had penetrated her chest, heart, and back, and the next day she was well.

Jim took roots of black haws, crushed their bark with sage, made a paste with spit, and rubbed it on the chest and back. He then sucked from the chest side. Afterward he wrapped a hot rock in sage and applied it alternately to the chest and back.

This treatment was not effective if the disease had run two or three days. By then, the disease was almost incurable.

Medicine: Curing: Pneumonia {Hoebel}   A girl had one more day to live (by white doctors). Post Oak Jim took her home and applied his Elk Medicine. He sucked the poison out of her; it seemed like a needle going through her back.

It was a strong medicine; the black thorn bush has thorns on it (to warn people off).

(Post Oak Jim's method). He took black thorn root and sage leaves and chewed them. He applied them over the heart and on the back. He sucked over the heart and on the back. He heated a stone (covered with a cloth) and applied it over the heart and on the back.

Medicine: Curing: Pneumonia   Another young boy was given up by white doctors, but cured in a peyote meeting by Jim of pneumonia. The cure was seen by Wagner.[2]

Medicine: Peyote   A peyote meeting might end in the morning, or at noon, at the leader's discretion. There were no individual variations in the altar.

Water and breakfast were brought in, sometimes by a married women, other times by a single woman.

One man had the entire tipi floor and fixtures of concrete, including a small stand for the peyote button.

Relations with Other Tribes: Osages and Omahas: Peyote   The Osages had frame peyote "tipis" with doors to the west and electric lights.

---

1. Wedel calls this the "Deer Dance." See previous note.
2. Presumably, Günter Wagner. See Introduction.

The Omahas used frame tipis in winter because of the hardness of the ground. [The Omahas also used a frame building in the winter, a tipi in the summer.]

Omaha sure could cook hog. They didn't give you any forks, because the hand was made before the fork. They just grabbed chunks of meat and went to work.

NIYAH
July 25, 1933[1]

Life Story: Niyah   Niyah lived with an old lady, Ya'ai.[2] She was no particular kin. His father was dead and his mother had remarried, but Niyah lived with this other woman.

Ya'ai made him a saddle (with low horns).

At fifteen years of age, he returned to his mother.

He was whipped [by his mother's brother] for going to another camp. [He said people would get the idea they were not feeding him.]

Life Cycle: Marriage: Bride Service   Niyah gave presents to his father-in-law.

[All males in one's wife's parent's generation were eligible for presents. Niyah gave only to his father-in-law or his father-in-law's brother.]

Animals: Birds   A war party wanted feathers for arrows, so they killed a cow and [a captive] got inside of the hide with his arms left protruding but covered with blood. When a bird came down [for carrion], he grabbed it and broke its wings; it was then released it to flutter about [they collected them in the evening]. Sometimes they got many birds (hawks) this way.

They also caught birds with horsehair snares set with bait, but less often.

Kinship Relations: Joking   One can joke with a brother-in-law or sister-in-law.

Life Cycle: Death: Disposition of Property   Treasured possessions (e.g., a valuable horse), were not always killed at death, one might be kept as a keepsake. [They seemed to keep one horse for a keepsake.[3]]

Life Cycle: Childhood: Orphan   There were two cases where a father's death made the son an orphan, although the mother was still living.

Camp Organization   Sometimes a family camped alone.

Kinship Relations   A man called his wife's first husband "brother."

[A former husband was called "brother" by an absconder.]

Life Cycle: Marriage: Restrictions   A man could marry his stepdaughter, also his actual mother-in-law after his wife's death, also his wife's brother's daughter [or his wife's sister's daughter].

---

1. Wedel's notes date this interview as July 24. However, inasmuch as they follow Post Oak Jim's interview on July 25, they may be misdated.

2. Otherwise unidentified.

3. Wallace and Hoebel 1952:152 (?). Hoebel's note card identifies this as being from Herman Asenap, who was the interpreter.

Life Cycle: Marriage: Remarriage {Wedel}   Case: a man's brother-in-law's wife died. So the man gave his daughter to the widower to keep him in the family.

A man could marry his wife's sister or his wife's sister's daughter if it wasn't his own daughter.

Life Cycle: Marriage: Remarriage {Hoebel}   Case: a man had a brother-in-law (a very good man). His sister died (leaving his brother-in-law without a spouse). He wanted to keep this good man in the family. The man gave him (the brother-in-law) his daughter (and became his father-in-law).

The attitudes changed (he could joke no longer).

A man could marry a close affinal relation, but not a blood relation.[1]

Relations with Other Tribes: Arapahos   The Sianaboo,[2] striped feathers, were the Arapahos.[3]

War Story: Comanches and Arapahos   Eight Arapahos went on a war party. One had bullet-proof medicine. Kiowas and Comanches were at the fork of a creek together. The Arapahos sneaked up early in the evening and got all of their horses. Early the next morning, the Comanches and Kiowas went out and saw their horses were gone. There was a great hullabaloo. They rounded up strays and went after them. (Choice horses might be staked near the tipi.)

The Comanches and Kiowas trailed the Arapahos for two days and nights. They battled and finally killed seven of the Arapahos. Two Kiowas on one horse rode up. One had a muzzleloader, the other had a bow and arrow. The last Arapaho's medicine was not proof against a certain metal (brass) and they had a (brass) cinch-strap buckle. The muzzleloader bullet hit him in the head and stunned him, so he fell off his horse. Other Kiowas and Comanches rode up and cut him up before he could recover. Years later, the Arapaho's father found out from friendly Kiowas and Comanches what had happened.

Life Cycle: Childbirth   When confinement began, the woman went to a special tipi. The bed was on the west side. Beside it was a pole for her to hold on to. When the pains began, the woman's mother or her maternal grandmother was notified. When labor began, the woman grasped the pole, knelt, and was grasped from behind under her breasts. Pressure was applied downward on the floating ribs. The mother picked up the child with her right hand, and laid it on her right side. The mother was the <u>first</u> to touch the child. Other women sat by but didn't assist. The baby was washed and dried by the mother and grandmother.

The umbilical cord was cut about three inches long. A circular piece of buckskin was cut with a hole in the center, and this was placed against the abdomen with the umbilical cord through the hole. A bandage of soft buckskin was wrapped around the child's body every time the child was washed.

Material Culture: Cradles: Night Cradle   The *habikʉni* was the night cradle.

Life Cycle: Childbirth   They inspected the cord and in several days it dropped off.

The afterbirth was wrapped in buckskin and laid aside.[4] The woman was washed. They dug a pit and built a fire, about thirty inches long, and put sage in it, and then a blanket.

---

1. Hoebel's notes are on two separate cards, with the second duplicating much of the first.
2. *sia* 'feather', *naboo* 'marked, striped, spotted'.
3. This ethnonym was usually applied to the Cheyennes.
4. Contra Wallace and Hoebel 1952:144.

In the summer they built a fire, then raked the coals away and the woman laid on this. She stayed until the blood stopped flowing, then went to bed for about ten days. Then she went to the creek, washed, and put on good clothes.

The newborn child was painted with grease mixed with red ocher, with especial attention to the armpits, thighs, and neck, to prevent chafing. This was kept up until the shedding of the first skin. Then ashes of cattails were used as a powder to cure body sores, etc.

After ten days, a carrying cradle was made. Some children hated the cradle and cried and kicked when they were put in.

The navel cord was wrapped and tied up in a hackberry tree.[1]

The father stayed outside the tipi and was notified as to the sex of the child. The child's maternal grandmother gave a feast to the attendant women, with the dishes distributed. Then the mother went home and the father saw the child for first time.

It was a man's duty to look after the child while the woman got up first and prepared breakfast and made the beds. Then, the child was bathed, greased, and powdered, and put in the carrying cradle and carried until the child was asleep. Then the cradle was set against a tree.

Material Culture: Cradles   A boy baby had his penis out through the lacings, held by a leatherlike stirrup, so he urinated out of the cradle. A girl baby had a wooden trough for her buttocks, with a pipe leading down between her legs. It was not as efficient as a boy's cradle.[2]

Life Cycle: Childhood: Nursing   A child was nursed whenever it cried, with a wet nurse if the mother's lactation was inadequate. Either grandfather then gave the nurse a present. The nurse had no claim over a child. If a wet nurse kept a child too long, other children (usually her son) would become jealous and get sick. If a child nursed more than year, it became cross.

Children were weaned on the juices of half-cooked meat at one year or less.

They were carried in the carrying cradle on the move, hung off the saddle horn while the mother mounts, then slung on the mother's back and secured by lashings about the mother's body to the saddle horn.[3]

---

1. Wallace and Hoebel 1952:144.
2. Wallace and Hoebel 1952:120.
3. This is the end of Wedel's Notebook 4.

UNIDENTIFIED CONSULTANT
Undated

Words   Words[1]:

ura	'thank you' (in Comanche)
aho	'thank you' (in Apache, etc.)
⟨mabuina⟩	'work is done'
Mamsookawat	85 years
sootipuhihwi[2]	'lots of money'
Johnson Porhwi[3]	
tekwoka*[4]	
penatek[5]	
yellow face[6]	

FRANK CHEKOVI
Undated I[7]

Life Cycle: Childhood   A child raised in a cradle was stouter than the present noncradle ones. A pillow was used to keep the child's head from flattening. Bedding was packed about the child to keep his head up.

The child slept with its mother for three to five years, then bunked with other children. A child was dressed at about five years.

{They were} very proud of their sons, they could protect their fathers.

Adornment: Earrings {Wedel}   Ears were pierced by a young man when he wanted to dress up.

---

1. These words are on the cover of Wedel's Notebook 5. The first three and the fifth words are also listed in the August 8 interview with Nemaruibetsi in Wedel's Notebook 6.

2. *sooti* 'many', *puhihwi* 'metal', metaphorically 'money'.

3. Possibly the man known as Johnson Pahrowdeup, thirty-two years old in 1933. This may also be a reference to John Poahwah, also called Woosedad, about forty-eight years old in 1933.

4. Asterisk in original. Herzog and McAllester (1939) identified one of their consultants as Tekwaki; otherwise unidentified.

5. Possibly a reference to the Penatuhka division. There were several individuals who had Penatuhka as a personal name.

6. If this was intended as a personal name, it is otherwise unidentified.

7. This is the beginning of Wedel's Notebook 5. In contrast to the other five notebooks, this first page lacks any headers or dates. Although that might imply that this was a continuation of the interview with Niyah from Notebook 4, other internal indications, particularly the reference to "Frank's" family (see below) and the parallel cards from Hoebel indicating Informant 7, show that it was with Frank Chekovi. Whether it was from July 24 or 25 is unknown. Below, there is another set of undated notes from Frank Chekovi recorded by Wedel, and a third set recorded by Hoebel.

He went to a confinement tipi and someone who knew how pierced them (it was not necessarily a relative). They used a red-hot needle. The piercer was not paid. A greased straw was inserted and renewed often until the wound healed.

There was one case where a men used cactus thorns to bore the ears; he then broke them off and left them for straws.

If more than one perforation was wanted, all were done at once so they healed simultaneously.

One ear was pierced all around and the hair was cut off. The other ear was partly covered with hair and partly decorated.

A favorite ornament was conch columella, often several in each ear.

Adornment: Earrings {Hoebel}   A young man might see other men who had their ears pierced. He came home and wanted it too.

He went to a place where a women had had a baby easily, and there, one of his female relatives pierced his ears for him (not necessarily a relative); (there was no payment).

It was in late adolescence.

Process: a red-hot needle; a greased straw in the hole, which may be re-greased and put back until the wound healed.

Case: a cactus-bored hole; in winter (ears numb).

They had them all done at once, so he could wear all his earrings at once.

He liked the long thin shell beads (from Mexico).

One ear was pierced for rings along the entire edge. The hair was shaved above so they would show. The other ear had only three or four rings. The braid came down over top of them.

Adornment: Hair Care: Hairbrush {Wedel}   Yucca leaves were pounded to get the fibers only. A number of leaves were bound together with a buckskin to give a brush effect on one end. The spines on the other end make a comb; they were singed off to make them scratch less.

Adornment: Hair Care: Hairbrush {Hoebel}   The large yucca variety was pounded to get the fibers out; they gathered them up and bound them with a buckskin thong.

The thorns at the end of the fibers stuck out and made a comb-like brush.

They singed the ends off the thorns so they were not so sharp.

Material Culture: Containers: *oyóotʉʔ* {Wedel}   A mother took care of her young son's dress clothes in an *oyóotʉʔ* of rawhide. The clothes are placed in the *oyóotʉʔ*; {the ends} were folded over and then the {sides} were brought down and laced together

Material Culture: Containers: *oyóotʉʔ* {Hoebel}   A young man had one suit of his best clothes cared for by his mother. They were kept in a buckskin bag (painted) [rectangular, rawhide; *oyóotʉʔ* (ends folded in, sides folded down to the center)].

Also packed in it were the leggings, moccasins, blankets, and braid wrappers—all but his feathers. It was painted by women with walnut dye and perfumed.[1]

1. Hoebel's note card cites both Frank Chekovi and Post Oak Jim as the source of this information. However, I can find no parallel in any of Wedel's interviews with Post Oak Jim, and so I have left this note here.

Material Culture: Containers: *tunawosa* {Wedel}   The *tunawosa*[1] was a rawhide satchel for paint and toilet articles, mirror, hairbrush, etc. It was canister-like, with an open top flap.

Material Culture: Containers: *tunawosa* {Hoebel}   The *tunawosa* was used to carry personal articles. It was circular and had a rounded bottom. It carried brush, mirror, paint, feathers (wrapped in cloth) (all wrapped together in cloth). It was carried on the left side of the horse when moving. The shield was on the right. The tool kit was also on the horse ridden by a woman.[2]

Material Culture: Feathers   Feathers were separately wrapped in cloth, accordion style, and placed in a small bag longer than the feathers. It was very stiff and protected the feathers.

Material Culture: Containers: War Bonnet Case   A war bonnet was placed in a rawhide [cloth] case with a drawstring at the top. It was slung at a warrior's waist [when they went out to raid].

[If they stopped for a long rest, they took it out to see how they were.] If the feathers were [split or] soiled or disarranged, the warrior spurted water over them and [smoothed them out] and put them in the wind to dry.

Material Culture: Clothing   It took two hides to make leggings, two for the trimmings, two hides for the shirt, one each for the sleeves, and one for the V-shaped fringed neckpiece. The thickest part of the hide was used for the upper sleeves, the thinnest for the fringes. There were short fringes at the cuffs, long fringes at the elbow and shoulder, and short fringes around the bib on front and rear; all were twisted.

Legging fringes were about six to eight inches long, also twisted. At the knee on the outer seam was a strap, swallow-tailed at the end. Next to it was a thin braid of hair with bells. At the bottom of the legging were conical tin bangles. There was a line of beads at the bottom of the legging.

On moccasins, there were two rows of narrow beading from toe to instep, and fringe at the heel and along the outside of the beaded strip.[3]

Adornment: Hair Care: Scalp Lock   The scalp lock went to the back. A strip of otter skin was fastened at the end to hang still farther down, almost to the ground. At the top of the lock was a downy eagle feather, erect, white or dyed yellow.

The hair was usually parted in the middle, with a thin earlock on the left side and a silver button just to the left of the part over a four-ply buckskin braid going down alongside of the ear lock. These were clamped together by silver bands at intervals. At the end of the thongs were four little "earrings."

A man might wear a buckskin bracelet with silver clamps.

The main hair was not braided. There were two thongs to tie the otter skin to the top of the hair, then the otter skin was wrapped very tightly about the braid. There was a band of beadwork with bangles at the top.

When mounted, the feather was removed and an otter skin cap substituted with a feather sewn on. There were very few beads on men's clothing.

---

1. *tuna* 'straight', *wosa* 'bag'. Robinson and Armagost (1990) identifies this as a "war-bonnet bag."
2. Hoebel's note card cites both Frank Chekovi and Nemaruibetsi as the source of this information. However, I can find no parallel in any of Wedel's interviews with Nemaruibetsi and so I have left it here.
3. Wallace and Hoebel 1952:78.

Material Culture: Clothing   Kiowas adopted the Comanche's cut of clothes.

There was no measuring for the shirt. Leggings were marked out. The gee-string was worn with a dangling tail fore and aft [almost to the ankle], ornamented with applique leatherwork. [(This was not supposed to come this far west); unusual.]

Material Culture: Clothing: Headdress: Roach   The roach was not old Comanche; it was worn at dances.

Material Culture: Clothing: Dance Bustles   Bustles were worn also at dances.

Material Culture: Clothing: Headdress: War Bonnet   There were not many in the old days. [They were worn by only a few. They were never worn except in battle.]

War: Weapons: Lance   The {headdress} wearer also had to use a spear in battle.

Material Culture: Clothing: Headdress: War Bonnet   A wearer who rode by a dismounted friend in war would lose his bonnet. When he got back to camp, he gave it to someone else. [A brave man who saw him do this could upbraid him with it. He might take the bonnet and give it to someone else who deserved it.] A man could refuse a bonnet because he felt wasn't qualified.

The bonnet might be kept secret until the battle began (cf. POJ[1]).

Camp Organization: Breaking Camp   Scouts were sent out in advance when the camp was to be moved. Sometimes they went twenty miles ahead. They didn't stop until they set up the new camp. The announcer would be the chief of the band, who called out and announced the move. Moves were seldom over one day long.

*aratsi*ʔ? =Wheel Game: What is it?

Social Organization: Family Groups   Frank's father and mother, brothers and sisters and cousins formed an extended family group. There were three tipis in the group.

Life Cycle: Marriage: Residence   An old married couple took care of the bachelors after a battle.

A younger brother might live with his older unmarried brother.

Pemmican?[2]

Medicine: Night Power   Power from the night, from darkness. They might blow smoke up and call on *tukaanItu*, the spirit of darkness.

---

1. Abbreviation in original; the specific reference to Post Oak Jim is unclear.
2. Possible a comment by Wedel. See Frank Chekovi, Aug. 10.

Post Oak Jim
July 26, 1933[1]

Names: Naming   Jim's baby name was given by his father's nephew.

Material Culture: Crafts: Hide Work   A buffalo hide was fleshed and rubbed with a buffalo tongue, then with brains.[2]

Material Culture: Containers   Meat was packed in the *oyóotɨ*. [It was undecorated.]

The *natɨsakɨna* was a small parfleche used to carry broken-up dried meat.

When they got back to camp, pemmican was mixed with fat and put in the rawhide bag.

Food: Sweet Meat   *tɨrahyapɨ* was sweet meat.[3] It was still used in peyote. Pemmican was mixed with sugar. Before they had sugar, they used mesquite pods.

Food: Food Preparation: Dried Meat   Meat was dried in long slabs and packed in a parfleche.

Food: Food Preparation: Stone Boiling   The Yapai were the only band to use skin boiling.

Long ago, the Mexicans early sold them brass buckets.

Food: Food Plants: Fruits

Dried plums (*sɨkɨ²i*) were eaten. Pack rats were tracked to their dens and their storehouses robbed. Their nests were very clean. Also, the seeds were extracted from plums, dried out, and stored for winter use. They were boiled sometimes with fat.

wokwéesi was prickly pear fruit. They wiped off the spines, extracted the seeds, dried them and mixed them with fat, and ate them.

Mesquite beans were boiled and mixed with corn meal to make a drink ⟨pihi sawana[4]⟩.

nɨmɨnɨɨ puhihuubA[5] was a Comanche drink. A gray weed (not sage) was made into tea. The reddish-brown berries from a bush near rain puddles were made into tea.

mitsonaa², pounded hackberries,[6] were mixed with grease and sugar and roasted like sausage on a stick.

tɨbitsiwaapI,[7] juniper berries, were eaten green and raw. The leaves were used in peyote.

Food: Food Plants: Nuts

⟨makine⟩, acorns, were boiled and stored. They were eaten when they were hungry. It was just plain oak.

tuhuupit,[8] blackjack acorns, were eaten at once.

⟨pibi[9]⟩ *tuhuupit*, white oak acorns, had three layers over the nut. It was eaten fresh.

---

1. Wedel's manuscript notes state "per C. Lockett," suggesting that these notes were copied from a solo interview conducted by Lockett. They are only minimally paralleled in Hoebel's notes. Wedel's typescript left out the first manuscript page of this interview.

2. Hoebel's only note card on this process has "c. Flesh scraped off with bull tongue" and "d. rubbed with brains."

3. Robinson and Armagost (1990) gives this as 'meatball'.

4. *pihi* 'heart'.

5. Carlson and Jones (1940) identifies *puhi huubA* as *Lespedeza capitata*, 'bush clover'.

6. Wedel's typescript has "blackberries" rather than the "hackberries" of the manuscript. *mitsonaa²* is 'hackberry'.

7. Literally, 'real cedar'.

8. *tuhupI* 'black', *huupit* 'wood'. Wedel's typescript omitted the description and jumped to the next entry.

9. Possibly *pivia* 'big' (pl.).

nakkɨtabʔI,[1] pecans, were picked and stored in sacks.

mubitai,[2] walnuts. The skins were taken off when green. The nuts were dried and stored.

Hunting   Young boys hunted small game, rabbits, quail, squirrel, etc.

Life Cycle: Sex   Jim's first sexual affair was at age ten while playing house.

Games   Boys would go to the swimming hole, build a big fire, and put in a rock. The rock then exploded. They got a big thrill from this.

Horses   Horses were guided by slapping on the cheek.

Hunting: Birds: Turkeys   Turkeys nested under driftwood. Eggs of these were boiled and eaten, as were those of the ducks, quails, and prairie chickens.

[If they spotted one or two, they stalked until they came to the flock. If they flew, they followed them until they tired, and then herded them out with long poles and struck them down with clubs.]

Medicine: Peyote   Women put up the tipi for the peyote meeting fifty-seven years ago given by Post Oak Jim's father.

Games: *aratsiʔ* {Wedel}   They fastened a two-and-a-half inch willow hoop in the center of a six-inch willow hoop, supported by rawhide lacing.

It was an individual game. Each man had fifteen or twenty ordinary arrows.

He also had a large five-foot arrow, forked at the butt and fire-hardened; it was sometimes feathered. The umpire rolled the hoop between two opposing lines of players. Each threw his long spear as the hoop rolled by. Someone had to put the large arrow through the small hoop. They may have to roll it several times. The successful man was out for the inning. Then, each of the others threw his arrows at the hoop from where he stood. When a man hit the hoop, the first man got all of the arrows he had thrown at the hoop.[3]

Games: *aratsiʔ* {Hoebel}   (Two accounts.)[4] The hoop was willow with rawhide webbing in two circles.

The arrow was hardened in a fire. A feather was fastened to the barb. It was five feet long.

To start the game, a man had to hit the center with his special arrow (each man had one special arrow).

Each man then stood in place until he hit it. If he hit it on the first round, the winner got one arrow; if the player had to shoot ten times, the winner got ten arrows.

After the winner hit the mark, he was through throwing.

---

1. Carlson and Jones (1940) identifies this as *Carya illinoiensis*.
2. Carlson and Jones (1940) identifies this as *Juglans nigra*.
3. Wallace and Hoebel 1952:115. This is possibly in answer to Wedel's question from July 25.
4. Apparently only one account was given.

FRANK CHEKOVI
Undated II[1]

Games: *aratsi* {Wedel}   A hoop of chinaberry[2] and an arrow about three feet long.

There were four players on a side, in two opposing lines. Each man had two arrows. If one arrow from each side went through, it was a tie and didn't count.

When the hoop fell, the striker marked the spot where he had stood when he hit it. Opponents then went over and threw arrows at the hoop. When one hit the hoop, the one who first speared the hoop got all the misses. The first spear was thrown low, the others over the shoulder.

Games: *aratsi* {Hoebel}   (It was a young man's game.) The target was a wood frame (bent willow) about four to five inches in diameter. It had sinew spokes and a hole one or two inches in diameter, wrapped in sinew.

The arrow was made from chinaberry (hard), about three feet long.

They threw the arrow at the target. If it went in the center hole, it caught on the barb and stuck in.

They played with two men on each side. The four men stood five or six steps from the wheel.

The starter rolled the wheel between four men, two on each side. They aimed from the side. Each man had two special arrows. They threw them all together as the wheel rolled by. When a man hit the mark, he put a mark on the ground to mark the spot at which he stood when he threw. The other two men stood at that point and threw at the wheel, which had now fallen down. They used ordinary arrows when the hooked ones are gone.

If they failed to hit it, the other man won and got all the arrows. If they succeeded in hitting the hole from there, they retrieved that arrow. For each arrow thrown and missed, he lost a regular arrow (the special arrows stayed with the game).

They might agree to shoot for either the center holes or the spokes.

Spectators bet on one side or the other (they gave the man the arrows to throw). The partners divided the take.[3]

Games: *naro'toneetsi* {Wedel}   *naro'toneetsi* was a slender arrow thrown for distance like the javelin.

Each man threw four arrows high up to stick near a marker arrow. If one man stuck one arrow nearest to the marker, he got all of the other contestants arrows. *nanatsue* were the rivals in one of the games.

Games: *naro'toneetsi* {Hoebel}   *naro'toneetsi* 'distance', *tiro'woka*, 'mark'.[4] They threw especially long and light arrows. The feathers were trimmed closer than an ordinary arrow.

---

    1. Wedel's notes at this point merely state "Frank," without the usual header and date. Hoebel's parallel notes confirm the consultant's identity. The date is uncertain, but probably July 26.
    2. Carlson and Jones (1940) and *Webster's New World Dictionary* (1951) gives soapberry as an alternative name. Carlson and Jones (1940) identifies it as *Spanindus drummondii*, Comanche *otɄmitsona'a*, but that term is not attested in the notes.
    3. Wallace and Hoebel 1952:114.
    4. Robinson and Armagost (1990) glosses this as 'throwing arrows'.

They might throw at a mark or throw for distance. A good throw was 200 yards. If a mark was used, the mark was an arrow thrown high (so it stuck upright in the ground). (Spectators bet on the outcome.) Each contestant threw four arrows. The loser had the privilege of throwing the <u>marker</u> arrow for the next game. The winner in throwing won the other's arrows unless they bet otherwise.[1]

War: Weapons: Lances {Wedel}   The *tsikarehi* was a lance with an eagle feather on a string at the butt.

The *haikorohkO*[2] had crow feathers in a fringe just in front of the grip. It was carried with a bonnet as insignia.

The *tsikarehi* was carried only by brave men.

It was made when a man thought he was brave, then he had to prove it. Nobody gave it to him. It was not used with a bonnet. The possessor couldn't retreat unless he had run up and used the spear on an enemy.

Frank's brother[3] was injured at Adobe Walls, retreated, and lost his spear.

War: Weapons: Lances {Hoebel}   It was not decorated in the old days as much as now.

Near the top of the handle was a bunch of crow feather pieces and one eagle feather decoration. It was fastened on with a buckskin string. It was called *haikorohkO*. In the old days, it had no other decorations. It didn't have a beaded handle like Quanah Parker's.[4]

Only a brave man had a spear, because it meant hand-to-hand combat (it was not thrown).

One couldn't lay it down and retreat like a war bonnet. One must stay and die. It was used without a bonnet.

Frank's brother gave up his spear after the Battle of Adobe Walls. People were glad; it was a big responsibility.

Anyone could make a spear like this if he wanted to live up to it.

Material Culture: Clothing: Loss of Rights   A man who lost his bonnet because he rode by a fallen comrade was called 'elder sister' thereafter.

[A man who failed to help, lost his bonnet and was called *pabiʔ* 'elder sister.'[5]]

Social Roles: Contrary {Wedel}   The *pukutsi* was a warrior who carried a roll of cloth under his armpit, fastened to his shoulder. In battle, he would unroll the sash and shoot an arrow into the end. Thereafter, he couldn't retreat unless a friend pulled out the arrow. Also, he did everything backwards. (Cf. the Crazy Dogs of the Crow.[6])

There was no vision before doing it.

1. Wallace and Hoebel 1952:114.
2. *hai* 'crow', *korohkO* 'necklace'.
3. Todoessy, born about 1847; he died after 1905, but before 1917. On the 1879 census, his name is translated as 'My Dear Child', but that translation has not been confirmed. In 1879 he was a associated with Tomichicut's Kwahrenʉʉ local band. The 1892 census implies that he was the leader of a small local group of about thirty people.
4. There are several photographs of Quanah with a fully beaded lance. A similar beaded lance is at the Panhandle-Plains Historical Museum at Canyon, Texas.
5. Hoebel 1940:35. Both Hoebel's synthetic note cards and Wallace and Hoebel (1952:273) gloss *pabiʔ* as 'elder sister', when, in fact, it means 'elder brother'. Elder sister is *patsiʔ*.
6. This comment is probably by Linton. See also Lowie 1913:175 and Part Two, below.

He would shoot an arrow into a pot of meat,[1] clowning, backward talk, etc.

Social Roles: Contrary {Hoebel}   The *pukutsi* was a warrior who had a long cloth fastened to his shoulder, a long sash rolled under his arm. In battle, he unrolled the sash and stuck it with an arrow. He couldn't go any farther than the sash would allow him. Only a friend could come and free him. He couldn't free himself.

He did everything backwards.[2]

Life Cycle: Death: Disposition of Property   The father of a dead man led his horse in its war outfit to his comrades. He asked someone to ride it before the enemy until it was shot from under him so it could join the deceased son. Frank's brother rode the horse. It was shot, finally it staggered and died. The rider was rescued.

Medicine: *nunupi*: War: Shields   A dwarf medicine man carried a saucer-sized shield.

[A medicine man Frank knew had this medicine. He had the little shield, arrows, etc. The Nunupi made the little stone arrows that they found all around.]

Horses   The Comanches raided into Texas for horses. They also broke wild ones. They rode horses on a raid to within the last day or two, then they walked so they could take more horses.

Were dogs eaten?[3]

Games: *wuhkeru* {Wedel}   *wuhkeru*[4] was a game. They set a marker arrow and they shot at it from about forty or fifty feet. Alternatively, two rivals shot arrows.

Where the arrow was {when it hit} was what counted, not where it stopped. Easy shooters were matched against hard shooters.

Games: *wuhkeru* {Hoebel}   Each contestant had four arrows. One shot ahead to be the mark. The target arrow was shot by the loser as in the Arrow-Throwing game.

They shot in turn. The arrow counted as where it finally landed.

One with four arrows closest won (as in horse shoes). The winner got the bets (arrows or other stuff). They bet with sticks to represent the goods (like chips). Spectators also bet.[5]

Games: *naro°toneetsi°* {Wedel}   *naro°toneetsi°* was distance arrow shooting. They used a bow guard. One camp might challenge another and pit their best respective marksmen against each other. The contestants picked out the best bow. They used dogwood arrows, heaviest at the center, to get distance and to eliminate quivering in flight. They also trimmed the feathers closer. A good man might shoot a quarter mile. Men were stationed at intervals to keep track of the arrows.

Games: *naro°toneetsi°* {Hoebel}   Each contestant had two arrows. Each contestant had a wristguard of rawhide for protection.

They shot with a bow and a special arrow. Spectators offered their bows for use. The contestant picked out a strong, springy one.

The arrows had no spike at the point or barbs. It was a plain point. The diameter was larger in the center to steady it. The feathers were cut closer.

---

1. Hoebel (1940:33–34) attributes his discussion of *pukutsi* to Nemaruibetsi, but there are apparently no extant notes from Nemaruibetsi about the *pukutsi*.

2. Wallace and Hoebel 1952:275. See also Frank Chekovi, August 10.

3. The source of this question is unknown.

4. Robinson and Armagost (1990) glosses this as 'to aim'.

5. Wallace and Hoebel 1952:114.

There were judges alongside the course.

They shot about a quarter mile.

Weapons: Lance   The single feather lance was carried by the *tekwʉniwapI*.

An underhand thrust was used with the spear, an overhand thrust was apt to break the shaft [point].

[It was thrust from under the arm because if it was thrust over arm, it might hit a bone and break the point, or frighten the horse.]

War   Some men went into battle totally naked because they didn't expect to return alive.

War: Shields   Shields were carried on the back while fleeing or shooting with the bow and arrow. There was a long sling on the shield that the warrior grasped next to the shield and braced it with his forearm.

Horses: Breaking   A horse was roped for breaking. They put on the bridle; also a loose rope surcingle. A captive got on the horse, slipped his feet through the rope, and was led to a creek. The captive took the bridle rope and the horse reared and rode off with the Mexican on top. He returned about noon broken and fit to ride.

War: Battle of Adobe Walls {Wedel}   The medicine man who started the Adobe Walls battle had Sun Medicine.[1] His body was yellow, and his horse had a yellow stripe from his mane to the tip of his tail.

War: Battle of Adobe Walls {Hoebel}   A young man notified the people that he had medicine, that he was impregnable to bullets.

It was in the spring. The band was drifting west to the Plains. Frank was living with his mother and two sisters and brother after the soldier's raid in which his father was killed.[2] They had few horses. A woman gave his brother one. They went to get the horse near Saddle Mountain.[3]

The horse was wild. They roped it and handled it until near evening. Then they took it home. At home, they were staying with another family. They had a captive Mexican who was good at breaking horses and they asked him to break this one.

The next morning, the horse was roped for breaking. They put on a bridle, also a loose rope surcingle. The captive got on the horse, slipped his feet through the rope, and was led to the creek. The captive took the bridle rope, and the horse reared and rode out of sight with the Mexican on top. They returned about noon, broken and fit to ride.

Frank's brother was glad. He put the saddle on, and a blanket over the saddle, to get the horse used to it. He tied the horse to a log with its head pulled back. This was the way the Mexican broke horses. It got to be a gentle horse.

His brother had a *tekwʉniwapI* spear.

They came to a new campsite where there were adobe cabins. They prepared for the attack on the cabins. This young man's body was painted yellow and he was riding a white horse with a yellow stripe from mane to tip of tail.

The medicine men was all naked and painted yellow. They were making war medicine for each other. This young man told them to wait until daylight, and he made them wait

1. This may be the basic linkage between Isatai's ceremony and the Sun Dance.
2. It is not clear what battle this refers to, possibly the 1872 Battle of McClellan Creek.
3. Saddle Mountain is at the northwest end of the Wichita Mountains.

until sunup so he could talk to the sun. There was a crowd of spectators on a hill to the north. They thought it was time to go, and they ran to their enemies. Frank's brother was among them with his spear. There was a stockade around the cabins.

His brother was hit with a buffalo gun from the walls, and he fell off his horse; the horse bridle was fastened around his waist and the rope pulled the horse back.

A Cheyenne rode past him (without helping) and through the gate. He got shot. He had a war bonnet. There was a covered wagon there. An Indian charged it and was shot from inside the wagon as he reached it. Others came and killed the white man inside. The Indians decided to ride away; they were badly shot with buffalo guns.

The young Cheyenne's father came to this medicine man and threateningly told him that if he had any power against bullets to go and bring his son out of the battle. The medicine man refused.

Frank's brother came to, got on his horse, and got away without being killed. He had a blue spot in the temple where he had been hit.

Two Cheyennes went to get the Cheyenne warrior; they were shot at, but got there and carried him off safely, dodging bullets. They buried him by the creek and moved from the area. One brother was shot in the ear.

Niyah
July 27, 1933

Social Roles: Friendship {Wedel}   Most true friendships had a captive as one member. They talked rough to each other, etc.

A warrior led a war party out and, in a fight, another man was killed. The second warrior's friend heard of it and came to talk to the first. He said he didn't think much of him and was going to whip him. So he whipped him. The friend also said it was wrong for the warrior to return alive when one of his men had been killed.

⟨nimɛnanawohaitsnap⟩[1] was this sort of friendship.

Another war party was out prowling around and one of the men was killed. The leader returned and was sitting in camp. He sent his wife to call his friend over. His wife went but the friend refused to come. He sent his wife again to urge his friend that it would be just too bad if he didn't come. That time the friend came.

The warrior was seated on the south, others were on the west. The warrior seated his friend at his side; he said he wanted very much to ask him some questions concerning the other man's death. The warrior who led the party in the earlier story got up, said the same thing had happened to him, and he had been whipped for it, {so} he should also be whipped.

So his friend beat the leader of the party about the face and nose until he was all bloody.

Other friends pulled him off his unresisting friend.

---

1. Except for the element *haitsI*, 'friend', this word is unattested.

His wife then led the warrior out and washed him up. He returned and sat down beside his friend, but dodged every time the latter moved. The friend told him he needn't dodge, that everything was settled. They stayed friends. There were never more than two men in a friendship.

There was another kind of friend. These were not blood relations, they wouldn't joke together. They would lead a war party jointly.

While one such party was out, they found some horses and began driving them away. The owners of horses trailed them and finally caught up with them; they had a fight. The two friends were in the fight. The horse of one was shot from under him and the unhorsed warrior was surrounded. Another man of the party saw this and told the other friend. He turned and rode back, while the raiding party went on. Both were killed. When the rest of party reached camp, they told the parents of the two friends. The parents were sorrowful, but proud of their sons.

If a man rode past his friend without helping him, the friendship was ended.

Friendships might begin when two youths took up with two young girls who were friends. Women also had these friendships.

If two friends collected *nanuwoku*, they split it between them.

Social Roles: Friendship {Hoebel}   ⟨nimɛnanawohaitsnap⟩ There was usually a full blood and a captive or a half-blood. They talked rough with each other, but didn't really mean it.

A man whipped his friend who led a war party in which a man was killed. He told him he should not have come back alive if he were really brave.

The same thing happened to the first man. The friend was sitting in camp. He sent his wife to go get this leader. The man refused. He was fetched again by his friend's wife. That time he came.

He entered the tipi and sat beside his friend in the west. Other guests were around the side.

He told his friend, "Now, the same thing has happened to you. You whipped me. Now we gotta get even."

He punched him all over his face until stopped by the visitors. The man offered no resistance.

He had his wife take him out, wash him, and give him clean clothes.

Howard White Wolf had such a friend. They talked mean about each other to other people.

Those friends went together as leaders of a war party. They located a large bunch of horses and made off with them. They were pursued and overtaken. In the fight, one of them was shot off his horse.

The other Indians had gone on; one told the friend that his buddy was down. He went back to help and both were killed.

They must stand by each other through thick and thin. Failure would bring disgrace. If a friend lived through it, the friendship was ended.

Matsuka[1] failed his friend who was thrown from a horse.

Friendships usually started by wooing together.

Story: Comanches and Utes {Wedel}   Two warriors were on a war party. They were close to an enemy settlement and they sent out scouts to look over the situation. One scout went up on a hill. He didn't notice anything and got sleepy, so he got off his horse and lay down on his belly to sleep, without removing his shield and quiver.

While the warrior was sleeping, Utes camped on the creek below. They sent several men up on the hill. They sat down around the sleeping warrior, who was covered with a blanket like the Utes used. They thought it was one of their men.

When the warrior awoke, he heard strange voices. He peeked out and saw the strangers, so he lay down again very quietly, pondering on what to do. He heard another noise in the distance. It was women, as if chasing a deer, so the young Ute warriors jumped on their horses and rode off, leaving the old men there. The sleeper got up and started toward the Ute camp, walking like a cripple and wrapped in his blanket. The old men started to make fun of him.

The warrior walked on, looking for a horse. He came to one with a deer dewclaw "bell" about its neck and dragging a rope. About this time, the sounds of the deer were coming on, so the warrior jumped on the horse and rode as though to head off the deer. The nearest pursuer of the deer was a woman. Before she knew it, he had hold of her horse's bridle rein and was leading her off. He took her home.

In the old days, when a man had such a lucky escape, people gave him a special ceremony. Members of the war party would form a circle about a pile of manure, then the successful warrior rode through, scattering it and leading the captive. Then he had to tell the story of his escape.

The leader of the war party was satisfied and they went home to have a victory dance. Some of villagers didn't believe the story, but they just disputed, never openly challenged his story.

Story: Comanches and Utes {Hoebel}   They were closing on their objective. A scout was out in front. He climbed a hill, but saw nothing. He got sleepy. He left his arms on his horse, dismounted, and dozed off.

Utes came and camped below him. Ute braves came up the hill. They thought he was a Ute, as he had the same kind of blanket over his head. They sat down to smoke about him.

He finally woke up. He heard the Utes talking, and he peeked out. He tried to figure out what to do.

Young people below were chasing a deer. The braves got to their horses and rode off; there were just some old men left.

The brave got up and limped toward the Ute camp. The old men saw him and laughed.

He saw a horse with a deer hoof necklace (dewclaw) (for favorite horses).

They were chasing the deer the way he wanted to go. He rode off as if to head the deer off. A woman was closest to the deer. He took her bridle and rein and led her off.

---

1. Otherwise unidentified.

When a man had such luck, they had a special ceremony. People stood in a circle with a pile of buffalo chips in the middle. The man rode across it and scattered the pile. He must tell everything from the beginning.

The leader of the raid was satisfied: a captive was taken with no losses.

They went back to the camp. Some warriors didn't believe it, but they never had any test.

They gave the Victory Dance.

Story: Comanches and Utes {Carlson}   Some warriors were going on a war party. They approached a settlement. They picked one man out as a scout.

The scout went out to see what he could see.

The scout was now on a hill, looking in all directions; he saw nothing.

He got sleepy. He got off his horse and dozed off to sleep on the ground.

While he was asleep, some Utes coming along, camped at the foot of the hill. Some of the Ute warriors went to the top of the hill.

They saw the man; he was covered with a Ute blanket. They thought he was one of their own men, so they sat around him in a circle and began to smoke.

Finally, he woke up. He heard talking and didn't recognize his own language. He peeked out from underneath the blanket and saw the enemy. He didn't know what to do. He meditated.

He heard a noise in the distance; it sounded like young men chasing a deer. Some of the Utes got on their horses and ran to help in the deer chase. Just some very old men remained near the Comanche scout.

The scout was a cripple. He got up and headed for the Ute camp so as to not attract attention. The old men looked at him and made fun of him, as he walked funny as he was a cripple.

He kept a lookout for a horse.

He finally spotted one which wore a necklace of deer dewclaws and was dragging a rope.

He got on the horse and circled around the hunting group to head the dear off.

It was a woman who was closest to the deer.

He got close to the woman and took hold of her bridle reins, led her off, and took her home with him.

When a man had such great good luck, a ceremony was held for the man.

The people stood in a circle, singing. In the center, they piled up bull manure. The man in question took his captive wife and rode across the manure pile, spreading it out. As he did this, he must recount the details of his escapade. The leader of the war party was then satisfied that they had made a conquest, so they returned home.

When they got home, they spread the news abroad. Some of the old warriors in the camp were skeptical about the man's story, but they said nothing about it in public, but they talked about it in public {*sic*}.

They had a Victory Dance.

Horses   Horses were mounted from the right. (Whites mount from the left because of the old military custom of wearing swords on the left—R. Linton.[1])

War Story: Comanches and Utes {Wedel}   A war party traveled two or three days and stopped. The leader sent out a scout. It was a cold and foggy winter night. The scout wanted to climb a mountain to find shelter for the night. Finally, he crawled into a cave and went off to sleep. The Utes also had a scout out looking for shelter. He found the same cave and lay down on the other side to sleep. Both slept soundly.

The Comanche woke first, got up, and saw that it was daylight. He saw the blanket move on the other side. The Ute got up at the same time. They noticed one another and spoke in sign language, each asking the other's business. The Comanche said he was scouting for Utes, the Ute said was scouting for Comanches.

The Ute said they shouldn't do anything to each other. They should have an arrow contest with four arrows each, with the winner to take the other's scalp.

The Comanche said, "OK," but even if he lost, he still meant to shoot the Ute. So both went out to find a bank to shoot against. They stuck a mark in the bank. The Ute shot, then Comanche, turn-and-turn-about. The Comanche won the first two games and let the Ute win the third, and won the fourth, for a total of sixteen arrows.

The Ute knelt and told the Comanche to tie something about his head and then take the scalp. So the Comanche put his knee in the Ute's back and took his scalp. Then they agreed on a place where the parties should meet within two days. The Ute told the Comanche he was going to ride a black-spotted horse. The Comanche was to ride an iron-spotted horse with a red rag about his neck.

So they parted and went to their respective camps. When the Comanche reached camp, he saw men standing about a manure pile. So he walked into it, scattering the manure. Then he told the story and threw out the scalp as proof. He told them where they were to meet the Utes, described the Ute scout and his mount.

At the specified time, they met. The Comanche clashed with the Ute scout and killed him with his spear. He had already killed him because he had scalped him.

War Story: Comanches and Utes {Hoebel}   A scout was sent out. It was winter, misty, and getting cold. He climbed a mountain and found a cave. He made a bed and went to sleep.

A Ute scout was out. It was cold and he was looking for a cave. He came into the same cave. He went to sleep on the other side.

The Comanche scout woke up first, the Ute right after. They asked the business of each other in sign language. Each was looking for the other people.

The Ute suggested, "Today we won't do anything to each other. We will have an arrow contest with four arrows four times. The winner will take the other's scalp."

The Comanche agreed.

They set the mark against a bank.

The Comanche won the shoot. He took the first two, blew the third so the Ute wouldn't get mad, and took the fourth.

The Ute got on his knees and asked to be blindfolded.

The Comanche cut across the front and ripped off the scalp, his knee against the neck.

---

1. This is the only aside in the notes that is specifically attributed Linton.

They agreed to meet in two days. The Ute said he would be riding a spotted horse. The Ute asked the Comanche what he would be riding. The Comanche said a gray horse, and it would wear a red blanket for a hood.

The Comanche saw his people around a pile of manure. He scattered the manure. Then he told them the whole thing from the beginning. He threw the scalp in for evidence. {He told them} of how they would meet in two days.

Then came the battle. The two scouts met and the Comanche killed the Ute with his spear.

He didn't get a coup for this because the Ute was scalpless.

War Story: Comanches and Utes {Carlson}   A war party was on their way. They had traveled two or three days. The leader sent out a scout when they were camped. It was in the winter, quite foggy. The scout looked for a place to sleep, a cave in the rocks or something. Finally, he located a cave, made himself a bed, and fell asleep immediately.

The Utes were nearby and they had a scout out who also got cold and sought a place to sleep for the night. This Ute found the same cave. It was dark. He crept into the cave; he did not see the Comanche.

They both slept soundly. The Comanche woke up first and it was daylight. He noticed something lying in the cave.

They both got up; they stood at the same time. They noticed each other. In sign language, they asked the business of each other.

The Comanche said, "I am scouting for you Utes."

The Ute said, "I was out to locate the Comanches in preparation for battle."

The Ute made the suggestion that they not try to harm each other. The Ute suggested that they have an arrow contest for the other's scalp. Each must use four at a time and shoot four times (sixteen arrows).

The Comanche agreed, but he had it in mind that if he should lose, he would shoot the Ute anyway.

The Comanche was a good shot.

They found a place with a high bank that they could shoot against. They put up a target.

The Ute shot first, then the Comanche.

The Comanche won the first two rounds; the Comanche didn't want to make the Ute {mad} by winning by too large a margin, so he let the Ute win the third round. The fourth round the Comanche won.

So the Ute got down on his knees and told the Comanche to take a rag and tie over his head tightly, "After you do that, take the scalp."

The Comanche cut the scalp; he put his knee against the Ute's back and pulled it off.

They agreed then that the two sides should meet on the battlefield in a certain place in two days. The Ute said, "In that battle, I'll ride a red-spotted horse."

The Comanche said he would ride a gray horse with a red blanket as a hood.

They parted and returned to each other's camps. When the Comanche returned, they were standing in a circle with a manure pile in the center. He scattered the manure and recounted his escapade. He threw down the scalp also.

Some of the people didn't believe him.

On the appointed day, the battle took place. The two scouts met and the Comanche used his spear and killed the Ute.

Oaths: Scattering Buffalo Chips   If a returning scout had no news, he wouldn't scatter the manure. If he had news, he scattered the manure as a sort of oath [as a sign he was telling the truth].[1]

Exclamation: Karáho   Karáho was a Mexican exclamation.[2]

War: Sentries   There was no punishment for sentries who went to sleep.

War Story: Comanches and Mexicans {Wedel}   A war party went out and set up camp on a mountainside after circling the mountain. They sent two scouts to the summit as lookouts.

The next morning, one of the Indians got up. He was making his toilet when, in his mirror, he saw Mexicans approaching. He shouted, "Karáho."

The Mexicans attacked and killed some of the Comanches before they could scatter.

The sentries weren't punished for laxity.

War Story: Comanches and Mexicans {Hoebel}   Sentries were not punished for sleeping on duty.

A party went halfway up a mountain to camp.

They sent two men to the top. They slept.

A warrior got up in the morning. He was looking in a mirror and saw Mexicans on them.

Several Comanches were killed, but nothing was done to the sentries.[3]

War Story: Comanches and Apaches {Wedel}   See Carlson.[4]

Thirty Apache warriors were camped in a small grove on a hillside. The Comanches sent three warriors down afoot as decoys with one horse. The others stayed up on the hill and watched. Presently, they saw a cloud of dust and knew the Apaches were attacking.

The three boys jumped on the one horse and fled back to the hill. The rest of the Comanches were ready and met the Apaches, killing twenty of them.

The Apaches decided to make peace with the Comanches.

(The Utes were regarded as the best fighters by the Comanches.)

So they sent two groups of ten men each to find the Comanches and establish peace, to ask to make a great camp together and cement their friendship. The Apaches (*esikwita*[5] 'gray scabby butt') promised to give their young women to the Comanche men as dancing partners.

One of the Apache parties met a Comanche war party of ten men. The Comanches prepared to fight, but the Apaches ran up a white flag. They told the Comanches they wanted to make peace, to camp together at certain place and have a good time.

1. Wallace and Hoebel 1952:248.
2. "Caramba"?
3. Hoebel's note card attributes this note to Informant 1 (Herman Asenap), but there is no apparent parallel in Wedel's notes of Asenap's interviews. There is, however, a minimal parallel with Niyah's comment, and so it is placed here.
4. There is no apparent parallel in Carlson's extant notes.
5. Literally, 'gray excrement'. It is a generic term for the Mescalero Apaches.

The Comanche war party was led by Keβasuwake,[1] one of the leading chiefs of the tribe. ⟨Tenoyɛkwe⟩[2] was a base of operations for war parties.

The Comanche chief suggested they all go back to the base.

The other Apache party saw the base and turned back.

The Comanche and Apache parties got down to the base and agreed to make peace, especially when the Apaches mentioned the young women.

Two of the Apache delegates were sent back to their main camp to call the rest up for the peace celebration. So the Apaches and Comanches all gathered. The Comanches were very anxious to meet the Apache women.

The Apaches built a big fire. The Apache woman were on one side, the Comanche men were on the other. Two women would come out and pick partners.

One old sick man came out to watch and was grabbed off by two attractive Apache girls. He smelled very bad, so girls had to hold their heads aside, but they kept on until the song ended. Every time he jumped, he let out bad air. After the song ended, the man disappeared. This was an *otsinɨhka*[3] dance.

War Story: Comanches and Apaches {Hoebel}   The Apaches raided in Comanche country; they killed people.

The Comanches trapped a party of thirty and killed twenty of them.

The Apaches decided they wanted peace so they could hunt without trouble.

The chief selected ten delegates to go to the Comanches. "If you meet the Comanches and they want to fight, tell them you don't want to fight. Offer to have a big dance for both sides. We will give young women to dance with."

Then Apaches took up with the Comanches. The Comanches got ready to fight. The Apaches showed a white flag. The Apaches made their proposition.

Keβasuwake was the leader of the Comanche band. He suggested they go to a rendezvous point for Comanche parties, ⟨Tenoyɛkwe⟩.

The terms were agreed to, especially when they were told of the women.

They sent the Apaches back to inform the tribe.

The tribes met at the place. The Apaches built a big fire and made the dance (*otsinɨhka*).

Story: Comanches and Tonkawas {Wedel}   A young Comanche girl died and was buried. Her mother didn't want to stay around her friends, so she persuaded her husband to move away with the family of seven. While drifting around, the Tonkawas attacked their camp and killed all, save one old woman and two children.

The Tonkawas wanted peace with the Comanches, so after holding the woman a year or so, thirty of them proceeded to the Comanche locality. They camped there one night.

The Tonkawa leader had a wife. They saddled up their horses and started out one day with his wife and the captive to find the Comanches.

A Kiowa-Comanche war party on the warpath met the trio at the top of a hill.

---

1. This name is otherwise unattested. Robinson and Armagost (1990) translates *suahketɨ* as 'to breathe', suggesting that, with *ke* 'not', ⟨keβasuwake⟩ is 'not breathing'. It is also possibly a mishearing of *kebakoweʔ* 'Doesn't Go in Water', a nickname for Coyote.

2. *kuʔe* 'hill, point'. This toponym is otherwise unknown.

3. Knee Dance. See Post Oak Jim, July 11.

A certain Comanche rode up and shook hands with the Tonkawa chief. The captive then said she was glad he had done this because the Tonkawas were on their way to make peace.

While they were talking, some of the Comanches and Kiowas had gone on and reached the Tonkawa camp. Soon they heard shots from the direction of the Tonkawa camp about a half mile away.

The Tonkawa chief said, "It's too late," wheeled, and started for his camp, but he was shot with an arrow in the back. His wife took his lance and charged the Comanches, scattering them. Then they turned and hurried to the camp.

The Tonkawas got the upper hand, killing quite a few Kiowas and some Comanches. The main Tonkawa warrior played an important part in the battle.

While the Tonkawas were chasing the Comanches, one of the latter, Quassyah's father, was unhorsed. The Tonkawa chief rode at him and the Comanches shot his pinto from under him.

A certain Comanche woman's horse gave out and she begged her son-in-law to give her his horse, but he refused, saying his horse was about played out. The woman told him that he couldn't live with her daughter when he got home.

The Tonkawas won this battle.

The Tonkawas said the Comanches were very brave until they began fleeing, then they were just like cattle.

Some Tonkawas used to live near Anadarko.

A neighboring people began to miss their children and finally decided that the Tonkawas were eating them. So they ganged up and drove the Tonkawas away.[1]

The Tonkawas were called *nʉmʉrʉhka* 'man-eaters'.

Story: Comanches and Tonkawas {Hoebel}   A girl died. The mother wanted to leave the tribe so she would see no more young Comanche girls. The family of seven left.

The Tonkawa attacked them; they killed four and captured the woman and two children.

The Tonkawa decided that they wanted peace with the Comanches. Thirty warriors escorted the woman after two years.

They came to Comanche territory and camped one night.

The Tonkawa chief and one warrior took the woman to look for the Comanches.

A Comanche war party with Kiowas met them on a hilltop. The Comanche chief came and shook hands before anything was said.

The woman said she was glad. "That's what the Tonkawas wanted."

Some of the Comanche-Kiowas had drifted on and found the Tonkawa camp. The group above heard a gun fired. The Tonkawa chief said, "Well, it's too late."

He whirled and rode off. A Comanche shot him in the side with an arrow.

His wife took a spear and scattered the Comanches. The Tonkawas got away. The Tonkawas beat up the Comanche-Kiowas. They chased the Comanches a long way.

One Tonkawa was outstanding. Quanah's brother shot his horse.

A woman was fleeing and her horse was about to give out.

---

1. This is apparently a reference to the attack on the Tonkawa village at the Washita Agency, October 1862 (Nye1969:30–33).

She came upon her son-in-law (*monahpʉ̓*). She asked for his horse but he refused. She said, "When we get home, you don't live with my daughter."[1]

Social Control: Theft {Wedel}   Niyah's sister's husband, a captive,[2] became pretty handy at picking up other people's things. So the man who captured him told the Kiowas that if he stole from them they should go ahead and kill him. He was ashamed of him.

The man went off by himself to see what he could get. He stole a good horse, a saddle, a nice blanket, and a spear from some enemies. While returning, he camped near some Kiowas.

One of the Kiowas went over and saw him, and then returned to the camp and told his friends that he had seen the man they were to kill. Several warriors then went over to see what he looked like. He invited them in to talk. They asked his name. He gave them the name of another brave captive.

So the first visitor went over to see him and called him by his right name, saying he was a thief. When the Kiowa got back to his camp, they asked the first visitor why he had told them that this was the thief. He had nearly caused a brave man's death.

The latter then rode back to see the man, but he had left as soon as the Kiowas were gone. He dodged the Comanche and went to the Kiowa {*sic*, probably Arapaho} and Cheyenne.

The Mexican owner of the horse came in search of it. He got no information from the Comanches, but among the Cheyennes, he finally found him and took the horse away.

Social Control: Theft {Hoebel}   Niyah's sister's man (*tetsI*), a captive, was a pretty handy thief. His captor got tired of the disgrace. He told the Kiowas to kill the man if they caught him at it.

The man went off and stole a horse, blanket, and a spear off of some enemies.

The Kiowas were out camping; one of them saw this man. They called the captive over and asked him his name. He gave the name of a brave captive who also belonged to the same band.

The man who first saw him came in and told them the fellow's right name, how he was not respectable.

They went down and upbraided the fellow.

The captive had been hunting. He shot himself.

Men took him in and fixed him up. He gave the fellow a horse and gun to get some game. The fellow rode off. That was when the Kiowas saw him.[3]

Captives {Wedel}   Young captive boys were raised; they seldom ran away.

Full bloods usually treated them pretty square. Other captives might treat them pretty rough, however.

If a captive had a family, he kept the horses he stole. If he was living with a captor, the latter might take over his loot. But if the captive was brave and treated his captor and family with respect, he generally had full rights as a warrior.

---

1. Wallace and Hoebel 1952:279.
2. It is not clear who this would have been.
3. Wallace and Hoebel 1952:240 (?).

Captives {Hoebel}   Captives were more cruel than full bloods.

Frank Chekovi's father-in-law[1] would throw captured babies in the air and then catch them on his spear.

Rights: If a captive had a family, he might keep booty, otherwise it went to the captor. Status was given if he was brave and good.[2]

Story: Comanches and Caddos {Wedel}   Four warriors went southeast on a raid against the Chickasaws. Near Snake Creek[3] there was a Caddo camp. The Caddos were hostile to the Comanches at the time.

A Caddo man was out stalking antelope on foot. The four Comanches got to his horse. They looked around and saw the Caddo approaching them. The leader of the Comanches could talk Caddo. He hailed him as the Caddo approached and reassured him.

The Comanche asked the Caddo where he was camped. He pointed north and invited them to eat with him. They accepted. They dismounted on the opposite side of the creek from the camp.

One of the Comanches had a Caddo haircut.

They went with their host; they saw almost no men in camp, and went in to dinner.

As they were eating and resting, some of the Caddo men returned and began discussing the Comanches. They decided to have a handgame.

The youngest Comanche was left with the horses, so they could escape if the Caddos attacked them.

The Comanches lost some arrows on the first night in the handgame.

On the second night, the Caddos asked why the fourth Comanche was out with the horses. A Comanche replied that he was part Caddo. One of the Caddo men asked them to bring the boy in the next day.

The Comanches planned out what he should say; they said the Caddos might ask him to stay with them, but he should put them off with promise of a visit until they were nearer the Comanches.

The next morning the Caddo came out, saw the Comanche, and embraced him as the long lost son of his uncle.

The Caddo was familiar with the country, so he gave them directions for finding horses. He told them to go only as directed or else they would find the people prepared. Then he got all the arrows that the Comanche had lost and gave them to the youngest boy.

So the Comanches went straight east and got army horses from a post and drove them back. The youngest man saw a beautiful sorrel in a barn and decided to take it. They drove the horses all day and came back past the Caddo camp. There were more strangers there than on the other trip.

As the Comanche passed by about sundown, the Caddo rode after them and called to them to come back and camp with them overnight.

So they left the horses and returned to the camp. The youngest boy thought he would sneak around and see what had become of the three older ones. One of the Comanches had

---

1. By 1933, Frank had had five wives, thus it is not clear which father-in-law this refers to.
2. Wallace and Hoebel 1952:260.
3. Location unclear.

been riding the army sorrel and a Caddo recognized it. He asked for it and was refused. The youngest boy could see the proceedings by firelight.

The three Comanches were killed and the youngest fled toward his people. He reached a swollen creek and shot his arrows across to keep them dry, then he swam over.

On the second night, he slept on a high hill. He saw an Indian camp, but dodged it, and went on northwest until he reached a Kiowa camp. He stayed with them until the Comanches drifted in, then he took up with his own people.

Story: Comanches and Caddos {Hoebel}   Four Comanches went off on a raid to the southeast. They found a Caddo camp at Snake Creek.

A Caddo was stalking an antelope.

The Comanches got to his horse.

The Caddo was returning. They asked for his camp. He pointed north.

The Caddo asked them to come in to dinner. They came to the camp and noticed that the men were gone.

Four or five men returned; they talked about the Comanches. One of them suggested a handgame for the evening.

The Comanches left the youngest across the creek with the horses in case of an attack.

They played for two nights. The Comanches lost some arrows on the first time. On the second night, the Caddos asked why they had left the boy across the creek. The Comanches made up a story; they said he was part Caddo.

The Caddo said his uncle lived with the Comanches and wanted to see the boy.

The Comanches coached the boy not to refuse an invitation to stay with the Caddos, if given.

They brought the boy over for breakfast. The Caddo fell on the boy and wept; he called the boy, "Brother" (uncle's son).

He told them how to find horses to the southeast and gave them back all their arrows.

The leader didn't follow directions and went east. He came upon a fort and stole the army horses. They drove the horses all day and came back to the Caddo camp.

There were strangers in the Caddo camp; they were going on.

The first Caddos went out and brought them back.

The boy snuck around the camp.

The Caddos asked the leader for his sorrel horse. He refused. The Caddos killed him and the others.

The boy headed for home. He came to a flooded creek; he shot his arrows across and swam the stream.

P.M.

Story: Panther, Bobcat, and Buffalo {Wedel}   A panther climbed a tree and lay on a limb where the buffalo came for water. The buffalo were getting water while the panther picked his prey. As the buffalo filed by, the panther sprang on a yearling heifer's back and bit her in the throat. The heifer ran along trying to throw off the panther. Finally, she fell dead, and the panther began to eat on it, commencing by ripping open the belly. After the panther was full, he dug a hole and buried the rest of the meat.

A bobcat saw this and decided to try to imitate it. He crawled up into the tree and picked out a buffalo bull and pounced as the bull came by. The bull began to buck and finally threw off the bobcat, breaking its hip, and it finally died.

Story: Panther, Bobcat, and Buffalo {Hoebel}   A panther set an ambush from a tree. The buffalo went to water. The panther picked out a fat heifer. He lit on its back and sunk his fangs in its throat, his claws in the back.

The buffalo started off and fell dead.

The panther surfeited itself, then dug a hole in some leaves and buried the remaining parts.

A bobcat saw this. He wanted to try it. He picked out a buffalo bull. The bull threw the cat and broke its back. The cat died of the attempt.

Story: Panther, Bobcat, and Buffalo (Carlson)   A panther was laying for some buffalo. He was hiding in a tree above the path by which the buffalo came to water. While the buffalo were getting water, the panther laid in the tree looking for the fattest one in the bunch.

As they were coming away from the water hole, the panther leaped upon a yearling and grabbed him by the throat. The buffalo were frightened and ran and jumped about.

Finally, the buffalo fell dead. As soon as the buffalo died, the panther began to eat the stomach. He ate his fill. The panther dug a place in the leaves and buried the rest of the meat in the leaves.

A bobcat saw what had happened, so he thought he would try to do the same thing. The bobcat followed a herd like the panther had done, hid by the water hole, and picked out a buffalo bull.

As a bull was coming away from the spring, the bobcat jumped on the buffalo's back and the bull shook him off and broke the bobcat's back. The bobcat died of this injury.

Story: The Caddos and the Panther   A True Story. The Caddos were once camped in the Wichita Mountains, hunting game. One had a wooden whistle that resembled a young deer's call to lure does. Once, he made a noise like a young deer and a panther answered. The Indian was seated on the ground blowing the whistle and the panther sprang from behind, seized and killed him, but didn't eat him. Later, the Indian's people were worried and came out to look for him. With the aid of dogs, they finally found the body. Then they trailed the panther west on the north side of the mountains and caught up with him near Snyder.[1] There they killed the panther.

Hunting: Snares   Snares of twisted horsehair were baited with liver and used to catch hawks and small birds, but not eagles.

Animals: Birds: Eagles   Eagles were caught in the winter when the ice got so heavy on their wings that they couldn't fly. Also, they were shot out of trees on moonlit nights with long spike arrows.

Material Culture: Arrows   Niyah straightened arrows with his teeth.

Weapons: Bow Guard   Niyah never used bowguards, although some Comanches did.

Medicine: Curing: Teeth   There was very little dental trouble in the old days. Tree fungi was gathered and heated, then applied directly to an aching tooth; it was sometimes bitten

---

1. A small town about ten miles west of Indiahoma.

between the teeth. For cavities, they took mushroom spores and applied the dust to the ailing tooth.[1]

Medicine: Sorcery {Wedel}   Pertooahvoniquo[2] (Looking After His Son) was a medicine man. If he was within a quarter mile of a man at whom he was angry he could harm him. He bragged about his power.

A certain person became sick and the medicine man was accused of being responsible. A relation of the sick person one evening went to visit him. He was very glad the visitor had come. He said, "We'll tell stories tonight."

So they sat and talked and smoked.

After midnight, when the visitor said that it was time for him to be going, but first he wanted to ask him a question that he must accept and answer.

He said that some of his relatives had accused the medicine man of using evil power to cause people's deaths and were threatening to kill him.

The medicine man said that they must withdraw the charges under oath to the sun or else he would kill the visitor. The latter swore that the charges would be withdrawn. Then he went home to bed.

Early the next morning, he went to see his people about the promise he had made. He pleaded with them to retract the charges.

A sick person probably got well when they found out who was responsible for the sickness.

The medicine man never admitted his guilt, but was probably guilty.

Medicine: Sorcery {Hoebel}   A medicine man (Pertooahvoniquo, Looking For His Son). He told people his medicine could kill anybody he got mad at within a quarter mile.

People got to suspect something. He heard they were accusing him, "kind of threatening him."

A relative of a sick man went to the medicine man one evening. The medicine man was very glad; he said, "We'll tell stories tonight."

They talked and smoked.

At midnight, the man said, "It's time I go home."

The medicine man said he had a certain question and the other must "accept" it. "I understand your relatives say I caused them death. They make threats about me."

He wanted this man to swear he would stop his relatives; if not, the medicine man would get him. The man swore.

Early the next morning he went off to tell his kin to lay off. He pleaded with them. They desisted.[3]

Herman: The medicine man never admitted guilt but was probably responsible.

---

1. Wallace and Hoebel 1952:170.

2. *pɨ* 'his', *tuaʔ* 'son', *punitɨ* 'see'. This name has been rendered a number of ways besides Wedel's Looking After His Son, including, Goes to See His Children (1879 census), Goes to See His Son (Hoebel 1940:142), and Been to See His Son (Robinson and Armagost 1990).

In 1879 and 1880, he was listed as a member of Honetosavit's (White Badger) Yapainɨɨ local band. The 1892 list implies that he had become a local band leader. The 1895 census lists him as fifty-seven years old; he must have died soon thereafter as he is not listed on any subsequent census.

3. Hoebel 1940:91; 1954:141.

Medicine: Curing: Payment {Wedel}   Another time, a person was sick and Pertooahvoniquo was given a horse and called in to doctor the patient, but the patient died.

The doctor was riding the horse in a race. A kinsman of the patient came and demanded the horse back, but the medicine man refused to give him up. Thereupon, the kin drew a pistol and shot the horse in the head. There was no comeback for the medicine man.

Medicine: Curing: Payment {Hoebel}   Pertooahvoniquo was called on to doctor a sick person. They gave him a nice horse, but the person died.

The medicine man was riding the horse in a race. A relative demanded the return of the horse. The medicine man refused. The relative pulled a pistol and shot the horse dead. There was no retaliation.[1]

Oaths   A broken oath would result in a slow death, like tuberculosis.

Medicine: Sorcery {Wedel}   A man once fell sick and several doctors tried unsuccessfully to cure him. Finally, they got the last medicine man. This doctor worked on him and found out that someone was using evil medicine. It was detected and they exposed the guilty man.

The sick man had two or three brothers who wanted to question the guilty man. They asked the discoverer whether it would be all right. The latter offered to confront the accused if they got him.

So they sent the wife of one of the brothers to call him. He came and entered the tipi of the sick man and sat down. He was then told of the charges made by the last doctor. They pleaded with him to withdraw the sickness. Their brother got well.

The medicine man asked who his accuser was. They told him it was a Mexican captive medicine man. Thereupon, the accused became angry and said the accuser had lied.

So a woman was sent after the accuser. He came in, sat down beside the sick person, and was told that the medicine man had denied the charges.

The latter quizzed the accuser how he had detected him. The medicine man answered that while doctoring another patient he had repeatedly seen someone just like the accused come before him in a vision.

One of the patient's brothers then spoke up and asked the medicine man whether he had anything more to say.

He still denied the charges. Finally, he said, "If these charges are true may the first lightning this spring strike me down."

The brothers thereupon said they couldn't do anything more.

The medicine man and his family drifted away from camp. In the spring, he was struck by lightning and killed. The patient had died before the medicine man.

Medicine: Sorcery {Hoebel}   A person was sick; they tried lots of doctors. Finally, one found out the sorcerer. He came out with it.

Three brothers of the patient heard it. They asked the doctor if it was OK to bring the sorcerer to call. He said, "OK."

They sent a woman to bring him in.

He came up. They talked nice. They told him they had a very peculiar thing in mind they

---

1. Hoebel 1940:126–27; Wallace and Hoebel 1952:167. The latter attributes this story to Post Oak Jim.

would talk with him about. They told him of the charge of the other medicine man. They pleaded with him to let their brother get well.

The medicine man asked who had told them. They told him, a captive. The medicine man got mad; he said "That follow's medicine makes him lie."

The brothers said, "We'll prove it."

They sent a woman for the medicine man. The medicine man came in. They told him to sit in a certain place. He said, "No, I have my place," and he sat by the patient.

The proof: the medicine man said, "While I was doctoring, you always appeared before us."

The sorcerer didn't have much to say.

A brother spoke up, "Now you've heard what he said, what about it?"

The sorcerer denied it again. "If I used medicine against this person, the first lightning of the spring will get me."

The brother said, "If you say such a thing, we can't dispute you. We drop it."

During the winter, the medicine man's family drifted away. The first lightning got him early in the spring. The sick person had died first.[1]

Medicine: Buffalo Medicine {Wedel}   A man with Buffalo Medicine was called in to cure bloody injuries. He used a buffalo tail. Sometimes he merely waved the tail like a mad bull; other times he held the tail in his mouth.

A certain man was shot through the chest in battle so that his fat was sticking out. Different doctors failed to cure him, so finally one was found who could.

The wounded man suffered from unconscious spells.

First he stopped the bleeding and pushed the fat back into place. Then he singed the spines off a cactus pad, warmed it, split it, applied half to each opening, and tied it on with a rag.

The bleeding was stopped by holding a buffalo tail in his mouth, shaking it with the hand over the patient, then blowing on the wound, and making sound like a bull.

Medicine: Buffalo Medicine {Hoebel}   A man was wounded in battle; his guts were sticking out. The doctors failed.

They got a special medicine man. He stopped the bleeding. He put a tail in his mouth and blew on the wound.

He pressed the fat back in.

He burned the thorns off a prickly pear. He split the cactus and put it on either side of the wound and bound it up.[2]

Medicine: Curing: Cactus Pad   A cactus pad was good to draw out pus and prevent infection.

Medicine: Herbs   A certain Arapaho Indian was selling sneezeweed to Indians. He said it was good for everything, including childbirth and the elimination of the afterbirth.

He traded some to an old Indian woman for meat. When her daughter came home, she scolded her mother for buying weeds that grew all over their place.

Story: The Man Who Captured A Ghost {Wedel}   There was a certain camping place for Indians where they were always scared by ghosts.

1. Wallace and Hoebel 1952:239 (?).
2. Wallace and Hoebel 1952:170.

A war party once camped there and called on one of the young men to go get some water. The young man hung around until one of the older men asked him whether he was afraid. He answered, no, he would go.

They had built a windbreak with a fire inside; it was fall.

The young man was using the paunch of a cow for a bucket. He got water and, on his way back, he began pondering on what the people who camped there had seen.

Presently, he heard a noise behind him, so he walked faster. Soon, he noticed someone put his arms about him from the rear, and the arms were nothing but bones. The young man grasped the ghost by the wrists and carried it and the water into the camp together.

The warriors heard the returning footsteps and the creak of bones. So the taunters called into the darkness to ask what the young man was doing. He threw the skeleton into the camp and the warriors fell all over one another trying to get away. Then the ghost disappeared.

That night, the ghost returned to the young man in a dream and gave him invulnerability in battle.

He instructed the man to make a ball of white lead clay paint.

He should never appear first in battle, but to follow his friends. Then, when his friends were in retreat, he was to come forward in costume and paint and he would not be killed.

The next day, the party stopped at a creek and the young man got his clay and rolled it into a ball as instructed. The party went on into Mexican country; they had good luck and got lots of horses.

They started back, and were chased by Mexicans, who overtook them. The young man went off by himself and painted up.

Another young man appeared and asked him for power, so he painted the second man up like himself. He told the young man to wait until the enemy drove their friends back past them, then to go and fight. The Indians retreated and came past the young men who rode out, killed some Mexicans, and drove them back. Thus he got power of invulnerability from the ghost and transferred it to a companion for this battle only.

Story: **The Man Who Captured A Ghost** {Hoebel}   They camped near a haunted spot. The people asked a young man to go get water. The young man stalled. One asked him if he was scared; he said he wasn't.

He went out with a cow paunch. He was thinking of ghosts. He heard something behind him. He felt arms around his neck. He saw they were only bones. He seized the arms of the ghost and carried him back.

The people heard him coming. They heard the squeaking of the bones. They called to him, "Coward, what are you doing out there? Bring in that water!"

He threw the skeleton in at them. They all fled and fell in a heap. The ghost disappeared.

The ghost came to the man in a dream that night. The ghost gave medicine. "You will be hard to hit, bullets will never kill you. Keep a ball of white clay. Never go into battle first. Wait until your friends retreat, then go in."

They went on the next day. They made a good raid on Mexican horses.

Mexican pursuers caught up and a battle started. He went off to prepare himself.

A young man came up and asked him for the protection of his medicine. He gave it, and told him to wait.

He became a famed warrior.[1]

Story: **The Man Who Captured A Ghost** {Carlson}   There was a certain place where a ghost always hung out.

Some Indians were camped at this place. They asked one of their young men to go after water. He kind of delayed; he sort of waited around. One of the old men asked him if he was afraid; he said no, he would go.

It was fall. They made a windbreak and the men were sitting around the fire.

The young man went for the water. On his way back, he wondered why people always got frightened at this place.

As he was going along, he heard a noise behind him. He felt someone put his arms around him from behind. He noticed that the arms were nothing but bones.

He grabbed the ghost by the arms and carried it on his back into camp.

While he was approaching, they heard his footsteps and the creaking of bones. Before he came into view, someone at the fire called out "coward" to him. They hollered for the water and he threw the ghost down instead.

This scared all the Indians. When the ghost hit the ground, he disappeared suddenly.

When the young man went to sleep that night, he saw the ghost in a dream. The ghost said to him, "I give you my power. From now on you will be hard to kill."

The ghost told the young man to get white earth paint and roll in into a ball. "Let your mates enter battle first. When they retreat, get ready and paint up and go out and fight and you will never be hit."

The next morning, these Indians moved camp. The young man went out and got some paint and rolled it up into a ball.

These Indians finally reached Mexican territory and captured a lot of horses. Before they got home, the Mexicans overtook them and gave battle. The young man did as the ghost told him to do in battle. As he was painting up, a young man came to him and asked him if would give him power and protection. The young man agreed and painted the other fellow too. He told the young man that they would have to wait until their people retreated before entering the battle.

The Indians retreated. The two young men fought the Mexicans. The Mexicans shot at them, but couldn't hit them. The young men killed many Mexicans. After this, the young man who had captured the ghost was well known for his bravery.

---

1. Wallace and Hoebel 1952:173.

HOWARD WHITE WOLF
July 31, 1933

Material Culture: Clothing: Headdress   A war bonnet might be awarded after two or several battles in which a warrior distinguished himself.

Camp: Tipis: Windbreak   A fence of willow withes or tall weeds (like sunflower stalks) was erected about tipis.

They set poles in the ground, then stretched three or four cords between them and lashed willows or heavy stalks upright to the cross cords. The fence would be about six or eight feet high, with the entrance to the east. Twigs and foliage were left on the stalks so as to form a windbreak. It was used in winter, principally since the end of the nomadic life. It was erected by the women, all helping each other.

Camp Organization: Sentries   In the old days, a lookout was sent out every day or two to scout about camp for hostile signs [about ten miles out].

If traces were found, the scout reported to the *paraibo*, who then called out loud that the scout had reported enemies near and that he wished to consult with the leading men. So they were always prepared.

Camps: Tipis: Windbreak   They had no time to raise a windbreak because they might have to move on short notice. The Arapaho and Cheyenne were great users of such breaks.

Camps: Brush Arbors   [Arbors were used only after the surrender.]

Material Culture: Crafts: Hide Work   They killed buffaloes, skinned and cleaned the hides very carefully. The spleen was cut and used with the brain (boiled and ground fine) to rub into the hide.

Material Culture: Tipis: Construction   The hide was pegged out for dressing and scraped first. Wood ashes were rubbed into the hair side. The hide was then scraped with large stone scrapers to remove the hair; it came out easily. The ashes were not moistened.

One woman acted as boss to direct the work.

The woman for whom the work was being done cooked meals for the helpers.

A steel blade was set adzelike to a bone handle, and used with hoelike motions to scrape the hide through. After the brain and ash treatment, sinew was then tied to the top and bottom of a pole about six or eight feet high and the hide was drawn back and forth through this loop to soften it up. The women had to stay with it until the skin was very soft and thin, white, like cloth.

The hide was then laid out and left to dry in the sun. Then the master worker laid the hides out and cut each one to a standard size and pattern with a knife. Then the hides were laid out and sewn with sinew, each woman being assigned a place to sew. When dinner time came, each woman left her sewing just where it was and the "manager" went around to check up. The tipi cover was never given another dressing; it was never greased. It was good for two or three years. It was never rolled when wet.

The cover was cut in panels.[1]

Method of folding: {It was folded into a rectangle, then rolled.}

---

1.   Wallace and Hoebel (1952:96) cites Kills Something (Mirsky; see Appendix A) and Nemaruibetsi as the sources for the information in this note.

Horses: Packing   Tipi poles were carried as follows: three or four long rawhide cords were fastened to each side of the saddle. The front cord passed through the holes at the top of the poles. The middle and rear cords fastened about the poles to keep them from spreading. A cross cord behind the horse's tail keeps the two bundles from spreading. All the poles from one tipi were carried on one horse, about ten to fifteen poles on each side of the animal. Thus, all the poles were kept even and safe from slipping in travel.

Baggage was packed in a long oblong bundle pack and placed one on either side of the animal, under the tipi poles. Each bundle had a wide strap near either end, passing about the poles. The bundle was secured to the poles, and acted as padding. The poles were fastened to the saddle with the cords. Two women were usually required to pack a horse, although one might do it. The tipi poles were tied together at the bottom of each bundle.

Horses: Whips   A rawhide whip was used when on the move.

Horses: Pack Horses   Pack horses were used for the same sort of load on successive trips.

Horses: Travois   The Comanches never used the travois, although Howard knew of its use among the Cheyennes.

Horses: Invalids   Invalids were probably carried on horseback, supported by another person and padded with pillows.

Life Cycle: Childbirth   An expectant mother always stayed with the camp when on the move; she was never abandoned in childbirth.

Horses: Saddles   The forks of an elm tree were cut so as to fit the horse's back, one fore and one aft. A flat piece was cut to go on each side, under the forks. The side pieces were pierced and lashed to the forks. The entire saddle was then covered with rawhide that shrank and held everything tight. There were two belly girths, a crupper, and a breast band, all lashed on by perforations and cords.

There were brass-headed tacks on the women's saddle horn; it was also painted red. A man's saddle was unpainted, although it maybe had tacks. Women threw a blanket over the saddle, fastened by a strap over the saddle and under the horse's belly.

Deerhorn bow saddles were the same as the other but with horn instead of elm forks.

Men made all the saddles; there were special [men] saddle makers.[1]

There was no definite arrangement of furniture on a saddle.

Weapons: Tomahawk   The tomahawk was used in close fighting. It was carried by the bravest men; there were very few of them in the tribe.

Social Organization: Societies   The Tuwi was the Yapai "regiment"[2] (Raven Dancers). There were about sixty or seventy men with officers.

The Piviapukunuu was the Kwaharunuu regiment. They danced like the Ravens, but used gourd rattles.[3]

The Yapai would erect a great tipi; they put two or three together. The dancers gathered and the drums begin to beat when the leading men arrived. One man had a serrated club

---

1. Wallace and Hoebel 1952:96.
2. Hoebel 1940:39; Wallace and Hoebel 1952:224.
3. In 1912, Wahkinney told Robert Lowie that the Big Horses used dewclaw rattles. See Part Two, below.

with a gray fox tail. This man was the high man of the regiment. The leader was on a painted horse, with its tail tied with red cloth and an eagle feather. The horse understood it.

All of the warriors sat in a line. They were supposed to dance together. If one hesitated, the leader struck him with the whip and he had to dance. A man who failed to dance must give a good reason. If he had done more brave deeds than the leader he could get out of it; otherwise, he paid a fine.

Once a man refused to dance. When his shirt was torn off and he was struck by the club, he said he was poor dancer. He told of a hard battle where he had killed several men. He said if the leader could boast of more brave deeds, he would dance as best he could. The leader admitted that he was beaten.[1]

Raven dancers moved with a slight up-and-down motion and chanted, imitating the raven.

The Yapai were the best of all the dancers. The women left everyone else when the Yapai men danced.

Large oval tipis, like a camp meeting tent, were erected for the big dances. They had no fireplaces. Maybe five or six tipis were used to build the large one, but details of its construction were unknown.

Camps: Tipis: Painted   Howard never knew of Comanches painting their tipis or otherwise decorating them.[2]

Material Culture: Crafts: Hide Work   Robes were painted as directed by a leading man when the man was well known. For example, he might draw pictures of the wearer's war exploits. The owner had to swear to the truth of the exploits before he could wear the robe. He swore by the Sun at the chief's demand, asking for long life for himself and his children if his deeds were true.

Women never painted their blankets to suit their vanity.

Material Culture: Pictographs   Pictures were drawn [on rocks] to tell who had been at a certain spot, for example a white wolf, black eagle, and red bird might be pictorially represented at a certain spring to inform later comers. A painted finger indicated the direction of springs or other localities.[3]

Signals   If men had been killed in war, returning scouts would signal the number of fatalities by raising and lowering a blanket on a hilltop visible from the camp.

Social Organization: Societies   A man could belong to one "regiment" only. All [most] of the men of a band belonged to its regiment, and could not switch band affiliations.

[Members were not supposed to switch from one regiment to another. That would mean switching bands.]

---

1. Wallace and Hoebel 1952:271 (?).
2. Contra Wallace and Hoebel 1952:89.
3. In 1848, Seth Eastman copied a "Comanche Inscription on the Shoulder Blade of a Buffalo," illustrated in Schoolcraft 1851–57, 4:153; the original drawing is in the National Anthropological Archives, Smithsonian Institution, item no. 08530904.

In June of 1875, after agreeing to surrender, Isatai left a pictographic "letter" on a buffalo hide for some absent hunters stating where they were going. The next day, some of those hunters caught up with them, showing that the message was successfully transmitted (Sturm 1875).

Social Organization: Bands: Nokoni   "Those who turn back before reaching their destination."

Dances: Scalp Dance   [Victory Dance] On the return of a successful war party, two good (female) dancers were selected and dressed up. The scalps were placed on a pole. The two women wore war bonnets.

Dances: Peace Pipe Dance   The Pipe Dance (came from the Pawnees or Wichitas). Wichitas sent word to Quanah that they were going to give him and his family a Peace Pipe Dance.

Two young Comanche women were selected.

It was fall.

The Wichitas came to the Comanche camp. They brought some gifts of money, blankets, etc.

The two Comanche women were told to be at the Wichita tipi. They prayed for them. The women were brought to the tipi, painted up, given gifts, seated on a blanket, and carried to the dance tipi.

There were two young men in the dance tipi, representing the black and white eagles respectively. Both were naked. They carried gourd rattles like in peyote. The young men danced backwards in opposite directions. The Wichitas were seated about the tipi.

Before each woman was a pile of goods, blankets, pipes, otter skins, etc. A Comanche would come in, select the goods he wanted, and give a horse in exchange.

The warriors were about two hundred yards away on horses.

A man would come out and tell his war deeds. At each deed the drum was struck. The man would attack and knife a life-size human effigy.

The dance was to give Quanah's daughter and her companion long life and a good start in life. They prayed before the girls left home. The ceremony was repeated four times.

The dance came first from the Wichitas.

[One of the girls was Quanah's daughter.] The second girl was Herman Asenap's half-sister's mother (?).[1]

If any of the war deeds were untrue, the man's children would be punished, etc.

Quanah Parker   Quanah Parker was disliked because of his influence with whites, somewhat because of his white strain.

Social Organization: Bands: Band Lists   Band List[2]

Penatᴈka   'honeyeater band'

Noyɛka

Nokoni

Yapai

Social Organization: Societies   These same companies or regiments gave other dances also, for example, the Crow and other dances.

Hunting: Buffalo Horses   Buffalo horses were trained to watch while its owner skinned buffalo. The horse would stand by, waving its ears alternately while buffalo and coyotes

---

1. Herman's half-sister was Hokup or Kitty Nipker, the daughter of Nipker, who was, in turn, the daughter of the Wia'nᴜᴜ local band chief whose name is variously spelled Wissiche, Waysee, and other variants (*wesi-* 'curly').

2. These spellings are as given in Wedel's notes.

were around, and pitching both ears forward if a man approached. This saved many lives, because by observing his horse, the owner knew of danger if any approached.[1]

Social Organization: Societies   When the leader of a regiment was killed, nominees were set up by the members. Their war records were considered. The man with the best record was selected as successor.

Tabenanaka and White Wolf   Tabenanaka and White Wolf were the Yapai leaders. They jointly succeeded Ten Bears.[2]

Story: Comanches and Utes   A Comanche woman was captured by Utes. The Comanches heard that she was still living with Utes and had children, so she made friendship between the Utes and the Comanche.

Social Organization: Societies: Tuwikaaʔnʉʉ   The Raven Dancers swore to stay together in war and fight side by side.

Dances: 49 Dance   Once some young men went to a white dance. They saw a number 49, so afterward, when they wanting to attend a dance, they said, "Let's go to the 49 Dance," hence the origin of the name. It was staged the night before a war party left.

Political Organization: Chiefs: Authority   A chief couldn't stop a war party from leaving.[3] The *paraibo* had advisory powers mainly.

He could be whipped by a dance leader if he joined a regiment [and didn't want to dance].

He decided when to move camp, and would go out and announce, "Listen, listen, we are going to move camp. The grass is getting short and we must move to the next creek. The place has already been chosen."

The camp moved whenever everyone was ready, in a body. The men kept together in a group or in small groups, the women and baggage in another body.

Scouts were always sent out ahead to select the new site when grass and fuel became scarce. It was always the same men as scouts.

Hunting: Opossum   The Comanches never ate opossums. [It was supposed to feed on corpses of the dead.]

Material Culture: Utensils   Leaves were used for table cloths in the old days. There were coffee pots (from Mexico). Knives came in Howard's father's time (ca. 1800–1830).[4] Wooden platters were made by burning or hollowing out with tools.

Material Culture: Crafts: Horn Work   Horn was boiled to soften it, then worked into long-handled spoons, buffalo horn.

1. Wallace and Hoebel 1952:61.

2. Esarosavit and Tabenanaka were brothers-in-law, the former married to the latter's sister. The two were also leaders of separate local Yapainʉʉ local bands in both the prereservation period and the later reservation period. But though there is documentary evidence that the two, along with Tabenanaka's distant relative, Cheevers, and the latter's uncle, Esananaka, competed for the position of Yapainʉʉ principal chief after Paruasʉmʉno's death in 1872, the historically documented role of Esarosavit is minimal. There is no documentary evidence that Esarosavit and Tabenanaka were "joint" *paraibo*.

3. Hoebel 1940:19.

4. Metal knives, in the form of the Spanish *cuchillos*, were reported as trade items as early as 1735 (Kavanagh 1996:67).

Relations with Other Tribes: Shoshones Howard's paternal grandmother was a Shoshone. When the Shoshones split, his grandmother went north with them, while his father remained with the Comanches.

Relations with Other Tribes: Enemies Comanches fought Mohaves, Kiowas, Apaches, Penatʉhkas [band separated][1] and almost all other tribes.

The leading men of the different tribes finally got together, smoked the long pipe, blowing smoke up, and swore peace.

Relations with Other Tribes: Kiowas Intermarriage with the Kiowas [one case] led to the peace treaty. They had to smoke the pipe, thereby swearing by the Sun to keep the peace.

The Comanches were camped near Lynchburg[2] with some soldiers. One man went out on a mule to get game. He met ten Kiowas under a very brave warrior coming south just before a Sun Dance. The Kiowas wanted to kill the Comanche. Finally, they decided to go and eat dinner with him because he said there were only a few of them. The Kiowas made a break for their horses when they got into camp and overheard that they were to be killed, but were all shot down. This was after they had made peace.

Relations with Other Tribes: Utes [A Comanche Woman was captured by the Utes. The Comanches heard that she had children by a Ute. She made peace between the Utes and Comanches.]

Relations with Other Tribes: Sign Language The Sioux were "cut throats."

For the Arapaho, they touched the right side of the nose.

For the Cheyenne, two lines were drawn across the left forefinger to indicate markings[3] (?).

For the Comanche, they made a rippling motion of the forefinger backward, meaning snake.

Material Culture: Clothing: Decoration The Comanche decoration on costumes meant nothing.

Political Organization: Chiefs The *paraibo* was not necessarily the man with the most war honors; they preferred a kind, generous, good man as chief.

Disputes were referred to the chief, whose word was final.[4]

Medicine: War: Transfer In a big battle, one Comanche gave his shield to another man, chewed a remedy, and blew it over the shield to turn bullets.

Power, but not actual war honors, could be transferred. The only way a man could share these war honors was to touch or strike the former's victims.

Hunting: Cougars Cougars were not hunted in the old days.

Antelopes were sometimes run down by horses, with several men pursuing in succession.

Buffalo was the main game, the others were very minor.

1. There is a persistent theme in the Comanche literature that the Penatʉhka were sufficiently distinct from other Comanches that there was active hostility between them. There is, however, little documentary support for this charge.
2. Apparently Lynchburg, Texas.
3. That is, the feather markings.
4. Hoebel 1940:19.

Material Culture: Clothing: Children's   Children's clothes were made of antelope skin, often with the fur on to give a spotted effect (especially on shirts).

Material Culture: Bow Case   Panther skin was used for bow cases occasionally.

Games: Arrows   An arrow was shot and set for the mark in shooting contests.

Material Culture: Arrows   Arrows were identified by their feathers. There were three feathers on each arrow, about one quarter of an inch wide.

Material Culture: Bow Case/Quiver   The quiver was made of panther tail skin with a longer bow case beside it.

Material Culture: Containers   A small pouch to carry flint, steel, and dry wood tinder was fastened by a sling to the belt. The awl was likewise attached.

Medicine: Sun Dance: Kiowa   The Kiowa Sun Dance lodge had a wall of willow across the back for placing the image and for the resting dancers.

Medicine: Peyote   Only old people used peyote in the old days. There were no all-night ceremonies because of the danger of attack while participants were recovering the next day.[1] It was used only in the morning and evening.

Medicine: Sun Dance   Howard knew of no case where a medicine man handed down to his son the right to give a Sun Dance.

There was no image doll in the Comanche dance. The Kiowa doll must be made by the leader.

NEMARUIBETSI
July 31, 1933[2]

Story: Life Story   Her name, Nemaruibetsi, meant 'She Invites Her Relatives'; *nemarui* is 'relatives'.[3] She belonged to the Penaŋʉʉ band and was over seventy years old. She was born up north[4] but doesn't remember her father. Her mother died when she was small. She was raised by her grandmother [*kaku*] until she was about ten years old.

Her grandmother's brother was away on a war party. A relative was sick, so they called for a medicine man. Her grandmother's brother had left a red blanket with a white stripe around the edge; [they gave it to the medicine man] who put it up as the door to his tipi. On his return, her uncle was angry that they had given his blanket to the medicine man. He sent the grandmother and this girl (now about twelve) away. They had no place to go.

---

1. La Barre 1975:58.

2. The content of this interview is from Hoebel, while the dating and variations are from Carlson. Except for Hoebel's numbered topical cards, the order is arbitrary.

3. '[our] lady friends'; see Introduction.

4. Although the Penaŋʉʉ are usually called "Southern" Comanches, Nemaruibetsi here states that she was "born up north." It may be noted that in 1862, when she was born, most of the Penaŋʉʉ were located near Fort Cobb, about forty miles north of Indiahoma, having been forced out of Texas in 1859.

Her grandmother told her she must marry to make a home for them. Soddyocoom[1] 'Male Dog' was a captive about thirty-five years old.[2] Her grandmother wanted her to marry him. She didn't want to, but her grandmother insisted. She finally consented. Her grandmother said she'd marry him otherwise.

Her grandmother went to see Soddyocoom. He agreed, but instead of their going to his place, he came to them. He didn't stay long; he told the grandmother that the girl was too young and he wanted to return. The grandmother insisted on his staying. He left for awhile.

She was about twelve or thirteen years old. She had never gone with any boys her age at the time.

Soddyocoom left awhile and then returned. He left two horses for them and left again. He liked to be with the Yapainʉʉ.

Her grandmother went to stay with a relative (her grandmother's uncle) called Mowway (the chief of a band).

The girl said she'd go to the Yapainʉʉ with her husband.

Mowway was glad to take care of the grandmother, but didn't like the way Chonip[3] (her mother's brother) had treated her. Mowway went to Chonip ('bone') and told him he hadn't treated his mother's sister (Nemaruibetsi's grandmother) right. He agreed to take her back.

Nemaruibetsi went to live with her husband, but neither was satisfied with the arrangement. She asked him to take her back to her grandmother. He did. He gave her a horse and took her back to her grandmother.

The husband returned some time later and asked for her, and her grandmother sent her with him again.

They had no home of their own but stayed with other people.

He again sent her back, and she told him she didn't want him to come back again.

Her husband was better at women's work than men's work. He liked to tan hides, etc. He was not good at hunting. Captives might do women's work, as tanning hides, but Soddyocoom was the only one of which she knew.[4]

Therefore, they had no home of their own, but lived with other people, especially Waunavani,[5] who called him "son." Waunavani told him that he should make a home for his wife; he was not treating her right. Soddyocoom said she was too young for

---

1. *sariiʔ* 'dog, *kuhma* 'male'. Soddyocoom is the agency spelling. agency records list him as a captive, born about 1833, and, from 1879 to 1883, a member of Neithkawoofpi's (*neki* belt', *kwibukitʉ* 'whip', Belt Whip) Penanʉʉ local band. He was later associated with Coby's and Tooahvonie's Kwaharʉnʉʉ local bands, 1892–95.

2. This would place this episode as about the year 1868. However, if Nemaruibetsi was born about 1862, she would have been only five at that time. Given the uncertainties with the dates, the early 1870s is probably as close an estimate as is possible.

3. Chonip, *tsuhniʔ* 'bone', was born about 1853. He had been a member of Terheryahquahip's Nokoni local band in 1879, and by 1889, he was the chief a small local group. The transition of Nemaruibetsi's residence from Soddyocoom to Chonip is unclear.

4. This note is on a separate card, outside the sequence of the story.

5. Hoebel spells this name Wonabanai. Waunavani is listed on the censuses, 1879–1885, as a member of Cheevers' Yapainʉʉ local band. It was variously translated as Wants To See A Woman and Big Belly. Neither has been substantiated. The kinship relationship between Waunavani and Nemaruibetsi is unknown.

responsibility. Waunavani told the girl that Soddyocoom wasn't satisfied with her and that her grandmother shouldn't send her with him again. She was then about fifteen years old.

She was now interested in other boys.

She would send him away when he would come to see her. She wouldn't let him sleep with her. Her feelings were hurt at the beginning because he told her she was too young for him to bother to work for her and take care of her.

People noticed that Soddyocoom left her alone for a long time. They told her he wasn't a good husband. He wouldn't do a man's work.

The last time he came for her, he brought a horse for her. She told her uncle she wouldn't go; she was engaged to another man. While Soddyocoom was there, she went to the creek (and met her lover. They ran away together.)

Chonip, her uncle, sent her to a hunting party to get some meat. On her return trip, she met him (her future husband). (She was on a horse and he stopped her by holding the bridle. It was the first time he had spoken to her.) He said he'd take her on a raiding party. She accepted (not seriously); she was in a hurry. When the occasion arose, she went with him in order to shake Soddyocoom, although she didn't know her lover very well. The lover was older than her; she was about sixteen.

She didn't know he would be at the creek and was surprised.

Her uncle and Soddyocoom went to the creek to find her. They looked until dark and finally gave up and Soddyocoom went away.

When she and her lover left, she didn't know where they were going. They were really going on a raiding party. Her lover came back and got clothes and a horse for her from his own home (his mother's or his sister's). When she got to know him, she found that he was already married.

On the raid, only three went—Nemaruibetsi, her lover, and another man, a friend. They met no enemies, but got six horses. She helped capture the horses. On their return, she gave a horse to her grandmother.

On their return, Soddyocoom was angry. Her lover went to visit some Penanʉʉ. While he was there, Soddyocoom and two other men came to see him. She hid in the tipi and heard everything.

They told the men that the lover wasn't there. Soddyocoom wanted certain horses. Her lover's brother said he didn't think that the lover would give them any.

The people she was staying with (the lover's brother) told her to go back to her own people to avoid trouble. She went to the creek at night; she was called for by her *araʔ*, her mother's brother, called Aku.[1]

She was covered with a blanket and taken back. While she was gone, Soddyocoom returned with his friends and the lover paid him the four horses.

Aku's brother asked the lover if he was going to marry her or not. If not, Soddyocoom was going to give her to another man (a brave warrior).

The lover said he'd like to keep her.

---

1.   Otherwise unidentified. There are three individuals named Ahko on the census lists, 1879–1923—two females and one male—but the male was too young to be Nemaruibetsi's *araʔ*.

Nemaruibetsi said nothing about the other wife she had learned about, and decided to stay with him until it was blown over anyway.

Her lover was going on a war party. He went to see chief Quanah Parker, who was taking a married woman with him, to see if he could go too and take her along. He was afraid of Soddyocoom's friend, who was a big warrior.

Question: What about the lover's first wife?

He said he was leaving her; she would go back to her own parents.[1]

Nemaruibetsi's uncle's brother wanted the lover to keep her and not let Soddyocoom get her back, as his friend was mean. They had to be careful, as their place was being watched by Soddyocoom.

Two days later, her lover came and said they would leave on the war party in two days and she should be ready to go. They came at night with Quanah and his wife. Quanah's woman's husband was a brave warrior, Тана3а,[2] and Quanah was already married to an Apache. Quanah's Apache wife saw him come for his clothes and had chased him on foot with a big knife. She wanted to do damage to the woman, but she couldn't catch up. They heard her later stop and cry, but they went on.

They traveled all day and the next night. They were afraid of the husband of the woman Quanah had along. They all traveled rapidly, with nothing to eat. They saw buffaloes and Quanah rode down after meat. They saw some horses on their way to the buffalo, so he killed a horse. He called them down. She didn't notice it was a horse until she was cleaning the gut and found horse not buffalo manure.

The buffalo were too far away, and the horses were near, and they were in a hurry. They took the horsemeat to the creek, where they sliced and cooked and loaded it. The men made a fire and cooked some. They spread leaves on the ground to eat on. This was the first time she ate horsemeat. She didn't like it and nearly vomited. Quanah's woman was used to eating horsemeat.

That night they camped. Quanah went on a hill to look around. He saw a man riding towards the creek. He told them to put their meat up in a tree away from coyotes and wolves (but coyotes got half of it).

They went to bed, all huddled close.

Quanah went to find the horseman to see who it was. He found it was three men, two women and some children, Comanches. They had left their camp. They had trouble sometime before.

Story: Ta'si'woo' {Hoebel}   It was Ta'si'woo' and his son and grandson. *ta'si'woo'*[3] means 'buffalo'.

The marriage set-up was this: {see fig. 5}

Ta'si'woo' and Isawura shot their father and grandfather through the abdomen with a bow and arrow and ran off with two of his wives (not their own mothers).

Old Ta'si'woo' was not killed. He pulled the arrow out and kept the arrowhead.

---

1. This is the only instance of a question in the notes with a direct answer.
2. Otherwise unidentified.
3. *ta-'* 'with the foot', *si'woo'* 'paw earth', commonly translated as 'drags his feet'. The man Ta'si'woo' is otherwise unidentified.

Both pairs had a child. Isawʉra's son was called Kata[1]; he was later called Taʔsiʔwooʔ 'Buffalo' also.

They left camp immediately after the deeds because they were afraid of the old man, and the people didn't like it. Old Taʔsiʔwooʔ's captive "brother," Tabeʔitsi, went with them. On their return they camped on the edge of the camp, ashamed.[2]

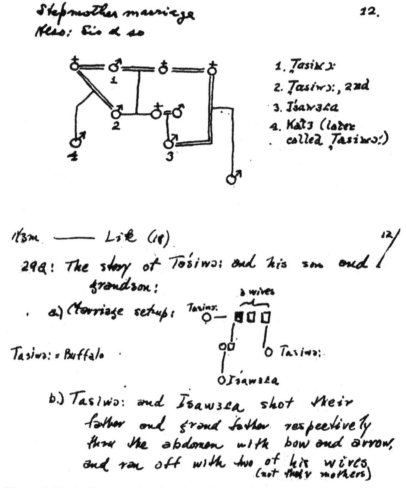

Figure 5. Hoebel's notes showing the relationships in the story of Tasiwo from Nemaruibetsi.

1. The 1892 census lists a Kahta, age thirteen, no parents given, as an alternate name for a man called Chimebitty. The Family Record Book lists him as the twenty-one year old son of Tahbeasche (possibly Tabeʔitsi) and Nem-a-roo-e-che (possibly Nemaruibetsi herself, although the Family Record Book also states that his mother was deceased).

2. Hoebel 1940:71; Wallace and Hoebel 1952:140. This note is within the narrative flow of Nemaruibetsi's life story.

Story: Taʔsiʔwooʔ {Hoebel}   A son and grandson shot their father and ran off with two of his three wives (those not their blood mothers).

The father recovered. The pairs returned with children later.

No action was taken because they were blood relatives (also clouded by the Quanah Parker case[1]).

They were ostracized by all of the people and were forced to live apart on the edge of the camp.[2]

Story: Taʔsiʔwooʔ {Carlson}   A man named Taʔsiʔwooʔ had three wives. By his first wife he had a son and a daughter. The son's name was also Taʔsiʔwooʔ. The daughter had a son named Isawɨra.

The son and grandson fell in love with the old man's other two wives.

They shot the old Taʔsiʔwooʔ in the stomach with an arrow, inflicting a grazing wound from which he recovered eventually.

They then eloped with old Taʔsiʔwooʔ's other two wives.

Old Taʔsiʔwooʔ's *haits*, a captive named Tabeʔitsi, went along with the four.

The five stayed away from the camp for a considerable length of time.

Isawɨra's son, who was named Kata, but later named Buffalo, died only recently.[3]

Finally, the group returned with Quanah Parker.

The people in the camp were still angry with him. They said they should have taken pity on an old man, and if they had not been his kinfolks, something would have been done to them.

Young Taʔsiʔwooʔ and his wife, and Isawɨra and his wife, always had to camp a little way away from the general camp ever after, because people didn't want to have anything to do with them.

Life Story (Cont.)   The two parties joined up and continued on their way. They went for two days and camped.

They left the two women and two children and Taʔsiʔwooʔ for protection. The others (four men and two women) went on. The next night they located a bunch of horses.

Quanah, Tabeʔitsi, and Isawɨra went to the horses. They told the others to wait at a certain place and not to leave it.

The women, etc., waited. They heard a shot and knew Quanah and his party had shot the guard. They heard horses coming and heard a whistle. Quanah was riding a new gray horse. He told her lover to get her a good horse as they must travel faster now.

They all picked horses from the bunch. She got a pacer. Her lover tried it first to see if it would buck. It was moonlight. She told her husband she liked that horse and wanted it. The next day the horses were divided. Another man {. . . [*sic*]}.

The division of horses was this: Quanah's first choice (his gray).

Tabeʔitsi and Isawɨra were next: they took the two women's horses. (Nemaruibetsi was disappointed.)

Nemaruibetsi's husband was next.

---

1. This reference is unclear.
2. This note is from a typewritten synthesis card labeled "Murder—Attempted."
3. The Family Record Book states that Kahta died May 29, 1906.

Then it was her turn; she got a bay (it was wild and mean).

Quanah's woman was next.

On Quanah's second choice, he took a mule.

The men got three apiece. The women got two apiece. They saved one for Ta'si'woo', and later gave him a second one.

They returned to camp where they remained for four days. Her husband broke her horse and gave her a gentle one in place of it. He said he would trade this one off to an Arapaho or Cheyenne.

Ta'si'woo' told her lover and Quanah that they were just getting horses for their wive's old husbands, as they'd get them on their return.

They started towards home. It was the first time Ta'si'woo' and his party had been home in four years. Quanah said Nemaruibetsi and her lover were through with their trouble, but Quanah was not through yet.

On their return, they rode into camp and dismounted.

Nemaruibetsi's lover gave two more horses to help Quanah with the *nanuwoku*. Nemaruibetsi gave four of her five horses to her grandmother. Isawura gave Quanah two horses.

Тана3а and three friends were out guarding Quanah's horses the first thing after he got back. They came to Quanah and said they wanted Тана3а's wife back (she was very good looking).

Quanah refused. He offered them ten horses.

One friend said he'd go take her.

Тана3а walked up to take her but was stopped by the crowd. People said he had another wife, to let her go.

The woman's uncle came up and offered him more horses and clothes, etc., to let her go.

Тана3а received about fourteen horses altogether and other goods. Quanah gave six horses, the lover two, Isawura gave two, and her uncle gave four.

The excitement over Quanah prevented everybody from noticing what happened to Ta'si'woo' and his party. The old father was still there in camp. They lived on the outskirts of the camp thereafter; they were ashamed, and people would have nothing to do with them. Old Ta'si'woo' couldn't hurt them, as they were kin.

Nemaruibetsi and her lover had no further trouble with Soddyocoom. His former wife went back to her relatives in the Penanuu band.

A man could have as many wives as he wanted to, but might send former ones home if he wanted to.

She lived with her lover for a long time, but they had no children.

Nanuwoku: Champion-at-Law {Hoebel}   Ekamurawa[1] 'red crooked nose' lost his good-looking wife to a young good-looking man. (She went on a raid with four men and a woman.) She never came back for two years.

---

1. *eka* 'red', *mu* 'nose'. The 1879 census lists a man named Eckimodawau as a member of Terheryaquahip's Nokoni local band. In 1885, he was recorded as forty-four years old, but in 1892, his age was given as seventy-seven. He is not listed on any later census. None of the censuses lists any children.

Hunters out one day found their camp. They came back and told Ekamurawa where they were.

Ekamurawa got a brave warrior to go with him to get her. (He couldn't get her alone, he didn't have enough war deeds.)

The woman heard they were coming. She told her {new} husband she didn't want to go with them. The husband recognized the brave warrior and said they had no chance to keep her.

Ekamurawa picked up a quiver of arrows outside the door. She told him to put them down, "You can't do any better with them than the young husband." He had to put the arrows down.

The husband offered food and asked them what they wanted. They said they wanted her.

The husband had his servant serve them and get her horse (this servant was a full blood).

Ekamurawa would accept no *nanɨwokɨ* (he needed his wife as he had a young child by her).

She dressed up. The horse had a good saddle, silver-braided bridle, good blankets, etc.

The young man said, "Take everything nice that belongs to you; this old man can't get anything like these for you." This shamed him.

The woman cried; she didn't want to return.

They started home with the woman and fifteen horses. She trailed behind, angry. She wouldn't ride with them.

When they left, her young husband broke camp and came in. He passed them. As he passed them, Ekamurawa killed one of the young fellow's horses, and called the others to take the meat he'd shot for them.

The young man said his feelings were not hurt. He can get plenty of horses. "They were like the grass, so many."

But he knew that Ekamurawa did it because the warrior was there to protect him; otherwise the young fellow would wipe him out.

While in camp there, he heard that the enemy was coming. The woman rode away. The men prepared to meet the enemies. The *tuibihtsiʔ* got on his war paint, bonnet, and war horse in preparation. He rode by with feathers flying into the fight. He was shot, the only one killed. The warrior said they caused him to be killed. They must go (Ekamurawa and the warrior) to get him. "I know you are a coward, but you have to go walk out in front of the enemies while I get the body."

The two brought the young man in. They put the body over the horse of another man, who took it to where the people were.

The women mourned him. The young woman saw him. She tore her dress apart, cut her body all up, cut her hair off. She embraced his dead body, and they couldn't tear her away.

Ekamurawa and the warrior came up. They told each other to mourn; both mourned him.

She wanted to throw away her bracelets and silver-braided belt. People told her to keep them in remembrance of him.

They wrapped him in a blanket and buried him by the creek.[1]

---

1. Wallace and Hoebel 1952:230–32.

Nanɨwokɨ: Champion-at-Law {Carlson}   Ekamurawa had his wife stolen by another man. Ekamurawa means 'red crooked nose', and he was ugly, with a good-looking wife.

The young man who took her was good-looking. They never came back.

One day, a hunter discovered the camp where they were staying, along with the men who had gone out on the war party with the young man. The hunter told Ekamurawa about it. Ekamurawa called a brave warrior to assist him. He never could have gone by himself. They went off together.

The couple knew them from a distance. The woman whispered to her new husband not to let her go. The young man said that the man with Ekamurawa was braver than he, and they could not help themselves.

They asked the two men to get down off their horses.

Ekamurawa picked up a bow case made of bobcat skin. His friend made him lay it down again, saying he was no braver than the young man.

The warrior asked for food. The young man asked whether he would like buffalo meat or horsemeat, they had both. The warrior said he would like to have both, so the young man's servant fixed a meal.

The two said they were coming after the woman. The young man told the servant to catch the woman's horse.

The woman was well dressed. There were Mexican blankets hanging around. She had a silver belt, a silver mounted bridle, and a leather saddle. The young man told the woman to take everything nice that belonged to her, as Ekamurawa wouldn't be able to furnish her anything to replace the stuff if she left it. All the time, the woman cried.

The two men started home with the woman and fifteen horses *nanɨwokɨ*. She lagged behind as they rode along.

In the meantime, the young man and his followers had no more reason to hide out, so they packed and started back to the main camp. As they got into camp, they passed Ekamurawa, who shot one of the young man's horses.

The young man said, "You thought you would hurt my feelings by killing that horse. My feelings are not hurt. I can go out and get all the horses I want. Also, you would never have got your wife back if you had come to me alone. It was because of the other warrior that you have her."

Soon after, the word was brought that the enemy was coming. The woman got on her horse and rode away. The men fixed up to meet the enemy. The young man put on his war bonnet, mounted his horse, and went out to meet them. He went out fighting. The woman kept an eye on him. The young man was shot.

An observer rode up to where Ekamurawa was talking to his warrior friend and told him that his brother was shot, that he must go get the young man. The warrior friend said they must go, that they were the cause of the young man's being shot, that even if Ekamurawa was a coward, he had to go out now.

They went out on foot. The warrior distracted the attention of the enemy while Ekamurawa picked up the body and started to carry it off on foot. A man came out on horseback and told them to sling the body over the horse that he'd brought out. They brought the body to where the woman stood. She tore her clothes off, gashed herself, and cut her hair. She hugged the dead man and cried. The other women tried to pull her away, but she told them not to interfere.

Ekamurawa and his old warrior friend came up. Some of the people asked them what they were going to do. The two men began to mourn. The woman wanted to throw away her twelve bracelets and her silver belt, but the people wouldn't let her. They told her to keep them for remembrance. The body was wrapped in two blankets and buried by the creek. After this, the woman went back to Ekamurawa. Nothing satisfied Ekamurawa but having his wife back. There was a small child at home that needed her.

Nanuwoku {Hoebel}   There was a hill, *wamutsikuʔe*,[1] where a woman went to get power. She got her parents to fix her a special tipi to go to when she returned from the lonely place to rest.

Her husband suspected something and followed her. He found her horse down by the creek. He went to a young man's tipi. He heard his wife inside. He looked in and saw them lying together.

He went home and asked his mother to remove the tipi; she refused. He asked his sister to remove it; she couldn't refuse.

The woman returned and asked where her tipi was. He invited her in and cut her hair off to the scalp, cut her skirt short, and drove her through the camp with a whip.

On their way, they passed her lover's tipi. The husband had her call him out to see her. She did, but he didn't appear.

The husband sent her to her lover *nanuwoku*ing, to call for six horses, a saddle, bridle, war costume, etc.

She went to him in that sad state. He said, "You look so pitiful, sister, you can have anything you want that I have."

His mother loaded his horse with all his belongings and the wife led it back through the camp where all could see her.

Her husband kept her after that.

Nanuwoku {Carlson}   There was once a woman who used to go every day to a hill called *wamutsikuʔe*, saying she got medicine from it. She had her husband's *kakuⁿ* {maternal grandmother} fix her a special tipi to rest in when she came down.

One day her husband followed her and found her horse tied in the creek bottom just outside the camp. He went to a certain young man's tipi. He could hear his wife's voice, and peeped in and saw her lying with the young man.

He went home and told his mother to take down the special tipi. She said she wouldn't do it, that it was his wife's medicine tipi. He told his sister to take it down. His sister couldn't refuse.

When the wife came back, she asked why the tipi had been taken down. The husband told her to come in the other tipi. She did, and he told her to sit by him. He cut her hair, slicing it away with a knife so that the scalp bled. He cut her dress off above her knees. Then he drove her through the camp with a whip. When they came to the young man's tipi, he had instructed her to call the young man out to see her.

---

1. Possibly *waa-* cedar, *mutsipʉ* 'points, pointed', *kuʔe*, 'hill', Cedar Point Hill. Its specific location is unknown.

She did as she was told, but the man would not come out.

When they got back {. . . [*sic*]}.

Life Cycle: Marriage: Polygamy {Hoebel}   A man had two wives. He got a beef and took it to one wife's parents. The other wife noticed him. She took a club and beat the other wife's horse, and then he beat her.

The one beaten was the younger wife.

He wanted to please the younger one by gifts.

The older one was the *paraibo* and could beat her.

Life Cycle: Marriage: Polygamy {Carlson}   A man could have as many wives as he wished, but he ran the risk of having family trouble. Wives got jealous of one another.

Once a man got some beef, and he was going to give some to his younger wife's parents. The other wife rushed up to the younger wife and beat first her horse and then her.

Wives called each other *patsiʔ* {older sister} and *namiʔ* {younger sister}. The *patsiʔ* would be the boss.

Story: The Woman Who Betrayed Her Husband {Hoebel}   Two brothers had one wife. She told them they couldn't get a scalp so she could dance in the Victory Dance. She wanted to go off with another man who could get a scalp for her.

The younger brother told her to get ready to go on a war party. He didn't tell the older brother about it. It hurt his feelings to take the wife thus, without his older brother's knowledge.

They traveled day and night to Ute country. They came to a timbered place to hide. He was still worried about taking her thus.

They sat down and saw smoke. The horses looked. They looked and saw a Ute coming. He asked the Ute to get down.

The Ute asked him what he wanted. The Comanche said he wanted to die. The Ute said he was returning to an old camping place to get a dog left there when they moved (recently).

He and the Ute decided to have a fight; the one who was thrown would be killed.

The Comanche told his wife to help him with a spear if he needed it.

They fought. The Ute got the best for awhile. She used the spear on him instead of the Ute.

Then the Comanche got the best of the Ute and overcame him.

He asked his wife why she had used the spear on him, did she like the Ute better?

He scalped the Ute. The young husband told her she could now have a Scalp Dance, although she had done him wrong.

They left the spot in a hurry and traveled day and night. On their arrival, he put his wife on the Ute's horse, put the scalp on the bridle, and shot as they entered the camp victoriously.

They inquired where they tipi was; the camp had moved in their absence.

The older brother was happy to see them; he hugged them.

Other people came into the tipi.

The young man told the story of their raid, their reasons for going, etc., how she had speared him.

Her two brothers were outside and heard the story. They called her out. They said she had disgraced them and that this was her last day to live. They killed her with a gun immediately.

Her brothers returned to their parents and told them how the sister had disgraced them, how she had missed the honor of helping to kill an enemy.

The parents mourned her, but upheld their actions.

Her husbands did nothing either; they didn't mourn her.

Story: The Woman Who Betrayed Her Husband {Carlson}   Once there were two brothers who shared a wife. The wife wanted to be able to hold the pole in the Scalp Dance. She had it in mind, and kept pestering the brothers to take her off on a war party. She was going to go off on a war party with another man.

At last, the younger brother told her to get ready, they would go on a war party. The elder brother was not around, so nothing was said to him about this plan. It hurt the *tami?*'s feelings to go off with his brother's wife without explaining it to him.

They traveled day and night so as not to be gone any longer than they had to. At last, they got to the Ute territory. They hid in the woods.

They saw smoke, so they got off. A man came towards them on horseback. It was a Ute.

The Ute made signs to the Comanche, asking him what he wanted. The Comanche said he was {. . . [*sic*]}.

The Ute said the smoke was from a recently abandoned Ute camp, and if he had been there sooner, he could have found death easily.

The Ute said he had been sent back to get a little dog belonging to his children that had been left.

They arranged to have a fight. The one who was thrown would be killed. The Comanche told his wife that if he was getting the best, she should take the spear and help. The Ute was a good-looking man. They fought and the Ute was getting the best. The Ute motioned to the woman for her to spear her husband. She tried to, but finally, the Comanche threw the Ute and killed him.

He took the scalp, saying to his wife that she could have the dance, even though she had done him wrong, but if it hadn't been for that, she would have had a better time.

They started home with the Ute's horse. They traveled day and night. When they got close to home, the man let the woman ride the Ute's horse. He put the scalp on the bridle. Early the next morning, they came into the camp shooting a gun. Everybody noticed them.

They inquired where their tipi was. The *pabi?* was there, and was very glad to receive the two. He hugged them. People came into the tipi.

The *tami?* told the story of how he tired of his wife's nagging about a scalp, how he decided to get her one, how worried he was about going without his *pabi?*'s knowledge, how they met the Ute, and how the wife tried to stab him in the back.

The woman's brothers heard this. They called the woman outside and told her she had disgraced them, so this would be her last day to live. Then they killed her.

Then they went home and told their mother and father how their sister had missed the honor of killing a Ute and had tried to kill her husband. She had disgraced them, so they killed her.

The father did not say much. He said if she disgraced them, it was alright. The family mourned her death, but did nothing to the two brothers. There was no Scalp Dance. The husbands said nothing. They did not mourn the wife.

Nanɨwokɨ {Hoebel}   Chonip[1] (Nemaruibetsi's *araʔ* {mother's brother}) had a brother. There was one wife between them (Tɨtaatɨ[2]).

They needed wood; the wife went for some. She stayed away a long time.

Chonip sent his small sister (about ten years old) to find her.

The small girl found wood piled up and the woman in a nearby tipi. She peeked in and saw her in bed with a man.

The small girl called her and asked what she was doing; her brother wanted her. She said she went in to smoke.

Chonip asked where she had been. The small girl told him about the adultery with Komahseet.[3]

On her return, Chonip said they wouldn't eat, but go hunting. He told his wife to bring the canvas to carry the game in.

Chonip threw her down and asked her what she was doing in the tipi. She said the small girl had lied.

Chonip took her by the throat and forced a confession. He cut half her nose off.

In the meantime, the old mother woke up in the morning and asked the young girl what had happened. She told her. The mother scolded the youngster for telling on her daughter-in-law; she said her (daughter-in-law's) mother loved her as she loved the youngster.

The young girl said she told because she was afraid of Chonip.

The young brother returned carrying her clothes. The mother asked why. He said they had killed a deer and she didn't want to soil her clothes with the blood.

The mother asked again.

He confessed that they had cut her nose off and left her at a certain place.

The mother sent the small daughter to Tɨtaatɨ's grandmother to tell her about it. They went and got her and took her home.

They went *nanɨwok*ing to Komahseet and got six horses and most of his clothes.[4]

Nanɨwokɨ {Carlson}   A man named Chonip was married to a woman, and his brother shared her. Once the wife went out to get some wood, and stayed a long time. Chonip sent his sister, a young girl, to look for her.

---

1. 'bone'. Born about 1842, in 1879 Chonip was a member of Terheryahquahip's Nokoni local band and by 1889, the headman of a local group of his own.

2. Hoebel spells this T₃:ta and translates it as Little (1940:145). Robinson and Armagost (1990) give *tɨtaatɨ* as 'small size, unworthy, pitied.' Otherwise unidentified.

3. The agency spelled this name both as Komahseet and Komahceet, and in 1885 it was translated as 'dry throat', but that seems unlikely. Hoebel spells the name Comatsi:t in his notes, and "Komahsit" in his 1940 work, where he notes (without citation) that it was a "Mexican name" (1940:97). Casagrande (1954–55, II:230) suggests that it is a captive name derived from *kuhmahchitO*, the diminutive of the Spanish "Comanche," in which the *ch* would reduce to *s*. There is, however, no historical evidence that Komahseet or his parents were captives. It may also be derived from *kɨhma* 'male'.

He was born about 1842. In 1876, he was listed as a member of Esihabit's Penatɨhka local band, and, by 1885, he was headman of the group.

4. Hoebel 1940:97.

The girl found the wood piled up by the creek, but didn't see her sister-in-law. She heard a woman laughing in a nearby tipi, so she peeped in and saw her sister-in-law lying with a young man.

The girl called her by name. She said, "Tʉtaatʉ, what are you doing?"

Tʉtaatʉ said she would be out soon, that she just went in for a smoke. The girl told her to hurry, that her brother wanted her.

When the girl got back, Chonip asked what Tʉtaatʉ was doing. The sister said she was lying with Komahseet.[1] When Tʉtaatʉ returned with the wood, the sister asked if she should build a fire. Chonip said, "No, we're going out hunting."

He told Tʉtaatʉ to bring along a canvas to carry the meat back in. The woman and her two brothers went out.

They threw the woman down and Chonip asked her what she meant by having intercourse with Komahseet.

Tʉtaatʉ said that the sister lied, that she only went in for a smoke.

Chonip grabbed her by the throat and choked her until she confessed. Then he cut her nose off. This happened in the early morning.

After the brothers had gone with Tʉtaatʉ, their mother got up. She asked the girl what had happened and the girl told the whole story.

The mother didn't like it. She was very fond of her daughter-in-law. She told her daughter she shouldn't have told on her. She said Tʉtaatʉ's mother loved Tʉtaatʉ as much as she loved her daughter, and it was not right to get her in trouble.

The girl said she was afraid not to tell, because Chonip would have hurt her if she didn't tell the truth.

Chonip's younger brother came back, carrying Tʉtaatʉ's clothes. The mother asked him why he was carrying the clothes. He said they had killed a deer and Tʉtaatʉ was carrying it and didn't want to soil her clothes. The mother persisted, and finally her son told the truth. She told him to notify Tʉtaatʉ's *kakuʔ* telling her where they had left her. Her *kakuʔ* and other relatives found her and carried her to the *kakuʔ*'s tent. The two brothers went to Komahseet for *nanʉwokʉ* and collected six horses and most of his clothing.

Kinship Relations: Brother-Sister {Hoebel}   A sister was afraid of her brother. He had complete power, even unto death, before her marriage. He could whip her. His treatment was much harsher than that given by her father.

Kinship Relations: Brother-Sister {Carlson}   A sister had to do what a brother told her. She was afraid of him. He might whip her, or even kill her, if she disobeyed. Only a man's real sisters obeyed him. If a young boy or girl was mischievous, they would bring in an older woman who was the child's classificatory *patsiʔ* to scare him.

---

1. Carlson spelled the name "k)matsi:t."

Kinship Relations: Joking   Nemaruibetsi didn't joke with her [second] husband's brother. She had known him before, and called him *ara⁷* [as a courtesy title]. Therefore, after marriage she didn't joke with him. He was old and did not call her *kwᵿhᵿ⁷*.

Kinship Relations {Carlson}   One went to one's *ara⁷* in trouble.[1]

NEMARUIBETSI
August 1, 1933[2]

Kinship Relations   A grandson could get anything he wanted from either grandfather, including the grandfather's medicine. The old man would tell him, "This is your living, abide by the rules."

Kinship Relations {Hoebel}   A boy went to his *ara⁷* {mother's brother} when in trouble, Nemaruibetsi maintained. The uncle would give him almost anything he wanted, even if the uncle's wife objected.

When the uncle was in his old age or poor, and the nephew (*ara⁷*) got horses on a raid, he would give them to his uncle.

This was true also of nieces and maternal uncles.

This was also true of nieces versus their maternal uncles as may take up with *ahpᵿ⁷* not so likely.[3] The *ahpᵿ⁷* {father's brother} helped sometimes too when a nephew "son" or niece "daughter" got into trouble.

The paternal *ara⁷* was not a real *ara⁷* as above.[4]

Kinship Relations {Carlson}   A man went to his *ara⁷* when in trouble.

If the trouble was over a woman, all the *ara⁷*'s horses were at his disposal in settling the *nanᵿwokᵿ*. He usually got anything the *ara⁷* had, even though the *ara⁷*'s wife objected. When the *ara⁷* became old and poor, the nephew gave him horses.

Herman Asenap's sister's children would listen to him when they would not listen to their own parents.[5]

The father's sister's husband was not in the same class. He was not a real *ara⁷*.

Sometimes a *paha⁷* will take great interest in the children. If she was childless, she may raise some of her brother's children. The same was true of the mother's sisters.

---

1. This sentence is duplicated in a note dated August 1. The relation between the two notes is unclear.

2. Most of the notes for this interview are from Carlson, with variations from Hoebel. The order is arbitrary.

3. This sentence is as written by Hoebel. Its meaning is unclear.

4. There are three of Hoebel synthetic note cards that begin, "A boy/man went to his *ara* when in trouble." I have combined them into this note.

5. It is not known if this was an observation by Nemaruibetsi or a statement by the interpreter, Herman Asenap.

When a man came back from a war party, he gave horses to his *ara*ʔ. The *ara*ʔ might divide with the father and father-in-law if he wished.

If a boy was living at home and brought in meat, he gave it to his mother to divide. She would give a good supply to his *ara*ʔ and his *nʉmʉtokʉ*.

Life Cycle: Marriage: Levirate/Sororate   If a man had it explained to him at marriage that he had no claim on the other daughters, he could not collect *nanʉwokʉ* if they married someone else. If a second daughter was neither promised nor refused to marry a son-in-law, it was alright to marry her to someone else, and the son-in-law would have no right to object or claim *nanʉwokʉ*. However, it was pretty hard to avoid the son-in-law if he wanted the girl, so they had to marry her off in a hurry.

Life Cycle: Death: Disposition of Property   Piarʉpsima,[1] Big Fall by Tripping, had lots of property, particularly horses. When he died, they rounded up his stock; his nephew [*ara*ʔ] rounded them up. He had in mind to kill all the horses [the wild ones]. He was killing horses right and left, when four [disinterested] men came up and said, "You mustn't kill all of them. You have children and friends. Give them to your children and maybe to your friends."

So the nephew gave horses to all of his friends and saved some for his children.[2]

The uncle had left two wives. Before the nephew began killing their horses, he picked ten of the gentlest, five for each widow. There were no children. If there had been, they would have taken charge.

Life Cycle: Death: Disposition of Property: Medicine   Sons and nephews could inherit medicine without having to ask for it with a cigarette.

Material Culture: Crafts: Hide Work {Hoebel[3]}   The hair was scraped off with a *tʉsibe*ʔ[4] (a handle with a metal edge) [an adzelike scraper used to remove hair from hides].

It was rubbed with beef brains, then put in a bag and immersed in water.

Then it was tramped on, up and down in the bag.

The green hide, with holes around the edge, was stobbed {staked} down to dry. The meat was cleaned off with a tool. They took a piece of [the blue-green tongue from] (between the liver and gall) and rubbed the hide [back and forth] with it. This prevented hardening.

The hide was worked with a flat rounded stone to soften it farther. The edges [peg holes] were trimmed with a knife. The entire inside of the skin was rubbed with fat. Then, a hoelike [adze] tool was used on it to clean it further and cut it down.

It was rubbed with brain; it came out white and clean.

It was soaked in water with some sinew. They took the sinew out and pulled it into strips and braided it to make a [3-ply] rope, about one quarter of an inch in diameter.

---

1. Possibly based on *pia* 'big', *nʉʉhpisi*ʔ*maitʉ* 'trip and fall'. Robinson and Armagost (1990) spells this name Piarʉtsima.

2. Hoebel 1940:124.

3. The next three notes are from Hoebel, with the variations from Wedel's worked-up pages. Those worked-up pages are not paralleled in Wedel's manuscript or typescript pages. Moreover, the order of steps generally follows the order on Hoebel's cards. This suggests that Hoebel provided Wedel access to his notes. The dating is from Wedel.

4. Robinson and Armagost (1990) has this as 'carpenter's plane'.

The hide was left in the water overnight, and rubbed occasionally to make it supple. The hide was hung on a forked pole and beaten it with a stick (like beating a rug). While it was still wet, it was gone over with a sawlike scraper [four inches by two inches], and then with a flat stone [four inches square, not a very sharp edge].

[The robe was then getting dry. It was pulled back and forth through the sinew loop. It was scraped on a pole by drawing it taut by stepping on the edge.] It was worked back and forth with the hands in a crosswise pulling motion.

It was as soft as a blanket when finished, even the edges. [An industrious woman made it soft as a blanket, with smooth edges.] Then it was rubbed with brains and it came out white and clean. Finally, it was laid outside in the dew overnight and rubbed with a rock [round stone] in the morning for a final polish.

The whole hide was used, not split and sewn together.

[A man's robe was split and sewn up again after the final tanning. A narrow red stripe, about a quarter of an inch or slightly more in width, was put down the center to hide the seam.]

Material Culture: Crafts: Hide Work: Robe Decoration {Hoebel}   Robes were worn the long way, with the head and tail on the sides.

Coup marks were ten or twelve inches long. The border design was one and a half inches from the edge and about one and a half inches wide. [The center design was a short foot across.]

A brave warrior might paint his brave deeds on a robe. It was worn by his chief wife. [A man's chief wife had both center and border designs. Other wives had no center design.] "You could tell which was the chief wife of the family by the one who wore this robe decorated with her husband's war deeds."

Unmarried women or other wives could wear a robe with a border but without the war deeds.

Material Culture: Tipis {Hoebel}   [Buckskin and tipi covers were treated somewhat differently from robes. The hair was removed with the *tʉsibeʔ*; no wood ashes were used. Brains were rubbed on the inside of the hide; the outside was scraped, then rubbed with brain. It was soaked in water. They had a bag made of hide into which the hide was put, then they tramped it in water.

There was no painting on tipis.]

Before painting, they took rubbings from a hide and put them in water. It became thick like glue.[1] This was rubbed on the hide [over the place to be painted] and painted over it. It preserved the paint so it wouldn't rub off. [Glue was put over the painting too.] It was spread out and three or four women did the work. One special woman was called on usually to block out the design and direct the others. It was usually given to a younger sister on the owners' death.

---

1. Wallace and Hoebel 1952:100 (?).

HOWARD WHITE WOLF
August 1, 1933[1]

Medicine: Sun Dance   Tooahvoniquo 'Big Medicine'[2] (Yapai) gave the last Comanche Sun Dance. It was near the Wichita Mountain filling station.[3] It was held in June. Everyone was notified to be there. The camp was built in a great semicircle open to the east. The dance arbor was in the center of the circle. Only cottonwood was used for the arbor. Tooahvoniquo was camped in the center of the crescent.

Camp Organization   There was no fixed camp circle in usual camps. The chief was always in the center. Relatives always camped together.

Material Culture: Wood Pack   In packing wood, women brought the strap up over the head and across her chest, and then it passed up under her arms. By holding the rope ends, the load was secure. Loosening the ropes let the wood drop.

Camps: Tipis: Fireplace   The fireplace was in the center. A forked stick was set into the ground at an angle and the kettle was suspended from it.

Camps: Tipis: Beds   There were three beds, one each on the north, south, and west.

Material Culture: Containers   *natɨsakɨna* was the soft, dressed buckskin parfleche for packing clothes, blankets, etc. It was painted in blue, yellow, and black linear decorations by some woman who was a good painter.

The ⟨pomawus⟩[4] was a rawhide envelope like a saddle bag with a flap. There was a rope at the top to hang it on a saddle horn. It was used to carry plums, fruit, etc.

natɨsakɨna also meant the stiff parfleche, like the one for carrying clothes, but undecorated. It was scraped clean, but not softened.

Food: Bread   Bread was baked in coals. There was no oven of any sort used. After baking, the coals were scraped away.

Camps: Tipis   The north ear was lowered for a south wind, the south ear for a north wind.

A special cover was used in an east wind to close the vent.

To reach the top-most pins on a tall tipi, a tripod was used as a stepladder; the poles were always carried along.

On a smaller tipi, one woman got on another's back.

Meals were taken while persons sat on the beds. There were no regular mealtimes.

Grass was spread for the mattress, with blankets and robes over it. There were no raised beds in the old days.

Tipis were trenched to keep out rain.[5]

Every family staked one horse beside the tipi at night to use in rounding up the stock the next day.

1. Although there are a few parallels to these comments in Wallace and Hoebel (1952), there are no extant Hoebel notes from this interview.
2. That is, Pertooahvoniquo. Although he was a noted medicine man, and one of his daughters was known as Matilda Big Medicine, there is nothing in the name itself that specifically refers to "medicine."
3. On present Oklahoma highway 49, between Lawton and Medicine Park.
4. Robinson and Armagost (1990) gives *pomarɨ* as 'pick fruit'.
5. Wallace and Hoebel 1952:88. It is possible that one tipi in the 1872–73 Medicine Creek village was trenched (Kavanagh 1991).

Horses: Breaking   Horses were ridden through the sand in breaking.

Cosmology: Star Lore   War parties traveled by North Star, named ____?[1]

Story: Piamupits   Piamupits was a great giant living on the earth. He was very strong; he lived by eating men. He used a cottonwood tree for a cane. Everyone was trying to kill him.

A family was living in a certain place. The father and mother disappeared, so the three children started off. The little child was carried by the oldest sister. The child was crying; the sister cautioned it, saying that Piamupits would hear and eat them. A little while later, the child cried again. This time Piamupits heard them and called to them. So they started through the woods and presently they came to a big fire.

Piamupits asked if they were hungry. They said "Yes," so he fed them, then told them where to sleep.

Piamupits was a big man, covered with fur.

He came and killed one of the children.

The oldest child then told her dog to watch, and if Piamupits came again, to scratch her foot. The dog did so and the sister woke and asked Piamupits what he wanted. He said he wanted to see whether the children were comfortable.

The next day, the children went down to the creek to wash the small child. The sister saw a bullfrog and told it to answer for them if Piamupits called, and that they were fleeing. Piamupits called and the frog answered; he called again and the frog said that they were cleaning the little child's clothes. Piamupits was angry and threatened to get them if they didn't come soon. Meantime, the children were fleeing.

Piamupits went down to the creek, saw the frog and tried to catch it, but the frog escaped. Piamupits started after the children. They saw him coming right behind them.

They came to a big river and at the edge they saw a crane. Sister said, "You're a wonderful bird, will you help us escape?"

The crane said, "You put one of my lice in your mouth and don't spit it out." The lice were very bitter, but the girl did as she was told. The crane laid himself across the river and they crossed.

Then they came to a buffalo herd and asked them for help. A big bull told them to stay right behind them.

Piamupits arrived at the river. The crane told him the same as the children, but when he spit out the louse, he fell into the water. On his second attempt he got across.

He continued on with his *wɨpitapuʔni* (stone-headed club). The buffalo bull bellowed and pawed the dirt, charged, and was killed by Piamupits, who killed other bulls.

Finally, he came to the buffalo calf. The calf pawed up dirt and tossed Piamupits away, up in the air, twice; on the second time, he landed on the moon. He's there now, cooking his meat (the Comanche Man in the Moon).

Now, children point to the moon and say, "Look at Piamupits."

This story has been handed down for many generations.

---

1. The blank is in Wedel's original. See Howard White Wolf, August 3.

Medicine: Curing: Piamupits' Bones   *tsoabits*[1] were large fossil bones used as remedies for broken bones, etc. They were said to be Piamupits' bones.[2] The bones were ground up and rubbed on the injury.

Social Control: Piamupits   Comanche children are still silenced when crying by threats of Piamupits.

Howard's wife's parents once dressed themselves in buffalo robes and carried axes and frightened children when they refused to come home. The children were much frightened.

Medicine: Foretelling   Once, a number of women and children were captured by soldiers and imprisoned for some years. The people didn't know where they were. The medicine man was called in by their kin to tell where they were.

The man who went to call the doctor had to approach him with eagle feathers and tobacco—a rolled cigarette of leaves—which was smoked. Then he stated the purpose of his call. If he agreed, he then told the leaders to erect a special tipi apart from the village. The medicine man said he would have to consult his friend, a ghost.

The leading men went in, sat down, and smoked.

They had no fire or other light.

The medicine man then went out from the tent and called aloud. Presently, those in the tent heard a strange noise in the distance. Then the medicine man came back in and said the ghost was coming.

The hollering noise was repeated twice more. The doctor told everyone to shut their eyes. Then, they heard a rushing noise like a wind and the ghost came in through the top of the tipi. The doctor then told the ghost what they wanted to know. The ghost said that the people were still alive and would be returned shortly.[3]

There was a sickly man among those present who couldn't be cured, so the doctor asked the ghost what would become of him. The ghost said the man would be cured. Everything happened as the ghost said. The people returned and the man was cured.

One man peeked and the ghost threw dirt in his eyes, blinding him for a time.

Then the ghost said, "I'm going home," and left through the top of the tipi and the men were left alone.

1. Although Wedel's notes imply that *tsoabits* refers to the bones, that word is the equivalent of the Shoshone *dzō'avits*, which was their name for the ogre, not its bones (St. Clair 1909; Lowie 1909). Jones (1944), based on some of Carlson's now lost original materials, gives the phrase "tsɔɔβit' sitsuni", that is, *tsoabits* *tsunipꟻ* (*tsunuipꟻ*, 'bone'), thus providing the missing bones.

2. Wallace and Hoebel (1952:171) attribute this to Medicine Woman and Yellowfish, both consultants of Ernest Wallace in 1945. There are fossil bone beds over much of southwestern Oklahoma, e.g., the Domebo mammoth find north of the town of Stecker on the old reservation (Leonhardy 1966).

3. On September 29, 1872, 132 Comanche women and children were captured at a Comanche village on McClellan Creek in the Texas Panhandle. They were held at Fort Concho, Texas. In the ensuing months, a number of leading Comanches traded their captives for their relatives. The prisoners at Fort Concho were ordered released in April 1873, and reached Fort Sill in June (Kavanagh 1996:434–37).

Medicine: Curing   Piwana[1] was a blind medicine man.

There were a number of sick men always in the camp. One day, about an hour before sundown, a mass of coyotes began barking about the camp. The men tried to figure it out, but couldn't.

In the old days, a coyote howling near a tipi meant either something good or bad was about to happen. You had to throw meat out to them to avert the evil.

So the leading men went around to Piwana and asked him what it meant; he understood coyote talk. So they set up a special tipi, and Piwana called out the names of those to attend the meeting. Then Piwana said, "I'll tell you what the wolves say. They're happy. We're going to have a great sickness (*tsotsoo²nI*[2]). It draws you up double, no matter how well you are, and you die very soon. Then the coyotes will get much food from robbing the graves."

The sickness came and people died, and mourning relatives became sick and died.

Skunk scent mixed with clay in a half cup of water was the only cure. This was finally revealed to Piwana in a dream and he cured all of the people who were sick.

This remedy is still used; it is taken internally, a spoonful at a dose cured at once. It was discovered by Comanches about 100 years ago.

Medicine: Curing: Cactus Pad   Prickly pear pads were thrown into the fire to singe the spines off, then split and applied over gunshot wounds, boils, and other injuries to draw out the infection.

Medicine: Vision Quest   To get medicine, a man went to a medicine man's grave, sat down and smoked. Then he talked to the grave as though it was the man himself, and asked for power. A man might go out three nights and, on the fourth night, the medicine man might reveal himself and give directions to observe: abstention from menstruating women, greasy hands, etc.

Medicine: Curing: Buffalo Medicine   To get Buffalo Medicine, a man would go and sleep beside a buffalo skeleton, and act just as in the preceding case. He should smoke and talk to it.

Story: A man was once shot in the arm in a battle. He was bleeding profusely, and was weak from the loss of blood and not expected to live.

A medicine woman took smoke, put on a buffalo robe, carried a buffalo tail, and circled the patient three or four times, bellowing like a buffalo. Then she put the tail in her mouth halfway and shook it over the patient, covering him with blue paint. Then she got hold of his arm, worried it for a brief spell, and the bleeding stopped. Then she raised him, put a finger under either arm and sort of pushed him along like a buffalo bull pushing something.

Medicine: Curing   Story: In the old days, a bad fever once killed off many people. A spirit appeared to a man and told him to look very closely at a certain strong-scented weed which grew around prairie dog holes. It directed him to take this weed, boil it, pour off the

---

1. Otherwise unidentified.

2. Robinson and Armagost (1990) identifies *tsotsoo²nI* as meningitis. Casagrande (1954–55, II:235) has meningitis as *n+m+tsa²toponi²eet+* 'makes you round, doubled up'.

liquid, cool, and drink it. It cured the fever, and was still used today. It was called *tuʔrukúu pahmo* 'prairie dog's tobacco'.

Food: Plants: Sage leaves were gathered in the fall, dried, and used in making tea in the winter. Tea was made like among whites. Sugar and sometimes cream was used in the tea, depending upon individual taste.

Fallen plums were gathered, dried, and stored for winter use, then boiled for eating.

A potato-like tuber, *payapI*,[1] was gathered in the old days. It grew in the west, and looked like a sweet potato, with small leaves like a sunflower. There were many on the Red River.

suhu tsitsinaʔ[2] was {. . . [sic]}. It looked like a potato. It was a vine that grew up a tree with a longish root. It grew on the Red River and on the creek just east of Stecker, the next station north of Apache.

Both above roots were boiled.

Food: Buffalo   Buffalo meat was cut in thin strips, especially in the fall, and hung up and dried. The fat was cut into slices and packed with the meat in a *natUsakUna*.

The meat was either eaten raw or boiled.

The brisket was always roasted.

Ribs were removed from the side and the meat roasted.

In buffalo butchering, the side meat was cut off from the neck to the hind quarters in two pieces.

The rump and brisket were cut off in one chunk, then {. . . [sic]}.

Material Culture: Crafts: Baskets   Comanches never made baskets.[3]

Material Culture: Fire Making   Fungi were used as tinder. Flint and steel were used to start the fire. Howard did not recall the use of the fire drill.

Material Culture: Bows: Bowstrings   Two extra sinew bowstrings were always carried.

Material Culture: Bows: Bow Making   There were specialized bow makers.

Mulberry wood was favored. It was cut and shaved and greased to prevent cracking, then placed in the fork of a tree and bent into shape.

The bow was carried unstrung, with the string removed in wet weather.

Material Culture: Bows: Wrist Guard   There was a rawhide wrist guard.

Material Culture: Arrows   War arrows were poisoned by applying a mixture of skunk scent (?) and something else.

Eagle feathers were used primarily for war arrows.

Cottonwood sap was used as a glue to fasten the feathers to the arrow shaft.

Political Organization: Chiefs: War Leader   War parties were always led by two leaders.

War: War Parties: Pursuit: Dogs   If there were dogs, Indians threw them some meat to quiet them.

1. *pa* 'water', *yapI* 'root'. Robinson and Armagost (1990) has both *"paiyapI* plant with edible fruit (name unknown; grows in Apache, Okla. area; seeds not swallowed; roots roasted or boiled and eaten)" and "*payaape* aqueous, wild tuber (grows above water, producing rich-flavored potato-like tubers in clusters each about three inches long."

2. Robinson and Armagost (1990) gives this as *suhu* 'willow', *tstsinaʔ* 'root'.

3. Contra Wallace and Hoebel 1952:91.

(Some Indians were once pursued by bloodhounds after stealing horses. They knew they couldn't escape, so the leader detailed two expert bowmen to fall behind and ambush the dogs. Thereafter, the Indians got away.)

Political Organization: Chiefs: War Leader   The *nomʉne*[1] was the leader of a war party. There were always two in number [leader and assistant?]. They had to agree on the course. If they disagreed, the party might split. If one had more experience, he would get the best following.

War: Division of Loot   They divided the loot as soon as they were safe from immediate pursuit. The bravest fighting man had the first choice, the others followed, with the *nomʉne* usually last. [Maybe he got nothing.]

War: Coup: War: Victory Parade   The bravest fighting man in each battle was always placed in front of the returning party. When they arrived near the village, the leading men rode back and forth in front of the party and they all fired their guns in the air.

Material Culture: Clothing: Headdress   If a man rode back and rescued a comrade who had been unhorsed while the party was in retreat, he was singled out for a war bonnet.

A bonnet could be inherited by a son if he was a brave warrior.

Political Organization: Chiefs   The *paraibo* was selected by all the men for bravery, kindness to children and other people, generosity, and general high character.

There were two *paraibo*s, one for war, other for civilian duties. The latter decided on moving camp, maintaining camp peace, etc. The former was in command when the tribe was at war.

Tabenanaka and White Wolf divided the duties of war and peace *paraibo*.[2]

FRANK CHEKOVI
August 2, 1933[3]

Life Cycle: Childhood: Disabilities   The Comanches kept crippled children, even when they were born crippled.

Life Cycle: Marriage: Home   Before Frank's father's death, Frank's married brother camped with his wife's people and not with his own relatives.

Life Cycle: Marriage: Polyandry {Carlson}   One brother was always the real husband, but he let the other brother share. No one could replace a man's brother, so a man would give his brother anything. The husband would send the wife to go sleep with the brother. The woman could not go on her own will.

If the wife and brother had a connection without the husband's permission, he'd be angry. If a woman objected to going to the brother, her husband would tell her he had only

---

1. Robinson and Armagost (1990) glosses *nomʉnewapʉ* as generalized 'leader or officer'. *-wapʉ* is an agentive suffix.

2. See Howard White Wolf, July 31.

3. The content of this interview is from Carlson, with variations from Hoebel. The dating is Carlson's, and the order of the notes is arbitrary.

one brother who was irreplaceable, but he could easily get another wife.

Life Cycle: Marriage: Polyandry {Hoebel}   Two brothers had one wife. "One is really her husband, of course."

He loved his brother. He knew that if his brother died, no one could replace him. He gave him everything he can.

The brother, therefore, sent her over to him occasionally as a gift.

She couldn't go of her own will.

They couldn't meet clandestinely or he would be angry.[1]

Nanuwoku {Carlson}   If a married man went on a raid with another woman, the husband of the other woman would get someone who was as brave as the abductor to run off with the abductor's wife.

This happened once, and the second pair went to the place where the war party would camp on their way home. They came up and camped a little ways off from the war party. The young man noticed the pair and said, "It's so-and-so's wife."

The husband had his brother along. He told his brother to go over and investigate, to find out if it really was his wife.

At first, the brother refused to go, saying that the man wouldn't let the woman go with him even if he did go over.

The husband insisted, though, so the brother went. He got there as the two were cooking dinner.

The man spoke to the brother as a friend, telling him to come down and eat with them.

The brother said he wouldn't sit down, that he just rode over to see what was going on.

The man asked him what he wanted.

The brother said he wanted the woman.

The man refused to give her up, saying that the husband thought more of the woman he had with him than of his wife. The man told the brother to go back and tell the husband not to interfere.

When the brother got back, the husband asked if it really was his wife and was told that it was.

The husband then asked who the man was, and the brother told him it was a *tekwʉniwapI*.

The brother repeated the other man's message.

The husband sent his brother back again. Again, the man asked him what he wanted and the brother said he had come for the woman. The man said he would not let her go and told the brother not to come back again.

The husband wouldn't believe this, and asked the brother to go back a third time.

The brother didn't want to go; he was rather afraid. However, when the husband insisted, he went.

This time, the man came out to meet him.

He told the brother to stop, to go back and tell the husband that if he was looking for trouble, to come himself.

---

1. Wallace and Hoebel (1952:138) attributes this information to Tahsuda.

The brother went back and told the news.

The husband acted surprised. He picked up his weapons and buckled his belt.

The other members of the party did not think he would do anything, so they let him go.

The man and the wife were still sitting at the spot where they had eaten. The man was combing the wife's hair. The man quit and stood up. The wife ran behind him.

The husband grabbed the woman by the hair, jerked her back and stabbed her. He said, "Friend, I have killed our wife. It's up to you. Do you want to do anything?"

The man said nothing.

The husband continued, "You talked so brave and said you wouldn't give her up. Now you have caused her death, are you doing anything?"

The other man said nothing; he didn't reach for his weapons.

The people in the other camp heard them weep and knew the woman was dead. The two men buried her.

Nanuwoku {Hoebel}   A woman ran off with a married man.

Another man got a warrior to go off with this married man's wife.

They went to the place where the other group would return.

The other party asked, "Who is over there?"

Answer: "Your wife is over there with _____" {*sic*}.

He sent his young, unmarried brother to verify the story. He came to a bank and looked down on the camp. The young fellow said he was just out looking around. They invited him into the camp.

They asked him what he wanted; he said he came for their deserted wife.

They told him that they preferred the one they had to this wife, so they'd keep her.

The young fellow returned. He said she was there with a brave warrior. He told him what he had heard.

The first husband sent his younger brother again. They invited him in again. He said he was coming for her again. They sent him back with the same statements. They told him not to come back again.

The older brother was angry. He sent the younger brother again.

The brave was watching for him. He stopped him at a distance. He told him to tell his brother to come himself if he wanted to cause any trouble.

The young brother returned and told the news. The old brother acted surprised.

He put on his war clothes and started out. People didn't think he'd really go.

He came to the camp and found the warrior combing his former wife's hair.

The old husband grabbed her by the hair and stabbed her dead.

He told the warrior that it was his turn to do something. He said he had caused the death of their joint wife by not sending her back to him. The warrior did nothing. They buried the woman and moved.

Gambling {Carlson}   Frank was in a gambling game with an old man. The old man was losing consistently. He had lost his money, clothing, tipi, and all the contents of the tipi. Finally, he wanted to bet his sister.

Frank refused to allow it. He said he had never heard of betting a human being. Frank's classificatory brother said, "Go on, allow something on her; a sister is just like a dog." The old man insisted, saying his mother wouldn't care what he did with his sister.

Frank allowed him 250 cartridges on his sister; the old man lost.

The next day, Frank sent his mother to collect all the winnings, but the man's wife wept, so he never collected.

Gambling {Hoebel}   Gambling was often done with (permanent) partners. Frank had a gambling partner named Kasese,[1] an older man.

The Indians drifted westward for meat. They camped on a creek. Then they started to gamble; they bet rings and cartridges. Frank and his partner were present. Frank bought some cartridges to hunt with. He hadn't gambled with this man before; this was the first time.

Frank went to the windbreak of the camp. He saw the men gambling there. He wanted to play.

He went in, bet and won, bet and won again. The old man told him to sit down and play. The old man had won everything.

Frank played. They all won everything back from the old man.

At this point, Frank had a large pile of one-point sticks and many ten-point sticks. The cartridges all went gradually to the other players. Thus, in the end, Frank got only the blanket (cartridge tally sticks and other articles were not redeemed).

The old man and Frank played each other, and Frank won consistently. The old man was broke. Frank won twelve hides that his wife hadn't tanned yet, then the man's tipi and everything in it, and two horses—everything he had.

The man bet his sister; Frank refused. His cousin said, "It's nothing, she's just like a dog."

The old man said her mother wouldn't care, what he said went.

Frank had tally sticks counting ten cartridges each. He allowed the old man 250 points for his sister. Frank won his sister.

The next day, Frank sent his mother after the goods he'd won. The wife cried and said those things weren't his to gamble. He took pity on them, and gave them all back but the blanket the man had on. So he lost his new-won wife.[2]

Story: Contest Between Cheyenne and Comanche Medicine Men {Hoebel}   Arapaho and Cheyenne medicine men sometimes used their medicine in evil ways.

The Cheyennes and Comanches were camped together.

They pointed out a medicine man who was using his medicine to cause deaths (a Cheyenne).

A Comanche medicine man heard of it and decided to go see him.

He got on his war horse, without a bridle, and rode to the Cheyenne medicine man's camp.

The Cheyenne came out and asked what he wanted. He said he wanted to smoke.

The Cheyenne invited him in and sat on the north side. He put the Comanche on the south side next to the sun.

---

1. Possibly the man named Kasaseah (*kasA* 'wing', *sia* 'feather') who was a member of Quanah's Kwaharʉnʉʉ local band in 1879. Apparently he died shortly after 1883, for his name does not appear on later censuses. If this was the case, Frank, born about 1861, would have been in his early twenties.

2. Wallace and Hoebel 1952:117–18.

The Cheyenne got his long pipe, filled it, and lit it with a coal from the fire.

He asked how the Comanche wanted the pipe passed; he said, any way. The Comanche took the pipe with two hands, inhaled four times, and got Cheyenne poison out of it on the fourth time; he could feel it.

He blew in the pipe and handed it back. He felt his belly and blew a yellowhammer feather out of his mouth. He asked the Cheyenne what he meant by that; he said he found it in the pipestem.

The Cheyenne said he could do whatever he wanted with it.

Then the Cheyenne medicine man smoked three puffs and on the fourth, he felt a pain in his side. He wiggled and blew and blew out an eagle feather into his hand. He asked what he meant by that.

The Comanche answered that he knew nothing about the feather, but since it was the Cheyenne's pipe, it must belong to him. The Cheyenne said he'd give him the feather.

The Comanche smoked again three times. On the fourth, he felt pain, blew out a black bug.

"What is this?"

"I don't know. It must be yours."

"It's not mine. It must be yours, the pipe belongs to you."

The Cheyenne smoked, and on the fourth puff he blew out a tarantula. "What is this? It must belong to you."

"No, it's your pipe. It must be yours."

The Comanche again smoked, and blew out a cockleburr.

The Cheyenne smoked and got a barrel cactus, but he couldn't blow it out. That was the fourth exchange.

The Comanche said it was a pleasant day and went home.

When he got home, the Comanches heard cries from the Cheyennes; the medicine man had died. (He had found a better medicine man than he was, and died of the cactus in his throat.)

The next day, the Cheyennes brought the Comanche medicine man a horse loaded with presents for killing the bad medicine man.

Story: **Contest Between Cheyenne and Comanche Medicine Men** {Carlson}   (This story starts out in the same manner as the one we had before[1] about the Comanche medicine man and the Arapaho medicine man, except that the other man was now a Cheyenne.)

The Cheyenne medicine man asked the Comanche to come in his tipi.

The Cheyenne sat on the north, the Comanche on the south. The Cheyenne asked how he should pass the pipe to the Comanche, and the Comanche answered that he should pass it any way he chose, and he would take it from him any way he pleased.

The Cheyenne extended the pipe, holding it with one hand in the middle of the stem.

The Comanche took it with two hands, one immediately above, and one immediately below the Cheyenne's hands.

The Comanche took four puffs. On the fourth puff, he grunted as he felt the medicine enter him. He blew into the pipe and handed it back to the Cheyenne. He felt himself and

---

1. See Niyah, July 6.

rubbed his belly. The middle tail feather of a yellowhammer had entered him. He blew (the illustration was more of a cough than a blowing) it out in the palm of his hand and asked the Cheyenne what he meant by doing that. He said he had found it in the pipe stem, and what should he do with it.

The Cheyenne said he could do what he pleased with it.

The Comanche said he would give it back.

The Cheyenne took four puffs on the pipe. On the fourth puff, he felt pain. He rubbed his chest and blew out an eagle feather in the palm of his hand. The Cheyenne asked the Comanche what he meant by that.

The Cheyenne {*sic*, Comanche} said he knew nothing about the feather, but he did know that the pipe belonged to the Cheyenne, and anything that came out of it must be from the Cheyennes.

The Cheyenne said, no, he had nothing like that. It must belong to the Comanche, and he handed it over.

The Comanche took the pipe again, and on the fourth puff was struck by something. This time he blew out a black bug.

He asked the Cheyenne what he meant by that.

The Cheyenne said he had never seen it before, that it came out of the Comanche's pipe, and so it must be his. The Comanche said he never owned a bug, that it must be the Cheyenne's, and handed it back over to him.

The Cheyenne smoked. On the fourth puff, something hit him. He blew out a tarantula. He asked the Comanche what he did that for.

The Comanche said he had nothing to do with it, that it came out of the Cheyenne's pipe, so it must belong to him.

The Comanche again took the pipe. He smoked, and on the fourth puff got hurt.

He rubbed his stomach and blew and out came a cockleburr.

Again, the Cheyenne smoked. On the fourth puff, he got a needle case cactus.

Then the Comanche thanked the Cheyenne for a nice time and went home, having had his four smokes.

Before he got home, he saw the Cheyennes running around and heard weeping. News reached the Comanches that the Cheyenne medicine man had died. The Comanche had shot the cactus crossways in his throat and he couldn't get it out.

The Cheyennes were glad that someone had killed this evil medicine man, so they gave the Comanche medicine man presents.

HOWARD WHITE WOLF
August 2, 1933[1]

Games: ⟨nasʉpe⟩   ⟨nasʉpe⟩ was the women's kickball game.[2]

Hunting: Prairie Dogs   Prairie Dogs were drowned out by diverting water from a buffalo wallow into a burrow. They were also caught by laying a noose over the burrow's mouth and lassoing the animals as they came out. [They were also shot with bow and arrow.]

Social Control: Murder: Liability   Two boys went turkey hunting. They were stalking turkeys when one stepped on a dry stick and scared the birds away. The other became angry and shot him in the side of the body. [He was frightened], then left him and went back home.

He got home and his father asked where his friend was. The boy pretended to be surprised; he said the other boy had left him to go home an hour before. The injured boy's mother and sisters got suspicious and went out to the mountains, calling out the son's name. Finally, they heard a low moaning, and followed it to where the boy lay among the rocks.

The boy told them what had happened. He asked his mother not to kill his friend because it had been accidental and revenge wouldn't bring him back. So the parents of the survivor paid all the funeral expenses and provided gifts for the body. The victim's fifteen-year-old sister cut and gashed herself, and cut off her hair in mourning. The killer was not punished.[3]

Social Control: Murder {Wedel}   Two men were married to each other's sisters. One woman wanted to borrow something from her sister-in-law, but the latter refused and spoke roughly. So the offended woman's husband went around and killed his sister.

The latter's two sons decided to kill their uncle, a very brave warrior. The latter was warned that the boys were after him, but he laughed. Finally, he tied a horse near his tipi, to get away on if attacked. The warrior was a sort of a medicine man.

The nephews and their friends couldn't hit him for a long time. (Quitsquip[4] led the avenging party and finally shot the warrior with a muzzleloader.) Finally, he began to retreat when one of their men shot him with a gun. This ended the trouble. The warrior's people did nothing about it.

Social Control: Murder {Hoebel}   Two men were married to each other's sisters. One woman wanted to borrow something from her sister-in-law, but the latter refused and spoke roughly. The offended woman's husband went around and killed his sister.

The dead woman's two sons decided to kill their uncle in revenge. The uncle was a very brave warrior. He was warned of their intention, but laughed. Finally, he tied a horse near his tipi, to get away on if attacked.

---

1. Wedel's notes merely state "August 2." The consultant identification comes from the parallel notes of Hoebel and Carlson.

2. Wallace and Hoebel 1952:115.

3. Hoebel (1940:76) attributes this to Post Oak Jim.

4. Quitsquip, *kʉtsʉkwipʉ*, usually translated as Chewing or Chew-up, sometimes as Elk's Cud or Chewing Elk, was a prominent Yapainʉʉ local band leader.

A warrior named Quitsquip led the boys in the attack on him, but they couldn't hit him (he was protected by his medicine). They started to retreat. One man hit him with a bullet from a muzzleloader. It killed him. The feud was over.

Social Control: Murder {Carlson}   Two men were married to each other's sisters. One went to borrow something from her sister-in-law. The sister-in-law spoke harshly to the woman who went back and told her husband. The husband then killed his sister.

His sister's sons were going to kill their uncle, but were afraid because he was a very brave warrior.

Someone told the man his nephews were after him, but he just laughed, saying they were only boys who had never been on a war party. However, he finally consented to tie a horse outside. In case trouble started, he'd then have it handy.

The boys came along with some of their friends. They shot at each other. The uncle was a medicine man and they couldn't hit him. Finally, the avenging party began to retreat.

There was a medicine man in this group named Quitsquip. Quitsquip stepped up and shot the uncle with a muzzleloader, killing him.

The uncle's surviving relatives did not carry the feud any further. It was purely a family affair.

Games: *natsihtóoʔetu̱* *natsihtóoʔetu̱* was a women's hockey game.

It was played by teams from different bands.

The game was announced by men.

There were ten to twelve women on each side. The best runners are selected for each side.

Poles were set up at each end of a field, about like a football field in length.

It was played when the grass was short.

There was a woman umpire on each side.

The spectators encircled the field.

The players wore light moccasins and short skirts.

There was a rawhide rope about twelve inches long with a heavy knot at each end.

Each woman had a stick with a hook at the end.

The rope was dropped between two of the women by one of them, and each made a grab. The best player would get it and throw it toward her goal. The other side tried to keep them from scoring. They couldn't use their hands on the rope. To score, the rope had to be thrown over the goal.

Heavy bets were placed on each side. The highest score won.

(Women's foot races were from a hundred yards to a mile.)

They played until one side won; there were no ties. The game took a long time.

The bets were paid after each score, the players themselves bet, and the game ended when one side had nothing more to wager.

The umpire would call out, "Have you anything more to bet?" and the women would admit that they had nothing more and were beaten. Clothes, jewelry, etc., were the stakes.

Sometimes a woman had her teeth knocked out.

Games: *tohpeti*   *tohpeti*[1] was a female and male gambling game. There were eight or ten sticks called *tohpeti*, each differently marked and about six to eight inches long. A cloth was spread out, and a flat rock about eight inches was laid on the cloth.

A pile of sticks were cut and laid side-by-side, maybe a thousand sticks.

Each player might bet a good shawl, and take two hundred sticks and place them by her as chips. The player threw her sticks down on the stone and let them fall apart. The high number won the throw.

Maybe twenty or so chips were bet at each throw.

Men also played this.

Women sometimes gambled their tipis; the tipi was the woman's property and couldn't be gambled away by her husband except with her consent.

-⟨keswat⟩ was the highest play.

-seven the next highest.

-six the third highest.

-⟨nebekʉ⟩ was the lowest play.

If all the sticks were laid with the highest value, painted-side up, it was called keswat.

If the four longest sticks lay thus, and a shorter one lay marked-side down it was "seven."

A player would holler "keswat" before she threw, amid much noise and excitement.

⟨narowait⟩ meant shooting the works.

The winner of a throw got the same number from her opponent as she had in her pile.

There were two players for this game. They had four long sticks painted black and marked with high numbers, and the other four were varicolored. If all the sticks fall red-side up showing highest number {*sic*}. If four short sticks lay one way, it was ⟨nabekʉ⟩, counting nothing. After narowait, the person who won had the right to bet her winnings against any new stakes put up by the loser, not risking the loss of her own goods.

A woman might carry one or two extra bunches of playing sticks; if her luck was poor, she might use a different set of sticks.

Games: Arrow   Throwing arrows were heavier than shooting arrows. They threw at a mark and for distance.

aratsiʔ[2] was a young man's game. There was a six-inch hoop, crisscrossed with sinew, and a four-foot long spear with feathers. The two players stood together; each chose the best players from among the others. The ring was thrown and the contestants threw their big spears. If one speared it, he then threw his small arrows, five or six of them, at the hoop. If he threw a small arrow into the hoop, he won the bet. He didn't really have to throw it through, if his big arrow had gone through. The other contestant had no chance until the hoop was thrown again.

Gambling   Two good players once played *tohpeti*. They bet property. One man finally won the other's tipi, saddle, moccasins, and thirty head of horses. The loser finally wanted to bet his shirt. They played two days without stopping and the man lost everything he had. This was the greatest match ever played.

---

1. Wallace and Hoebel 1952:116 (?).
2. Wallace and Hoebel 1952:115.

An unlucky man might call a friend who was a good player to play for him. Such men didn't gamble their own belongings, and winnings belonged to man for whom he played. There were some professional gamblers, both male and female, who were looked down upon by others.

Gambling: Gambling Debts   A man who gambled under false pretenses, putting up stakes he didn't have, was discredited.

Story   A young man had gone on a war party. They had a battle with another tribe, maybe Utes. When the enemy attacked the village, the boy got {. . . [sic]}.

Medicine: Shields; War: Medicine   Shields had a loop for slinging about the neck and shoulder. It was held out to the front against the left forearm to turn bullets.

Wild geese gave a medicine man the power to escape bullets The geese appeared to him in a dream, and said, "We fly high, bullets don't hit us. You'll be like us, no matter where you go." So he got immunity from bullets. He had geese painted on his shield.

Bears were painted on shields to turn bullets.

Children couldn't carry meat near a shield. The owner couldn't touch it with greasy hands and menstruating women stayed away.

Eagles were drawn on shields sometimes, as were sparrowhawks, because they flew fast and could kill anything they attacked.

The prairie chicken also, because if you don't get it on the first shot, it gets away; so too with the owner of this medicine.

Medicine: Transfer   A medicine man would spend several days with a young man, blow on him, chew up some seeds and spit them into his mouth, and the latter would swallow it. The medicine man painted a shield for the young man. This protected the young man for the one battle only.

Medicine: Tree   In the old days, before the Comanches surrendered, an old medicine man gave war power to a young man. He set up a young cottonwood where he gave him power. Years later, the Indians passed the spot and the tree had grown large. Thereafter, every time they passed the place they tied gifts to the tree so their children could have long lives.

Medicine: Vision Quest   A seeker for power at a medicine man's grave had to know his deeds.

Medicine   Way back in the old days, people knew of medicine men in other tribes.

The Comanches had a big battle with another tribe. Every one of the enemy was slain, save for a single medicine man, although they shot at him with bows and arrows, guns, etc. Finally, at sundown, they threw him down and killed him.

Years later, a man went to his grave for power and stayed all night. The medicine man's appearance was very terrifying. He carried a big rattlesnake. No one had ever stayed out the night.

The leader of these three Comanches was very brave; he said would stay by the grave, and he sent the others away to where they could hear him. He told them not to come, even if he hollered. They took his horse.

It was about 10:00 P.M., and the companions sat up to see if the medicine man would scare their leader away. Toward midnight, they heard a whooping and knew the medicine man had attacked, but they stayed away. Finally, everything became quiet.

The next morning they went over and found their companion dead.

Medicine: Transfer   A man could get power from a medicine man of another tribe.

P.M.

War Parties: Parade   When a war party was getting ready to leave, the warriors beat on a rawhide with drumsticks and sang; then they got on horses, one *nomUne* in front, the other behind, and they rode from one end of camp to the other and back. All the women came out and sang as they went by.

Political Organization: Chiefs: War Leader   The *tekwUniwapI* was any brave warrior.

Hunting: Deer: Decoys   Deer were stalked by hunters who held a bush up before themselves and gradually moved to within killing distance.

Cosmology: Star Lore   They had a name for a certain fixed star that was used in travels (North Star_____),[1] also the Pleiades. The same was for the circular constellation ("smoking stars"_____).[2]

Story: War: Rescue   A young man was on a war party. After a big battle, he failed to return; he was either dead or captured.

The other warriors said he had fought bravely when last seen. So, a few days after, his friend said he was going to look for his friend.

He found out where the battle had taken place, so he went there and he found the enemy camp.

It was a moonlit night with clouds.

They were having a Sun Dance.

So the young man took his weapons, threw a blanket over himself, and went into the camp.

Presently, he got to the dance arbor. He heard someone groaning on top so he went up to see who it was. When the people sang and the clouds covered the moon, he climbed; otherwise he lay still. It was his friend who had been tied up. He had a broken leg.

They got down and the rescuer carried his friend back to his horse and they rode back to the top of hill and watched.

When the enemy warriors saw that the captive was gone, they trailed him a ways, then gave up.

The next night, the two Comanches rode on home. These men were very close friends.[3]

Medicine: War   In actual battle, warriors fought naked, with their bodies painted as directed by their medicine power. They carried weapons and shields always. Some wore only a breechcloth, others only moccasins. Their horses were painted.

Musical Instruments: Drums   The Comanches beat the drum only before going to war or for dancing, never at the start of a battle.

The drum was about the size of a cheese box. A green hide was stretched over the frame, with crosspieces on the underside for grasping.

1. The blank is in Wedel's original; see Howard White Wolf, August 3.
2. The blank is in Wedel's original. There is no other reference in the notes to this constellation.
3. Compare with Niyah, July 10.

Drums were beaten by a returning war party. The warriors were painted black and carried the scalp like a flag.

If a member of party had been killed, warriors didn't paint or beat the drum. They just came back quietly.

Captives   Captives belonged to the captor. In the old days, captives were subject to the captors. If they married a Comanche, they got the same rights as full bloods, children the same. They had slave status until marriage.

Material Culture: Clothing   Warriors wore calico shirts, save in battle, a g-string, leggings, moccasins[1]; it was regular apparel.

Leggings were decorated with fringes and beads. They were fastened to the belt with a string at the outer edge. They were cleaned every morning by the women. They scraped the shirt and leggings first with a bone tool, then rubbed them with yellow clay and a little water, and hung them up to dry. When dry, the surplus dirt was removed; if an article was still stiff or dirty, it was again treated. Some of the clay went in and colored it.

The scalp lock passed through a silver or iron ring.

A small silver disk was fastened to the ear lock, (always over the right ear). Also, a bear's ear was painted and decorated along the edge with beads. The lower part of the ear lock had otter skin attached.

The *korohkO*[2] was the bone or shell bead breastplate worn by wealthy young men.

They wore buckskin shirts with fringes and beads. There were no beaded vests among the Comanches.

Quassyah was a good dresser.

At the upper end of the otter skin[3] was attached a beaded disk, to which were fastened colored ribbons.

The whipcord fringes that ran down the sleeve seam of a shirt were periodically rubbed with white clay.

Valuable blankets were made by sewing two different colored cloths together.

Necklaces of Mexican beads passed over one (left?) shoulder and under the other arm.

Dress moccasins had two lines of beads from the instep to the tip of the toe. There was a painted line between the beads. Along the outer edge of the outer beads were short fringes with conical bangles of metal. Sometimes the beads extended along the top of the moccasin to the rear. The lower edges of the side flaps were beaded and the flaps were sometimes painted. There were fringes at the rear seam, four to six inches long. They were painted one color; ⟨taseyuke⟩ were the bangles.

Quassyah had an otter skin cap with a single eagle feather.

Clothes were stored away with sage (?) leaves to get a good odor. "Without it, we smell awful strong."

A poor man's moccasins usually had no beads or fringes; warrior's moccasins were the same.

1. Wallace and Hoebel 1952:77.
2. *korohkO* is generic for 'necklace'.
3. The hair or braid wrap.

Rawhide "overshoes" of buffalo hide, furside inside, were for snow and winter rains.[1]
Buffalo robes were worn by old people in the winter, blankets by the younger set.

A "dandy" might wear an otter skin cap. In winter, warriors sometimes wore gray fox caps.

War Story: Comanches and Navajos   Three Navajos stole a lot of horses from the Comanches early in the evening. The Comanches chased them the next day. The Navajos stopped and began racing the horses. The Comanches caught and killed them.

(The Navajos frequently raided into Comanche territory; they were great fighters, as were the Pawnees and Osages.)

Medicine: Peyote: Origins   A returning Comanche war party stopped among some mountains where the White Mountain Apaches lived. After midnight, they heard a drum beating.

The head man said he was going over to see what it was. If he hadn't returned by sunup, they would know he had been killed and that they should continue on their way.

The people (Apaches) had been eating peyote. One of them told their leader that a Comanche, their enemy, was coming. [An Apache had had a dream that the enemy Comanche would appear.] The leader said that they should bring him in [when he came].

An hour later, the Comanche arrived and was met and led into the tent. The Apaches asked what he wanted.

The Comanche said he had heard the drums and wanted to see what it was.

The Apaches explained that peyote was big medicine. They told him to watch closely, then go back to his own people. They said they stopped at daybreak because enemies might attack them.

The next morning, they gave the drum [and a button] to the Comanche and he went home. Thus, peyote came to the Comanches.

The men eat no salt meat, stay away from their wives, etc., during peyote.

Later, Pawnees, Osages, etc., got peyote.[2]

[This was told to White Wolf (who was about 80[3]) when he was a small boy, by an old man who had been told it by an old man.]

Material Culture: Clothing: Women's   Women wore high moccasins with beads down the side seam, and brass headed buttons in a double row down the lower one-half to one-third of the seam. The upper was sewn to the moccasin above the ankle. The seam was beaded. The drawstring was just below the seam.

The sole was cut out first (and fitted on the foot).

The uppers were also fitted.

Any woman could make moccasins, but some were better than others.

Fringes hung down from the top like on a shawl.

They were scraped like the men's moccasins to clean, but no water was used. Moccasins were carefully watched. If they were left in the sun too long, they would be ruined.

A woman could paint her own moccasins.

There were large disks, sometimes in a single row, down the side.

---

1. Wallace and Hoebel 1952:78 (?).
2. Wallace and Hoebel 1952:334; La Barre 1975:25. The variations in this note are from Hoebel.
3. See Introduction.

There were plainer, beaded moccasins for everyday wear.

Women wore cloth belts with brass cartouches and a tail hanging down in front, terminating in a silver or brass triangle. A small bag containing paints was beaded; the flap had a button and was edged with bangles, and was hung to the belt. A pocket knife was also in a small pouch at the belt.

(Belts were traded from Mexico, for men, silk belts of cloth; belts of cloth over one shoulder.)

The buckskin dress was fringed at the sleeves, bottom, and sides. Elk teeth {illegible} were sewn at the breast and back sometimes, by the wealthy only. It was beaded about the neck, sleeves, and bottom. There were colored ribbons tied to the arms, breast, etc., if desired, and the dress was finished.

Bangles were fastened to the bottom fringes. The dress was painted the way the owner wished, for instance, yellow from the waist up or down, etc.

There were special dressmakers, but any woman could make a dress if she wished.

There were wide brass wristlets of wire terminating at the wrist with a silver ring; there were silver earrings.

Adornment: Hair Care   The hair was permitted to hang free at dances, etc.

They ordinarily wore two queues tied with string, but they were not plaited like the Cheyennes.

Dances; Adornment: Face Paint   When a dance was announced in the morning, men and women painted their faces.

Material Culture: Soap   The roots of *mumutsiʾ*, yucca, were peeled, pounded, and placed in water, and used to wash the hair and skin.

Adornment: Hair Care: Combs   Pointed weeds were cut and bound together with sinew, then trimmed off even to make combs.

Games: ⟨nasʉpe⟩   ⟨nasʉpe⟩ was a women's kick ball game.[1] There were three variations:

a) Two teams of, say, four players each. A woman hopped along on her left foot, bouncing a ball of deerskin stuffed with grass on the instep of her right foot. When she dropped the ball, another woman took it over and continued until she dropped it. The team that went the farthest won the game. Sometimes a very good player could outdistance the entire other team.

b) An individual woman stood on her left foot, with her body bent slightly forward, her hands cupped behind her back. The ball was kicked over the player's own head and caught behind her back, and then thrown forward, without unhooking her hands, and caught on her foot. It went on back and forth. The winner was the one who completed the most bounces over her head. The ball couldn't touch the ground.

c) The player hopped along, alternating her feet. The ball bounced from her right thigh and was caught on the left, bounced back, and so back and forth on alternate thighs. Great dexterity was required.

Games: Children's Games   On moonlit nights, children played all sorts of games.

They never mixed sexes.

---

1. Wallace and Hoebel 1952:115.

Both sexes would run foot races; blind man's bluff and hide-and-seek were popular. They were the same as with whites.

The hand game was also popular.

Games: Wrestling; Boxing   Young man never boxed, but often wrestled. Wrestlers would put their arms about one another, each trying to put opponent on the ground. The winner was the man who stayed on his feet longest; he won as soon as the opponent was down.

Games: Bear Game   In the Bear Game, boys lined up behind one another, facing the same way each with their arms about the one in front. The "bear" was in front of the leader, facing the boys, and trying to get at the boys in the line. The leader tried to prevent their capture. There was much excitement and hollering.

The boys sat side by side, drumming on their thighs, repeating "nꭒe, nꭒe, nꭒe" ("me, me, me") in a loud monotone.

Older boys would come along. The first boy took the loudest shouter, slung him over his back, head down and with his feet over his shoulders, and carried him as far as he could. Each of others carried a boy. The winner was the one who carried a boy the farthest.

Old people watched games, and sometimes participated.

Dances   Men and women dancers never embraced.

FRANK CHEKOVI
August 3, 1933[1]

Kinship Relations: Brother-Sister   A brother ruled over a sister. He could claim her property.

Kinship Relations: Uncles   There was nothing definite as to whether the paternal or maternal uncle would be of more assistance. It depended upon which had the closest bond of sympathy in any case.

Kinship Relations: Joking; Social Relations: Friendship   Parꭒakuhma and Ebiyꭒri[2] were friends. They were not real friends, but it came out in battle.

At a dance, Parꭒakuhma was telling his war deeds. Ebiyꭒri elbowed his way through the crowd and held his hand up. Every one thought he was going to tell one of his war deeds. He said, "Listen, I know what he's going to tell. He's going to say that when the Mexicans captured him, they buggered him."

Kinship Relations: Affines   Brothers-in-law usually get along well together.

A question might arise between them, concerning the wife's property. A brother could claim all the property a sister owned before marriage, but he could not claim property she acquired through her husband. A woman went to her husband with just her clothing.

Life Cycle: Marriage: Levirate/Sororate   If a widow was left with children, a grown son would try to keep his mother single, but if all the children were young, she would probably remarry.

---

1. The content of this interview is from Carlson, with a single variation from Hoebel. The order is arbitrary.

2. *ebi* 'blue'. Otherwise unidentified.

If her husband's brother wished to marry her, it was hard for her to refuse. He could collect *nanuwoku* on her.

The brother asked her in a good, kind way, and if she refused, and started taking up with some other man, he would get angry.

If a brother claimed a widow, he could collect *nanuwoku* on her even if he never laid with her.

A friend had the advantage over him in collecting *nanuwoku*, but could not collect *nanuwoku* from the brother.

A man died, leaving two wives. His brother, Kaibubi,[1] claimed one {wife} and his friend the other. Both took their women home. The friend was already married and his new wife did not stay with him long. His first wife mistreated her and she ran off. Kaibubi was a widower. He lived with his wife for a long time.

Life Cycle: Death: Disposition of Property   In the old days, when a person died, they killed as many horses as they could, and left the rest to the widow.

When Piarupsima died, his widow could get no help in moving the body,[2] so he was buried in the tipi, and when they moved, they left the tipi standing. This was an unusual thing.

Property went to the widow, and perhaps the children might get a share.

Kinship Relations: Incest   The Wo'anuu[3] were called *nahma'sunuu*, meaning 'something together',[4] because it was said they practiced incest.

Incest was bad: the family decreased and the children were not strong. The Comanches were a bashful people. They thought it a disgrace to marry your relative.

The Wo'anuu were decreasing, probably because of incest.

It was worst to marry your sister, daughter, or niece.

It a man married a pregnant woman, the child was not his own, but it could not marry a child of that man by another wife.

Paternity   Paternity was established, in case of doubt, by who the child resembled.

HOWARD WHITE WOLF
August 3, 1933

Medicine: Herbs: *tohpotsotsii*   *tohpotsotsii*[5] was a slightly spiny plant whose root was boiled. The decoction was drunk as a tuberculosis cure in the old days. The fruit was spherical or very slightly elongated.

1. Otherwise unidentified.
2. Wallace and Hoebel 1952:40 (?).
3. 'Wormy People'.
4. Robinson and Armagost (1990) glosses *nahma'ai* as 'together (with each other)'.
5. Robinson and Armagost (1990) and Carlson and Jones (1940) identify this as nightshade, *Solunum* sp., "used in a general tonic and tuberculosis remedy" (1940:524).

Games: Tops   Sticks were put through these {*tohpotsots`ii*} to project on either side and were used as tops by boys. They were set spinning by rolling between the hands. The winner was the boy whose top spun the longest.

Material Culture: Containers: Water   Water was carried in buffalo paunches by warriors or when moving camp. Paunches were sometimes sewed into bags.

Cosmology: Star Lore   *tatsinoke'mia*[1] was "the star that never moved," the North Star.[2] Warriors on devilment watched this star as a guide.

War   Mexicans said that in the old days roosters warned them of raids, because they called "Comanche, Comanche."[3]

Camp Organization: Breaking Camp   Camps were moved every week, or more often, to escape enemies. [Ordinarily they camped three or four days in one spot.]

Scouts were sent out by the *paraibo* to locate the next campsite. It might be fifteen or twenty-five miles distant. When the scouts returned, the *paraibo* called the leading men to his tipi and informed them that they were moving.

That evening, he set out and announced it publicly. The camp was broken early; loading might take till noon. The *paraibo* led. At the new site, he pitched camp first, then the others camped around him.

The horses were rounded up and brought into camp. The first pony was loaded with the tipi poles, the next one with the cover, then came two or three loaded with blankets, robes, and furniture. A man's shield was carried by his wife while on the move, his spear also. Sometimes she carried his bow and arrows. When everyone was ready, the fires were extinguished and the *paraibo* gave the signal to start.

The warriors rode on either side of the party. There were no stragglers allowed. [If any woman fell behind, they stopped the whole bunch.]

Scouts were always in advance and on all sides. While women set up the tipis and established the new camp, the warriors indulged in horse races, etc.

A scout appointed by the *paraibo* went out daily from camp and circled it at ten miles or so. If he struck a trace, he followed it to a camp to find who had passed, then returned and reported to the *paraibo*.

If the trace had led toward a camp, the horses were brought in and kept near the tipis for emergency use.

Story   After the Comanches surrendered, about twenty warriors with their families broke away and fled to "No Man's Land," the Llano Estacado, and some died of thirst. A few knew of a spring and managed to reach it and live.[4]

Social Control: Fighting   Men never fought with fists. They tried to pull each other's hair and scratch their faces, etc.

---

1. Robinson and Armagost (1990) gives this in reverse, *kemi'arɨtatsino*. See also Frank Chekovi, August 11.

2. This is perhaps in answer to a question from the previous day. See Howard White Wolf, August 2.

3. The last three lines of this page of Wedel's manuscript notebook are torn off, but it does not appear that any information was lost.

4. There were several attempts to flee the reservation in the first few years after 1875, so it is not clear to which particular event White Wolf was referring.

Story: The Woman Who Betrayed Her Husband   The Comanches fought a big battle with an enemy tribe. The Comanches were camped in a creek before the battle.

A scout was sent out, and he took his young wife along. Presently, they reached a barren hill, where they tied their horses, and the husband crawled to the top.

Meanwhile, a scout from the enemy camp came to the same hill. The two scouts reached the top at the same time. One suggested that they wrestle, the winner to take the other's scalp. These men were leaders of their respective war parties.

They laid their weapons aside and went at each other. They were both fine, strong men. The Comanche's wife came up. She saw the other man was better looking than her husband, so she got in and grabbed her husband's leg and tried to throw him down.

Finally, the Comanche threw the other down. The vanquished man sat down. He had fine long hair. He asked the Comanche to tie a rag tightly about his head so he wouldn't bleed to death. The Comanche took a knife and scalped him. Then each rode back to his party. Afterwards the Comanche killed his wife for disloyalty.

The next day, they had a big battle. Each leader was riding a special horse. They had told each other how they would dress. They fought each other and the Comanches finally won the fight.[1]

War Story   Howard's aunt was in a certain camp; a captive Mexican woman was also there. The name of the *paraibo* was not known.

One morning, Mexican traders came with goods on *muura?*,[2] burros. They told the Comanches to trade at once because they were in a hurry. U.S. soldiers were coming to attack the Comanches.

The captive was a poor interpreter; she warned the Comanches that the Mexicans were trying to get away.

The soldiers got to the Comanches before the latter were expecting them. The Comanches ran for their lives.

Two young men were still in bed when the attack was made. Their mother and father told them the U.S. Army was attacking, but the boys refused to get up. They told their parents to let them sleep. The father turned his horse loose because he wouldn't leave the boys.

Many people escaped to the hills. The next day, some of the warriors came down. The camp had been burned, tipis and all. They never camped there again.[3]

The same thing happened near Mt. Scott.[4]

War Parties: Organization   Each warrior on a raid had an extra pack horse. He carried spare clothes, supplies, etc.

When they were three or four days distant from the enemy, they left the pack animals. Each man took his best horse, a blanket, and went on, leaving three or four guards for the

---

1. Compare with Nemaruibetsi, July 31.
2. Specifically, 'mule'.
3. The specific historical referent of this story is not clear.
4. Mount Scott is just north of Lawton in the Wichita Mountains Wildlife Refuge. The closest battle site to the old reservation is Rush Springs, about thirty miles northeast east of Lawton, where, in 1858, Texan soldiers under Earl Van Dorn attacked a Comanche village (Kavanagh 1996:375).

horses. If the raiders didn't return in a set number of days, those guardsmen returned to their village.

Medicine: Foretelling: Badger's Mirror   Sometimes before a war party left, they killed a badger, laid it on its back, cut its belly open, and spread the skin apart. They let the blood coagulate to form a mirror.

Then, the men dressed in their war costumes, with paint and weapons, and gathered in a little group, each man holding his shield in fighting position.

They danced forward to the badger (maybe twenty feet away) making the quavering sounds the same as when they were going into battle.

As he approached the animal, an old man at one side recounted the young man's war deeds; they had to be true. [If he missed one, or any were untrue, there was no reflection].

The man stooped and looked into the blood. [There were three possible results:] If he saw himself with gray hair, he would live long; if he saw blood, he would be killed; if he was thin, he would die of tuberculosis.

It took a brave man to look into the blood mirror. Warriors usually did this, but anyone who wished could look in.

A special man had to kill and prepare the badger.

Medicine: Curing   Years ago, a young man on a war party was nearly blind; he came to the mineral spring near Carnegie.[1] That night in a dream he was told to wash his eyes in the spring. He did so and was soon cured. *pisikwana*[2] 'smells bad' was the name for the spring. It had power to cure sores.

Food: Salt   Yavini's wife,[3] who lived near Post Oak Mission, said salt was gotten in lumps from the bottom of a creek, whose name was unknown. Some salt came from the creek banks, but it was not so good.

Material Culture: Paint: Pigment   Red paint was made from a rock found east of Ft. Sill. Some were softer than others. It was used on the face in the summer to prevent sunburn.

There were two red paints: a dull red (hematite) for sunburn, and a brilliant red (cinnabar).

Yellow ocher came from a creek bank.

White paint for buckskin was also from creek banks. It was soft, like flour, molded into a ball, and stored. It was also used on faces. One source was about a mile from Howard's home.

Black was also used; its source was unknown.

Howard knew of no vegetal pigments.

Food: Alcohol   No intoxicating drinks were made by the Comanches.

Medicine: Curing   A broken leg was set as follows: cactus pads were singed in a fire; they were split and fastened on the break by cloth wrappings as hot as the patient could stand. After a couple of changes, the pads were left off.

---

1. Carnegie is on the Washita River west of Anadarko.
2. *pisi* 'infected', *kwana* 'odor'.
3. For whatever reason, Yavini (no translation given) does not appear on any census before 1899, where he is listed as twenty-three years old. In 1933, his wife was Aseniyoko (given on the 1885 census, somewhat indelicately, as Gray Screwing, *esi* 'gray', *yoko* 'intercourse'). It is not known if the Field Party actually talked to her, or whether White Wolf was referring to her knowledge.

Piamupits' bones were ground up and smeared over the leg, and then {it was} set with splints and allowed to knit.

A cross of walnut wood was worn about the neck, although the exact purpose was unknown.

The {Medicine} Man generally tied a small piece of medicine up in buckskin, and tied it to a braided thong about the neck, often with a bear or eagle claw and some beads. Sometimes there was a small metal figure of a woman or man suspended, if directed so by the spirit.

Colds in the head were cured with sneezeweed. The leaves were dried and stored, *natsaakɨsi*.[1]

kunanatsu[2] was called 'fire medicine'. The root was chewed and rubbed on a burn to prevent blistering and to alleviate pain. It could be boiled and the decoction drunk to break colds. The weed used to grow here but doesn't any more.

A green, round, strong smelling fruit growing on the ground. The vine was used to produce vomiting to break chest sickness, tuberculosis, etc.

Howard's son once had a nosebleed for most of a day. The doctors couldn't stop it, so they went to one of his relatives and was referred to a medicine man. He took tobacco and went around to see the doctor. The boy was beginning to get very weak and his parents were worried.

The doctor began to pray. He had a small ring with his medicine, and he doctored the patient about the nose and stopped it at once. Howard did know the medicine.

Headaches were cured by making a small cut on each temple with a flintstone and allowing it to bleed for a time. This always cured it.

A prairie dog showed a rheumatism cure to a Shoshone visiting the Comanches. He told the Shoshone to kill a prairie dog, cut out his fat and squeeze out the soft oil, and to mix that with red paint and rub it on the affected limb, always with downward motion. Then, get a hot rock and hold it over the part to make the grease penetrate to the bone. They used prairie dogs because they never suffered from rheumatism.

A certain Osage was suffering from tuberculosis. He went to Texas to get a cure because the doctors couldn't cure him. He was walking along when he stumbled over a vine with round fruits. He walked on, then turned back, and smelled the fruit. It was very strong smelling. He took a nibble, then a bite. Finally, he ate it. An hour later, he had to vomit; he vomited nearly a bucketful. It was all black, blue, green, and awful smelling stuff. He felt weak for a while, but soon got stronger. Before he had been unable to eat much, now he ate a hearty supper and began to recover. He was now a strong man. The Comanche use the same cure for bronchitis, not yet for tuberculosis.

1. Carlson and Jones (1940) identifies this as *Helenium microphalum*.
2. *kuna* 'fire'. Carlson and Jones (1940) identifies this as *Zanthoxylum americanum*, prickly ash or toothache tree.

p.m.

Plants:

wo^ʔanatʉsʉ^ʔ[1] (ragweed) was a worm medicine. The leaves were stripped off, pounded, and boiled. It was poured over open fly or worm sores to keep the flies away. It was used on animals.

pohóobi[2] (wild sage) leaves were boiled and used for sore eyes. It was strained into a cup, then taken up in a cloth and a drop or two squeezed into the eye. It was also used in peyote meetings, about the wall, to sit on, etc. Another, more bushy form along the Red River was made into tea.

pesotai[3] was used for the gambling sticks in *tohpeti*. The twigs were split to give the flat side for markings.

ekawoni 'red burning'.[4] It had a small seed. For a practical joke, spit on or wet the plant, then have the victim rub it on his wrist or body; it burned liked fire.

wokwéesi[5] ⎫ cactus pads used to reduce swelling, to stop bleeding, and to prevent
wokweebi[6] ⎭ infection.

Constipation was cured by some sort of salt (see Yavini's wife[7]); it was drunk before breakfast.

Diarrhoea was cured by drinking a decoction from a certain weed.

pibiarona were plums.[8]

natsomɄ were dried plums.

kuupɄ[9] were nuts or fruit stored up by rats.

wokwéesi, prickly pear fruit, was pounded fine and mixed with fat.

Mesquite beans were picked ripe, boiled, and the seeds removed. The pods were crushed and the juice strained off. Sugar was added, then boiled like jelly. Sometimes corn meal was added to make ⟨maxyan⟩. The pods, when squeezed out by hand, were called *namabitsoo^ʔni*.

natsohkwe^ʔ wohi^ʔhuu "to pound mesquite."[10]

puhi huwa[11] or *puhi tuhpaa*[12] was a weed used for tea. It was gray like *pohóobi*. It was better than the white man's tea.

mitsonaa^ʔ was pounded hackberry and grease and sugar. The berries were pounded out into a thin cake, about eight inches wide by twelves inches or more long. Sugar was

---

1. Carlson and Jones (1940) identifies this as *Amrosia psilostahcya*, western ragweed.
2. Carlson and Jones (1940) identifies this as *Artemesia ludviciiana*, lobed cutweed or white sage.
3. Carlson and Jones (1940) identifies this as *Cephalanthus occidentalis*, button bush.
4. Robinson and Armagost (1990) gives this as 'smartweed'.
5. Robinson and Armagost (1990) identifies this as both barrel cactus and prickly pear cactus.
6. Robinson and Armagost (1990) has this as 'peyote plant or button, thorn, thistle.'
7. See above, Food: Salt.
8. *pibia* 'big' (pl.), *tona^ʔ* 'stinger'? In contrast, Robinson and Armagost (1990) has plum as *sʉkʉ^ʔi*.
9. Robinson and Armagost (1990) glosses *kuupɄ* as simply a 'cache'.
10. *na-* reflexive prefix, *tsohkwe* 'pound', *wohi^ʔhuu* 'mesquite'.
11. Carlson and Jones (1940) has *puhihuβa*.
12. Carlson and Jones (1940) identifies this as bush clover, *Lespedeza capitata*. Robinson and Armagost (1990) has bush clover as *puhi tubi*.

seldom added because the berries were naturally sweet. Grease was added, and it was kept in a *natʉsakʉna*. When one was hungry, he rolled out a ball of it and roasted it over a fire.

kusiwaapokopl[1] gray juniper berries. The small blue berries were not eaten; the leaves were <u>never</u> used in peyote.

waapokopl were the larger, reddish, cedar berries. They grew mostly toward the east. The berries were eaten raw.

Berries from the *tʉbitsiwaapl*[2] 'cedar tree', leaves were used in peyote meetings.

pibiahuupi[3] 'real oak', white (?) oak; the acorns were removed from the cup, but they were too bitter to eat.

paʔsa ponii were any kind of acorns.

tʉbitsihuupi[4] was a large acorn from dwarf trees growing far to the west.

tʉbitsipaʔsa ponii were small round nuts. They were hard to crack. One had to use a hammer. Inside was a small kernel, round like a marble; they were sweet (filberts?). They grew on small trees three or four feet high, along creeks. Sometimes they were boiled; they were also eaten fresh. They grew far to the west.

⟨tibapt⟩ were pinon nuts gathered by the Comanches far to the west; they were eaten fresh.

nakkʉtabaʔi—'crack it with your teeth'[5]—pecans were gathered and stored for the winter.

mubitai, walnuts, were cracked with a hammer or rock. The kernel was extracted with a pointed bone pick about five inches long. There was no regular name for it.

Material Culture: Utensils: Spoons   Buffalo horn was boiled to soften it, then the spoon was carved out with a knife. They went from teaspoon size to a meat ladle. Howard's wife's family had many of them, as well as wooden platters for eating.

Food: Food Plants: Roots: *pihtsamuu*   *pihtsamuu*[6] was a reddish, sweet root, eaten raw or boiled.

Medicine: Curing: Toothache   Tree fungi was heated and used to reduce the pain in toothache; it was also as tinder by warriors.

Games: *tohpeti*   The sticks were flat on one side, all painted red on the flat side. The four long ones had notches on the edges and were marked on the back. They painted the four short ones but they were not marked.

If they all fall one way, it was ⟨keswat⟩; five and three was the lowest throw ⟨nabekʉ⟩. (See Henepeti,[7] a woman near Blue Beaver). Four and four was no score (?). Either side counted; if they were all the same way it was ⟨nahiru⟩. (See Yavini's wife also.[8])

---

1. *kusi* 'gray', *waa-* 'cedar', *pokopl* 'berry'.
2. Literally, 'true cedar'.
3. Literally, 'big wood'.
4. Literally, 'true wood'.
5. Robinson and Armagost (1990) gives *nakkʉtabaʔi* as the nut, with *kʉtabarʉ* as the verb, 'crack with the teeth'.
6. Robinson and Armagost (1990) translates this as a 'milky-rooted plant'.
7. The closest name on the census rolls is Hemabitty, a woman who lived on Blue Beaver Creek near Indiahoma. The Field Party apparently never went to see her.
8. See above, Food: Salt.

Games: Hand Game *nahiwetʊ*   *nahiwetʊ* was the hand game.

The game was announced a day beforehand.

Heavy bets were placed.

It was played when different bands came together.

A special large tipi was erected, generally in the fall or winter. They gathered a lot of wood because the game usually lasted through the night. Each side had a number of men as follows: one guesser, *wuhtekwawapI*[1] who, if unlucky, could turn the job over to another man.

The men of each band might bet blankets, leggings, *korohkO*, etc., against the men of the other band.

Two men came out from one side; everyone sang, and they advanced toward the guesser, chanting. Each of the two men had a bone cube ⟨taki⟩ in one hand. They held their hands behind them, then put them forward.

If the guesser missed one of the two hands, he tried again. If he missed the bone again, both had the right to play again.

There were eight tally sticks. If the guesser missed both hands, that side got two sticks. When they missed one, they got one stick, and the guesser had another chance at the person who got by. If he missed again, both sides had the right to resume play. If he guessed both right, the bones went to other side. When one side had all the sticks, the first bets were paid off and new bets were made.

The ⟨teritsiwapI⟩[2] was the scorer on each side.

A side might win three or four sticks, but when they lost the bones, the sticks were replaced and they had to start over again the next time.

The guesser would spit on one hand, rub his hands together, then point to where he thought the bone was hidden in each of the two players hands.[3] If one of the players who was trying to hide the bones was consistently guessed out, one of his friends had the right to take his place, as was the case of a poor guesser.

The spectators and players all sang a chant and clapped their hands, especially when their side won all the sticks. They yelled and clapped their hands repeatedly over their mouths as a sign of victory. There were no drums or rattles.

Relations with Other Tribes: Pawnees   A Pawnee war party once came down for devilment during a hand game. Some of the Pawnee warriors went and looked into the gaming tipi. One Pawnee came up, laid a hand on a Comanche man in friendly way, and looked in, but the other Comanches saw him, recognized him as an enemy, and killed him; the other Pawnees got away.

kwitarai meant 'big anus'. *witsa* was a later term.[4]

---

1. From *tekwawapI* 'talker'.

2. Possibly *tebitsi* 'true', *-wapI* agentive suffix.

3. In modern Comanche hand games there are four possible positions of the bones: in both right hands, in both left hands, in the inside hands, or in the outside hands.

4. These are Comanche terms for the Pawnees. The former is derived from *kwitapʉ* 'excrement'; however, "big anus" would be *piakwitarai*. Robinson and Armagost (1990) has both *witsapaii* and *witsapainʉʉ* for Pawnee, but gives no etymology.

The Pawnees always howled like coyotes when their warriors were scattered, as a signal for gathering. Sometimes Pawnee warriors sent out scouts dressed as wolves to spy on Comanche villages. The Pawnees were very tricky. Sometimes they slipped into Comanche camps and cut horses loose from the tipis and drove them off. The old people said there were no people as tricky as the Pawnees.

Hunting   The Comanches had no animal calls.

Names   *isa* was 'wolf'; Esarosavit was 'white wolf'.

Names: Naming   A certain woman couldn't raise children beyond a certain age. So she went to a brave warrior and told him she wanted to save her last child. The warrior had shot and felled *tupʉ*,[1] an enemy in battle. He recounted this event and named the child Topetchy.[2] The Sun and Earth were called on as witnesses. The child was still living as a deacon of the Baptist church at Deyo Mission.[3]

Women were named after their father's deeds.[4]

Games: Hand Game   In later days, women became participants in hand games, and the drum was used by each side. It was played in the daytime now.

Relations with Other Tribes: Ethnonyms

wasási[5]		Osages
sianaboo[?6]		Cheyennes
sariitʉhka	'dog eaters'[7]	Arapahoes
nʉmʉrʉhka	'man eaters'	Tonkawas. They were mostly killed on Tonkawa Creek near Anadarko, but a few escaped.[8]

Medicine: Curing: Eyes   Indians, when they had something in the eye, put a small seed in the eye to make it water, thus washing out the foreign substance.

---

1. Robinson and Armagost (1990) gives *tupʉherʉ* as 'fall away'.

2. The name Topetchy is on the 1885 census as 'knocking down', consistent with White Wolf's translation. Under *topehtsi*, Robinson and Armagost (1990) has "'pass it on' (outstanding deacon, a strong Christian Man)." Casagrande (1954–55, III:15) has *topehciʔ* 'after . . . he . . .'.

Topetchy was the son of Mihesuah, *mihe* 'war', *suʔakʉtʉ* 'like someone, something', given in 1879 as Raider. (His descendants give it as First To Fight [Mihesuah 2002].) His mother was Voneite (from *punitʉ* 'see'), glossed in 1879 as Looking and Running. Topetchy was a member of Cheevers' Yapainʉʉ local band.

3. In 1933, Topetchy was the Deacon of Deyo Mission.

4. Wallace and Hoebel 1952:123 (?).

5. *wazaze* is the Osage's own name for themselves.

6. *sia* 'feather', *naboo* 'marked, striped, spotted'.

7. It is possible that the Plains Apaches were also referred to as "dog-eaters" (Thurman 1988).

8. This is apparently a reference to the attack on the Tonkawa village at the Washita Agency in October, 1862 (Nye 1969:303).

FRANK CHEKOVI
August 4, 1933[1]

Life Cycle: Marriage: Divorce   If a couple disagreed, and the man sent the woman away, maybe his parents knew nothing about it. His father sent his mother to the girl to get her back; she was a nice girl. Maybe the girl refused because she was now mad.

[A man sent his wife away. Her father-in-law sent his wife to see the daughter-in-law. The mother-in-law went to see the daughter-in-law to persuade her to go back to their son. They settled it among themselves; it was a family matter.[2]]

Life Cycle: Marriage: Go-Between   A young man might give up all hope of talking with an unmarried girl. Then he would have a female relative[3] whom he thought could keep a secret to take a message to her. He would not pick his own sister, for they might suspect, but he would use a distant relative. The girl's parent's wouldn't suspect a strange woman talking to their daughter. If things were agreeable to the girl, she would appoint a meeting place. If the young man hung around the watering place, he might get to talk to a girl.

[The go-between—a kinswoman (a distant relative; he didn't want to arouse suspicion[4])—she made rendezvous plans with the girl. Usually, they met at a water place.]

Life Cycle: Marriage: Elopement   When a young man and a girl were in love with each other, they might marry without the consent of the girl's father. The young man might prowl around the camp at night, and wait until the girl slipped out. Then he would take her to his own tipi. If the girl was not afraid, he might take her on a war party with him.

[They usually married without the consent of the parents. The young man might prowl around her tipi at night. She tried to get away. He might ask her to run off on a war party.]

Life Cycle: Marriage   When the man took her to his tipi, the girl's parent's could not object to the marriage.

If they went off on a war party, the girl's parent might follow them if they had no confidence in the man. If they failed to catch up, the marriage stood. In a run-away marriage, the girl was more likely to be satisfied with her husband, and it had a better chance of lasting.

[A boy and girl might run away and marry. Her parents might follow them to bring her back. If they couldn't catch them, it was too late. There was nothing to do when they returned. If a boy and girl took up in his tipi without the parent's consent, it usually stood. Those marriages were the happiest and the most common.]

People in general approved of a runaway marriage over an arranged one. In an arranged marriage, the wife was likely to become angry on the least provocation and leave.[5]

People in general did not approve of a father giving his daughter to someone she did not like. If he did it more than once [several times], the people would talk [they would begin to talk about him[6]]. It would not look right.

1. The content and dating of this interview are from Carlson, with variations from Hoebel.
2. Hoebel 1954:141.
3. Contra Wallace and Hoebel 1952:135.
4. Wallace and Hoebel 1952:134.
5. Wallace and Hoebel 1952:138.
6. Wallace and Hoebel 1952:138.

The runaway marriage was more common. The people in general did not approve of a man giving a daughter to a man she did not like. If he did more than once, the people would talk. It would not look right.

A man does not have to make a gift in recompense for a runaway marriage. Sometime later, he would probably make some gift to his father-in-law, but a man who had a woman given to him would be under more compulsion to make a gift to his father-in-law to show his appreciation.

An attempt to get a story of a runaway marriage was met with the statement, "But there's nothing to tell about that. They just got married, and lived together happily."

Story: Quanah and Tonarcy {Carlson}   Tonarcy was a woman of the Woʔa band that Quanah Parker was interested in.[1]

He invited a bunch of Indians to make a trip to Texas with him.

The young women all rode on horseback, so they could make side excursions for berries and wild grapes.

Tonarcy was riding horseback.

Quanah Parker was in a buggy, but he had a horse tied behind. Maybe he had his plan in mind. A short distance before the camping ground, Quanah stopped and got out. He got on his saddle horse and told his wife[2] to drive on, he wanted to ride awhile. He rode in the direction the women had gone.

Tonarcy and her sister {Erksey} were married to Cruz.

Quanah came over the hill and saw the women in the grapevines and plum trees, but he didn't see Tonarcy. He went on and found her some ways off. That was how he got to talk with her.

When the Indians got back from this trip to Texas, Tonarcy's father[3] was sick and the medicine man was doctoring him. The father lived by Cache, and her husband lived a long ways away from there.[4] It was a good excuse for Tonarcy to leave her husband.

Quanah Parker visited the sick father a lot. The Woʔa suspected something when they heard about this.

The father died.

The Woʔa wanted to question Tonarcy about what she had been doing, but she didn't return to Cruz. She stayed with her brother.[5]

Finally, she heard that the Woʔa intended to question her. That night she disappeared. She walked over to Quanah Parker's house and knocked on the door. He spoke to her in

1. The Family Record Book implies that Quanah took Tonarcy around 1891.
2. It is not clear who this might have been, as Quanah had several wives at this time, the early 1890s.
3. The father was Tenamaki (sometimes spelled Tenawaki), glossed in 1879 as Man with a Forehead (possibly *tenahpʉʔ* 'man', *kaʔi* 'forehead'). He was a local band chief, although his divisional affiliation is unclear. He died about 1890.
4. There is apparently no extant data on Comanche residential locations between 1879 (Hunt 1879) and 1897 (Long 1897). However, in contrast to Frank's comment, Cruz probably did live fairly close to Quanah. In 1897, Cruz lived on the "southwest side of Post Oak Creek twenty miles west of Ft. Sill" (Long 1897), that is, within ten or twenty miles of Quanah's original house site. There is apparently no specific data on where Tenamaki lived.
5. Peetsueni (no translation given), born about 1866.

English through the closed door. She said she was an Indian, so he asked in Comanche who it was. She said, "It's Tonarcy, open the door."

He let her in and she told him what she had heard. Quanah got his hired man {David Grantham} and told him to hitch the buggy. He took her across the river to Texas and left her with a white rancher who was his friend. Quanah came back the same night.

The next morning, he went to town. Cruz came to get his wife. Her relatives said that she had disappeared the night before and that they hadn't seen her since. Cruz sent two of his friends over to Quanah's place to see if they could find her. They asked for Quanah, and his wives said he had gone to town. They came back and told Cruz that they couldn't find the woman and that Quanah had gone to the traders. The Cruz bunch figured that Quanah had left Tonarcy with the trader near Fort Sill.[1] He sent two men to the trader. One man was to watch for Quanah from the timber. Those at the store were supposed to ask for goods from upstairs so they could look there.

{Hoebel[2]} Quanah came along and talked friendly to the men. He asked what they were doing there. He loaded the buggy with clothes for her and went home. The man came to the timber later, and guarded all night after Quanah had gone. They watched Quanah for four or five days, and then decided that she had gone off with someone else.

One night, when he was no longer being watched, he went down for her. They went on to Arizona to the Mescalero[3] Apaches. Her husband and his party came up, with Pahighpeop[4] and Isarekwini[5] with them. They were told about Quanah. They were mad. "Now it's time to kill that white man," meaning Quanah. "He's caused enough trouble, and now he's getting worse."

Cruz was a captive,[6] not well known among the Comanches. He lived with some Mexicans. When he heard the warriors talking big about killing Quanah, he said, "You don't dare do what you say." They said that they meant it. Cruz said he'd abide by their decision in the matter.

Frank's brother was Isarekwini's brother-in-law and a good friend of Quanah's. He wanted to avoid trouble and to help Quanah. He decided to wait and see Quanah on it.

1. The Red Store, so-called because of its red-painted false front. It was established in 1886 by the firm of Collier and Sneed (Hagan 1976:175), just south of Fort Sill, on what is now Rogers Road on the north side of Lawton. The building itself still exists at Eagle Park in Cache.

2. The second page of Carlson's story is missing, but the details are filled in here from Hoebel.

3. Given that they were going to the Mescaleros, their destination was New Mexico, not Arizona. A number of Comanches apparently fled to Mescalero after the Battle of Palo Duro Canyon in 1875. The 1889 Mescalero census lists at least one family headed by Comanche John.

At about the same time—the early 1890s—a number of Lipan Apaches at Mescalero transferred to the Comanches, apparently at Quanah's request. These included Chebatah and his brother Penaro, later credited with bringing the Peyote ritual to the Comanches. They were listed on the Mescalero censuses as late as 1888, and on the Comanche censuses as early as 1892.

4. *hai*, 'crow', *pia* 'big', Big Crow. He was listed as a member of Mowway's local Kutsutɥhka band in 1879, but by 1883 he was recognized as a local band leader on his own. He was born about 1854.

5. This name is as given. It is possibly Isatakewon, *isapU* 'liar', *tekwa* 'talk', given in 1885 as False Speaker. He was born about 1865, the son of Tabbytosavit (White Sun) and Tarsip (no translation given). He was associated with Komah's Kwaharɥnɥɥ local band.

6. See Index.

When Quanah returned, he sent word out to his friends that he was back. The other group met at Frank's brother's to decide what to do. They decided they wanted eight articles in *nanuwoku* including a matched dun team, a buggy, a saddle, a gun, and half his pay from the cattlemen—twenty five dollars a month—to Cruz as alimony. If they wouldn't accept this, they could do what they want, he would meet them.

Of the six, there was Cruz, his nephews and friends, and Frank's brother as go-between. The two nephews didn't expect anything out of it, but they wanted to get the wife, too. {Carlson[1]} . . . because they couldn't keep her if they did get her, and if they kept on arguing, they might end up getting no *nanuwoku* at all. It was up to Cruz to decide.

He thought it was all right. He would take the money. Isarekwini would take the team and the buggy, and Pahighpeop and the other men would get nothing. They agreed.

Frank's brother went back and told Quanah Parker. Quanah thanked him, and said he'd saved bloodshed on both sides.

Isarekwini got the team and buggy, and Cruz had twenty-five dollars a month until he died.[2]

Cruz's *ara?*'s were along to protect him. Only brothers and close friends could share the *nanuwoku* payment. Other relatives got nothing.

{Hoebel} Frank's brother advised them to accept; if they got the woman, she wouldn't stay anyway. Cruz accepted. He offered the buggy to Isarekwini. Pahighpeop and the others would get nothing. Cruz got twenty-five dollars a month until he died. Quanah was told of their acceptance and thanked the go-between for settling the matter without bloodshed.

She later went to Washington with him.

HOWARD WHITE WOLF
August 4, 1933[3]

War: Battle of Palo Duro Canyon   When Howard was about eight or nine years old,[4] his uncle {Esarosavit} and Tabenanaka were jointly *paraibos* of the Yapai band.[5] They were still going on the warpath at that time. The Quaker agent[6] finally called the two men in and advised them to settle down and behave, or else the government troops would punish them. But they said they would rather go out in the old way, to hunt and raid. The agent said if they did, they would be taken prisoner and confined, and all their horses would be taken and shot so that they would have to walk on foot.[7]

1. Here Carlson's narrative picks up again.
2. Cruz died about 1905.
·3. The content of this interview is from Wedel, with variations from Hoebel and Carlson, as noted.
4. According to the censuses, White Wolf was born in 1867. His statement here implies an earlier birth year—1865 or 1866—but it could also be that his estimate of his age then was a little bit off.
5. See Howard White Wolf, July 31.
6. Lawrie Tatum; see Tatum 1899.
7. There is no direct documentary confirmation of this claim.

Some of the people remained under Black Beaver,[1] another brave leader, but the main part of the Yapai went out west under White Wolf and Tabenanaka to do some devilment. They combined with the Kiowas, Cheyennes, and Arapahos.

Finally, they found that soldiers were right behind them with ten Wichita scouts. Tawakoni Jim[2] was captain of the scouts.

The Comanche scouts came in one morning and said the soldiers were right on their track, camping where the Indians had camped. They brought back canteens, hard tack, etc., dropped by the soldiers. When the scouts had reported, one of the *paraibo*s got up and called to his people in a loud voice. He told them the soldiers were after them, and he advised everyone to tie their horses at the tipis so they could move fast and save the women and children if they were attacked. Then they fled to a big canyon west {*sic*, Southeast} of Amarillo, Texas.[3]

The army was about ten miles behind at last report. "The Wichita scouts sure knew tracks fine."

The Comanches were the last to make camp, and their tipis were the farthest to the front. About daybreak, they heard the first guns as the soldiers attacked the rearmost camp. A *paraibo* got up and yelled, "We are attacked by the army."

Everyone was all excited and yelling.

tuhkɄhunubɪ[4] 'deep creek' was the name of the canyon.

Everything was already packed for an emergency, and at the *paraibo*'s call, they all fled, while the warriors turned back and fought to cover the retreat of the women.

There was only one way out of the canyon. Everyone was fighting to get out, dogs barking, horses neighing, women yelling, children crying, all at once. The soldier's horses were about paid out from the long ride, and the Indians got away. They escaped to a big rocky hill. The next morning, the *paraibo* told them where to move, all in a bunch.

In the old days, the warriors were supposed to do the fighting, and any man who stayed with his family was a coward.

The tipis were left behind in the flight.

So they got away from the soldiers. They went on a certain distance, but the soldiers trailed them for maybe a month or two until the Indian horses began to give out.

Finally, they got up to Pecan Creek, west of Hobart, Oklahoma,[5] and there the soldiers caught up with them. A scout came riding up and told the people that there was no use going further because the leading men had been captured by the army, and they might as well surrender.

---

1. There is no documented Comanche prereservation chief named Black Beaver. There was a man in Cheevers' local band in 1879–81 named Honetohavit, Black Beaver, but nothing more is known about him. At the same time, there was a prominent Wichita man called Black Beaver.

2. As his name implies, Tawakoni Jim was a prominent man amongst the remnant Tawakoni division of the Wichitas. However, his role in the Palo Duro campaign is not clear. Nye's history of Fort Sill (1969) does not mention him, nor is there any historical documentation of him or any group of Wichitas serving as scouts in the 1874 campaign.

3. Actually, the Palo Duro ('hard wood') Canyon is about thirty miles south of Amarillo, east of the town of Canyon, Texas. The battle of Palo Duro Canyon took place on September 27, 1874.

4. *tuhkatɄ*, 'deep', *hunubɪ* 'creek'.

5. Hobart is a small town on the far northwest corner of the old reservation.

The camp was in a great bend of the creek. The people could look far across the prairie and saw the flash of metal. An Indian woman raised a white flag.

When the soldiers came up, they herded the men into one place, and the women and children in another. There were guards all around. The woman who had raised the flag (White Wolf's wife[1]) was appointed by the troops to direct the women; she alone had the right to talk to the warriors. The soldiers searched everyone and took away all the bows and arrows, knives, spears, shields, and guns, and threw them all into a great fire, and left the Indians helpless.

After a few days, they marched the warriors back to the post. They asked the *paraibo* how many more Indians had gotten away and were still loose; the *paraibo* said they were about all present, nearly everybody had surrendered. Wichita scouts scoured the neighborhood for strays and rounded up everyone.

At the post, all the names were taken and checked.[2] The leading Indians were kept in chains while on the march, and all the warriors, save the *paraibo*, went on foot to the fort. The women were under guard, camped on the creek east of the fort. The leaders were placed in the guardhouse, and the other men, maybe all of them, were placed in two other long buildings. The length of their confinement was unknown.

Cheevers was appointed as boss of the men; he recommended women to see their husbands. The men were released ten or fifteen at a time. The leaders were held to the last. The horses were shot on the site of the new post at Fort Sill.

Camp Organization {Wedel}   When the Comanche bands all camped together, one band camped, then each of others went a little farther ahead, so the last arrivals were the farthest ahead.

There was no set order of departure.

Camp Organization {Hoebel}   When the whole tribe gathered, as for the Sun Dance, they formed a circle. First one band moved up; the next went beyond, etc., forming a circle. In an ordinary encampment, no circle was formed.

Camp Organization: Tipis: Domestic Arrangements   Each wife had a separate tipi. There was a large tipi for sleeping, where the clothing, blankets, etc. were kept. The shield was close behind it. It was called the *tʉbitsikahni* 'real tipi'. There was also a smaller tipi for cooking, storing food, etc., called *tʉhkakahni*, 'eating tipi'.

Camp Organizarion: Adolescent Lodge   Young men got a separate tipi at about twenty years of age. It was wrong for a young man to sleep in the same tipi with his father and sister. Sometimes, a dome-shaped shelter was covered with canvas for the young man. Others put up a regular tipi. It was kept in order by his mother or sister.

A sister <u>never</u> went into a brother's tipi while he was there. There was no special name for this. [Food was never taken to his tipi.]

Life Cycle: Children   Boys were more respected than girls because they were liable to be killed at anytime.

---

1. Since Esarosavit had several wives, it is not clear which one this was.

2. Rather than a full census of the Comanches, this is possibly a reference to Richard Pratt's notebook list of prisoners (Pratt 1875–77).

Life Cycle: Marriage: Residence   When they married, the girl came to his tipi. They ate with the boy's family.

When a boy wanted to marry, he brought the girl to his tipi overnight. If she stayed until daybreak they were considered married. If she didn't want to marry him, she left before dawn.

His mother might object to the match if the girl was flighty, lazy, frivolous, or quick tempered. Boys preferred girls who were raised at home and didn't run around.

Girls married at [fourteen[1]] fifteen or sixteen. Boys, as soon as they could, got a wife. They didn't have to go to war first.

[A boy didn't have to consult his mother before marriage.[2]]

If his mother disapproved of her son's choice of a wife, he usually sent the girl home again. Sometimes he would leave his people and go to live with his wife's people rather than give up the girl.

Life Cycle: Marriage: Divorce   In the case of divorce, each party took its own property. When a girl came home alone with her bundle, her parents noticed it and asked her what the trouble was. She said she'd separated from her husband and that was all there was to it. The woman took the tipi only if the man consented [if he were generous[3]]; otherwise she took only her personal belongings. If there were children ____ {sic}.

Life Cycle: Marriage: Divorce   Howard's son {Russell White Wolf} married at age eighteen. He met his wife at Santee, Neb.[4] The girl's father was dead and her uncle was her guardian. She wrote of the engagement, but her uncle protested and said no. Also, the boy's mother didn't want him to marry too soon. When they separated, the child was adopted by its paternal grandparents.

Life Cycle: Marriage: Divorce: Custody   Sometimes parents divided the children: the mother took the younger, and the father took the older. It also depended upon the grandparents.

If a couple had children, and all the grandparents were still living, the father kept both children.

If the woman went home crying, her parents would consider the status of her husband's father [kaku[5]]. If he was a good warrior, they wouldn't try to recover the children. [But if not, the maternal grandfather, the tokoʔ, would probably take them away. The sex of the children made no difference in the division.[6]]

Food: Food Plants: Corn   haniibi was corn; *tosaniibi* was white corn.

Life Cycle: Marriage: Residence   Sometimes a family went off and camped by itself, with one or two tipis. This was very dangerous. Maybe they wanted to hunt, etc.

Story: False Incest Claim   Once, in a big camp, a man got away with his wife and sister and set up their own tipi some distance off.

---

1. From Hoebel and Carlson.
2. From Carlson.
3. From Hoebel.
4. There were two Indian boarding schools at Santee: the Santee Normal Training School, run by the Congregational Church to train teachers, and the Santee Industrial School, run by the BIA. It is not clear which one Russell White Wolf attended.
5. From Carlson.
6. From Carlson.

There were many enemies.

They had two tipis.

About midnight, a man went and lay with his sister. She didn't know who the man was. [She knew there were no other men about, and that her brother must have committed incest.[1]] The next morning, the man's wife said to his sister, "Eat," but the sister said, "I don't want to."

The wife asked, "Are you sick, sister?"

"No."

Wife: "Then why don't you eat?"

Finally, the sister said, "I hate to tell you."

The wife said, "Why? I'll help you if there's any trouble."

Then the sister said, "Last night a man came to my bed and lay with me all night. My brother was the only man here; he must have been the man; that's what hurts me."

The wife said she was glad to know.

The man went hunting and came back to supper. His sister didn't eat and the wife asked her why. She repeated the story, saying her brother was only man there.

The man swore that he hadn't done it. Finally, he called his sister and said he would rather die than lay with his sister. It must have been an enemy who had found the camp. "We will find out tonight when you go to bed. Tie a rope to your leg (or hand) and bring it over to my tent. When the man comes to lay with you, just pull the rope and I'll come get him."

So they did this and went to bed.

Presently, she heard another man come; he got into bed and had his way with her. She pulled the cord and her brother got up, taking his knife, went in, and killed the man. He was an enemy. [A Pawnee man in another version.[2]] The brother hadn't slept with his sister at all.

They had two tipis. They broke camp right away and traveled all night to get back to the main camp. They told the people what had happened. This was a true story.

Camp Organization: Tipis: Sleeping Arrangements   Children usually slept against the west wall, the parents on the north or south at will. Children up to six or seven slept with their parents. Later they slept in their own separate beds, with the sexes segregated.

Story: Comanches and Pawnees   Another man went off alone with his wife. Every night the man would light his pipe and blow the smoke upward toward the east, and he extended it up as though handing it to another man. He would say, "Take my smoke and bless me, TukaanItʉ."[3] (Comanche custom)

A large Pawnee war party was not far away. One warrior, the *paraibo*, wandered over and found the tipi. The Pawnee was named Tukabit.

When the Comanche said, "Take my smoke, TukaanItʉ," the Pawnee was standing at the door and he took the pipe. He said {with signs}, "Yes, I'll take your pipe. You have called on me; your life will be saved. There are many Pawnees (here raising both hands

1. From Carlson.
2. From Carlson. It is not clear what this "other version" was.
3. *tukanI* 'night'.

to side of his head and raising an index and middle fingers like a wolf's ears) and warriors nearby. Move your camp right away and you'll be saved."

They broke camp right away and traveled all night to get back to the main camp. They told the people what happened. This was a true story.

Political Organization: Chiefs   Howeah, Sumuno, Tipenavon[1] ('Painted Mouth'), Poyawetoyah[2] ('Iron Mountain'), Mowway, and Quitsquip[3] ('chewing') were Yapai[4] *paraibo*s.

Terheryahquahip and Onawia[5] were Nokoni *paraibo*.

[There were eight or ten *paraibo*s in the Yapainuu.]

Political Organization: Chiefs   One man was appointed to be camp *paraibo* when the band was all in one camp. He was chosen by all the *paraibo*. [When the band was in a single camp, this group as council would elect one as head chief.[6]] Ten Bears was the main *paraibo*.

A successful war leader would be made a war *paraibo*. He had to be consulted when peace was made.

Political Organization: Chiefs: Insignia   (The Kiowa war *paraibo* had a buckskin shirt with horsehair. There was no special badge of office for a Comanche *paraibo*.)

(*tekwawapI*[7] was an interpreter.)[8]

Political Organization: Chiefs: War Leader   A *tekwUniwapI* was a brave warrior. The *paraibo* had nothing to do with war.

Material Culture: Clothing: Headdress   Headdresses with buffalo horns but no feathers, a "rawhide with little fur on it" (deer roach), reached to between the shoulder blades. A wearer never deserted his men in battle. There were not many in a band. In case of a retreat, he was last to leave the field, covering the retreat.

A *tekwUniwapI* could also wear a bonnet of gray fox or otter skin.

If he retreated ahead of his men, a *tekwUniwapI* lost his headdress and was demoted and called "woman."

[He couldn't retreat directly. He must ride back and fourth behind the other's retreat as cover.]

Material Culture: Crafts: Hide Work: Buckskin Making   The hide was pegged out and treated like a buffalo hide with brains and liver or spleen and was soaked in warm water. The hair was scraped off with a rib beamer. The hide was laid over a framework of poles

1. *tupe* 'mouth', *naboo?* 'painted'. According to Joe Attocknie (MS), he accompanied Paruasumuno to Washington in 1863, although that has not been confirmed. He signed the 1867 Treaty of Medicine Lodge Creek, but he must have died before 1879, for his name does not appear on any census.

2. *puhiwi* 'metal', *toya* 'mountain'. He signed the 1865 Treaty of the Little Arkansas and is listed as a local band leader in the early reservation period, 1879–83, but he is not listed thereafter.

3. Quitsquip, *kutsukwipU*, usually translated as 'Chewing' or 'Chew-up', sometimes as 'Elk's Cud' or 'Chewing Elk'.

4. Mowway is usually considered to be a Kutsutuhka.

5. *ona* 'salt', *wia* 'worn away spot'. Known as Salt Gap, Onawia was Yapainuu.

6. From Hoebel.

7. Wedel's notes has "tekwɔwʌp" [*tekwawapI*], which Robinson and Armagost (1990) glosses as 'speaker, spokesman', while giving *tekwakutU* as 'interpreter'.

8. This parenthetical sentence is in the typescript of Wedel's Notebook 5, but not in the original manuscript. Its source is unknown.

and smoked over a fire of tree fungus to get the yellow color. The hair was removed by scraping with a buffalo rib beamer while the hide was stretched over a log.

Hunting: Traps   Old style traps were not known to Howard. There were no deadfalls.

Hunting: Fur   Beaver and otter are very sharp. One should never to be on dry land when setting traps, because they can smell you. The nature of the traps was unknown.

Beaver and otter were used for young men's hair dressing.

Medicine: Otter Medicine   Pregnant women wore a belt of otter skin, with the tail hanging down in front on the left side. They had fine beadwork as well, bangles attached at the end of the pendent portion. Sometimes two skins, with both tails hanging together, were worn.

Otter was very smooth and slick when it came out of the water, nothing hindered it. So too the child would be born easily if the woman wore an otter skin belt.[1] It was rarely worn as an ornament at other times.

Life Cycle: Childhood: Weaning; Animal Powers: Porcupine   When a child was about a year old, the mother was probably in the family way, so her milk was not good and the child's stomach was bad.

They took the quills (which the porcupine could throw at you) and put them in the fire and the child smelled the smoke. Then it quit nursing and took its own food. Sometimes six or eight quills were stuck in a buckskin thong that was then tied about a child's neck to hasten weaning.

Animal Powers: Porcupine   *yʉhnʉ* was porcupine. The mother porcupine always left the young as soon as they were born. This porcupine magic made children able to fend for themselves very early.

A man who deserted his family was called *yʉhnʉ*.

Life Cycle: Childhood: Weaning: Medicine   A man once had an eight-month old child. The mother was in the family way, and her milk was spoiling. The child was crying so much that the father was worried, he thought the child would die.

He had a dream. It asked him if he saw a horse that ate grass day and night, which had a good appetite. He was told to mix remedies and feed the child twice daily, and always to keep food under his pillow and feed the child when it cried at night, and finally it would forget about milk and eat meat. It would have an appetite like the horse.

The remedy was to take the "button" from inside the horse's front leg and the seed of *pawahkapʉ*,[2] grind it fine, and boil thoroughly, then strain it and feed the child. He was also to bathe the child with it and take some in his mouth and blow it into a child's rectum, on the kidney, and to place some up the child's nose; the child would be healthy and get fat.

Howard doubted this. He told his wife, who told another pregnant woman with a small child in a cradle. The child was very weak. The mother asked Howard to doctor it, even though he wasn't a doctor. Howard finally tried it; he doctored four times and very soon the child was crying for food, so he gave it some bread and the child soon forgot about milk and took solid food. Later, Howard doctored three other children and cured them all.

1. Wallace and Hoebel 1952:143.
2. Robinson and Armagost (1990) gives this as "an herb (name unknown; grows near creeks)."

Hunting: Birds   Comanches rarely ate prairie chicken, quail, or similar small game.

Hunting: Falls   Buffalo were once inadvertently driven over a cliff and killed.

Hunting: Fire   Fire was never used to get buffalo.

Medicine: Curing: Snake Bite   Howard heard of a few cases in the old days where the wound was cut and the poison sucked out.

Howard once attended a Cheyenne camp meeting where a Cheyenne woman was bitten. They tried rattles, but the Cheyennes said, "No go."

Finally, they came to Howard. He said, "Yes," his friend could cure it. So the woman's son or husband came to him with a cigarette. They said the woman was suffering and would die, and they wanted a cure. The man went to the missionary for permission to cure in the old way. The missionary said it was OK if he used herbs. So the Comanche cured her.

Howard's wife was bitten shortly after their marriage by a snake. They stopped at a white woman's place. She said to apply chicken; it was no good. The doctor gave alcohol; it was no good. Finally, they went to an Indian doctor and smoked with him. The doctor examined the leg; it was badly swollen. So he began to doctor. He drew a black mark about the thigh above the swelling. He said if the swelling passed the mark he had failed, that the medicine was no good. Then he began to suck on the wound on the ankle until they were opened. Soon they could see yellow stuff come out; it smelled bad. She was cured after a couple of hours; the swelling went down. The doctor said if Howard had good teeth, he could suck the poison out anywhere. The same was with spider.[1]

ATAUVICH

August 7, 1933[2]

Piamupits   The Comanches scared their children with threats of Piamupits.

Story: The Buffalo Hunter and Piamupits   Once a hunter went out alone for buffalo with a pack mule. He killed a buffalo and set it up to skin it. Piamupits came up, but the hunter didn't notice him. The hunter got the skin off one side and walked around to the other side. Then he saw Piamupits. The hunter was scared, but he was afraid to show it. He said, "*Haitsl*, just sit there. When I get this skinned, I'll give you some."

Piamupits said, "No, I don't want any of that meat. I'll eat you."

The hunter said, "Wait until I get the meat packed on the animals and start towards camp. Then you can do what you please."

When the hunter got the meat loaded on the pack mule, he whipped his buffalo horse to make it lively. When Piamupits was not looking, he jumped on and ran. Piamupits chased him, but couldn't catch him.

Piamupits called out, "I'll get you yet." He didn't try to catch the pack mule.

The next year, in midsummer, the camp broke up. The hunter could not find his horses,

---

1. This is the end of Wedel's Notebook 5.
2. These notes are from Carlson. The order is arbitrary.

so he was out looking for them while the rest of the camp was moving on. While he was gone, his little boy noticed something coming toward the camp. It was Piamupits. The woman didn't know what to do. She closed the smoke vents and lashed a stiff rawhide across the door.

By that time, Piamupits was sitting on the door trying to untie the knots. The man came home with the horses. He saw Piamupits. He said to himself, "Well, Piamupits said he'd get me. I'm a man. I'm a little man, but still I'm a big man."

He came towards the tent thinking what could he do to save himself and his family.

He took the pole holding the smoke flap. He broke off a fourth of it. Piamupits did not notice him, he had his back to the man. The man shoved the sharp end of the pole in Piamupits's anus. Piamupits walked away and lay down. The man called to his people that he'd hurt Piamupits, and for them to get out and away as fast as they could.

They ran out, caught their horses and got away as fast as possible. Finally, they caught up with the main camp and told them what had happened. The man said he thought he had killed Piamupits.

The announcer said they must go out and see what had happened.

The next morning, the men set out to investigate. The hunter's family went along to find what had happened to their belongings. When they got over the hill, they could see the camp as they had left it, and Piamupits, swollen up dead.

Piamupits looked like a giant man.

His skin was so tough you could not pierce it.

Kinship Relations: Incest   A boy and a girl who were not blood relations could marry, even though they were brought up together.

Kinship Relations: Terminology   Atauvich's first wife {unidentified} was raised with him and he called her *namiʔ*.

Kinship Relations: Terminology   *samohpʉʔ* was a brother-sister term used for a husband's brother's wife and a wife's sister's husband. It was not used to a person who was not related by marriage.

Captives   A captive could probably not marry into the family that had caught him. He would be considered a real son. If a captive wasn't much good, they'd sell him to another tribe.

One Kiowa, Sawekit,[1] was a Comanche captive who was sold to the Kiowas for four ponies. In this case, the people who captured him were very poor and needed the horses, so they sold him. It was a custom from way back to sell captives.

It was easier to sell a woman than a man.

If a man had three full blood wives and one captive wife, it was the captive who did all the work. A man could not sell a captive wife if she was the mother of his child.

Dances: Horse Dance   Atauvich's favorite dance was the Horse Dance.[2] When he was young, his *araʔ*, Woodauhaupith,[3] aged fifty-three,[4] was the leader of this group. He sang the

---

1. Otherwise unidentified.
2. It is not clear if this was the *tuepukunʉʉ*, Little Ponies, or another group. See Part Two.
3. *wʉraohapitʉ* 'yellow bear', was a member of Quanah's Kwaharʉnʉʉ local band.
4. He was about fifty years old in 1885, the last year he was listed on the census.

songs to Atauvich as a child and taught him how to dance, so Atauvich joined the group when he grew up.

Story: The Fox and the Doe   Fox was wandering around and he ran into a doe with fawns. Fox liked the fawns; he had young ones himself, and he thought the fawns were the prettiest children he had seen in a long time. He stood around and looked.

Finally, he asked the doe, "What did you do to make these little ones so nice and speckled?"

The doe answered, "I dug a hole in the ground and built a big fire in it. Then I put the fawns in it. The sparks flew up and burned them, and the speckles are the scars."

So Fox went home and talked with his wife. He told her how he saw some awfully pretty fawns, nice and speckled. He asked his wife, how about it. He liked the looks of the young fawns. The mother asked if he got information on how to do it and Fox said he did, so she said they could try it if he wanted to.

She built a fireplace and Fox talked to his young ones. He told them how pretty they were going to look. The little Foxes were glad. They hopped around anxious to get in the hole.

He put them in, one by one. Finally, all were in and he plugged the hole. After a while, the young foxes began to holler. It was hot and they wanted to get out. Fox stood at the door and held it, so they couldn't get out. Finally, there was no more noise. Fox looked in. All the little foxes were roasted.

The mother came up and they began an argument. They blamed each other. Mother Fox said, "You are always trying to cheat somebody, now you got cheated."

This story was also told of Fox and Wildcat.

Story: Fox and the Berries   Fox ate some berries, they looked so nice. The berries had warned him that they would give him an itch, but Fox wanted to prove it. It was a custom to rub some of the berries on the hind end, and Fox did. His hind end began to itch. He scratched it. Then he began to run it on a rock. He rubbed until you could see his backbone.

Finally, he met some of his friends. They asked him why his hind end was sore and bleeding.

Fox said he ate some berries that gave him an itch. The rest of the Foxes stood around and made fun of him.

Story: Fox and the Birds   Some little birds were throwing their eyes at a willow tree and they would fall back in place. Fox came along, and said that he wished he had the power to do that. He asked them for the power.

The birds gave him the power. They told him not to throw his eyes on grayish willows, only on yellow willows. They said they didn't have much confidence in Fox, and if he didn't mind the rules, he'd hurt himself.

He went along, trying the trick. He would throw his eye on a yellow willow and it would come right back. He had the power alright.

Fox said, "I can't see why I shouldn't try the other willows, maybe it would give me more power."

He pitched his eye on a grayish willow and the eye stuck there. He went on and came to some more little birds.

They saw Fox only had one eye and knew what had happened. One of them flew back to the first little birds to ask them to replace Fox's eye before sundown, when it would be too late.

Fox took them to where he had thrown the eye. One of the birds reminded him that they had said he would disobey the rules.

They got the eye for him and took him back to the yellow willows. He tried throwing his eye, and still had the power. They took the power away from him. They couldn't trust Fox.

Story: How Fox Showed a Man How He Worked Tricks   Once Fox was sitting by a crossroad. A man came by on a pacing horse. He asked Fox what he was doing, Fox said he was having a rest. The man asked Fox what his name was. Fox said, "Ohaahnakatʉ."[1]

The man said, "You are the person who likes to cheat people. How do you cheat people?"

Fox said, "Just any way I can."

The man sat there on horseback. He didn't get off. He said, "While I sit here on my horse, I want you to cheat me."

Fox said, "I can't do any cheating now, I left my medicine at home."

The man said, "I will lend you my horse so you can go get your medicine."

Fox got on and paced off. He went a little way and the horse stopped and backed. Fox said, "Probably the horse was not familiar with my clothes. Loan me your blanket."

Finally, Fox had all the man's clothes. Then he went off. When he got to the top of the hill, he called back, "That's the way I cheat people."

Story: The Owner of the Buffalo   Once there was a selfish man who penned up all the buffalo. He had plenty of meat and everyone else had none.

One day, this man was out walking around. He was carrying his bow and arrow and shield. At his shield, he had a piece of sinew fastened. While he was wandering around, he met some of the people. They were playing *aratsiˀ*.

While he was looking on, he felt the need to urinate, so he hung his bow and quiver on a bush and went out in the woods.

While he was gone, a crow came along. In those days, crow was white.

He looked at the quiver. There was some fat still on the sinew. He smelled it and rubbed it in his mouth. It tasted good.

He took a bit of fat off the sinew and showed it to the players. They all smelled it. They were hungry and had nothing to eat.

The people suspected something. This was fresh fat and the man must have got it somewhere. After the game, they watched the man, but he disappeared and nobody knew which way he had gone.

All the people and animals got together to have a meeting. They discussed things. They appointed two to watch, Alligator and Fox. They watched closely and saw someone up on a hill.

---

1. 'He has yellow armpits', usually a nickname for Coyote.

The people began to play a game to draw his attention. The person began to come towards them, and they saw it was the same man. He stood there a while, watching, then hung his bow and quiver on a bush and went off into the woods.

The people were watching him, particularly the two scouts.

The man came back and took his bow and quiver.

Finally, he thought no one was looking at him. He went straight up in the air. They watched him. He lit way up north at the foot of the mountains and they lost sight of him.

They selected two to go investigate. They chose Fox and Quail.

The two scouts went out and kept going and going. Finally, it got dark and they couldn't see. Finally, they saw a light in a camp. They discussed which of them could travel noiselessly, and Fox thought Quail could, so Quail went to investigate.

Quail went and located the tipi. There were three people inside, a man, a woman, and a little boy about four years old.

Quail motioned for Fox to come, and Fox crept up as quietly as he could.

Quail motioned for him to look and Fox saw the three people.

The Fox wanted to go back, but Quail wanted to stay and find out more about these people.

While they were waiting, they heard the boy cry for something to eat. The man said, "Well, we might as well eat."

The woman took down a parfleche full of dried meat all pounded and ready to eat. The Fox had stepped away, but Quail saw this. Quail motioned for Fox to come. When Fox saw the meat, he couldn't stand it.

The man asked the woman how much they had left. She said the parfleche was only a quarter full. The man said they must kill another beef tomorrow.

That was what Quail and Fox wanted to know, so they started back. Fox was anxious to get back, but Quail still wanted to stay and find out more about these people.

When they got back and reported what they had seen, the people discussed it. Finally, they decided that these people must have all the buffaloes penned up somewhere. They decided to move the camp down by this tipi, and they did.

The woman saw them coming and told her husband. He said, "What do you mean by coming here?"

The man suspected they must have found something out and told his wife and son not to give anything away, to keep things quiet.

The people got through setting up camp. They selected several men to visit this man. The man told them to come in and asked what they wanted.

They said they were hungry and asked for something to eat.

The man told the visitors that they had nothing to eat, they were hungry too.

The visitors stayed there, but he gave them nothing to eat.

Every once in a while, one of them would get discouraged and get up and go home. Some stayed until sundown before they gave up and went home.

The three people didn't want to kill a buffalo while the people were around, so pretty soon they ran out of meat and began to get hungry.

Fox came to camp and visited an old woman. The old woman asked what he wanted. He said he wanted something to eat, he was hungry. The old woman said she was hungry too, but she said that the tipi down there had been there a long time and they probably had plenty to eat.

Fox went down there but he couldn't get anything to eat.

Fox asked the chief when they were going to move. The chief said they had given up hope of getting anything here and were going to leave. Fox said he'd get meat if they let him have his way. He would lay around as a little puppy when the camp moved.

The next morning, the announcer cried that they were going to move, that there was no meat supply there, and somewhere else they might find some roots or herbs.

Fox turned himself into a little puppy.

The tipi that had been there before was still there.

When the people were gone, the woman and the little boy came out to pick up what things might have been left behind. They poked under bedding to see if they could find anything.

They found the puppy under a bush. The little boy picked it up. The mother didn't like it. She thought that the pup might give away the secret of the meat supply, but the little boy cried, so the mother didn't say anything more about it.

The boy took close care of the puppy, for fear that his mother or father might kill it. He took it to bed with him.

The father was away at this time. When the man returned, the boy showed him his pup. The man was afraid, and told the boy to throw it away, but the boy held it close.

That night the boy went to bed with it. The father and mother said that when the boy got to sleep, they'd kill it.

Fox kept the boy awake by tickling him, so they had no chance.

The next morning, the father and mother left the boy in camp alone. The boy was anxious to show the puppy the buffaloes. He had the pup in his arms and opened the gate.

Fox could see the buffaloes crowded up inside. There was nothing in sight but buffaloes. It was a trap in the ground.

The boy sicced the Fox, trying to make him bark, but Fox was tricky, he acted afraid, and tried to back away. The boy took him back to camp.

That night the boy told his father and mother that he'd shown the puppy the buffaloes. So they got after him, asking him what he meant, that the dog might give away the secret. The boy said, "No, he was afraid, he tried to back away."

The parents told him not to take the puppy there again. The boy said, "Oh, I want to have fun with him. Those buffaloes aren't cute like my little dog."

The next day, the boy played all day with the Fox.

That night, the man and woman lifted the cover. They were going to get the little dog, but Fox scratched the little boy's ribs and woke him, so they had to give up.

The next morning, the father went away again and the mother was out working around. The boy decided to show the pup the buffaloes again. He opened the trap door. Fox backed off as if he were afraid.

Suddenly, he jumped through the door among the buffalo. The boy was afraid his dog would get hurt and cried for help, but no help came. The mother scolded the boy and said that when the man came home, they'd probably both get a whipping.

It was nearly noon when the man got back. His wife told him what had happened. He went to look. He opened the trap door and could hear someone yelling. The buffaloes were milling around inside, and suddenly they came through the gate like water going over its banks.

Inside, Fox kept yelling to the buffaloes that there was better land above and that they should go and investigate.

It took the buffaloes all day and a part of the night to go through the door; by dawn most of them were out.

The woman was crying all this time. She hated to lose all this good meat. Finally, the man got her to stop crying. They got clubs and went to the gate. They were going to kill Fox when he came out.

The very last buffalo to come out was an old bull whose hair was loose, and who looked scabby. It was Fox. They didn't know this, and expected to see Fox come out behind the bull. When Fox got a ways off, he turned back into himself. He called, "Now I've worked you. When you want meat, come to our camp."

The buffalos then scattered all over.

Fox was anxious to spread the news. He went down to the camp to tell them. He looked up the old woman and asked her if she had heard any news. She said, "No."

He asked her for something to eat, but she said she had nothing. Fox told her that there were now plenty of buffaloes, he had worked the family that had them. He told her to tell the chief.

When the chief heard it, he didn't dispute, he believed. He had the announcer tell what Fox had done, and tell everyone to fix up their hunting horses.

The people went out and killed all the buffaloes they wanted and came back to camp. The women sliced the meat. That was all the food they had, just the meat.

Three or four days passed. At first, the white crows didn't notice them. Then they saw that they had plenty of meat. They came back and cried "*tutsukamaru, tutsukamaru,*"[1] 'it don't taste good', thus spoiling the meat.

Fox was proud of himself. He wouldn't go to the old woman's to eat. He went to the chief's tipi to eat.

The chief told Fox that he was a wise person and he wanted information from him: Why wasn't the meat tasting good?

Fox went out and ran around, wriggling his tail. He came back and said the crows were spoiling the meat. They must catch two.

The chief asked, "How?"

Fox said they would do it with a horsehair noose where a buffalo was killed.

They caught two crows and tied them in the smoke vent. The crows cried, "*tutsukamaru.*" After four days, the crows had turned black and were saying "*ka?ka.*"

These crows were a little larger than the crows of today.

---

1. *tutsu* 'bad', *kamaru* 'taste'.

They asked Fox what he was going to do with the birds. Fox told the crows that from then on, they were not to say *"tʉtsʉkamaru,"* but *"kaʔka."* They were to be black for as long as the Indians had meat. They would say *"kaʔka"* and the meat would taste good. Crows would only be allowed to eat the fat inside the eyes, and the guts.

(This story was sometimes told as "How The Crows Got Black.")

NEMARUIBETSI

August 8, 1933[1]

Medicine: Herbs   *pohóobi*, sage, was pounded, soaked in water, and strained; it was used for the eyes. Sometimes salt was added.

Medicine: Eye Trouble   There was very little eye trouble in the old days.

Medicine: Teeth   If an old person had a loose tooth, they heated a bone and placed it against the tooth to remove the pain. There was no pulling. The tooth was usually good.

A tree fungus was used for toothache; it was not heated. It was a small brown toadstool.

Medicine: Herbs

wapokopI was spread on a blanket and dried for winter use.

seheriabi[2] was a tree root used for constipation [or urinal stoppage]. It was like a willow. The root mainly was used. It was pounded, boiled, strained, and drunk cool. It was either for constipation or diarrhea.

It was good for swelling. The cure was revealed to Nemaruibetsi's husband while very sick. [Nemaruibetsi's husband was sick with a swollen penis. A medicine man had a dream and learned of this medicine; he used it the next day and reduced the swelling.]

Sage was pounded, made into tea, and fed to children with colic. It was sweetened with sugar.

pesotai[3] bark was peeled off and the inner bark scraped out and made into tea. It was fed to children with constipation. [They peeled the willow bark very thin. They took the layer of tissue between the bark and the tree, and made a tea of it and drink it.]

Medicine: Curing: Sore Throat   *kuitsyan*[4] were swollen tonsils in children. They stuck a finger on a hot coal, then touched the sore in the throat, and it went down.

The Kiowas once had much trouble with this sickness and came to the Comanches for a cure.

When a grown person had throat trouble (e.g., as in smallpox), they cut a narrow strap, about six inches long by a quarter of an inch wide, wrapped it with cord or sinew, and

---

1. This is the beginning of Wedel's Notebook 6. Variations from Hoebel.
2. Carlson and Jones (1940) identifies this as *Andropogon scoparius*, false indigo.
3. Carlson and Jones (1940) identifies this as *Cephalanthus occidentalis*, buttonbush.
4. Robinson and Armagost (1990) has *kuitsI* as 'throat', *kuitsiwatʉ* as 'sore throat'. The Comanche Language Committee (1993) has *kuitswai* as 'medical treatment in the throat'.

soaked it in water until it was soft. Then they stuck it into the patient's throat to clear the throat.

nakuitsiwai was the leather gadget.[1]

A necklace was made from the bone of a turkey's windpipe; the bone was cut into segments, strung alternately with beads, and worn to protect children against throat trouble.[2] It was called *korohkO*.[3]

Adornment: Breastplate   The bone breastplate was called *tsuhni korohkO*.

The beaded necklace with two small pouches of medicine tied at the bottom as a charm against sickness was ⟨mata⟩. It came from the inside of a horse's leg; it was used for weaning children.

Medicine: Charms   Crow feathers were put in a child's forelock for protection against ghosts (spasms).[4] Ghosts were probably afraid of crows.

Adornment: Hair Care   The forelock was braided and left hanging, just for pretty.

Animals: Birds: Crow   *tuwikaaʔ* was the crow.

War Parties: Full Moon   War parties went on raids at the time of the full moon. There were no beliefs about the effects of the moon on meat, etc.

Animals: Dogs   They were afraid to kill dogs in the old times, they might lose some children if they did. [This still held. Howard White Wolf tried to get Waldo to kill one for him. His sister had a flock of dogs and he was afraid to kill them.]

Sometimes all the dogs in camp would go out for a communal hunt.

A childless couple might take care of a dog, feed it, carry it on horseback when on the move.

Nemaruibetsi had a large dog [she had no children]. Once, when moving camp, the dog, which was used to riding, sat down and began to howl. The dog was in the family way. Nemaruibetsi finally got her grandmother to let the dog ride on a packhorse. The pack got disarranged and Nemaruibetsi's horse ran away. The dog was beaten by an old man. That night the pups were born and all but two were drowned by her grandmother.

Cats were *waaʔooʔ*; there were none in the old days.

Nemaruibetsi knew of a pet raccoon that was kept for a long time. A coyote pup was also kept for a short time. The raccoon dug the marrow out of soup bones with a stick.

They put a beaded necklace on the coyote. They took meat out to where they had caught it and finally let it go.

[They caught a baby coyote. It was not kept long. They were afraid of bad luck. They put a bead necklace around its neck. They put it back and talked to it. They left meat there for its mother.]

paruukuʔ was raccoon.

pahtsikwasi,[5] opossum, was not eaten.

pisunii, skunk, was eaten. It was first roasted with the hide on or on a rack. You had to

1. Wallace and Hoebel 1952:169–70.
2. Wallace and Hoebel 1952:169.
3. *korohkO* is generic for 'necklace'.
4. Wallace and Hoebel 1952:160.
5. *pahtsi* 'slick', *kwasi* 'tail'.

be careful in skinning it.

Material Culture: Clothing: Robes   Skunk skins were used for robes. It was cleaned up until very white inside. It took a lot of skins.

Skunk, coyote, and bear were used for robes.

Two bears (*wasape*) would make a robe.

It took about four gray wolves, if large, or eight coyote hides[1] to make a robe.

Robes of rabbit skin were made for children, but they tore easily. There were no twisted rabbit-fur robes. Rabbit tails were fastened to the belt to keep a child from bed-wetting.

Material Culture: Clothing: Winter: Overshoes {Wedel}   There were rawhide overshoes, hairside inside, with a strap over the seam as a welt. *puhurasubua*[2] 'overshoes' were worn with a sort of cloth sock. The sole was larger than the sole of the foot. It was turned up about the edges. The sole and the lower shoe were slightly greased.

Material Culture: Clothing: Winter: Overshoes {Hoebel}   Hide boots, *puhurasubua*, with the hair on the inside (to the knee).[3] There was a piece of skin sewn across the seams to keep them warm and to make them watertight. They were loose fitting, not tight like moccasins. The soles were folded up higher on the sides. Cloth was folded over the feet for socks. The soles and foot, but not the legs, were greased.[4]

Material Culture: Clothing: Winter: Caps   They used caps of buffalo calf skin, coyote skin, etc. in the winter to cover the ears.

War Parties   War parties went out winter and summer, and fought in the raw.

Animal Powers: Wolf   The Lobo wolf gave a man medicine against cold. [With power from a wolf, a man won't feel cold. On raids in the winter, they took a Wolf Medicine Man along.]

When they met the enemy, they undressed and painted up. The medicine man had to howl four times like a wolf to give the resistance to cold to his comrades [in transferring his medicine on raids].

He needed no shoes or other clothes, no matter how cold. [A Wolf Medicine Man could walk in snow barefooted.[5]]

Ticeahkie[6] had Wolf Medicine. He got it from a woman named Yohya[7] ['hurry'].

On his inner shield was a picture of a coyote. The cover had seven spots about the periphery. There were two eagle downy feathers and two scissortail feathers in the center spot. It had a plain white background.

Bullets couldn't kill a wolf, but an arrow could. You would find bullet marks on a wolf if it was shot with an arrow.

Medicine: Wolf Sickness   A certain man was killed in war. His daughter went away from the

---

1. Contra Wallace and Hoebel 1952:194.
2. *puhu* 'wooly', *ta* 'foot'.
3. Wallace and Hoebel 1952:78.
4. Wallace and Hoebel 1952:79.
5. Wallace and Hoebel 1952:203.
6. This is the agency spelling. Wedel spells the name Taisɔkai, Hoebel spells it Tisikai. It is translated on the censuses as Corn Planter, but that is unattested. The Family Record Book lists him as "age 51 . . . Mexican captive . . . Parents unknown . . . Captured by Comanches when four years old."
7. Robinson and Armagost (1990) gives *yohyakatu* as 'hurry' (-*katu* 'possessor'). She is otherwise unidentified.

camp, weeping.

Near a tree, she saw a wolf coming toward her. She tried to climb the tree. The wolf got her by the leg and pulled her down and was biting her leg. She called for help and the people came out. The wolf fled.

But every time someone touched her she made a sound like a wolf. They took her to a medicine man. He said to go out and kill the wolf, skin it, and bring it back.

The people went out, shot at the wolf with guns but didn't kill it. Finally, they shot it with bow and arrow. [They found powder marks on the skin from bullets.]

They skinned it and painted the tip of the nose red. They removed the cover of the tipi door, and put the wolf skin over the door, with its head down and facing inward. They asked the wolf to take the sickness from the girl. The girl had been getting worse, hollering like a wolf. She quieted when the skin was brought in.

The medicine man continued doctoring. The patient was out of her head, She came to when the hide was brought in. She spoke and said she felt better and asked for a drink.

The medicine man demanded a gray horse, saddle, blanket, and a silver-mounted bridle as pay. They always ask for four things.

Whatever was used for the door belonged to the medicine man always, so he took the wolf skin in this case. His wife tanned it, and he drew a wolf at the top of the hide. He used it as a shield cover.

The shield was always put facing the sun, on a forked stick turned during day to follow the sun.

The medicine man put the wolf skin over his shield, with the head hanging over the face of the shield, the tail over the back side.

It was Ekarərə[1] 'blush' who was bitten by the wolf in the above case.[2]

Medicine: Wolf Medicine   Wolf Medicine was given to very few; probably by going to a lonely place?

Kawertzene[3] 'Doesn't Get Enough to Eat' had the Wolf Medicine in the above case.

Medicine: Transfer   Wives could prevent men from getting medicine.

Medicine: Medicine Women   Medicine women could get power only after the death of their husbands. Medicine women were usually widows. A brave man who expected to die anytime {soon} would teach his wife his power; she had no power until his death, then

---

1. *eka* 'red'. Otherwise unidentified.
2. Wallace and Hoebel 1952:167.
3. This is the agency spelling, where it is translated as 'Long Hungry'. Both Wedel and Hoebel spell it phonetically as kewɜtsəmi and translate it as 'Doesn't Get Enough to Eat' and 'Not Enough to Eat' respectively. Mooney (1898:195) spells it Ka-ati-wertz-ama-na in the caption of a William S. Soule portrait, and, in an undated "Additions and Corrections," commented:

This name, as written on the photograph furnished by former agent Lawrie Tatum, seems to be a corrupted Comanche form, but neither the name nor the picture can be identified by the Indians to whom it has been submitted. He is described in the inscription as "a brave man, not afraid of any Indian." [Mooney 1898:445]

Perhaps he was unidentified because the photograph was shown only to Kiowas.

Kewertzene was the son of Mowway. He is listed as a local band leader on the 1879 and 1885 censuses, but he must have died sometime between 1885 and 1889 for he is not listed thereafter. He was the father of William Saupitty, a long-time member, and later chairman, of the Kiowa-Comanche-Apache Business Committee.

succeeded him.

If the wife went to the deceased husband's grave, she could get his power; he might tell her how. A widow could get power easier than a single woman. A husband might take his wife to a lonely place, so she could get power direct instead of through him.

Words   {Word List[1]}

ʉra	'thank you' in Comanche
aho	'thank you' in Apache, etc.
⟨mabuina⟩	'my work is done'
sootipuhihwi[2]	'lots of money'

Marriage: Polygamy   When a man had several wives, they were usually related. Such wives were generally peaceful and didn't make much trouble.

If unrelated, they often had arguments and fights. One wife was usually the favorite.

Marriage: Adultery   A certain man suspected that his favorite wife [the eldest of three sisters] had a paramour, so he put an arrow under her bed, unbeknownst to her, and then went off to a smoking party [Smoke Lodge]; he was quite old.

When he returned, he found the two lying in his bed. He went up and asked them what they were doing.

The man [*tuibihtsi*] asked for assistance. They couldn't get apart. He offered the husband some presents. The husband went out, got a switch, and came back and used the switch on the guilty man. They did everything they could to get apart but couldn't.

[He wanted to go to bed.] The husband asked another wife to come and help. She seized the wife's legs, he seized the man's, and they dragged them out into the open.

The next day, the camp was to move. In the morning, the young man's [*tuibihtsi*'s] people missed him. They looked all through the camp but couldn't find him. The parents were still looking when the man's father passed by and saw the couple lying. He went over and found his son.

The father begged the medicine man to take off the medicine, but he refused. He said he loved his wife; she had done this to him and he wanted her to get enough of it, so they could lie there until they died.

The father called other warriors [of influence] and had them intercede for him. He was willing to pay the medicine man an indemnity. After a long talk, the medicine man consented, went into his tipi, pulled the arrow out from under the bed, and they got loose.

This was the oldest of three wives; they didn't know he had such powerful medicine. This was why wives were usually faithful to husbands. They feared some similar predicament.

[The *tuibihtsiˀ*'s father paid him.]

The woman's father came to pay the medicine man so he wouldn't divorce or maltreat her, but he refused the gift. He said he would treat her as a captive [slave] instead of as a favored wife. She would have to serve the other two.[3]

---

1. These words, along with others, are also on the cover of Wedel's Notebook 5.
2. *sooti* 'many', *puhthwi* 'metal, money'.
3. Hoebel (1940:101) attributes this account to Tahsuda.

Life Cycle: Marriage: Polygamy: Favorite Wife   The favored wife did practically no work; she would make her own clothes, but she didn't have to cook, carry water, etc. The favored wife was usually the first married.

In the above case, she lost all her fine clothes, jewelry, etc., and the second wife was promoted.

The *paraibo kwuhu?* was the chief wife.[1] When the favorite wife died, the second was promoted.

In one case, when the head wife died, her sisters wanted to buy all her fine clothes, etc., but the husband refused to allow it. [The {new chief} wife got the good clothes of the other and all of her privileges.]

The chief wife in the above story had refused to let the other wives sleep with her husband; the new chief wife was more lenient.

Younger wives never succeeded the first wife in status. Most of the dirty work went to the wives in between.[2] The chief wife above usually had the right to say which one should spend night with the husband, especially if they were sisters.

Younger girls must obey their older sisters, even before marriage.

As a man grows older, he never refused a proffered wife: the more wives, the more *nanuwoku*. A younger man might turn down a woman.

Sisters usually stuck together to deceive their husband. Where the wives were not related, it was "dog-eat-dog."

A man who married several sisters was more highly regarded than one who married unrelated women.

Life Cycle: Marriage: Polygamy: Jealousy   The first wife had a boy. [The husband brought a second wife home.] The second wife had no children.

The man went on a buffalo hunt and took the second wife, because she had no children.

The first wife's older sister told the wife she better go or she wouldn't get her share of the meat. So the first wife said she was going. The husband said, "No, it is too hot for the boy."

She insisted, and he pushed her away.

She turned to the second wife standing nearby, seized her by the hair, twisted her head, and walked away. The husband got angry, threw his knife, and hit her above the kidneys and killed her.

Her sister saw it, began crying, and took the young son.

The husband felt bad about it; he hadn't meant to hit his wife with the blade, he only meant to scare her. He blamed his wife's sister for the trouble, but couldn't prove anything. Her parents did nothing about it.

The husband wanted to "get" the sister, but was persuaded not to. She took the boy of her deceased sister.

Life Cycle: Death: Custody   If a woman died leaving children, and the other wives were unrelated, her children usually went to her parents.

---

1. Wallace and Hoebel 1952:141.
2. Wallace and Hoebel 1952:141.

Life Cycle: Marriage: Polygamy   Women didn't ask their husbands to bring in additional wives; there was not enough economic need for them.

If a second wife was promoted, the first one might walk out. [She wouldn't stand for it.]

There were more women than men in the old days, due to war casualties. There were no old maids, and there was only one man known who was too mean to marry.

Life Cycle: Marriage: Jealousy: Sorcery   There were two [unrelated] wives. One went around to her father (a medicine man) and asked him to get rid of the other wife because they couldn't get along.

So the father used medicine and the woman sickened and finally died. The disgruntled wife was apparently a demoted first wife [she was appointed above her]. Her husband accused the second wife of conniving with her father to cause the other's death, but he didn't send her away.

Life Cycle: Marriage: Polygamy: Less Favored Wife   There was a separate tipi for the less favored wife.

A Mexican and a full blood woman were both married to a certain man. They could {not} get along, so they had separate tipis. Finally, the Mexican had a son, and the husband elevated her to first place and lived with her. The other wife remained living beside them.

Life Cycle: Marriage: Divorce   Women were not divorced for unfruitfulness.

Gambling: Gambling Debts   A woman usually paid up if her husband gambled her tipi away, and vice versa if the woman lost.

Medicine: Love Medicine   A man wanted a certain woman very badly, but couldn't get her. [He heard of a medicine man with power over women.]

Finally, he went around to a medicine man, rolled a cigarette, and smoked with him. He said he must have the woman. The medicine man gave him a medicine and he got the woman. After marrying her, he gave a horse to the medicine man.

The woman knew nothing of the medicine man's actions.

There were also love medicines for women to catch men. [Nemaruibetsi didn't know the details.][1]

Material Culture: Tipis: Housekeeping   Tipis were swept out with a certain weed [with yellow flowers], *ohayaaʔ*.[2] There were small openings [depressions] below the door to sweep out the dirt. The floor was watered and tramped down. [They sprinkled the ground in the tipi to lay the dust.]

Marriage: Polygamy   Two women lived in one tipi, but were separate; when the man spent the night with one, she had to feed him.

The wives were always fighting. Each cleaned half of the tipi, tanned hides for her side of the tipi, [cut half the tipi poles, put the wood each got on her side of the fire], etc. There was only one fireplace.

1. Wallace and Hoebel 1952:134 (?).
2. Robinson and Armagost (1990) gives this as 'sunflower'.

Nasutipe[1] "to give up to someone else," the younger of them, had two children, then became the big shot.

If all the wives had children, the favorite wife and her children slept with the man and the others had separate tipis nearby.

Material Culture: Tipis: Cover   The bottom row of hides on a tipi cover were rectangular. The others narrow to form a wedge. There are about twelve hides per tipi.[2]

Material Culture: Clothing: Cleaning   Soapweed and white clay were used to clean buckskin suits.[3]

Material Culture: Containers   The *tetsakɨ* was the rawhide from which the *oyóotɨ'* was made. The *naboo oyóotɨ'* was soft, not like buckskin, for clothes, etc.; the decorated suit case, *natsɄakɄne*, was stiff, for meat.

[Clothing: the *natsɄakɄne* (it was not the same as an *oyóotɨ'*). It was envelope shaped, tied shut, and there was a hole to hang it by.

The *oyóotɨ'* had decorations in blue, black, or maybe red, but there was no meaning to it. It was roughened before painting with a beef tongue to make the paint stick.]

POST OAK JIM
Undated[4]

Medicine: Herbs   *ohahuupi*, Osage orange root bark, was boiled, strained, and put in the eye. It was pounded before boiling.

Food: Fruits: Persimmons   They ate persimmons on war parties in Texas.

Material Culture: Containers: Water was stored in a buffalo paunch or in a skinned-out leg of a horse with the attached hoof.

Food: Food Preparation   *kuˀenawapU*[5] was a tripod of forked sticks beside the fireplace; green poles were leaned against it over the fire and a slab of meat was laid on the leaning poles and roasted.

On a hunt, they laid the poles close together on the ground and laid the meat slabs on them. There were no raised racks.

---

1. This is the agency spelling. Wedel spelled it Nasutaip; Hoebel spelled it Nasɔti:p. The 1879 census translated it as Charitable. Robinson and Armagost (1990) gives *nasutarɨ* as 'surrender, give up'. She was born about 1827, and in 1879 she was a member of Quanah's Kwaharɨnɨɨ local band. On all of the censuses, she is listed as single; however, the Family Record Book lists her as the mother of a daughter, Pihe 'heart', born around 1868, with the father recorded as Noko (otherwise unidentified). No other children of Noko or Nasutipe are mentioned. Pihe married Chebatah (Chivato), the Lipan Apache.
   2. See Kavanagh 1991.
   3. The bottom three lines of this page of Wedel's notebook 6 are torn off, but there does not seem to be any data lost on this side or the next.
   4. These undated notes are in Wedel's notebook 6 at this point.
   5. Robinson and Armagost (1990) has *kuˀe* as 'top, summit'.

Material Culture: Clothing: Headdress   The beaverskin cap had a tail piece (like a coonskin cap), with mirrors around the cap and down the rear strip. There was a feather at the rear of the cap.

ATAUVICH

August 9, 1933[1]

Social Relations: Intergenerational Attitudes   An old man was cared for by his daughter after he got too old to care for himself. If the daughter was too old to do this, it was up to her daughter.

There was an old man who was dependent on his daughter. His sister's daughter paid no attention to him. The daughter died, and the son-in-law had no way of taking care of him. A man could not care for an old man by himself. He told the sister's daughter she'd have to take care of the old man. The woman's husband told her it was her duty, so she took him in and he lived with her until he died. She kept him pretty well contented.

Tekwaka[2] did not stay at his daughter's much. Probably he didn't get along with his son-in-law. Tekwaka had property, too, and could help with the finances. His son-in-law called him *tetsI*,[3] instead of *nɨmɨtokU*, which showed he didn't care much for him.

In the old days, you respected your father-in-law because you were expecting a second marriage. Nowadays, you can't marry two women and you don't respect your father-in-law.

You got more favors from your *araʔ* than from your paternal uncle. A brother loved a sister, so he would do things for her son. Atauvich's *araʔ*, Yellow Bear,[4] did lots for him. He was sick and none of his father's three brothers would help him, but Yellow Bear paid all his doctor's bills and got him well. Your *araʔ*, either way, was the closest friend you had.

A man treated his sister's children like his own, but did not treat his brother's children so well.

Atauvich knew of no case of a brother marrying the widow {of his brother} but has heard of several cases where they collected *nanɨwokɨ*.

Life Cycle: Marriage: Residence   A man generally brought his wife to live with his parents. He might live with his wife's people later.

Life Cycle: Death: Disposition of Property   A wife would probably inherit property if she survived. She might divide with her husband's mother if she was still living.

---

1. These dated notes are from Carlson. They are in an arbitrary order.
2. Possibly the man named Takewaker, Outside Talk. He would have been about 73 in 1933.
3. A man's brother-in-law.
4. Woodauhaupith, *wɨra* 'bear', *ohapI* 'yellow'. He was associated with Quanah's Kwaharɨnɨɨ local band.

Yellow Bear's property was divided among his children.[1] Most of it went to his daughter. Atauvich got five head of cattle. Weckeah[2] got three cows. A man named 'Coffee',[3] Yellow Bear's half-brother, got five. Atauvich's *kaku?* got some. A white man did the dividing. No one objected.[4]

Paternity   If a woman went on a raiding party and nine months later gave birth to a child, the man who took her on the raiding party was the legal father, even though the woman was pregnant at the time she left. The woman would declare it to be his son.

Comanche Jack's[5] mother was pregnant by her husband, and another man took her off on a raiding party, afterwards taking her home to her own people. He didn't go to see her. Her brother inquired what was the use of keeping her when she was married. They took her to the man who took her off. The child was born and the woman claimed that this man was the father.

Kinship Terminology: Adultery   You called a man who has stolen your wife "brother," but you would not pick him up off a battlefield as soon as a real brother. A man must observe sister taboos with the sister of a man whose wife he had stolen.

Kinship Relations: Joking   You mostly joked with your *haipia?*. A man might accuse her of having relations with a certain man.

If a man saw his *haipia?* with a young man, he would take something from her, such as a ring. He would keep it for a while, and then usually return it.

One might joke with the *tetsI* the same way, but not so frequently.

You could tell a story like Fox and Raccoon[6] to your sister-in-law. You could not tell it to your sister or to your father-in-law.

Kinship Relations: Joking   You don't call a tribal member "brother." In formal times, he was *haits*, in joking *nɨmɨtɨi*.[7]

Two men who called each other *nɨmɨtɨi* would call each other cowards. You would tell people your *nɨmɨtɨi* was bashful with women. You did not accuse him of being with a certain woman. You would say, "My friend went visiting and farted so badly that they couldn't stand the smell," or "My friend went to a place for dinner and ate everything himself," or "He visited the Osages and stole six blankets."[8]

Life Cycle: Marriage: Divorce   The wife would probably take the children in a divorce, or they might divide them between them.

1. Woodauhaupith died between 1885 and 1889. He was listed as 50 years old in 1885.

2. Weckeah was one of Quanah Parker's wives. Her relation to Woodauhaupith is unclear.

3. There were several men named Coffee, but the genealogies do not go back far enough to determine which one this was.

4. Hoebel 1940:121.

5. Also known as Permamsu. Born about 1854, he was a member of Tahpony's Yapainɨɨ local band. The censuses translate his Comanche name as both Hairy and Afraid of Hair. Casagrande (1954–55, III:14) transcribes the name as *pɨhɨmahmsu?*, which he translates as 'one who rejects a bunch of hides', but he does not provide an etymology.

6. See Naiya, July 8.

7. *nɨmɨtɨi* 'our relative'.

8. The first line of this note is from Hoebel, the remainder from Carlson.

Life Cycle: Illegitimacy   Once there was a brother and sister. The brother had a family. He went on a raid and got killed. His mother couldn't care for her granddaughter, so she gave her to her daughter, the girl's *pahaʔ*. The aunt mistreated the girl.

As the girl got older, she wanted to get away. She had an illegitimate child, and the aunt still continued to be mean to her.

One day, the aunt threatened to kill her. The girl ran off with her baby. They looked for her, but couldn't find her. The girl had gone to the tipi of a brave warrior, where she hid under the bed. She stayed there four days. The aunt said she'd kill her if she found her.

On the fourth day, the wife of the warrior found her, and asked what she was doing. The girl told her troubles and said she knew the warrior could take care of her. The wife told her to come out. She called her husband. She said, "Do you remember our son who died at this age. I have taken pity on this child. How can we save them."

The husband said the only way was for him to marry the girl. The wife agreed.

The aunt heard the girl had been found and came looking for her. The warrior asked what she wanted, and she said she was looking for the girl. The warrior said he would not let her go, that she was his wife. The aunt asked the man's wife if this was true, and the woman said it was.

The wife wanted the girl to work for her, and that was why she acted like she had taken pity on the child. The girl was the warrior's wife, and gave birth to two children by him. The girl's name was Petsatasai.[1]

The husband cared for the bastard like it was his own son. The bastard could probably not marry his step-sister, the parents would not have stood for it. If the mother had died and the boy had left, living with someone else, he might marry his step-sister, but as long as he made his home there it would not look right.

When a girl had an illegitimate child, her parents tried to get a husband for her. They would probably have to marry her to an older man, a young man probably would not have her.

{Carlson} Also see Herkeyah's life story for Toyop's illegitimate child.[2]

Life Cycle: Death: Disposition of Property   You might give things away at death, instead of destroying them, even in the old days.

Life Cycle: Death: Custody   When a widow with children remarried, her new husband might live with the children for a while, but he would soon want to get rid of them. They would probably let the mother's sister take care of them. It might be the *kakuʔ*. It wouldn't be any of the father's relatives.

There was a woman related to Atauvich whose husband died, leaving her with young children. She remarried, and the children got along with the stepfather for a while, but fairly soon hard feelings arose. The stepfather didn't care for the children and they didn't take care of him. The children were given to the mother's sister.

If the mother died, the father would get some of his relatives to help care for the children.

---

1. Otherwise unidentified.
2. The specific reference of this note is unclear.

A man with more than one wife may have the remaining wife take care of a deceased wife's children, if she was a good woman. If she was a flighty woman, who was always going off to dances, she may not do it.

Life Cycle: Marriage: Polygamy   When a man married an older sister, he was likely to marry the younger sister. He would not give her to his younger brother. You did not act to your wife's brother's wife as to a sister.

Life Cycle: Marriage: Polygamy   A man could marry his wife's sister's daughter.

Mamsookawat had two wives at once who called each other *paha*.[1]

Mamsookawat was married to two women at once, an aunt and a niece. The two women got along together fine. When one died, the other inherited her property as a relation. Children of *tsoo*[2] could probably marry.

It was not only real sisters, but also classificatory sisters that a young man must not be alone with. This was taken on when a young man got old enough to begin going around with girls.[3]

Story: Fox and the Prairie Dogs   Fox came to a prairie dog village. He acted disturbed.

He said to the prairie dogs that there was a very dangerous sickness coming. He said the only way to prevent it was to have a "scare dance."

He asked where the chief lived and they showed him a big tipi.

He told the news to the chief. They fixed a place to dance and the announcer went around with the news of the dance.

Fox told the prairie dogs to close their doors tight, for fear that thieves might break in. Everyone was invited to dance.

They built a big fire to dance around and started to dance in a circle, clockwise, around the fire.

Fox told them to dance with their eyes closed. He began to club them.

One prairie dog didn't trust Fox, so he danced with his eyes half open. He called out, "Fox is killing us with a club, run for your lives."

The prairie dogs ran, but their doors were closed, so Fox killed them all.

Fox took the dead ones away and built a fire. He put them in the fire with just their tails sticking out.

As they were cooking, another, smaller fox came along. The small fox said, "I want something to eat. Look at my belly."

The big fox looked, and its belly was all drawn up. The small fox hadn't eaten for ten days. The big fox said, "The only way you can get something to eat is to race me. If you can beat me, you can have all you want."

The small fox said, "No, you are bigger, you can beat me."

The big fox said, "I will tie a rock to my feet." etc.

The little fox returned to find that all the prairie dogs were already eaten.

1. The 1879 census lists Mamsookawat with three wives (all unnamed); on all later censuses he is listed as having only one wife.

2. Great-grandparent/great-grandchild.

3. This note is based on two separate notes from Carlson, one labeled "Polygamy," the other "Incest Rulings," but clearly they refer to the same incident.

Story: Fox and Meat   The little {*sic*} fox went on. He saw ahead of him a big ball of meat and a big ball of fat, so he laid down like he was all starved. He asked them if they'd give him something to eat, and they said he could have just four bites. The small fox told them they'd find starving people all along the line. etc.

The fourth time the fox asked for something to eat, the two balls could see his full stomach. They asked him to open his mouth. They saw chunk of meat on his teeth. They said they wouldn't give him any more, so the Fox chased them. They ran away and fell in a creek. The fat left the surface of the water covered with grease. The small fox went to get a dipper to skim off the fat, but while he was gone, wildcat came along and skimmed it and ate it, so when the fox came back there was nothing left.

Story: The Thrown-Away Children   Once a man and his wife drifted off by themselves to get a supply of meat. The woman had a baby.

Buffalos were scarce and hard to locate. The man was going to try to get some by going out at night. He told his wife to fix up the tipi, that he had going to leave her. He told her not to stick her knife through the side of the tipi, because someone might see it and know someone was inside, and not to open the door, no matter how much anyone called. Then the man went off and killed his buffalo.

When the man was gone, the woman stuck her knife out the tipi door. Piamupits was passing and saw it. He begged the woman to open the door. The woman wouldn't do it for a long time.

Finally, Piamupits got angry and threatened the woman. She recognized Piamupits' voice and was scared, so she finally opened the door.

Piamupits walked in.

The woman asked what he wanted.

He said he wanted something to eat. He was hungry.

The husband had not come back.

The woman asked if it would be alright to fix him something to eat.

Piamupits said that was what he wanted.

The woman asked how she should fix a place to serve him.

Piamupits said the only place he ate was off a person's belly.

The woman said, 'Well, I guess I'll have to lay down and let you eat off of my belly."

After Piamupits finished, the woman asked if she should get up and get him a rag to wipe his hands. Piamupits said he would wipe on her belly. In wiping the knife on her belly, he cut her stomach open.

She had twins in her. Piamupits threw one down by the door and one in the water of the creek.

He took the woman's body outside and propped her up as if she were alive. He fixed a smile on her face.

The husband came up and saw the woman by the door. He got close and stopped. He talked to her.

He said, "I'm tired of riding. Why do you stand there? Why don't you help me?"

She kept on smiling.

He said, " Come around and help untie this meat."

She said nothing.

He said, "Come around and help untie this meat."

She said nothing.

The husband got mad. He went to the woman and jerked her. He pulled her down and saw that her insides had been cut out. He cried, and dumped the meat on the ground and ran away.

He went back to the main camp and told the news. The people talked about it and decided it was Piamupits' work.

The people wouldn't do anything, so the man decided to go back to his own tent. If it had been Piamupits who did it, he would probably come back. The man stayed all night at the tent where his wife was killed.

The second night, he went to bed. All was quiet. Towards morning, he heard coyotes howling, and could hear someone taking arrows.

He uncovered and saw someone running towards the door. He didn't think at the time of his family being killed there. He didn't think it might be a ghost.

The next morning, he went out and watered his horses. When he got back near the camp, he saw a little boy playing near the camp. The boy saw him and ran in the tipi. The man hurried to the tipi as fast as he could, but there was no one there.

The next night, he intended to watch.

Night came, and he went to sleep. A bit before daylight, he awoke, but kept his head covered. He heard someone trying to get arrows out of his quiver. Slowly he uncovered his head.

The little boy was standing on tiptoe trying to reach the arrows.

He tried to grab the boy, but the boy was too quick and ran through the door. When the man got to the door, there was no sign of the boy anywhere.

The next morning, the man again went off to water the horses. Coming back, he again saw the boy playing in front of the tipi. But when the boy saw him, he ran into the tipi. The man jumped from his horse and ran in the tipi, but it was empty.

The next night, the boy again tried to get the arrows, and the man lay in wait. Again, the boy ran to the door and disappeared.

The next morning, the man went out to locate his horses. He came back and rode into the yard on horseback. The boy ran underneath the horse.

The man told the boy that this was their camp, and they'd have something to eat.

So the man cooked food while the little boy watched. When the man sat down to eat, the little boy sat beside him.

That night they went to bed. The boy told his father that he had a brother down by the creek. The father asked him if he couldn't get the brother to come up to the camp. The boy said he could, but the brother wouldn't come while the father was there, so he would get him when the father went off to round up the horses.

The next morning, the father went for the horses. When he came back, he saw the two boys playing together. The one started to run for the creek and the other tried to stop him, but the first ran too fast and jumped in the water.

The father told his son, they'd better get the brother. He said, " Come out, we'll shoot bows and arrows."

Then he caught his brother, and the father got his two sons. Then they packed things, and drifted back to the main camp.

{Carlson} "Atauvich volunteered the statement that he thought there were more stories about these twins, but he didn't know them."

Story: Terrapin's War Party   Once a bunch of people were having a dance. They were getting ready to go on a war party.

Terrapin told his mother that he would like to go with them. The men said that anyone who wanted to join the party could do so. They would wait at a certain place for several days to give latecomers a chance to catch up.

Terrapin had his mind set. He told his mother that he wanted to have a war party, and she must get his things ready and saddle his horse. His mother got the things ready and left the horse saddled outside the tent.

Terrapin's legs were too short to get on a horse in the regular way, so he led it into a ditch so he could get on. He tried and tried to get on the horse, but couldn't quite make it.

That night the women were talking about the boys on the war party. Terrapin's mother said she didn't know how her boy would get along, as he never had learned how to get on a horse.

Just then, Terrapin came up. He called his mother.

When she came over, he said he had been trying all day to get on his horse to go on the war party. Terrapin asked his mother to put him on the horse. His mother wouldn't put him on the horse, so Terrapin couldn't go on a war party.

Story: The Substitute Prisoner   Fox had been stealing around, getting things that didn't belong to him. So they arrested him and put him in jail. They were going to keep him for four days and have a trial.

So they kept him four days, had a trial, and found him guilty.

They were going to punish him.

They put him in a box with holes bored in it and nailed him up.

They were going to throw him in the water and let him drift away.

Before this time, a wealthy man came around. He saw the box there with something in it. He kicked the box, but couldn't move it.

The man called out, "Is that a human in there?"

"Yes."

"Who are you?"

"I am the Fox."

"Why are you penned up?"

"These people have it in for me. It won't be long until they throw me in the river and I'll take my punishment."

The man asked, "What shall I do to save you?"

Fox got to thinking that maybe he could get things fixed up, so he said, "The way I understand it, there are two options. Some want to punish me and some want to turn me loose and give me a nice-looking woman. If you want a wife, you can get in this box and you can have the woman. They may turn you loose. When you get in and I get out, I'll go free."

The man didn't believe Fox. He said, "No, you said they'd throw you in the water."

But the man had the woman on his mind, and finally decided to take a chance. The man got in and they put the lid back as before. Fox changed clothes with the man. Fox got on the man's horse and rode off with his cattle.

When noon approached, the man began to get uneasy. They were announcing that it would soon be noon. Soldiers were drilling, and they came to the spot where the box was. They lifted it up and swung it back and forth, as if they were about to throw it in the water.

They heard a voice inside. The head officer told them to wait a minute. He didn't understand what the person in the box said, and he didn't want to do anything until he heard for sure. They took off the lid and saw the man.

They asked how he got there.

The man said, "Fox told me that the army officers would turn me loose and the general would give me a good-looking woman, so I got in."

So they discovered that Fox had got off, and they turned the man loose.

FRANK CHEKOVI
August 10, 1933

Bows   Bows were simple arcs. The grip was not wrapped.

Material Culture: Utensils: Spoons   *kuhtsutue'aawo, aatue'aawo*[1] were buffalo or horn spoons. The horn was scraped smooth, placed in boiling water to soften it, then cut in the desired form with a knife. The core was removed after boiling. Sometimes the core was loosened by holding it over a fire for a short time, then tapped and removed. The tip was used for the handle. Buffalo or beef horn was used; there was no special shaping.

Wooden spoons were *hutue'aawo*.[2] Large ones and dippers were made of the wart on a tree. They were split off, with a sliver running down to form the handle. Smaller ones were made by hollowing a slab of wood with an adze.[3]

The wooden vessels were meat grinders mostly. The stone pestles, about ten inches long, were made of schist. The meat grinder was *tuhkatayu'ni*.[4]

The stone maul, with a green hide and stick handle, was used for pounding tipi stobs {stakes}.

There was no anvil and rawhide mortars.

Pecan blocks were cut out, split, then hollowed out with an adze. About one inch thick was hollowed out first, then the outside was trimmed; it was used for a meat pan. It was

---

1. *tue* 'little, *aawo* 'container', *kuhtsu'* 'buffalo', *aa* 'horn'.
2. *hu-* 'wood'.
3. Wallace and Hoebel 1952:91.
4. Literally, 'pounded meat'; *tuhka* 'meat. Robinson and Armagost (1990) has *tayu'neru* as 'crush, pound with a pestle (cause to be crushed)'.

called *huʔtɨsoona*.[1] It was a few inches deep, about two feet in diameter, and oval. It was very hard to make. It had no decoration.

The Osages liked to paint things. The Comanches got the idea of painting the *oyóotɨʔ* from the Osages.

War   Warriors on a raid usually carried no food, but they lived off the country.

Food: Pemmican   *taʔooʔrɨbayapɄ*[2] was pemmican mixed with fat and stored in the parfleche. It was used as emergency rations. Only the only choice meat, the loin, was used. Ordinary meat was not ground for storage, but was sewed up and stored.

Material Culture: Containers: oyóotɨʔ   *oyóotɨʔ* were used for ordinary meat. One was packed on each side of the horse.

Food: Food Preparation: Pemmican   *taʔooʔrɨbakipɄ* was carried on top of the pack.

To make *taʔooʔrɨbakipɄ*, they gathered mesquite beans when they were ripe. They took only the sweet ones. They put them on a big rawhide, then crushed them with a pestle until it looked like meal. Then they separated the pods and used them; the seeds are no good. They might get a small sackful.

A dry buffalo paunch, stretched over a bent limb, was perforated and used to sift out the finer meal. This was mixed with lean meat and sewed up in the bag, then stored for later use. *taʔooʔ* was meat.

Social Roles: Club Man   The *pianɨʔɨpaiʔi* was the war club. It was straight, like that carried by dance leaders, but set with spikes along one edge. It was carried by very few men. The user had no other weapon, but had to fight hand to hand. The user was braver than a man with spear or gun. Parɨakuhma, He Bear, owned one of these; so did Esahabit, Gray Strip in the Sky.[3]

Only a man who used this club in war could carry the "peace club" and make warriors dance. He had to display the war club whenever he recited his deeds.

Social Roles: Contrary   The *pukutsi* "doing things backward." He was a warrior who unrolled a red strip from his belt, then shot an arrow into the end. Then, he couldn't retreat unless a friend pulled it out.[4]

Animals: Birds   The *piakini*[5] was the kingbird (hawk). Its tail feathers, maybe a dozen or so, were stuck in the scalp lock. It was a bird that swooped and caught its prey; it never missed. It was probably a goshawk or sharp shin, a "fast moving bird," gray in color.

Hunting: Otters   Otters were sometimes dug out if their dens were found. After a flood, otters would be intercepted as they returned upstream to their dens. They were very vicious and dangerous to tackle by hand.

Animal Powers: Otter   Otter skins were used for pregnancy belts, because an otter gives birth to its young very easily; they're slippery. It was sometimes worn for decoration. They were prized because of their rarity, "not everyone has 'em."

1. Literally, 'wood pan'.
2. Wedel spells this da:oriβakip. Robinson and Armagost (1990) gives *taʔooʔ* as 'dried or pounded meat'.
3. See above, Quassyah, July 5.
4. Wallace and Hoebel 1952:275.
5. *pia* 'big'. The other part of the word is unattested.

Animal Powers: Beaver   If person was mean, you came up behind him, took some dried beaver lung, and threw it away, thus discarding the meanness.

Medicine: Nuts   Nuts[1] were cut off, dried hard, and a piece cut off and wrapped in a kerchief, then soaked in water. The water was then rubbed over *tohpeti* sticks for luck.

Animals: Birds   *kwihnaikwasi*[2] was a big bird with very fine feathers. It was not known in this country.

Hunting: Birds   They couldn't catch them. Finally, they killed a beef, gutted it, and put a man inside it. The birds were very greedy. The man waited awhile, then birds began swooping. Finally, they lit and began to eat on the viscera. The man reached out, grabbed it by the wing, and broke the wing. Then he hid again. He caught two birds, breaking the wing of each so it couldn't fly off. It was impossible to catch these birds otherwise; they are very timid.

Hunting: Birds: Eagles   There were no eagle-catching pits.

Hunting: Birds: Hummingbirds   *wʉʔkʉʔbuuʔ*, hummingbirds, were very hard to hit. They were so small you could hardly see the bird. They put a crosspiece across the tip of an arrow. This knocked the bird cold. It was then picked up and skinned. The skin was stuffed with buffalo hair to look like a live bird, and put on a shield, it made the owner hard to hit.

Animals: Buffalo   *takwi*[3] was a yearling buffalo.

Social Roles: Contrary   A *pukutsi* went through camp, entering tipis and singing.

One old lady heard him and told him to get her a *takwi* to make a robe. He went on singing as though he didn't hear.

That night he went on a war raid alone. Near an enemy camp he met and killed an Osage. He skinned him out, leaving the head, hands, and feet on, then he hurried back.

People didn't hear him around camp and wondered where he was. Finally, they heard him coming, singing. He went on to the woman's tipi and said he had brought her the robe. He left it by her door and went away. The woman came crawling out and reached up. She felt the hairless skin. She was scared, and called her husband. He brought a light and saw it was a human skin, and recognized the tribe from the hair dressing. The Osages wore their hair clipped short and powdered with red in the old days; maybe they had a crest down the center of head. They looked terrifying.[4]

Life Cycle: Life Stages {Carlson[5]}

tuinʉhpʉʔ	was a boy until adolescence.
tuibihtsiʔ	a young man.
tenahpʉʔ	a man.
tsukuhpʉʔ	an old man.

1. It is not clear if this reference was to tree nuts or to testicles.
2. Literally, 'eagle tail'.
3. Robinson and Armagost (1990) gives this as 'wrinkled'. The linkage to a yearling buffalo is otherwise unattested.
4. Wallace and Hoebel 1952:275.
5. The final three dated notes of this interview are from Carlson, paralleled in Hoebel; they have no parallels with Wedel's notes. It is not clear if Carlson or Hoebel conducted a separate interview with Frank Chekovi, or if Carlson's dating was in error.

muʔwooʔ   was a substitute term for *tenahpɨʔ* used by some people on account of the taboo placed on the other because of a relative by that name.

narabɨ   was a joking word for 'old man'.

Kinship Terms {Carlson}   One always called a person by a relationship term. It was more polite. This held true even if there was no actual relationship.

nɨʔnanamɄsuʔnɨɨ[1] were (my progenitors), male or female speaking, ancestors in a direct line.

For *haipiaʔ*[2] (male speaking), one might substitute *kwɨhɨʔ* (wife); for *kuhma* (brother-in-law, wife speaking), one might substitute *haipiaʔ*. Both these terms were equally possible, but the alternatives in each case were not used as frequently. A man called his wife's *tɨe haipiaʔ*[3] and she reciprocated with *kuhma*.

Social Organization: Intergenerational Relations {Carlson}   A grandfather stood outside his granddaughter's confinement lodge and asked the girl the sex of the child. They said, *ɨhaitsIma*[4] "it's your *haitsI*," for a boy. For a girl, they said *ɨsamohpɨ*[5] {it's a girl}. They might say *tuinɨhpɨ* {(it's a) boy}, if it was a boy.[6]

FRANK CHEKOVI
AND PEDAHNY[7]
August 11, 1933

Dances: Crow Dance   The Raven Dance was held outside. There was a special dressing tipi, but no large composite tipis.

Material Culture: Tipis   The domed boy's tipi was made of small brush, arched, tied together at the top, and then covered with leaves and robes.

There were no brush arbors on buffalo hunts.

Small tipis were used on buffalo hunts. The large ones were left at home.

Adornment: Face Paint; Tattooing   There was no tattooing, but there was face painting: red paint around the eyes, two vertical finger lines each two inches long in front of the ears.

---

1. Robinson and Armagost (1990) gives *nanamɄsuʔ* as 'in-law'. *nɨʔnanamɄsunɨɨ* is *nɨ-* 'my', *nanamɄsu* 'in-law', *-nɨɨ* plural.

2. Opposite sex sibling-in-law.

3. *tɨe* 'little'; presumably 'little sister'.

4. Literally, 'it's your close friend'.

5. Literally, 'your sibling'.

6. Wallace and Hoebel 1952:144. Hoebel's note card has no consultant identification, but its information is identical to Carlson's note from Frank Chekovi dated August 10. The relevant paragraph in Wallace and Hoebel (1952:144) credits "Medicine Woman, Kills Something, and Post Oak Jim." Medicine Woman and Kills Something were among Wallace's 1945 consultants; there are apparently no parallel comments in Post Oak Jim's various interviews.

7. Although Wedel's manuscript notes attribute this entire interview to Frank Chekovi, both he—in his worked-up papers—and Carlson attribute the section on hide work to "Mrs. Frank Chekovi," i.e., Pedahny.

There was a small red dot on the cheek. This painting was for dress. Also, there was some red on the ears.

Adornment: Face Paint: Peyote   There were red stripes over the eyes and on the hair, yellow stripes on the eyes and hair on the other side. They were made by putting stripes first on the hand, then pressing the hand over the face and hair.

Women painted a red triangle on each side of her head or a red dot on the cheekbone.

The hair part was painted red by both sexes.

Animals: Buffalo Hair   Buffalo hair was not woven.

Horses: Saddles: Saddle Blankets   A hide with the hair left on and tanned was used as a saddle blanket.

Material Culture: Ropes   The best rawhide ropes were braided. Straps were used to fasten packs. They were three-ply braided ropes.

Material Culture: Crafts: Hide Work   Vertical frames on fixed poles for hide dressing were not used.[1]

The deer was skinned by splitting the hide down the belly and along the inside of the legs, then peeled off. The hide was stretched over a rounded and smoothed post top [with the worker on one side and an assistant on the other to hold the skin taut]. It was fleshed [of clinging fat] with a toothed scraper [held in the hand like a dagger], and then soaked in water. The hair was scraped with a horse rib beamer, sharpened [with a stone] like a knife. ⟨eno⟩ was the thin hide under the hair. It was then [stretched] over a leaning [slanting] pole [post] for beaming.

[When the hair was removed], it was dried in the sun, pegged out on the ground.

It was again soaked in water. Beef brain was then smeared all over.

A horse rib was used to dehair deer or antelope hide.

It was again placed in water. It was wrung out by twisting with a stick while the hide was over the pole. It was laid in the sun for a while and then in the shade. It was held with the feet and pulled with the hands to stretch it. It was put out in the sun again.

The hip part was thick, slow to dry.

It was trimmed off on both sides with a *tohtsiyuʔ* (a quartzite or sandstone scraper, c.f. Pawnee[2]). [It was about five or six inches across, to remove any last traces of flesh and to ensure evenness.] The ⟨tiratsike⟩ was the large dehairing stone slab for dressing rawhide.

A hole eighteen inches deep by ten inches in diameter was dug and the skin was sewn on the legs of the stand to retain the smoke. The forepart of skin was up, with the tail down.

Six poles were set about the hole, converging at the top.

The skin was placed over the poles so as to hold all the smoke.

Chips were used for fuel.[3]

---

1. Contra Wallace and Hoebel's "laced to upright saplings" (1952:94). Also contra George Catlin's painting of a Comanche village (reproduced as an engraving, plate 164, [1841, 2: opposite page 64]) which shows several skin-working frames. There are, of course, several other problems with Catlin's Comanche ethnography.

2. This parenthetical comment is probably from Wedel, based on his archaeological work in Nebraska.

3. Wallace and Hoebel 1952:90 (?).

A wagon sheet was put about the skin to keep the wind off.

Green bark was used first; they didn't want any fire.

The skin was watched to prevent scorching.

A long smoking gave a dark brown, a short smoking gave a yellowish.

In the old times, buffalo chips were used by the Kwaharʉ especially. Dead pine was used after the reservation days; [other bands often used] oak bark for fuel.

Material Culture: Clothing: Sewing   Awls were used for sewing, sinew for thread. There were no needles.

Material Culture: Containers: *oyóotʉʔ*   *oyóotʉʔ* painting was not Comanche, and was seldom done; it came from the Arapahos and Cheyennes.

Adornment: Face Paint   There were no bone paint brushes; they used their fingers to paint the face.

War: Armor   There was no armor.

Material Culture: Utensils: Digging Stick   The pooro was the digging stick.[1] It was made with a flattened point at one end and a knob (knot) for grasping. It was used for herbs, roots, etc.

Food: Food Plants: Seeds   There were no seed beaters, long poles used to shake down nuts, etc.

Comanches used few seeds.

Food: Food Plants: Berries   *tonopI* were black, round, berries. The bushes had no thorns. It was sweet.

Currants were eaten raw when ripe.

Camps: Moving: Fog   They followed the wind to get out of fog.

Cosmology: Star Lore   They used the star that never moves, *kemiʔarʉtatsinuupI*, 'not moving star'.[2]

The morning star was *tatatsinuupI*.

UNIDENTIFIED CONSULTANT
August 10–12, 1933[3]

Material Culture: Clothing: Men's Shirt   It was made of white or yellow buckskin. There were long fringes (six to eight inches long) appended at the seam where the sleeve was sewn to the shirt proper. In some cases, Mexican red beans[4] were fastened at the base of alternate fringes, but generally they were left plain. Long fringes also were fastened at the elbow along the seam, but only for two or three inches. Cuffs, folded up for an inch or two,

---

1. Wallace and Hoebel 1952:91. The Comanche Cultural Committee (2003) gives *pooro* as 'club, weapon, or tool'.

2. See also Howard White Wolf, August 3.

3. This note is from Wedel's worked-up pages. No consultant is named. Wedel interviewed Frank Chekovi and Pedahny during those days. It may also be a direct observation of Chekovi's shirt.

4. Mescal beans (*Sophophora secundiflora*).

had short fringes (one or two inches) along the edge. A triangular bib hung down front and rear, reaching about halfway to the belt. The edges of the bibs were also decorated with short fringes. There was no beadwork or other ornament on the shirt

---

HERKEYAH
August 13, 1933[1]

Social Control: Rape   There was a man named Pooʔaikʉ[2] with whom the women wouldn't have much to do.

He had a bad habit of breaking into a tent at night and feeling around a woman. The woman wouldn't let him get anywhere, though.

He also used to rape women whom he caught away from the camp in the daytime, forcing their legs apart with his elbows [and was successful].

No one ever caught him raping a married woman, so nothing was done to him.

One night a big, heavy woman felt Pooʔaikʉ feeling her. They fought and the women got him down. She took off his breech clout and grabbed his penis. She started to pull him out of the tent by his penis. Her son begged her not to do it, but she said she was going to teach him a lesson. She dragged him out in front of all the people. That broke him of his habit. Nobody had ever done anything to him before this [and the last time he offended].

HERKEYAH
August 14, 1933

Names   *parʉanakItsaʔnikaʔ*.[3]

War: Armor   A vest of steel armor was worn by Mupa 'hair in nose'.[4]

Relations with Other Tribes: Tonkawas   Herman Asenap's mother was fleeing from Tonkawa scouts. She tied a knot in her horse's tail, drove it into a stream, hung on to the tail, and safely crossed the flooded creek.

---

1. This dated note is from Carlson, with variations from Hoebel. However, August 13 was a Sunday, and since no other interviews were made on weekends, it was probably on August 14.

2. Hoebel (1940:111, 145) gives this name as Blow It Away. Robinson and Armagost (1990) also has *Pooʔaikʉ* as "(name) Blow-it-away," presumably from *poʔ ayaahkʉtʉ* 'blow away'. He is otherwise unidentified.

3. *parʉa* 'bear', *nakItsaʔnikaʔ* 'earring'. The word is on one line, and its relation to other comments is unclear. In Hoebel's undated notes from his interviews with Herkeyah, below, this name is associated with "a warrior."

4. *mu-* 'nose', *papI* 'hair'. According to Joe Attocknie (MS), this was the Comanche name of the man the Texans called Pohebitsquasso, *puhiwikwaso* 'Iron Shirt'. See Kavanagh (1996:365ff).

Names: Tasobakwitsi   Tasobakwitsi 'got wet for nothing'.[1]

Life Cycle: Death: Burial   There were individual burials.

Names: Makera.[2]

Life Cycle: Death: Disposition of Property   The deceased's property was destroyed. A mourner erected a dome-shaped *mutsikʉni*,[3] made by fastening willows to stakes circularly arranged, covered with buffalo hide or canvas.

Food: Plants: *toʔroponiiʔ*   *toʔroponiiʔ* was a round bulb with yellow flowers. It was dug by children and eaten.

Social Roles: Friendship   Children of true friends were brothers and sisters.

Medicine: Sun Dance   In the Kiowa Sun Dance, the arbor was open at the top. There was wet sand on one side where the tired dancers lay down to rest.

Life Cycle: Death: Mourning   Men sometimes cut their hair short in mourning, but they never gashed themselves.

War: Trophies   There were no finger necklaces among the Comanches.

Life Cycle: Death: Mourning   Women sometimes cut off their earlobes in mourning.

Medicine: Foretelling   There was a powerful medicine woman once among the Comanches.

The Osages had captured a Comanche woman. Her mother went to the medicine man {*sic*} for help. He told her that her daughter would be home in two or three days. They could hear the Osages dancing across the river.

The man who had captured the Comanche woman finally left her alone in the tipi. She ran out, got a bridled black horse beside the tipi, and fled. Her captor met a friend at the dance and told him to go stay with the woman awhile. He went, but he failed to find her. Then he returned and told the captor of the woman's escape. They stopped dancing and went in search right away.

The woman was chased by two Osages, but got across the river safely. There she met the Comanche man, who told her of the medicine being made for her return. The medicine was made in a small brush hut.

When the girl got home, her mother told her to give the black horse to the medicine woman. The girl refused, offered other horses, but the medicine woman declined any other. On the way home that night, the black horse died.

Social Organization: Bands   Herkeyah switched from the Noyʉhka to the Kwaharʉnʉʉ band.

Life Cycle: Death: Mourning {Carlson}   Tasobakwitsi did not stay around camp during the period he mourned his wife. He went off in a lonely place and mourned. He cut his hair. He kept up the mourning for two years.

Kinship Relations: Affines   Tasobakwitsi had intercourse with his d.d. {*sic*, ?} co-wife.

---

1. Robinson and Armagost (1990) gives *pakwihtsikʉrʉ* as 'dampen'. The word and gloss are on its own line in the notes and its relationship to the other comments is unclear. It would seem to go with the note directly above it, and Tasobakwitsi was Herman Asenap's mother's name, referring to her crossing the creek. However, the censuses give her name as Tahchockah. Moreover, in comments below, Tasobakwitsi is referred to as a man, otherwise unidentified.

2. Otherwise unidentified. This name is on a line by itself with no immediate context. The name reoccurs below.

3. *mutsi* 'point, *kahni* 'house'. Robinson and Armagost (1990) glosses it 'a wigwam made of curved sticks'.

Life Story: Herkeyah {Hoebel}   Herkeyah belonged to the Noyʉhka.

Her name meant Holding Something Up For Shade.[1] She received the name from a brave warrior, PitUwetʉ.[2] He said she would never be killed by enemies and that she would have a long and happy life. When she received the name, she and the warrior were out in the sun. When she picked up "something for shade," he named her thus.

Her former home was near the highest mountain in Mexico. It took three to four days to reach the camp at the top. She didn't remember her parent's name.

It was the custom among the Indians to cache stuff on that mountain when on a raid, and also to leave the captives there while gathering more.

She was captured in the summer by a *tekwʉniwapI*, Toyop, who was himself a captive. "It's funny, they had no pity on their own people."

She was going to school. She had heard of another girl who was captured and never returned. One day, she saw an Indian push the fence down. She was in her grandmother's arms, sitting on a log. Toyop rode up, grabbed her from her *kaku's* arms, and put her behind him on the horse. She was the only one in her family captured (her parents were absent).

They came to a group of Indians. It was nearly night. They killed a boy sheepherder and ate his lunch.

The next morning, Toyop put her on another man's horse. They heard a wagon at the foot of the mountain and sent four men to investigate. They heard shots and soon the men came back with some food and Mexican blankets. (Thus she knew that the men were Mexicans.)

They rode on to the high mountain; it was a four-day trip to go up the mountain. They were out of food so they killed a horse. It was raining hard, so they went to bed soaking wet.

When they reached the camp, the Indians ran up and snatched her earrings and clothes for souvenirs. The other little captive girls told her not to be afraid, they wouldn't hurt her.

On the mountain, the girls ate apart so they wouldn't disturb the men's medicine. They learned to eat horse meat. They stayed there in the camp quite a while; the warriors made more raids for horses and captives. They had a large camp there. She didn't seem to be afraid.

On the last raid, the whole camp, including the women, went. They left a man (a captive) in charge of all of the captives.

He told them to go for wood and had them dig a pit in the ground. He built a fire in the hole, and put crosspieces across and rocks on the top. He killed a horse, put it on hooks, put wet grass on it, dirt on top, and then built another fire on the top (the stomach hole was fastened together with sticks). The next day, they all ate as much as they could. The raiding party returned with more horses. They prepared for their return (this was probably in September).

On the return, each family drove its own bunch of horses. Each family camp started individually when it got ready.

---

1. See Introduction.
2. Robinson and Armagost (1990) gives *pitUwetʉ* as 'limp'. Otherwise unidentified.

Toyop was not satisfied with his horses and he wanted more, so he didn't break camp with the others (there were about thirty in his group).

A man, Wahaomo, {Two Legs} from another group rode back to get something. He rode by Herkeyah.

Toyop told him that they were going on another raid and that she was in the way, so they intended to kill her. He felt sorry for her and thought of his own children (his wife was dead), so he picked her up and put her on his mule. Toyop gave the man three blankets and gave her one to ride on. The man gave Toyop a few arrows.

En route, they passed a girl lying in the road about to die (she had been raped). Later, they passed a boy captive, dead.

The man told her that when she grew up she would be his wife; his niece was running his camp (his wife was dead). He told his niece to be good to her (sometimes they were very mean to captives), and to look after her so no men would harm her.

When they were in camp, a *tuibihtsi*ʔ came along and led her away. One night while her uncle was out looking after the horses, he pulled her against her will. The young man lay down; he had a diseased scrotum. She stood around.

Her captor saw her and ran to her. He scolded the fellow and took her back. After that, he took her along when he went places; he tied her on the horse and he led the horse.

They came to a Kiowa camp; there was peace between them at the time.

They needed food. Wahaomo sent her and her niece after food. They went and looked for the largest camp. Wahaomo was dressed in a blanket with his face painted. They asked if she was a warrior's wife. (She said, "No, a captive.")

The Kiowas loaded them up with dried meat and told them of a Comanche camp near by.

They went there and found the fires were still smoking at the old camp site.

They traveled all the next day following the trail. Finally, the next evening, they came upon them. She noticed that his wife's parents' and sister's hair was already long; he must have been gone several years.

He took her into their tipi; it was all fixed up with blankets. He put her at the west side of the tipi; her regular place was next to the door. The women struck her with whips as was the custom upon the arrival of a captive in the camp.

The care of his children was her job. She must carry the crippled one on her back and take the other one with her. She went wherever they went to play.

Wahaomo slept regularly with his former wife's younger sister, Puki. The grandmother of the children was PahmukUsi.[1]

A party left on a hunting trip. In their absence, the camp had trouble keeping horses. There came a snowstorm and it covered some of the horses completely.

The people on the hunt were in the storm (their location was somewhere north of here).

The people in the main camp were running short of wood and food. The captive boys got wood and cut paths through the snow. They ate frozen horses when they could find a corral.

---

1. Both of these women are otherwise unidentified. The latter is probably *pahmu* 'tobacco', *kusi* 'gray'.

The people on the hunting trip <u>invented</u> *waraatsu*,[1] 'snow shoes'. They were made of woven sinews.

They couldn't find any game and nearly starved.

Once, one man made some *waraatsu* and went hunting. He shot an arrow at an animal and then slid right on past it.

Others borrowed his snow shoes to get the meat, as he couldn't carry a big load on account of the weight of the meat, and hadn't enough sinew along to make many pairs.

They fed the horses cottonwood shoots and bark. It was good feed, but if frozen it would cut the horses' mouths.

They used the wood afterwards as fuel.

The hunting party returned after a month on account of the big storm, bringing some meat, but they had lost many horses and some had to return on foot. It was a hard winter. They couldn't make any more snowshoes as they had no more sinew. (It was necessary to go on another raid to get more horses.)

She learned to hunt from Wahaomo. On their return from a hunt, they must give to all who came asking for meat. "It's a custom."

It was hard on the families of generous men.

Wahaomo hadn't married her yet, but was just kind to her. The wife would take a stick from the fire and poke it at her in jealousy to scare her (to make her cry). The children would help her against her step-mother.

By the fall of the second year, she knew the language and was familiar with the customs. The Kiowas were about to have a Sun Dance.

Toyop and his brother, Tokemi[2] Black Horse, played hand game and lost everything.

They wanted to move out of camp. They drifted away; the two camps had no salt. A man, Tasobakwitsi,[3] and his captive wife came back for salt; they had a baby. He also had a full-blood wife. On their return, the full-blood wife found the man sleeping with the captive wife. She threw water in their faces. The full-blood wife went outside, mad.

When the man went out to her, he saw a herd of buffalo coming towards them. They ran to the horses and both mounted; he killed a buffalo.

The buffalo were being driven by the soldiers and Tonkawas. They didn't see him, but {they} went to the camp and captured the captive wife and children, and Toyop's wife. The full-blood wife was killed after a fight with one.

Toyop and Tokemi had been out to the buffalo and had seen the enemy; they got away. A man returning to the main camp jumped into the creek with the enemy following him. He ran towards the warriors camp with the news.

---

1. Robinson and Armagost (1990) gives this as 'sandals', which they cite as from the Spanish *huarache*.

2. *tuhkuhma*, literally 'black male', commonly translated as Black Horse and spelled Tokemi. He was one of the Comanche prisoners sent to Fort Marion, Florida. After 1885, he was called Tabeko (*tabe* 'sun'), although his name was still translated in the records as Black Horse. He was the leader of a small Kwaharunuu local group.

3. Robinson and Armagost (1990) gives *pakwihtsikuru* as 'dampen'. Otherwise unidentified.

A warrior, ParᵾanakItsaʔnikaʔ,[1] got ready; others joined him and they went to meet the enemy. They went to Toyop's camp, but the enemy was guarding it. A man wanted to attack, but they told him to wait until dark.

The soldiers had also killed a man in another camp nearby to the west. Herman's mother was there; she was captured and a Tonkawa took a little boy from her, but Prenhub[2] shot the Tonkawa and got the little boy.

Then the Comanches attacked the soldiers and Tonkawas, but failed to get the captives. They fought through four days, but were unsuccessful.

On the fourth day, Herman's mother (lying between two Tonkawas) saw a horse outside, so she slipped quietly outside, got on the horse and got away. She rode for several days without seeing anyone. Finally, she saw a horse with a saddle. She went to get on, but found worms in the saddle, so she left it and went on. She came to a creek and swam over, hanging on to the horse's tail. She ultimately found the main camp safely, but heard her mother had been killed. The main camp then moved over by the isolated ones to bury the dead. The soldiers had left the dead there and cut up the tipis.

The camp drifted on towards the Kiowa Sun Dance. Toyop asked how she was getting along. Toyop begged Wahaomo to give her back to him to care for his aged classificatory father, Tasobakwitsi, because the women were all killed. Wahaomo agreed, and he went to get her; they all cried. She was now about twelve years old.[3]

That night Makera,[4] a grandchild of the old man, came for her on a horse. They took her to the old man. He had nothing, and she slept on the ground. He was living in a small mourning shelter; everything else was destroyed in the mourning.

In the morning, the camp moved on towards the Sun Dance. She helped guide the pack horses. That night, they gave her nothing to eat. She went to dig roots to eat, which she took to the old man to divide. She found a woman inside with him. It was Pᵾhᵾwa.[5] She was also a wife of Ohiwi.[6] Thus, the women were Makera, Pᵾhᵾwa, and one other.

The next day, she wanted to go back to Wahaomo; he left, and she went with a friend of Wahaomo, Tereyeka.[7] Toyop was mad that she had left Tasobakwitsi. He rode up and lifted her off her horse by her hair. This made Tereyeka mad, and he went over and pulled Toyop off by the hair too, saying, "I'll sell you for tipi poles." Others around prevented a fight.

Toyop got her and drove her ahead of him, whipping her along. Toyop's friend, Tosamareah,[8] came along and heard the tale. He suggested they kill her on the spot, but they decided to wait and ask his father. A man came along and shamed Toyop for being a coward in the battle, running from the Tonkawas, and he took Herkeyah with him.

1. *parᵾa* 'bear', *nakItsanʔnikaʔ* 'earring'. Otherwise unidentified.
2. Otherwise unidentified.
3. About 1870.
4. Otherwise unidentified.
5. *pᵾhᵾ* 'hairy, furry'; also possibly *pᵾhᵾwahtᵾ* 'prairie'. Otherwise unidentified.
6. Otherwise unidentified.
7. Otherwise unidentified.
8. *tosa* 'white', *muʔwoo* 'grown man'. A man, Tosamareah, translated as White Husband, was listed from 1879 to 1892 as a member of Waysee's Kwaharᵾnᵾᵾ local Wiaʔnᵾᵾ band. There is no other evidence to connect him with this story.

A girl who had escaped from the camp looted by the Tonkawas came along and told them to leave her alone; that saved Herkeyah's life this time. This girl was respected because she had been in the Tonkawa fight and had a hard time.

She was sent back to Tasobakwitsi; she was beaten by him and Makera. They made her care for the horses.

They came to the Kiowa Sun Dance. She was afraid to look much for fear of being beaten. They tied her up at camp without food or water when they went to see the dance. Puhuwa came and loosened her and let her go to the creek and drink. They made her cook the meals.

After the Sun Dance, they drifted on with some Kiowas. The scouts caught an Osage man that the Kiowas wanted and they quarreled. Watchsuah[1] (a captive) came up and shot him in the head, settling the quarrel. Other Osages heard the shot; some Osages were willing to make peace, but the young man's relatives refused and split off from the group.

Then an Osage warrior rode up and the Comanches sent a captive out to him (the captive had only one leg). The Osage said he'd go back and get two representatives to meet two from the Comanche-Kiowa group to make peace. The four men made peace on certain conditions, particularly that they wouldn't cross a certain river to hunt. Wahaomo and his wife and daughter crossed the river. They were caught by the Osages. The man and wife were scalped and the other woman was captured.

Wahaomo's wife was unconscious; she came to. She said they hadn't taken the whole scalp. She was found and taken back to camp; her head healed up. Wahaomo's wife was now alone. She went to see a medicine woman who told her that her daughter, captured by the Osages, would be back in two or three days. The girl escaped from the Osage camp while her captor was at a dance. He had sent a friend to stay with her, but she escaped. They hunted for her and didn't find her. The next morning she rode to the crossing in the river. Two Osages shot at her. She got across safely and met a Comanche man on the Comanche side. He told her about the medicine woman. When the girl returned to camp, she noticed the sweat lodges for the medicine to get her back. Her mother told her to give the medicine woman the black horse she had ridden back, but she refused, saying they'd give other horses. The medicine woman didn't want the other horses. That night the black horse died. (This was a custom of this medicine woman. Once before, a warrior had refused to give her a horse from a successful raiding party and that night the horse died.)

Herkeyah then drifted off to the Kwaharunuu band. PitUwetu organized the band to retake the captives from the soldiers and Tonkawas. There were probably ten or more camps going. He intended to negotiate for the captives. On the first night, they stopped at Petakaruhka's[2] ('eat by self') camp.

Some people went over to see the Penanuu. Five were selected: PitUwetu and his wife; a girl, the daughter of Pasuwakitsu[3]; and Tutsiktoke[4] and his wife. The Penanuu were friends with the soldiers and Tonkawas. Wutsita,[5] their chief, gave a good answer and said

1. See above, Introduction and Post Oak Jim, July 25.
2. *peta* 'alone, solitary'?, *tuhka* 'eat'. Otherwise unidentified.
3. Otherwise unidentified.
4. Otherwise unidentified.
5. Otherwise unidentified.

he would go to the Tonkawas. PitUwetʉ would go back to his camp with Penanʉʉ rations to get his second wife. Herkeyah stayed alone. PitUwetʉ returned again. The first three or four trips to the Tonkawa failed to find the girl they were looking for. The Penanʉʉ chief went with PitUwetʉ's wife. The last time, they were gone a long time.

PitUwetʉ's nephew had them move the camp to make a more advantageous defense in case of attack; they left behind a marker showing a false direction. The girl was finally located, but the Tonkawa refused to give her up.

Herkeyah and her man were out looking for that borrowed horse {sic, ?}. They saw a smoke sign below their old camp, and saw Weseka[1] out hunting. She thought he was an enemy and fled back to camp. But she started playing with the children without telling the news.

At dark, the people asked her where her husband was. She told them he had gone down to see about the smoke, and how a man on a mule had chased her. The people got excited, got on their horses, and rode up the hill. A boy came back and helped her catch a horse. PitUwetʉ and his party came back bringing the lost girl.

On their way back, they saw a covered wagon. Her husband went up to it to see what it was about. They talked a long time, and caught up with the horses. They got crackers and green coffee. This was the first white man she had seen with whiskers.[2]

Life Story: Herkeyah {Carlson}   Herkeyah was a Mexican who was captured as a child by Toyop, a Comanche warrior, who was a captive himself. When the band that had captured her started home, Toyop decided to stay for one more raid before going home. There was a group of about thirty that stayed with him.

While the rest of the camp broke up, they stayed eating breakfast. Herkeyah sat to one side, with no one paying any attention to her. One man, Wahaomo, came back to pick up something he had lost. On starting back to rejoin the party, he saw Herkeyah.

The men who were eating called to Wahaomo that they had no way of taking care of this girl, that they were going on a war party. They said they thought they had better kill her. Wahaomo had two young children, one sickly and the other crippled. His wife was dead and there was no one to care for his children. He thought of his children and thought it wouldn't be nice to kill this little girl.

He picked her up and set her on his yellow mule. Toyop got up and picked up some blankets. He gave the girl one to sit on and gave three to Wahaomo. Toyop asked Wahaomo if he had any arrows to spare. Wahaomo gave him a handful from his quiver, then rode on with the girl.

On their way towards the main group, they saw one of the captive girls laying by the roadside. She was bleeding at the genitals. She had been raped and was dying. A little further, they saw a captive boy dead in the road.

As they went on, Wahaomo told Herkeyah she would be his wife when she was grown. He wanted to take her home to care for his children.

---

1. *wesi-* 'curly'. Otherwise unidentified, although he could have been the Wiaʔnʉʉ local band chief whose name was spelled Wissiche, Waysee, and other variants.

2. Wallace and Hoebel 1952:261–63. The dating of Herkeyah's life story is from Carlson (see next note).

After a year with Wahaomo where she was well treated, having nothing to do but care for the children, Toyop asked to have her again. The soldiers had raided his camp, killing or capturing the women of the group, and there was no one to care for his adopted father, the brother of the man who had captured Toyop. The father's name was Tasobakwitsi.

Toyop begged Wahaomo to let him have the girl again. That day, she was out playing with the children. Wahaomo came down and told his children that their mother was going to leave. The two children and Herkeyah began to cry. Herkeyah was then about twelve years old.

Makera, who was Tasobakwitsi's *toko?* {maternal grandmother}, came for her that evening, and took her to the old man.

HERKEYAH
August 15, 1933[1]

Kinship Relations   There was a passing reference in Herkeyah's life story to a boy who was raised by his *huutsI* when his mother abandoned him.[2]

Kinship Relations: Cousins   Black Horse[3] threatened Tuhuub,[4] his classificatory sister, so she ran off and lived with her *ara?*.

Tuhuub and Tokemi called each other *samohpʉ?*, although they could have used sibling terms, being cousins.

---

1. From Carlson.
2. The specific reference of this note is unclear.
3. See p. 382, note 2, above.
4. Robinson and Armagost (1990) gives *tuhUbʉ* as 'hide'. Otherwise unidentified.

FRANK MOETAH
August 16, 1933[1]

Relations with Other Tribes: Tonkawa {Carlson} The Extermination of the Tonkawas[2]

Many tribes of Indians were camped at the Anadarko region, near Fort Cobb[3] and Big Corn Creek—Comanches, Delawares, Caddos, ⟨Khiticharri⟩,[4] ⟨Waponakai⟩,[5] Tukahninuu,[6] and Tonkawas.

The Tonkawas were reputed to dig up corpses and eat them.

Bodies began to be missed.

In a regular meeting one day, the son of the Comanche chief said he would go deer hunting the next day. He went off to shoot deer, but he never came back.

When he was gone a day and a night, his father and five others discussed the disappearance.

"Tonkawas or other enemies must have got him," the father said. The boy's five brothers and six old men talked about what must be done. Finally, they decided on a plan.

They got a lot of calico cloth, and three old women were to carry it through the Tonkawa camp the next morning to see if they could find any trace of the young man in any of the pots. They would seem to be selling the cloth and that would get them into all the houses of the Tonkawa.

The next day, this plan was carried out. The three old women went through the Tonkawa camp trying to find out what each family was having for dinner.

One old woman went into a Tonkawa house, and when she looked into the soup pot, while the people of the house looked at her cloth, she saw the head of the young man in a pot of corn, boiling for soup. The eyes were there in the head and a certain bad tooth which she knew the young man had, making her absolutely sure that it was the head of the young man.

The old woman ran outside immediately and went back to the father of the young man.

In his tipi, she reported her find. The two younger brothers of the young man got mad. They wanted revenge right away, but their father said, "No, that would cause bad trouble later. The best thing to do was to take it to the law."

So the father and the two brothers went to the Indian agent.[7] They said they had come merely to tell him the cause of the disappearance of corpses and of people, that the

---

1. The first note is from Carlson and titled, "August 16, Walters, Norton, Frank Moetah." The rest of this interview is from Hoebel's undated cards. Since there is no other evidence of another interview with Moetah, I have placed them all here. The order is arbitrary.

2. This apparently refers to the Tonkawa Massacre of 1862 near Anadarko (Nye 1969:30–31).

3. Fort Cobb is a small town on the Washita River. The original post was established in 1859, then abandoned in 1862 following a raid by Federal Indians. It was reoccupied in late 1868, but soon abandoned again in favor of Fort Sill. The present town of Fort Cobb was established after the opening of the reservation in 1901 and was named after the nearby ruins.

4. Possibly the Kitsai.

5. An otherwise unknown ethnonym.

6. Literally, 'dark houses', Wichitas.

7. In 1862, the Confederate agent at Fort Cobb was Matthew Leeper; such papers as do survive from the Fort Cobb Agency (Abel 1915) do not contain any mention of this visit.

Tonkawas had been eating the people, even the whites. The Indian agent replied that if the Indians could prove it, he would find a way to fix it up.

So the Indians told him about the disappearance of the young boy and how the three women were sent out to look for him, and how the one old woman found the head boiling in the pot of corn, and that the boy was identified by the bad tooth set to one side in his head. They said that they were going to get all the Indian tribes in the neighborhood together and wipe out the Tonkawas before they were all eaten up.

So the Indian agent told the Indians to summon all the chiefs of the tribes to his office. When the chiefs were assembled, the Indian agent told the story. He said he believed the Tonkawas were guilty and asked for opinions from the Indians. They said they all agreed, that they had suspected this for some time. Now they had the proof, their suspicions were confirmed. The Indian agent said that this message should be delivered to all the people: all those who live near the Tonkawa camp should move a safe distance away immediately, and all the Indian warriors should assemble the next morning near the Tonkawa camp. Then he sent for some soldiers from Fort Cobb.

At sunrise the next morning, the soldiers and Indians surrounded the Tonkawa camp and began the attack. The women and children ran away, even the chief of the Tonkawas ran. The Caddo chief came up to the Tonkawa chief and bullied him for running; he said they should stand their ground and shoot and kill each other. They fought and both died.

There was one Tonkawa warrior who was the only brave man in his tribe. He was on horseback and he continually rushed out and shot at the soldiers. He wounded many, but was not touched. The Tonkawa group was pushed across the creek now called Tonkawa. The Tonkawas were surrounded. The brave young warrior's horse was shot from under him, but he went back and got arrows from his friends and rushed out again on foot. He danced around in front of the Tonkawa band.

This went on until evening. Finally, he came out no more, he must have been killed or have given up. Thirty or forty Tonkawas must have escaped and went down into Texas, for they acted as scouts and guides later down there. But all the rest of the tribe was slaughtered. There were dead everywhere.

N.B. Later, when the Comanches were on a war party into Texas, they lost some men while fighting against the soldiers. When they went back to bury their dead later, they found that all the flesh had been stripped from the bodies. So they knew that the Tonkawas had been there.

Social Roles: Contrary   Any man brave enough and with the desire could become a *pukutsi* on making up his mind.

He could never retreat in a raid. With a bow in one hand and his rattle in the other, he would take his position and sing until victory or death. Should he give way after the fight was done, the other warriors would taunt him in an attempt to egg him into an overt action so they could kill him.

He carried a rattle made from a buffalo scrotum. He would go through the camp singing no matter what else might be going on. He was never molested because he was so recklessly brave, no matter what his action.[1]

---

1. Wallace and Hoebel 1952:275.

Medicine: Duration   The only time medicine weakened was because of broken taboos.

In such a case, the medicine was dropped; there was no attempt to restrengthen it, but he could try for a new vision for new medicine.

He might be successful in getting the same medicine all over, or he might get a new medicine, or he might be informed that he was unworthy.

Medicine: Peyote   The four whistles at midnight by the leader outside the tipi were to notify all things in all directions that they were having a meeting there at the center of the cross.

When the whistle was blown inside at midnight, it was calling the great power to be with us while we were drinking, so that it could hear our prayers and bless us.[1]

Medicine: Peyote: Menstrual Taboos   Menstruating women should not go into a Peyote meeting. If she did, she should tell the leader beforehand. Otherwise, her pain would come back on him after the meeting.

Oaths: Sun Killing   Someone might try to cause a medicine man to break his taboo.

The medicine man might see in a dream that this was being done to him and see the image of the offender.

The medicine man would confront the offender and accuse him of the act.

In case of denial, he could then force him to swear by the sun. To admit the deed would endanger one's life.

QUASSYAH
August 1933[2]

Material Culture: Clothing: Headdress: Victory Dance   Women wore feather headdresses if their sons or husbands had returned from war.

Material Culture: Clothing: Headdress: Roach   The roach was introduced from the Osages, Pawnees, and Otoes. It was made from the mane of the elk, also from deer tail or skunk, and dyed.

Social Organization: Bands: Parʉhya   Parʉhya was the Elk band ('water horse').[3]

Material Culture: Clothing: Headdress: Roach   The braided scalp lock passed through the holes, and the roach was tied to the lock at this point. The thunder bird was at the top and bottom. It was called *kuʔeksitsanike*.[4]

Material Culture: Clothing   There was a beaded sleeve holder {*sic*, arm band?} with pendent ribbons.

---

1. La Barre 1975:51.
2. Wedel's notes do not indicate a specific date.
3. Wallace and Hoebel 1952:30. On the spelling and etymology of the name, see the section on Tahsuda in the Introduction.
4. *kuʔe* 'pointed', *tsinikarʉ* 'insert into something'.

Adornment: Necklace   There were necklaces of blue paste beads, with a single plain grizzly bear claw as pendent. There was red paint in a groove on the underside and in a hole near the base.

A medicine man alone could wear a bear claw.

There was a beaded circlet worn over the ear lock at the top.

Medicine: Peyote: Motifs   The motifs on a Peyote drum stick represented lightning and an alligator's back. When beaten, the drum represented the thunder.

The alligator was the water monster.

The peyote button at the top of the gourd rattle represented the earth.

There was no significance to the beadwork.

The rattle sounded like a whistle when the peyote worked.

Animals: Birds: Waterbird   ⟨haiβex⟩ feathers were used for the fan. It had long legs and a long neck; it flew high and fast; it was a loon. The ripples on the feathers represented waves.[1]

The fans were made by wrapping cloth at the base of each feather and tying them together with thongs from several feathers. There were long beaded strings from the bottom.

Material Culture: Bows   Bois d'arc was used at any time of year. It was cured for about two weeks. It was cured before a fire only if it was needed urgently.

The wood came mostly from one corner of the state.

Mulberry was used out west, where the former was rare. *tamutso²I*[2] was also used. It had thorns and leaves like pecans.

Bows were about three-and-a-half feet long.

The {plain arc} was preferred for war. It was harder shooting.

The other {recurved} was for hunting.

The wood was selected for straight grain.

It was smoothed with sandstone in the old days.

It was greased with beef fat, then warmed by the fire to soak in.

The heart of the tree was always used for bows.[3]

The upper end was sometimes decorated with dyed horsehair. There was a notch for stringing.

The other end was the same, but was without the peg for decoration.

Bear gut was preferred in the old days for the string. It was unaffected by wet weather.[4]

Material Culture:Arrows: Arrow Release   The arrow was held between the thumb and index finger, the ring finger catches the string also, not the middle finger. There were three feathers, sinew fastened at the top and bottom.

⟨patsənai⟩ (awkward), shooting on the right of the bow, was wrong for a right-handed man, he should shoot over his bow hand.

1. *Anhinga anhinga*, commonly called the water bird.
2. Robinson and Armagost (1990) gives *tamutso²I* as 'green briar'.
3. Contra Wallace and Hoebel 1952:100.
4. Wallace and Hoebel 1952:101.

Material Culture: Arrow Smoother   *pahtsasuʔne*,[1] arrowshaft smoothers, were used in pairs
for the final smoothing after first drawing through holes in a tin can.

Material Culture: Arrows   Arrows had two or three shallow grooves; wavy snake arrows
went "quick as lightning."

They had steel blades; the basal tongue fit into the split shaft. It had barbs to hold it firm
in the sinew wrapping.

Wooden pointed arrows were occasionally used.

The tips were greased, then hardened in the fire.

There was a tuft of colored feathers at the lower end of the shaft feathering.

Arrows were marked with identifying marks.[2]

The *nanopuata* (*karisu*) to the west used bone-tipped arrows.[3] The Comanches also.

The Navajos used arrows with a foreshaft.

⟨pakətusas⟩ was a poison put all over the arrow, not only on the point. It made the body
swell. It was made by rubbing leaves on the arrow. It smelled sweet.

Arrows were deadly up to twenty-five yards on all but the largest game.

There were special arrow makers.

Buzzard and hawk feathers were used.

Weapons: Lances   The blades were about twelve inches long, made from large knives. They
were not notched or barbed save where they fastened to the shaft.

They had a straight slender blade, fastened like arrows in a slot in the shaft. The shaft
was about six feet long by one-and-a-half inches thick.

The spear was ⟨woinutsik⟩[4] with a fringe of *nahaikorohkO* (crow feathers). {see fig. 6}

The spear was wrapped up and laid away in warrior's tipi when not in use. It was
sometimes kept by the shield outside.

The lance was carried in the hand, not in a scabbard. It was not thrown. A young man
once threw one at his affines and was discredited.

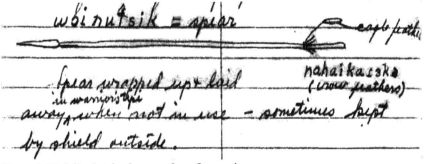

Figure 6. Wedel's sketch of a spear from Quassyah.

1. Robinson and Armagost (1990) gives *pahtsi* as 'smooth', and *tsasuʔnerʉ* as 'scrape smooth'.
2. Hoebel 1940:120.
3. The referents of these ethnonyms are unclear. The "to the west" reference suggests the Carrizo
(Cibicue) Apaches.
4. Possibly *wohihɄnutsikarʉ*. Robinson and Armagost (1990) translates *wohihɄ* as 'mesquite' and
nuutsikwarʉ 'give pain'. For *tsik* as 'spear', see Lowie's notes in Part Two, below.

Weapons: Pistols   Pistols were worn on the wrist in a loop.

War: Shields   Shields were *topʉ*.

They killed a buffalo bull and cut the hide from its neck, the thickest part, a little larger than the desired size of the shield. It was stobbed {staked} to the ground and dried hard.

When it was hard, they took out the stobs and had someone who was good cut out a good circle. It was cleaned well on the inside before trimming. They varied according to the size of the individual.

A buckskin cover, *topʉtsoʔnika*,[1] was put over the rawhide, fastened at back with sort of drawstring "like a laundry bag."

The painting on the buckskin was of buffalo, bear, a man with gun, etc.

The carrying case was ⟨haiʔkem⟩ with feathers about the edge; it was also painted. When going into battle, part of the haiʔkem was thrown over on the front like a flap. It looked like a war bonnet. It {shield} was slung at the side or back on a long loop. It was held in the hand by the loop in battle. It had two small loops at back as hand grips, in addition to the carrying loop.

Material Culture: Clothing: Headdress   The war bonnet was carried in a circular, flat-bottomed, cylindrical case with a rawhide cover called ⟨titsomoi⟩[2] or *piatsoʔnikaʔ*.[3] It was used on war parties.

War Story   Quassyah's father asked another warrior for his horse, which was very fast. Quassyah's father wanted to be the first to meet the enemy. The other thought he wanted to flee.

They went out and met the Utes. A dismounted Ute, who had a bonnet like Quassyah's father's, came up and started to shoot, but changed his mind and ran. Quassyah's father shot him in the back of the neck. The Ute tried to pull out the arrow while fleeing; he also tried to throw off his bonnet. The Utes were shooting, but couldn't hit them. The Comanche warriors rode in and used spears on them.

Hubia,[4] a young man, claimed an important part in the fight. He came along and struck dead men and got war honors, but he didn't kill many. The killer had first honor; if he was killed, the second coup counter could claim the former's honor.

The Ute threw off his bonnet and fled back to his fellows. Another Comanche picked it up and brought it away.

Quassyah's father had the same name as Quassyah.[5]

The other warriors said he was braver than Paruakuhma.

Weapons: Knives   Knives were used in close fighting; also spears.

Social Roles: Club Man   White Horse[6] used the *pianʉʔʉpaiʔi* only. It was a club with spikes, no other decoration whatever. White Horse also used the "peace club" in dances.

---

1. Robinson and Armagost (1990) gives *tsoʔnika* as 'hat'.
2. See next page, where this is described as the war bonnet itself.
3. Literally, 'big hat'. Robinson and Armagost (1990) has it as 'headdress'.
4. It is not clear to whom this refers, either Huubaʔ or Howeah.
5. See Introduction.
6. It is not clear to whom who this refers; there was no known Comanche named White Horse, although there was a famous Kiowa by that name.

Material Culture: Clothing: Headdress   The feather bonnet, without a train, was more honorable than the *pianɯʔɯpaiʔi*. There were only two in the Kwaharɯ, both medicine men. The others were by Ekawokani.[1] There were several "peace clubs" in later times in the Kwaharɯ.

Ekawokani had a nephew, Pirirakoniwop,[2] who wanted a similar bonnet. Ekawokani had no confidence in him, because if you retreated with a bonnet, you were disgraced. Ekawokani found he was serious, so he put his bonnet on his nephew.

Soldiers were coming and the people were waiting for them. Pirirakoniwop couldn't wait and started toward the enemy ahead of every one. An old man who had lost his son went through the camp leading a horse belonging to his son. He wanted someone to ride the horse in battle, but no one volunteered.

Finally, a poor boy took it and rode out. He was the second to close. Pirirakoniwop speared a soldier; the second boy got off, took the scalp, and then went back. Pirirakoniwop rode around in front of the soldiers and was shot at, but missed, then he rode back to his people. The nephew was brave man, but he just wanted to show off with the bonnet.

Story: Nappywat   Nappywat[3] was another brave warrior. A Tonkawa scout with the troops would ride across line of battle and taunt the Comanches. Nappywat rode out finally to clean up on him. They rode toward each other, but the Tonkawa turned back before they closed.

Material Culture: Clothing: Headdress   ⟨titsomoi⟩[4] was the feather headdress. There was tail of silk ribbons, beaded around the front, about a one inch wide band.

Eagle feathers were used before this. In the old times, they used a long trailer on the headdress; it was more honorable than these.

Signals   A lost person might set fire to the prairie; people would come out to see what was wrong and find him.

Smoke signals were used.

They also imitated animal calls when they were in hostile territory.

Material Culture: Clothing: Moccasins   There were no heel fringes among other tribes.[5]

---

1. Hoebel (1940:146) gives Ekawokani as Red Young Man. While the *eka* is clearly 'red', the *wokani* part is unclear. He is otherwise unidentified.
2. This is as written by Wedel. Possibly *pibia* 'large', *kuʔina* - 'roasted meat'. He is otherwise unidentified.
3. See Index.
4. See previous page, where this is described as the war bonnet case.
5. This is the end of Wedel's Notebook 6. All further notes are from either Hoebel or Carlson.

RHODA ASENAP
Undated[1]

Life Cycle: Marriage: Wife Desertion   "Several women were killed for running away."

When her husband came for her and she wouldn't go back, he shot her; nobody did anything about it. The man she ran away with was seldom hurt; the punishment fell on her.

Rhoda's father's cousin went with a raiding party. Her husband told Rhoda's father to be ready to go for her on their return. They returned during the night. Her husband and several other men went for her. The woman saw them coming and ran behind her new husband.

Her old mother greeted them and asked what was wrong. Her father's cousin explained that he wanted his wife back. Her old parents advised their son {i.e., son-in-law} to give her back, they had "been together long enough."

The man didn't want to give her up. There was a long discussion. Her old husband promised not to harm her. They finally let her and he took her back. His promise was not worth much, the woman was bound to be treated roughly.

"Girls try every way to get rid of an old man."

As for going on a raiding party, she might be in love with the leader. He might be a better warrior than her husband and can therefore protect her. On their return, she might stay with the leader if he was strong enough to keep her and her husband wouldn't dare come for her. Her husband might try to claim her if he has the power, "and sometimes it causes much trouble and maybe death."

If she was the wife of an important warrior, they were afraid to go, no one would be able to protect them. None of Rhoda's father's wives ran away[2]; everyone was afraid of him and his brothers.

If she was mistreated she could leave and go to her parents, if her parents would protect her. Those without parents had a harder time. Some other relative might stand by them to prevent their being mistreated.

Life Cycle: Marriage   Rhoda's mother's sister was given to an older man by her brother, who owed him a debt. The man had another wife, who was jealous, and she made life miserable for her, she made a slave of her. "Somehow she got rid of him."

She ran off with a raiding party. On her return, she wasn't forced to go back to him because it was known that he was too mean. She went back to her parents.

Life Cycle: Marriage: Ceremony   There was no marriage ceremony. He asked a girl to marry him. If they arranged it, he called for her at night and took her to his tipi. They were married from them on.[3]

Life Cycle: Marriage: Polygamy   Women liked to marry a warrior for his name, and because he had many horses. Therefore, Pahdopony was popular. He had three or four wives[4]; Rhoda was the daughter of his last wife.

---

1. These notes are from Hoebel. The order is arbitrary.
2. Wallace and Hoebel 1952:236.
3. Wallace and Hoebel 1952:136 (?).
4. Wallace and Hoebel 1952:236.

Life Cycle: Marriage: Divorce   If a woman's parent's didn't like a marriage, they could break it up. They went to the boy's tipi and took their daughter back. Therefore, the couple usually had the consent of the parents first. This was most likely to take place when a man was already married.

Life Cycle: Marriage: Levirate   On the death of a brother, his wife or wives went to his brother if he wanted them. If he didn't, the women were free.

Medicine: Shields   Rhoda's father had a shield, but she never saw it (he was "very precious about it"). She wouldn't have seen it normally, if she lived in an old camp. It was hung outside, but she couldn't have gone close enough to see the design.

Social Roles: Gender Roles: Female Warriors   Women sometimes went along for the fun of it, but they never went on the hardest raids. Some could shoot bows and arrows.

Medicine: Sun Dance   A pile of sand was brought into the arbor and wetted down for the dancers to lie on when they were exhausted. They flopped on their stomachs and dug down into the damp sand. It cooled them.

Material Culture: Crafts   Beadwork woven on a wooden loom was used on belts and as decorative pieces for the dress of men and women. There were medicine patterns, such as dragonflies. Beadwork was sewn on in small rows of five beads.

Moccasins were made of three pieces, the sole, top, and tongue. Beads were sewn on moccasins in a zigzag pattern.

Life Cycle: Menstruation   She slept with old people (her family) to avoid hurting her husband's or her father's medicine. They all had some kind of medicine, but the medicine of the old people was too weak to be harmed.

POST OAK JIM
Undated[1]

Medicine: Peyote   Jim's uncle traded a fine horse for 500 peyote buttons from a Mexican.[2]

The Comanches were tickled over the surveying[3] so they had a meeting to celebrate. The women put up the tipi.

The meeting lasted as long as the chief wanted it to. He sang the midnight song and the morning song at the time he wanted them. Some {sang it} at nearly morning, some at noon. He dictated who would bring in the midnight water and breakfast, whether single or married, and he might choose either one.

One man had an entire tipi floor of cement with a special place for the fire and the road medicine built of cement.[4] There was a fence to keep the stock outside. This was the only one Norton Tahquechi had ever seen like that.

1. From Hoebel.
2. La Barre 1975:64.
3. Presumably for allotment.
4. La Barre 1975:76.

The Osages had one in a frame building, with electric lights in it. They had beds in it, and smoked cigars and had spittoons. It was different from all others. They stew the {. . . [*sic*]}

Language: Baby Language   There were baby talk terms for certain words; these were used by anyone talking to babies and by babies when they learned to talk.

tsisti	visitors
kok?o	candy
tata	meat
mama	horse
ana	hurt
muma	owl
kwasino	coyote
tata	shoes
tsitsinʉ	mother
ahpʉ	father
kaku	either grandmother

Shields   Jim once saw his father's shield; he looked under the cover from the bottom. The decoration was a peyote with green leaves and red flowers. There were thirteen marks (stripes), and a cow head. Jim's mother would carry it; when Jim grew up, he carried it for his father.

Medicine: Curing: Lice   Cut off all the hair, wash with yucca root, and then have a woman remove the eggs with her nails.

Medicine: Curing: Harelip or Twisted Limbs   Kill a crow, pound the fresh meat with brains, rub this on the afflicted part.

Medicine: *puhakatʉ* Conquers Buffalo Bull   A *puhakatʉ* was out hunting buffalo with his brothers. The medicine man stumbled (horse) in loose sand and he was thrown. The buffalo fell too.

His partner came up. The medicine man told him to take off the horse, but to stay away from the bull.

The bull was getting his dander up. The medicine man rubbed sand four times with his hands, then stood up straight up like a tree. The bull charged full into him, but bounced back. The bull charged again and lifted him bodily. This happened four times. On the fourth time, the medicine man rubbed sand four times and took up a handful. He threw it at the bull, hitting him on the head; a cloud of smoke came out of his nostrils.

The bull fell down on its knees. The medicine man took his whiskers, ran his hand upon its head, and turned it over. He put his hand down the buffalo's throat to its stomach, and pulled out some foamy stuff and swallowed it.[1]

Medicine: *puhakatʉ* Cures a Child   An unknown fever broke out in the encampment. A couple had an only child and it got sick. The child was in the tent. They brought up two pintos for the funeral. They washed, painted, and dressed the child, and set it down to die and started mourning.

---

1. It is not clear if this story, or the next one, are supposed to be autobiographical.

The medicine man sent his wife down to see what they were about. She held up her hand to stop the mourning. She said, "You who are bleeding, go out and get coals for a cedar smudge."

The woman went back to get her man. He circled and entered. He asked for a clay cup with water.

The child was facing east with the medicine man at its feet. He took out an eagle feather, wet it in his mouth, and waved it over the child; the child showed a little life. He waved it three more times; on the fourth time, they could hear an eagle song and the child opened its eyes. The medicine man sprinkled the child on the head with water.

He spoke to the mourners outside. He told them to wash their wounds in lukewarm water, take red clay and mix it with water, and smear it on the wound. Those who had no red should take gray clay and apply it dry. "Now come in, I'll talk."

The medicine man said, "This sickness has caused no death, but would make a long sleep; that was how many were buried alive."

He told the parents to wash the paint off the child. It woke up, and said, "Gee, I'm hungry."

It was fed with cornmeal mush.

The medicine man said, "This was all I will do; I'm going now." The family gave the doctor the two ponies, just as they stood ready for the funeral, loaded with gifts for the grave.

Hunting: Antelope Drive   If the whole camp was out of food, someone went to a medicine woman, smoked, and told her the trouble. They all went outside, lined up with the medicine woman in the center, on foot, facing east. On either side of her was a mounted warrior. All the rest of the people in the camp were unmounted. Her medicine was two antelope hoofs on sticks. She crossed her arms halfway down her forearms and blocked the antelope. She opened her arms and gave one hoof to each horseman.

The horsemen rode, one northeast, one southeast. They crossed their paths about a mile to the east, and returned on the other's path.

The people followed the horsemen on foot until they were standing in a huge circle, all singing. The antelopes were then inside the circle. The people closed in on them, shouting. The medicine woman chose an antelope in a bunch with one horn down; she pointed her hoof at him and he died. The people then piled in and killed them all.

Food   Marrow from buffalo bone was mixed with sugar (sweet meat); it was used in peyote. Before they had sugar, they used to mix the marrow with mesquite beans.

They put the meat into a parfleche, cut up in long pieces the length of the bag.

Wild grapes were dried like raisins. They were wet and mashed, mixed with grease, and kept over the winter. They were toasted in chunks.

Mesquite beans were boiled and mixed with cornmeal as a drink.

Comanche tea was boiled from either a gray weed, or the reddish brown berries of a plant.

Hackberries were pounded and mixed with grease in a form like a sausage; it was toasted.

Cedar berries were eaten raw.

Acorns were picked and boiled, and eaten when you wanted to. (They were stored.)

They were "regular oak."

Walnuts: take the skins off when green; dry and store.

Prickly pear: clean the seeds out, rub the stickers off on grass, dry, and cook with fat. They were kept for winter.

Medicine: Curing: Hemorrhage   Jim's (*puhakatʉ*). He never used it when menstruating women were about, or else the sickness would come back on the medicine man. Jim didn't like to use it.

Jim obtained it at about age twenty-five. As a young man, he was out hunting bird feathers for a bouquet for himself. He felt dopey so he lay down under an *otʉmitsonaaʔ*[1] ('mountain ash').

A dream came to him. It told him where to find a root and warned him of the taboo. An alternative was also given, which was not so dangerous. It gave him a bulb wrapped in buckskin. It told him to bury it in a creek, if he wanted to get rid of the power, and thus, bury evil thoughts (fear of the medicine) with it. He should go back to the tipi and burn cedar.

He went back for the bulb, which was under water.

The spirit kept talking; it said, "From now on, you'll be a medicine man," and told him to wake up.

He went back to his wife. He told her not to hide any love affairs from him; he had the power to see all, and if she doubted, he would prove it.

He told her to get a mirror and he wiped it on his knee. He blew on it four times and told her to look in it; she saw herself with a former swain.

The medicine was also good for urinal stoppage.

A woman swallowed a needle at Anadarko. She coughed blood and couldn't breathe. She called on this medicine man. He got ready, washed, combed his hair, took a clean sheet and the center feather of an eagle tail. He circled the tipi and entered. He faced the woman to the east, crouching. He dusted the woman three times with the feather. He put it in his mouth to wet it, and cried like an eagle. He put it down the woman's mouth, then pulled it out; the needle was standing on the end of it. The medicine man stuck the needle in his scalp lock. The woman drank water, spit it out, coughed, and was OK.

Games   The children played house by the creek.

Jim would be the chief.

They made a windbreak to sleep in.

They hunted squirrels, etc.; they got food in the camp to cook.

One day they played at being married; Jim did his best to make a baby with "his wife."

They swam in the creek.

They gathered in the ponies with the girls and rode together.

They picked berries, mulberries, and gooseberries.[2]

Life Cycle: Marriage: Adultery   A handsome young man had a plain wife. The husband went off on a raid. The wife adultered. A sister-in-law saw her lying with another man.

---

1. Literally, 'brown blackberry'. Robinson and Armagost (1990) gives *otʉmitsona*, as 'soap berry'.
2. Wallace and Hoebel 1952:128.

The girl's father was bragging about what a good daughter he had, what a faithful wife she made her husband.

The sister-in-law remarked that she was not so good, and that she was going to tell her brother what she had seen of his wife.

The husband returned and slept with his wife the first night.

The next morning, the husband's sister came to talk to him. She told him she wanted to tell him something and he shouldn't take it too hard.

His uncle added that what she was going to tell him was true, but he was a good, honorable man, brave, a good man; he should keep his reputation good. The husband took the news easy. He merely told his wife he was going to leave her. He GAVE HER 8 HEAD OF HORSES {sic}. He picked himself another wife right off. He started to take the woman back to her band, the Kwaharʉnʉʉ.

The first wife carried a muzzleloader. When the ex-husband got off his horse to do something, she shot at him and missed.

"Now are you trying to take my life?" he cried.

He pulled her from her horse, threw her down, cut off her nose, and left her lying there. He returned to his own camp with his wife.

The woman recovered and got back to her people. Her family was pretty mad. Her mother went to a sorceress for help.

This medicine woman went to lonely place, and, cutting a piece of flesh from her shoulder, asked for the power to kill this man.

A few days later, the husband organized a war party again and went off. The enemy could not be found. The leader had bad dreams, so he turned the band back.

They were attacked by white soldiers.

The leader and many others were killed.

Two of the party survived to get back with the news.

The people could not understand why a plain woman had so thrown down her husband.

There was no revenge or punishment for this sorcery.

Medicine: *puhakatʉ* Kills a Mule   An army unit from Anadarko was camped across from the Comanches.

A medicine man said to his wife, "I have had a beautiful dream. I must do this in your presence."

"See that beautiful mule hitched to that wagon?"

"When my life is done, I want to look pretty."

He was going to kill that mule, "so I'll have it to ride when I go to meet sorrow."

He sat down and made a smooth place on the earth. He put in a knife, and moved it around. His wife could see the mule stiffen. He pulled the knife out and the mule fell dead; blood flowed on the ground.

Political Organization: Chiefs: War Party   The chief would always comfort the survivors of a casualty on his party and would sometimes give them a horse or other gift.

Captives: Ransom   A man or child was sometimes released for a horse or cattle.

War: Raiding Parties   People were told not to wait for missing men, but to go ahead and move the camp. If they came back, they would follow the trail of the camp and catch up. It was dangerous to wait for them.

Medicine: Sun Dance   The general site was selected in advance.

The camp was broken and groups moved by easy stages to this locale.

There were four stops with overnight camps made on the way.

The time was usually late summer.

The ceremonial camp was pitched in a semicircle about the site of the dance arbor.

It officially began with the bringing in of the materials for the arbor. All the materials must be brought in before work began.[1]

Hunting: Preparation of Buffalo   They left cows lying on their sides. Bulls were set with fours spread. They were cut down the back for buffalo quilts.

War: Coup   A small boy was told by the medicine man to go out and strike the ten Utes he'd killed (that the medicine man had killed), so that when he was grown up, he could tell about it at all the dances.[2]

Animal Powers: Coyote   A Coyote Medicine Man showed his power by walking barefoot in the winter.

He painted the web of his foot red, because coyotes had red between their toes and under their arms in winter.

Life Cycle: Marriage: Forced   Where a girl became pregnant, the man may marry her willingly, or the girl's parents went and talked friendly to persuade him. They got results without trouble.

Animal Powers: Beaver   Most Beaver Medicine Men were bad, although some could cure wasting-away sickness.

Medicine: Honey for Meal   Wʉsawi[3] was a medicine man and leader. It came mealtime. Someone said, "I wish we had some honey."

Wʉsawi said, "That's easy."

He waved a buzzard's wing and saw where it was. He called some old people to get their horses and ride up to Giant's Cave.[4] There the king (*paraibo*) bee would come out. It worked as promised. The king bee flew off to a dead oak.

They went to it with axes. It was rotten, so they pushed it over. There were eleven thick layers of honey, the finest stuff. They smeared honey all over themselves so as not to get stung. They cut the honey out in hunks.

Life Cycle: Childhood: Girls   {Girls} would gather turkey, duck, quail, and prairie chicken eggs in their aprons (also berries). They also gathered roots.

Food: Taboos   They didn't kill ravens.

The Walters Indians didn't eat pounded meat.

Life Cycle: Marriage: Polygamy   The permission of the wife's parents was not necessary. In the first place, the man had rule over the woman.

Kinship Relations: In-Law Obligations   The mother helped the girl make her tipi. Her brother and husband produced the hides. A son-in-law was treated as a son. Parents-in-law

---

1. This typewritten note seems to be a synthesis of Post Oak Jim's information from other dates.
2. The antecedents of this story are unknown.
3. Otherwise unidentified. There are several names on the census lists spelled Woosuwy or some variant, but they are all female.
4. Location unknown.

respected each other, there was no joking between them. Brothers-in-law usually got along together.

Nanɨwokɨ   A man's close friends were called upon to go with him on a *nanɨwokɨ* mission. It was very dangerous, but they were willing to die for him. It was not so likely to call upon one's relatives.

They might ask for his special keepsake, such as a favorite horse. If he won't give it to them, they can kill the horse. This was not done if the man had more war deeds than they.

If a man took another man's wife, the injured man may take the other's horses; he may kill the other's horses; he may kill the other man (?); he may kill the woman, or both.

He did not kill the offender's brother; he alone was responsible.

If the man who took the wife was a brave warrior, the injured man went to talk it over; if there was no agreement, "war broke out between the families."[1]

Medicine: Duration   Medicine did not work all the time. A medicine man might be invulnerable in one battle and sieved with bullets in the next.

Life Cycle: Illegitimacy   Illegitimacy was rare. The girl was not usually married to another for a long time. The father could claim his child at any time.

Life Cycle: Marriage: Sororate   A worthy man, a young man, married to a daughter of a polygamous family, might get all the daughters all of the wives of his wife's father.

Life Cycle: Marriage: Exchange   If a man slept with another man's wife, the second man squared it by sleeping with the other man's wife. "Then they both had done wrong."

Life Cycle: Courting   Boys seemed to stay pretty much to their own tipis.[2] It was the girl's place to come to him.

A girl might spend the night before a raid in the boy's tipi and then go on the raid with him.

Kinship Relations: Joking   One could joke only with an elder sibling's mate.

One could joke with the spouse of the opposite sex of cousins, called brother or sister.

Social Roles: Friendship   Jim has one. They met in Lawton. They made out like they were fighting and the police took them.

They must stand by each other in warfare. They had great respect for each other.[3]

Beliefs: Moon   The moon was the mother, as was the earth. She was the guardian of the raid. They laid a rope on the ground and sat on it and smoked. They prayed to the moon, the mother: "If it is your will, let this rope take away many horses."[4]

Medicine: Buffalo Call   The buffalo were scarce. The people gave a pipe to the old medicine man. They smoked, and he made medicine in secret at night.

He sang four buffalo songs, either alone or with others.

Whatever animal he had power over would drive the buffalo in. He sent out bucks as scouts to report the appearance. This was Buffalo Medicine.

1. This may have been from July 24; compare with Wedel's notes from the interview of Post Oak Jim of that date.
2. Wallace and Hoebel 1952:133.
3. This note card starts with number 2 indicating that the previous card is missing.
4. Wallace and Hoebel 1952:197.

He walked around to the south side, he cut off the tail and came back to the head.

He got on his horse and rode off with his partner.

He told his partner not to glance back until he was told to.

Finally, he gave the sign, and his partner saw buffalo running off to the west.[1]

Medicine: Buffalo Call   A medicine man named Puhakatʉ,[2] who had great power over buffalo, was about to die.

He called all the medicine men to his bed. He told them they might call his name, and the wind and the birds would bring the message to him and he would get them buffalo.

Life Cycle: Death: Burial   If not too inconvenient, a medicine man would be buried at the spot where he first got his medicine.

Material Culture: Clothing: Cleaning   A grayish clay was used on buckskin suits and moccasins, etc. They put water on the skin, then rubbed the powder in, then washed it off. It cleaned the skin.

Beliefs: End of the World   White people predicted the end of the world. It would get dark and all the people would die. It ain't never happened. It was just like predicting a big storm in the paper.

Medicine: Jim's Philosophy   He thought he was man enough to doctor himself. He came to a case he couldn't cure. He asked how the power came. He learned from peyote that the power of the Almighty alone can do. It rests on the will of God, not in the power of Jim to cure. He first became conscious of medicine at about sixteen, when he first saw doctors perform miracles.

Food: Food Preparation: Stone Boiling   The Yapai used to cook in skins (paunches). Then they got "yellow"—copper—pots from Mexicans.

Beliefs: Ghosts   There was no necessity of absolving a killer from the spirit of his victim.

Medicine: Charms: Bat   A stuffed bat was put on the end of a baby's cradle to protect it. "He's little, but he's really a man."[3]

Never kill a cyclone bat or you could bring on a cyclone.

Case: George's wife killed one and brought on a cyclone.

Material Culture: Clothing: Headdress: Doctor's   It was worn in combat while doctoring the wounded.

Ceremonial installation was necessary. A young man might demonstrate talent. His father or brother recommended him to the doctors, who might select him for the honor.[4]

Horses: Names   There were no war names for horses.[5] They were named by peculiarities of their hoofs, ears, blemishes, etc. For example, 'buffalo horse'.

---

1. Wallace and Hoebel 1952:61 (?). This note is from two cards, one numbered 1–6, the other 7–8, but it is not certain that they go together.

2. This is the generic name for a medicine man, 'possessor of power'.

3. Wallace and Hoebel 1952:160.

4. These notes are from a card, apparently a synthesis of notes about Doctor's Headdresses from July 25 and some other date.

5. Contra Wallace and Hoebel 1952:46.

Life Cycle: Life Stages

{Males}	*ɰkɰruibihtsiʔ*[1]	a young boy
	nahnapʉ[2] *tuibihtsiʔ*	a man in the prime (about my age, said Post Oak Jim)
	tsukuhpɰʔ	old man
{Females}	*ohnaʔaʔ*	baby
	tɰepetɰʔ	young girl[3]
	naiʔbi	young woman
	hɰbi	woman (about fifty years old)
	⟨puʔstɰ⟩	old woman (about eighty years old)[4]

Medicine: Sorcery   A nice young man was bewitched by an old Beaver Medicine Man (sorcery); he wasted away. Someone asked another medicine man what was wrong. He told them of the sorcery. He also attributed other such cases to the same cause.

All the men in the tribe had a conference and decided to kill the sorcerer.

They set up a beaver lodge and put the sick boy in it. They went and smoked with the sorcerer and asked him to perform the Beaver Ceremony. He did so.

They left two young warriors outside the lodge to kill him when he came out.

He came out and started home (he lived a long way off) with a small boy. When they were halfway home, and the women were all asleep, they sent the small boy away and killed him.[5]

TAHSUDA
Undated

Names: *Tahsuda*   After his birth, his grandfather walked in and said, "*Tahsuda*," 'That's It'.[6]

Social Organization: Bands: Band Lists

The Noyɰhka had three names:

Nokoni, 'Those who turn back.' They turned back from raids.

Tɰtsɰnoyɰhka, 'Wandering around they camped in bad places'.[7]

Noyɰhka, 'Wandering around'.

Other bands were:

⟨Pananaitɰ⟩[8] 'Those who live higher.' They lived on the higher side of a creek.

---

1. *ɰkɰ* 'young'.
2. Robinson and Armagost (1990) gives *nahnapʉ* as 'eldest child, grown son or daughter, adult kinsman'.
3. Literally, 'little daughter'.
4. Wallace and Hoebel 1952:145.
5. Hoebel 1940:78.
6. See Introduction.
7. *tɰtsɰ* 'bad'. On his note card, Hoebel has struck out the phrase "they camped in bad places" and placed it after the next entry, but it belongs here.
8. Robinson and Armagost (1990) gives *panihputʉ* as 'high'.

Woʔanʉʉ[1] 'Lots of maggots there'. They were named from a good looking *tekwƗniwapI* who got the venereal from a woman.[2]

Tʉtsahkʉnʉʉ[3] 'Those who make bags while moving'. They manufactured parfleches while on a march. They were located west of Apache; it was a pretty large band.

Otʉtaʔooʔ,[4] 'Burnt Meat'. In the fall, they made a big buffalo hunt. The women dried the flesh and sewed it up in parfleches (pounded). As it was used, they would rip open the corners of the parfleche and dig it out. Chunks of fat were also enclosed. By spring, the meat would be dried out and tasted like it was burnt. They would dump the surplus when they went off for the spring hunt.[5] Other Indians who saw these people's dumps called them by this meat.

Penanʉʉ. When captured, they would scout for the whites against other Comanches.[6] They were hated for it. Their chiefs included Wichitai.[7]

Wiaʔnʉʉ 'Hill Wearing Away.' They always stuck together. They lived in a gap between a large and a small hill. There was fast erosion. A Mexican came through and said, "You people are like me. I don't see why you can't make a living like me."

He plowed a level strip and gave plots to the Indians. They named him Nasokomaka[8] 'gave land away'. There were only six or seven families, but they are increasing today.

Tasipenanʉʉ 'The Tasi'[9] were an Apache band to the west of Anadarko. They joined with the Penanʉʉ and formed a separate band.

Kwaharʉnʉʉ lived mostly in the mountains, where the deer and antelope were. They believed the water was better there.

⟨Mutsanʉʉ⟩ meant 'undercut bank'.[10] Tahsuda didn't know how the name came about. Long ago, they were named after some hills, *tumutsi*,[11] about 200 miles to the northwest.

Story: In a camp, the people were having a good time; they were at peace. They saw cavalry coming along the flats. They were outnumbered and most fled in fear. But some stood their ground. A joker there said, "What are you gonna do? Grab your guns, you ain't gonna smoke your pipes too long time if you don't." Tahsuda believed they were extinct.

Parʉhʉya 'Water Horse'.[12] The name was given by other Indians. They were all tall, thin, and fleet of foot. The cause of tallness was that when two bands gathered for games, they would bring up great bundles of goods for wagers, put at the stake, and matched piece for piece. They played *natsihtóoʔetʉ*. They beat all the other bands until the others refused to play them.[13]

1. Robinson and Armagost (1990) gives *woʔaabI* as 'maggot, worm'.
2. Wallace and Hoebel (1952:30).
3. *tʉtsahkʉnarʉ* 'sew'.
4. *otʉ* 'brown, *taʔooʔ* 'pounded meat'.
5. Wallace and Hoebel 1952:30.
6. Although this was a common charge, I have found no documentary evidence to support it.
7. This name is unknown. Tahsuda may be implying that some of their chiefs were Wichitas.
8. *na-* reflexive, *soko* 'land', *makarʉ* 'give away'. Otherwise unidentified.
9. *tasi* is the Comanche name for the Kiowa-Apache (Plains Apache).
   10. Wallace and Hoebel 1952:30.
   11. This is apparently *tu-* 'black', *mutsi* 'pointed'. Possibly the Antelope Hills on the Canadian River in the Texas panhandle.
   12. For the etymology of this name, see the section on Tahsuda in the Introduction.
   13. Wallace and Hoebel 1952:113.

Political Organization: Chiefs: Paraibo   "I hardly know how to tell about them. They never had much to do except to hold the band together. When there were family troubles, he hardly ever entered in."

He was a father, "kind to the people; he didn't try to be brave; he was generous."

{Hoebel} (Note: this was in contrast to the story of his uncle, the "war chief," which was remembered in great detail.)

Among the Parʉhʉya, people just recognized him as a friendly man. A war leader, however, got a special tipi.

{Hoebel} (Tahsuda had a hard time getting the meaning to the inquiry concerning accession to position of *paraibo*.)

They hold a council of warriors to raise someone to the rank of *tekwʉniwapI*. "There was nothing to it, but that he was our peer."[1]

Nanʉwokʉ   If a man was too poor to pay, they give him a beating. They stripped and tied him to a tree. This was done to Tahsuda's brother; they gave him four strokes.

Nanʉwokʉ   A man went on the warpath.

A young man stole his wife and followed along. They came to a separate camp on the opposite side from where the husband was. Some person squealed. The husband said he would look into it in the morning.

The husband took his younger brother along. He told the younger brother to get off his horse.

He called to the father, who answered, "What do you want?"

"Oh, I want to see you; I come to make *nanʉwokʉ*."

"Who's it on?"

"That boy of yours."

The husband told the boy to sit down next to him and he called on his brother. He said he didn't want much, he would take four horses. The boy wanted to know who it was on; they said, "You." {. . . [*sic*]}.

Nanʉwokʉ   A young man dated the wife of another man early one evening. The husband came home early and found them near the tent. The young man ran off. The husband asked his wife the name of the offender. She told him. He said tomorrow he would go get *nanʉwokʉ*.

He went right after breakfast. The boy was still in bed. The boy said he thought the man was wrong. His father asked his son if it was true. The boy denied it and said the man lied.

The husband got mad. He pulled his knife and slashed off one side of the boy's long hair. He said "I wasn't going to do this, but if you insist on lying like a coyote, I'll sure make you look funny."

He threw the hair at the boy's feet. He said that was all he would do, he wouldn't take any horses, "But you sure look funny."

The boy sulked in his tent.

Then, an alarm spread through the camp that whites were coming. All the people rounded up their horses and mounted for battle. The youth saw a chance for a distinguished death—he looked too ridiculous to live—but the whites made terms and there was no fight.

---

1. Hoebel 1940:13; Wallace and Hoebel 1952:211–12.

Nanɨwokɨ   A man had a handsome grandson. The boy was playing at the stick game. The grandfather came in and nudged the boy. He said that woman over there looked like the woman he had the other night. The boy looked up and told his grandfather to go away. The old man said he had said nothing wrong, it just looked like her. The grandfather repeated it several times. Her husband was sitting there; he said yes, that's the fellow. The old man left and the game broke up.

The husband got on his pony and went up and shot the red mare, the favorite of the old man. He also shot the boy's pony. He was letting the matter ride until he was tweaked by the old man.

The boy said "Grandfather, you sure done wrong. Look what you got us into."

The old man went off and wept.

Life Cycle: Marriage: Divorce   There were two ways to answer. A man could tell his wife, "You and I are done; you go your way."

If she wanted the children, she must ask for them.

Or, they "do the best they can. Most likely some old man came in and advised."

The chief was not active.

Isatai   Returning from a raid on which they found no enemy, ⟨Tarenamo⟩.[1]

He told the young men that he would make a medicine man of one of them, and that they would have a big celebration. He invited them all, the girls, and the people. Isatai volunteered. It was known all over the camp that Isatai would be the big medicine man.

Isatai asked Kobebababe,[2] the medicine man, who was known for his white horse.

He painted it up and showed off in front of the people. They would say, "There's that man they're talking about. He's so powerful."

The people were told that he could stop guns from shooting. All the people talked about it. Other camps moved in to join his.

Isatai made his announcement. He wanted all to follow him. They were going to a certain place and clean up on the soldiers. Somebody suggested that they clean out a certain white settlement first.

He made all sorts of fiascos later. He got to be a chief under white influence, but he never could have been in the old days.[3]

Ordeal   ⟨papitson⟩ A young man or woman talking to another of either sex might say, "I heard you been intercoursing with so and so."

It was denied. Then the other says, "Well, we'll prove it."

They picked up some dirt in their two forefingers and put it on the denier's hair. If the claim was true, the hair would fall out shortly.

Or it may be put on the tongue, causing loss of speech. It was used in joking relations.

Norton[4] saw a man do it to a woman in Lawton in 1933. The woman fled through the streets to escape. It was not used for serious matters.

---

1. Possibly an ethnonym, but otherwise unidentified.
2. Perhaps *kobe* 'face' or *kobi* 'mustang', *papI* 'head'. Otherwise unidentified.
3. Isatai seems to have been the principal chief of the Kwaharɨnɨɨ who met with J. J. Sturm in 1875 (Sturm 1875). In 1879, he led the fourth-largest local group on the reservation, after Cheevers, Coby, and Quanah.
4. Norton Tahquechi was the interpreter for Tahsuda's interview (Wallace and Hoebel 1952:160).

Camp Organization: Scouts   A scout was selected for the permanent job by the four bravest men in the band. For a false report he lost the job, but there was no punishment.

Food: Birds: Duck   It was death to eat duck. They could have killed thousands.

But the eggs were highly prized as food. Tahsuda knew no reason for the taboo.

(In answer to a question as to whether they eat ducks now: "I've seen plenty of white people eat them. I'll do my share anytime.")

Social Control: Theft: Captive Killed Horse for Food   A man had a horse of quality. The man was killed and a close relative claimed it. It could be ridden only in battle.

Captives were herding the horses and noticed this fat one that was never ridden. They were hungry for fat meat, so they cut out the horse and slaughtered it. A Comanche from a strange band saw the smoke and located the gang cooking the meat. He snuck up and scared them off, and the leader dove in a pool.

The Indian told him to come out or get killed, and then offered him a choice of getting killed or having his hair cut. The captive took the hair trim. "Ya, you cowardly thief."

The Comanche cut a small scalp from the front, back and sides of his head.

Tahsuda thought a full blood would have gotten the same.

Life Story: Paruasumuno   A family went out on the warpath and got separated. They had a son and a daughter. The daughter got hungry and the father went out for meat. They saw a large number of Indians on the warpath and had a battle. The daughter was hit and got as far as a creek where she died. (She had her small son with her.)

The Indians that remained went to the creek for a drink. They saw buzzards and found her and her small son. The little boy motioned them to come and they took him away. He was adopted and grew up. His father died and later his mother died. He was an orphan.

Paruasumuno gave his horses away. He cried and wouldn't come into the camp. Finally, he got hungry and went into the camp. They told him he should have come sooner. He was adopted again by this family.

They met Utes on the warpath and his father got killed again {. . . [sic]}.

Oaths   Where denial of guilt was sustained, the resort to oath was demanded. False swearing would result in death, unless removed by a doctor.

Oaths: Sun Killing   A man blamed his wife for adultery. The wife denied it. The husband made a Sun Killing. So his wife said, "You are going to make a smoke. You want to kill me. I deny it. But you listen, I'm going to make smoke too. If you are putting the lie on me, the Sun will get you."

The husband backed down, he "gave her sugar words."

This was not possible in the old days.

Tahsuda thought that some medicine man put her up to it; it was not her idea.

Today, both would bring smoke and one must die.

Think it over before trying now.

Oaths: Scattering Buffalo Chips   A scout was sent out alone.

He might run into the enemy unexpectedly and, perhaps, kill one.

The band watched for his return.

On his appearance, all would line up.

They would pile three or four buffalo chips on end. If the scout had killed a man, he speared a chip for each man, and said *ahe*, I claim it."

If none were killed, he walked around the pile.

Tahsuda never heard of kicking the chips.[1]

War Honors   Among the Parɨhya, the first to arrive after a kill made by another struck with his weapon and called "*ahe,*" and claimed half of the honor.

The killer must kill with a spear. If a gun or bow was used, the counter got more honor than the killer.

Life Cycle: Marriage: Polygamy   PakikƱni[2] had ten wives. The first two slept in his tipi. The other (younger) wives, slept in pairs with their children in separate tipis. They were slaves of the center group. The two favored wives did no work. Two slave wives committed adultery. He killed them.

Social Control: Adultery   PakekƱni found one of his wives in bed with a man. He killed her on the spot. The man ran off. There was no *nanɨwokɨ* in such case.

Origin: Shoshone   They had no horses, and dogs were used for pack horses. They would come down to visit. They were very poor, and would sell their children for horses. They spoke the same language, but so fast that no one could understand it.

War: Scalps   The Parɨhya took the entire scalp and stretched it on a willow frame. They combed out the hair.

It was carried on a long pole.

After the Victory Dance, the scalp was split in two. When a man took more than one, the second coup-counter was most likely to get the parts.

Dances: Victory Dance   In the Parɨhya band, they stopped outside the camp and painted their faces and bodies black.

They drew a white line on their face by scraping off the paint with their fingers. They sang the Victory Songs with the hero out in front. They rode around the camp, dispersed, and went to their tents. In the evening, they built a big fire.

Life Cycle: Illegitimacy   An unmarried woman had a child. She said she would never be able to raise the child. So she took it to a grove. She washed it up and laid it in on a bed of sage leaves. Then she went off and left it.

A young man going out to tend horses found the baby. He wrapped it in a blanket and took it home.

Just as he walked in the door, the baby cried.

His mother said she thought she heard a baby. The youth said, "Yes, here's my son."

His mother objected, "What a burden."

The boy insisted on keeping it. He took it to a wet nurse and gave presents in payment. Later, he bought corn off Mexicans and raised the baby to three years of age on it.

The father told his parents he now wanted to go on the warpath. He was gone for a year.

The true mother wanted to come over on the day of his return. She hesitated three times, then came over at breakfast the next morning. She was invited in to eat and sat next to the boy. She told the grandmother she would do the dishes and clean up everything.

1. Wallace and Hoebel 1952:248–49.
2. *paki* 'dry, *kahni* 'house 'Dry Tipi'. Otherwise unidentified.

She sat down next to the grandmother. They asked her how come she visited them, when she had no connection with them. She told her story and begged to be allowed to stay in any capacity.

The old man said, "OK, it's up to the mother."

The grandmother said, "OK, it's up to the father and son."

The man said, "OK, she could take care of him."

She said she would take care of him. They named the child Pohóonʉʉkema,[1] 'covered with sage'.[2]

Life Cycle: Marriage   Sometimes they did not ask for parental consent. Sleeping together until daybreak was a sign of marriage.

Life Cycle: Marriage: Framing Girl with Pants   Tahsuda never heard of a horse offering, but something like it.

A boy hid his leggings under his chosen girl's blanket.

The frame-up was set in a gambling game. The boy lost but didn't have enough to pay all. He told his friend to go over to such and such a tipi and get some money out of the pocket[3] in the leggings under the bed.

The friend asked the girl's father for those leggings. The father was ignorant of the pants, so the youth went in and pulled out the pants. The father called in the girl and asked her, "How come I didn't know you were married?"

The girl denied it, but her mother said "You're old enough, you might as well go with your husband."[4]

Political Organization: Council: Smoke Lodge   The Smoke Lodge had a special tipi.

No young men or women were allowed, just the old men.

They smoked four times during the night.

They talked all night between rounds. The matters discussed were unknown; as a young man, Tahsuda could never get close.

The chief gave the first command for the smoke. They built up the fire. The chief filled the pipe. He held the pipe to the sky and laid a pinch from the pipe on the ground. All must be silent. Should someone break the taboo, all the tobacco must be dumped from the pipe on the ground and the pipe refilled.

The fire tender brought the coal. He could go to the chief from any side. The tender went out first at the end and they all followed around to the north. When smoking, they may leave from either side.[5]

Political Organization: Council: Smoke Lodge Mischief Makers   Way back when, there was no foolishness, but in Tahsuda's day, he remembered a stunt.

A young fellow pushed a wild colt in there; it tore things up. The old men were awfully sore and began to talk about what they should do to the young man when they caught him,

---

1. *pohóobi* 'sage', *nʉʉkʉnarʉ* 'cover.' Otherwise unidentified.

2. Hoebel 1940:107–8.

3. Wallace and Hoebel has "I have some money in my leggings" (1952:137), thus avoiding the problematic fact that leggings do not have pockets. That anachronism suggests that this story may date from the reservation period.

4. Wallace and Hoebel 1952:137. This note title is from Hoebel.

5. Wallace and Hoebel 1952:147.

"What law they should give him."

An old man spoke up, "Now, you old fellows, you were boys once. When the sun was shining, you were mighty nice, but when the sun went you were devils. Don't you remember how you were? Boys will be boys."

They all laughed and let it drop. Tahsuda didn't know what kind of law they'd give him, but he did know they would have gone to talk to his parents.[1]

Captives   They adopted the young ones into the family. They made slaves of the older boys. They captured so many women there are only a few full bloods left.

Wahatoya   Wahatoya[2] (Two Mountains) was chief of the Parʉhʉya band; he was Tahsuda's father. He was the oldest man, a "fine gentle fellow, never looking for no trouble; whatever they did, he was the leader of all."

There were four in the family, the father, uncle and two sisters. Wahatoya was the peace chief, *paraibo*.

Ʉʉtsʉʔitʉ (Cold) was the war chief, *tekwʉniwapI*.

The grandfather was EkamakwʉUsa (Red Sleeve). He was a real *tekwʉniwapI*; he was also a *paraibo*.

The war chief was the boss of the *paraibo* on a raid.

Ʉtsʉʔitʉ   They were returning from a horse raid in Texas, and some were anxious to get ahead. Ʉtsʉʔitʉ always stayed behind to see that no stragglers were lost.

He saw a pursuit group of ten Mexicans with short spears and gold daggers.

He mounted his men and gave orders for them not to charge without orders. When the Mexicans were a few yards off, he gave the charge order.

He picked out the Mexican captain. He missed his spear thrust and got struck under his left arm. He pulled the spearhead from the wound, made a quick turn and killed the Mexican chief. The Mexicans broke and fled. Ʉtsʉʔitʉ fainted from loss of blood.

{Card(s) missing}

The advance group turned back to meet them. While talking over the first scrimmage, they saw the Mexicans returning.

Ʉtsʉʔitʉ said, "I'm glad we will have more fighting." They saw the soldiers with rifles.

He gave instructions to meet the Mexicans halfway off from the horses and women. He rode four circles and then plunged into their midst with a war whoop. That was the signal for attack.

He took out for the leader, and drove him right through his men into the open, then back into the troop, but his horse stalled. Ʉtsʉʔitʉ struck him there. The Mexicans broke.

Ʉtsʉʔitʉ received a wound in his side. His horse ran off towards their camp. Ʉtsʉʔitʉ fainted again, and was cured.

He told the people to go ahead, but he was still in danger and too weak to travel himself. He would hide out in the hills until he was strong enough to go.

The *paraibo*, his brother, said, "No, we won't leave you."

OK, he got on a pacing mule and brought up the rear.

1. Hoebel 1940:43; Wallace and Hoebel 1952:149.
2. *waha* 'two', *toya* 'mountain'.

They met with a friendly band of Apaches. Some time before, he had ridden off with all their horses.

The Apaches had killed his fattest horses to eat. The Apaches were playing the arrow game. The Apaches said it was their honor to take the fattest horses. They took the chief's mule.

Utsʉʔitʉ called for a horse and went down with a bow. The Comanche called to the two Apaches to leave the mule alone, but they didn't heed him. Utsʉʔitʉ shot a grazing blow on the shoulder of one. The Apaches fled.

The Apaches were mad. They intended to kill them.

A Comanche ran up and began to talk: "You should have asked for this. The chief was not right, but you took things in your own hands."

The Apaches got scared and began packing. Patchoconi[1] told them not to be scared, but to stay there and not to break up the friendship. The Apaches stayed, but stole off in the night. Utsʉʔitʉ decided to pull out before the Apaches came back for trouble.

The band returned from the pursuit. They found the chief and took him from near death. They called a Buffalo Medicine Man. He blew four times on his arm and on the wound. The blood stopped. He blew four times on his heart and he recovered strength.

Utsʉʔitʉ refused to let a man help him ride on his horse. His brother, his sister's son, mounted behind him.[2]

Life Cycle: Death: Disposition of Property   If the son was old enough to care for the herd, then OK. A women was not able to take care of many horses. The elder brothers must share their horses with others. Tahsuda never heard of any case of an older brother chiseling.

Norton[3] said this was the thing nowadays.

The chief would try to smooth it out.

Personal belongings may be asked for by friends, otherwise they went in the grave.[4]

Social Control: Murder: Leader Killed Over Horse   A party on a raid headed towards Mexico. They were disappointed. "They couldn't find no trouble."

They were about to camp. One young fellow said, "We ought to make our main camp."

He was easygoing. Another fellow said, "No, it's too far and the water holes are too sparse."

The horses were already loose and the bunch wanting to go on started to round up their horses. The colt of a conservative got loose and ran into the herd of the people going and they couldn't cut it out. The leader said to let him be. "He'll come with us, you can get him tomorrow."

The gang stopped at a water hole and got hungry. They decided to kill a horse, but they couldn't find a fat horse, so they killed the colt. They said they would give the owner the

---

1. *paatsoko* 'otter', *neki* 'belt', Otter Belt; Patchoconi is the agency spelling. In March 1872, he was chief of a large Nʉmʉkiowa camp at Muchoque; the following September, the village had moved to McClellan Creek (Tipi Creek) where it was attacked by the Tenth Cavalry (Kavanagh 1996:429ff). Patchoconi died after 1883, but before 1889.

2. This story is presented in the order of Hoebel's cards. Some of the episodes seem out of order.

3. Norton Tahquechi was the interpreter for Tahsuda's interview (Wallace and Hoebel 1952:160).

4. This note begins with number 4b, indicating that earlier cards are missing.

choice of any two of their best horses. The other group came along and missed the trail. They camped on the other side of the hill. The first group sent a scout up the hill. He saw the camp and hastened down to explain to the chief.

He got sore. He hadn't expected this. The scout asked if it was OK to give him two horses. The chief bowed his head and said, "Yes." (He didn't look him in the face.)

He told him to come over right away, as they going to break camp. The chief came over the hill with a bow and arrow, but instead of coming right up, he rode around to the south. He looked up the herd and shot two horses. Then he turned around and rode back.

One of the owners got mad. He said, "Gee, that's a mean man. He makes me mad. I'm going to kill him for the way he shot those fine horses down like dogs."

He told his captive to mount and go with him. He gave instructions to his captive to draw him out to fight: "Whatever he does, you give him back, then I'll shoot him with the bow."

They went up to the chief's tipi and got behind the chief. He stopped and asked what they wanted. "Oh, we just came to see you."

"Fine."

He turned to face them.

"Well, we came to kill you, such a mean fellow I never saw."

The chief turned on the Mexican. "What fellows, you Mexicans. You can't do nothing."

He swung at his head with his bow, but missed. The Mexican returned the blow and also missed.

The chief grabbed the Mexican's hair; the Mexican retaliated. They tussled and fell from their horses; they struggled on foot.

The other Indian got down and shot the Indian through the body. The Indian said to the Mexican, "See how easy."

They returned to camp.

The chief asked how they made out; "OK, we've got him."

"Where was he?"

"Over the hill there."

He went over to mourn. The dead man's servant came out and saw his friend dead. He buried him in a draw. The captive of the victim joined with the first bands.

The murderers said they were going by themselves. When the party got to the main camp, they turned his horses and belongings over to his parents, and they told them who had killed him. The victim had been married just before the raid. The child was born when the band returned. They made a special gift of a horse to the wife for the baby to ride on.

The mother died while the child was still young. She was raised by an old lady to the age of womanhood. She married, had a child, and died. The old woman put the child in school (fifty-three to fifty-five years ago). The same thing happened again. This child was still living. The Mexicans killed the murderer before the relatives could get him.

Medicine: Sorcery   KwihnainakI[1] used the spears of dwarfs on people.

Kutu[2] had three wives.

---

1. Possibly *kwihnai* 'eagle', *nakI* 'ear'. Otherwise unidentified.
2. Otherwise unidentified.

KwihnainakI put (shot) spears into the spines of Kutu and PahmokutU[1] paralyzing their legs.

Kutu said he would doctor himself. His wives put up a tipi with backrest stakes. He sat by a peyote button. He ate four buttons and sang four songs. He heard people outside.

He stopped the meeting to ask what they wanted. They said they had PahmokutU there. He told them to take him on, he was busy fixing himself.

In the morning, he walked out himself. As soon as he stepped over the tipi door, he felt better.

People told him that PahmokutU was dead. He was his *ara?*, and said he would revenge him.

Kutu went on a buffalo hunt. Just before sundown, KwihnainakI shot him in the eye again. Water streamed from his eye.

He fixed up a peyote lodge for doctoring.

Kutu was singing his song when KwihnainakI came up to the lodge and looked in. He shot Kutu in the elbow. Kutu grabbed his rattle with his left arm and finished. He said to the next man, "Gee, that fellow's mean; he's still after me."

Later, KwihnainakI came into the lodge. He had his head covered and held a black eagle feather in front of his face. Kutu asked where he generally sat; he said on the north side. "OK, go over there."

He gave him four peyotes, and he later took the extra button Kutu had put by the road medicine. Kutu gave him the last button later on.

KwihnainakI began to groan. He broke up his feather. He asked Kutu if he could go out. "Sure."

He went out and felt a lot worse. He asked if he could smoke. "Sure."

He asked Kutu to smoke too and cure him: "I'm just an old man. I didn't know what I did. Be a friend of mine."

Kutu fixed him up OK.

The next morning, KwihnainakI got up early. He felt fine. He was walking around. Suddenly, he coughed, shot blood, and fell over dead. Kutu had evened things up.

Social Roles: Warrior Class: Parɐhya Band   There were two young brothers; one was sixteen and the other was twenty-five years old. Neither was a medicine man.

In the old days, lots of trouble began over women.

The oldest brother was out wandering about camp. He came on a cow path. A young woman was coming down. She proposed to him that they go on the warpath together. They had seen each other in dances. The girl had plotted the meeting.

He said, "I am a young man. I take orders only from my people. You are beautiful and married. If we do this, there will be trouble."

They met again later at the same spot. She said, "For a young man, you're an awful coward. Come on, let's go."

He was kind of sore, and he answered, "Well, you come at sundown with your stuff. I'll bring two horses."

---

1. *pahmo* 'tobacco', *kutU* 'possessor'. Otherwise unidentified.

Her husband was in the habit of having old men in for a smoke in the evening. He told her to clean up the tipi; he told her to bring a fire stick, and to lie down and listen.

The sister of the boy brought over a rare blanket and slipped it to her. She told her own sister she wanted air, so she put the shawl over her head and walked right by the smoking men outside. One man noted her as a boy with a beautiful blanket. She met her lover and rode off.

The husband missed her in the morning and inquired about her. He went up to the boy's tipi and asked the father where the boy was. The father said he was not in all night. The husband said, "He's run off with my wife."

They told him they were sorry and he went away. He came back later and said what he wanted. He said he wanted *nanɨwokɨ*. The father offered the pick of all of horses. The younger brother said, "OK, if you leave my favorite."

The husband said, "OK," and laughed, and said, "That's just the very horse I want."

The boy said, "It's just as good as yours. But I'll keep it until my brother gets back."

His mother pleaded the same as the boy, and the husband agreed to let the *nanɨwokɨ* go until then.

A war party was organized. The sixteen-year-old asked his father for permission to go. His father said, "OK, take this pony and lead it from the mule. When you're in enemy territory, ride this pony fast a ways and then stop. Do this four times and he will never tire."

People wondered when he did this.

They camped and sent a lookout up a hill. The lookout saw two tipis on the other side. He went down and reported that three people were returning to those tipis and had seen him.

The party went around the hill and saw three families fleeing, three women ahead of three women.[1] They chased them and shot. One man on a fast horse carried on the rear guard action.

The sixteen-year-old boy drove at him on the next sally and speared him. The other two dismounted and started shooting with guns. He speared them both. He looked back and saw his party coming all strung out. The first man up counted coup. They took scalps and mounted them on long poles and returned to camp and gave the Victory Dance. Women took the war honors. It was a ⟨tusoetsekin⟩, a Shakedown Dance.

The next morning, the women dressed like warriors (men) and came to the hero's tipi and danced. Some lifted up the sides of the tipi and saw him sitting there. His relatives and parents brought gifts and piled them outside. The leader of the women dancers went in and took the first gift, then she distributed the gifts saying, "We're seeking for something that you threw away, or are going to throw away."

His father gave two horses.

The boy went off on another war party as leader. He worked his horse as before. The party met another band "looking for war like they were," Utes.

The parties faced each other. The boy rode out and made a circle before the other band.

---

1. This sentence is as written by Hoebel. Wallace and Hoebel has: "The women were in front. The three men were riding behind them to cover their flight" (1952:219).

Their chief chased him back. Then, he had one of his followers repeat the tactic. When their chief followed up, the boy rode up and speared the chief of the enemy. He rode into the enemy and killed two more. His band followed him in and they broke up the enemy. They returned to the dead and took scalps and looted the bodies. They took anything they wanted, and then returned to the main camp.

There was a big Victory Dance that lasted almost until morning, and a Shakedown Dance in the morning at the boy's tipi. His father gave three horses this time.

After the Horse Dance, they went on a raid again. They clashed with the Osages. There were three chiefs with the Osages. The boy charged and killed the three. There was a general melee and the Osages fled. They took the scalp locks off the Osages.

There were more dances, and the father gave four horses.

There was a war bonnet induction ceremony three years later, when the boy was nineteen years old. They had a buffalo-hide tipi set up and painted with white clay. The floor was all smoothed out. There were buffalo-hide robes and blankets spread out. The warriors entered. The leader was in the west. They went to the north of the door and filled back. They entered according to the seniority of their status. The neophyte entered and took his place at the left of the leader.

The chief got up and made a talk: "So-and-so has done brave deeds. What's more, I honor him ahead of myself. Hereafter, he is chief in my stead. This is merely a bunch of feathers given by your friends."

Then, they gave him a bonnet on his head. There were two rows of feathers as a special honor. The boy went to the first position instead of the usual place to the south of the door. Then the group was dismissed. He rolled up the bonnet and walked out. They "consider themselves like a club."

They met to decide on war by the entire band. This was the only function of the group.

Ten years later, they went on another big raid to the Mexican border. They came to an elbow hill. There was a large camp unnoticed behind the crook. They met unsuspected resistance. The leader was surrounded and forced into a draw. He killed many and was himself shot in the limbs. Finally, the gang broke away from him.

But his band had left. He followed slowly. After eleven days he could not catch up, so he put in at a creek at sunset. He climbed a hill and saw some horses and located fires. He left his horses behind and snuck up on a brush lodge and heard a man speak to his wife in Comanche. He took off his weapons and walked up. The man greeted him and fixed him up with clothes and a blanket to sit on. The old man was glad to see someone to talk with. Supper was served.

When it was finished, they began to tell stories. The chief said, "You told your wife you were going to shoot a hawk for your son. I've got some feathers over here. Go get him some."

The man sent his wife over to get them. She was surprised at his war materials. She brought them back. The man saw he had a chief with him, and he asked for the name of the chief's father. "Well, my father was nobody. I'm ashamed to tell you about him. But I got those feathers, etc.", and he told of his brother running off, and of his own deeds.

His brother asked what had been done about *nanɨwokɨ*. He took his family and went back with his brother. The lookout met them and told them to wait while he rode in and warned their parents. The chief had been given up for dead, and mourning was done by his family. His mother fainted. When she recovered, she washed the gashes, dusted herself with red powder, and they were reunited again.

Their father traded two horses for a large tent from some Kiowas. He got two tents for four horses.

He wondered why the old man hadn't come up for *nanuwoku*, so they sent down for him to come up and get his wife back from the brother. The old man couldn't get another woman. The brother was young, and the chief would take care of the children himself.

Their mother talked to the elder brother and told him that his brother was now a big *tekwUniwapI* and that what he said must go.

The old man didn't want to go, but one of his wives (he had four wives) egged him to go with the messenger.

The "young chief dictated things."

The old man entered. The chief told him to sit between his brother and his wife. The old man hesitated, but the husband said it was OK. The old man hugged the children; he was really pleased.

The chief said, "Wait until tomorrow to take the children and your wife. Bring another wife, and we will have a meal."

The old man and the woman were not as one until they were on horses and ready to go on the next day.

Thereafter, the old man told the two brothers to pitch their tipis in back of his. His wives were theirs for the asking evermore. Names: {. . . [*sic*]}.[1]

Omens: Locust   When the locust sang to himself until he burst, that meant something was ripe. Then the Indians went out and picked whatever was in season.

Kinship Terminolgy: Respect   The relationship terms must always be used. One never used the name to relatives.

Kinship Relations: Incest   In the old days, close relatives could never come near each other. Tahsuda never heard of a case of incest.

Life Cycle: Childhood: Child Training   Paruhya children were taught never to look about, always to keep the mind forward.

Names   A man might simulate a brave man's name. Paruhyatai[2] meant 'elk's twaddle'. Isatai wanted also to have great name; *isatai* meant 'wolf's twaddle'.

Medicine: Sorcery   When a feather was shot into a person, a medicine man "could see, just like reading a newspaper, who put it there."[3]

But if the sorcerer had more powerful medicine, he would not touch it. Yellowhammer and redhammer were the best feathers.

Medicine: Desacralizing Objects   Before letting another person handle a medicine object, the owner must take the power off. He passed it under his arm, or talked to it.

1. Wallace and Hoebel 1952:217-23. The subject heading for this note is Hoebel's.
2. Otherwise unidentified.
3. Wallace and Hoebel 1952:239.

Relations with Other Tribes: Apaches: Intermarriage   Quanah was the first Comanche to marry an Apache. Also, Patchoconi, Nappywat ('Without a Leg'), and Isaroi.[1]

War Story: Comanches and Utes   Comanches and Utes were in a fight.

A Ute woman was with the Comanches (a captive). She had a son among them. She got scared for her son.

She rode out between the fighters, held up her hand, and called them to stop. She said she was on both sides. She was Ute, her son was Comanche.

The Ute chief rode up. The woman wanted to shake hands. The chief said "No, not until I know if your chiefs sent you."

Her son came up. He was a war chief. He was willing. So a truce was made. The Utes camped on one side of a hill, the Comanches on the other.

A group of returning Comanche hunters was ignorant of the truce. They killed and scalped one of the Utes, and went into the Ute camp by mistake, singing the victory song. The chief of the Utes said, "OK, we're at peace, we won't get mad."

They went back and found their own camp. The Comanche chief went over to the Utes and told their chief that since a Comanche was killed first, things were even.

A council of ten Ute chiefs called at the Comanche camp to visit the Ute woman. They found she was the sister of one of them. They took her and her family back to see her parents, who were still living. They gave her a special tipi with an antelope skin tied to a pole for a sign. The Utes said, "Four days are up, now we will separate."

The Utes wanted the woman's son to go with them. He refused.

Left alone, he finally followed them up. He came to the Ute Camp and asked for the chief. The chief invited him to dismount, and told his wife to give him supper. He got a Comanche woman captive to serve as interpreter. He told the chief of his desire to become a Ute. The chief said, "OK, you can be my son. But these Utes are bad. They might kill you sometime."

The chief named him Wasape Semanete, gave him a pack horse, and sent him back. The Comanches renamed him Parɨasɨmɨno.[2]

Oaths: Sun Killing   A woman, Tɨsɨtsaponi,[3] was caught in adultery. She denied it. Her husband laid the case before the supernatural. He smoked to the Sun.[4] "You, Father, know the truth of this matter. As you look down on them, don't let them live till the fall. You, Mother Earth, as you know what was true, don't let them live a happy life on you."

The husband gave the pipe to the woman to swear. Although guilty, she swore to the powers, "Sun, if you don't believe me, let me perish. Mother Earth, if you don't believe me, let it be true that I won't live right on you. Whatever he says, let it be."

After a few months, she began to waste away. She had fainting spells. After three or four days, a doctor came to her and said he believed the charge to be true.

---

1. A man named Esaroi, translated as Rising Wolf, is listed on the censuses 1879-1895, although conflicting ages are given. There is no confirming evidence that any of these latter three had Apache wives.

2. Wallace and Hoebel 1952:277.

3. Hoebel's notes spell this name "Tɜsɜtsagóni"; Hoebel (1940:145) spells it "Tɜsɜhtsapóni" and translates it as 'Looking for Fun', based on *punitɨ* 'see'. Otherwise unidentified.

4. Wallace and Hoebel 1952:195.

The woman owned up, and said she couldn't confess because she was afraid of her husband. Besides, she didn't believe in the power of the oath.

The medicine man recommended a certain doctor, a specialist in such matters.

The girl asked the medicine man to tell her mother.

The medicine man went over and told her mother that it was a good time to get this doctor, the girl's husband was on a war party and wouldn't know.

The doctor said, "Yes, he could cure her. It was good that they came at that stage, as it was incurable later on."

There were two alternatives: they could sacrifice someone else in the family, or eight horses to kill instead. He said he would prefer not to take the life of a human being.

They broke camp before the husband returned. While driving the eight horses, one of them dropped dead. The others followed, one after another.

They had been told that if the eight horses didn't die, it would be a sign that the doctor could not save her.

The doctor could be paid with anything but a horse.

The husband returned from the raid. They told him that they had broken camp and lost eight horses on the way, no one knew why. That's all the husband ever learned.[1]

Medicine: Sorcery: White Man Tries Medicine   The Indians were settled at Anadarko (before the time of the city).[2]

A medicine man, a white man, was out looking over the young men.

They saw a stalwart youth and picked him out.

He said, "Young man, I like your build. Let me give you a new shirt."

He took measurements and had a coat of Prince Albert cut made from a gray blanket, a material popular at the time. The youth wore it among his friends and was very proud.

The next morning, on wakening, he felt dull. There was a pain in his heart. It got worse, until his whole body was wracked. All the medicine failed. He thought he would die before sunset.

The people said, "You've got peyote medicine. Why don't you use it? We will have a meeting tonight."

They set up the tipi, and drove in two stakes for his backrest.

They came to the meeting. The youth was too weak to sing. He took four buttons and passed up his turn. On the second time around, he still didn't sing, but took four more buttons.

An old man sitting behind him egged him on. "You've got power, what ails you?"

On the third time, he sang one song, but barely made it. The old man said, "That's better."

He sang a second song, and followed up with other songs, and was getting better.

He said he would tell them what was wrong, come morning.

His wife brought water for the pause. He told her to go home and get him the new shirt and a knife. She brought them and handed them in to the fire tender.

1. Hoebel 1940:100; Wallace and Hoebel 1952:196.

2. Although there had been an agency settlement at Anadarko since 1879, when the agency moved there from Fort Sill, the city itself was not established until the opening of the reservation in 1901.

The youth told them to watch while he showed what pained him. He turned the coat wrongside out. There was a small patch on the inside, over the heart. He ripped it out and revealed a black spider, bad medicine. He rubbed the spider on the palm of his hand and blew on it, and his cure was effected.

He announced to all that he was going turn the pain back on the sorcerer. He went alone to a lonely spot and drew an effigy of the man on the ground with a heart. He stuck a pin into the heart. Blood appeared. He returned to the people.

They heard that the white man was about to die. He wanted to see this boy before he died.

The boy went down.

The white man said he had done wrong. The Indians knew all his power, but being new, he had to try it. "Please cure me up."

The Indian said he had no medicine. The white man asked four times.

The Indian said maybe, if the man had faith, he could do it. He blew once in his closed fist and placed his hand on the patient's body.

The man took a deep breath and felt better.

The patient promised $100 in cash and a $10 grocery credit. He blew and blessed him four times. He was not fully cured and asked the medicine man not to stay away long. He still had a pain in his heart. The medicine man went up to the effigy, pulled out the needle, and the man was OK.

Medicine: Sorcery *puhabehkakarʉ* was medicine killing.

Oaths: Sun Killing *tabebehkakarʉ* was sun killing.[1] It was a good deal like consumption. It was not considered evil medicine.

Medicine: Charms Crow feathers tied to a child's bed would keep away evil spirits. It was taboo to use them as arrow guides; one absolutely could not hit anything with such arrows.[2]

Material Culture: Arrows Norton[3] hunted game all winter with arrows, and he had tried crow feather guides. "It did something to the shooter so he couldn't can't hit nothing."

Games: *natsihtóo°etʉ* There were ten players from each band, women. The goal was a stick at each end of the field, about one-and-a-half inches by three feet. They threw a rawhide thong, *wʉtako*, one-half inch thick and one-and-a-half feet long. It was knotted at the ends when green. They used a stick with a hooked end for throwing. The thong couldn't be touched with the hand. It was played like lacrosse.

They started with the centers in the middle and the others paired off. One center threw the thong upward, two caught it. The hooks caught on the end knots, pulling on it. Then the referee stopped them; if they broke loose first, then it was OK.

Then they tussled the thong loose with the stick. The one who got it loose must throw it.

If they were blocked, they threw it to a teammate, or threw it ahead and caught it himself {*sic*, herself}.

---

1. Wallace and Hoebel 1952:195.
2. Wallace and Hoebel 1952:160.
3. Norton Tahquechi was the interpreter for Tahsuda's interview (Wallace and Hoebel 1952:160).

They threw the thong at the stake; when it was wrapped about the stake, the game was won.

War Honors   War honors were never sold. They might be given away at a dance.

They called in the entire band and gave a dance to attract people. They stopped the dance, and the giver made an address.

He swore before Sun and Earth, who had witnessed the killing, "I now give this to my brother."

It might be {given} to any person.

The receiver stood. "I now take this deed; Sun Father, Moon above, and Earth Mother, witness it was mine. I killed this man."

Then the drum was struck. He said, "You people recognized my deed."

It was given only to brave men to help them towards a grade; also to a *paraibo* who had no war honors.[1]

Social Control: Murder   Raiders took off with the horses. A boy jumped on the favorite buckskin of Wutsuki.[2] He overtook them and killed a raider. The rest got away. He overrode the horse on his way back and the horse died.

His mother went over to Wutsuki and said, "My boy has done great things, but at the same time, he has had misfortune—the horse is dead."

The man got mad.

He said he loved it better than anybody; why did he have to pick on that horse, when so many other fast ones were about.

The mother got mad. "What are you talking for. You couldn't do nothing. You do no brave deeds. If you love the horse better than me, why don't you kill me?"

He said, "Tʉpiwokwe,[3] do you mean that?"

She answered, "Yes."

He went and got his bow and shot her twice.

Wutsuki decided to move outside camp before the raiding party returned. He said, "If they are going to kill me, let them do it away from camp."

An old man, his best friend, went along.

The party came in that night and heard of the deed. In the morning, five warriors, relatives, went over. He saw them coming and went in to get ready. He came out with a knife to meet them. They shot, but he got right up to them before an arrow pierced him. It was shot by Quitsquip.[4] All of the men were the mother's brothers in this case. It happened over seventy years ago.[5]

1. Hoebel 1940:29; Wallace and Hoebel 1952:242, 250.
2. Hoebel has this name as Crowding a Person, then later in the same work as Crowds Someone (1940:70, 145). Robinson and Armagost (1990) gives wʉtsʉkitʉ as 'crowd'. Otherwise unidentified.
3. *tʉpi* 'rock', *wokwe* 'cactus, thorn'. Hoebel (1940:70) gives this as Rocky Thorn. Otherwise unidentified.
4. Quitsquip, kʉtsʉkwipʉ, usually translated as 'Chewing' or 'Chew-up', sometimes as 'Elk's Cud' or 'Chewing Elk', was a prominent Yapainʉʉ local band leader.
5. Hoebel 1940:69–70.

Story: Bear Shelters A Woman {Hoebel}   A war party was all slain, save one woman. She had plenty of supplies, but they all ran out. The weather turned cold, so she went up to a stream bank to look for shelter. There she found a cave. She felt heat coming out, and she sat down.

Soon, bear cubs came out and played about her. She picked them up and talked nice to them. They went to sleep. They were awakened by the father bear prowling around. The bear snorted and walked by sideways without bothering her.

He came out in the morning to forage as usual. He told the woman that since she had been nice to his little ones, he would get her some game.

The bear would go a little way, then come back and look at the woman, and then look away. The woman decided he wanted her to follow.

He led her to a big fat deer. He looked at the woman, then looked at the deer. The woman asked the bear if he wanted her to quarter it. He answered, "Yes."

Then the bear pulled down dead limbs, and the woman asked if she should build a fire; the bear answered, "Yes."

The woman began cooking slabs of meat. She gave a raw piece to the bear. He ate it and said, "This ought to be enough for my children."

He went home.

The woman decided she might just as well go back too. There she saw a smooth grass mat in front of the cave. She thought, "This ought to be for my meat."

The bear lined up his cubs. He regurgitated food for each one.

The bear talked best to the woman in her dreams.

Come spring, the bear told her it was time to go back to her camp. He licked her hands and feet and told her he would take her back tomorrow. They would have to travel fast because Mrs. Bear would be back tomorrow.

They started the next morning. The woman got tired and the bear took her up on his back. The bear had told her in a dream that they would meet the first Indian at noon on a hill, and he asked the woman to be sure to warn the Indian not to hurt him.

The Indian went down the hill to get his horse. The bear told the woman she was in safety now, and he would go so as to take no chances.

The Indian wanted to know where the other one was. The woman stalled and said she was alone, then said he had gone back. Finally, she admitted it was a bear, and told her story. The woman got on the horse with the man. They went back to camp. The people were glad to see her.

Story: Bear Shelters A Woman {Carlson}   A party went on the warpath. A woman was along. All the men were killed; she was alone. She had provisions, but soon they went.

It was beginning to get cold. She was hungry and cold. She went up to a high cliff for protection. There she saw a large hole—large enough for her to stand in.

As she stood at the entrance, she could feel heat from within.

She sat down in the entrance; a great deal of heat came out.

A little while later, some young bears came out and began to play around her. She picked up one of the bears and petted it. She did this to each of them. The little bears liked her.

Night was coming on. She lay back to sleep.

After a while, she heard something. It was the father bear. He stood on his hind feet, as if in preparation for an attack. He never even touched her, but went on back into the cave.

The next morning, the papa bear went past her again without harming her. He was gone all day. The next night, he came home again.

During the night, the bear spoke to her in a dream, and said, "You love these little bears as I do. You have been good to them. Tomorrow, I'm going to get you something to eat, a buffalo or something."

The next morning the bear went out. He was gone only a short time. Then he came back and acted funny, as if he wanted her to follow him. She did.

They went down to the creek and there was a large deer. The woman said to the bear, "Do you wish me to cut this deer up?"

The bear said, "Yes."

When she was almost through cutting up the meat, the bear went a short distance and began tearing the limbs off a tree. "I'll bet he wants me to make a fire," the woman said.

She asked, and he said, "Yes."

She built the fire. She cooked some meat and gave the bear some raw meat. The bear ate until he was full, and then said, "The rest of this raw meat is enough for my children."

The bear returned to the cave and she returned soon after. She saw grass placed near the entrance—she knew it was set up for her meat. She placed her meat on it.

The father lined up his children and kept throwing meat in the air and the young ones would catch it.

(The only time that the bear spoke to her was through dreams.)

The woman lived with the bears until spring.

One day the bear said, "It is spring, you should be able to get home. Your camp is only over there a short way. I'll go with you to see that no harm comes to you. I'm going to travel pretty fast, as my wife will soon be back."

Early the next morning, they started off. They went so fast that the woman got tired, so she got up on his back and he carried her.

In the night before, in a dream, he had designated a certain hill where they would meet some Indians. (He told her to do him a favor and tell the Indians not to shoot him, and that he was just bringing her back to her people.)

When they came to the hill, they saw an Indian who was hunting. The woman and the bear saw him.

The bear said, "You're OK now, I'll leave and go home."

The Indian then came up and asked where was the other one. She replied, "There was no other."

"Yes, there was," he said, "I saw him."

"Well, he's gone back," the woman said.

The Indian was determined to find out who the individual was. Finally, the woman confessed and said, "All he was was a bear."

She told the Indian how the bear had brought her back.

"Where are your folks?" said the Indian.

Then the woman told of her experiences. The Indian then put the woman on his horse behind him and they went back to camp. Everybody was overjoyed to have her back again.

Life Cycle: Suicide   A boy was four years old. They were moving camp. His mother strapped him in a little saddle. She happened to drop behind.

A young man proposed marriage. "OK," said the mother, "and don't be bothered by the child."

She tied his horse to a tree in the midst of a grove and left him to starve.

Some hunters, after a bobcat, came on the grove. One hunter said to the others, "There's a horse standing there."

They all came in and watched the boy sleeping. Someone said to wake him up, so they woke him up and asked of his mother. He told them the direction she had gone.

They followed the band, and gave him to the band to keep until the mother might show up. His grandfather raised him. He grew to manhood and married.

His mother blew in one night. She went to his tipi, took his arm, and asked him to get up and get some bison before they moved camp; they were going to a place where the bison were scarce. The boy woke up, and asked if she called him "Son."

He said he didn't have a mother. "You tell me you're my mother, you don't know what you're talking about."

The mother groaned, left, and went back to her own tipi.

The mother committed suicide. She threw a rawhide rope over a tree, stood on a log by the creek, kicked the log out in the stream, and hung herself. Her body was discovered by a hunter. The people ran down to cut her down, and they buried her not far from the creek.

The brother of the woman said he would kill his *ara*ʔ*'s* wife; he said she must have had something to do with it. The young man and wife fled until the trouble was forgotten.[1]

Story: Fox Gets Water Horse   Kawos[2] was opossum.

Water Horse lived by a creek with his wife and children.

Fox's wife said she was hungry, so Fox went out and got some food. Fox came on a bunch of water horses.

"Oh, what a good time we'll have. First we play your game, then you play the games I want to," Fox said. "Today is your day. We had a fine time running up and down this bank. Tomorrow we will play my game. Where will you be at?"

They told him it would be at the same spot. Fox went home and sharpened a stick, two or three feet long. He came back early the next morning, made a mud slide, and planted the stick at the bottom.

"Now come on and play my game. We all start at once and go together."

He had the fattest sit next to him and aimed it at the stake. He just missed the first time.

"How did you like that game, hey?"

"Oh, that's fun."

They tried again. Fox told the others to give his friend and him room. Down they went and the water horse was impaled through his rectum. The horse was groaning.

---

1. Hoebel 1940:114–15.

2. This name is from a separate typewritten summary card. Casagrande (1954–55, III:9) has *kawos* as 'coyote' and notes that it was "given by one informant as something like 'has a bag of tricks'." Robinson and Armagost (1990) gives *kaawoosA* as 'fox, jackal', and *pahtsi kwasi* (literally, 'bare tail') as 'opossum'. The Comanche Language Committee (2003) lists both *kaʔwosa* and *kaawosa* as 'coyote'.

"What's the matter?" said Fox.

"Oh, down here" he said, pointing with his leg.

Fox looked, and instead of pulling the stick out, he pushed it in the whole way. The horse lay there suffering.

Fox was at his side lamenting the accident. "I'm so sorry such a misfortune came on him. I love him so, this friend of mine. It makes me sad to think how he was hurt while we were having such a good time. I hate to think of those birds flying over and eating him. It makes me sad to think of those animals getting him. I sure don't like the way this thing happened."

The horse died.

Fox said, "Well, we decided we can't leave him here. Push him in the water where those beasts can't get him."

They did that. "It's not enough to leave him just floating around here, we've got to get him out in the current where those animals can't eat him."

That done, Fox said he didn't want to play more, he felt so sad for his close friend. He would come back and play some other day. "Will you be here?"

"Yes."

"I'll go home and cry myself to sleep."

Fox went over the hill and whooped. He got home and told his family to look for meat coming down the stream. His wife hollered, "Here comes something black, it's a big one."

Fox jumped in and pulled out the water horse. "Now, we ain't going to string this up, there are too many Indians about who might tell the water horses."

So they stripped the meat and buried it in a hole between layers of hay. (This was not a Comanche practice.)

They ate plenty. Then Fox trimmed off the hair of his young and rubbed them with gray ashes.

The next morning, Fox told his wife to get out some of that meat for breakfast. There came a bird. The water horses came down in a stampede, they were so mad. (Same sequence as first version.)[1]

The next morning, Crow came out and sat on a tree. "Hey, Kawos, give me something to eat."

"Shoo, get along, you ain't got no business there, you with them big whiskers. Besides, you stink like a dead cow anyway."

Crow said he would go tell. Fox said, "Aw, go on."

Fox cut off his hair and smeared ashes on himself. Down came the water horses in a cloud of dust. (Same result as before.)

Story: Fox Marries His Daughter   The next morning, Fox woke up his children. They were now all grown and Fox fell in love with his oldest girl.

He told his wife, "You might as well know it. I'm sick. I'm dying. Cover me over with sand except for my head down here. I want you to move camp. Go over that hill. You will find plenty of Indians there. You've got two fine daughters. Marry one of them to a fine

1. It is not clear to what this refers.

industrious brave I know over there. He'll take care of you with plenty of game. His name is Yixhanait."

"After you bury me, don't look back, because if you do, I will to take one of you with me."

They went on. Before they got to the hill, one of the boys looked back. "Oh look, my father's crawling on his hands and knees."

His mother reprimanded the child.

The hero, Yixhanait, was to be identified by his short, otterhair bands and wristlets, and he was always laughing. It was Fox himself in disguise. He circled around and got into the camp.

The mother asked in camp for Yixhanait. The people said they didn't know him; he must be that newcomer.

Fox came back and talked to an old woman. She said that lady down there was asking for Yixhanait. "What's your name?"

"That's just it."

"Well," she said, "if you have no objections, you can marry her eldest daughter and take care of their little camp."

He went over and sat down, and accepted the daughter. The next morning he went out and brought in game. "There it goes, just like he said, he would take care of this family."

The mother asked him if it looked like her red mare was picking up weight, "Yes, she's coming up fast."

The next day, he went down to see and found her bloated up and dead. The old woman went down and checked. She got mad and began to suspect him: he covered his mouth every time he laughed.

She told her daughter to lift the man's lip and look at his teeth that night. He would have no front teeth. She also told her to pull up his right pant leg and see if he had a scar.

The mother called them to breakfast. Her daughter told her the signs were right for her father. The mother took a club and hid it by her side. When Fox came in to breakfast, she rapped him on the shin and he ran off.

Story: Possum and The Raccoons   This is the story of the animals who pulled roots from the ground with their tails. He {Possum} pulled and jerked and ripped the skin off his own tail. He went back and asked the raccoons how to fix it up. They replied, "No can do."

Story: Turkey's War Party   A raiding party was returning from the west. They saw something walking back and forth on a hill, and thought it was an Indian. They heard a war whoop on the other side and got ready for combat.

From over the hill came a big turkey and his flock, running back and forth. The chief said, "Get ready for trouble."

They started shooting. No one could hit any, but they broke the wings of the leader and the rest of the turkeys turned and fled.

Not one got killed. Another party, under Quanah, out for meat saw this battle. They thought they were fighting Indians. If the leader hadn't got shot, those turkeys would have cut the Indians up.

Story: The Owner of the Buffalo {Hoebel}   The Comanche's knowledge goes only to the point where men and the earth were already here.

The Indians were playing three kinds of games: wheel games, throwing arrows, and shooting with the bow. A strange man appeared in their midst. He talked to no one, but just looked on. He kept his quiver always on his shoulder.

He said, "I'll go to punkle over here." He laid down his quiver and jumped in the creek. A young man came up and looked in the bag. He found a nice piece of fat. He took it up and showed it to the other Indians. They all wondered where the man came from, with plenty of game.

They plotted to stop the game at dinner time. They left the old man alone in the field, walking back and forth. He jumped back in the draw while the people watched. The old man came out as a bird flew up and over the mountain.

The people wondered how they could get over the mountain to see it. They thought of two birds, *pohkóo?*[1] Owl (it flies quietly) and *tʉebasuu?* Quail (it walks quietly).

Those two went over the top of the mountain. They saw a single tipi facing east. They landed nearby at sunset.

After dark, Owl said, "That's what we're here for."

Owl lit on a tipi pole. As he touched it, the old man said, "Uh, there's an Indian."

Owl flew back to Quail and told him, "He knew I landed, and when I flew away, he said, 'Uh, the Indian is gone'."

Owl and Quail went up. They could hear someone talking. There was no sound for a long time. Then Owl told Quail to go up. Quail went up and peeked. Three times he looked. Then went back to Owl. He said, "There are three people there, the old man, his wife and daughter."

They waited a long time again, until midnight. Then the daughter spoke, "Mother, let's have something to eat."

Owl said, "There they go, there's plenty of meat."

They waited a long time. The girl asked again, and her mother warned "Shh, don't talk like that. You can't tell how those Indians travel."

Owl nudged Quail, "She means us."

This was repeated three times. Finally, the old man said they should eat. The woman opened a parfleche. {When they were done} she swept up the suet and meat chunks to the back of the tipi.

The people went to sleep. Quail went up and snitched pieces and took them to Owl, "Here's your meal." They took the meat in their claws and flew back to the Indians.

The people said, "My, they got lots of meat."[2]

Story: The Owner of the Buffalo {Carlson}   There were only Indians here. They were playing *aratsi?*, throwing spears, and shooting with bows and arrows.

A strange fellow came up. He was an old man. He was dressed like an Indian. He had arrows with him. He spoke to no one and watched the game. Never before had he taken his quiver off his shoulder.

This time, he took off his quiver to go to the toilet. He made some dirt, and then jumped into the creek and disappeared.

1. Robinson and Armagost (1990) has this as specifically a burrowing owl.
2. Wallace and Hoebel 1952:51.

When he was gone, a boy came up and saw the quiver. He found a piece of meat. He took the meat and ran back to the camp leaders.

"He must have lots of meat," the boy said.

The men decided that they would follow the man in order to find out where he lived.

When everyone quit the games to eat, only the man was on the field. He walked up and down the field. Suddenly, he jumped into the same hole where he had done his toilet. In a short time, he came up out of the hole as a bird. He flew high into the air and towards the mountains.

The people wondered how they could find out about the home of this bird in the mountains.

"We will need a bird that flies very quietly and one who walks very quietly," they said. Finally, they got Owl as the quiet flyer, and Quail, who was a quiet walker.

The two birds flew away together to the mountains, where they got to a gully. The two birds flew down to a place near the tipi just at sundown.

When it got dark, Owl flew to one of the tipi poles. Just as Owl lit on the pole, the man inside said, "There is an Indian up there on our tipi pole."

When Owl heard this, he flew back to his friend, Quail. He told Quail that he had been very quiet, but the old man had known when he lit and when he left the tipi; when he flew, the old man said, "The Indian is gone from up there."

Quail and Owl then went up to the tipi together. They stopped to listen for conversation, but could hear none after a very long time.

Hearing none, Quail decided to go up and peek in. So, very quietly, he went up to the tent and peeked in. The people did not hear him.

He went back to his partner, Owl, and told him that there were three people in the tent, the father, the mother, and the daughter.

They waited and listened. Finally, after a long time, they heard the daughter say, "Give me something to eat."

When Owl heard this, he nudged his partner and said, "There you go, lots of meat, lots of meat."

The mother replied to the daughter, "Ssh, keep quiet, there might be some Indians around."

Owl nudged his partner and said, "That means us."

The girl asked again, and her mother answered her as before.

A third time.

Finally, the father said, "It is time to eat," and the mother dragged out the bag of meat. She dropped a piece on the ground, unnoticed.

After they were through eating, the mother swept the floor, and swept the meat over close to the wall. Finally, they went to bed.

When all was quiet again, Quail crept quietly up and took the meat. He brought it back to his friend. The two of them took the meat in their claws and flew back to the Indian camp. When they got there, they dropped the meat on the ground.

The people remarked, "My, they must have a lot of meat."

Episode 2 {Hoebel}   They decided to go over around the mountain. They moved their camp. They packed ten horses representing each band.

The old man saw them and came out. "What do you want?"

"Oh, just a visit."

He marked a line from a tree to a stump and told them to camp on the other side and not to cross the line. For three days, he visited them and kept them from coming to his tipi. He always said, "I don't know where we could get some meat to eat."

Kawos[1] was an Indian who could turn himself into any form. The Indians told him to figure out how to get some meat. "He ain't ever gonna give us any."

He said, "There's only one way, leave it to me."

He had them break camp. Then Kawos changed to an opossum.[2]

The old man followed the people to see where they went. After a while, his daughter came out to scavenge in the camp site. She heard a little dog. "Oh you poor little dog, you're mine from now on."

The pup backed off. "You'll never be hungry, I'll prove it to you."

She opened the door to the tipi. Kawos saw a hundred thousand buffalo under there.

The old man came home. He said, "Take that dog back. I can see from the look in his eyes that it's a grown person. I will kill it if you don't."

The old man followed her out with him as she put down the dog. Her father went on to see if the Indians had turned back, and the girl took the dog back.

She showed him the buffalo again. "You'll never get hungry."

The dog got nervous and jumped from her arms, shouting like a human, stampeding the buffalo. The door broke down and out they poured.

The dog was still inside. The girl took a club to kill the dog when it came out. The dog turned back to human. He hung on the side of a bull and rode out and made for the hills. Then he saw the mess of buffaloes.

He went back to his people. They asked him how he made out. He said "At sunrise, those buffalo will be right at our door."

{**Episode 2**} {Carlson[3]}   The camp decided to go around the hill for meat. They had ten horses with them. On their way, they met the old man. He asked what they wanted. They answered that they had come for a visit.

The old man laid out an arbitrary line beyond which they were not to go.

They camped on the outside of this line. They did not get a chance to visit the tipi of the old man, as each day he would come to them before they had a chance to visit his tipi. He would always say on these visits, "Isn't it too bad that we can't get any meat."

Within the group of Indians was a man who had the ability to change himself into anything. The Indians came to him and said, "You're a smart man, tell us how we are going to get some meat. We'll never get any from that old man."

The man said he would do his best, but that all the rest must break camp and leave. When they left, this man turned into an opossum.

    1. Wallace and Hoebel describe Kawos as the "Culture Hero" (1952:51). However, in Hoebel's and Carlson's versions of Tahsuda's story (see below), there is confusion between Kawos, another unnamed hero, and the hero's dog, Kwasi 'tail'. Robinson and Armagost (1990) has *kaawosA* as 'cheater'.

    2. Both Hoebel and Carlson (see below) recorded this as opossum; Carlson includes the note that he then turned into a puppy.

    3. Carlson's notes do not have the episode breaks.

The old man followed these people, leaving his wife and daughter behind. After a while, his daughter decided to go to the old camp site and see if she could find anything.

When she got near the site, she heard a dog. The man had turned himself into a little dog.

She reached for the dog, but it drew back at first. Finally, she caught him saying, "Come with me, I promise you'll never be hungry as long as you live."

She took the dog home. When they got home, the girl showed the dog a trap door through which they looked. Within a corral, they saw thousands of buffalo.

After a while, the father came home. He saw the dog and was angry. He said, "That dog has a grown-up look in his eyes; he's dangerous. Take him right back to where you got him."

The daughter obeyed; she put the dog where she found it. Her father followed her, and went up to where the Indians were. When the father had disappeared, the girl went and got the dog again. She took him home again. She said again, "As long as you are my dog, you shall not go hungry."

She took him to the door leading to the secret corral. She was holding the dog in her arms. When they were within the corral, the dog began to get uneasy in her arms. Suddenly, he sprang out of her arms and yelled like a human and ran around the corral. The buffalo were stampeded and ran to the outer world in all directions.

(This was the origin of the buffalo. This was how they came to the Indians. Prior to this time there were no buffalo.)

The girl stood by the gate and waited for the dog; she held a club in readiness to kill the dog when he came out.

He changed to a human again, clung to the side of one of the buffalo, and got out of the corral that way.

When he got some distance from the corral, he got off his horse and ran for the hills. He got back to his people and told them of his success. "Tomorrow, we shall have plenty of meat."

Episode 3: How the Crow Got His Call and Color {Hoebel}   The old man had servants, white crows. He told them to fly over the bison and, whenever they killed one, to fly down and say to the Indians, *"tʉtsʉkom"*[1] 'bad meat'. Thus, they spoiled the meat. The only way to foil them was to cut a piece off before the crows got there and hide it in the brush.

A strange young man came to camp. He went to an old lady and asked for food. The woman said, "There are plenty of buffalo, but no meat. Those white birds spoil it."

The young man went out and got some. The woman cooked it over the fire. The young man said, "Tomorrow, I will get you plenty."

"You will have to work fast before those birds see you," she said.

The young man went out bright and early. He skinned and butchered a buffalo, and crawled under the skin on the skeleton. The crows come over to look at the dead buffalo. One landed and the man seized it.

The man took the meat and the bird up to the woman. They tied the white crow tight to the tip of a tipi pole alive. The woman lit the fire and the smoke came out of the hole while

---

1. *tʉtsʉ* 'bad'.

the crow said, "*tʉtsʉkaka.*" Pretty soon the smoke hurt its voice, and it could only say, "caw, caw," and his feathers got black.

The young man took the crow down, and said, "From now on, you're black, you don't pester these Indians no more. You'll get the leavings of butchered bison, but you can't spoil the meat."

The other white crows circled around the black crow and gradually changed their voice and color.

{**Episode 3**} {Carlson}   Losing the buffalo made the father mad. He had some white crows. He told these crows to fly around and guard the buffalo. If there was one killed, they should light near it and say "*tʉtsʉkom*" 'bad meat', and then the meat was spoiled. This was just as bad as not having any buffalo.

So the Indians, as soon as they would kill a buffalo, they would cut off a piece and throw it in the brush before they heard this voice; this would preserve the meat.

There was a strange young man who came into the camp. He came to the tipi of an old woman and asked her for something to eat. She told him there was plenty of buffalo, but because of the birds, the meat was all spoiling.

The young man said, "Wait, I'll go out and get some meat."

He went out and returned in a little while with some beef. She cooked it for him. He then told her that the next day, he would go out and get her all kinds of meat.

Early the next morning, he went out and killed a buffalo and cut it before a single bird came up. He took the hide and crawled in. Soon a white bird came and lit on the hide. He then reached out and grabbed the bird.

He took the meat home to the old lady. Then he took the bird and tied him up on top of her tipi pole. The old lady built a big fire and began roasting the meat and the smoke began coming out of the top. The bird was still saying "*tʉtsʉkaka,*" etc. Finally, the smoke got thick and the crow turned black and all you could hear was the crow saying, "Caw, Caw, Caw."

After a while, the man took him down and said, "From now on, you'll be black and always you will get what is left."

When the white crows saw the black crow, they began to chase him. They followed him around in a circle; each time they circled, their color and voices kept changing until they were all black and said, "Caw, caw."

This young man was a stranger to the Indians. He told them that now they could kill all they wanted. Then he disappeared and no one know where he went.

Episode 5 {Hoebel[1]}   The young man went away, no one knew where. He had a staff (*pawahkapʉ*[2]); a dog was his only other belonging.

He went to another bunch of Indians. He asked an old woman for food, but no one could give it. They said, "That hill up there swallows people alive. You can't leave camp."

The young man said, "Old lady, I will go get meat tomorrow."

The woman said, "Don't go, I'm used to being hungry."

---

1. There is no Episode 4 in Hoebel's notes.
2. Robinson and Armagost (1990) identifies *pawahkapʉ* as "an herb (name unknown; grows near creeks)."

The young man went up, and the hill opened up and swallowed him, stick, dog, and all. There was a path over the hill and you could get across between the openings.

The young man landed on a pile of ribs of people who had thirsted to death. There were others there who were alright. He asked the people if there was anyplace in the cave which was sensitive to the touch. A man answered that when you touched one rib in the wall it moved.

The young man stuck his stick in the rib. He sicced his dog on the next one and broke them. They each took two more apiece on that side, then they broke six on the other side and the walls sprang open. All the people got out.

The young man got back to the old woman and told her to send the people who had lost relatives in there up with water for them. Now they could always go on the hill. The young man went away, no one knew where.

{**Episode 5**} {Carlson}   This young man had a long black stick called *pawahkapƲ* and a dog called _____ {*sic*}. This was all the property the man had. He killed all the game with this stick.

This young Indian then went to another tribe. He went to the tipi of an old woman and asked her for some meat.

She said, "My dear young man, I would like to give you some, but we don't dare leave our tipis because that hill over yonder swallows people."

The young man said, "In the morning, I will go out and get meat for you."

The next morning, he went directly to the hill. When he got there, the earth opened up and he went down in there with his dog and stick and was covered up.

There was only one trail which you could take over the mountain; by watching your steps, you could hurry over between openings and closings.

Down in the earth, there were many people who were suffering from thirst. The young man asked them if the sides of this cave seemed to react when they touched it. They answered, "Yes."

The young man then took his stick and broke one of the ribs (the inside was like the inside of a person) and his dog took another; alternating thus, they broke all of the ribs (twelve). And when the last was broken, the lid flew open.

The man then got out and went to the old lady and told her to tell all those who had relatives in the hill that they should run to their assistance with water.

Those who had disappeared lately were already on their way home.

He told the Indians they could shoot all the buffalo they wanted and they would not be swallowed up.

The man disappeared and no one knew where he went.

Episode 6 {Hoebel}   The young man went on to another old lady.

He said, "Old Lady, give me some meat."

"I ain't got no meat."

"Well, I'll get you some."

The old woman said, "There's only one way to get meat. There's a single gap to the buffalo range, guarded by a medicine man who takes all the meat away from you. You must get by while he isn't looking."

The young man went in and drove a buffalo up to the medicine man's tipi and killed it there. A man rode up on his horse and demanded the meat. The young man said, "Says who? I'm hungry."

The servant of the medicine man said, "You're as good as dead if you don't."

The young man said, "Go along. Tell him I'll keep my meat."

The medicine man had a pile of polished granite which he would throw. His medicine was from there, in the form of the stone.

All of the stones fell short.

The young man came up closer to give him a better chance.

He threw the final stone.

The young man held his staff in front of his face. The rock hit it and fell to the ground. He picked it up and threw it at the medicine man, killing him.

{**Episode 6**} {Carlson}   The man went to another old lady in another tribe. He asked her for some meat. She told him that they had no meat. So he went out and got some beef. He said, "Tomorrow, I'm going after buffalo meat."

The old woman said that that was impossible, as there was only one passage to the buffalo area, and that was guarded by a medicine man who took every bit of meat that you tried to bring back. The only way you could get meat past the medicine man was when he was sleeping.

The young man went after a buffalo, and he chased it to near the medicine man's lodge and killed it. While he was cutting up the meat, a man rode up and asked for the meat. This man was a servant of the medicine man. "You are as good as dead if you don't turn over the meat."

The young man told the servant to tell him that he was hungry, and he had killed the buffalo and intended to keep it.

When the medicine man heard this, he climbed upon a pile of stones which was nearby, and threw stones at him; this was throwing his medicine at him.

He threw one big stone at the young man, but the young man held his stick in front of him. The rock hit the man in the chest and bounced off without hurting him. The young man then picked up the stone and threw it back at the medicine man and killed him.

The young man then returned to his people and told them they could now hunt and not fear the medicine man, as he was dead.

Episode 7 {Hoebel}   The young man went on to another bunch of Indians. He heard a woman crying hard. He asked her what was wrong. She said, "My time was come."

She was between thirty and thirty-five years old. "Piamupits eats us when we get this old."

Mupits had eight heads.

"We'll go along and see what he's like; come on, Kwasi."[1]

They went up. Mupits stuck out his eight heads. He knocked a head off with his stick. He said, "Kwasi, do your stuff."

The dog took off another head.

---

1. *kwasi* 'tail'. His dog.

Mupits ducked. He came up after awhile, and they took off two more heads. He had four more, and they got all the heads.

He told the girl to go home. "If your father asks how come, tell him; if he wants to know who, tell him I will be at a certain place by the tipis."

Kawos wanted credit, "Take me, take me."

He told her to tell her father he did it. Her father said, "How come you're back here, I thought you were supposed to let Mupits eat you."

The girl told her story. "Well, bring the young man in."

He told Kawos that he could have his daughter tonight, or what he would.

Before her father had finished, Kawos grabbed her around the waist and fell in bed with her. She banged him in the ribs and threatened to expose him. She told her father he was not the man and Kawos fled.

They brought in the young stranger. Her father said if he was the hero, he could have her. He slept with her that night and disappeared the next morning.

{**Episode 7**} {Carlson}   The young man disappeared again and came to another bunch of Indians. This was a large camp. He came upon a tipi where a woman was crying.

He walked up to her and asked what was wrong. She said, "My days (she was thirty-five) are over with, because when you get to be my age, Piamupits eats you."

Piamupits had eight heads.

He said to the woman, "I will go along with you, and we will go and see this Piamupits."

They came to Piamupits' cave. Piamupits stuck his eight heads out. Then alternately, he (with his stick) and his dog, knocked off all eight heads. Each time Mupits would stick up a head, one or the other would hit and take off the head.

The young man told the woman to go back and tell her father that Piamupits was no longer. If her father wanted to see him (the young man), he would be at a certain tipi.

It happened that this tribe was the tribe in which the man who brought the buffalo lived. When he heard that Piamupits had been killed, he wanted to be the one that had killed him. So he went to the girl and told her to tell her father that he was the one who had killed Piamupits. He said, "I will be waiting here."

So the girl went to her father and her father said, "What are you doing here, you were supposed to have been eaten by Piamupits."

The girl answered, "Piamupits is no more; he is killed."

The father said, "Who killed him?"

The girl said, "He is out here."

"Go get him," father said.

The girl went and got the dog-man.[1] When they came back to the tipi, the father said, "I'll give you my daughter as wife for your services."

He had no sooner said this than the dog-man grabbed the girl and fell on the bed with her. The girl kept nudging him, telling him to stop; if he didn't stop, she was going to tell her father the truth. He didn't stop, so she told, at which time the young man jumped up and ran out of the tipi.

She then went out and got the right man and brought him back.

1. Probably Kawos.

The father said, "You can have my daughter for as long as you want."

So the young man took the woman and went to bed with her that night. During the night he disappeared and no one knew where he went.

Episode 8 {Hoebel}   The next morning found the young man with two different bands of Indians; one band worked, the other did no work. One bunch was sorting out pin feathers; one bunch was working in charcoal. They were all dusty.

Another bunch worked on glue. He stopped to watch this bunch. He said he would like to help with the glue.

The leader said, "You're a fine looking man, it wouldn't do to get you smeared up like this."

The young man got them to change his clothes for work clothes. He liked to work in glue.

While working, they called his attention to a big tipi and told him the chief and his daughter lived there. They pointed out both. "That was where the girl comes down to the spring for water."

It was a private spring for the chief alone.

He saw the girl pick up her blanket and get water. The boy made a bone. He sharpened it at both ends and smoothed it off.

They told him she always came back at sunset.

The boy placed the bone across her path and went off. The girl came down and noticed the bone. She rubbed her foot over it, but didn't pick it up. She went on to get water. When she came back, she picked up the bone and rubbed it between her hands.

She put it down between her breasts. She forgot about the stick. After nine months, she felt funny. She said to her mother, "I believe I'm pregnant."

At the beginning of the tenth month, she got a child, a boy. All her relatives were tickled to death.

Come four years, there came a crying spell. It cried until it was cried out, for four days straight. The grandfather got the medicine men from the drone camp to find out the trouble. There were ten in number. They talked it over. The medicine man sitting next to the grandfather held up his hand. He said that the matter was that he wanted his pappy. They told the boy to look for his father among the medicine men, but the boy still cried.

The grandfather got the drone camp to come in groups of ten. Kwasi was in the last group; he wanted that woman. He made the boy a bow and arrow and gave them to him. The boy was shooting around. The grandfather said, "Ah, there's his father."

Kwasi started getting next to the girl. The boy threw down the arrows and cried. Kwasi had failed.

They began with the laboring band. They lined the featherpickers up in four tens; no soap. Then they lined up the charcoal workers. Still the boy cried.

Then, they lined up the glue workers. There were four tens with one man over. The hero stood apart. The boy still cried.

Grandfather thought, "I guess we didn't find his father."

The hero walked in, and the boy ran to him and ceased his crying. "My son," said the hero.

The chief was so mad—he didn't like the stranger—that he had bumped his head on a tipi pole, but the others were glad to find the father. The chief disowned his daughter. He told her to clean out a chicken coop and sleep with her husband there.

Indians came in and stole horses off them; only the chief had horses left. The daughter said to the chief, "Father, my husband is active. Why don't you give him a horse to enjoy?"

"OK, he can't handle horses, I'll give him one."

A three-legged critter was turned out for him.

He took out in pursuit of the horse thieves. He didn't want to pass the pursuit, which was on foot. He went to cross a creek and the horse slipped and fell and could not get up.

The raiders were getting farther away, so he changed his dog into a white horse and passed everyone. He rode up on the two raiders, tapped them with his staff, and they fell dead. Then he rode back to the creek and changed his horse back to a dog.

The people went on and drove back their horses and helped him get up his three-legged critter.

The big chief asked the people how they had done it. The people said a man on a white horse went by so fast, "We couldn't see who it was. He did his deeds and returned, and disappeared down the creek bank. There was this fellow with his three-legged horse and we helped him out. That's all we know."

They had a victory dance, but they didn't know to whom the honor should go.

Later on, two more came in and stole horses with a repeat of the previous episode. This happened a third time.

On the fourth time, the chief called the four bravest men on the four fastest horses. They would file through their spearpoints and charge this hero, breaking off a spearpoint in his hip. "Then we will see who does us these favors."

They fared as before. As he rode back, the first three warriors tried, and the fourth got him.

The chief called in the four warriors. "Well, we got him, but how we gonna find him? We've got to wait."

After four days, the point began to hurt him. He told his wife to go up and get her father to come down and take out that metal. He dressed himself in his good clothes, washed up; he was "as fine looking as you ever saw."

The father said, "I'll take my time."

He hated him for being such a dirty-looking man with his fine daughter. The father entered, all pleased with this good-looking fellow. He called the man his son-in-law for the first time. The chief called in the warriors, who brought along the broken spear. "How did you get such a point?"

The hero told them to cut a cross on the wound and to pull out the point. The point fit the spear.

The chief invited his son-in-law to move up to his big tipi. They stayed where they were, however. The wound healed and the scar disappeared.

He said to his wife, "I'm going to leave you. My friend lives over the hill. I'm going to go see him and bring him back. You look me over close, he looks just like me. If you pick him as your husband, he'll always be."

She said, "I won't miss. There's that sore."

You could just see it.

He returned with his friend. They stood outside the tipi and called, "Here we are, come out and find your husband. If you go back in without choosing, we will never talk to you."

She looked him over carefully. They were both alike in all parts of the body; both had wounds. She made up her mind and took one by the wrist, the other one. Her husband said, "Well, I guess that leaves me out. I've got to go now. I hope you live happy forever. Good luck."

He went away and was never heard from again.

{**Episode 8**} {Carlson}   He came, the next morning, to a group of people who were divided into two classes. One class worked and the other one did nothing.

The first group he saw were separating pin feathers from big feathers, and they were all covered with feathers. He didn't stop here, but went on to a second group that was working with charcoal; they were all black and covered with charcoal. He didn't stop there, but went on to a {third} group that was working with glue; he stopped here. These people were all sticky with glue.

He told these people that he was interested in their work and wanted to join in and make glue. One of the men told him that he was a fine young man, too nice to work with glue.

The young man said, "Never mind, I'll change my clothes and work with you," which he did.

He was given some sticky clothes. While he was working, someone pointed out a lone tipi to him saying, "In that tipi a great chief lives with his daughter, and that trail is the one she takes when she goes for water for the chief. At that spring, she is the only one that gets water."

When this was being said, a girl came out, went to the spring, and got some water.

After this, the young man took a piece of bone and whittled at both ends. He knew that she came for water during the evening. The young man went to the path and put the bone crosswise on the path, and then hid in the woods.

When the girl came for water, she saw the bone in the pathway, but she didn't pick it up. She rolled it back and forth with her foot and then moved on to the spring. She got her water and started back. This time she picked up the bone, rubbed it in her hands, and then put it down her bosom. After she took the bone, she forgot all about it.

After nine months she began to feel funny, and she went to her mother saying, "Mother, I am pregnant." A short while after, she gave birth to a child (a boy). The girl's father was very happy. They took good care of him.

At the age of four, he would sit down and start to cry, and cry and cry and stop when he had enough. He cried for four days straight.

This worried the grandparents. The grandfather decided to call in the aid of some of the medicine men. The medicine men talked it over. Finally, one medicine man said, "I know what is wrong with the child. He is crying for his father."

The grandfather decided that the only thing to do was to find the father of the boy. The grandfather lined up the medicine men (ten of them) and told the boy to look for his father in that group.

The father was not there, so the boy began to cry.

The grandfather sent out word that all the men should arrange themselves in groups of ten, and the boy looked at them all but would start crying, so the father was not found out.

Finally, in the last group was the dog-man,[1] and he was anxious to get the boy's mother. He planned to try to make the boy think he was the father. He made bows and arrows for the boy. The boy was pleased and started to play. The grandfather saw this and said, "Surely, he is the boy's father."

The dog-man heard this and was much pleased. He kept edging up towards the boy's mother.

However, the boy soon started to cry, and they knew that the dog-man was not the father.

After all the non-working group was checked on, they started on the working group. The first group checked was the feather bunch. They took them in lots of ten, of which there were four. The boy cried still.

Next, they took the charcoal bunch in four lots of ten each, but the boy still cried.

Finally, the glue bunch came. There were four groups of ten each, with one extra (our hero). This man came up and the boy stopped crying. He took the boy on his knee and said, "Yes, this is my son. He is puny, but he is still my son."

The old grandfather was angry because he didn't know the young man. The old man was so sore that he kept hitting his head on the tipi poles. He turned to his daughter, saying, "You take your bedding and go and clean out that tipi (chicken house) and sleep there. You cannot be in the same tipi with me any longer. And take your man with you."

Just about the time that the couple was to move into their apartment, someone stole all the horses from the camp except those of the chief. The daughter went to the father and asked him for a horse for her husband. The father finally gave the young man a three-legged horse.

The man took his horse and rode along, but the horse fell in a ditch and couldn't get out.

The horses that were being driven off were getting farther and farther ahead.

The man then took his dog and changed him into a white horse and rode after the herd. He caught up with the raiders. There were only two of them. He touched each of them with his stick and they fell off their horses, dead. He then left the catching of the herd to those of his camp who were chasing the herd on foot.

He rode quickly back to his three-legged horse in the ditch, changed his white horse back into a dog, and then proceeded to get the three-legged horse out. By that time, those on foot had caught the horses and were returning.

When the gang got back, the grandfather asked them how they could possibly get the horses when they were so far behind. The men then told that, while following, someone on a large white horse rode by going so fast they couldn't see who it was. He touched the thieves with his stick and they fell dead. He then rode away and disappeared down by the creek. "When we came back, all we saw was this fellow trying to get his three-legged horse out of the ditch."

1. Kawos.

Before they had gotten back to the camp, they sang, and shot, and celebrated. They didn't know who the honor should go to, as they didn't know who killed the men. The honors finally went to the whole camp.

After everything had quieted down, two men again stole the horses. The young man's entire performance of before was repeated.

This act was repeated four times, but on the fourth time, the camp was determined to find out who this person was that was doing all these favors. The chief reserved four of the fastest horses to find out who this person was. The chief chose four men who he instructed to take spears and whittle around the point until they were almost ready to come off. With these spears, they were to stab the white horse man in the leg as he went by.

But when he went by, they all missed. He rode up to the herd, and repeated his earlier performances and started back. The first three warriors missed him, but the fourth drove his spear into his leg, but the man kept riding back to the ditch.

When the four warriors came back, they had a meeting with the big chief. They told the chief that they had done as he instructed, but they didn't know how they were going to find out who it was.

At the end of four days, the pain got so bad that the young man told his wife to go to her father and get him to come over and take the steel out of his body. The young man changed from his dirty, gluey clothes he always went around in to his really nice clothes. He was very handsome.

FRANK CHEKOVI
Undated III[1]

Nanuwoku   One time, a bunch drifted away from the main camp. While they were gone, a man died in the party, leaving a widow. The widow took up with one of the men in the group. On arriving at home, the (classificatory) brother of the dead man and a friend demanded *nanuwoku* from the brother of the present husband. They went to him on the grounds that the husband was propertyless. The brother refused. He said he didn't know his brother was married to the woman. He told them to get the brother's shirt, if nothing else was available.

The pair went to the husband. He told them that he would like to do the right thing, but he had nothing, he just drifted from camp to camp. The pair demanded the woman back in lieu of *nanuwoku*. The woman refused. She said that there was no case, that she didn't intend to live with this man, but had come to him for protection on the way home and had already left him.

She picked up a bucket and went to the creek for water. When she didn't return, they looked for her and found the bucket lying near the creek. The pair then went home and let things be. The husband went to a prearranged place near Cache to meet her. From there,

---

1. Except where noted, these notes are from Hoebel.

they walked to Saddle Mountain to Frank's camp with the Yapainʉʉ. Frank was distantly related to the woman and called her "sister."

The man was bashful, so he sent the woman in to talk to Frank. Frank asked her what the trouble was, [saying that he had heard that she was married, and asking where her husband was. The woman said her husband was outside, he was afraid to come in, and told all the trouble they had got into through the *nanʉwokʉ* case, saying they wanted Frank's assistance.[1]]

[Frank told her to bring her husband in, that they could stay with him as long as they wanted. He would help them settle the affair.]

Frank met up with one of the two men at the trader's place north of Lawton.[2] [Both of the men who were trying to collect were friends of Frank's.] Frank told him that the couple was with him, and that if they wanted to see the man, they should come up. This man said to Frank that they had already heard that they (the couple) were at his place. [They didn't want to cause Frank any trouble, so they sent a message by him that the trouble was over, that they would no longer try to collect *nanʉwokʉ*. Frank said he was glad they had got out of the notion. When he got back, he told the news to the couple. He told them that when they decided where they wanted to set up housekeeping, he would be glad to move them there and would give them some dishes. He brought them back.]

[Mamsookawat was camping in Tumotsukatʉ's {Black Moustache} band east of Cache, and Frank took them there. He gave them dishes. The woman cut some tent poles and got some canvas. Then they had a household. They lived a long time together until finally the man died. They were very wealthy towards the last.]

A classificatory brother doesn't collect *nanʉwokʉ* very frequently.

Nanʉwokʉ {Carlson}   Tokwia[3] and Yutaibo[4] were friends, they called each other brother. When Tokwia died, Yutaibo claimed his wife, but the woman refused [the woman refused him].

The woman was Wifeper,[5] aged thirty-five. Yutaibo never lived with her and finally she took up with Frank and they lived together. Yutaibo heard of this. He was living with another woman at the time. Yutaibo told two friends, Tasiabokurawa[6] and Atsaci,[7] to go to see Frank [to collect *nanʉwokʉ*].

1. The variations in this note are from Carlson.

2. The Red Store; see next page.

3. *toh-* 'with the hand'. Hoebel (1940:146) gives it as Touched with a Closed Fist; he is otherwise unidentified.

4. *yuhu* 'grease', *taibooʔ* 'non-Indian', the Comanche ethnonym for Mexican. Casagrande has *yu-* as 'common' (1954–55, II:227). As an individual, he is otherwise unidentified.

5. *waʔihpʉ* 'woman'. Wifeper is the agency spelling; it is also spelled Wahper. In the censuses from 1879 to 1902, there are at least twenty entries identified only as 'woman', and it is not clear how many of these may be duplicates. By cross-checking the parentage listings in the Family Record Book, however, this particular individual can be identified as the daughter of Hightosa (*hai* 'crow, *tosapI* 'white') and Pettyoden (*petʉ* 'daughter', *urarʉ* 'to find'). Wifeper was born about 1875. She was married to George Koweno and known as Mary Koweno.

6. Hoebel (1940:47) and Wallace and Hoebel (1952:228) give this as Mangy Coat, possibly derived from *taʔsiʔwoo* 'buffalo'. Otherwise unidentified.

7. Hoebel (1940) did not translate this name.

Frank and Wifeper were camped [living] at the Red Store.[1] The men came up and said they were collecting *nanɨwokɨ*. Frank asked them which of the two had a claim on the woman, and they said Yutaibo. Frank asked Wifeper if she was married to another man. She said "No," that she had nothing to do with the man who claimed her.

Frank asked what Yutaibo wanted.[2] They said he wanted a certain horse that Frank had gotten from a dead friend of his, and another horse, a saddle, and a Winchester. Frank said he couldn't part with the first horse, but he would replace it with one equally good. Atsaci said that was not satisfactory, that Yutaibo had asked for that particular horse and they must have it. Frank tried three times to get them to agree on another, but they refused. Finally, Frank said that if they insisted on taking the horse, they would get nothing else in addition.

Frank told Atsaci that he wanted to say something to him when they were through arguing. Atsaci was married to two daughters of Frank's brother. Frank said to Atsaci, "Remember, you are married to two of my daughters. If I accept these terms and you insist on that horse, you can have it, but you will lose your wives. I will take back my daughters from you. You are my *monahpɨʔ* {son-in-law} and yet you are not caring what you say. You are trying to get the horse I love."

Tasiabokurawa said that Atsaci was not thinking of what he was saying. He said they would be willing to take another horse in place of the one disputed about.

Atsaci hadn't much to say. He was older than Frank and had forgotten he was a classificatory son-in-law. [Frank asked Atsaci what he had to say about the arrangement. He answered that since Tasiabokurawa was older, then it was up to him. Frank was willing to do the right thing, so he gave them a gray mare, a bay horse, a saddle, and a gun. Eventually the gray horse became a very good race horse.

[Felix Kowena was the son of Frank and Wifeper.][3]

Life Cycle: Marriage: Wife Exchange   Pahighpeop[4] was the man; Takama[5] was the woman; Namiquaya[6] 'where you undress' was the other man. The two men were friends, but were unrelated.

Takama had children; she was the wife of Pahighpeop. Namiquaya's wife had no children. She liked to gamble. They exchanged wives; the husbands stayed friends. The

1. The Red Store, so-called because of its red-painted false front, was established in 1886 by the firm of Collier and Sneed (Hagan 1976:175), just south of Fort Sill, on what is now Rogers Road on the north side of Lawton. The building itself still exists at Eagle Park in Cache.
2. Wallace and Hoebel 1952:37.
3. Hoebel 1940: 56-57; Wallace and Hoebel 1952:228. Variations are from Hoebel.
4. See above, Frank Chekovi, August 4.
5. The censuses spell this name several ways: Tahkumah, Tahcomah, and Tahconah. The 1885 census translated it as 'sweetening'. Robinson and Armagost (1990) gives *kamatɨ* 'taste'.
6. This is one agency spelling; it is also spelled Namiquau. Hoebel spelled it Namakweyei. The 1879 census translated it as 'undressing', but according to Robinson and Armagost (1990), 'undressing' is *natsakweʔyarɨ*. His father was said to be a Crow Indian. Namiquaya was a member of Tahpony's Yapainɨɨ local band.

man who got the children got the best of it (they got money from the government for each child.).[1]

Medicine: Transfer   When a medicine man transferred his medicine to another man, he didn't tell the initiate about the medicine, but let him find out for himself (by a vision from the medicine) whether he had the power.[2]

Medicine: Transfer   Frank's half-brother got a gift of medicine from an old medicine man, who gave it to his four sons at the same time. He went to lonely places to find out more about it.

He demonstrated it to Frank. He swallowed an eagle breast feather. He drew a figure of a man on the ground. He blew out four times. On the fourth time, the feather came out and stuck in the breast of the figure. Medicine men sometimes had a shield that went with the medicine, but this man didn't have one.

Frank's brother wanted Frank to have his medicine. Frank refused twice. He didn't want to have to follow the taboos. Finally, his brother forced it on him. Frank was married and had children. His brother said he would especially need it then, so he wouldn't have to hire another medicine man if anyone was sick. It would save him money and trouble.

Frank was living with his mother and two sisters. He was a young man. His half-brother and wife were living in another tipi.

His brother's wife called in the early morning from outside. She said his brother wanted him in the tipi, and that he should bathe in the creek and come over.

He heard his brother singing in the tipi, so he bathed and went over.

He found his brother sitting on a blanket on the west side of the tipi. He told Frank to sit on the north side. His brother painted his own face and started to paint Frank's face in the same way.

His brother had previously wanted to pass his medicine on to Frank, but Frank had refused. His brother had done this twice. Each time, the brother painted him according to a dream he'd had during the night.

Frank had since gotten married and had a daughter. His brother wanted him to have the medicine, especially now.

His brother again called him in. He took a stick and bent it in a circle {about two inches in diameter}; he strung white beads and covered the circle. Two strings were in a cross in the center, one hanging down.

---

1. The censuses provide some verification of the relationship between these three people—and others—but the details are difficult to sort out. This case does point out some of the difficulties in working with the censuses.

   The 1885 census, the first census to list all spouses and children rather than just the head of the family, gave Pahighpeop—then a local band chief—as married to a woman named Mahkersey. They were listed as having two children, a girl Hauvah, age sixteen, and a boy, Pauau, age thirteen. That same year, Namiquaya—in Tahpony's local band—was married to two women, Moosook, who had one child named Tahkonywup, and Tahkumah, who was listed with no children. In 1889, Pahighpeop was still married to Mahkersey, and they still had Pauau in the family. Hauvah, now an adult, was listed with Tahkumah, who had separated from Namiquaya. However, the Family Record Book listed the parents of Hauvah as Pahighpeop and Tahkumah rather than Pahighpeop and Mahkersey.

   2. Wallace and Hoebel 1952:162.

His brother fastened this gadget and an eagle feather to his side medicine lock. He told Frank his medicine taboos, not to eat beef heart, not to eat beef leg muscle. His brother gave Frank his power, put it in him. He said the medicine would come to him in a dream since Frank had refused to take it from him.

Frank knew this medicine would be bad for him; it was borne out later. When Frank felt his power, he could swallow it.[1]

Medicine: Curing   People soon found out that Frank had his brother's medicine.

They came to smoke, etc., for help. He went with them. He came dragging a rope, which meant he wanted a horse as payment; there was no need to mention it.

He doctored a person and he got well.

He was successful, so he set up a separate tipi as an office,[2] the other to live in. His medicine articles were kept in the separate tipi.

He doctored a patient four times on two days. If there was no success, he might be re-engaged for four days. If he wasn't cured, he sent for another medicine man.

Medicine: Curing: Specialization   A medicine man doctored a man with pneumonia, but couldn't cure him after two days. He finally went to Frank for assistance (he sent his wife to get him in the night). Frank went. The medicine man had a cigarette ready for him. He said he'd like his help. Pneumonia was Frank's specialty; all medicine men specialized.

When they smoked together, they were as one doctor.

The first medicine man doctored the patient, then Frank. The next morning, Frank went over and found the man better. They doctored him again—the first medicine man, then Frank—for two days. He was cured.

The pay went to the first medicine man. All Frank got was the smoke and the agreement that Frank could call on him any time he needed assistance.[3]

Medicine: Tipi   Frank's medicine tipi was set up with the fireplace in the middle. There was a pile of dirt on the west. Over it was a forked pole with a piece of brush leaning against it (about one-and-a-half to two feet high). The feathers were kept in the brush.

Medicine: Taboos   Frank could not eat leg muscle, beef liver, beef heart. A woman could not stir his food with the point of a knife. If she did, bullets would enter as the knife was stuck in the meat.

The taboos were also kept by the medicine man's wife.

Medicine: Taboos: Breaking   A mean woman who didn't like her husband could break his medicine taboos to get rid of him.

A man received medicine from a medicine man. If he got sick and could get no relief, he might see another medicine man who might advise him to go back to the one who had given him his medicine. The old medicine man might suspect that he had broken the taboo of his medicine. They would go to lonely places, perhaps several of them, until they learned what he had done wrong. This old medicine man had the power to cure him.

1. Wallace and Hoebel 1952:162–64.
2. Wallace and Hoebel 1952:166.
3. Hoebel 1940:126.

Once Frank was cutting timber on Washita Creek. He cut his instep with the ax; his foot was covered in blood. Karisu[1] ran up to him and helped pull his boot off. He lifted him onto the lumber wagon and took him to the agency at Anadarko and called a white doctor.

He couldn't stop the bleeding. Frank covered his head with a sheet to avoid seeing the blood; he dozed off. He thought he was dying.

When he came to, he found women there crying; they thought he was dead.

He lay in his house a long time while it healed. The doctor said he could ride to the timber now and then for air.

A Kiowa invited Frank to dinner on his way home one noon. He was still weak (also another man).

He sat down on a bed.

The man's wife got the meal. He washed and sat down to eat. They had beef heart, but he couldn't eat it (because of his medicine taboo), the other man also.

Their host tried to call their attention away so he would eat the meat.

They joked. Frank had a piece of bread. He stuck it in the meat gravy twice. When he noticed it, he felt cold chills up and down his back. When the woman came for the dishes, she said, "Those men weren't hungry, they wouldn't eat."

The Kiowa ate no meat or gravy whatever.

When they got home, he felt all right for three nights. On the next night, he felt a pain in his stomach; a knot formed. He decided to go see his half-brother from whom he received the medicine. He got to his brother's camp at about three o'clock in the afternoon. At sundown, his wife removed all the dishes.

They put Frank on the west side of the tipi and smoked. His brother stood at the foot of the bed, holding eagle feathers, and found out what was wrong.

He sat down and told Frank he shouldn't eat beef heart. Frank denied eating any. His brother said the beef heart had formed a knot in there. He said he'd cure it the next morning, early.

The next morning, Frank came out and found a sweat lodge built, with a fire outside. His brother told him to squat down on the west side. Frank couldn't squat, so he lay down with his head towards the sun, facing the fire.

The ceremony was this: His brother told his wife to bring in the hot stones. His brother dropped the stones in a bucket of water, singing, and stirring it. His brother fanned the steam around. Frank nearly smothered. His brother removed the rock from the bucket and put it in the fireplace inside, and asked for another rock from outside. She brought in four more rocks, poured water over them in the fireplace, and prayed. Frank wished he were elsewhere.

His brother's wife opened the door a minute for air, and then closed it again.

His brother poured water on the rocks three times. His brother sang. He took the last red-hot rock in his hand, and rubbed the knot in Frank's stomach with it. It felt like ice to Frank. His brother told him this hot rock would melt the knot and the pain away; it had the power.

---

1. Otherwise unidentified.

Frank staggered out; he couldn't see. He rode to a creek nearby and lay in the water until he was cool. The knot was gone and there was no more pain.

He went home and felt all right for a month. Then he got the pain again (it came up through his legs). He lay on his stomach on a grass clump and the pain went away. He still occasionally got the numbness in his legs and pain. He always lay on grass clumps to cure it.

He heard about peyote; a brother who knew about his trouble invited him to a meeting. His brother said the sweat lodge medicine given him by his other brother had caused him lots of sickness.

Medicine   Frank was camping by Saddle Mountain with the Yapainʉʉ. He got a job as a cowboy. He worked back by the Red River.

He was asleep one night and had a dream. He saw a woman lying on the south side of a tipi. She spat up blood. It {the dream} said that if he got to her in time he could cure her. He went home after some blankets and his wife told him there was a sick woman with pneumonia, who spat up blood. Chills ran all over his body.

It was at night; he heard footsteps outside; he invited the person in. When she came in, she was bearing smoke and sage. Frank bade her be seated on the south side of the tipi. It was the mother of the sick woman. Before she lit her cigarette, he told her he consented, for her to go ahead and he would follow. They would smoke on their arrival.

Part of Frank's medicine was that a person must go around his tipi before entering, and then he couldn't refuse.[1]

The patient was lying on the south side. He stood to the west of the patient, the mother stood to the north of him. He told her to lay the lower end of a feather towards the sun, with the bird facing the sun. He said he was ready. She lit the prepared cigarette with a match. Frank usually used the fire, but he didn't want to bring a coal over the feathers. She asked which hand to use in passing the cigarette. He said the right hand. He smoked and prayed and placed the cigarette to the west of the fire. He took the sage, stripped it, and rubbed his hand and body with it. He put the sage down by the feather and picked up the feather, and blowing on it, he fanned himself. He got up and went around the fire to the south side. He sat down by the patient. He moved the feather like an eagle flying over her.

He noticed where her pain was and returned to it. He came back to the patient, picked up the flesh where the pain was and sucked it, blowing the pain out into the fire, and blood appeared on his hand.

He fanned the place four times. The bird appeared to fly away, and the pain then disappeared. He asked the patient to move around to see if any pain was still there. She said there was a deep pain, but not very bad. He doctored her thus four times, once in the morning, once in the evening for two days. She got well and was still living.

Medicine: Curing: Epilepsy   A medicine man with power over ghosts was called in to look at a patient. He said this disease had nothing to do with ghosts; it was not in his line and must be something else. The medicine man couldn't help this sickness, it "seemed to be inside of him."

---

1. Hoebel 1940:126.

Frank knew a man who had spells often, until he was old; he finally died of it. He would make for his tipi when an attack was coming on.

The treatment was this: his friends took his scalp lock and shook him with it, and threw water on him, then laid him down until he came to again.

An epileptic could marry. Frank knew an epileptic, ⟨Puwakaib⟩.[1]

Medicine: Vision Quest   To get ready to go, you took a bath. You took a sheet to cover your head, and rode a white or gray horse. The medicine man might receive you at the hill with pleasure; you might hear a voice of welcome.

You smoked and mentioned the medicine man's name.

You tied up your horse and went to the place (not necessarily the grave). There you slept[2] and had a vision right away if the medicine man was friendly. He gave you power or instructions as to how to get well. There was no pay to the medicine man, only smoke.

You must know in advance what power you wanted to receive, or you wouldn't receive any at all.[3]

You didn't necessarily go to the grave of a medicine man. You might just have some special medicine Man in mind, on the way.

anahabikwai[4] (*anáabi* 'hill', *habi* 'lie') was the name for a lonely place when a person was sick.

puhahabikwai (*puha* 'medicine') was the man who wanted medicine.

If two men were on the same hill for a vision without knowing it, their vision would tell them of the other's presence and one would be directed to go to another hill. Only one man could receive a vision on one hill at one time.

Case: *anahabikwai*. A man laid down, covered his head, and slept. He felt a cool breeze and heard leaves rustling. The man held fast to his head cover (he was not allowed to remove it). He heard thunder and he was afraid it would storm. He looked out and saw the moon and stars. He decided to wait and try again, and not look this time.

He heard groaning by his head. Towards morning, he fell asleep, and he heard the wind and saw the ghost of a scalped man. He started up in fright, and he gave up and went home.

Such a person hadn't sufficient faith and he received no power; he got bluffed out.

Frank went for a vision. He already had medicine, but he was sick and wanted help.

He covered himself with a sheet, lay down with his head to the west and feet to the sun. In such cases, the man couldn't move after he lay down.

Frank had a dream. He heard two men talking at his feet. One came around and said his pain was nearly gone (stomach); the other came and noticed the pain was all gone. They told him he was well.

They instructed him to leave his feather on the top of the hill, the feather was causing the trouble. They told him then to go home and wash in the creek and he would be well. (He was given instructions about where to find the pool of water.)

1. Wallace and Hoebel 1952:174. Puwakaib is otherwise unidentified.
2. Contra Wallace and Hoebel's "watch" (1952:158).
3. Wallace and Hoebel 1952:157 (?).
4. Robinson and Armagost (1990) gives *anahabitniitʉ* for the vision quest.

Realization: he left the feather, bathed, rested, and was then well.

Medicine: Sorcery   If a young man went around with a medicine man's wife, the medicine man might put sickness on him, paralyze him out of jealousy. The life of such a young man was very dangerous.[1]

Case: A young friend of Frank's lost the use of his legs. He didn't know why, it was either sickness or as above.

Medicine: Taboos: Feathers   If a medicine man dropped a feather, he couldn't pick it up himself, someone else picked it up and spoke to the bird through the feather.

He addressed the bird, saying, "I found a feather of yours."

If he didn't want it, he gave it to the medicine man, as though he had found it outside. As the medicine man accepted it {. . . [*sic*]}.

If a person out wandering around found a feather, he could keep it.

One person was not supposed to kill more than four eagles in his lifetime. After pulling out the feathers, the eagle was placed on a tree facing the sun; it was never put on the ground.

In the disposition of feathers among several hunters, the tail feathers were laid out in a row. The first man was asked if he wanted a feather and he took his choice. The next man must then take the mate to that feather, he had no choice.

Frank killed an eagle one evening. It was sighted against the moon. He picked out the tail feathers and laid them in a row. Frank's friend took a speckled one from the outside. The others were all white. Later, another man chose the mate to the speckled feather, leaving Frank with the ten white ones.

Medicine: Peyote   This was a story told by Mamsookawat.

Kuhtuubi ('charcoal') was directing a party where to find peyote. The Apaches knew where it was and directed them.

On the road, Kuhtuubi noticed the place described by the Apaches. They spread out to look. They had never seen it growing before. Mamsookawat found some and called the rest to see.

They all gathered and took a peyote meeting formation. Kuhtuubi was the leader. Kuhtuubi smoked to the peyote, spoke to it. They were going to take it for protection against enemies.

He cut it off just below ground level. He cleaned the dirt off, wrapped it in a clean cloth and put it in his pocket over his heart. Kuhtuubi told the rest to cut what they needed to take along too. They planned a meeting for that evening.

That night, they cut brush and made a windbreak of blankets, tipi-like. Kuhtuubi made a fireplace. They all prepared for the meeting. They all took a bath, and returned to paint up and get dressed. They entered the tipi, circled it, etc. He asked Mamsookawat to be fire tender.

Kuhtuubi used the first button he cut as the road medicine.

Kuhtuubi lit a cigarette with a coal, and told the peyote he had heard that it had power. He was going into enemy territory and intended to carry it for protection. He put the cigarette down, charred wild sage and rubbed it over his body. The other men did also.

---

1. Wallace and Hoebel 1952:236.

A bag of buttons was brought in. Kuhtuubi took four, and each man was given four buttons. They chewed the peyote, spit it in their hands, and made a circular motion around the fire four time. Then they swallowed it. They spit again and rubbed their head, arms, and ears (to hear better).

Kuhtuubi used his bow for a staff.[1] He had a rattle and drum along. The rattler and drummer sang together. They sang four songs around clockwise (each one a new song). Kuhtuubi asked if they wanted more peyote and passed them out.

Kuhtuubi spoke up, "Mamsookawat, stir the fire. I have learned that tomorrow we will be killed."[2]

They smoked again; he told the peyote he didn't expect anything bad like this. Now he was in a very dangerous place. "Tomorrow we will go over a certain hill. There we will meet two companies of soldiers. We might as well as die now, eat a lot."

Kuhtuubi ate more and more buttons with tears in his eyes.

Mamsookawat didn't eat so much. He was younger and didn't realize the danger so much.

At the midnight water, they took four swallows each and they smoked. While smoking, the fire went low. Kuhtuubi again upbraided the peyote for treating him thus. He ate again many buttons. Each time Kuhtuubi smoked and spoke. The rest must be quiet and listen.

He gave another speech. "We will meet enemies, but no harm will be done. We will go on and get horses. We will return safely. We will find a gray horse for Kuhtuubi."

In the morning at breakfast, they prepared to leave. They went up the hill and saw two companies of soldiers on the opposite hill across a creek. After drill, the soldiers left. The Indians went around to the southwest. At night, they came to the enemies and found the horses. They found a gray one. Kuhtuubi said, "That's my horse."

They gathered the horses and rode home, with Kuhtuubi riding the gray horse. "This shows the wonderful power of peyote. It all came true."

Kuhtuubi was sick when he was old because he had probably eaten something the peyote didn't allow.[3] He still had the famous peyote button. He gave it to a friend who knew the peyote ways. It was still possessed today by Mamsookawat.[4]

Medicine   Tsuʔiʔ[5] was a gambling partner of Kuhtuubi. One night, Kuhtuubi put his gun in the center and wrapped his head up. Tsuʔi went out and shot his arrow. Kuhtuubi's cover was off; he said he'd find this arrow to show his power. He returned with Tsuʔi's arrow. Kuhtuubi's power was from peyote.

Medicine   Frank found out in a dream how to combat a situation when someone else tried to disturb his medicine and make it turn against him. He must go back to the person who gave him the power.

1. La Barre 1975:46 (?).
2. La Barre 1975:50, 73.
3. La Barre 1975:97.
4. Wallace and Hoebel 1952:335–36; La Barre 1975:47.
5. Otherwise unidentified.

Medicine   A medicine man and his wife were living together. When someone worked against his medicine, the medicine man would climb up his tipi poles and make a noise like a bear. He was so heavy that he broke several tipi poles.

He had a close friend who heard about it.

His wife didn't have enough tipi poles, so his wife traded a horse to an Arapaho or Cheyenne for more poles.

His friend ran to the medicine man's wife to find out what to do to break those "climbing spells." The wife said the medicine man had told her to have someone shoot him when he was in the spell. The friend went home for a gun. He loaded it and put a spear in it. He asked the woman if she was sure. She said, "Yes, shoot him."

The medicine man called down that she was wrong and promptly climbed down. He had no more such spells.[1]

Medicine   A medicine man sometimes hid out so as not to be there when someone called for assistance, when he knew there was little likelihood of his being paid. The person wanting help then asked his wife how he can get to the medicine man. She told him. The medicine man often received nothing for his services; he went to help the people out.

Medicine: Vision Quest   The time for going out for a vision was early spring and fall. Winter was too cold. Summer was too much danger from "snakes and other insects."

Medicine: Feathers   Feathers that have cured people gained additional power therein and were used later.

Medicine: Curing   For a bloody wound, they used a tourniquet.

Medicine: Sorcery   A medicine man could be hired to harm the abductor of a man's wife.

Medicine   Frank was bashful about his medicine; he wouldn't dare go to face an evil medicine man as in the Comanche-Cheyenne sorcery case.

Medicine: Sun Dance   The people who cut and carried the pole were a captive man with war deeds or a virtuous woman.

The Mud Men were *sekwitsi*.[2]

There were four buffalos[3]; brave warriors.

The buffalo put on the pole was not stuffed, just the hide.

The lodge was left open at the top, only the sides were filled in. The screen was of cottonwood.

A dancer could get permission to quit; his place was taken by another man.

The dancers were all painted yellow. They washed at the creek every night. The medicine man set a guard over them. They were painted fresh every morning. They didn't dive in, but sat in the water and washed.

On the way home, they camped four times, as done before the dance.

The feast was given by relatives of the dancers to honor them. Only the relatives, drummers, singers, and the medicine man were invited.

It was held in the summer.

1. Wallace and Hoebel 1952:169.
2. Otherwise given as *sekwitsipuhitsi*, *sekwi* 'mud', *puhipʉ* 'leaf'.
3. Presumably this refers to the mock buffalo hunt. See above, Post Oak Jim, July 17.

Material Culture: Clothing: Breechclout   The ends hung nearly to the ankle. It was appliquéd.

Kinship Relations: Brother-Sister   Small boys were teased by their "sisters," not necessarily their real sisters, but also their sisters' friends and distant relatives who were called "sisters." Small boys were afraid of them. Herman said so too.

    For example, Frank's mother was making mush. Frank wanted some and cried. His mother called for one of those "sisters." She put a rawhide strap around his neck and dragged him into the tipi and said she'd hang him to the top of the tipi if he was not good. Frank was very frightened.[1]

Life Cycle: Childbirth   The navel was wrapped in buckskin and tied on a hackberry tree.[2]

Life Cycle: Childhood: Learning to Ride   The child sat behind its mother on the horse on moving. At about five years, it had its own horse, maybe strapped on. At seven years or so, it could ride alone.[3]

Beliefs: Physical Deformities   Some children were born paralyzed (legs). They were not killed. They were raised and might marry later. Tɜmɜwɔki's[4] legs were paralyzed from birth. (He was still living, but he can't walk.) He married a widow with children.

Adolescent Lodge   The adolescent lodge was usually placed to the west of the parent's tipi. The reason was that the young man might have his shield or other medicine articles around, and it was dangerous to have them any place where a person with greasy hands might touch them. They were placed farthest to the west to protect his medicine. Several sons might live in one special tipi, but not sons of different families.[5]

Medicine: Sweat Lodge   The fire was built about a foot deep. Rocks were heated and lifted out of the fire with a forked stick, an "Indian Fork." They were handed in by a woman to the men in the sweat lodge. They were plunged into water, removed, and put in the fireplace inside. Three more times, rocks were put in the fireplace and water was poured over them, four times together. They sang and prayed. They placed a hot rock on the sick parts.

Life Cycle: Marriage: Polygamy   They probably would kill a chief in the old days if he took many men's wives. This was not likely to happen. An old man *paraibo* had enough wives of his own.

    If parents gave their daughter to an older man she didn't like, people didn't like it. If he {*sic*, they} did it once, nothing was said, but if he did it often, people didn't like it.

Life Cycle: Marriage   When a young pair married without the consent of their parents, the young man made presents to her parents (not at the time). When parents gave a daughter to a man, he <u>must</u> give them gifts or the parents would take their daughter back.

---

1. Wallace and Hoebel 1952:124.
2. Wallace and Hoebel 1952:144.
3. Wallace and Hoebel 1952:126.
4. This spelling is given. A man, Tenawaki (sometimes spelled Tenamaki), appears on the 1879 census as Man with a Forehead (possibly *tenahpʉ* 'man', *kaʔi* 'forehead'). He was the father of Quanah's wife, Tonarcy. He died before 1892. There is no indication that he was a cripple. However, Tenawaki's son, Tomeatooah (given on the 1885 census as Young Colt, *-tue* 'little'), born about 1870, is listed in the Family Record Book as a "cripple." Thus, Chekovi may have confused father and son.
5. Wallace and Hoebel 1952:130.

Quanah Parker   Quanah Parker went to the Cheyenne camp for a peyote meeting. He got sick on the way home and died on his return.[1] People thought he had been poisoned.

Political Organization: Chiefs: Paraibo, TekwUniwapI, and Announcer   One chief, the camp chief, didn't go anywhere. He was an old man, the *paraibo*. He decided when to move camp, etc. The *paraibo* was called "father" by all men in the tribe. He called them "son."[2]

He settled disputes by advice, if possible. He couldn't use force.

There was also the announcer.

The announcer-chief said who might go out with him to hunt buffalo in the morning. He rode through the camp announcing important news, not daily events.

The other chief was the war leader, *tekwUniwapI*. There may be several of them.

Material Culture: Clothing: Cap   A man wore a cap to save his scalp eagle feather; it was made of otter skin with a feather sewn on top.

Horses: Borrowing of Horses   The people were drifting out west. The young men were out in front, hunting.

Frank's brother asked for a gentle horse of Quassyah's mother. He saw a tired deer, an easy shot, but it was on the wrong side so he turned the horse. The horse stumbled and jammed its head in a coyote hole. He fell off and broke the stock of his gun. He beat the horse with the barrel until its head was bloody. Then he rode the horse back to the general herd and turned it loose.

Quassyah saw the horse the next morning and berated his mother. She went over to see Frank's brother. He told her what had happened. Everything was all right because Frank's brother didn't know the horse turned opposite from the touch.

Kinship Relations: Brother-Sister   A brother may claim property owned by his sister before marriage, but not however, any acquired through her husband after marriage.

Nanuwoku   The reason for going *nanuwok*ing was to protect their relative. Brothers and friends usually went together.

Only brothers and close friends could share the *nanuwoku* results. The other relatives got nothing.

A husband's brother could collect if his {the husband's} widow remarried without his {the brother's} permission, even if he never slept with her, or married her.

Medicine: Sorcery   Kwitawowoki[3] used medicine in a bad way against Paruakuhma, who got sick. Various doctors were called on to help Paruakuhma. No success; they gave up.

They called on a captive medicine man, Noboʔik ('On the Highway').[4] He acted as though he was flying over the patient (feathers). He saw who had put the evil spell on him. Noboʔik doctored him three times.

---

1. Quanah died February 25, 1911.
2. Hoebel 1940:18.
3. Hoebel's note cards, and Hoebel (1940:89, 145), record this name as Witawowoki and translate it as Barking Buttocks; this is seconded by Robinson and Armagost (1990) in the form Witawooʔooki. However, inasmuch as 'buttocks' is *kwita*, this probably should be *kwitawooʔwooki*, the form used by the Comanche Cultural Committee (2003). Otherwise unidentified.
4. Hoebel (1940:89, 146) gives this name as Traveler's Road (*pu'e* 'road'). Otherwise unidentified.

Two of his four brothers came and asked what he found out. Noboʔik said he thought Kwitawowoki had put the bad medicine on him. The brothers promised not to do Kwitawowoki harm, but to ask him to withdraw his evil medicine. They asked Noboʔik how he knew. He said that when flying over their brother, he saw the shadow of the bad medicine man.

The next day, they told the patient's wife to ask Kwitawowoki to come to their tipi. He came. The brothers were sitting on the east. They moved apart for him to sit between them. Both brothers had weapons.

They talked to him kindly. They said they had a question to ask him. "Our brother is sick, you caused it. Please take pity on him. He's old, like you are. Let him live."

The medicine man denied his guilt. He asked who told them he was responsible. The brothers told him it was Noboʔik.

Kwitawowoki said this captive had no sense. "Bring him in and let me talk to him." The wife went for Noboʔik.

He came. They placed him at the foot of the sick man. One brother explained to Noboʔik that Kwitawowoki had denied the charge. Noboʔik pointed at Kwitawowoki, "How can he deny it? He knows he did it."

Kwitawowoki called him, "Captive, *taibo*[1]" in a slurring voice (he was a full blood). Noboʔik said he saw his shadow over the man.

One brother was annoyed. He asked Kwitawowoki, "What about it?"

"Very early in the spring, the first lightning and thunder will take my life if this is true." The brothers were satisfied.

The next spring, Kwitawowoki moved out of camp.

He went hunting one day with his nephew-in-law. On their return, a cloud came up. The fourth lightning struck Kwitawowoki dead.[2]

NORTON TAHQUECHI
Undated

Life Cycle: Death: Burial   The bands living on the Red River away from the mountains used scaffold burials.[3]

Omens: Coyote   Norton's mother made a prediction.

She heard a coyote howl one night. At breakfast, she said the coyote was telling the tribe that they were going to get a lot of money pretty soon. His uncle laughed and said, "How do you know?"

---

1. The implication here that 'captive' and *taibo* were equivalent is probably unwarranted.
2. Hoebel 1940:89, 1954:141; Wallace and Hoebel 1952:239. Hoebel (1940) attributes this story to Tahsuda. However, the note cards clearly have a "7", which was Frank Chekovi's number.
3. Wallace and Hoebel 1952:150.

His mother said, "You wait and see. If the Old Man talks again before the week is out, it sure is coming true."

On Friday, they heard him again. The very next day, there came checks for $180 at the agency for every member of the tribe.[1]

Beliefs: Revealing Dreams   A bad dream, if told to any person before four days passed, would come back on the dreamer.

Norton's experience: On Friday, Post Oak Jim told of the medicine man who took foam from the buffalo's stomach and ate it down.[2] He also remarked that Indians would eat anything but shit.[3]

On Monday, when we went to work with Tahsuda, Norton was sick to his stomach and said he had been very sick over the weekend. I {Hoebel} doctored him with spirits of ammonia. He said he couldn't have gotten through the day without it.

On Wednesday morning, driving out, Norton said, "Well boys, I'll tell you what was wrong with me."

He had dreamt of that medicine man eating the stomach foam. It had made him so sick that he had awakened and vomited. His stomach was upset for three days. He was not so sure it was true, but he was taking no chances of telling before the four days were up.

Norton went on to tell of his skeptical uncle. His uncle dreamed of a man who had damaged his thumb to the point that it was almost torn from his hand; the man came to him for medicine doctoring.

The uncle was telling them the dream at the breakfast table. His mother told him to stop, it would sure be bad for him if he didn't.

His uncle laughed. That week he went out hunting squirrels. The squirrel kept on the other side of the tree from him, so he finally shot it straight up the trunk.

He saw some quail across the creek, so he went over and looked in the brush but couldn't flush them.

He came back to the creek and saw a forty-five-pound catfish in the pool. He wondered how to get it. He stuck the muzzle of his shotgun in the water and pulled the trigger. The barrel exploded and nearly ripped off his thumb.

He went home and Jim's mother doctored it. It required nine days to heal.[4]

Omens: Coyote   Norton was staying with an old man north of Medicine Park. The old man asked him one night, "Well, have you heard our friend yet?"

Norton had heard nothing. The old man said, "Well, you'd better listen good now. I believe he's coming about pretty soon."

They were talking one night, about ten o'clock, when the dogs began to bark. The old man said, "You'd better shut those dogs up. I believe there's our friend."

Sure enough, there was a coyote howling.

Norton couldn't interrupt. The old man said, "You'd better start saving up your bread."

1. Wallace and Hoebel (1952:202) attributes this story to Yellowfish, one of Wallace's consultants in 1945. There were several "per capita" payments made before 1933 from various funds, but I have not found any specific references to a $180 payment.
2. See Post Oak Jim, Undated.
3. This is not recorded in the notes.
4. Wallace and Hoebel 1952:155.

He said, "There's going to be a pretty hard winter this year. We ain't going to have too much to eat."

Sure enough. The winter before, all the Indians had more flour than they knew what to do with, but that year there were hardly rations enough to give them what was coming.[1]

Social Control: Theft   Norton's uncle had two sets of harnesses stolen from his barn.

He saw moccasin tracks and knew who had done it. He charged the man with the deed, but got a stout denial.

One morning, a few days after, that man came driving up the road with a load of hay. His uncle called them all to come out on the porch, he said he would show them something.

He was going to get even with that fellow. His aunt tried to dissuade her husband; she said he would make trouble.

He said he was going to fix that fellow anyhow.

He put his hand to his mouth and drew out a puff of breath in a sharp motion towards the wagon. Immediately, the wagon burst into flames.[2]

Hunting   For hummingbirds, they used a vertical split in the arrows, also for bull bats. Boys might spend all day chasing one bird.

Bats were shot with a horizontal split.

Grasshoppers were shot with vertical split arrows. They ate the long legs.[3]

Games   They would catch the "shit roller" beetles, tie a thread with a straw to its legs, and watch it fly.

They would put straw up the anus of a horse fly and turn it loose. They would tie grasshoppers together with short thread. The first one to fall on its back lost.

They would have a mud fight with balls slung from a stick.[4]

TENEVERKA
Undated

Medicine: Foretelling   Three warriors went to a medicine man to find out where band members captured by Utes might be {. . . [sic]}.

Life Cycle: Death: Disposition of Property   Piarʉpsima had about three thousand horses.[5] He had no relatives but his wife. He told the tribe that on his death he wanted each of his three hundred arrows to kill one of his best horses. No one should have his best horses.

1. Wallace and Hoebel 1952:202.
2. Wallace and Hoebel 1952:240 (?).
3. Wallace and Hoebel 1952:128.
4. Wallace and Hoebel 1952:128.
5. Hoebel has "more than a thousand horses at a time" (1940:15); Wallace and Hoebel has "1,500 horses at the time of his death" (1952:39).

He had three quivers of one hundred arrows each. The rest of the horses should be divided among the tribe. He died and was buried inside a hole in his tipi. The tipi was left standing over him. His wife moved out.

The next day, the *paraibo* called for the best marksmen to kill his horses with those three hundred arrows. The remainder were divided among the tribe.[1]

Esasʉmʉ,[2] a Kiowa Chief, knew of Piarʉpsima's case. He built his house right over Piarʉpsima's tipi, the place where he was buried.

Every night a ghost would come and knock on the windows and doors. Someone would get sick.

Esasʉmʉ went to Piarʉpsima's grave. He said he didn't come to show he was greater, he just liked the place. He said he might talk it over. "Come and tell me."

That night there came a knocking on the door. He said he talked it over with his wife, and he decided to dig up the grave. He did so and put the remains in a casket in the cemetery. They were all right after that. Piarʉpsima didn't like being tramped on.

Nanʉwokʉ   Teneverka was with a boy friend down by the creek. A woman came down for water. She was sister to the stepmother of the boy. Teneverka proposed that the two of them seek intercourse with the woman. Teneverka went down to see her. She was willing, but wanted to take the bucket of water up to the camp first. She went and the two got excited by the prospect.

Teneverka demanded first chance for himself. While they were having intercourse, the woman's sister came up and saw them, and slipped quietly back into the brush. Then Teneverka's partner took his turn with the woman, and the sister spied on this escapade.

The sister went to the woman's husband and informed on the adultery. The old man came down to the father of Teneverka's pal and asked how about it. The boys were called over and the charge was put to Teneverka. He vigorously denied it. When they asked the other boy, he acknowledged it with a boast, "Sure I did it. It was an honor to be able to do such a thing as that."

The old man demanded *nanʉwokʉ* and got two good horses in satisfaction.

The elder brother came home and was angry that the horses had been given up. He went to the herd of the old man and shot down two horses with his bow and arrow. The younger brother of the old man was incensed with the treatment of his brother and the action of his brother's wife; he cut off the nose of the beautiful sister of Teneverka's pal.

Beliefs: Rainbows   If you point at a rainbow, whatever you point with will drop off.

Social Organization: Bands: Band Lists

The KwahihʉʉkI,[3] Carrying Sunshade on Their Back, very rarely came south of the mountains. They held a stiff square of hide over their heads.

The Kuhtsutʉhka[4] were Meat-eaters. They always had plenty of buffalo meat. They were from the Red River up from Burkburnett, Texas.

---

1. Hoebel 1940:124.
2. Literally, 'one wolf' in Comanche; he was known in English as Lone Wolf, and in Kiowa as Guipago. There were several Kiowa men with this name, sons, or stepsons of the antecedent. The first Lone Wolf died in 1879, so this story probably refers to the second.
3. *kwahi* 'back', *hʉʉkI* 'shade'.
4. *kuhtsu* 'buffalo', *-tʉhka* 'eater'.

They had about six hundred people.

There were more adults than children.

They were noted among the bands as warriors out looking for trouble, always going on the warpath, but they were not distinctive from others.

Medicine: Sun Dance   The occasion of the Sun Dance was revenge for the death of warriors. During the dance, they discussed how to get revenge. Then they went off on a raid. If they captured a man from the band that did the killing, they slew him by himself. If not, they must make a general attack.

They held a dance against the Cheyennes. It was a five-day dance, and then they went off on the raid. The chief selected four braves to go out and show themselves to the Cheyennes as a signal that the band was there. The Cheyennes sent a man out to see what was wanted.

It happened that the warriors were out on a raid. The Comanches said to themselves, "Just what we want."

So they drove at him and shot him. They turned back satisfied. The man later got away on a white man's horse.

No arbor was built. It was held out in the open. They put on their best clothes and painted up. The dance was for four or five days. Then they went on a raid to revenge the death of a brave. There was no taboo on food or drink during the dance.

War: Armor   Paruakuhma wore a rawhide jacket laced up the center of the breast.

War   They were camped at Dark Creek.[1]

A girl married an Apache. She was disowned because they hated the Apaches.

The camp moved. They left her behind with her husband. The Apache husband wanted her to go home with him, but she didn't want to, so he whipped her. She left him and walked towards the Comanche camp. She got a horse and rode in. She told her mother about it. Her mother called on Teneverka during the night.

Teneverka went out for a horse, but couldn't catch one, so he started back. On his return, he heard a bunch of horses; the leader was belled. He went in and told his mother about it. His mother sent him to bed.

The next morning, he went out and found their horses were gone. He went back and had the announcer tell the camp. They all chased the horses. [Teneverka found that the horses had been filched. He came back to camp and told it to the "loud speaker" to tell to the camp.][2]

They saw the horses in the distance with four men driving them. They all disappeared into the valley. The Indians charged. Two of the men on horses got away. One on a horse and one on foot were left. They got on one horse, but the horse wouldn't leave the herd. The Indians circled them. The old leader, Paruakuhma, came up and shamed the young braves for not having killed the three men yet. "When he was a boy, they wouldn't leave their enemies unharmed so long."

Paruakuhma dismounted and started towards the three men. He had on his buffalo jacket as protection. His only weapon was a whip, a part of his medicine. He knocked down the

---

1. Location unknown.
2. This variant is from a separate card entitled "Crier."

fellow who had the bow and arrow. The other fellow shot Parʉakuhma clean through the breast, but he didn't die because he was a medicine man, a buffalo doctor. The arrow penetrated the laced opening down the center.

Medicine: Buffalo   Parʉakuhma lay down by a bleached buffalo skeleton for two days and nights. He had the power to treat wounds on himself and on others in time of war.

War Story   Two friends, Horseback {Terheryahquahip} and ⟨Sorsi⟩ Cold Head,[1] always tried to see who could do the best deed.

They went out together for horses. On the raid, they camped near to an enemy camp. They rode up together. They found a white pair asleep in their underwear. {One[2]} walked in, picked up the woman, still asleep, and carried her out to his partner. She awoke. They carried her off.

The next morning, they wondered what to do with her. Horseback was going to kill her. His friend said, "No," so Horseback cut her hair all off and set her loose near her camp.

Later, it was Cold Head's turn. The whole band was out on the warpath. They were going south. They came to a creek by San Antonio in flood. Sorsi crossed over the creek to do his deed, while Horseback waited for him. Sorsi heard singing late that evening and came to a hand game in an arbor. He put a buffalo robe over his head and snuck up, singing too.

He began to play with them and won everything. They called for him to come out and he beat it. He got on a horse with a bell and ran. He got to the creek. He heard horses coming and prepared to meet his enemies. It was just the horses and mules following the bell mare. They all swam the creek. He met his friend and they rode home.[3]

Life Cycle: Death: Disposition of Property   Horses went to the nearest relative—father, mother, elder brother, all other relatives. If there were no other relatives, to best friend. There was no fixed rule.

In polygynous marriages, only the wives who have children by the husband could inherit. The first wife administered the distribution.

Social Roles: Club Man   The *pianʉʔʉpaiʔi* was obtained through a dream. "There will be lots of danger," said a voice, "you will need protection."

It told him how to make the whip. There was a lash on the big handle. He was the only possessor.

There were two forms of war clubs. One was the tomahawk, owned by Ekatotakape.[4] It was obtained in a dream and there was only one of these in the band.

Material Culture: Clothing: Headdress   The buffalo scalp bonnet was worn by a brave man, but not necessarily a *tekwʉniwapI*.

It was a buffalo scalp with the horns still attached. There was a row of eagle feathers that reached to the waist, with breast feathers tied to the end of each feather. There was a bunch of magpie feathers at the center of the back of the head.

---

1. Hoebel's notes for this story give this name both as So:esi and Sorsi, translated as Cold Head. He is otherwise unidentified.
2. By implication, Terheryahquahip.
3. Wallace and Hoebel 1952:246–47 (?).
4. *eka* 'red', otherwise unidentified.

In battle, the war bonnet owner couldn't hit the ground or be captured. A man wearing a bonnet must be protected or helped at all cost if he was wounded; it was parallel to our flag.

Case: Comanches and Utes were fighting. They fought over a territory of sixty or seventy miles. A *tekwƗniwapƗ* was wounded in the leg. He was weak from loss of blood. Another *tekwƗniwapƗ* got on his horse to hold him, giving his horse to a woman.

The Utes drove the Comanches back about sixty-five miles. The *tekwƗniwapƗ* who was wounded died, but was tied on the back of the horse and was carried to avoid his being captured. The pair was protected by a group of warriors. He was buried when the battle was over.

The owner could never retreat. If he could not hold his place, he must throw the bonnet down and abandon it. Anyone who saw it and was willing to assume its obligations could pick it up. No spear or bow was necessary. The bonnet was assumed by those who felt worthy. There was no ceremonial gathering or bestowal. It might be given by friends to a brave man. One friend would suggest it to another and together they would get the feathers and make up the bonnet to present to the mutual friend as a token.

Teneverka could have had one, but he felt he really wasn't brave enough to wear one. He wore a buffalo scalp hat that he hung on a tree and left when they submitted to the whites.[1]

Animal Powers: Wild Goose   The wild goose gave protection from bullets. It appeared in a dream to a man. It could fly high and was hard to hit. Its holder painted a goose on his shield.

Animal Powers: Chicken Hawk   The chicken hawk was proof against bullets. They flew fast and could kill anything. Some men painted them on their shields.

War Story: Comanches Trick Some Confederates   They were camped west of San Antonio where there were lots of buffalo. Over the hills there were some gray soldiers. His brother was chasing buffalo around the hill and spotted the camp. He dashed back and told the chief. The chief called in all the warriors (some were out butchering bison). He sat on a buffalo hide to talk. They talked over how to get these fellows. The chief asked one man what he suggested.

He offered that they should send their English-speaking halfbreed to go over and parley. They could invite the soldiers to come up and camp with the Indians; they would be good friends.

He did so and the soldiers accepted. They moved their camp over there. Then the chief suggested that all the young men do something. A bunch of soldiers were sent for wood, another bunch were sent for water.

When the soldiers were all gone, the Indians gathered and took the guns that were in a pile in the center of the camp. An officer ran forward. The chief shot him. The soldiers all ran toward their camp. The Indians shot all but three out of thirty-three, and wounded two others. They left one unwounded to go back and tell the tale.[2]

---

1. Hoebel 1940: 29; Wallace and Hoebel 1952:272.
2. There is no other record of this fight.

War: Teneverka's Story　　At age seventeen, he went on his first raid, against the ⟨Aboʔeʔnʉʉ⟩[1] in the Southwest. An epidemic of *tsotsooʔni*,[2] paralysis, hit them while they were in New Mexico. The band split. Half went to the band of a Mexican for protection and doctoring, but he couldn't help, so they went on.

They were attacked by Utes and all but three were killed or captured.

Mowway, Parʉakuhma, and ⟨Watur⟩,[3] a captive, went on a private raid to get back some of the captured Comanches from the Utes. They made an agreement with the Utes and got back all of the captives except Norton's grandmother. The agreement lasted four years and was then broken.

Medicine: Vision Quest　　It was necessary to recite the dead man's deed to get medicine from the grave.

NEMARUIBETSI
Undated[4]

Social Organization: Bands: Differences in Dress　　The Kwaharʉnʉʉ in the west were poor and not fancy dressers. They got a little from Mexicans. They learned fancy dress from the Penanʉʉ later.

The Penanʉʉ, Penatʉhka, in the southeast, were wealthier, and wore fancy clothes. The women wore red {triangular} insets in the sides of their dresses, and had red sleeves, *ekawewek*,[5] which were very fashionable. There were also small bands of red over the shoulder and as sleeve trim; it was very distinctive.

The men wore red cloth leggings with four or five inches of beading up and down the leg; also very distinctive.

Material Culture: Clothing　　Wives of brave warriors had a special decoration on the tongue on the back of their dresses; one 'l' for each war honor, in dark blue. There was a fringed, rounded tongue in the front.

Dances: Victory Dance　　The warriors came in early in the morning to greet the people. They rode in with shots, carrying the scalps on a pole. They held a Victory Dance with those scalps.

Dances: Scalp Dance (Give Away Dance)　　It was a social dance and honored the women who held the scalps obtained by their husbands.

They made a big arbor in the summer time. The dancers came into the arbor and sat down. The drummers and songleaders sat near the center of the arbor.

---

1. An unknown ethnonym.
2. Robinson and Armagost (1990) identifies this as meningitis. Casagrande (1954-55, II:235) has meningitis as *nʉmʉtsaʔtoponiʔeetʉ* 'makes you round, doubled up'.
3. Otherwise unidentified.
4. The order of these notes is arbitrary.
5. *eka* 'red'. Otherwise unattested.

One or two of the oldest women in the tribe, "who want to dissipate in this dance," held two poles with the scalps on them. (They could use old scalps.) They oversaw the dance. They came to the dancers and told them to get busy and dance together, even if a married woman, or she would strike them with the scalp pole.

The *tuibihtsiˀ* were all dressed up inside {the arbor} singing and dancing before the women arrived. The women came in pairs up to the young men and asked them to dance. They expected presents from the men. A man's sister or mother brought a present over to her (it could be any one of his relatives). A fellow might give a girl a stick (representing a horse). It was a disgrace for a man's kin not to give her a gift.

Adornment A man's hair was daubed with yellow from the forehead to the scalp lock. It was put on with the finger. A woman braided his scalp lock for him. A long leather strip was fastened to the scalp lock, hanging down to the ground and decorated with fifty-cent pieces.

Men wore several earrings.

Side locks were worn on either the left or right, usually left; they were twisted, with a piece of silver up near the scalp.

A man might wear some of a woman's hair fastened to his scalp lock as a remembrance. A man might use a mourning woman's hair at the bottom of his side locks; he might splice it on to make his hair appear longer. When she cut it off in mourning, he would ask her for it. He might fasten an eagle feather to the side lock, or a bear's ear, or scissortail feathers (or any medicine article).

There was a gathering, a big dance. One fellow was dancing; everyone was watching him. He was a *tuibitsiˀ*. He threw his side lock over his shoulder and the attached end came off. The people all laughed at him; he picked it up and went home.

Women painted the part of their hair red, and let it hang loose. Her eyes were painted with a red line above and below the lid which might cross at the corners. They also might use yellow.

Adornment: Face Paint The cheeks were painted solid red-orange on both cheeks. There was a solid triangle on the rear of the cheek back by the ear.

The ears were painted red inside.

Two women friends might dress alike.

Adornment: Earrings If a man wanted his ears pierced, he went to have it done in the lodge where a woman had recently had a baby easily; it would hurt him less.

There were holes all up and down the helix. There were so many worn that the ear bent over from the weight. There were shell dangles tied on with sinew. Long shells were perforated and fastened high up on the ear; they had silver trimming. They wore five or six in one ear.

Material Culture: Bows and Arrows Women sometimes used bows and arrows; they knew how to make them.

They made special little bows and arrows for the children.

Food: Drinks: Tea *puhi huubA* was a tea; it was not medicinal.

Medicine: Inheritance Medicine was inherited from father to son, or from uncle to nephew. An uncle might then give his nephew his shield.

Shields were put away (probably in water): they were not passed down.

Social Roles: Friendship   Friends might go on a war party together (one might serve the other), one might wait on the other.

They might be a full blood and a captive. The servant was given a choice from the horses after a raid. But Nemaruibetsi never heard of a full-blood serving a captive thus.

They call each other *haitsI* 'friend'. They couldn't desert each other in battle. They might go *nanɨwok*ing together (if they were brave enough).

Etiquette: Hospitality   Families might scatter away from camp alone in hard times to avoid having to offer hospitality to so many people who would come around to eat with them, so they'd have enough to eat themselves.

Hunting: Division of Hunt   When a boy brought meat home, his mother dictated how it would be divided. She would probably give the uncle {her brother} some meat, and her father-in-law, and her father some too.

Life Cycle: Marriage: Polygamy   An oldest wife wouldn't let the younger ones spend a night with the husband; she regulated it entirely.

After she got let out for adultery, the next one got the chief place. She let her younger sister sleep with him, whenever she wanted to.

A man would pay more attention to younger wives; he would try to make work light for them. The work then fell on the middle wife.

When several wives were sisters, they stuck together against the husband. When several wives were not sisters, they worked against each other to get the leadership. It was more honor for a man to have several sisters as wives. This proved his father-in-law liked him and was satisfied.

If a man had three wives and liked them all, they might all live in the same tipi. If a man had three wives, but liked one less than the others, she might have a separate tipi alone. Wives with children might have separate tipis, but the *paraibo* stayed in the husband's tipi.

Example: A man had two wives who couldn't get along, so they had separate tipis. When one had a son, he felt better and she got to be head wife. The husband favored her and lived with her.

Life Cycle: Marriage: Adultery   Wives of medicine men were very careful about adultery; their husbands could do them damage with the medicine.

If a man talked to the wife of a medicine man, she would say she didn't want to because she was afraid of the medicine man's magic. The magic would do more harm to the man than to the wife.

Life Cycle: Marriage: Spinsters, Bachelors   Nemaruibetsi never heard of a woman who lived without a man her whole life. She heard of one man who never married; he was so mean that no one would marry him.

Nanɨwokɨ   After a *nanɨwokɨ*, the husband could still try to get his wife back.

The custom was to go *nanɨwok*ing if the wife went with another man (even if he[1] didn't care).

A man's sister may not live with him at all, but if she ran away with another man, he was expected to go *nanɨwok*ing anyway.

---

1. It is not clear who this refers to, though presumably it would be the wronged husband.

A son-in-law had a claim on his wife's younger sister. Parents may say, "Son-in-law, when she grows up, she will be yours."

If she wanted to marry someone else later, the man must settle with him, especially if she was good looking. If a girl grew up and refused to marry her older sister's husband, the only way she could avoid it was to run away on a raid with someone. This was also settled by *nanɨwokɨ*.

A man had the same privilege with his younger step-sisters-in-law {*sic*}.

Old men married young girls in expectation of *nanɨwokɨ*. An old man never refused younger wives when they were offered to him; he might get a chance for *nanɨwokɨ*. Younger men might refuse extra ones.

Medicine: Medicine Women: Transfer   A woman had a powerful medicine for curing.

She wanted to give it to her young male relatives. She called them together. She showed them her power by blowing blue paint, which gave invulnerability,[1] on her hand. She asked each to swallow some in turn.

One of these young men was Nemaruibetsi's deceased husband. His power was to cure paralysis (stiffness and slobbering), spasms, the ghost sickness. A man was sick. He made a fire and took a coal from the fire and put it in his mouth. He blew sparks out. He blew sparks on the sick man. Then he chewed the coal and rubbed the man; he got well. This occasion shows that her husband really got power from this medicine woman.

Medicine: Medicine Women   Such women could only use their power after their husband's death.

A brave warrior, if he was kind and sensible, would show his wife how to use his medicine, so that when he died, she could use it in his place and keep his clientele.

The wife of a medicine man might go to his grave after his death to receive his power. He might come and give it to her. It was impossible for a single woman to get power.

A medicine man might also take his wife to a lonely place so that she could get the power directly, instead of giving her directions himself.

Her power was as strong as that of a medicine man. There were not many of them. She could get a good income through her medicine, but there was no jealousy on the part of her husband.[2]

Medicine: Curing: Hemorrhage   They hung a red blanket with a white border up over the door; these special blankets came down from the north. When cured, they gave the blanket to the medicine man.

Medicine: Curing: Cattle   *woʔanatɨsɨʔ*, worm medicine (ragweed), cured worms in cattle cuts. It was pounded and put into the cut.

Life Cycle: Death: Custody   At a mother's death, the children most likely went to their mother's parents, instead of being brought up by an unrelated stepmother.

Kinship Relations   The eldest sister was the head of the younger sisters in the family. This carried over when they were all married to the same man.

1. Hoebel's card has the comment "gave vulnerability," but this is probably the intended meaning.
2. Wallace and Hoebel 1952:166.

The father's sister might take some of her brother's daughters to bring up, if she was kind and didn't have too many of her own. The mother's sister also helped in the same way.

If a boy was very mischievous, they called on his "sister," not a blood sister, to tease him. His older sister, *patsi*, sometimes treated him rough.

If a girl was mischievous, they called on a "brother" in the same way to straighten her out, a *pabi*. Older boys couldn't be bluffed out by an older "sister" as could a young one. He might get mad and may shoot a blunt arrow at her. No one tried to control him after that.

A father was kind to his daughter, not like her brothers; brothers were usually mean to their sisters. A daughter did not have the same terrified obedience to a father that she gave to a brother. The father was kind. The daughter doesn't need to obey him out of fear of punishment.

The father and father's brothers both disciplined children. The maternal uncle was more their friend. This was borne out by Herman; he went to his *ara* for help after trouble with a woman. The maternal uncle helped him out, and gave horses for the *nanʉwokʉ*.

A boy could get anything he wants from his *toko* {maternal grandfather} and *kʉnu* {paternal grandfather} (the same as with his *ara*). This held also for medicine.

The *kaku* (maternal grandmother) had more respect from a child than *huutsI* (father's mother).

The maternal uncle was considered more of a friend than the paternal uncle (*ahpʉ*).

kuhmtoko, the maternal grandfather, was respected more than *kʉnu*, paternal grandfather.[1]

A young man could marry his stepmother when his father died. In such a case, the children of both were "brothers" and "sisters." Such stepbrothers and stepsisters could probably marry each other. Nemaruibetsi never heard of a case in which they did.

Daughters-in-law usually respected their parents-in-law, but some didn't. Some helped them, but some hated their in-laws and did nothing for them.

Social Relations: Joking   A man might take a girl's bridle and ask her to go on a raid with him in a joking way. This was like saying that he loved her.

HERKEYAH
Undated

Economy: Hunting   They shot deer and antelope near the camp during her first hard winter.

The custom was to divide up the meat on their return with all who came for some. If a man wouldn't give it away, they camped on him until he did.[2]

---

1. Wallace and Hoebel 1952:127.
2. Hoebel 1940:119.

Captives   When the women captives were brought to a man's camp, the women in that camp came out and struck her on her arrival.

Captives   If a man got tired of a captive, he might tie him to a saddle and drive the horse with the general herd; eventually he was killed. If the saddle turned, the boy would be trampled.

Medicine: Miscarriage   Certain foods, such as plums, could cause miscarriage.

Medicine: Contraceptives   Herkeyah knew of none.

Camp Organization   The tipis were placed according to whim, but they were bunched for protection against attack.

A strung out camp would have been ridiculous; it would have been three to four hundred miles long {*sic*}.

On the plains, where there was no timber, the Kwaharʉ camped around a pond.

Beliefs   A man dreamed long ago that Indians and whites would be friends. "Here we sit now; it has come true. It is good."

Political Organization: Chiefs   Among the Noyʉhka, he announced plans for the day each morning.

Material Culture: Clothing: Winter   In the winter, they wore buffalo boots with the fur inside. Well tanned was good; rawhide was untanned.

Buckskin leggings were worn under the boots; they came up to the hips.

Poor people got pretty cold[1]; they had no skins for leggings, no boots, only plain moccasins and trade cloth wrapped around the legs.

People wore a cap of coyote fur (never of buffalo hide). They wore buffalo robes, but there was nothing for their hands (it made it hard to shoot).

Life Cycle: Death: Mourning   They destroyed everything after death in mourning. For shelter, they might put a willow stick in the ground and cover it with hide or brush; it was called *mutsikʉni*.[2] Tesobakwitsi cried during the day for two years. He cut his hair off and lived in a mourning tipi mourning for his wife (the one who threw water on him and the captive wife).

People in mourning always avoided the graves of their close relatives if it could be helped.

They might cut off their ear lobes.

Nanʉwokʉ   Kohiʔ.[3] Eksiakoro[4] had three wives. Kohiʔ ran off with the youngest wife. After a long time, they returned. Eksiakoro and six friends came *nanʉwok*ing. Kohi asked what they wanted; they told him, "The wife."

Kohiʔ asked if they would take something instead. One of the friends said ten horses. The settlement was made on this basis; saddles and blankets.

Nanʉwokʉ   Parʉakuhma took a woman on a raid. They went on a mountain top to rest while the rest of the party stayed at the foot. An Apache warrior snuck up; Parʉakuhma killed

---

1. Wallace and Hoebel 1952:79.

2. 'pointed house'; see above, Herkeyah, August 14.

3. Hoebel (1940:146) gives this as Narrow Gut. Robinson and Armagost (1990) glosses it as 'small intestines'. Although Kohiʔ is included in the Hoebel (1940) list of names, this case does not appear in the book. Otherwise unidentified.

4. *eka-* 'red'. Otherwise unidentified. Possibly EkakorohkO, Red Necklace, father of Teneverka.

him in hand-to-hand fight. The husband of this woman (Wanakwada[1]) had neglected her, so she ran off with Parʉakuhma. The husband demanded four horses, a quiver, and blankets. Parʉakuhma paid up and the husband released her.

Nanʉwokʉ   *nanʉwokʉ* must be paid in all events, even if the absconder was braver than the husband. Parʉakuhma ran off with the wife of Eksiakoro (who had no special standing). He got tired of waiting for Parʉakuhma. He went up and killed four of his best war horses. On his return, Parʉakuhma said nothing.

Nanʉwokʉ   On moving his tipi, Ohawura[2] found a man's red bead necklace under his bed. He questioned his wife in a lonely place; his *haitsI*, Téʃowakat[3] went along to help. She confessed that Tokwia[4] had lain with her. Téʃowakat shot her dead and left her lying there for her mother to care for. They *nanʉwok*ed Tokwia for three horses.

The price was in scale to the wealth of the correspondent.[5]

Nanʉwokʉ   Youniacut found Tippanah[6] lying with his wife. Tippanah was too poor to pay, so Youniacut beat him with a quirt until his back was raw. He didn't have to tie him up, he had to stand and take it. In later years, Tippanah would tell how he got beat up.[7]

Nanʉwokʉ   Esiʉrʉhka's[8] wife, Nanasʉyʉ,[9] was caught in adultery with a man. Her husband started to cut off her nose. She got angry with him and he managed to get only a slice off. He later went and collected four horses off the man.

Oaths: Sun Killing   A woman, Tsihtara, was charged by her husband, Kóhiʔ. He smoked, and said, "Sun, if she did that, let her die when the geese fly from south to north." She died.

This was done in a lonely, secret place. He brought her along, but she didn't smoke.

The woman must place her hands flat on the earth while her husband smoked and avow her denial by the earth.

A woman was not likely to try to throw it back on a man; she was afraid of the man and "ain't got the nerve."

Herkeyah knew of only one woman who did it; her husband died. Otherwise, nothing happened if she was innocent.

1. Possibly *wana* 'cloth, blanket', *kwaharʉ* 'antelope'. It is not clear if this was the wife or the husband. Otherwise unidentified.

2. *oha* 'yellow', *wura* 'bear. Hoebel (1940) does not give a translation.

3. Possibly *tʉe* 'little', *puhakatʉ* 'medicine man'. No translation of this name is given in the notes, but Hoebel (1940:145) gives it as Little Medicine. Otherwise unidentified.

4. Hoebel gives this both as Touch A Person With A Closed Fist (1940:98) and Touch With A Closed Fist (1940:146). Otherwise unidentified.

5. Hoebel 1940:97.

6. Tippanah, 'cliff', was a young man (twenty-four years old in 1885) in Youniacut's local Yapainʉʉ local band, later in Pequeohaupith's (Yellowfish) Kwaharʉnʉʉ local band. He is not listed on any later census.

7. Hoebel (1940:58) attributes this story to Tahsuda.

8. Possibly *esi* 'wolf', *tʉhka* 'eater'. Otherwise unidentified.

9. There is a Nanasuyo listed as a member of Tokemi/Tabeko's local band, but that person was a male.

TetsI[1] heard a false report about his wife Ohapia's[2] infidelity. She swore by the sun that it wasn't true; she said, "If he cuts my nose off, grant that he won't live long."

He cut her nose off and within a month he got sick and died.[3]

War: Armor   Some wore iron vests.[4]

Material Culture   To keep awake while riding, put a small sharp stick between the gums.

Animal Liability   There was none for a dog bite. For a horse kick, there were usually no damages, but a quick-tempered man might kill the horse; there were no damages for killing the horse.[5]

Life Cycle: Puberty or Menopause Ceremonies   Herkeyah knew of none.

Life Cycle: Menstruation Taboos   Such women were not allowed to touch their hair or comb it, or they might get gray hair when still young. They were not allowed to wash their face, or they might get wrinkles when still young.

They couldn't eat meat. The reason was that it would make them sick to the stomach, and make them flow more and get weak. There were no sanitary napkins, but they wore heavier dresses.

The taboos were completely removed after menopause.[6]

Medicine: Sorcery: Retaliation   Kwahi[7] wanted to make love to Onawia's wife,[8] but she refused him. He got angry and put medicine on her twelve year old daughter. He used a black handkerchief and caused a hemorrhage.

They brought her over for Herkeyah's husband to doctor. Having no success, they called Herkeyah to come in from her playing. They told her to breathe on the patient. She did this four times and the bleeding stopped. They repeated this again and the girl was all right.

They told Onawia to bring his tipi down close to where they could look after her in the night. They had finished the cure just as the sun was rising.

Her husband had a copper medicine bucket, and he said he would show them what he found. The bucket had a painted rim, plain red. He filled it with water and made passes over it. They looked in and saw the reflection of Kwahi with a black handkerchief. When he moved it, it caused the hemorrhage. They called the girl's mother to look in. He told her he had dreamed the night before how she had refused Kwahi's advances.

Onawia was afraid to approach Kwahi, either to plead or to threaten. He was not a *tekwᵾniwapI*, but was a coward. The girl was never completely free of illness. Onawia

1. 'brother-in-law'. Otherwise unidentified.

2. A woman named Ohahpeya (*oha* 'yellow', *pia* 'mother') was in Tosawa's Penatᵾhka band in the late 1870s.

3. Hoebel 1940:99.

4. There were at least five Comanche men in the eighteenth and nineteenth centuries known by some variant of the name 'Iron Jacket.'

5. Hoebel 1940:119; Wallace and Hoebel 1952:241.

6. Wallace and Hoebel 1952:145.

7. *kwahi* 'back, shoulder'. Hoebel (1940:146) spells this name Kwahiɜa, translated as Robe on His Back. Robinson and Armagost (1990) has it as Kwahira. Otherwise unidentified.

8. *ona* 'salt', *wia* 'worn away spot'. Known as Salt Gap, Onawia was Yapainᵾᵾ. The wife in question is not known.

stayed with Herkeyah's husband for a whole year; she was not bleeding anymore. Then he said he would go north to join a northern band.[1]

Story: Revenge on Innocent Mexicans   A band of women, with a man, set off to trade with the Mexicans. White soldiers took their horses and shot a woman; they left her behind.

After the return of the group, the band decided to send a rescue party for the girl.

Onawia's daughter had died after she split from the band. Some young braves, out chasing a coyote ahead of them, found the body exhumed by the beasts.

They recognized Onawia's daughter by her bracelets. The next day, they found a Mexican who told them the woman they sought was dead. They had a council to see if they would go further to find her. The next day they were sore, so they took everything off of the Mexicans—cattle, sheep, and goods. They couldn't handle them all, so they killed some.

Social Control: Adultery   Tokasai married Wihimatsai.[2] He went on a raid shortly after. Out of jealousy, some of the girls he had gone with told him falsely that she was unfaithful. He nearly choked her to death trying to force a confession.[3]

His folks took his knife away to forestall action. He took his wife to bed and bit her nose off.

Wihimatsai's mother called Tokasai down to her tipi. She was mad. She told him to kill her. "You have no war honors; you are too cowardly to kill an enemy. Try to kill me!"

His brothers restrained him.

Life Cycle: Marriage: Divorce   Whenever a husband cut off a woman's nose, he never took her back. Adultery was the sole cause for nose-cutting. He may also mutilate her in other ways and mistreat her without divorce.

Life Cycle: Marriage: Divorce: Disposition of Property   The children usually went with the mother; also if one was a young man {*sic*}. Both took their personal property. The woman was entitled to the tipi.

Herkeyah knew of no disputed cases.

Social Roles: Contrary   Herkeyah knew of only one. He went around the camp with a rattle, singing. He went into a tipi with a pot boiling over a fire, shot some arrows into the fire, and helped himself to whatever was in the pot. He ate it and went to another tipi. He was sure always to do just what you don't want him to do. He wasn't brave, but wasn't afraid to do anything.

A *pukutsi* was going through camp, singing as usual. An old woman stopped him and said, "*Pukutsi*, I want you to kill me a buffalo to use for my saddle; I have no boys to do it for me."

He went and was gone a long time. Finally, he came back at night with a human skin, with the feet and hands on it (Pawnee); he hung it standing on her arbor. He told the old lady her hide was on her arbor. She got up early and found it and was frightened.

---

1. Hoebel 1940:92; Hoebel 1954:141
2. *wihi* 'knife' or *wihI* 'grease'. Both are otherwise unidentified.
3. Wallace and Hoebel 1952:234 (?).

A man told her she shouldn't have asked a *pukutsi* to do such a job; he was afraid of nothing. She said she didn't ask him to bring her an enemy. But the old lady jumped and sang, she had an enemy scalp, which she kept.[1]

Medicine: Sorcery: Exile   An old woman, Kapewaitʉ,[2] and her daughter had powerful medicine. They had a taboo against yellow paint. Anyone they dreamed about they must put a curse on; they had nothing else against the victim. They cursed a young man and he "wasted away."

People suspected her. A medicine man found her out. He asked her to doctor him {the young man}. She refused, saying she had no power. It was almost too late. A man was bringing her up, but when they heard the mourning cries, they knew the boy had died. "She knew she was guilty," and she turned and fled.

She fled into the tipi of Esihabit, chief of the Penanʉʉ. She hid behind the chief and threw her arms about him, begging for protection.

The chief asked her what ailed her; she said they would kill her. The chief settled it there, he told her he would protect her there. He told her to leave the country. "Those people will kill you."

He arranged to sneak her and her daughter out that night. They left their tipi and belongings standing. They lived out their lives with the Caddos.

When a dream came upon her, she had to put a curse on the person dreamed of or sickness would come on her. She had such a dangerous power that they just gave up when she worked against a person. The power was obtained at a grave. She lived to an old age and died only recently. The daughter still lives; she has the power but not so strong. It was inherited through generations, mother through daughter.

After long years, she returned to the Comanches. She was very kind to an old man; she fed him. The old man, Panukanop,[3] got a sickness from the meat. He didn't suspect trickery, since she was so nice to him. A medicine man came down to doctor him. He discovered Kapewaitʉ was guilty and charged her; she denied it. The medicine man told Panukanop to paint his body all over with yellow paint. The next morning, she called him to come over and get meat. He refused, so she brought it over herself. He threw it out. This paint caused Kapewaitʉ to get sick and die; Panukanop recovered.[4]

Signals   If a man some ways off had news, not urgent, he would ride back and forth slowly on a hilltop. If it was urgent, he would ride rapidly. If it was sad news, he would wave his blanket to the ground once for each death; a white blanket was preferred.

Grave Robbery   Herkeyah never heard of it being done.[5]

1. Wallace and Hoebel 1952:275.
2. Robinson and Armagost (1990) gives *kahpe* 'bed', *waitʉ* 'lacking'. Hoebel (1940:146) gives this as Kapewat, No Bed. A man named Kapihewite is listed on the 1881 census as a member of Esihabit's Penatʉhka local band; he is not listed on any other census. There is no woman listed with this name.
3. *pahmu* 'tobacco', *tenahpʉ* 'man'. Probably the man named Pownitannup, Tobacco Man, listed on the 1881 census as a member of Esihabit's local band. In1889, he was listed as being a leader of a small group himself.
4. Hoebel 1940:93.
5. Wallace and Hoebel 1952:240 (?).

Names: Taboo   There was circumlocution of names after death[1]; after Tuhutuhuya's (Black Horse's)[2] death, all black horses were called *esitutuhuya*.[3]

Medicine   One medicine man could never leave his fire in case of attack on the camp. He would walk about it in a circle until the enemy came up to him.

Life Cycle: Childbirth   A medicine man was called upon in especially hard births.

Herkeyah's husband was called in for a case when the midwives couldn't succeed. He asked for a buffalo hide with a tail on it. He rubbed a stripe of white paint down the center of it with his fingers and used it for the doorway of the tipi. The expectant mother and father had to wear buffalo robes with the hair outside and tails.

The medicine man came into the special childbirth tipi holding a buffalo tail. He waved the tail in front of her face and made a motion like he was going to vomit. He breathed in the patient's mouth, and spit in the midwive's hand and had her rub them together and rub the patient's abdomen; then he walked around the fire and out the door. The child should be born when he put his second foot outside the door; it was successful. The people were poor, but gave him their best horse.[4]

Herkeyah was out playing with other women. A pair came to her and offered her a bowl full of pounded meat. Their child was having trouble in childbirth and they wanted her husband to come and help them.

Herkeyah took it home and gave it to her stepdaughter. She went to her father; he said they probably wanted him to help them. He sent Herkeyah back with the empty bowl to ask them what they wanted. They wanted him to save their daughter. He gave them instructions (as in the other case). He went through his medicine practices, but when he left, the child wasn't born; the reason was that they hadn't come to smoke in the regular ceremonial way.

They heard that the child wasn't born. Her husband called Herkeyah; he said he would fix her to go and help the woman. She didn't want to go, but he and his daughter made her go. He gave her the buffalo tail, and breathed on her, and spat on her hand and made her swallow it; thus he made her go and doctor the mother.

She went and breathed on her four times, spat on her hands and rubbed the woman's abdomen. She spat on the midwife's hands and had her rub the abdomen. She told her to walk around the pole as she left the tipi. When the midwife was halfway around the pole, the baby came. Herkeyah heard the birth cry as she left the tipi. Her husband wanted to give her his medicine, but she refused it. There were too many taboos, and she might get killed.[5]

---

1. Wallace and Hoebel 1952:123 (?).
2. While Tuhutuhuya is literally 'black horse', the man historically known as Black Horse was apparently never designated by that name in documents.
3. Literally, 'gray horse'.
4. Wallace and Hoebel 1952:143.
5. Wallace and Hoebel 1952:143.

HOWARD WHITE WOLF
Undated

Life Cycle: Marriage: Polygamy {Carlson}   Three wives at once was the normal maximum.

OHATAIPA
Undated

Cosmology {Hoebel}   The earth was above the water level which formed the clouds in the sky of the underworlds, where the dead live. When the sun was furthest north {*sic*, south?} in winter, there were red sunsets caused by the underearth people dancing in celebration of the change of seasons. The red was the dust kicked up by their dances.

UNIDENTIFIED CONSULTANT
Undated

Story {Hoebel}   There was a Noyʉhka man on a war party by himself. He had lots of horses. There was another Comanche war party nearby, made up of half-Shoshone men. They had lots of horses too. A couple of the Noyʉhka's horses got mixed up with the other bunch. The Shoshones were talking. They told a couple of men to go ahead and kill a horse at the camping place. There was a Mexican captive along. He was the cook. One of the horses that got mixed in was a mare. She was nice and fat, the smallest, and a mare, so they said to kill her. They would give the owner another horse. They killed it and cooked it.

The Noyʉhka came and made camp a little ways off. He was a real mean man. After he finished pitching camp, he sat there. He smelled something cooking. He went over, so they told him to get off and make himself at home. He looked at the meat and it was all fat. He knew it was a horse that had gone astray.

The leader said, "Yes, that's your horse."

The Noyʉhka turned to the Mexican and said, "You killed him {*sic*}; when we get on a ways, I'm going to kill you."

They left camp. They offered to give the man another horse, but he wouldn't take it. They rode on. The man came up and pulled the Mexican from his horse and whipped him.

The leader said, "Wait a minute."

The man said, "No, he's not worth anything," and went on whipping him.

The leader put an arrow on his bow and walked over.

First, he talked in a friendly way; then he walked over and said, "If you don't stop I'll kill you."

The man went on whipping the Mexican. The leader finally came up and shot an arrow through the man and he died. They took his horses.

When they got close to the main camp, the leader got to feeling bad because he had killed the man. He came home and said he had killed his friend, so he left camp and went away. He went off and was bringing horses down to camp.

A bunch of white people came along, caught, and killed him. It was their horses he had. He had gone out looking for death and was glad to die.

Nanuwoku {Hoebel}   If the offender was a boy, the husband might go easy. If crossed by the boy, he might make him ridiculous by cutting his hair.

They might ask for his special keepsake, such as a favorite horse. If he wouldn't give it to them, they could kill the horse. This was not done if the man had more war deeds than they.

Material Culture: Beadwork: Loom {Hoebel}   They used a double thread in the needle. The thread was tied to the left warp thread. Then, string all the beads across and place in position between the warp threads. Then string them back through on the top of the warp. It was tied again on the left side to hold the first row. This was continued, tying all knots on the top side. For a new thread, a knot was caught in the third bead from the left, then it was run through these three beads and continued.

Story: The Blind Man and the Foxes {Carlson}   Some Indians were going on war party. There was one blind man in the group. A young man took care of him.

As they were going along, they met a fox.

They were camping at a certain place that night.

Toward morning, they were attacked by enemies. The young man was around by his father. He ran out and forgot his blind friend.

The fox came into the tipi and saw the old man. He led him out to a draw and watched over him. All of the members of the party were killed. The fox went to the camp and discovered this.

He returned to the blind man and told him this. The blind man cried. The fox said, "Stop crying," and the man did. They left that place.

As they were going, the fox said, "Would you like to go home?"

The man said he would, but he couldn't see. The fox called out and other foxes came. They started on their way. After a while, they asked him if he wanted something to eat. He said yes, but there was no one around who could cook for him. The foxes went out and killed a young calf. They led the old man up and let him take his knife, cut it open, and eat the insides. When he was full, the foxes started to eat.

This man stayed with the foxes so much he knew their ways. They camped and got wood for the old man so he could have a fire to cook the fresh meat that they had got for him.

After eating, they continued on their way towards the man's camp. They went up a hill. When they got on top of the hill, they noticed some of the man's people chasing buffalo. They saw one man riding toward them. So the foxes left the man standing there and hid in the brush nearby. They said if the man didn't see the blind man they would take him nearer to home. But the man saw the blind man and was surprised to see him. He asked the blind man how he got back, and the man recounted his experiences. To show their appreciation for the foxes' behavior, the Indians killed some buffalo and left them there for the foxes to eat.

Story{Carlson} Once there was a woman and two sons. One of them was a young man, the other a boy.

The oldest son took someone else's wife with him and eloped (a very brave man). The man from whom the wife was stolen had four wives, of which this one was the youngest.

They stayed away six years from the tribe.

The people at home thought the couple had been killed. They began to mourn, destroying the couple's property, etc.

The man's mother kept the warrior's white war horse, however, for the younger son to ride. The younger brother grew up to be a very brave warrior.

About thirty men organized a raiding party. The younger brother joined the party. They were going north, which was the direction the couple had gone.

The boy led the brother's white horse as an emergency horse.

They got to the Osage people and attacked some of the Osages. The Osages got the best of the battle, and the Comanches had to run. Many of the Comanches were on foot.

The only one left on horseback was the boy. He fought hard for those Comanches who were on foot. They fought all day until sundown, when the young man's horse was shot.

The boy continued to fight on foot. He was wounded, but not seriously, and continued to fight until it got too dark, when the fighting ceased. Many of those who were on foot ran back and continued to run until they reached their tribe.

They brought news back that the group had almost all been killed, and they told the young man's mother that he had been killed.

When it got dark, the young man walked, trying to get home. After traveling half the night through the forest, he saw a light in the forest. He decided to seek aid from those who lived in the tipi, regardless of the consequences. He listened to the conversation and heard the woman speak to a child in Comanche. The young man was overjoyed at this.

The people within heard footsteps, and the woman told her husband that she thought someone was coming. The husband told her to look out, which she did, She saw the man and told her husband. He then told his wife to ask the man if he was an Indian (meaning Comanche).

The man answered back that he was.

The lady told the him to come in, which the man did. The man questioned him about the reasons for being out in such a condition, without the proper clothes, no horse, blanket, etc.

The young man recounted his experiences to the man of the tipi.

They asked him if he wanted something to eat. He answered, "Yes."

The tipi man told him that when he was through eating, he would question him more as to his relatives, the occasion for the raid, etc.

When he finished, the man asked him who his parents were. The boy said he really didn't know. "But I do remember that I had a brother older than myself who ran off with a woman and we never did see him again."

The tipi man asked his name and the boy told him. It was his own brother. They were overjoyed. They embraced and kissed each other.

The young man said, "I think back home, the news is that I've been killed."

The older man said, "Your mother will be worried. I'd think we better return."

They returned that very night. They drove the remainder of the night.

The next day, while en route, they overtook some of the raiding party members on foot. They got one member of this group to take one of their horses and ride ahead with the news that both of the boys were alive and coming back. They promised the messenger that if he would do this, they would give him one of their best horses.

The messenger was too late. The mother already had the news. He drove up to the home. He saw a man nearby. The man pointed to the tipi saying the mother was already cutting herself in mourning.

The men drove to the woman's tipi. She asked what they wanted. The messenger told her, "Your sons are alive and are coming home. You may not believe it, but it is the truth. They will be here at noon. Go to the creek and wash the blood from your wounds."

A little after noon, the mother, who had cleaned up, watched for her sons. They arrived and the mother was so happy.

The older brother said to his mother to take gifts—horses, blankets—to the first husband. If he refused and wanted his wife back, he could have her.

The woman brought the presents and told the man everything.

The former husband said he was pleased with the gifts and the young man could keep the wife.

Story: Origin of Horses {Carlson}   A group was returning from a war party without much success.

The horses were getting tired.

They stopped to camp near a canyon. One man walked away from camp. He noticed a man there with lots of hair down in his eyes; his eyes sparkled.

He called to his friends and told them what he had seen, but when they came up, the man had disappeared and all they could see was a cloud of dust.

The group decided to find out what was in the hole. They took a mirror and shone it into the hole and saw a large stallion within.

They set a rope trap in front of the cave to catch the stallion. They hid. Soon, a stallion came out and they caught him. The people then pulled him away. As they did this, all kinds of horses came out—mares, colts, antelopes, etc. This was how the Indians got horses, antelopes, etc.

The man in the early part of the story was a stallion with a large mane.

Story: The Animals' War Party {Carlson}   Eagle was in charge of a band. In the band were Opossum, Wolf, Redbird, Bear, and Turtle. The Turtle was the mightiest of them all.

They were on the warpath. They traveled a whole day before they sighted a camp. They met a band of Indians, also on the warpath.

They had a battle. The Eagle was killed and the Turtle took charge. "Follow me" he said.

The Indians killed all but the Turtle. The Turtle said, "They won't kill me," and he drew his head under his shell.

Finally, the Indians ran short of ammunition. "Let's capture him," but they couldn't get hold of him.

Finally, someone said, "Let's burn him."

They got hold of his tail and the turtle began to lead them toward the fire.

"We can't put him in the fire," some said, "he likes it. He is leading us toward it."

Then someone suggested that they throw the turtle in the creek. At those words, the Turtle drew his head under his shell. "Look," said one, "he's afraid of it; he is drawing his legs and head in."

"He's afraid of the water, that's where we will put him, in the creek."

As they led him along to the creek, he fought and struggled to get free. They finally got him to the creek and threw him in. The Turtle went down in the water and swam underwater for a long time, and then crawled out on the opposite bank, free.

(The Turtle in this story was the rear guard.)

Story: **The Boy Who Was Whipped** {Carlson}   A man had a boy ten years old. He always whipped the boy. The boy got tired of being whipped so he ran away from home.

The father waited three days for his son to come back, but the son did not come back.

The father then went though the camp, asking about his son. Finally, a man spoke up and said, "Yes, I've seen your son. He is over there by the creek, playing with those little foxes."

The father went right down there. Sure enough, there was his son, playing with the little foxes. He ran up, and before he got there, all the foxes ran into their hole. The son followed them into the hole.

The father stood out by the opening, calling to his son. But the son would not come out. Finally, the father said "If you don't come out, I'll smoke you out."

Hearing these words, the son came out and his father took him home.

He had lived with the foxes all this time.

Story: **Fox and the Kettle** {Carlson}   Fox had a fire. He ran an underground tunnel from this fire. At the opening of the tunnel, a little way from the fire, he was boiling some stuff.

Some Indians came along and were surprised to find that he was boiling meat with no fire. They asked him how he did this.

Fox said, "You should have one of these kettles; they are very good. When you are out, all you have to do is put water in it and the water will boil."

The Indians asked Fox to sell it to them.

Fox said, "No. If I sold it, I'd starve."

The Indians were anxious to get the pot and offered Fox two good horses.

Fox finally gave up his pot for the horses. He said, "I'll probably starve now."

Fox then told the Indians how to use the pot. He said, "Just stop, clear a place on the ground, put water in your pot, and it will boil."

The Indians and Fox then parted.

Toward sundown, the Indians made camp and were anxious to try their new pot. They cleared a place, put water and meat in the pot, and set it on a cleared place. They waited a while, they watched patiently, but the meat did not boil.

After a while, the one who had made the bargain knew that he had been fooled. They decided to go back to the place where they had made the bargain with Fox. They looked the place over and saw the Fox's trick. The Indians knew then how they had been cheated.

Story: **The Fox and the Young Girls**   One time, two foxes were out walking. They met six young girls picking berries.

One fox got in a cradle as if it were a baby, and the other pretended to be his mother.

They joined the girls and all picked berries together.

When evening came, the leader of the girls said, "Let us make windbreaks and camp here tonight. Then we can have another day picking berries."

Two of the girls and the foxes slept in one windbreak, and the other four girls in another.

During the night, the girls wanted to play that they were with men. Fox said that he would be the man. He did it to one of the girls.

The fox in the cradle said, "How about giving me a turn?"

"Be still, or you will give us away," said the other.

He then did it to the other girl. The two girls called over to the other camp, "Girls, come on over. This woman is as good as a man."

Fox left. When he got to the top of the hill, he called back, "Hey, you girls, I got what I wanted of you."

Story: The Story of Nasituinʉhpʉ?   After Fox left, he came to another band of Indians.

The chief of that band was telling his people where to go to find a certain kind of fox (*waani*). He was giving his people orders to go out and hunt this *waani*.

In this band of Indians there was a young boy called Nasituinʉhpʉ?[1] ('boy who always wets his bed'). This boy lived with his grandmother. "Grandmother," he said, "make me a trap so I can go and trap some animals."

His grandma said, "Ah! What do you want with a trap, you are too young to have a wife."

(The chief had two daughters; the person who got the *waani* had his choice of either daughter.)

Finally, the grandmother made a trap for the boy and said to him, "Be sure to put this trap right at the side of a bank, as you will more likely get them there."

She put a buffalo robe on him, as it was cold. She gave him a stick and got him started early in the morning. He went to his trap and found *waani* there in the trap.

He hit the fox on the head, stuck it under his robe, and took it home and showed his grandmother.

Just at dinner time, the chief got up and asked if everyone {*sic*, anyone} had got the fox. The chief then made the rounds of the tipis and looked in. When he came to the tipi of the boy and grandmother, he found the fox all skinned and stretched out.

He said, "This is just what I want."

He took the hide and went to his own tipi. The oldest daughter of the chief, after a while, came to the tent of the boy with some meat. They ate the meat, and finally the girl said, "Let's go back to my tent for supper."

After supper, she wouldn't let him go back to his tipi.

The boy was restless.

After supper, the younger sister looked at the boy and said, "Oh, sister, let me have this man as a husband, he is just my size."

The older sister said, "Nothing doing. I went all the way down to his tipi to get him and I am going to keep him."

---

1. *tuinʉhpʉ?* 'young man'; *nasi* is unattested.

After a while they went to bed; he was sleeping between the two sisters. The elder sister held him tight and he wet her. She pushed him out of bed. The younger sister said, "What is wrong?"

The older sister said, "Oh, he peed on me."

The younger sister said, "That is nothing, it's only water."

So she took the boy into bed with her, saying, "I'll take him for a husband."

The next morning, when he got up, the younger sister told her father that the boy was her husband.

The young boy left the tipi and went up the hill and sat facing the east, crying.

After a while a bird (eagle) came along, saying, "What are you crying about?"

The boy said, "Oh, I peed on my wife last night and she threw me out."

The bird said, "Oh, don't worry about that."

He then plucked a feather from his body and gave it to the boy; it changed into a fine suit of clothes for the boy. The bird said, "I'll give you my size and wisdom."

Then the bird left; he began to fly off.

He began to cry again. Soon a turkey came along. He asked him what was wrong. The boy told him. Turkey plucked a feather and gave it to the boy and made him even more handsome than before. The turkey said, "I will give you power to grow," and caused the boy to grow to full size.

The turkey left.

After this, two water horses came, a male and a female. Each of them plucked a hair from their fur and thus made him a pair of moccasins.

After this, a little bird came along. He asked what was wrong. The boy told him. The bird gave the boy a beautiful Spanish shawl.

Just as the boy was ready to return, a redbird lit on the top of his head and said, "I'm your friend. I'll be with you always."

He then went to his grandma's tent, and his grandma was surprised at the change in the boy. He told his grandma to go and call the younger of the two sisters.

She did this, and the younger sister came. She, too, was surprised.

He told her to come and sit by him.

She did; he took out a fine buckskin dress and gave it to her, then moccasins, and finally, the shawl. Then he combed her hair and parted it.

"Now," he said, "go back to our tipi and I will come in a short time."

The girl got back to the tipi. When the older sister said, "Where did you get all those lovely things? I want some," the younger sister told her where.

The older sister went to the boy's tipi. He gave her stuff, but it was not nearly as nice as the costume that he had given the younger girl.

The older sister said, "He didn't treat me right, look at the funny outfit he gave me."

She got mad. It was about that time that Fox came to the camp. He was a person as proud as could be. The elder daughter went to see Fox about it. Fox told her to make a date with the young man. Fox said, "Dig a hole in the tipi, and when he comes in, have him stand in it and I will do the rest."

She did as instructed and that night, when the young man came, he stood in the hole and the sand came in and held him tight. He began to sink, and his wife tried to get him out, but it was no use.

He sank up to his knees. At this time, the elder daughter ran out to where the Fox was and told him. The Fox said in reply, "Don't forget, you are going to be my wife."

The girl said, "Yes."

The next day the camp was to be broken. The man was still up to his waist. He told them to leave him behind, as the one who had done this dirty work would "let me out afterwards."

When all had gone, the Fox (Opossum) came up and said, "Brother, I sure hate to see you in that condition. I sure would like to help you."

He said, "I would like that bird on your head."

He took the bird and put it on his head. "I think I'll try to pull you out."

He put his tail around the man and pulled him out up to his knees, and then up to his ankles. He got him out, finally. He was very glad.

Kawos began nudging him with his elbow. "Oh, my poor brother, if I hadn't got you out, you would have died. Just think, you nearly lost your two wives."

He went along like that for a long time. They came to the deep hole where the fellow was buried. The boy pushed Kawos in.

Kawos wanted to know how he was going to get out. The boy suggested he go off to camp and get some rope. He would need four days to make the trip.

Kawos said, "No, I'll die in the meantime."

The boy could see no other way. Kawos finally agreed.

The camp was only a couple of hours off, but he spent four days with his wives.

He came back. He hid part of the rope behind his back. The rope was too short, Kawos couldn't reach it.

The boy said he must take another four days to the camp for rope. Kawos said he was dead, sure.

"Well," said the boy, "if I get you out, you do what I want hereafter?"

Agreed.

The boy asked for the redbird on Kawos' head. Kawos said the bird was dead, starved to death.

The boy told him just to take it off, shake it, and throw it up. The bird flew up to the boy.

The fellow went off and played out the rope. He came back and pulled him out.

"Don't forget our agreement."

Answered, "You bet. I'll do anything."

Boy: "Then take that road and keep on going. I'll go back to camp. We don't want to see you about no more."

Kawos said, "But I'm pretty nearly dead for food."

"Well, you keep on going to our old camp, you'll find plenty of bones there. Maybe you can get some rabbits. From now on, you're a fox."

Story: Turtle's War Party   All the animals in the world, and all the people in the world, were gathered together in one place. At this place, the people named their life occupations.

The turtle spoke up and said that he wanted to be a warrior and go on the warpath.

One day soon after, he went to his mother and told her that he was going on the warpath, and she should prepare some clothes for him and to make two pairs of each, as he was taking a woman with him.

There was a log near camp. Turtle led his horse and tried to mount from one side, and his girl from the other, but they couldn't make it. They were too short.

He and his girl friend spent a month trying to get on the horse, but they could not make {it}.

One night, turtle's mother heard the girl cry out; she thought they were returning with horses from a raid. Come to find out, they hadn't even started.

The mother had a sack of food. She put her son and his girl friend in the sack and left them there to eat all they wanted.

NOTES ON DANCES
AT WALTERS
AND APACHE
UNDATED[1]

Dances   Occasionally, a dancer would give a specialty dance, such as the Skeleton Dance.[2]

In one dance, young women joined the war dancers in a round dance; the men's step was slightly more complicated than the women's.

At the four-day picnics[3] they lived in canvas tents or brush arbors.

The man who gave the picnic furnished the beef for the crowd.

At Apache, there were about fifty families with about eight persons to each family; at Walters about {. . . [*sic*]}.

At Apache, two cattle were killed each day. The distributed meat was hung on racks near the arbors to dry.

The order of the dances was: nine o'clock to ten or eleven: Brush Dances; two o'clock to five or six: social dances; eight-thirty to eleven o'clock: War Dances; eleven o'clock until indefinitely, 49 Dances. There was considerable gambling in between.

Dances: Brush Dance {Hoebel}   A group of old men and women gathered about 200 feet from the dance circle. The song leader (Post Oak Jim) took his place on the west side of the drum, grasping the drum by the leather thongs attached to the sides. Seven other men ranged themselves about the drum, also holding the thongs. The balance of men stood on the east facing the drummers. All the women formed on the west behind the drummers.

---

1. This information is from Wedel, Hoebel, and Carlson. The order of the notes is based upon modern dance schedules. The Walters dance took place on August 16, 1933.

2. Otherwise unidentified.

3. In the early twentieth century, Comanche and other Oklahoma dances and celebrations—later called powwows—were called picnics.

Post Oak Jim started the songs, the rest joined in. As they sang, they slowly danced toward the dance circle or arbor, entering it on the east. Short rest stops are made between the songs. When they had reached the circle, the dance was finished.

According to Clay, at Apache the group danced to the center of the arbor before stopping.

After arriving at the arbor, they sang four songs. During this dance, one woman dragged a cottonwood limb; according to Clay, this was placed on top of the arbor afterwards. All the women carried in their right hands a bunch of leaves, sage, cottonwood, pecan, "Indian perfume," or poplar. The women also wore a crown of the same leaves; they kept time with leaves, shaking them. The men were attired in nothing special, no costumes.

Clay reported that on the second morning, the men carried eagle feather fans in their left hands that they waved in time to the music, and one carried a rattle.[1]

Dances: Social Dance   These were performed in the afternoon. The drummers were to the west. When the music started, the women danced out into the circle in a loping step. There they joined in pairs and loped up to a man, each taking him by one hand. He got up and danced forward with them while they danced backward, or all three danced forward together. A woman might go alone for a partner, or she might accost a drummer (e.g., Post Oak Jim). When the song was finished there was a pause, then the men took their seats again.

The women were supposed to be paid by the man, unless his female relatives came for him (e.g., Linton). This was repeated with the next song.

The social dances were held before a raiding party goes out as a general party in celebration.

Dances: Social Dances: Round Dance   The round dance was a social dance. It took place in the afternoon. Young girls started dancing first; two or three locked arms and danced around the center pole. The step was a side-step to the left, bringing the right foot over the left on alternate beats. There were separate songs for girls, boys, and mixed groups, which varied from time to time. The dance generally lasted about two hours.

Social Roles: Club Man   Owned by Pinedapoi.[2]

Dances: Buffalo Dance   The Buffalo Dance was given the night before a war party. Men and women danced up by stages from opposite sides. After they progressed a few minutes, the music stopped. Then the drums beat fast and the dancers and singers whooped; then the dancers relaxed and the dance continued.

After several such shifts, after reaching the center, it was over, and they turned and danced back towards their places.

The leader carried a coup club and could make people dance with it.

There were four men dancers out front. One carried a gun and shot it occasionally. There were eight drummers and s ingers, including women, who followed close behind the

1. This note is apparently a synthesis of observations at the August 16 dance at Walters, and the dance witnessed by Clay Lockett in Apache (see Introduction).
2. Also known as Penaro, Dinero, and Dinero's Boy. The latter is the source of Hoebel's spelling, Pinedapoi (Nancy Minor, p.c. 2004). Wallace and Hoebel 1952:189.

singers. There was a row of women in costume, some wearing war bonnets and carrying spears.

They danced slowly into the dance circle. The man with the club was on the horse. When in the center of the dance circle, the leader raised his hand and counted the coups on his club with the dancers standing around him.[1] There were then four more songs and they disbanded.

Dances: 49 Dance   Drummers danced in the center of a milling group of young men and women (all singing). Women danced in groups covered by a single blanket. Boys linked arms in groups. All moved slowly in a circle, with a shuffling step. At intervals, the drum was raised high, then lowered, and they continued.

Dates were being constantly made between couples, who dropped out and met at a rendezvous, to return later to the dance.[2]

Music: Songs: Round Dance Song   "I don't care if you're married, I still love you, I'll get you yet, hai yo oh hoy noib haiba . . ."[3]

Music: Songs

⟨tomimodyai⟩[4] *tuibihtsiʔ* ⟨me:kanakakubix⟩

young man listen to this and loud over

Itesa ⟨eninmroyain⟩ *naboabekʔem*[5]

these here that you have they killed discovered

⟨etto nauɨ tso⟩ *haits*

that's your boyfriend's friend

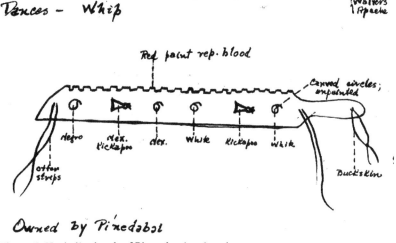

Figure 7. Hoebel's sketch of Pinero's *pianɨʔɨpai*.

---

1. This refers to the scalp symbols on Penaro's *pianɨʔɨpai* (see fig 7).
2. This material appears on one of Hoebel's note cards attributed to Howard White Wolf, but it is unclear as to whether the linkage should be by consultant or subject.
3. This is a 49 Dance song.
4. Probably based on *tɨmahyokɨrɨ* 'listen'.
5. Robinson and Armagost (1990) gives *nabehkakɨ* as 'kill'.

PART TWO

Robert Lowie's 1912 Field Trip

Introduction

During the initial stages of gathering the Field Party notes, I visited the American Museum of Natural History (AMNH). While there, I asked if there were any extant notes from Robert Lowie's 1912 research trip to the Comanches, the basis of his 1915 publication, *Comanche Dances*. I was shown his small notebook and made a manuscript transcription. In 1995, the AMNH provided a copy of Wahkinney's drawing of the "otter wrapped crooked stick" from those notes for use in my *Comanche Political History* (1996).

In 1999, while editing the Field Party notes, I began to consider other original sources that might also be suitable for publication. I concluded that although Lowie's notes were too brief to warrant a separate publication, they were still important in their own right. The AMNH granted permission to publish the notes and provided a photocopy of the original manuscript for comparison with my earlier transcription. Their cooperation is most appreciated.

ROBERT LOWIE'S 1912 FIELD TRIP

In early June, 1912, Dr. Robert Lowie spent about a week (his notes are unclear) among the Comanches. Lowie's trip was part of the AMNH's investigation of Plains Indian men's societies, begun by Franz Boas and continued by Clark Wissler (1912–16). This was a broad-ranging field project with many collaborators.

Lowie's notes of his Comanche trip are in a small pocket notebook, about four inches by six inches. The first page is dated June 8 (Saturday), noting "I have been here several days"; the last dated page, page 9, is dated June 12. There are seventeen more pages of notes, some attributed to consultants, some not.

It is not clear whether the notes were immediate inscriptions or whether there was some interval between interview and inscription. That the latter may be the case is suggested by several points: there are a number of changes of writing implements, e.g. from pencil to pen and back, and there are several pages of apparent doodles. Though it does seem likely that most of the notes were written after the fact, it was probably not that long afterward.

In formatting Lowie's notes, I have used the same normalizing protocols as with the Field Party notes: full sentences, past tense, Comanche names as spelled on the censuses, normalized spelling of Comanche words in italics, and unattested Comanche words in angle brackets.

Since Lowie did not supply note headers other than date and consultant name, I have not inserted any. However, I have indexed his notes in the same format as the Field Party notes. The bolding of consultants and dates and the insertion of Lowie's page numbers in braces are my own.

Lowie identified four Comanche consultants by name: Quassyah,[1] Isatai,[2] Wahkinney,[3] and Cavayo.[4] In addition, there was at least one other, unnamed, Comanche consultant, and two non-Indian consultants, Hope M. Fulbright and Dr. James Rowell.

Along with his notes on the societies, Lowie recorded comments on a number of other topics, including personal hygiene, buffalo hunting, the organization of war parties, and the value of coups.

Lowie's 1912 Field Notes

{Page 1}

Lawton, Oklahoma, June 8.

I have been here several days waiting for Harrington's[5] interpreter, Mr. Hope M. Fulbright.[6]

Dr. Rowell,[7] who is married to a Kiowa woman, told me that all the K{iowa} women pull out their eyebrows, by which token they may readily be distinguished from the Comanches (?). He also says (as does Mooney[8]) that the K{iowas} had a Rabbit society that must be entered before any other. Whether the other societies were also graded, he does not know, but he will inquire.

The claw hammer[9] type of pappose board is said to be common to both the Kiowas and the Comanches.

I myself saw a Comanche man today whose eyebrows had been completely removed.

1. See Introduction to the 1933 Field Party.
2. See Introduction to the 1933 Field Party.
3. Wahkinney (*wakarée*, 'turtle') is listed in the Family Record Book as forty-five years old in 1901, but he is not listed on any census before 1892. He was a member of Tischecoddy's Kwaharʉnʉʉ local band.
4. Cavayo (from the Spanish *caballo* 'horse') was a born about 1860 and a member of Tahpony's Yapainʉʉ local band.
5. Presumably, this refers to Mark R. Harrington (1882–1971), who, a few years earlier, had made collections in western Oklahoma for Gustav G. Heye's Museum of the American Indian. John Peabody Harrington of the Smithsonian did not visit the Kiowa Agency until 1917, and he worked only with the Kiowas.
6. Hope M. Fulbright was born in Texas in 1876, and came to Fort Sill and the Kiowa Agency in 1892, where he served in various positions. He also worked at the Red Store. Fulbright learned the Comanche language quickly, serving, as noted by Lowie, as interpreter for Mark Harrington. He was also one of the early interpreters at Deyo Mission. My thanks to Wahnee Clark for this information.
7. Dr. James Frederick Rowell (1874–1951) arrived at Anadarko around 1900 to serve as the Kiowa Agency physician. He married a Kiowa woman, Mahbone. Their descendants include Dr. Everett Rhoades, who, from 1982 to 1983, was United States Assistant Surgeon General and head of the Indian Health Service. Again, my thanks to Wahnee Clark.
8. Mooney 1898:230 (?).
9. I know of no other published description of Kiowa or Comanche cradles as "claw hammer." The more recent term is "lattice back."

{Page 2}

I am informed by the traders at Lawrence's store[1] that, of the Indians about Lawton, only the Apaches now make beadwork.

Mr. Hope M. Fulbright, who inquired about the print for Mr. Harrington,[2] said the Comanches never had a Sun Dance, so far as their recollection goes.

June 10
Isatai[3]

Long ago, the buffalo was the source of all supplies. It was very important to hunt them. The leaders said, "No one was to advance before the rest."

In preparation, scouts were sent out in different directions; they might be gone for a day. The chief and council would tell them where to go. The scouts looked for the trail {Page 3} of the bison and determined their appropriate number. They came back, smoked, and told their observations.

In the morning, the council men would call out for men of age to get ready to go at an early hour. The chiefs said, "This is for all of us. It is not for one man. Don't run ahead to kill for yourself, we must all stay together."

They got their arrows and bows and were commanded not to break {illegible}.

They rounded up the buffalo.

If some y{oung} man did run in, they would tell him he was crazy, and reprove him, and tell him he'd have to be in want if he acted that way.

The Comanche never punished a man by whipping or tent tearing. If he was really bad, his horse was killed on the second or third offence. And he was reproved by the leaders.

The Comanche do not seem to {Page 4} have <u>had a regular police</u>.[4]

(Isatai has plucked out his eyebrows, ditto a visitor.)

Songs were more important than <u>dances</u>.

Other informant[5]:

Other tribes policed the buffalo hunt, not the Comanches, however.

June 11
Quassyah

⟨nā´wapinàr⟩[6] (= challenge of enemy or calling of volunteers).[7]

Dogs

Spokesman and chief of ceremony[8]

---

1. Arthur D. Lawrence ran a general store in Lawton that catered to Indians.
2. The details of this inquiry are unknown.
3. Although Lowie must have known that Isatai was the 1874 prophet (Mooney 1898:201), he asked no questions about that ceremony.
4. See also Naiya, July 7, 1933.
5. The unnamed visitor.
6. Joe Attocknie (p.c.) suggested to me that this word was 'stir-up', but I have not been able to confirm it.
7. Lowie 1915:810.
8. These latter two notes were scattered across the bottom of the page. The reference to dogs may be to the prohibition of dogs during the Tuwikanᵾᵾ ceremonies.

{Page 5}
{diagram of dance}
Horses   Crows   Colts   Drum-dancers Buffalo ~~chaparral bird~~
(very swift)
⟨waⁿtsi⟩[1]

The spokesmen asked the rest who was to be manager.[2] If they made any mistake, they might be deposed for the afternoon performance.

Spokesmen were also suggested in the same way.[3]

{Page 6}

If a man danced as Horse in the morning, he might change to Crow in the afternoon.

There were four hand drums.

Dogs that had entered the Crow Dance were killed with arrows. They were supposed to be especially offensive to the Crows. But sometimes a man who especially liked his dog was requested to sacrifice it.[4]

Comanches never ate dogs.

(Comanches used four tipi poles; Kiowas, three.)

Before going into {a} buffalo tipi,[5] they had a horse parade. The managers pretended to strike laggards with clubs.

{Page 7}[6]

{Page 8}[7]

The Comanches regarded as brave a man who, though dismounted, made his escape and even killed or wounded an enemy, and a man who challenged to single combat and overcame an enemy. Horse stealing was regarded as an art rather than a bravery exploit. Scalping was not prized.

{Page 9}

Use of quirts by managers?

Name of dance group in ⟨nā´wapinàr⟩?

Women dance?[8]

---

1. On June 12, below, Lowie noted that "another informant says that *wotsi* is not a bird (chaparral) but the swift fox." This explains the strikeout, and suggests that the words ⟨waⁿtsi⟩ and ⟨wotsi⟩ are *waani* 'fox'.

2. Position noted on diagram.

3. Lowie used the terms "manager" and "spokesman" throughout. Despite the lack of collaborating contemporary evidence, it is tempting to suggest that the "spokesman" corresponds to the modern powwow announcer, and the "manager" is either the head man dancer, and/or arena director.

4. Lowie 1915:811.

5. It is not clear what this refers to.

6. This page consists of a line of doodles, which may include the outline of a soft-soled moccasin and a tipi frame.

7. The top two-thirds of this page has a sketch of what might have been intended to be a travois, although travois are not mentioned in the text.

8. This seems to be a list of questions to ask.

June 12

Another informant said the *wotsi*[1] is not a bird (chaparral) but the swift fox. He said all the dance names given by Quassyah alternated; they were not simultaneous.

The <u>Yapai</u> band always danced the Crow dance. There was no special costume.

Bands[2]:

1. Yamparɨhka
2. Kwaharɨ   Antelope
3. Penatɨhka   Wasp Honey eaters
4. Noyɨhka   Travelers; they had an older name: Nokoni

Most marriages were within the same band. Children were counted in the father's band.

{page 10}

Wife's sister and brother's wife were called wife and treated familiarly.

Brothers-in-law were chums. They played jokes on each other.

nanɨwokɨ = confiscation of goods.

Comanches cut off an adulteress's nose.

Today, I saw some shade lodges {brush arbors} of rectangular plan, rather similar to the Shoshone type.

Practically all the Comanche men have no eyebrows. Today I also saw an old woman without them.

Wahkinney

patso'ikowe kwitubi[3] otter wrapped stick and hook. {see fig. 8}

{Page 11}

Figure 8. Wahkinney's sketch of the *patso'ikowe kwitubi*.

---

1. See above where this was written with a superscript 'n'.

2. In the three band lists in Lowie's notes, the ethnonyms are spelled essentially the same, although they have been normalized here. Lowie's original spellings were Yápairē`ka, Kwãare, Pēnatēka, Nóyeka, and Nókōni.

3. Robinson and Armagost (1990) has *paatsoko* 'otter', *nɨɨhkwiitubitɨ* 'wrap around and around'.

There were two pairs of eagle feathers on the top and bottom of the hooked part. Certain men only had these sticks. They were warriors. They were also carried in dances.

When a man had lost a son through a hostile tribe, he felt badly and wanted revenge and invited neighbors to join in a dance (⟨nā´wapinàr⟩). Then he, and others who had these hooked poles, would use them in the dance on that occasion.

The Big Horses had a little different song from other songs. They never danced by themselves.

The Big Horses took *ekwipIsa*ʔ (red body paint) and painted their bodies down to the waist. They had rattles, and shook them. They took {Page 13} hawk and sparrowhawk feathers tied to the back of their heads so they would flutter as they moved.

The Big Horses remained in office every time the people were on the march, as long as they pleased. They had no function outside of marching.

W{ahkinney} saw them in action himself. Big Horses were never young men. Wahkinney never saw more than twenty.[1] Their main function was to make peace with another tribe.

{Wahkinney} never saw the sash (cf. Big Dogs of Crow[2]).

{Wahkinney} never saw notched rasps.

Dauntless men were called Piarekaekapit[3] (a Large Red Buffalo Meat).
{Page 14}

⟨nai' imea paikit⟩ uncommunicativeness was practiced by Piarekaekapit.

There was nothing distinctive in the dauntless men's garb. A blue or other cross was painted on the quiver of one of these men. They acted very quietly. The cross man had a singular tomahawk with a long blade, looking powerfully different from others. An eagle feather was tied to its handle (with a dark tip). He was killed by the Navajos.[4]

Dances[5]

1. Horse

2. Colt

3. Crow

4. Drum

5. Horn (or Buffalo) is not so common. {Page 15}

6. Fox (not so common)

The Horse Dancers had a rawhide rattle. {Wahkinney} danced the Horse and Colt and Fox dances. The Horses carried spears (*tsik*) with eagle feathers.

1. Lowie 1915:812.

2. Lowie 1913:175.

3. *pia* 'big', *tɨhkapa* 'meat', *ekapitI* 'red'. Other than Lowie, there is no ethnographic or ethnohistorical mention of this as a status or a group name. However, there is historical mention of an individual, a Nokoni local band chief, with the name Red Food, or Big Red Food (Kavanagh 1996:431, 448). Based on that historical evidence, I favor the interpretation that the reference is to a single individual rather than to a social status.

4. If Piarekaekapit was a single individual, rather than a social group, then he died after the winter of 1875, the last time his name appears in the historical record (Davidson 1875), and before 1879, since his name does not appear on any census list.

5. This is given as a numbered list. Here Lowie, as did others before and after, confused the names of dances with the groups that danced them.

Wahkinney danced the Horse Dance usually, but the Colt Dance was started and Wahkinney said he was willing, but didn't know what his own manager would say about it.[1]

The Horse Dancers never met specially for feasts by themselves.

{Page 16}

~~Cabello~~ Kabē′yo[2]

Comanches had the ⟨nā′wapinàr⟩.[3]

A man who lost a relative passed a pipe around from one to another to get people's help. He then selected the site to which people would come for assembly. This initiator was the master of ceremonies for that particular occasion.

Yamparᵾhka
Nokoni   } 3 bands of the whole tribe
Kwaharᵾ

They all assembled at the site.

Each band had its own dance and officers, the others only watched. But any might {Page 17} dance the Buffalo Dance.

Some were on horseback, as captains or war chiefs. The number was rarely more than ten. They became leaders on account of war honors. They knew who was the best of all and he came last in line.

The people filed out a certain distance. The drummers got out also, and the people formed an arc and the captains bade them halt.

The drummers were simply good singers.

The captain (the bravest) called the halt. The dancers did not talk at all, only the drummers and the captain. The captain stuck his spear into the ground; then all drummers at once beat their drums. Then they, the drummers, made remarks. And the captain told what the injury to the tribesman was. The captain pretended three times to put his lance in the ground. Then {Page 18} he told the offence. They all moved some distance. Then the second highest man repeated the same performance. These leaders were very rarely over six.

(Clans had nothing to do with it.)

Buffalo Dance was *aanᵾhka* (Horn D{ance}). Sometimes small horns were used on bonnets. This could be danced by any clan. Jack[4] said it was the greatest dance. They never danced two buffalo dances in one day.

{drawing}

            Spectators --------------------Women
                    \ \ \ \ \ Drummers
                 \ \ \ \ \ \ \ \ \ \ \ Dancers

                | | | | Mounted Men | | | |

1. This implies a relatively late origin for the Colt Dance.

2. Lowie's original transcription of this name is closer to the agency spelling of the name, Cavayo, than is his insertion. Cavayo was born about 1860 and was a member of Tahpony's local band.

3. Much of the following information appears in Lowie (1915:809–10).

4. A number of Comanches named Jack were alive in 1912, but Cavayo, the last-named consultant, was apparently not one of them; thus it is not clear to whom this referred.

All of the row of dancers would go a considerable distance in the dance step.
{Page 19}

The privates wore practically the same costume in all dances, but in the Buffalo Dance anyone having a horned headdress could use it.

The dancers filed out in couples, with an officer on either side carrying a heavy war club and a waist-loop of swift {fox} skin and tassels. Each officer stayed on one side. These officers asked certain men to act as guards for the march.

The best dancers were asked to take the lead. They marched in pairs some distance, forming the arc of a circle.

When the dance started, perhaps only two advanced at first, then others followed.

The managers would bid the dancers to stop, and they would tell about the fight they were going to make, or other public announcements.

At the same time, they would make motions several times {Page 20} while drummers struck their drums.

Crow Dance = *tuwikaaʔnɨhka*. The custom was that no dog must advance before the dancers, and that if he did, he would be shot. Women told their children to look out for dogs prized by them.

Only the Yapai danced the Crow Dance.[1] In each dance, the dancers marched through the entire camp. The dancers imitated the motion of a crow bird.

The Honey, or Wasp Eaters, occupied the border of the Rio Grande, which is a great bee district. The Penatɨhka {Page 21} were on the plains part of Oklahoma. On the panhandle of Texas and Colorado were the Kwaharɨ. The Nokoni occupied the mountain region of Oklahoma; the Yapai were further north.[2]

Yamparɨhka = *ɨtsɨʔitU* ⟨tiwowa⟩ (cold territory).

Kwaharɨ = *kuhtsutɨhka* (Buffalo Eaters).

Penatɨhka = *tɨhkapUwaatɨ* (without any meat to eat).

Nokoni = *ta nɨmɨ* (our people).[3]

The Kwaharɨ danced the Colt Dance (*tuepukunɨhka*) and Horse Dance.

The Nokoni danced the Fox Dance (*waaninɨhka*).

The Penatɨhka also danced the Fox Dance preferably.

All clans had their favorite, but not exclusive, dances.
{Page 22}

Even the Buffalo Dance was danced separately by each band with its own officers.[4]

When the Master decided that it was time to stop dancing and take action, they acted accordingly.[5] This general council and dance might last weeks or a month.

The Master has been injured in some way by an enemy.

This was given for preparation for the warpath.

---

1. Lowie 1915:810.
2. Lowie 1915:809. The distinction between the "Honey Eaters" and the Penatɨhka is unexplained.
3. If analyzed as given, this appears to be *tahɨ* 'our', *nɨmɨ* 'people'. This accords better than the usual translation 'liver eater'.
4. Lowie 1915:810.
5. Lowie 1915:811.

The day before they started, the clans were called out and they all came out on horse. At the head, they rode two by two, otherwise single file in general. The women had a buffalo hide brought out and sticks for some men to beat (⟨ni´otsāīt⟩).

They have a special song for the occasion. The men were on one side, the women were on other. They held the hide and beat with the sticks.

{Page 23}

The Master sang alone at first, then all joined.

The next day, they were ready for their journey.

The Master of Ceremonies led in front.

Big Horses, Horses, Little Horses were different company's names. Clans have nothing to do with this.

Crows, Foxes, Drum, were other companies. The Buffalo was not a special company.[1]

If nothing special happened in war, a man would stick with his first chosen company. In council, they might join any friend they wanted to join. There was no special relationship of friendship between members of one company.

{Page 24}

Dew Claw[2]

As they approached a hostile camp, they appointed scouts or guides to look for the enemy. When they came back, they called people to nearby. Then the leader sang one.

Buffalo dung was piled up. The leader, in front of it, sang a war song. The dung was an oath that the camp was really located at certain place. Also, a place for the Com{anches} to return to.[3]

(The Big Horse dance was associated with dewclaw rattles.)

There was an inquiry as to who killed the enemy, and there were public thanks for those who thus avenged the injury. Scalps were put on a pole. The main chief stripped to the waist and painted himself black. He carried the scalp and they {page 25} returned home. He rode ahead. A war song was sung. He held the scalp aloft. The women, etc., saw the scalps and knew that they were revenged. The returners fired guns.

Horse and Little Horse had rawhide rattles with yellowhammer feathers and buffalo sashes not with head slit.

Mr. Fulbright told me the following story illustrating the confiscation proceedings mentioned above page 10. A man had been guilty of adultery with another man's wife, and the offender's brother-in-law confiscated the culprit's horse, one of his hogs, and some other property. All comprised under the term *nanɨwokɨ* to the offended husband. However, each property was regarded as undesirable and the new owner disposed of the horse for $5 and the

1. Lowie 1915:809 (?).
2. These words are in the upper margin of the page, along with other doodles. They may be related to the reference to the Big Horses using dewclaw rattles farther down on the page.
3. Lowie 1915:811.

hog (really worth $10) for $2 to Mr. Fulbright. As Mr. Fulbright saw nothing about the horse to prevent him from riding it, he did so freely, but all the Indians looked down on him for it, so that he finally exchanged it for another belonging to another white man. Against this, the Indians had no objection.

Dr. Rowell's remark on page 1 was not confirmed by Mr. Fulbright, who said both Kiowa and Comanche women plucked out their eyebrows.

Appendix A

Sources of Ethnographic Information in Hoebel (1940)

In Appendix A, I have attempted to link specific ethnographic statements in Hoebel's *Political Organization and Law-Ways of the Comanche Indians* to specific entries in the Field Notes. This analysis revealed a number of possible relationships:

- Ethnographic statements whose cited sources can be confirmed in the notes; in these cases, no further comment other than the reference is made
- Ethnographic statements with cited sources, but which are attributed to a different consultant in the notes; in these cases, the cited consultant is listed in plain text, the proper consultant in braces, and the date given is the correct date
- Ethnographic statements with cited sources, but whose source cannot be identified in the notes; these are noted as "Not Found"
- Ethnographic statements without cited sources, but whose sources can be confirmed in the notes; no further comment is made
- Ethnographic statements without cited sources whose sources are provisionally identified; these are noted as "?"
- Ethnographic statements without cited sources and which cannot be confirmed in the notes; these are cited as "Unattested"
- Ethnographic statements based upon the notes of Dr. Jeannette Mirsky[1]; these are cited as "Mirsky"

HOEBEL (1940) CONCORDANCE

PAGE	SUBJECT	SOURCE	DATE
6	"Horned Toad's Wife"	Unattested	
11	Esananaka	Quassyah	July 5
12	Life Cycle: Marriage	Herman Asenap	June 30

1. Mirsky visited the Comanches around 1935. Her primary consultant was a Comanche named Talker, who is otherwise unidentified. Extensive search has failed to turn up any of Mirsky's notes.

PAGE	SUBJECT	SOURCE	DATE
55	Case 8: Land Dispute	Quassyah	July 5
56	Case 9: Levirate Claim	Frank Chekovi	Undated
58	Case 10: Buffalo Robe vs Cliff	Tahsuda {Herkeyah}	Undated
58	Case 11: Whipping Waived	Post Oak Jim	July 24
60, n.12	". . . fighting with rifles . . ."	Post Oak Jim	Not Found
62	Case 12: Wife Absconding	Nemaruibetsi	July 31
66	Case 13: Murder	Mirsky (Talker)	
68	Case 14: Horse Slaying/Murder	Tahsuda	Undated
		Mirsky (Talker)	
69	Case 15: Horse Slaying/Murder	Tahsuda	Undated
71	Case 16: Brown Robe vs. Crazy Bear	Tahsuda	Undated
		Nemaruibetsi	July 31
	Story of Taʔsiʔwooʔ	Nemaruibetsi	July 31
	"His feeling for his son . . . "	Mirsky (Kwasi[1])	
72	Murder: Patricide	Tahsuda	Not Found
73	Wife Desertion/Murder	Rhoda Asenap	Not Found
	Murder	Nemaruibetsi	Not Found
74	Case 17: Murder	Post Oak Jim {Howard White Wolf}	August 2
75	Case 18: Wife Destroys Husband	Mirsky (Talker)	
76	Case 19: Accidental Homicide	Howard White Wolf	August 2
78	Case 20: Sorcery	Post Oak Jim	Undated
79	Case 20a: Sorcery	Naiya	July 6
	Case 20b: Sorcery	Mirsky (Talker)	
80	Case 21: Sorcery Contest	Frank Chekovi	August 2
81	Sorcery Contest	Quassyah {Niyah}	July 6
82	Cheyenne Dog Soldiers/Comanche tipi	Howard White Wolf	Not Found
	Premature Hunting: Watchers	Niyah	July 7
	Premature Hunting: Case	Niyah	July 7
85	'No Bed'	Nemaruibetsi{Herkeyah}	Undated
	Medicine Competition	Passim; See Index	
86	Beaver Ceremony as Divination	Post Oak Jim	July 14
	Peyote as Sorcery Divination	Post Oak Jim	July 11
88	Case 22: Repelling Curse	Post Oak Jim	July 11
89	Case 23: Sorcery	Tahsuda {Frank Chekovi}	Undated III
91	Case 24: Sorcery	Quassyah {Naiya}	July 27
92	Case 25: Sorcery	Herkeyah	Undated
93	Case 26: Sorcery	Herkeyah	Undated
94	Case 27: Sorcery	Mirsky (Talker)	
97	Case 28: Adultery	Nemaruibetsi	July 31

1. Kwasi is otherwise unidentified; perhaps Quassyah.

PAGE	SUBJECT	SOURCE	DATE
97	Adultery: Ohawura	Herkeyah	Undated
98	Case 29: Adultery; Denial of Guilt	Naiya {Tahsuda}	Undated
99	Conditional Curse	Herkeyah	Undated
100	Case 30: Adultery; Conditional Curse	Tahsuda	Undated
101	Case 31: Adultery	Tahsuda {Nemaruibetsi}	August 8
102	Ordeal	Tahsuda	Undated
103	Ordeal: Example	Norton Tahquechi (in Tahsuda)	Undated
	Buffalo Tongue Ceremony	Mirsky	
105	Case 32: Coup Sustained by Oath	Tahsuda	Undated
106	Oath: Scattering Buffalo Chips	Passim; See Index	
107	Case 33: Illegitimacy	Tahsuda	Undated
108	"they did not know about the harm ..."	Herman Asenap	Not Found
	Case 34: Incest	Mirsky (Talker)	
110	" . . . niece-uncle marriage . . . "	Unattested	
	Rising Sun/Wide Feet	Unattested	
	Incest	Herman Asenap	July 7
111	Case 35: Rape	Herkeyah	August 13
	Grave Robbery	Unattested	
112	Case 36: Grave Robbery	Naiya	July 8
	Suicide	Post Oak Jim	Not Found
	Suicide	Post Oak Jim	Not Found
113	Case 37: Adultery and Retaliations	Teneverka	Undated
114	Case 38: Suicide	Tahsuda	Undated
115	Case 39: Suicide	Mirsky (Talker)	
119	Animals; 'Mákutavai'	Post Oak Jim	July 18
	Killing dogs "Bad luck"	Post Oak Jim	July 18
	Animal Liability: Dog Bite	Herkeyah	Undated
	Horse Kick	Post Oak Jim	July 18
	Division of Hunt	Herman Asenap	June 30
		Niyah	July 7
		Herkeyah	Undated
	" . . . hard winter . . ."	Nemaruibetsi	Not Found
120	Arrow marks	Quassyah	August
	Arrow makers	Quassyah	August
	Women saddle makers	Herman Asenap	June 30
	Saddles	Post Oak Jim	July 18
	Divorce: Ownership of tipi	Howard White Wolf	August 4
	Inheritance	Herman Asenap	June 30
	Disposition of Medicine	Herman Asenap	June 30
	Disposition of Property	Atauvich	August 9
		Teneverka	Undated
		Tahsuda	Not Found
	Disposition of Property: Suicide	Mirsky (Talker)	

PAGE	SUBJECT	SOURCE	DATE
124	Case 40a: Estate: Piarupsima's Horses	Teneverka	Undated
	Case 40b: Estate: Piarupsima's Horses	Tahsuda	Not Found
	Case 40c: Estate: Piarupsima's Horses	Nemaruibetsi	August 1
	Case 40d: Estate: Piarupsima's Horses	Mirsky (Talker)	
126	Contract: Curing	Passim; See Index	
	Contract: Curing: circle to left	Frank Chekovi	Undated III
	Contract: Curing: consultants	Frank Chekovi	Undated III
	Contract: Curing: Pertooahvoniquo	Niyah	July 27
127	". . . glad to help out . . ."	Unattested	
	". . . certain woman . . ."	George Koweno	July 27
	". . . honorable man . . ."	Niyah	July 6
	". . . Medicine Men hid . . ."	Frank Chekovi	Undated III
	Medicine: Transfer	Post Oak Jim	July 14

APPENDIX B

Sources of Ethnographic Information
in Wallace and Hoebel (1952)

In Appendix B, I have attempted to trace the materials in Ernest Wallace and E. Adamson Hoebel's *The Comanches: Lords of the South Plains*, to information recorded in the Field Notes. I was able to connect 428 statements in Wallace and Hoebel to the Notes, although less than half are explicitly cited (192; see also Thurman 1982). The proportionate contributions of the various consultants are as follows.

CONSULTANT	STATEMENTS	PERCENTAGE
Post Oak Jim	107	25
Niyah	71	17
Frank Chekovi	52	12
Herman Asenap	47	11
Howard White Wolf	45	11
Tahsuda	24	6
Nemaruibetsi	22	5
Quassyah	18	4
Rhoda Asenap	11	2
Herkeyah	9	2
Norton Tahquechi	8	2
George Koweno	6	1
Teneverka	6	1
Atauvich	1	>1
Frank Moetah	1	>1
Ohataipa	0	0
Pedahny	0	0

In the concordance below, the same protocol applies as in Appendix A. In addition, counter instances—when a consultant directly contradicts published material—are indicated with an asterisk.

WALLACE AND HOEBEL (1952) CONCORDANCE

PAGE	SUBJECT	SOURCE	DATE
9	Story: Origin	Post Oak Jim	July 17
24	"That was [name of band] way . . . "	Unattested	
25	Bands: Penanʉʉ	Quassyah	July 5
26	Bands: Nokoni	Howard White Wolf	July 31
	Bands: Tʉtsʉnoyʉhkanʉʉ	Quassyah	July 5
28	Bands: KwaihuukInʉʉ	Teneverka	Undated
30	Bands: Otʉtaʔoo	Tahsuda	Undated
	Bands: Woʔanʉʉ	Frank Chekovi	August 3
	Bands: Pahʉrʉya	Tahsuda	Undated
36	"Some men loved their horses . . ."	Post Oak Jim	Not Found
	". . . demand favorite horse . . ."	Frank Chekovi	Undated
37	Nanʉwokʉ	Frank Chekovi	Undated
39	Piarʉpsima's horses	Teneverka	Undated
39–40	Piarʉpsima's size	Howard White Wolf	August 3
42	Lassoing Wild Horses	Niyah ?	July 10
	Lassoing Wild Horses	*Post Oak Jim	July 11
	Horses: Wild Horses	Post Oak Jim	July 11
44	Horse Raids	Rhoda Asenap	July 7
46	Horse Names	Niyah	July 10
	Horses: Mares	Niyah	July 10
	Horses: Gelding	*Post Oak Jim	July 11
47	Horses: Gelding	Post Oak Jim	July 11
	Horses: Care	Niyah	July 10
	Horses: Breaking	Post Oak Jim	July 11
	"Contemporary Comanches . . ."	Unattested	
49	Horse Race Medicines	Post Oak Jim	July 11
50	Horse Races	Post Oak Jim	July 11
51	Story: Owner of the Buffalo	Tahsuda	Undated
56	". . . unless moonlight . . ."	Post Oak Jim	July 17?
57–61	Hunting	Niyah	July 7
	Hunting: Premature Hunting	Niyah	July 7
	Hunting: Scouts	Niyah	July 7
	Hunting: Division of Hunt	Niyah	July 7
	Hunting: Claims on Meat	Niyah	July 7
	Hunting: Division of Labor	Niyah	July 7
	Hunting: Buffalo	Niyah	July 7
	Arrows: Marks	Niyah	July 7
58	Hunting: Danger	Niyah	July 7
59	Hunting: Falls	Niyah	July 7
	Hunting: Falls	*Howard White Wolf	August 4
60	Hunting: Butchering	Post Oak Jim	Not Found

PAGE	SUBJECT	SOURCE	DATE
60		Niyah	July 7
	Clothing: Sinew	Niyah	July 7
61	Hunting: Buffalo Horses	Howard White Wolf	July 31
	Buffalo Calling Medicine	Post Oak Jim	Undated?
	Omens: Horned Lizards	Post Oak Jim	July 13
67	Hunting: Antelope Drives	Niyah	July 7
68	Hunting: Antelope Drives	Post Oak Jim	Undated
69	Hunting: Coyote	Post Oak Jim	July 18
	Animal Powers: Coyote	Post Oak Jim	July 11
	Animals: Dogs	Post Oak Jim	July 18
	Animals: Dogs	Nemaruibetsi	August 8
71	Foods: Stone Boiling	*Herman Asenap	July 7
		Post Oak Jim	July 12
72	Food Plants: Berries	Post Oak Jim	July 12
		Post Oak Jim	July 26
		Howard White Wolf	August 8
72–73	Food Plants: Roots	Post Oak Jim	July 12
		Howard White Wolf	August 3
74	Food: Pumpkins; Corn	Niyah	July 6
	Food: Alcohol	Howard White Wolf	August 3
	Smoking: Tobacco	Niyah	July 6
	Containers	Passim; See Index	
74–75	Food: Mealtimes	Niyah	July 8
75	Etiquette: Hospitality	Niyah	July 8
77–78	Clothing	Howard White Wolf	August 2
78	Clothing: Moccasins	Quassyah	August
		Frank Chekovi	Undated
		Howard White Wolf	August 8
78–79	Clothing: Winter	Nemaruibetsi	August 8
		Herkeyah	Undated
		Howard White Wolf	August 8
79	Clothing: Scalp Shirt	Niyah	July 6
80	Utensils: Awl	Post Oak Jim	July 11
81–82	Clothing: Robes	Nemaruibetsi	August 8
82	Clothing: Fur Caps	Nemaruibetsi	August 8
83	Adornment: Hair: Braid	*Howard White Wolf	August 2
		Post Oak Jim	July 24
	Adornment: Eyebrows	Niyah	July 6
	Hair Brush	Howard White Wolf	August 2
		Frank Chekovi	July 25
	Adornment: Hair	Nemaruibetsi	Undated
	Adornment: Hair Care	*Howard White Wolf	August 2
84	Adornment: Face Paint	Frank Chekovi	August 11

Page	Subject	Source	Date
84	Adornment: Earrings	Nemaruibetsi	Undated
		Frank Chekovi	Undated I
85	Clothing	Nemaruibetsi	Undated
		Howard White Wolf	August 2
86	Adornment: Hair	Frank Chekovi	August 11
	Clothing: Children	Nemaruibetsi	August 8
	Containers: natᵾsakᵾna	Howard White Wolf	August 1
		Nemaruibetsi	August 8
	Containers: tunawosA	Frank Chekovi	Undated
86–88	Tipis	Niyah	July 6
		Howard White Wolf	August 1
87	Tipis: Tipi Cover	Nemaruibetsi	August 8
	Tipis: Furnishings	Howard White Wolf	August 1
	Container	*Post Oak Jim	July 26
87–88	Tipis	Howard White Wolf	August 1
		Herman Asenap	June 30
88	Tipis: Skins for	*Niyah	July 7
88	Tipis: Ear Flaps	Niyah	July 6
89	Arbors	Niyah	July 18
	Tipis: Painted	*Herman Asenap	July 7
89	Arbors	Niyah	July 10
	Fire Making	Post Oak Jim	July 11
		Howard White Wolf	August 1
90	Beds	Niyah	July 6
	Beds	*Howard White Wolf	August 1
91	Utensils: Pottery	Herman Asenap	June 30
	Food: Stone Boiling	Post Oak Jim	July 12
	Food: Stone Boiling	*Herman Asenap	July 7
	Utensils: Spoons	Frank Chekovi	August 11
	Utensils	*Herman Asenap	June 30
	Baskets	*Howard White Wolf	August 1
	Utensils: Digging Sticks	Post Oak Jim	July 7
		Frank Chekovi	August 11
94–95	Hide Work: Buckskin Making	Howard White Wolf	August 4
		Frank Chekovi	August 11
96	Tipis: Construction	Howard White Wolf	July 31
	Saddle Making	Howard White Wolf	July 31
97	Saddle Blankets	Frank Chekovi	August 11
	Women's Saddles	Post Oak Jim	July 18
	Horses: Stirrup	Post Oak Jim	July 8
	Smoking: Tobacco	Post Oak Jim	July 13
	Tobacco from Mexico	Post Oak Jim	July 13
	Cigarette Wrappers	Post Oak Jim	July 12

PAGE	SUBJECT	SOURCE	DATE
98	Smoking: Pipes	Post Oak Jim	July 11
		Herman Asenap	July 7
100	Bows	Post Oak Jim	July 11
		*Herman Asenap	June 30
		Quassyah	Undated
101	Bow and Arrow	Post Oak Jim	July 13
	Bowstring	Naiya	July 7
		Post Oak Jim	July 12
		Post Oak Jim	July 13
101–2	Other Tribes' Arrows	Post Oak Jim	July 11
104	Arrows	Herman Asenap	June 30
		Post Oak Jim	July 11
101; 105	Bows; Bow Making	Howard White Wolf	August 1
	Arrows: Straighten with Teeth	Herman Asenap	June 30
		Niyah	July 7
102	Arrow Smoother	Quassyah	August
102–3	Arrows: Grooves	Quassyah	August
103	Arrows: Fletching	Howard White Wolf	July 31
		Howard White Wolf	August 1
		Quassyah	August
104	Arrows: Arrowheads	Post Oak Jim	July 12
105	Arrows: Poison	Post Oak Jim	July 12
		Howard White Wolf	August 1
		Quassyah	August
106	Bow Guard	Post Oak Jim	July 13
		Niyah	July 22
		Howard White Wolf	August 1
	Arrows Across River	Post Oak Jim	Undated
	Shields	Niyah	July 6
		Post Oak Jim	July 13
		Quassyah	August
		Post Oak Jim	July 26
108	Shields: Medicine	Niyah	July 8
		Post Oak Jim	July 12
		Post Oak Jim	July 13
109	Shields: Medicine	Rhoda Asenap	July 12
		Niyah	July 6
	Medicine: Transfer	Niyah	July 6
	War: Shields: Painting by Peyote	Post Oak Jim	July 13
110	"Hooked Lance"	Lowie 1912; 1915:811	
	Lances: Size	Quassyah	August
	Lances	Frank Chekovi	Undated II
	Lances: Beaded	Frank Chekovi	Undated II

PAGE	SUBJECT	SOURCE	DATE
128	Hunting Hummingbirds	Frank Chekovi	August 10
		Norton Tahquechi	Undated
	Hunting: Bull Bats	Norton Tahquechi	Undated
	Hunting: Grasshoppers	Norton Tahquechi	Undated
	Fun with Insects	Norton Tahquechi	Undated
	Arrow Weed	Post Oak Jim	July 13
	Slings	Herman Asenap	June 30
		Post Oak Jim	July 14
	Games: Boys Horsing Around	Post Oak Jim	July 18
		Post Oak Jim	July 26
	Life Cycle: First Sex	Post Oak Jim	July 26
		Post Oak Jim	Undated
129	Games: Bear Game	Post Oak Jim	July 18
	Games: Guessing Game	Post Oak Jim	July 18
	Games: *nanipʉka*	Post Oak Jim	July 18
	Beliefs: Thunderstorms	Niyah	July 6
130	Brother-Sister Avoidance	Herman Asenap	June 30
		Nemaruibetsi	July 31
	Adolescent Lodge	Passim; See Index	
131	Medicine: Vision Quest	Post Oak Jim	July 13
	First War Party	Niyah	July 6
	Give Away/Shake Down Dance	Tahsuda	Undated
132	Wife Sharing	Post Oak Jim	July 19
	Marriage	Post Oak Jim	July 19
	Marriage: Brother-Sister	George Koweno	July 21?
	Marriage: Age	Herman Asenap	June 30
		Rhoda Asenap	July 12
133	Bride Price	*Herman Asenap	June 30
	Bride Service	Passim; See Index	
	"Boys seemed to stay . . ."	Post Oak Jim	Undated
	Courting	Herman Asenap	July 7
134	Marriage	Herman Asenap	July7
	Courting: Go Between	Herman Asenap	July7
		Frank Chekovi	August 4
	Courting	George Koweno	July 21
	Marriage: Bride Service	Niyah	July 7
	Medicine: Love Medicine	Nemaruibetsi	August 8
136	Marriage: No Ceremony	Herman Asenap	June 30
	Marriage: Residence	Herman Asenap	June 30
137	Marriage	Tahsuda	Undated
	Marriage: Framing Girl	Tahsuda	Undated
137–38	Marriage: Elopement	Frank Chekovi	August 4
	"In an arranged marriage . . ."	Frank Chekovi	August 4

PAGE	SUBJECT	SOURCE	DATE
152		Niyah	July 25
		Teneverka	Undated
		Nemaruibitsi	August 1
155	Revealing Dreams	Norton Tahquechi	Undated
156–58	Medicine: Vision Quest	Passim; See Index	
159	Animals: Eagles	Post Oak Jim	July 18
160	Charms	Tahsuda	Undated
	Crow Feather Charms	Post Oak Jim	July 24
	Crow Feather Arrows	Tahsuda	Undated
	Stuffed Bat Charm	Post Oak Jim	Undated
	Medicine: Transfer	Post Oak Jim	July 24
161	Masiitotopʉ	Post Oak Jim	July 14
162	Medicine: Bullet Proof	Post Oak Jim	July 12?
	Medicine: Transfer	Frank Chekovi	Undated
162–64	Medicine: Transfer	Frank Chekovi	Undated
165	Medicine Societies	Post Oak Jim	July 14
		George Koweno	July 21
166	"My office"	Frank Chekovi	Undated III
	" impossible . . ."	Nemaruibetsi	Undated
167	Curing: Payment	Niyah	July 6
	Pertooahvoniquo	Niyah	July 27
	Wolf Medicine	Nemaruibetsi	August 8
168–69	Curing	George Koweno	July 21
169	Climbing Spells	Frank Chekovi	Undated III
	Curing: Turkey Necklace	Nemaruibetsi	August 8
169–70	Curing: Sore Throat	Nemaruibetsi	August 8
170	Curing: Belly Wound	Niyah	July 27
	Curing: Headache, etc.	Post Oak Jim	July 25
	Curing: Toothache	Nemaruibetsi	August 8
	Curing: Cavities	Niyah	July 27
171	Curing: Mupits' Bones	Herman Asenap	June 30
		Howard White Wolf	August 1
		Howard White Wolf	August 3
172	Medicine: Rain Making	Niyah	July 6
	Medicine: Foretelling	Post Oak Jim	July 18
173	Man Who Captured the Ghost	Niyah	July7
174	Ghost Sickness	Frank Chekovi	Undated III
	Medicine: Nʉnʉpi	Passim; See Index	
175	Medicine: Beaver Ceremony	Post Oak Jim	July 14
		George Koweno	July 21
176	Bull Roarer	Post Oak Jim	July 14
181	Council: Smoke Lodge	Tahsuda	Undated
	Smoking: Cigarettes	Post Oak Jim	July 11

PAGE	SUBJECT	SOURCE	DATE
230	Ekamurawa	Nemaruibetsi	July 31
230–32	Nanuwoku	Passim; See Index	
233	Feud	*Post Oak Jim	July 24
	"killing a horse . . ."	Tahsuda	Undated
234	Forced Confession	Herkeyah	Undated
		Rhoda Asenap	July 12
236	Medicine: Sorcery	Frank Chekovi	Undated III
		Rhoda Asenap	July 12
		Herman Asenap	June 30
236–38	Medicine: Competition	Frank Chekovi	August 2
238	Medicine: Sorcery	Niyah	July 6
239	Medicine: Sorcery	Tahsuda	Undated
		Niyah	July 6
		Frank Chekovi	Undated III
240	Rising Sun/Wide Feet	Unattested	
	Rape	Herkeyah	August 13
	Control: Theft	Herman Asenap	June 30
		Quassyah	July 5
		Niyah	July 27
241	Animal Liability	Herkeyah	Undated
	Captives	Passim; See Index	
	Animals: Dogs	Post Oak Jim	July 18
242	Transfer of War Honors	*Howard White Wolf	July 31
		Tahsuda	Undated
243	Disposition of Property	Passim; See Index	
246	Scalps	Passim; See Index	
	Dances: Victory Dance	Niyah	July 6
247	War Story	Teneverka	Undated
	Suicide	Herman Asenap	June 30
248	Oath	Tahsuda	Undated
249	War Honors	Tahsuda	Undated
250	Transfer of War Honors	Tahsuda	Undated
251	War Parties	Passim; See Index	
253	Wife Desertion	Herman Asenap	June 30
	Gender Roles: Female Warriors	Post Oak Jim	July 12
		Rhoda Asenap	July 12
254	Wife Desertion	Rhoda Asenap	July 12
256	War: Revenge	George Koweno	July 21
260	Captives	Niyah	July 10
		Niyah	July 27
		Rhoda Asenap	July 7
261	Life Story	Herkeyah	Undated

APPENDIX C

Sources of Ethnobotanical Information in Carlson and Jones (1940)

In Appendix C, I have attempted to correlate the entries in Table 1 of Carlson and Jones' *Some Uses of Plants by the Comanche Indians* (1940) with their sources in the extant notes. Spelling of the Comanche botanical terms has been normalized to that given in Robinson and Armagost (1990) and the Comanche Cultural Committee (2003).[1] The list is in the order of the scientific name in Carlson and Jones.

Carlson's extant notes do not include any Comanche botanical materials. About two-thirds of the terms detailed in the Carlson and Jones article appear in Wedel's notes.[2] Presumably the remainder were in Carlson's now-missing notes. The missing terms are marked "Unattested." Most of them can be identified and normalized with the Comanche dictionaries. Those that are not in the dictionaries appear in roman type in angle brackets.

For four entries, Carlson and Jones lists the Comanche name as "Not Recorded." However, three of the four had, in fact, been solicited by the Field Party. They have been supplied.

CARLSON AND JONES (1940) CONCORDANCE

SCIENTIFIC NAME	COMANCHE NAME	COMMON NAME	SOURCE
Allium spp	*pakʉʉkA*[3]	Wild onion (large)	Post Oak Jim, July 12
	tʉekʉʉkA[4]	Wild onion (small)	

1. In one case, *Allium*, I have used a slightly different transcription; see the note on that entry.
2. Carlson did, obliquely, credit Wedel as their source: "Mr. Carlson is responsible for the field notes, native terms, and phonetics. Dr. Waldo R. Wedel coöperated with him in the collection of the field data" (1940:518).
3. Post Oak Jim (July 12, p.139) gives this as *pa* 'water', *kʉʉkA* 'onion'. Carlson and Jones (1940) has it as 'large onion'.
4. The Field Party was fairly consistent in transcribing the Comanche morpheme *tʉe* 'small' as some variant of "tidi." Thus, Wedel spells this *tɜdie kɜ:k* and Carlson and Jones (1940) transcribes it as *ťdiekø:k*, both translated as 'small onion'. I have given it as *tʉekʉʉkA*. Both Robinson and Armagost (1990) and the Comanche Cultural Committee (2003) give it as *tʉetʉtaatʉkʉʉkA*

Scientific Name	Comanche Name	Common Name	Source
Ambrosia psilostachya	*woʔanatsʉ*	Western ragweed	HWW,[1] August 3
Amorpha angustifolia	*seheriabi*	False indigo	Nemaribetsi, August 8
Andropogon scorparius	*ekasonipʉ*	Little bluestem grass	Unattested
Argemone intermedia	*pitsi tora*	Prickly poppy	Unattested
Artemisia filifolia	*pasiwona pʉhʉbi*	Silvery wormwood	Unattested
Artemisia ludoviciana	*pohóobi*	Lobed cudweed; white sage	HWW, August 3
Brayodendron texanum	*tuhnaséka*	Mexican persimmon	Post Oak Jim, July 12
Camassia escuelenta	*siiko*	Wild hyacinth; Camass	Post Oak Jim, July 12
Carya illinoensis	*nakkʉtabaʔi*	Pecan	Post Oak Jim, July 26; HWW, August 3
Celtis laevigata	*natsohkweʔ*	Southern hackberry	Post Oak Jim, July 12
Cephalanthus occidentalis	*pesotái*	Buttonbush	HWW, August 3; Nemaribetsi, August 8
Cirsium undulatam	⟨tsɜn⟩[2]	Thistle	Unattested
Cornus asperifolia	*parʉabi*	Dogwood	Herman Asenap, June30; Post Oak Jim, July 11; Niyah, July 27
Coryphanta sp.	*wokwe*	Cactus	Passim, see Index
Crataegus sp.	*tueamawooʔ*[3]	Thornapple; "red haw"	Post Oak Jim, July 12
Crataegus sp.	*tubokóo*[4]	Thornapple; "black haw"	Post Oak Jim, July 12
	wokwekatʉ[5]		Passim, see Index
Croton monanthogynus	*kapIsimawa*	Croton weed[6]	Unattested
Cymopterus acaulis	*tunʉhaa*	Cymopterus	Post Oak Jim, July 12
Diospyros virginiana	*naséka*	Persimmon	Post Oak Jim, July 12
Echinacea sp.	*tuhkunʉ natsU*	Purple coneflower	Unattested
Elymus sp.	*pui tsaseni*	Rye grass	Unattested
Eriogonum longifolium	*ekanatsU*	Eriogonum	Unattested
	⟨ekanaropa⟩		Unattested
Gutierrezia sarothrae	*sanaweha*[7]	Snakeweed	Unattested
	ohayaaʔ[8]		Post Oak Jim, Undated
Helenium autumnale	*tuʔrukúuʔ pahmu*[9]	Sneezeweed	HWW, Aug. 1

1. Howard White Wolf.
2. Robinson and Armagost (1990) has thistle as *poʔayaʔeetʉ*.
3. Robinson and Armagost (1990) has this as 'crabapple', while the Comanche Cultural Committee (2003) has it as 'thorn apple, red haw, little apple'.
4. Carlson and Jones (1940) has this as the fruit.
5. Carlson and Jones (1940) has this as the tree.
6. Also called 'prairie tea'.
7. Robinson and Armagost (1990) has this as 'broomweed, mormon tea.'
8. Robinson and Armagost (1990) has this as 'sunflower.'
9. Literally, 'prairie dog's tobacco'.

SCIENTIFIC NAME	COMANCHE NAME	COMMON NAME	SOURCE
Helenium microcephalum	*natsaakɨsi*	Sneezeweed	Post Oak Jim, July 12
Hoffmanseggia jamesii	*pihtsamuu*[1]	"Camote de raton"; rushpea	Post Oak Jim, July 12
Ilex sp.	"not recorded"	Holly	Unattested
Juglans nigra	*mubitai*	Black walnut	Post Oak Jim, July 26; HWW, Aug. 3
Juniperus virginiana	*ekawaapI*	Juniper; red cedar	Unattested
Lespedeza capitata	*puhi huubA*	Bush clover	Post Oak Jim, July 26
Liatris punctata	*atabitsɨnoi*	Button snakeroot	Unattested
Lophophora williamsii	*wokwe*	Peyote	Passim, see Index
Maclura pomifera	*ohahuupi*	Osage orange	Herman Asenap, June 30; Post Oak Jim, Undated
Malvastrum coccineum	*yokanatsuʔu*	Red false mallow	Unattested
Morus rubra	*etɨhuupi*[2] ⟨*soho bokopI*⟩[3]	Red mulberry	Post Oak Jim, July 12
Nelumbo lutea ?	*kɨrɨʔatsI*	Yellow lotus	Unattested
Nymphaea advena ?	*kɨraita*	Yellow pond lily	Unattested
Opuntia sp.	*wokwéesi*	Prickly pear cactus	Passim; see Index
Petalostemum purpureum	*pakeeso*	Purple prairie clover	Post Oak Jim, July 12
Prosopis glandulosa	*namabitsooni natsohkweʔ*	Mesquite	Post Oak Jim, July 12
Prunus angustifolia	*tɨahpI*	Chickasaw plum	Post Oak Jim, July 12
Prunus spp.	⟨*yusɨkɨiʔ*⟩	Early plums	Unattested
	parɨasɨkɨiʔ	Late summer plums	Unattested
	kusisɨkɨiʔ	Fall plums	Unattested
	natsomƲ	Dried plums	Post Oak Jim, July 26; HWW, August 3
	sɨkɨiʔ	Plum	Post Oak Jim, July 26
Psoralea hypogeae	*ekahkoni*	Indian breadroot	Post Oak Jim, July 12
Quercus marilandica	*tuhuupi*	Blackjack oak	Post Oak Jim, July 12
Quercus sp.	*paʔsa ponii*	Oak	HWW, August 3
Rhus glabra	⟨*duməyo*⟩	Smooth sumac	Unattested[4]
Rhus trilobata	*tatsipƲ*	Skunkbush	Unattested
Ribes odoratum	*poʔapokopI*	Wild currant	Post Oak Jim, July 12
Salix sp.	*ohasɨhɨ*	Willow	Unattested

1. Robinson and Armagost (1990) has this as "lit., milky root (*pitsipƲ* 'milky', *mu* 'root')." The Comanche Cultural Committee (2003) gives *pihtsamuu* as 'dandelion; milky-rooted plant'. Both also have as an additional gloss, 'legume'.
2. Robinson and Armagost (1990) has this as 'osage orange, hedge apple, bois d'arc'.
3. Robinson and Armagost (1990) has this as 'hackberry'.
4. See Post Oak Jim, July 13, for sumac leaves used for smoking.

Scientific Name	Comanche Name	Common Name	Source
Sapindus drummondii	*otɄmitsonaaʔ*	Soapberry[1]	Unattested
Smilax bona-nox	*tamotsoʔi*	Greenbriar	Post Oak Jim, July 11
Solanum sp.	*tohpotsotsii*	Nightshade	HWW, August 3
Sophora secundiflora	"not recorded"	Mescal bean	
Typha latifolia	*pisibuniʔ*	Cattail	Unattested
Vitus spp.	*natsomukwe*	Grape	Post Oak Jim, July 12
Yucca louisianensis	*mumutsi*	Yucca	Post Oak Jim, July 12
Zanthoxylum americanum	*kunanatsu*	Prickly ash	HWW, August 3
Unidentified	*ekamistaaʔ*	Barrel cactus	Post Oak Jim, July 12
Unidentified	⟨itse⟩		Unattested
	⟨timeyhǝ⟩		Unattested
Unidentified	*kusipokopI*		Post Oak Jim, July 12
Unidentified	*kusiwɄɄnɄ*	{black haws?}	Post Oak Jum, July 25?
Unidentified	⟨mawitsɔk⟩		Unattested
Unidentified	*nɄmɄ rɄassI*	[perfume]	Unattested
Unidentified	*paiyapI*		Post Oak Jim, July 12
Unidentified	*puhu natsu*	Red false mallow	Unattested
	peher		Unattested
Unidentified	*poiya*		Unattested
Unidentified	*ketanarɄhka*		Post Oak Jim, July 12
Unidentified	*sehetsitsina*		Post Oak Jim, July 12; HWW, August 1
Unidentified	*tabahko*		Post Oak Jim, July 12
Unidentified	*totohtu*		Post Oak Jim, July 12
Unidentified	*tsunIsu*		Post Oak Jim, July 12

1. Frank Chekovi (Undated II) and Webster's New World Dictionary (1951) gives "chinaberry" as an alternative name for soapberry.

APPENDIX D

Comanche Lexicon

natsomukwe, bot., 'grapes', 140

natᵾsakᵾna, 'leather bag', 264

⟨na'a⟩, 'matchbox' ?, 127

⟨nebekᵾ⟩, play in the stick game, 324

⟨ni'otsāīt⟩, 'pre-war social dance', 137, 491

⟨nimɛnanawo'haitsnap⟩, related to 'friendship', 266, 270

Nokoni, Comanche division ethnonym, Those Who Return, 348

nomᵾne, 'leader', 316, 326

nomᵾnewapᵾ, 'leader', 316

Noyᵾhka, Comanche division ethnonym, 13, 46, 56, 75, 129, 134, 194

nᵾmᵾkuhtsu', 'buffalo', lit. 'our meat', 81

Nᵾmᵾnᵾᵾ, ethnonym, Comanche, 45

Nᵾmᵾrᵾhka, ethnonym, Man Eater, Tonkawa 278, 339

nᵾmᵾtokᵾ, 'grandfather', 365

nᵾnapi, 'little people', 252, 253

oha esi, horse name, 'yellow gray', 115

ohaahnakatᵾ, 'he has yellow armpits', nickname for Coyote, 110, 353

ohaekapItᵾ, horse name, 'yellow-red', 115

ohahuupI, bot., 'yellow wood, Osage orange, 41, 364

ohanakI, horse name, 'yellow ears', 115

Ohapia, pers. name, Yellow Mother, 465

ohAsapU, 'yellow dye', 128

ohayaa, bot., 'sunflower', 363

Ohiwi, pers. name, 383

ohna'a', 'salt', 403

omotoi, 'straight pipe', 'bone pipe', 127

Onawia, pers. name, Gap In Salt, 50, 119, 465, 466

⟨oranansewekai⟩ ⟨ɔrɘnansɜwɜkai⟩, 'great spirit', 246

otsi, 'knee', 126

otsinᵾhka, 'knee dance', 126, 277

otᵾkUma', horse name, 'sorrell' lit. 'brown male', 115

otᵾmitsonaa', bot., 'mountain ash', 'soap berry', 398

Otᵾta'oo', Comanche band ethnonym, Burnt Meat, 404

oyóotᵾ', 'leather case' 364

Paaroponi, pers. name, Pahdopony, Water Measurer, (See How Deep the Water Is), 79, 394

paasitsI, 'sleet', 161

paatsasune, 'arrow shaft smoother', 391

Pahaipiap, pers. name, Big Crow, 440

paha', reciprocal father's sister/mother's brother, 308, 367, 368

Pahkeah, pers. name, Stiff Robe, 12

PahmukUsi, pers. name, Gray Tobacco, 381

pahtsikwasi, 'opossum', 358

paiyapI, medicinal plant, 139

pakeetso, root plant food, 139

PakikᵾnI, pers. name, Dry Tipi, 408

pakᵾᵾkA, bot., 'water onion', 139

⟨pakɘtusas⟩, 'arrow poison', 391

⟨Pananaitᵾ⟩, Comanche band ethnonym, Those Who Live Higher, 403

panihputᵾ, 'up' or 'above', 104

Panukanop, pers. name, Pownitannup, Tobacco Man, 467

⟨papitsoin⟩, 'ordeal', 406

paraibo, 'chief', 16, 26, 56, 58, 163, 187, 288, 293, 316, 332, 333, 343–345, 347, 348, 405, 410, 420, 449, 450, 454, 460

paraibo kwᵾhᵾ', 'chief wife', 362

⟨parewa⟩, 'marrow', 54

parᵾa, 'bear', 46

Parᵾakuhma, pers. name, Male Bear, 38, 46, 50, 54, 373, 392, 450, 455, 456, 458, 463, 464

ParᵾanakItsa'nika', pers. name, Bear Earring, 383

Parᵾasᵾmᵾno, pers. name, Ten Bears, 23, 30, 45, 47, 54, 47, 49–51, 118, 119, 407, 417

parᵾabi, 'dogwood', 46

Parᵾhᵾya, Comanche band ethnonym, Water Horse, 389, 404, 405, 408

Parᵾhᵾyatai, pers. name, Elk's Vulva, 416

Pasuwakitsu, pers. name, 384

⟨patarub⟩, bot., 'peyote juice', 198

Patchokoni, pers. name, Otter Belt, 411

patsi', 'older sister', 304, 307, 462

tonop, bot., a fruit, 140

topₑ, 'shield',66, 168, 339, 392

topₑtsonika, 'shield cover', 392

tosa, 'white', 115

Tosamareah, pers. name, White Husband, 383

tosaníibi, 'white corn', 346

Tosawa, pers. name, White Knife, 50

tosaʔesi, horse name, 'white gray', 115

totohtₑ, bot., a root, 138

Toyop, pers. name, 380–383, 385, 386

toʔroponiiʔ, bot., plant with yellow flowers, 139, 379

Tsakaʔai, pers. name, 207

tseena, 'fox', 192

tseenahaₑrₑʔ,'trap', 196

tsikarehi, 'spear', 267

tsipitoko, a snake 249, 250

tsisti, baby talk, 'visitor', 396

tsitsinₑ, baby talk, 'mother', 396

Tsiʔtsi, pers. name, 192

⟨tso:⟩, 7,

tsomonapU, 'beaded mocassin', 224

tsooʔ, 'great-grand-parent/child', 368

tsotsooʔni, 'meningitis', 314, 458

tsuhni korohkO, 'bone necklace', 358

Tsuhnip, pers name 'bones', Chonips, 307

tsukuhpₑʔ, 'old', 7, 374, 403

tsunₑsₑ, bot., root plant food, 139

tₑbitsikahni, 'real tipi', 345

tₑbitsinahaitsIna, 'real friend', 211, 212

tₑbitsipaʔsa ponii, bot., a small round nut; filbert?, 337

tₑbitsiwaapI, bot., 'juniper ' 364, 337

tₑebasuuʔ, 'quail', 426

tuekₑₑkA, bot. 'little onion', 139

tₑepetₑʔ, 'young girl', 403

Tuepukunₑₑ,'Little Pony Society', 351

tueʔₑtsₑʔimua,'getting cold month', 161

tₑhkakahni, 'eating tipi', 345

tₑhkatayuʔni,'meat grinder', 372

tuhkaʔnaaiʔ, 'night', 69

Tₑhkaʔwaatₑ, Comanche band ethnonym, No Meat, 490

tuhkₑhunubI, Dark Creek, 344

tuhna, bot., Plains springparsley, 138

tuhnaséka, bot., 'black persimmons', 140

tuhsanabo, horse name, 'black paint', 115

tuhunakI, horse name, 'black ears', 115

tuhuniya, horse name, 'yellow with black mane', 115

tuhunuhka, 'fear dance', 126

tuhupI, 'black stain', 160

Tuhₑpₑ, pers. name, Hide, 386

tuibihtsiʔ, 'young man' 301, 302, 374, 381, 403, 459, 479

tuinₑhpₑʔ, 'young man', 374

⟨Tukabit⟩, pers. name, 347

TukanItₑ, pers. name, 'night', 263, 347

tukuhma, horse name, 'black horse', 115

tumutsi, 404

tumutsi, 'black hill', 404

tunawosa, 'leather case', 262

tₑnoorₑ, 'hunchback', 214

tupIsikUmaʔ, horse name, 'dark bay', 115

Tₑpiwokwe, pers. name, Rocky Thorn, 420

tupokopI, bot., 'black haws', 139

Tupₑsahunuʔbi, Black Paint River, 128

tₑrahyapₑ, 'sweet meat', 54

tusanaboʔ, horse name, 'black paint', 115

tₑsibeʔ, 'adze-like hide scraper', 309

⟨tusoetsekin⟩,'shakedown dance', 414

Tₑtaatₑ, pers. name, 'little', 306, 307

Tutsanoyₑhkanₑₑ, Comanche band ethnonym, Bad Campers, 46

Tₑtsahkₑnₑₑ, Comanche band ethnonym, Sewing People, 404

Tₑtsiktoke, pers. name, 384

tₑtsₑkaka, sound made by crows, 430

tₑtsₑkamarₑ, sound made by crows, 356

tₑtsₑkom, sound made by crows, 429, 430

Tuwikaaʔ, Crow or Raven Society, 358

Tuwikaaʔnₑhka, Crow Dance, 490

Tuwinₑₑ, Crow or Raven Society, 485

tuʔarₑkaa, 'black deer', 86

tuʔrukúuʔ pahmu, 'prairie dog's tobacco', 315

ₑhaitsIma, 'your friend', 375

ₑkₑruibihtsiʔ,'young boy', 403

References

Abel, Annie Heloise
  1915   The American Indian as Slaveholder and Secessionist: An Omitted Chapter in the Diplomatic History of the Southern Confederacy. Cleveland: Arthur H. Clark Co.

Attocknie, Francis Joseph
  MS.   The Life of Ten Bears and Other Stories. Manuscript in Thomas Kavanagh's Possession.

Babb, Theodore A.
  1912   In the Bosom of the Comanches: A Thrilling Tale of Savage Indian Life, Massacre and Captivity, Truthfully Told by a Surviving Captive; Texas Borderland Perils and Scenes Depicted; The Closing Days of the Trying Indian Struggles upon the Frontiers of Texas. Dallas: Press of John F. Worley.

Bailey, Garrick A.
  2001   Osage. *In* Handbook of North American Indians, Vol. 13, Plains, Raymond J. DeMallie, vol. ed., William C. Sturtevant, gen. ed., pt. 1, pp. 476–96. Washington: Smithsonian Institution.

Berlandier, Jean Louis
  1844   Caza del Oso y Cibalo en Nordeste de Tejas. El Museu Mexicano 3(8):177–87. [Mexico City.]

Buntin, J. A.
  1926   [Report on Kiowa-Comanche-Apache Business Meeting, dated Jan. 2, 1926.] File 067-Business Committee, Apache, Kiowa, Comanche, 1926. Federal Archives and Records Center, Fort Worth, Texas.

Burton, E. F.
  1895   [Letter to Frank Baldwin, dated November 17, 1895.] Microfilm KA 42, "Kiowa Murders," no frame number. Kiowa Agency, Oklahoma Historical Society, Oklahoma City.

Butler, Pierce M.
  1846   [Letter to William Medill, dated March 4, 1846.] Microfilm M234, Roll 444, Frames 48–50, Miscellaneous Letters Received, Record Group 75, National Archives, Washington, D.C.

Butler, Pierce M. and M.G. Lewis

1846   [Letter to W. Medill, dated August 8, 1846.] Microfilm T494, Roll 4, Frame 259.
           Documents Relating to the Negotiation of Ratified and Unratified Treaties with Various
           Tribes of Indians, 1801–1869, Record Group 75, National Archives, Washington, D.C.

Canonge, Elliot D.

1958   Comanche Texts. Illustrated by Katherine Voigtlander; Introduction by Morris Swadesh;
           Edited by Benjamin Elson. University of Oklahoma, Summer Institute of Linguistics
           Series 1. Norman.

Carlson, Gustav G. and Volney Jones

1940   Some Notes on the Use of Plants by the Comanche Indians. Papers of the Michigan
           Academy of Science, Arts and Letters 25:517–42.

Carroll, H. Bailey and J.Villiasana Haggard, eds. and trans.

1942   Three New Mexico Chronicles: The *Exposicion* of Don Pedro Bautista Pino, 1812; The
           Ojeada of Lic. Antonio Barreiro, 1832; and the Additions by Don José Augustín de
           Escudero, 1849. Quivera Society Publications 11. Albuquerque: The Quivira Society.

Casagrande, Joseph

1954–55   Comanche Linguistic Acculturation I, II, III. International Journal of American
           Linguistics 20(2):140–51, 20(3):217–37; 21(1):8–25.

Charney, Jean Ormsbee

1993   A Grammar of Comanche. Studies in the Anthropology of North American Indians.
           Lincoln: University of Nebraska Press.

Clark, Edward L.

1881   [Report to William P. Clark, dated May 18, 1881.] Microfilm KA 11, Frame 513, Kiowa
           Agency. Oklahoma Historical Society, Oklahoma City.

Clark. William P.

1885   The Indian Sign Language; With Brief Explanatory Notes on the Gestures Taught Deaf-
           Mutes in Our Institutions for Their Instruction, and a Description of Some of the
           Peculiar Laws, Customs, Myths, Superstitions, Ways of Living, Code of Peace and War
           Signals of Our Aborigines. Philadelphia: L. R. Hamersly and Company. (Reprinted:
           University of Nebraska Press, Lincoln, 1982.)

Comanche Census

1876–95   Records of the Kiowa Agency. (Microfilm rolls DA 1 and 1a.) Oklahoma Historical
           Society, Oklahoma City.

1899–1938 (Microfilm Publication M595, rolls 211–23.) National Archives and Records Service,
           Washington.

Comanche Language and Cultural Preservation Committee

1993   *Taa Nʉmʉ Tekwapʉˀha Tʉboopʉ*. Lawton, Okla.: Privately Printed.

Corwin, Hugh D.

1959   Comanche and Kiowa Captives in Oklahoma and Texas. Guthrie, Okla.: Cooperative
           Publishing Company.

Detrick, Charles H.

1895   Comanche-English Dictionary and Vocabulary of Phrases. Native American Manuscript
           Resources, Western History Collection, University of Oklahoma, Norman.

Davidson, J. W.

1875   [Letter to J. M. Haworth dated January 9, 1875.] Microfilm KA 7, Frame 344, Kiowa Agency. Oklahoma Historical Society, Oklahoma City.

DeMallie, Raymond J., and Douglas R. Parks

2001   Tribal Traditions and Records. *In* Handbook of North American Indians, Vol. 13, Plains, Raymond J. DeMallie, vol. ed., William C. Sturtevant, gen. ed., pt. 2, pp. 1062–73. Washington: Smithsonian Institution.

DeShields, James

1886   Cynthia Ann Parker: The Story of Her Capture at the Massacre of the Inmates of Parker's Fort; of Her Quarter of a Century Spent Among the Comanches, as the Wife of the War Chief, Peta Nocona; and of Her Recapture at the Battle of Pease River by Captain L.S. Ross, of the Texian Rangers. St. Louis: Printed for the Author. (Reprinted: Naylor, San Antonio, 1934; also, E.L. Connally, Waco, 1972; also, Garland Pub, New York, 1976; also, S. Malone, Printer, San Augustine, Tex., 1986; and, Chama Press, Dallas, 1991.)

Emory, William H.

1857   Report on the United States and Mexico Boundary Survey under the Direction of the Secretary of the Interior. 34th Cong., 1st sess., H. Ex. Doc 135.

Family Record Book

1901–2   Anadarko Agency Allotment Record: Genealogical Book of the Kiowa, Comanche, Kiowa-Apache, and some Twenty-five Sioux Families in 1902. Oklahoma Historical Society, Oklahoma City. (For a typewritten transcription, see Murphy 1991.)

García Rejón, Manuel

1866   Dictionario del idioma Comanche. México: Impr. De Ignacio Cumplido. Mexico City.

Gatschet, Albert

1893   [Comanche Vocabulary from information from Philip Bloch, Indian Scout.] Manuscript No. 751, National Anthropological Archives, Smithsonian Institution, Washington.

Gelo, Daniel J.

1995   Comanche Vocabulary / Vocabulario del idioma comanche, compiled by Manuel Garcia Rejón. Trilingual ed., 1st ed. Texas Archaeology and Ethnography Series. Austin: University of Texas Press. (See also Garcia Rejón.)

Gregg, Josiah

1844   Commerce of the Prairies, or The Journal of a Santa Fé Trader. 2 vols. New York: J and H.G. Langley. (Reprinted, 2d ed. in 1845; also, in Vols. 19 and 20 of Early Western Travels, 1748–1846. Reuben G. Thwaites, ed., Arthur H. Clark, Cleveland, Ohio, 1905; and, Max L. Moorhead, ed.; University of Oklahoma Press, Norman, 1954.)

Hadley, J. Nixon, Robert W. Young, and William Morgan

1948   A Birth Certificate Tells the Facts! Give Your Child a Permanent Name! Washington: Dept. of the Interior, United States Indian Service.

Hagan, William T.

1976   United States-Comanche Relations: The Reservation Years. New Haven: Yale University Press.

Haley, James L.

1976   The Buffalo War: The History of the Red River Indian Uprising of 1874. Garden City,

N.J.: Doubleday. (Reprinted, University of Oklahoma Press, Norman, 1985; and, State House Press, Austin, Tex., 1998.)

Hardee, William J.

1851   [Letter to George Deal dated Aug. 28, 1851.] Microfilm M234, Roll 858, Frame 889, Letters Received from the Texas Agency, Record Group 75, National Archives, Washington.

Hebard, Grace R.

1932   Sacajawea: Guide and Interpreter of the Lewis and Clark Expedition, with an Account of the Travels of Toussaint Charbonneau, and of Jean Baptiste, the Expedition Papoose. Glendale, Calif.: Arthur H. Clark Co. (Reprinted in 1957, 1967; also, Overland Trails Press, Mansfield Centre, Conn., 1999; and, Dover Publications, Mineola, N.Y., 2002.)

Herzog, George, and David McAllester

1939   [Comanche Field Notes.] Manuscript 54-302-F, Archives of Traditional Music, Indiana University, Bloomington.

Hoebel, E. Adamson

1936   Associations and the State in the Plains. American Anthropologist 38:433–38.

1939   Comanche and Hɜkandika Shoshone Relationship Systems. American Anthropologist 41:440–57.

1940   Political Organization and Law-Ways of the Comanche Indians. Memoirs of the American Anthropological Association 54. Menasha, Wis. (Reprinted: Kraus Reprints, New York, 1969.)

1941   The Comanche Sun Dance and Messianic Outbreak of 1873. American Anthropologist 43:301–3.

1954   The Law of Primitive Man: A Study in Comparative Legal Dynamics. Cambridge, Mass.: Harvard University Press.

Hunt, Philemon B.

1879   [Location of Families and bands of the Kiowa Reservation, the number of people in the families or bands, and the distance and direction of each from Fort Sill. Enclosure in, Hunt to Hayt, dated January 15, 1879] Microfilm M234, Roll 384, Frames 693ff, Letters Received from the Kiowa Agency, Record Group 75, National Archives, Washington.

Jones, David C.

1966   The Treaty of Medicine Lodge: The Story of the Great Treaty Council as Told by Eyewitnesses. Norman: University of Oklahoma Press.

Jones, Daniel

1917   An English Pronouncing Dictionary (On Strictly Phonetic Principles). London, Toronto: J.M. Dent; New York: E.P. Dutton.

Jones, David E.

1972   Sanapia: Comanche Medicine Woman. New York: Holt, Rinehart and Winston. (Reprinted: Waveland Press, Prospect Heights, Ill., 1984.)

Kardiner, Abram

1945   The Psychological Frontiers of Society. With the Collaboration of Ralph Linton, Cora Du Bois, and James West. New York: Columbia University Press. (Reprinted in 1956, 1963; also, Greenwood Press, Westport, Conn., 1981.)

Kappler, Charles J., comp. and ed.

1972 Indian Treaties, 1778–1883. New York, Interland Publishing Co. (Originally Published as Indian Affairs: Laws and Treaties, vol. 2, Government Printing Office, Washington, 1904.)

Kavanagh, Thomas W.

1980 Recent Socio-cultural Evolution of the Comanche Indians. M.A. Thesis in Anthropology, George Washington University, Washington.

1985 The Comanche: Paradigmatic Anomaly or Ethnographic Fiction. (Haliksa'i. U.N.M Contributions to Anthropology.) Journal of the University of New Mexico Anthropological Society 4:109–28.

1986 Political Power and Political Organization: Comanche Politics, 1786–1875. Ph.D. Dissertation in Anthropology. University of New Mexico, Albuquerque.

1989 Comanche Population Organization and Reorganization, 1869–1901: A Test of the Continuity Hypothesis. In Plains Indian Historical Demography and Health: Perspectives, Interpretations, and Critiques. Gregory R. Campbell, ed. Memoir 23, Plains Anthropologist 34(124, Pt. 2):99–111.

1991 Whose Village? Photographs by William S. Soule, Winter 1872–1873. Visual Anthropology 4:1–24.

1996 Comanche Political History: An Ethnohistorical Perspective, 1706–1875. Studies in the Anthropology of North American Indians. Lincoln: University of Nebraska Press. (Reprinted, rev. ed., 1999, under title: The Comanches: A History, 1706–1873.)

2001 Comanche. In Handbook of North American Indians, Vol. 13, Plains, Raymond J. DeMallie, vol. ed., William C. Sturtevant, gen. ed., pt. 2, pp. 886–906. Washington: Smithsonian Institution.

La Barre, Weston

1975 The Peyote Cult. 4th ed., enl. New York: Schocken Books.

Laubin, Reginald, and Gladys Laubin

1977 The Indian Tipi: Its History, Construction, and Use. 2d ed. Norman: University of Oklahoma Press.

Leonhardy, Frank C.

1966 Domebo: A Paleo-Indian Mammoth Kill on the Prairie-Plains. Contributions of the Museum of the Great Plains, No. 1. Lawton, Okla.

Linton, Ralph

n.d. [Project for Ethnological Work Among the Comanches for the Laboratory of Anthropology, Santa Fe.] File 89FS 3.013.1. Archives of the Laboratory of Anthropology, Museum of New Mexico, Santa Fe.

1933a [Letter to Jesse Nusbaum, May 16, 1933.] File 89FS 3.013.1. Archives of the Laboratory of Anthropology, Museum of New Mexico, Santa Fe.

1933b [Letter to Jesse Nusbaum, June 7, 1933.] File 89FS 3.013.1. Archives of the Laboratory of Anthropology, Museum of New Mexico, Santa Fe.

1933c [Letter to Jesse Nusbaum, Aug. 3, 1933.] File 89FS 3.013.1. Archives of the Laboratory of Anthropology, Museum of New Mexico, Santa Fe.

1933d [Letter to Jesse Nusbaum, Sept. 2, 1933.] File 89FS 3.013.1. Archives of the Laboratory of Anthropology, Museum of New Mexico, Santa Fe.

1933e   [Letter to Jesse Nusbaum, Oct. 13, 1933.] File 89FS 3.013.1. Archives of the Laboratory of Anthropology, Museum of New Mexico, Santa Fe.

1935   The Comanche Sun Dance. American Anthropologist 37:420–28.

1936   The Study of Man: An Introduction. New York: Appleton-Century Co.

Linton, Adelin, and Charles Wagley

1971   Ralph Linton. New York: Columbia University Press.

Long, M. F.

1897   [Report on Indian Houses, dated August 21, 1897.] Manuscript in Kiowa Agency Records, Oklahoma Historical Society, Oklahoma City.)

Loomis, Noel M., and Abraham P. Nasatir

1967   Pedro Vial and the Roads to Santa Fe. Norman: University of Oklahoma Press.

Lowie, Robert

1909   The Northern Shoshone. American Museum of Natural History Anthropological Papers 2(2):165–206. New York. (Reprinted: AMS Press, New York, 1975.)

1913   Military Societies of the Crow Indians. American Museum of Natural History Anthropological Papers 11(16):143–218. New York. (Bound with other monographs in: Societies of the Plains Indians, Clark Wissler, ed., New York, 1912–16.)

1915   Dances and Societies of the Plains Shoshone. American Museum of Natural History Anthropological Papers 11(10):803–35. New York. (Bound with other monographs in: Societies of the Plains Indians, Clark Wissler, ed., New York, 1912–16.)

MacGowan, D. J.

1865   [Notes of a Brief Stay among the Comanche, Caddos, and Wichitas. Fort Smith, Arkansas, Sept. 1865] Copy by George Gibbs. Manuscript No. 1814, National Anthropological Archives, Smithsonian Institution, Washington.

McAllester, David P.

1949   Peyote Music. Viking Fund Publications in Anthropology 13. New York. (Reprinted: Johnson Reprint, New York, 1971.)

Mihesuah, Henry

2002   First to Fight. Devon Abbott Mihesuah, ed. Lincoln: University of Nebraska Press.

Mooney, James

1896   The Ghost-dance Religion and the Sioux Outbreak of 1890. Pp 641–1136 [pp. 1111–36. Vol. Index] in Pt. 2 of Fourteenth Annual Report of the Bureau of American Ethnology [for] the Years 1892–93. Washington: Smithsonian Institution; U.S. Government Printing Office. (Reprinted: rev. ed., 1965; Dover Publications, New York, 1973; also, with an Introduction by Raymond J. DeMallie: University of Nebraska Press, Lincoln, 1991.)

1898   Calendar History of the Kiowa Indians. Pp. 129–468 in Pt. 1 of Seventeenth Annual Report of the Bureau of American Ethnology [for] the Years 1895–96. Washington: Smithsonian Institution; U.S. Government Printing Office. (Reprinted, with an Introduction by John C. Ewers: Classics of Smithsonian Anthropology. Smithsonian Institution Press, Washington, 1979.)

1918   [Notebook] Manuscript No. 2537, National Anthropological Archives, Smithsonian Institution, Washington.

Murphy, Polly Lewis, ed.

1991   Anadarko Agency Allotment Record: Genealogical Book of the Kiowa, Comanche, Kiowa-Apache, and some Twenty-five Sioux Families in 1902. [Lawton, Okla.: privately published.] (Copy in Lawton Public Library.)

Neighbors, Robert S.

1852   The Na-ün-i or Comanches of Texas: Their Traits and Beliefs, and Their Divisions and Intertribal Relations. Pp. 125–34 in Vol. 2 of Historical and Statistical Information Respecting the History, Condition, and Prospects of the Indian Tribes of the United States. Henry R. Schoolcraft, comp. and ed. 6 vols. Philadelphia: Lippencott, Grambo, 1851–1857.

Nusbaum, Jesse

1933   [Letter to Ralph Linton, dated Nov. 8, 1933.] File 89FS 3.013.3. Archives of the Laboratory of Anthropology, Museum of New Mexico, Santa Fe.

Nye, Wilbur S.

1969   Carbine and Lance: The Story of Old Fort Sill. Norman: University of Oklahoma Press. (Originally published, 1937.)

Opler, Marvin

1943   The Origins of Comanche and Ute. American Anthroplogist 41:155–58.

Pettis, G. H.

1908   Personal Narratives of the Battles of Rebellion: Kit Carson's Fight with the Comanche and Kiowa Indians [1878]. Max Frost, ed. Historical Society of New Mexico [Publications] 12. Santa Fe: New Mexican Printing Company.

Powell, Peter J.

1981   People of the Sacred Mountain: A History of the Cheyenne Chiefs and Warrior Societies, 1830–1879; with an Epilogue, 1969–74. 2 vols. San Francisco: Harper and Row.

Pratt, Richard H.

1875-77   [Letterbook Regarding Indian Prisoners in Florida.] Manuscript 493a, Richard Henry Pratt Papers, Collection of Western Americana, Beinecke Rare Book and Manuscript Library, Yale University, New Haven.

Richardson, Rupert N.

1933   The Comanche Barrier to South Plains Settlement. Glendale, Calif.: Arthur H. Clark.

Robinson, Lila Wistrand, and James Armagost

1990   Comanche Dictionary and Grammar. Summer Institute of Linguistics and the University of Texas at Arlington. Publications in Linguistics 92. Dallas: Summer Institute of Linguistics.

St. Clair, Henry Hull

1902   [Comanche Texts]. Bureau of American Ethnology Manuscript 877, National Anthropological Archives, Smithsonian Institution, Washington. (Published in: Shoshone and Comanche Texts, Robert Lowie, ed., Journal of American Folklore 22(85):265–82, 1909.)

Schoolcraft, Henry Rowe

1851-57   Historical and Statistical Information Respecting the History, Condition and Prospects of the Indian Tribes in the United States . . . Philadelphia: Lippencott, Grambo. 6 vols. (Reprinted: Arno Press, New York, 1969.)

Slobodin, Richard

1966   Martha Champion Randle, 1910–1965. American Anthropologist 68:995–96.

Smith, Ralph

1970   The Comanche Sun Over Mexico. West Texas Historical Association Year Book 46:25–62.

Smithwick, Noah

1983   The Evolution of a State, or Recollections of Old Texas Days. Austin: University of Texas Press.

Stanley, Henry M.

1967   A British Journalist Reports the Medicine Lodge Peace Councils of 1867. Kansas Historical Quarterly 33:249–320.

Stecker, Ernest

1914   [Report on Kiowa-Comanche-Apache Business Meeting, dated November 14, 1914.] File 067-Business Committee, Apache, Kiowa, Comanche, 1914. Federal Archives and Records Center, Fort Worth, Tex.

1915   [Letter to the Commissioner of Indian Affairs, dated March 1, 1915.] File 067-Business Committee, Apache, Kiowa, Comanche, 1915. Federal Archives and Records Center, Fort Worth, Tex.

Steward, Julian

1938   Basin-Plateau Aboriginal Sociopolitical Groups. Bureau of American Ethnology Bulletin 120. Washington: Smithsonian Institution. (Reprinted: University of Utah Press, Salt Lake City, 1970.)

Stinchicum, C. V.

1916   [Letter to the Commissioner of Indians Affairs, no date]. File 067-Business Committee, Apache, Kiowa, Comanche, 1916. Federal Archives and Records Center, Fort Worth, Tex.

Sturm, J. J.

1875   [Notes of Travel in Search of the Quah-de-ru Band of Comanches.] Manuscript S248/2 in Letters Received, Department of the Missouri, Record Group 98, National Archives, Washington.

Tatum, Lawrie

1899   Our Red Brothers and the Peace Policy of President Ulysses S. Grant. Philadelphia: J. C. Winston & Co. (Reprinted: University of Nebraska Press, Lincoln, Neb., 1970.)

ten Kate, Herman F. C.

1885   Notes ethnographiques sur les Comanches. Revue d'Ethnographie 4:120–36.

Thomas, Alfred B., ed. and trans.

1932   Forgotten Frontiers: A Study of the Spanish Indian Policy of Don Juan Bautista de Anza, Governor of New Mexico, 1777–1787. Norman: University of Oklahoma Press.

Thurman, Melburn D.

1982   Nelson Lee and the Green Corn Dance: Data Selection Problems with Wallace and Hoebel's Study of the Comanches. Plains Anthropologist 27(97):239–43.

1988   On the Identity of the Chariticas (Sarh Rikka): Dog Eating and Pre-Horse Adaptation on the High Plains. Plains Anthropologist 33(120):159–70.

Wagner, Günter

1932a   Entwicklung und Verbreitung des Peyote Kultes. Baessler-Archiv, 15:59–141.

1932b   [Report on Research Work, July–October 1932, Letter to Franz Boas, dated October 21, 1932.] Franz Boas Collection, Library of the American Philosophical Society, Philadelphia.

Wallace, Ernest

1978   The Journal of Ranald S. Mackenzie's Messenger to the Kwahadi Comanches. Red River Valley Historical Review 3:227–46.

Wallace, Ernest, and E. Adamson Hoebel

1952   The Comanche: Lords of the South Plains. Based on Field Work 1933–1945. Norman: University of Oklahoma Press. (Reprinted in 1954, 1958, 1969, 1982, 1986, 1988.)

Wedel, Waldo R.

1977   The Education of a Plains Archeologist. Plains Anthropologist 22(75):1–12.

Wissler, Clark, ed.

1912–16   Societies of the Plains Indians. American Museum of Natural History Anthropological Papers 11. New York. (Reprinted: AMS Press, New York, 1975.)

Woodbury, Natalie F. S.

1987   Past Is Present: Amplification: The Death of Henrietta Schmerler. Anthropology Newsletter 27(6):3.

Index

In *Studies in the Anthropology of North American Indians*

Yuchi Ceremonial Life:
Performance, Meaning, and
Tradition in a Contemporary
American Indian Community
By Jason Baird Jackson

The Comanches: A History,
1706–1875
By Thomas W. Kavanagh

Comanche Ethnography: Field
Notes of E. Adamson Hoebel, Waldo
R. Wedel, Gustav G. Carlson, and
Robert H. Lowie
Compiled and Edited By Thomas
W. Kavanagh

Koasati Dictionary
By Geoffrey D. Kimball with the
assistance of Bel Abbey, Martha
John, and Ruth Poncho

Koasati Grammar
By Geoffrey D. Kimball with the
assistance of Bel Abbey, Nora
Abbey, Martha John, Ed John, and
Ruth Poncho

The Salish Language Family:
Reconstructing Syntax
By Paul D. Kroeber

Tales from Maliseet Country: The
Maliseet Texts of Karl V. Teeter
By Philip S. LeSourd

The Medicine Men: Oglala Sioux
Ceremony and Healing
By Thomas H. Lewis

A Dictionary of Creek / Muskogee
By Jack B. Martin and Margaret
McKane Mauldin

Wolverine Myths and Visions: Dene
Traditions from Northern Alberta
Edited by Patrick Moore and Angela
Wheelock

Ceremonies of the Pawnee
By James R. Murie, Edited by
Douglas R. Parks

Archaeology and Ethnohistory of the
Omaha Indians: The Big Village Site
By John M. O'Shea and John
Ludwickson

Traditional Narratives of the
Arikara Indians (4 vols.)
By Douglas R. Parks

A Dictionary of Skiri Pawnee
By Douglas R. Parks and Lulu Nora
Pratt

Osage Grammar
By Carolyn Quintero

"They Treated Us Just Like
Indians": The Worlds of Bennett
County, South Dakota
By Paula L. Wagoner

A Grammar of Kiowa
By Laurel J. Watkins with the
assistance of Parker McKenzie

Printed in the USA
CPSIA information can be obtained
at www.ICGtesting.com
LVHW081355210923
758924LV00006B/134